Exam 70-646: *PRO: Windows Server® Administration*

Objective	Location in Book
Planning for Server Deployment	
Plan server installations and upgrades.	Chapter 1, Lesson 1
Plan for automated server deployment.	Chapter 1, Lesson 2
Plan infrastructure services server roles.	Chapter 2, Lesson 1
	Chapter 2, Lesson 2
	Chapter 3, Lesson 1
	Chapter 4, Lesson 1
	Chapter 9, Lesson 2
	Chapter 10, Lesson 1
Plan application servers and services.	Chapter 4, Lesson 2
	Chapter 5, Lesson 1
Plan file and print server roles.	Chapter 6, Lesson 1
Planning for Server Management	
Plan server management strategies.	Chapter 7, Lesson 1
Plan for delegated administration.	Chapter 7, Lesson 2
Plan and implement group policy strategy.	Chapter 3, Lesson 2
Monitoring and Maintaining Servers	
Implement patch management strategy.	Chapter 8, Lesson 1
Monitor servers for performance evaluation and optimization.	Chapter 7, Lesson 3
Monitor and maintain security and policies.	Chapter 8, Lesson 2
	Chapter 9, Lesson 1
Planning Application and Data Provisioning	
Provision applications.	Chapter 4, Lesson 3
	Chapter 5, Lesson 2
Provision data.	Chapter 6, Lesson 2
Planning for Business Continuity and High Availability	
Plan storage.	Chapter 10, Lesson 2
Plan high availability.	Chapter 11, Lesson 1
	Chapter 11, Lesson 2
Plan for backup and recovery.	Chapter 12, Lesson 1
	Chapter 12, Lesson 2

NOTE Exam objectives

The exam objectives listed here are current as of this book's publication date. Exam objectives are subject to change at any time without prior notice and at Microsoft's sole discretion. Please visit the Microsoft Learning Web site for the most current listing of exam objectives:
http://www.microsoft.com/learning/exams/70-646.mspx

Microsoft

MCITP Self-Paced Training Kit (Exam 70-646): Windows Server® Administration

Ian McLean
Orin Thomas

PUBLISHED BY
Microsoft Press
A Division of Microsoft Corporation
One Microsoft Way
Redmond, Washington 98052-6399

Library of Congress Control Number: 2008923652

Printed and bound in the United States of America.

1 2 3 4 5 6 7 8 9   QWT   3 2 1 0 9 8

Distributed in Canada by H.B. Fenn and Company Ltd.

A CIP catalogue record for this book is available from the British Library.

Microsoft Press books are available through booksellers and distributors worldwide. For further information about international editions, contact your local Microsoft Corporation office or contact Microsoft Press International directly at fax (425) 936-7329. Visit our Web site at www.microsoft.com/mspress. Send comments to tkinput@microsoft.com.

Acquisitions Editor: Ken Jones
Developmental Editor: Laura Sackerman
Project Editor: Maria Gargiulo
Editorial Production: S4Carlisle Publishing Services Inc.
Technical Reviewer: Bob Dean; Technical Review services provided by Content Master, a member of CM Group, Ltd.
Cover: Tom Draper Design

Body Part No. X14-33190

About the Authors

Ian McLean

Ian McLean, MCSE, MCITP, MCT, has over 40 years' experience in industry, commerce, and education. He started his career as an electronics engineer before going into distance learning and then into education as a university professor. Currently he runs his own consultancy company. Ian has written 21 books plus many papers and technical articles. He has been working with Microsoft server operating systems since 1997.

Orin Thomas

Orin Thomas, MCSE, MVP, is an author and systems administrator who has worked with Microsoft server operating systems for more than a decade. He is the coauthor of numerous Self-Paced Training Kits for Microsoft Press, including *MCSA/MCSE Self-Paced Training Kit (Exam 70-290): Managing and Maintaining a Microsoft Windows Server 2003 Environment,* Second Edition, and a contributing editor for Windows IT Pro magazine.

Steve Suehring

Steve Suehring is an international consultant who's written about programming, security, network and system administration, operating systems, and other topics for several industry publications. He also speaks at conferences and user groups and served as an editor for LinuxWorld Magazine.

Contents at a Glance

Table of Contents

What do you think of this book? We want to hear from you!

Microsoft is interested in hearing your feedback so we can continually improve our books and learning resources for you. To participate in a brief online survey, please visit:

www.microsoft.com/learning/booksurvey/

What do you think of this book? We want to hear from you!

Introduction

This training kit is designed for server administrators who have two to three years of experience managing Windows servers and infrastructure in an environment that typically supports 250 to 5,000 or more users in three or more physical locations and has three or more domain controllers. You will likely be responsible for supporting network services and resources such as messaging, database servers, file and print servers, a proxy server, a firewall, Internet connectivity, an intranet, remote access, and client computers. You will also be responsible for implementing connectivity requirements such as connecting branch offices and individual users in remote locations to the corporate network and connecting corporate networks to the Internet.

By using this training kit, you will learn how to do the following:

- Plan and implement Windows Server 2008 server deployment
- Plan and implement Windows Server 2008 server management
- Monitor, maintain, and optimize servers
- Plan application and data provisioning
- Plan and implement high-availability strategies and ensure business continuity

---

Find additional content online   As new or updated material that complements your book becomes available, it will be posted on the Microsoft Press Online Windows Server and Client Web site. Based on the final build of Windows Server 2008, the type of material you might find includes updates to book content, articles, links to companion content, errata, sample chapters, and more. This Web site will be available soon at *www.microsoft.com/learning/books/online/serverclient* and will be updated periodically.

Lab Setup Instructions

The exercises in this training kit require a minimum of two computers or virtual machines:

- One Windows Server 2008 Enterprise server configured as a domain controller
- One Windows Vista (Enterprise, Business, or Ultimate) computer

You can obtain an evaluation version of the Windows Server 2008 Enterprise Edition software from Microsoft's download center at *http://www.microsoft.com/Downloads/ Search.aspx*. If you want to carry out the optional exercises in Chapter 4, "Application

Servers and Services," you need an additional Windows Server 2003 member server. If you want to carry out the optional exercises in Chapter 11, "Clustering and High Availability," you need an additional Windows Server 2008 Enterprise member server. These servers can be virtual machines.

All computers must be physically connected to the same network. We recommend that you use an isolated network that is not part of your production network to do the practice exercises in this book. To minimize the time and expense of configuring physical computers, we recommend that you use virtual machines. To run computers as virtual machines within Windows, you can use Virtual PC 2007, Virtual Server 2005 R2, or third-party virtual machine software. To download Virtual PC 2007, visit *http://www.microsoft.com/windows/downloads/virtualpc/default.mspx*. To download an evaluation of Virtual Server 2005 R2, visit *http://www.microsoft.com/technet/virtualserver/evaluation/default.mspx*.

Hardware Requirements

You can complete almost all practice exercises in this book using virtual machines rather than real server hardware. The minimum and recommended hardware requirements for Windows Server 2008 are listed in Table 1.

Table 1   Windows Server 2008 Minimum Hardware Requirements

Hardware Component	Minimum Requirements	Recommended
Processor	1GHz (x86), 1.4GHz (x64)	2GHz or faster
RAM	512 MB	2 GB
Disk space	15 GB	40 GB

If you intend to implement several virtual machines on the same computer (recommended), a higher specification will enhance your user experience. In particular a computer with 4 GB RAM and 60 GB free disk space can host all the virtual machines specified for all the practice exercises in this book.

Preparing the Windows Server 2008 Enterprise Computer

Detailed instructions for preparing for Windows Server 2008 installation and installing and configuring the Windows Server 2008 Enterprise domain controller are given in Chapter 1, "Installing, Upgrading, and Deploying Windows Server 2008." The required server roles are added in the practice exercises in subsequent chapters.

Preparing the Windows Vista Computer

Perform the following steps to prepare your Windows Vista computer for the exercises in this training kit.

Check Operating System Version Requirements

In System Control Panel (found in the System And Maintenance category), verify that the operating system version is Windows Vista Enterprise Edition, Business Edition, or Ultimate Edition. If necessary, choose the option to upgrade to one of these versions.

Name the Computer

In the System Control Panel, specify the computer name as **Melbourne**.

Configure Networking

To configure networking carry out the following tasks:

1. In Control Panel, click Set Up File Sharing. In Network And Sharing Center, verify that the network is configured as a Private network and that File Sharing is enabled.

2. In Network And Sharing Center, click Manage Network Connections. In Network Connections, open the properties of the Local Area Connection. Specify a static IPv4 address that is on the same subnet as the domain controller. For example the setup instructions for the domain controller specify an IPv4 address 10.0.0.11. If you use this address you can configure the client computer with an IP address of 10.0.0.21. The subnet mask is 225.225.225.0 and the DNS address is the IPv4 address of the domain controller. You do not require a default gateway. You can choose other network addresses if you want to, provided that the client and server are on the same subnet.

Using the CD

The companion CD included with this training kit contains the following:

■ **Practice tests**   You can reinforce your understanding of how to configure Windows Vista by using electronic practice tests you customize to meet your needs from the pool of Lesson Review questions in this book. Or you can practice for the 70-646 certification exam by using tests created from a pool of 190 realistic exam questions, which give you many practice exams to ensure that you are prepared.

■ **An eBook**   An electronic version (eBook) of this book is included for when you do not want to carry the printed book with you. The eBook is in Portable Document Format (PDF), and you can view it by using Adobe Acrobat or Adobe Reader.

■ **Sample chapters**   Sample chapters from other Microsoft Press titles on Windows Server 2008. These chapters are in PDF format.

> **Digital Content for Digital Book Readers:** If you bought a digital-only edition of this book, you can enjoy select content from the print edition's companion CD.
> Visit *http://go.microsoft.com/fwlink/?LinkId=112300* to get your downloadable content. This content is always up-to-date and available to all readers.

How to Install the Practice Tests

To install the practice test software from the companion CD to your hard disk, do the following:

1. Insert the companion CD into your CD drive and accept the license agreement. A CD menu appears.

   If the CD menu does not appear   If the CD menu or the license agreement does not appear, AutoRun might be disabled on your computer. Refer to the Readme.txt file on the CD-ROM for alternate installation instructions.

   ---

2. Click Practice Tests and follow the instructions on the screen.

How to Use the Practice Tests

To start the practice test software, follow these steps:

1. Click Start, click All Programs, and then select Microsoft Press Training Kit Exam Prep. A window appears that shows all the Microsoft Press training kit exam prep suites installed on your computer.

2. Double-click the lesson review or practice test you want to use.

Lesson reviews versus practice tests   Select the (70-646) Windows Server Administration *lesson review* to use the questions from the "Lesson Review" sections of this book. Select the (70-646) Windows Server Administration *practice test* to use a pool of 190 questions similar to those that appear on the 70-646 certification exam.

Lesson Review Options

When you start a lesson review, the Custom Mode dialog box appears so that you can configure your test. You can click OK to accept the defaults, or you can customize the number of questions you want, how the practice test software works, which exam objectives you want the questions to relate to, and whether you want your lesson review to be timed. If you are retaking a test, you can select whether you want to see all the questions again or only the questions you missed or did not answer.

After you click OK, your lesson review starts.

- To take the test, answer the questions and use the Next, Previous, and Go To buttons to move from question to question.

- After you answer an individual question, if you want to see which answers are correct—along with an explanation of each correct answer—click Explanation.

- If you prefer to wait until the end of the test to see how you did, answer all the questions and then click Score Test. You will see a summary of the exam objectives you chose and the percentage of questions you got right overall and per objective. You can print a copy of your test, review your answers, or retake the test.

Practice Test Options

When you start a practice test, you choose whether to take the test in Certification Mode, Study Mode, or Custom Mode:

- **Certification Mode**   Closely resembles the experience of taking a certification exam. The test has a set number of questions. It is timed, and you cannot pause and restart the timer.

- **Study Mode**   Creates an untimed test during which you can review the correct answers and the explanations after you answer each question.

- **Custom Mode**   Gives you full control over the test options so that you can customize them as you like.

In all modes the user interface when you are taking the test is basically the same but with different options enabled or disabled depending on the mode. The main options are discussed in the previous section, "Lesson Review Options."

When you review your answer to an individual practice test question, a "References" section is provided that lists where in the training kit you can find the information that relates to that question and provides links to other sources of information. After you click Test Results to score your entire practice test, you can click the Learning Plan tab to see a list of references for every objective.

How to Uninstall the Practice Tests

To uninstall the practice test software for a training kit, use the Program And Features option in Windows Control Panel.

Microsoft Certified Professional Program

The Microsoft certifications provide the best method to prove your command of current Microsoft products and technologies. The exams and corresponding certifications are developed to validate your mastery of critical competencies as you design and develop, or implement and support, solutions with Microsoft products and technologies. Computer professionals who become Microsoft-certified are recognized as experts and are sought after industry-wide. Certification brings a variety of benefits to the individual and to employers and organizations.

All the Microsoft certifications   For a full list of Microsoft certifications, go to *www.microsoft.com/learning/mcp/default.asp*.

Technical Support

Every effort has been made to ensure the accuracy of this book and the contents of the companion CD. If you have comments, questions, or ideas regarding this book or the companion CD, please send them to Microsoft Press by using either of the following methods:

E-mail: tkinput@microsoft.com

Postal Mail:

Microsoft Press

Attn: MCITP Self-Paced Training Kit (Exam 70-646): Windows Server Administration, Editor

One Microsoft Way

Redmond, WA 98052–6399

For additional support information regarding this book and the CD-ROM (including answers to commonly asked questions about installation and use), visit the Microsoft Press Technical Support website at *www.microsoft.com/learning/support/books/*. To connect directly to the Microsoft Knowledge Base and enter a query, visit *http://support.microsoft.com/search/*. For support information regarding Microsoft software, connect to *http://support.microsoft.com*.

Chapter 1

Installing, Upgrading, and Deploying Windows Server 2008

Great systems administrators do not show up at work in the morning, have some coffee and a biscuit, and then decide to install a server operating system because they have got a few spare hours before lunch. Great systems administrators work with a plan. They know how they are going to install the server operating system before the server hardware leaves the vendor's warehouse.

This chapter is about planning the deployment of Windows Server 2008. Lesson 1 covers deciding which edition of Windows Server 2008 is most appropriate for a given set of roles, what preparations need to be made to deploy features such as Bit-Locker and Server Core, and what you need to take into account when upgrading a computer from Windows Server 2003. Lesson 2 looks at automated deployment options, from creating and utilizing unattended installation files to scheduling the deployment of multiple Windows Server 2008 operating systems using Windows Deployment Services.

Exam objectives in this chapter:
- Plan server installations and upgrades.
- Plan for automated server deployment.

Lessons in this chapter:

Before You Begin

To complete the lessons in this chapter, you must have done the following:

- Have access to a computer with at least 20 gigabytes (GB) of unpartitioned disk drive space, 512 megabytes (MB) of RAM, and a 1-gigahertz (GHz) or faster processor. The practice exercises in this book assume that the computer that you are using is not connected directly or indirectly to the Internet, but is connected to

1

a network with a private IP address. It is possible to use virtual machines rather than real server hardware to complete all practice exercises in this chapter except practice 2 in Lesson 1, "Configuring BitLocker Hard Disk Drive Encryption."

■ Downloaded the evaluation version of Windows Server 2008 Enterprise Edition from the Microsoft Download Center at *http://www.microsoft.com/Downloads/ Search.aspx*.

No additional configuration is required for this chapter.

Real World

Orin Thomas

The vast majority of organizations that will deploy Windows Server 2008 won't have IT as the core focus of the business. In my experience, new operating system features are introduced very slowly in most organizations because most organizations are conservative and don't like messing around with what already works. This is most likely what will happen with BitLocker. Encryption can be tricky to explain to non-technical people and you are likely to have been deploying Windows Server 2008 for a while before someone allows you to use BitLocker to encrypt the hard disk drive of an important server. And that is where you will most likely encounter a problem.

As you'll learn in this chapter, if at some stage in the future you plan to deploy BitLocker, you have to configure hard disk partitions in a particular manner before you install Windows Server 2008. This means that you really need to set up all Windows Server 2008 computers to support BitLocker, even if there are no immediate plans to use it, because at some stage in the future that policy might change. Setting up an extra 1.5-GB boot partition prior to installing Windows Server 2008 and switching on BitLocker at some future point is much simpler than having to reinstall Windows Server 2008 from scratch after repartitioning the hard disk drive because your manager decides that implementing BitLocker is an idea whose time has come.

This is why planning is important. When planning server deployment, you have to take things into account that might never happen so that you have the flexibility to quickly respond if that which might not eventuate actually does.

Lesson 1: Planning Windows Server 2008 Installation and Upgrade

This lesson covers the various editions of Windows Server 2008 and the roles that they are designed to meet. You will learn about the new Windows Server Core, which you can think of as Windows without actual windows. You will learn about the Windows Server 2008 installation and upgrade process, and you will learn about BitLocker volume encryption and the steps that you need to take to implement it.

> **After this lesson, you will be able to:**
> - Plan for the installation of or upgrade to Windows Server 2008.
> - Plan for the deployment of BitLocker.
>
> **Estimated lesson time: 60 minutes**

Selecting the Right Edition of Windows Server 2008

Windows Server 2008 comes in several different editions, each appropriate for a specific role. One edition and configuration is appropriate for a branch office file server; another edition and configuration is appropriate for a head office Microsoft Exchange Server 2007 clustered mailbox server. On top of these different editions, there are different versions of most editions for different processor architectures as well as the ability to install the stripped-down Server Core version of each edition. In the following pages you will learn how all of these options fit into different deployment plans and how you can assess a set of requirements to determine which edition of Windows Server 2008 best meets a particular set of needs.

Windows Server 2008 Minimum Requirements

Before you learn about the different editions of Windows Server 2008, you need to know whether the computer you will be installing or upgrading is capable of running Windows Server 2008. Unless you are using Windows Deployment Services or are booting into the Windows Pre-installation Environment off a CD-ROM, you will need access to a DVD-ROM drive. This is because Windows Server 2008, like Windows Vista, is installed from DVD rather than CD-ROM. As you will learn in Lesson 2, you can still install Windows Server 2008 if no DVD-ROM drive is present; these options will be covered later in "Installing Windows Server 2008." Other than the optical media, and the ability to support basic VGA graphics, Windows Server 2008 has the minimum requirements outlined in Table 1-1.

Table 1-1   Windows Server 2008 Minimum Hardware Requirements

Hardware Component	Minimum Requirements	Recommended
Processor	1 GHz (x86), 1.4 GHz (x64)	2 GHz or faster
RAM	512 MB	2 GB
Disk Space	15 GB	40 GB

Although Table 1-1 says that 15 GB is required, the actual installation routine for the standard x86 edition will inform you that only 5436 MB is needed. On the other hand, Windows Server 2008 Enterprise x64 edition requires 10412 MB of free space for installation. 15 GB is specified as a minimum in Table 1-1 because this provides enough space for the operating system and additional space for the swap file, log files to be stored, and any additional server roles to be installed on the server at a later date.

NOTE   Varying documentation

You might find that reports vary on the specific minimum requirements of Windows Server 2008. This is not uncommon for new operating systems because the minimum requirements change as the operating system moves from beta to the release candidate stage to the final RTM version. The requirements outlined in Table 1-1 are not finalized. You might be able to get Windows Server 2008 to install on a computer that does not meet these specifications, but the experience will be less than optimal.

The maximum supported hardware varies with each edition. There is no upper limit in terms of processor speed or hard disk space, but each edition has a separate maximum amount of RAM and separate maximum number of processors that can be deployed in Symmetric Multi-Processing (SMP) configuration. In some cases these figures vary depending on whether the x86 or x64 version is installed. In general, the x64 version of a particular edition of Windows Server 2008 supports more RAM than the equivalent x86 version. When considering which version of a particular edition to install, remember that you can only install the x86 version of Windows Server 2008 on x86 hardware, but that you can install both the x86 and x64 editions on x64 hardware. If the hardware you are going to install Windows Server 2008 on has an Itanium 2 processor, you can only install Windows Server 2008 Itanium Edition.

Windows Server 2008 Standard Edition

Windows Server 2008 Standard Edition is the version of the software targeted at the small to medium-sized business. This edition of Windows Server 2008 is the one that you will choose to deploy most often to support Windows Server 2008 roles in your environment. The following Windows Server 2008 Standard Edition properties differ from other editions of the software:

- The 32-bit version (x86) supports a maximum of 4 GB of RAM. Supports up to 4 processors in SMP configuration.

- The 64-bit version (x64) supports a maximum of 32 GB of RAM. Supports up to 4 processors in SMP configuration.

- Supports Network Load Balancing clusters but does not support failover clustering.

When planning the deployment of servers, you are likely to select the standard edition of Windows Server 2008 to fill the roles of domain controller, file and print server, DNS server, DHCP server, and application server. Although these services are vital to your organization's network infrastructure, they do not require the increased features present in the Windows Server 2008 Enterprise Edition and Datacenter Edition. You should use Windows Server 2008 Standard Edition in your plans unless Enterprise Edition features, such as failover clustering or Active Directory Federation Services are required to meet your goals.

Windows Server 2008 Enterprise Edition

Windows Server 2008 Enterprise Edition is the version of the operating system targeted at large businesses. Plan to deploy this version of Windows 2008 on servers that will run applications such as SQL Server 2008 Enterprise Edition and Exchange Server 2007. These products require the extra processing power and RAM that Enterprise Edition supports. When planning deployments, consider Windows Server 2008 Enterprise Edition in situations that require the following technologies unavailable in Windows Server 2008 Standard Edition:

- **Failover Clustering**   Failover clustering is a technology that allows another server to continue to service client requests in the event that the original server fails. Clustering is covered in more detail in Chapter 11, "Clustering and High Availability." You deploy failover clustering on mission-critical servers to ensure that important resources are available even if a server hosting those resources fails.

- **Active Directory Federation Services (ADFS)**   ADFS allows identity federation, often used by organizations with many partners who require access to local resources.

- The 32-bit (x86) version supports a maximum of 64 GB of RAM and 8 processors in SMP configuration.

- The 64-bit (x64) version supports a maximum of 2 TB of RAM and 8 processors in SMP configuration.

When planning deployments, you are likely to use Windows Server 2008 Enterprise Edition in conjunction with Windows Server 2008 Standard Edition. Standard Edition will meet most of your organization's requirements and it will only be necessary to plan the deployment of Enterprise Edition when a server has unusual requirements, such as needing to be a part of a failover cluster or needing exceptional processing or memory capacity.

Windows Server 2008 Datacenter Edition

Windows Server 2008 Datacenter Edition is aimed directly at very large businesses. The key reason to deploy Windows Server 2008 Datacenter Edition over Enterprise Edition is that Datacenter Edition allows unlimited virtual image rights. Windows Server 2008 Datacenter Edition is likely to be the best choice for organizations that use virtualization to consolidate existing servers or simply require significant hardware capacity for application servers. Windows Server 2008 Datacenter Edition has the following properties:

- The 32-bit (x86) version supports a maximum of 64 GB of RAM and 32 processors in SMP configuration.

- The 64-bit (x64) version supports a maximum of 2 TB of RAM and 64 processors in SMP configuration.

- Supports failover clustering and ADFS.

- Unlimited virtual image rights.

Windows Server 2008 Datacenter Edition is available only through OEM manufacturers. A datacenter class server, colloquially known as *Big Iron*, will cost tens, if not hundreds of thousands of dollars, and is a significant capital investment. When deploying Windows Server 2008 Datacenter Edition, you are likely to work with the OEM during the operating system installation and deployment phase rather than popping the installation media into an optical media drive and doing it yourself. This is partly because a significant hardware investment that would justify the installation of Windows Server 2008 Datacenter Edition over Windows Server 2008 Enterprise Edition is likely to include a rigorous level of OEM support. For example, Datacenter Edition will be deployed on servers where the cost to the company of the server being down for an hour might be measured in the tens of thousands of dollars. In the event that a critical component such as a motherboard fails, the vendor is likely to send out someone personally with the replacement part. Not only will that person deliver the part, but he will also perform the replacement. This is not because anyone doubts your ability to replace a motherboard, but because a vendor that sells your organization a server that costs many thousands of dollars has a legal responsibility to ensure that this server functions correctly. This legal responsibility will not be discharged if the vendor merely sends out a replacement part by courier with a photocopied set of instructions allowing you to do it yourself.

Windows Web Server 2008

Windows Web Server 2008 is designed to function specifically as a Web applications server. Other roles, such as Windows Deployment Server and Active Directory Domain Services, are not supported on Windows Web Server 2008. You deploy this server role either on a screened subnet to support a Web site viewable to external hosts or as an intranet server. As appropriate given its stripped-down role, Windows Web Server 2008 does not support the high-powered hardware configurations that other editions of Windows Server 2008 do. Windows Web Server 2008 has the following properties:

- The 32-bit version (x86) supports a maximum of 4 GB of RAM and 4 processors in SMP configuration.
- The 64-bit version (x64) supports a maximum of 32 GB of RAM and 4 processors in SMP configuration.
- Supports Network Load Balancing clusters.

You should plan to deploy Windows Web Server 2008 in the Server Core configuration, which minimizes its attack surface, something that is very important on a server that interacts with hosts external to your network environment. You should only plan to deploy the full version of Windows Web Server 2008 if your organization's Web applications rely on features such as ASP.NET, because the .NET Framework is not included in a Server Core installation.

Windows Server 2008 for Itanium-Based Systems

This edition is designed for the Intel Itanium 64-bit processor architecture, which is different from the x64 architecture that you will find in chips such as the Intel Core 2 Duo or AMD Turion series of processors. This is the only edition of Windows Server 2008 that you can install on an Itanium-based computer and requires an Itanium 2 processor. Both application server and Web server functionality are provided by Windows Server 2008 for Itanium-based systems. Other server roles, such as virtualization and Windows Deployment Services, are not available. Up to 64 processors in SMP configuration and 2 terabytes of RAM are supported on Windows Server 2008 for Itanium-based Systems.

MORE INFO   Researching Itanium

Check the Windows Server 2008 product Web site for more details on the specific roles available for the Itanium edition at *http://www.microsoft.com/windowsserver2008.*

Windows Server 2008 Server Core

Server Core is a stripped-down version of an edition of Windows Server 2008. Rather than providing a full desktop, Windows Server 2008 is administered from the command shell, as shown in Figure 1-1. You can manage a computer running Server Core remotely by connecting through a Microsoft Management Console (MMC). You can also establish an Remote Desktop Protocol (RDP) session to a computer running Server Core, though you will need to use the command shell to perform administrative duties.

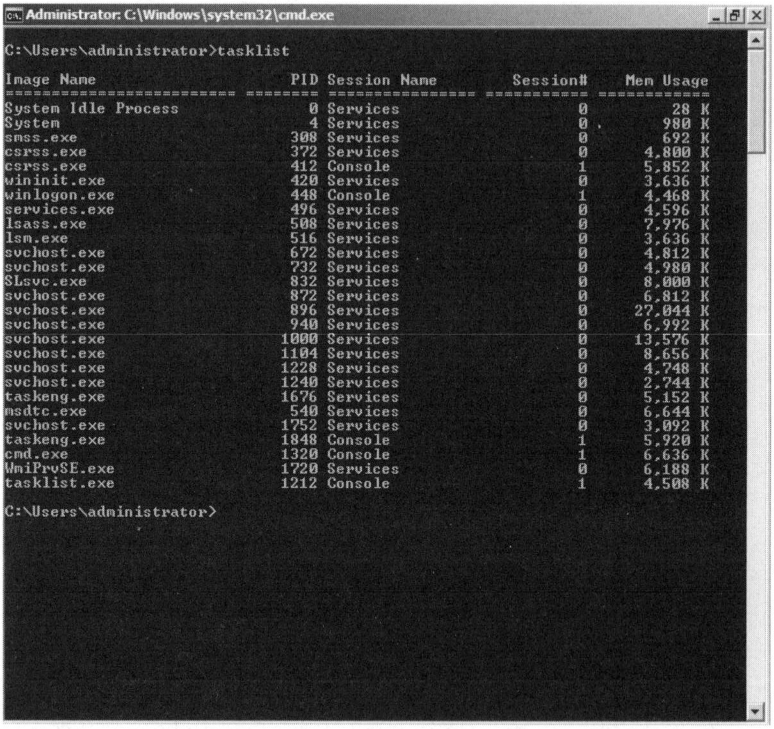

Figure 1-1   Server core desktop

Using the server core version of Windows Server 2008 has two primary benefits:

- **Reduced attack surface**   Fewer components are installed, which reduces the number of components that might be attacked by someone attempting to compromise the computer. A computer running only a small number of components to meet a specialized role also needs fewer updates.

- **Lower hardware requirements**   Because so much has been stripped out of the server core version of Windows Server 2008, you can run server core on a computer that would exhibit performance bottlenecks running a traditional full installation. A benefit of this is that it allows organizations to utilize older hardware, such as hardware purchased to run Windows 2000 Server as a platform for a Windows Server 2008 installation.

When you purchase a license for a particular edition of Windows Server 2008, you have the option of installing the full version or the scaled-down server core version of the operating system. Either way, the license will cost the same amount. If you license a particular edition, you can install that edition in either its full or server core configuration, as shown in Figure 1-2.

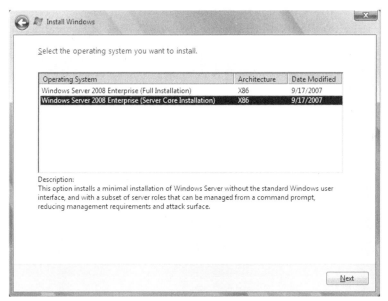

Figure 1-2   Installation options with a Windows Server 2008 Enterprise Edition license key

You use the same commands to manage server core that you can use to manage a fully featured installation of Windows Server 2008. You should examine the Windows Server 2008 Command Line Reference, available in Help, to learn how to perform common administrative duties from the command line. For example, to join a computer running a Server Core installation to the domain CONTOSO using Kim Akers' domain administrator account, you would issue the following command:

```
Netdom join COMPUTERNAME /domain:CONTOSO /userd:Kim_Akers /passwordd:*
```

This command will work on a fully featured installation of Windows Server 2008, but most administrators will join a computer to the domain using the GUI because this is the process that they are most familiar with. On a Server Core installation, you have to do everything from the command line.

One important area of difference in terms of command-line administration between a fully featured installation and a Server Core installation is that Server Core does not support PowerShell directly, although you can run some PowerShell commands against a Server Core installation remotely via WMI. It is possible to run Windows Script Host scripts on a Server Core installation just as it is possible to run the same scripts on fully featured installations of Windows Server 2008.

As shown in Figure 1-3, you can run several important tools graphically on a Server Core installation, including regedit and Notepad. It is also possible to invoke the Time and Date Control Panel and the International Settings Control Panel. These are invoked using the commands *control timedate.cpl* and *control intl.cpl*.

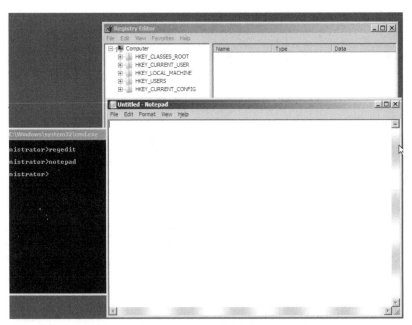

Figure 1-3   Regedit and Notepad are available in Server Core.

Two more important commands are *oclist.exe* and *ocsetup.exe*. *Oclist.exe* provides a list of all server roles that are currently installed on the server and what roles are available to install. Figure 1-4 shows the list of features installed by default on a Server Core installation of Windows Server 2008 Enterprise Edition. You can add and remove these features using the *ocsetup.exe* command. For example, to install the IIS-Webserver role, issue the command *ocsetup.exe IIS-WebServerRole*. It is important to note that the role name is case sensitive. The command *ocsetup.exe /uninstall IIS-WebServerRole* is used to remove the Web server role, although it is necessary to ensure that all of the role's services are shut down prior to attempting this.

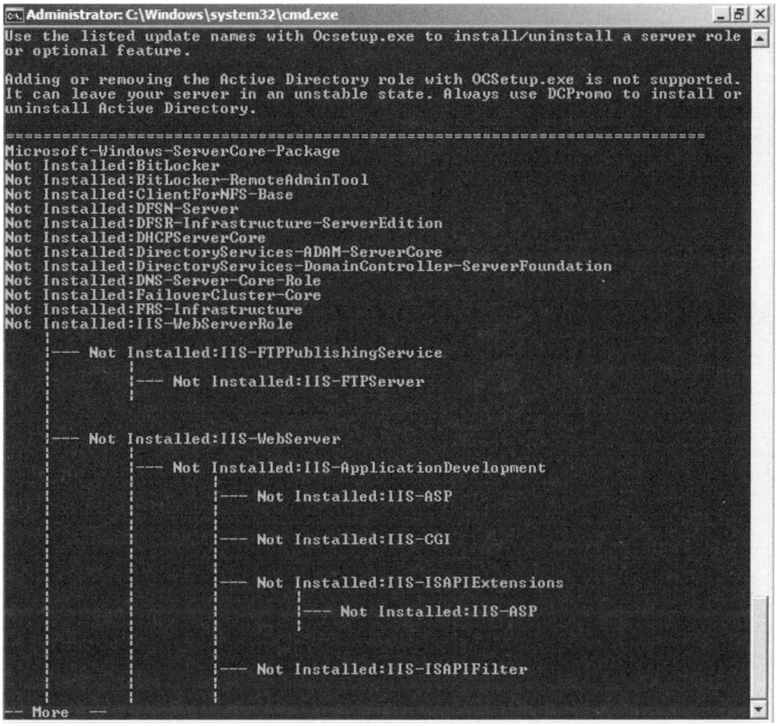

Figure 1-4   Viewing roles and features available on Server Core

It is not possible to upgrade a computer running the Server Core version of a specific edition to the full version, just as it is not possible to upgrade a computer running Windows Server 2003 to a Server Core version of Windows Server 2008. Although Internet Information Services (IIS) is supported on Server Core, the lack of the .NET Framework means that some Web applications that rely upon the .NET Framework will not work on Windows Server Core. Some roles, such as Active Directory Certificate Services, Active Directory Federation Services, Application Server, and Windows Deployment Services are not available on Server Core installations at the time of release, but might be included in later service packs. For this reason you should use *oclist.exe* on a test deployment of server core with the latest updates and service packs applied to determine which roles and features can be deployed in the server core environment.

NOTE Always check

During the initial beta period, a Server Core installation could not function as a Web server. By the time that release candidates of Windows Server 2008 became available, it was possible to configure a Server Core installation to function as a Web server. Therefore you should check with the *oclist.exe* command when attempting to determine which roles and features can and cannot be installed on a computer running Server Core.

> ## Quick Check
> 1. Which versions of Windows Server 2008 Standard Edition can be installed on a computer that has a Core 2 Duo processor and 4 GB of RAM?
> 2. What are the two benefits of deploying Server Core over a normal installation?
>
> ### Quick Check Answer
> 1. Both the Server Core and standard installation options with both the x86 and x64 versions.
> 2. Better performance and reduced attack surface.

Installing Windows Server 2008

Installing Windows Server 2008 is a relatively straightforward exercise. You start the installation media and select your language options, and are then presented with the option to enter your product key to determine which edition you are licensed to install. You do not need to input the product key at this stage, but if you do not, you might install an edition of Windows Server 2008 that you are not licensed to install. If this happens, you can either purchase a license for the edition you actually installed, or you can start over and install the correct edition.

NOTE Do not instantly activate

Although the default option is for activation to occur after the computer connects to the Internet, you might not get your configuration precisely correct the first few times you install Windows Server 2008. It is a good idea to use part of the 30-day activation grace period to let the server settle, ensuring that nothing drastic needs to change, such as upgrading the processor or RAM (which would normally lead to a reactivation) before the server undergoes the activation process. So remember to wait, ensure that the server does not require further hardware upgrades, and then perform activation.

You should review the section "Planning BitLocker Deployment" later in this lesson about configuring partitions to support BitLocker prior to performing the installation. The practice exercise at the end of the lesson also shows the steps necessary to configure the server so that you can deploy BitLocker at a later date.

In the event that the computer on which you want to install Windows Server 2008 does not have a DVD-ROM drive, you have several options. If the computer has a Preboot Execution Environment (PXE) capable network card, you can configure Windows Deployment Services, covered in detail by Lesson 2, "Automated Server Deployment," as a method of deploying Windows Server 2008 over the network. Alternatively, if a server does not have a PXE capable network card, or you do not want to use Windows Deployment Services, you can boot using the Windows Preinstallation Environment (Windows PE) and use operating system files hosted on a network share to perform a network installation. Windows PE is a free tool that you can download from Microsoft's Web site. It allows you to boot into an environment where you can perform certain maintenance on a computer in the same way that boot diskettes did back when all computers came with floppy disk drives. The standard installation process is covered in more detail by the first practice exercise at the end of this lesson.

MORE INFO   Windows PE 2.0

To learn more about Windows PE 2.0, consult the following TechNet Web page:

http://technet.microsoft.com/en-us/windowsvista/aa905120.aspx.

Upgrading from Windows Server 2003

Some organizations will want to upgrade their existing Windows Server 2003 computers to Windows Server 2008. You perform upgrades using the same media that you use to perform a normal installation. Unlike Microsoft's client operating systems, no cheaper upgrade version of the Windows Server 2008 installation media is available, and upgrades are almost always performed because the upgrade process is simpler than a migration. Upgrades to Windows Server 2008 from Windows Server 2003 are supported under a specific set of conditions, which are covered in the next few pages. The first thing to note is that you can perform an upgrade only if you start the upgrade process from within Windows Server 2003. It is not possible to perform an upgrade by booting from the installation media.

As shown in Table 1-2, you can upgrade only to an equivalent edition or a higher edition. This means that you can upgrade from Windows Server 2003 Standard Edition to Windows Server 2008 Standard or Enterprise Edition, but you cannot upgrade

Windows Server 2003 Enterprise Edition to Windows Server 2008 Standard Edition. This rule does not apply to Windows Web Server or the Datacenter Edition. You can only upgrade from Windows Server 2003 Web Edition to Windows Web Server 2008 and from Windows Server 2003 Datacenter Edition to Windows Server 2008 Datacenter Edition. You also cannot upgrade to Server Core from any edition of Windows Server 2003. Furthermore, it is not possible to perform a direct upgrade from any edition of Windows 2000 Server to Windows Server 2008. Finally, to perform an upgrade, Windows Server 2003 must have Service Pack 1 or later applied. This means that Windows Server 2003 R2 can be upgraded to Windows Server 2008 without the application of any additional service packs.

Table 1-2 Windows Server 2008 Upgrade Paths

Windows Server 2003 Edition	Upgrade Path
Windows Server 2003 Standard Edition	Windows Server 2008 Standard Edition
	Windows Server 2008 Enterprise Edition
Windows Server 2003 Enterprise Edition	Windows Server 2008 Enterprise Edition
Windows Server 2003 Datacenter Edition	Windows Server 2008 Datacenter Edition
Windows Server 2003 Web Edition	Windows Web Server 2008
Windows Server 2003 for Itanium Enterprise Edition	Windows Server 2008 for Itanium-Based Systems

NOTE **With and without Hyper-V**

You may notice that some Stock Keeping Units (SKUs) of Windows Server 2008 are labeled as being "Without Hyper-V." This labeling indicates that the files required to install the Hyper-V role are not included with the Windows Server 2008 installation media. The Hyper-V role can still be installed on a computer that is installed from media without the Hyper-V files, but the files required to install Hyper-V must be downloaded from Microsoft's Web site. You can find out more about Hyper-V in Chapter 5, "Terminal Services and Application and Server Virtualization."

It is not possible to upgrade to a different processor architecture. For example, if your organization is running Windows Server 2003 R2 x64 Standard Edition, you cannot perform an upgrade to Windows Server 2008 x32 Standard Edition. It is also not possible to upgrade a server from the 32-bit version of Windows Server 2003 to a 64-bit version of Windows Server 2008, even if the hardware supports it. For example: Ian has a 32-bit version of the Windows Server 2003 Standard Edition operating system configured to function as file and print server. This server has an Intel Core 2 Duo processor and 4 GB of RAM. Although the server has a processor capable of supporting a 64-bit edition of Windows Server 2008, Ian is only able to perform an upgrade to a 32-bit edition of Windows Server 2008 because the existing installation of Windows Server 2003 is 32 bit rather than 64 bit. If Ian wants to install a 64-bit installation of Windows Server 2008, he needs to perform a separate installation. It is possible to install Windows Server 2008 to a separate partition from the existing 32-bit Windows Server 2003 edition, re-create the shared printers, and re-create file shares that point to the existing shared data. Alternatively Ian could back up the server's data, format the hard disk drives, and then perform a clean installation of a 64-bit edition of Windows Server 2008. What is important to remember is that Ian will not be able to perform a direct upgrade, retaining shared printer and shared folder data, because it is not possible to upgrade between different processor architectures.

From a planning perspective it is not always clear whether you should perform an upgrade or back up an existing server, format the hard disk drive, install Windows Server 2008, and then restore the data and reinstall any applications. Upgrades are often implemented when the transition is simple, such as upgrading a computer that functions as a Windows Server 2003 domain controller to a Windows Server 2008 domain controller. When a server has a more complex role, such as a server hosting a large SQL Server 2008 instance, you need to carefully weigh your options. If you need to do a lot of post-installation custom configuration for the roles that the server hosts, performing the upgrade can be significantly quicker. Because prior to performing any upgrade or in-place migration you need to perform a full backup anyway, you should attempt the upgrade first and then look at other options, including rolling back to the original configuration if the upgrade goes awry. Rollback scenarios are covered in more depth in Lesson 2 under "Rollback Preparation."

NOTE Remember Itanium

Although Itanium is a 64-bit architecture, it is not the same as the x64 architecture. You cannot upgrade from or to an Itanium version of Windows Server 2008 unless your existing version of Windows is the Itanium edition of Windows Server 2003.

Prior to initiating the upgrade process, the Windows Server 2008 installation routine will perform a compatibility check, presenting findings in a compatibility report shown in Figure 1-5. The compatibility report will attempt to advise you of any problems that might occur if the upgrade commences, but the compatibility report can only inform you of problems that Microsoft is aware of. If the computer that you are going to upgrade has an unusual hardware or application configuration, the compatibility check might not flag the problem and you will be unaware of it until you encounter it directly. To ensure that the compatibility check is as accurate as possible, you should ensure that Windows Server 2008 is able to retrieve the most up-to-date installation files when you are queried about retrieving updated installation files at the beginning of the upgrade process. Also important to note is that upgrades require significantly more disk space than direct installs and you should ensure that at least 30 GB are free on the volume that hosts the operating system before attempting an upgrade. Contingency plans for the upgrade process are covered in more detail in Lesson 2, "Automated Server Deployment."

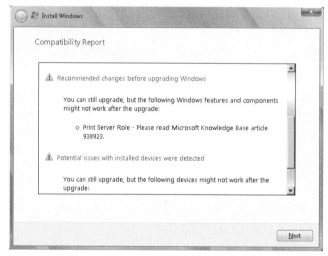

Figure 1-5   Compatibility report generated during upgrade

To summarize, keep in mind the following points about upgrades as compared to installations:

- You must initiate upgrades from within Windows Server 2003. You can initiate installations from within Windows or by starting from the installation media.

- An upgrade requires that more free space be available on the volume where Windows Server 2008 is being installed compared to a clean installation.

- Upgrades work best when a significant amount of customization is required that cannot be implemented simply by restoring backed-up data and installing applications on a new Windows Server 2008 installation.

- Implementing BitLocker on a computer upgraded from Windows Server 2003 is very difficult. For more details, see "BitLocker Volume Configuration" later in this chapter.

Planning BitLocker Deployment

Windows BitLocker and Drive Encryption (BitLocker) is a feature that debuted in Windows Vista Enterprise and Ultimate Editions and is available in all versions of Windows Server 2008. BitLocker serves two purposes: protecting server data through full volume encryption and providing an integrity-checking mechanism to ensure that the boot environment has not been tampered with.

Encrypting the entire operating system and data volumes means that not only are the operating system and data protected, but so are paging files, applications, and application configuration data. In the event that a server is stolen or a hard disk drive removed from a server by third parties for their own nefarious purposes, BitLocker ensures that these third parties cannot recover any useful data. The drawback is that if the BitLocker keys for a server are lost and the boot environment is compromised, the data stored on that server will be unrecoverable.

To support integrity checking, BitLocker requires a computer to have a chip capable of supporting the Trusted Platform Module (TPM) 1.2 or later standard. A computer must also have a BIOS that supports the TPM standard. When BitLocker is implemented in these conditions and in the event that the condition of a startup component has changed, BitLocker-protected volumes are locked and cannot be unlocked unless the person doing the unlocking has the correct digital keys. Protected startup components include the BIOS, Master Boot Record, Boot Sector, Boot Manager, and Windows Loader.

From a systems administration perspective, it is important to disable BitLocker during maintenance periods when any of these components are being altered. For example, you must disable BitLocker during a BIOS upgrade. If you do not, the next time the computer starts, BitLocker will lock the volumes and you will need to initiate the recovery process. The recovery process involves entering a 48-character password that is generated and saved to a specified location when running the BitLocker setup wizard. This password should be stored securely because without it the recovery process cannot occur. You can also configure BitLocker to save recovery data directly to Active Directory; this is the recommended management method in enterprise environments.

You can also implement BitLocker without a TPM chip. When implemented in this manner there is no startup integrity check. A key is stored on a removable USB memory device, which must be present and supported by the computer's BIOS each time the computer starts up. After the computer has successfully started, the removable USB memory device can be removed and should then be stored in a secure location. Configuring a computer running Windows Server 2008 to use a removable USB memory device as a BitLocker startup key is covered in the second practice at the end of this lesson.

NOTE   **Security is more than BitLocker**

Securing your organization's data requires more than just encrypting your server's hard disk drives. Ensure that your backup tapes are stored in a secure location. Although the data stored on a BitLocker encrypted drive is encoded, the data on backup tapes generally is not. Implementing BitLocker is a bit pointless if you store all of your backup tapes on a shelf in the server room!

BitLocker Volume Configuration

One of the most important things to remember is that a computer must be configured to support BitLocker prior to the installation of Windows Server 2008. The procedure for this is detailed at the start of Practice 2 at the end of this lesson, but involves creating a separate 1.5-GB partition, formatting it, and making it active as the System partition prior to creating a larger partition, formatting it, and then installing the Windows Server 2008 operating system. Figure 1-6 shows a volume configuration that supports BitLocker. If a computer's volumes are not correctly configured prior to the installation of Windows Server 2008, you will need to perform a completely new installation of Windows Server 2008 after repartitioning the volume correctly. For this reason you should partition the hard disk drives of all computers in the environment on which you are going to install Windows Server 2008 with the assumption that at some stage in the future you might need to deploy BitLocker. If BitLocker is not deployed, it has cost you only a few extra minutes of configuration time. If you later decide to deploy BitLocker, you will have saved many hours of work reconfiguring the server to support full hard drive encryption.

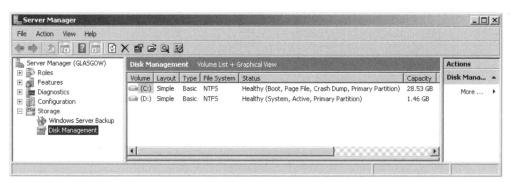

Figure 1-6   Partition scheme that supports BitLocker

The necessity of having specifically configured volumes makes BitLocker difficult to implement on Windows Server 2008 computers that have been upgraded from Windows Server 2003. The necessary partition scheme would have had to be introduced prior to the installation of Windows Server 2003, which in most cases would have occurred before most people were aware of BitLocker.

BitLocker Group Policies

BitLocker group policies are located under the Computer Configuration\Policies\ Administrative Templates\Windows Components\BitLocker Drive Encryption node of a Windows Server 2008 Group Policy object. In the event that the computers you want to deploy BitLocker on do not have TPM chips, you can use the Control Panel Setup: Enable Advanced Startup Options policy, which is shown in Figure 1-7. When this policy is enabled and configured, you can implement BitLocker without a TPM being present. You can also configure this policy to require that a startup code be entered if a TPM chip is present, providing another layer of security.

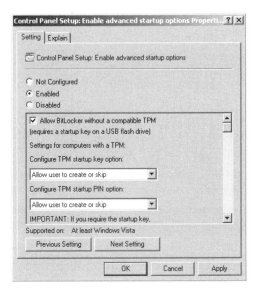

Figure 1-7   Allowing BitLocker without the TPM chip

Other BitLocker policies include:

- **Turn On BitLocker Backup To Active Directory Domain Services**   When this policy is enabled, a computer's recovery key is stored in Active Directory and can be recovered by an authorized administrator.

- **Control Panel Setup: Configure Recovery Folder**   When enabled, this policy sets the default folder to which computer recovery keys can be stored.

- **Control Panel Setup: Configure Recovery Options**   When enabled, this policy can be used to disable the recovery password and the recovery key. If both the recovery password and the recovery key are disabled, the policy that backs up the recovery key to Active Directory must be enabled.

- **Configure Encryption Method**   This policy allows the administrator to specify the properties of the AES encryption method used to protect the hard disk drive.

- **Prevent Memory Overwrite On Restart**   This policy speeds up restarts, but increases the risk of BitLocker being compromised.

- **Configure TMP Platform Validation Profile**   This policy configures how the TMP security hardware protects the BitLocker encryption key.

Encrypting File System vs. BitLocker

Although both technologies implement encryption, there is a big difference between Encrypting File System (EFS) and BitLocker. EFS is used to encrypt individual files and folders and can be used to encrypt these items for different users. BitLocker encrypts the whole hard disk drive. A user with legitimate credentials can log on to a file server that is protected by BitLocker and will be able to read any files that she has permissions for. This user will not, however be able to read files that have been EFS encrypted for other users, even if she is granted permission, because you can only read EFS-encrypted files if you have the appropriate digital certificate. EFS allows organizations to protect sensitive shared files from the eyes of support staff who might be required to change file and folder permissions as a part of their job task, but should not actually be able to review the contents of the file itself. BitLocker provides a transparent form of encryption, visible only when the server is compromised. EFS provides an opaque form of encryption—the content of files that are visible to the person who encrypted them are not visible to anyone else, regardless of what file and folder permissions are set.

Turning Off BitLocker

In some instances you may need to remove BitLocker from a computer. For example, the environment in which the computer is located has been made much more secure and the overhead from the BitLocker process is causing performance problems. Alternatively, you may need to temporarily disable BitLocker so that you can perform maintenance on startup files or the computer's BIOS. As Figure 1-8 shows, you have two options for removing BitLocker from a computer on which it has been implemented: disable BitLocker or decrypt the drive.

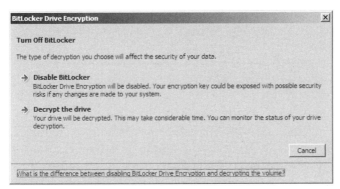

Figure 1-8   Options for removing BitLocker

Disabling BitLocker removes BitLocker protection without decrypting the encrypted volumes. This is useful if a TPM chip is present, but it is necessary to update a computer's BIOS or startup files. If you do not disable BitLocker when performing this type of maintenance, BitLocker—when implemented with a TPM chip—will lock the computer because the diagnostics will detect that the computer has been tampered with. When you disable BitLocker, a plaintext key is written to the hard disk drive. This allows the encrypted hard disk drive to be read, but the presence of the plaintext key means that the computer is insecure. Disabling BitLocker using this method provides no performance increase because the data remains encrypted—it is just encrypted in an insecure way. When BitLocker is re-enabled, this plaintext key is removed and the computer is again secure.

Exam Tip   Keep in mind the conditions under which you might need to disable BitLocker. Also remember the limitations of BitLocker without a TPM 1.2 chip.

Select Decrypt The Drive when you want to completely remove BitLocker from a computer. This process is as time-consuming as performing the initial drive encryption—perhaps more so because more data might be stored on the computer than when the initial encryption occurred. After the decryption process is finished, the computer is returned to its pre-encrypted state and the data stored on it is no longer protected by BitLocker. Decrypting the drive will not decrypt EFS-encrypted files stored on the hard disk drive.

Practice: Installing Windows Server 2008 and Deploying BitLocker

In this set of exercises you will install Windows Server 2008 Enterprise Edition on a computer or virtual machine and configure it to function as a domain controller in the domain contoso.internal. After this process is complete, you will deploy BitLocker on the computer.

Real World

Orin Thomas

Ian and I use virtual machine software extensively when writing Training Kits and we both recommend that you utilize this technology in your own certification studies. Although it is possible to complete all of the practice exercises in this book by installing the evaluation version of Windows Server 2008 Enterprise Edition that you have downloaded from Microsoft's Web site directly onto a spare computer, most exam candidates prefer to use virtual machine software to perform training kit practice exercises. Using virtual machines offers many benefits, including the ability to create restore points that you can roll back to in the event that something goes awry during a practice exercise. It is also simple to have multiple virtual machines active simultaneously, allowing interaction between these virtual computers to occur. Microsoft and other vendors have freely available versions of virtual machine host software available for download. You can obtain a free download of Virtual PC from *http://www.microsoft.com/virtualpc.*

▶ **Exercise 1: Install Windows Server 2008 Enterprise Edition**

In this exercise you will perform the installation and initial configuration of Windows Server 2008. You will start with a clean hardware setup, install the operating system, and then configure the server to function as a domain controller in a new Windows Server 2008 domain. You will do all configuration using the Administrator account. You will perform later practices using the Kim_Akers user account. To complete this exercise, perform the following steps:

1. Start the computer or virtual machine on which you will install the operating system from the Windows Server 2008 Enterprise Edition installation media that you have downloaded from the Microsoft download center at *http://www.microsoft.com/Downloads/Search.aspx.*

2. On the Install Windows page, select your language, time and currency format, and keyboard or input method, and click Next.

3. On the Install Windows page, click Repair Your Computer.

NOTE Unusual steps

It is necessary to perform these unusual steps to configure Windows Server 2008 to support BitLocker. This method allows for the creation of an active system partition that is separate from the partition that Windows Server 2008 will be installed on, allowing for the full encryption of the partition hosting the operating system later in this chapter.

---

4. Ensure that no operating system is selected in the System Recovery Options dialog box and then click Next.

5. In the Choose A Recovery Tool dialog box, shown in Figure 1-9, click Command Prompt.

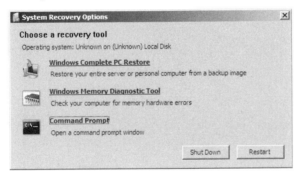

Figure 1-9   Choose a recovery tool

6. In the Command Prompt window, type **diskpart** and press Enter.

7. Type the following commands in order, pressing Enter after each one:

```
select disk 0
clean
create partition primary size=1500
assign letter=S
active
create partition primary
assign letter=C
exit
```

8. Typing **exit** terminates the diskpart utility and returns you to the command prompt. At the command prompt, type the following commands to format the partitions. Press Enter after each command.

```
format c: /y /q /fs:NTFS
format s: /y /q /fs:NTFS
exit
```

9. In the System Recovery Options window, click the close window icon located in the top right corner of the dialog box. This will return you to the Install Windows dialog box. Click Install Now.

10. On the Type Your Product Key For Activation page, shown in Figure 1-10, enter the Windows Server 2008 Enterprise Edition product key.

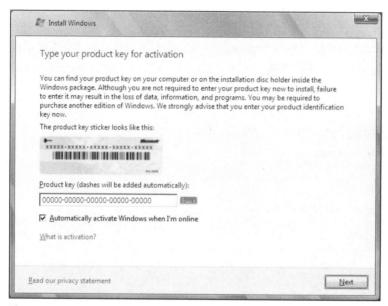

Figure 1-10 Enter the product key

NOTE Automatic Activation

The practice exercises in this book assume that the computer you are installing is not connected either directly or indirectly to the Internet. Therefore, you should clear the Automatic Activation option during installation and then perform activation at a convenient time later.

---

11. Click Next. On the Select The Operating System You Want To Install page, click Windows Server 2008 Enterprise (Full Installation) and then click Next.

12. On the Please Read The License Terms page, review the license and then select the I Accept The License Terms check box. Click Next.

13. On the Which Type Of Installation Do You Want page, click Custom (Advanced).

    Under which conditions would the Upgrade option be available?

    Answer: If you had started the installation from within a compatible edition of Windows Server 2003.

14. On the Where Do You Want To Install Windows page, click Disk 0 Partition 2 and then click Next.

15. The installation process will commence. This process may take up to 20 minutes, depending on the speed of the hardware upon which you are installing the operating system. The computer will automatically restart twice during this period.

16. You will be asked to change the password prior to logging on for the first time. This is where you set the password for the Administrator account. Click OK, enter the password **P@ssw0rd** twice in the dialog box shown in Figure 1-11, and then press Enter. Click OK when you are informed that your password has been changed and you will be logged on.

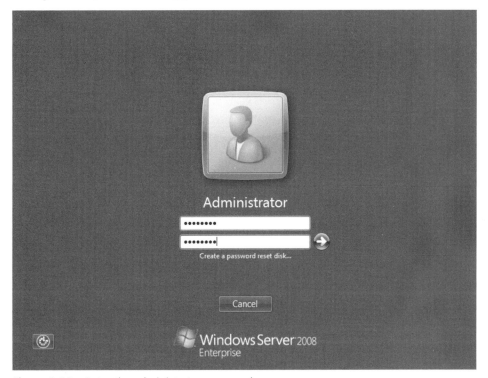

Figure 1-11   Enter the administrator password

17. On the Initial Configuration Tasks page, click Set Time Zone and configure the server to use your local time zone.

18. Click Configure Networking. Right-click the Local Area Connection and click Properties.

19. From the list shown in Figure 1-12, click Internet Protocol Version 4 (TCP/IPv4) and then click the Properties button.

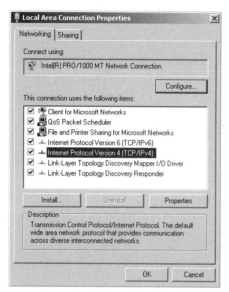

Figure 1-12   Configuring network properties

20. Configure the Internet Protocol Version 4 (TCP/IPv4) Properties dialog box as shown in Figure 1-13 and then click OK. Click Close to close the Local Area Connection Properties. Close the Network Connections window to return to the Initial Configuration Tasks page.

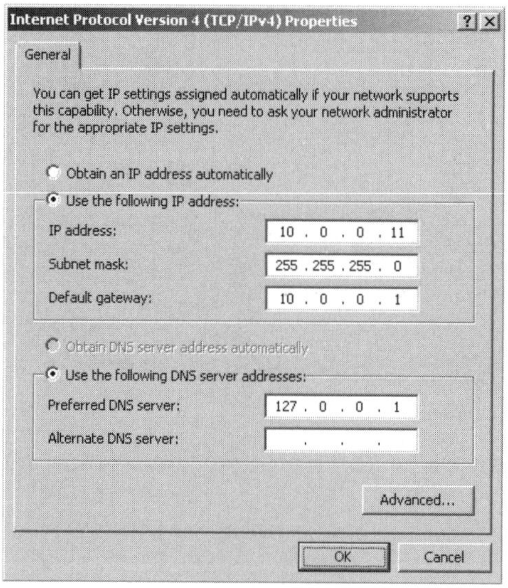

Figure 1-13   IPv4 Properties

21. On the Initial Configuration Tasks page, click Provide Computer Name And Domain. This will open the System Properties dialog box. On the Computer Name tab, click the Change button.

22. In the Computer Name/Domain Changes dialog box, set the Computer Name to **Glasgow** and click OK. Click OK when informed that it will be necessary to restart the computer and click Close to close the System Properties dialog box. Click Restart Now to restart the computer.

23. After the computer has restarted, log on using the Administrator account and the password configured in step 8.

24. Click Start and then click Run. In the Run dialog box type **dcpromo** and then click OK.

NOTE   Active Directory binaries

Issuing the *dcpromo* command will automatically install the relevant files on the computer prior to beginning the domain controller promotion process.

---

25. On the Welcome To The Active Directory Domain Services Installation Wizard page, click Next.

26. On the Choose A Deployment Configuration page, select the Create A New Domain In A New Forest option, as shown in Figure 1-14, and then click Next.

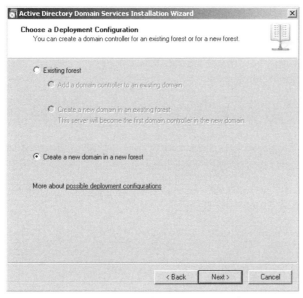

Figure 1-14   Create a new domain in a new forest

27. On the Name the Forest Root Domain page, type the name **contoso.internal** and click Next.

28. On the Set Forest Functional Level page, leave the default Forest Functional level in place and then click Next.

29. On the Set Domain Functional Level page, leave the default Domain Functional level in place and then click Next.

30. Verify that the Additional Domain Controller Options page matches Figure 1-15 and then click Next.

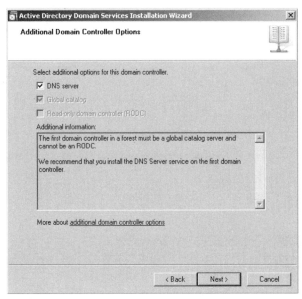

Figure 1-15   Additional Domain Controller Options

31. In the Static IP Assignment warning dialog box, click Yes, The Computer Will Use A Dynamically Assigned IP Address (Not Recommended).

    Why does the Static IP Assignment dialog box appear when you manually set the IP address earlier in the practice exercise?

    Answer: Only the IPv4 address was statically assigned. The interface has an IPv6 link-local address is automatically configured.

32. When presented with the delegation warning, click Yes.

33. On the Location For Database, Log Files, And SYSVOL page accept the default settings and then click Next.

34. Enter the password **P@ssw0rd** twice for the Directory Services Restore Mode Administrator account. Click Next.

35. On the Summary page, review the selections and then click Next. Active Directory will now be configured on the computer. When this process is complete, click Finish and then click Restart Now.

NOTE Adding a client computer

Several of the practice exercises in later chapters require that you use a client computer running Windows Vista or Windows XP to communicate and interact with the Windows Server 2008 computer named Glasgow. This computer can be configured to exist only in a virtual environment. Because you have most likely performed many Windows client installations, only basic configuration information is provided here. You should perform a standard installation, naming the computer Melbourne and giving it the IP address 10.0.0.21 with a subnet mask of 255.255.255.0. Set the DNS server address to 10.0.0.11 and join the computer Melbourne to the Contoso.Internal domain.

▶ **Exercise 2: Configure BitLocker Hard Disk Drive Encryption**

In this practice you will configure the server named Glasgow to use BitLocker full hard disk drive encryption. This practice can not be completed using a virtual machine because BitLocker is not currently supported for virtual machine clients. This practice assumes that the computer does not have a TPM 1.2 or later chip. Instead of storing the BitLocker startup key in the TPM device, a startup key will be stored on a removable USB memory device. After BitLocker has been configured and its functionality demonstrated, it will be removed from the practice computer to simplify subsequent practice exercises in this book.

To complete this practice, perform the following steps:

1. Log onto the computer Glasgow using the Administrator account.

2. From the Administrative Tools menu, open the Server Manager.

3. Right-click the Features node and then click Add Features.

4. On the Select Features page of the Add Features Wizard, select the BitLocker Drive Encryption feature, as shown in Figure 1-16. Click Next and then click Install.

5. Click Close to close the Add Features Wizard. When presented with the Do You Want To Restart Now dialog box, click Yes. The computer will restart.

6. After the computer restarts, log back on using the Administrator account and the password **P@ssw0rd**. The Resume Configuration Wizard will automatically start after the logon process completes. Click Close when the wizard completes.

7. Click Start and then click Run. In the Run dialog box, type **gpedit.msc** and then click OK.

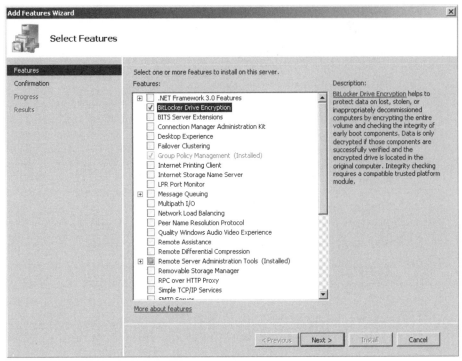

Figure 1-16   Add the BitLocker Drive Encryption feature

8. In the Local Group Policy Editor, navigate to the Local Computer Policy\Administrative Templates\Windows Components\BitLocker Drive Encryption Node.

9. Open the Control Panel Setup: Enable Advanced Startup Options policy, select the Enabled option, select the Allow BitLocker Without A Compatible TPM option, click OK, and then close the Local Group Policy Editor.

10. Open a command prompt and issue the command **gpupdate /force** to apply the policy. Close the command prompt.

11. Verify that a removable USB memory device is connected to the computer.

12. Open Control Panel and then open the BitLocker Drive Encryption item. Under volume C:\ click Turn On BitLocker.

13. At the Warning prompt shown in Figure 1-17, click Continue With BitLocker Drive Encryption.

14. On the Set BitLocker Startup Preferences page, click Require Startup USB Key At Every Startup.

15. On the Save Your Startup Key page, select your removable USB memory device and click Save.

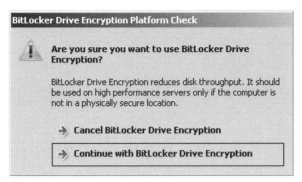

Figure 1-17   BitLocker warning

16. On the Save The Recovery Password page, shown in Figure 1-18, click Save The Password On A USB Drive and select the removable USB memory device that you saved the startup key data on and click Save.

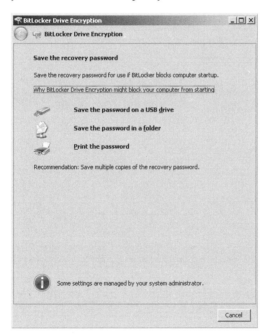

Figure 1-18   Storing the BitLocker Recovery Password

17. Once the recovery password is saved, click Next.

18. On the Encrypt The Volume page, shown in Figure 1-19, ensure that the Run BitLocker System Check item is selected and then click Continue. Ensure that the Windows Server 2008 installation media has been removed from the DVD drive and then click Restart Now. The computer will restart.

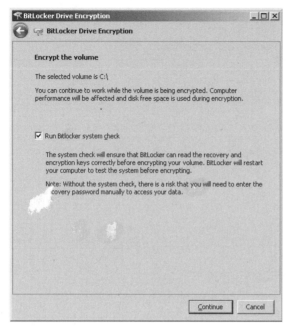

Figure 1-19 Encrypt The Volume

19. Log on using the Administrator account and the password **P@ssw0rd**. After logon you will be informed that your computer does not support BitLocker or that the operating system volume is now being encrypted. If your computer does not support BitLocker, you cannot complete this practice.

NOTE Long process

It is not strictly necessary for you to perform step 20 and decrypt the hard disk drive after the encryption process in step 19 is completed. Having a BitLocker-encrypted computer will not alter the functionality of the other practice exercises in this book. The drawback to retaining an encrypted hard disk drive is that it will be necessary to have the USB memory device present each time the computer starts and that restarts occur regularly during training kit practice exercises.

---

20. After the hard disk encryption process has finished, open the BitLocker Drive Encryption item in Control Panel and verify that BitLocker is activated. If Bit-Locker is activated, the Turn Off BitLocker and Manage BitLocker Keys options will be available, as shown in Figure 1-20.

21. Click Turn Off BitLocker and then click Decrypt The Drive. This will initiate the decryption process, which will take approximately the same amount of time as the encryption process.

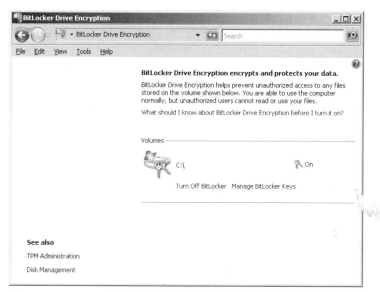

Figure 1-20   BitLocker Drive Encryption

Lesson Summary

- Windows Server 2008 comes in the Standard, Enterprise, Datacenter, Web Server, and Itanium editions. The Enterprise and Datacenter editions support failover clustering, Active Directory Federated Services, and more powerful hardware configurations.

- Server Core is an installation option that allows Windows Server 2008 to be deployed with a smaller attack surface and smaller hardware footprint.

- Upgrades can be initiated only from within Windows Server 2003.

- You cannot upgrade a 32-bit version of Windows Server 2003 to a 64-bit version of Windows Server 2008.

- To implement BitLocker on a computer, you must configure hard disk partitions prior to installing the operating system.

- Computers with TPM chips can use BitLocker to verify that the boot environment has not been tampered with.

- Using Group Policy, you can configure BitLocker to function on computers that do not have TMP chips.

- You can configure group policy so that BitLocker keys are archived within Active Directory.

Lesson Review

You can use the following questions to test your knowledge of the information in Lesson 1, "Planning Windows Server 2008 Installation and Upgrades." The questions are also available on the companion CD if you prefer to review them in electronic form.

NOTE Answers

Answers to these questions and explanations of why each answer choice is correct or incorrect are located in the "Answers" section at the end of the book.

---

1. Your organization has a Windows Server 2003 R2 Standard Edition computer that is used as an intranet server. Which of the following upgrade paths are possible for this computer? (Each correct answer presents a complete solution. Choose two.)

    A. Windows Server 2008 Datacenter edition

    B. Windows Web Server 2008

    C. Windows Server 2008 Enterprise Edition

    D. Windows Server 2008 Standard Edition

    E. Windows Server 2008 Standard Edition (Server Core)

2. Your organization has a computer with a Core 2 Duo processor that has the 32-bit Windows Server 2003 R2 Standard Edition operating system installed. Which of the following versions of Windows Server 2008 can this computer be upgraded to?

    A. 32-bit version of Windows Server 2008 Standard Edition

    B. 64-bit version of Windows Server 2008 Standard Edition

    C. 32-bit version of Windows Server 2008 Datacenter Edition

    D. 64-bit version of Windows Server 2008 Enterprise Edition

3. You have been asked to encrypt the hard disk drive of a Windows Server 2008 file server using BitLocker. The file server has two disk drives. The first disk has a single volume that hosts the operating system. The second disk has a single volume that hosts the shared files. The computer's motherboard has an activated TPM 1.2 chip and a TCG compliant BIOS. What steps do you need to take to enable BitLocker to encrypt the volume hosting the operating system and the volume hosting the shared files?

    A. Configure the appropriate group policy.

    B. Repartition the disk hosting the operating system volume and reinstall Windows Server 2008.

    C. Deactivate the TPM chip.

    D. Upgrade the TPM chip.

4. You are in the process of configuring BitLocker for a file server that will be located at a branch office. The server's hard disk drive is partitioned so that it starts from a system volume that is separate from the operating system volume. The computer does not have a TPM chip, so BitLocker will be implemented using a USB startup key. After the BitLocker feature is installed, you open the BitLocker Control Panel item and are presented with a screen identical to Figure 1-21.

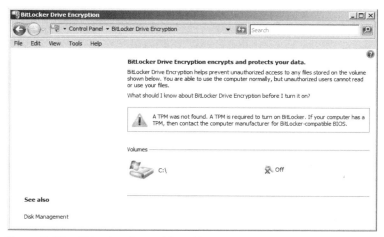

Figure 1-21 BitLocker Control Panel item

  Which of the following steps must you take so that you can enable BitLocker on this computer?

    A. Insert a removable USB memory device.

    B. Upgrade the computer's BIOS.

    C. Configure local Group Policy settings.

    D. Install the BitLocker feature.

5. Which edition of Windows Server 2008 would you choose if you wanted to deploy an Exchange Server 2007 clustered mailbox server, which requires that a failover cluster be configured prior to the installation of Exchange?

    A. Windows Web Server 2008 (x64)

    B. Windows Server 2008 Standard Edition (x64)

    C. Windows Server 2008 Enterprise Edition (x64)

    D. Windows Server 2008 Standard Edition (x86)

Lesson 2: Automated Server Deployment

As an experienced systems administrator, you probably have server deployment down to a fine art. Rather than having to sit down and click through a series of dialog boxes, you have probably performed the process so often that you could do it with your eyes closed. In this lesson you will learn what tools you can utilize to create XML answer files for the Windows Server 2008 installation process and how to install and configure Windows Deployment Services, a service that allows you to deploy operating system images to compatible clients over the network.

After this lesson, you will be able to:

- Create and use an unattended XML file to install Windows Server 2008.
- Schedule the deployment of Windows Server 2008 using operating systems and Windows Deployment Services.

Estimated lesson time: 40 minutes

Windows Server 2008 Answer Files

An answer file allows you to specify specific setup options such as how to partition hard disk drives, the location of the Windows Server 2008 image that is to be installed, and the product key. The Windows Server 2008 answer file is usually called autounattended.xml. This is the filename that the Windows Server 2008 installation process automatically looks for during setup in an attempt to initiate an unattended installation. As opposed to answer files used with previous versions of the Windows Server operating system, the Windows Server 2008 answer file uses XML format. As an administrator you will almost always create this file using the Windows System Image Manager (Windows SIM) tool. The Windows SIM tool is included with the Windows Automated Installation Kit (Windows AIK or WAIK). Although you can create an answer file using a text editor, the complex XML syntax of the unattended installation file makes the Windows AIK tools a more efficient use of your time. Another benefit of the Windows AIK tools is that they allow you to verify that an unattended answer file actually produces the desired result.

To create an answer file using the Windows System Image Manager, perform the following steps:

1. Start Windows System Image Manager. This application is included in the Windows Automated Installation Kit, which can be downloaded from Microsoft's Web site.

MORE INFO   **Download the Windows AIK**

You can download the Windows AIK from the following location:
http://go.microsoft.com/fwlink/?LinkId=79385.

2. Copy the file \Sources\install.wim from the Windows Server 2008 installation media to a temporary directory on the Windows Server 2008 computer on which you have installed the Windows AIK.

3. Click the File menu and then click Select Windows Image. Navigate to the temporary directory where you copied install.wim and select the file. This file contains all editions and versions of Windows Server 2008 that can be installed from the installation media.

4. You will be prompted to select an image in the Windows Image file. Select Server Enterprise and then click OK.

5. When prompted to create a catalog file, click Yes. When prompted by the User Account Control dialog box, click Continue. The Catalog file will be created.

6. From the File menu, select New Answer File.

7. By selecting the appropriate component in the Windows Image, you can configure the properties for that component. Figure 1-22 shows the configuration settings that allow the computer being installed to automatically join the domain contoso.internal with the specified set of credentials.

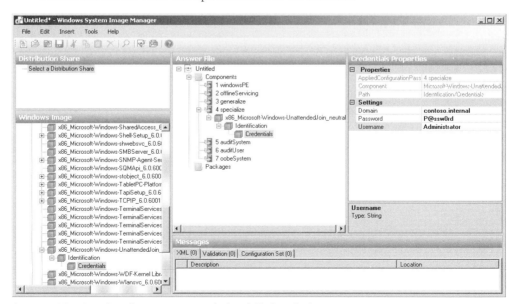

Figure 1-22   Creating the autounattended.xml file in Windows System Image Manager

8. When the answer file is saved, it is automatically validated against the operating system image that has been loaded.

MORE INFO   **Unattended files**

For more information on the creation and configuration of unattended installation files, consult the Unattended Windows Setup Reference, which is accessible from the Help menu in Windows System Image Manager.

Running an Unattended Installation

Traditionally, unattended installations used floppy diskettes that contained the unattended text file. Most modern server hardware does not include a floppy disk drive, so—as mentioned earlier—the Windows Server 2008 setup routine will automatically check all of the server's local volumes for a file called autounattended.xml. This automatic check also includes any removable USB memory devices attached to the computer.

In the event that the installation will use setup files located on a network share, it will be necessary to boot into Windows PE, connect to the network share, and then issue the command **setup.exe /unattend:x:\autounattended.xml** (where x:\ is the path of the autounattended.xml file). In "Windows Deployment Services" later in this lesson, you will learn how to use unattended answer files with Windows Deployment Services.

Quick Check

1. Which tool should you use to generate an unattended XML answer file?

2. When starting from the Windows Server 2008 installation media to perform a setup on a computer without a floppy drive, how can you ensure that the autounattended.xml file will be recognized by setup?

Quick Check Answer

1. Windows System Image Manager from the Windows Automated Installation Kit (WAIK or Windows AIK).

2. Place the autounattended.xml file on a removable USB memory device that is connected to the server. An alternative is copying it to the volume on which you will install Windows Server 2008, although this requires more preparation than using the USB device.

Windows Deployment Services

Windows Deployment Services is a role you can add to a Windows Server 2008 computer that allows remote deployment of Windows Server 2008 and Windows Vista. You can also deploy earlier versions of Microsoft's operating systems using Windows Deployment Services (WDS), but this lesson concentrates on deploying Windows Server 2008 using this technology.

WDS requires that a client computer have a PXE-compliant network card. If a client computer does not have a PXE-compliant network card, you will need to use another method—such as a network installation using Windows PE— to perform a remote installation. The process works when the computer with the PXE-based network card starts and then locates the WDS server. If the client is authorized and multicast transmissions have been configured, the client will automatically begin the setup process. Unicast transmissions, which are less efficient when multiple clients are involved are enabled once an operating system image is installed. If an autounattended.xml answer file has not been installed on the WDS server, this installation will proceed normally, requiring input from the administrator. The only difference between a WDS-based installation and a normal installation is that the server appears to be starting from the Windows Server 2008 installation media over the network rather than starting from the media located in a local DVD-ROM drive.

Windows Deployment Services can be installed on a Windows Server 2008 computer only under the following conditions:

■ The computer on which WDS is deployed is a member of an Active Directory domain. A DNS server is required, although this is implied by the existence of the domain.

■ An authorized DHCP server is present on the network.

■ An NTFS partition is available for storing operating system images.

You cannot deploy WDS on a computer running a Server Core edition of Windows Server 2008. After you install Windows Deployment Services, you need to configure it before it can be activated. You can do this by using the Windows Deployment Services Configuration Wizard, which is covered in practice 2 at the end of this lesson, or by using the WDSUtil.exe command-line utility.

If the WDS server is collocated with the DHCP server, it is necessary to configure WDS not to listen on port 67. If you do not do this, WDS and DHCP will have a conflict. It is also important to configure the WDS server to add option tag 60, as shown in Figure 1-23, so that PXE clients are able to detect the presence of a WDS server.

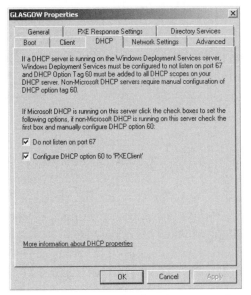

Figure 1-23   DHCP tab of WDS server settings

The Client tab of a WDS server's properties, shown in Figure 1-24, allows you to specify a default unattended installation file for each specific architecture. If the autounattended.xml file is not specified for the architecture of Windows Server 2008 that you are installing, the installation will require the normal amount of manual input.

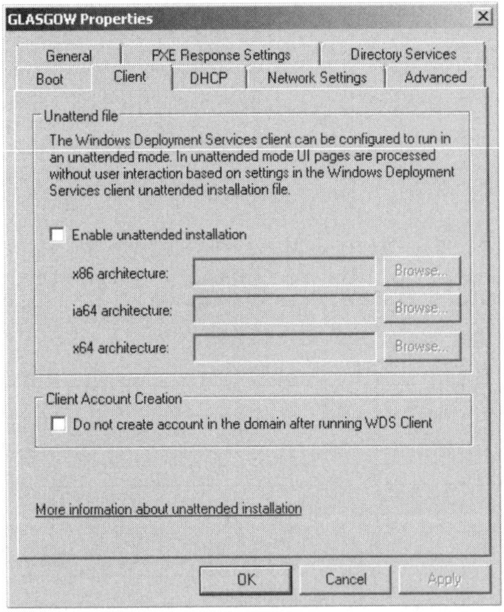

Figure 1-24   You can specify default unattended installation files on the WDS server

Some network environments will have services such as teleconferencing and video-casting that already use IP addresses in the multicast range. You can use the Network Settings tab, shown in Figure 1-25, to configure the multicast IP address range used by WDS and the UDP ports that will be used by the multicast server. You can also specify a network profile that will limit the amount of bandwidth that WDS multicast transmissions consume.

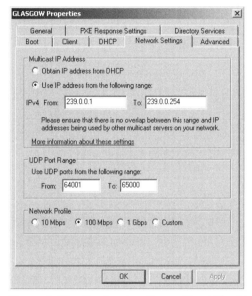

Figure 1-25   Configuring the multicast IP address

You can also configure the PXE response policy by configuring the WDS server settings. The first setting to configure is the PXE Response Delay. You configure this setting when you want to specify the order in which WDS servers respond to PXE requests. You can configure three PXE response settings:

- Do Not Respond To Any Client Computer. WDS does not respond to PXE requests.

- Respond Only To Known Client Computers. This option is used if clients have been pre-staged in Active Directory.

- Respond To All (Known And Unknown) Client Computers. This setting has an additional option allowing for administrators to manually approve unknown clients.

Multicast, Scheduled, and Automatic Deployment

Multicast allows organizations to more efficiently use their network bandwidth, allowing an operating system image to be transmitted over the network once to multiple installation clients. For example, if you are deploying 20 Windows Server 2008 computers, you save significant bandwidth in transmitting one installation image across the network (approximately 1.5 GB of data) compared to transmitting all 20 (approximately 60 GB of data). You can also configure multicast deployment to use only a specific amount of the network's bandwidth. Multicast deployment is supported only in network environments where the routers support multicast transmissions.

You can also schedule deployments. This allows the transmission of installation image data to occur at a predetermined time. For example, you could configure deployment to occur during off-peak hours when the transmission of a significant amount of data would have little impact on a network's day-to-day operation. Alternatively, you can configure a scheduled multicast to occur when a specific number of clients are ready to receive an image. You can also combine these settings. For example, Figure 1-26 shows a multicast transmission that will occur at 3:00 A.M. if 10 clients are ready to receive the image. When you combine WDS with an unattended installation file, you can power up a set of computers prior to leaving the office for an evening and come back the next day to find that each has been automatically installed and configured during the overnight lull in network activity. An auto-cast means that a multicast transmission will start as soon as a client requests an install image. Auto-cast is most often used for one-off deployments rather than large-scale deployments where scheduled-cast is more appropriate.

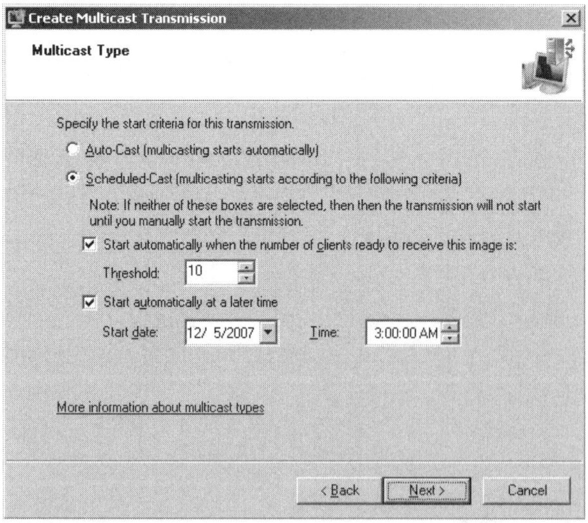

Figure 1-26   Configuring a multicast transmission

Exam Tip   Remember that a deployment scheduled to occur in the middle of the night needs an answer file; otherwise, the deployment process will stall when administrator input is required.

Windows Deployment Services Images

Windows Deployment Services uses two different types of images: install images and boot images. Install images are the operating system images that will be deployed to Windows Server 2008 or Windows Vista client computers. A default installation image is located in the \Sources directory of the Windows Vista and Windows Server 2008 installation DVDs. If you are using WDS to deploy Windows Server 2008 to computers with different processor architectures, you will need to add separate installation images for each architecture to the WDS server. Architecture-specific images can be found on the architecture-specific installation media. For example, the Itanium image is located on the Itanium installation media and the x64 default installation image is located on the x64 installation media. Although you can create custom images, you only need to have one image per processor architecture. For example, deploying Windows Server 2008 Enterprise Edition x64 to a computer with 1 x64 processor and to a computer with 8 x64 processors in SMP configuration only requires access to the default x64 installation image. Practice exercise 2 at the end of this lesson covers the specifics of adding a default installation image to a WDS server.

Boot images are used to boot a client computer prior to the installation of the operating system image. When a computer boots off a boot image over the network, a menu is presented that displays the possible images that can be deployed to the computer from the WDS server. The Windows Server 2008 boot.wim file allows for advanced deployment options; you should use this file instead of the boot.wim file that is available on the Windows Vista installation media.

In addition to the basic boot image, two separate types of additional boot images can be configured for use with WDS. The capture image is a boot image that starts the WDS capture utility. This utility is used with a reference computer, prepared with the sysprep utility, as a method of capturing the reference computer's image for deployment with WDS. The second type of additional boot image is the discover image. Discover images are used to deploy images to computers that are not PXE-enabled or on networks that do not allow PXE. These images are written to CD, DVD, or USB media and the computer is booted off the media rather than off the PXE network card, which is the traditional method of using WDS.

MORE INFO   **More on managing images**

For more information on how to manage WDS images, consult the following TechNet article: *http://technet2.microsoft.com/windowsserver2008/en/library/06fd5868-cf55-401f-8058-2339 ab1d4cbe1033.mspx.*

WDS and Product Activation

Although product activation does not need to occur during the actual installation process, administrators considering using WDS to automate deployment should also consider using volume activation to automate activation. Volume activation provides a simple centralized method that systems administrators can use for the activation of large numbers of deployed servers. Volume activation allows for two types of keys and three methods of activation. The key types are the Multiple Activation Key (MAK) and the Key Management Services (KMS) key.

Multiple Activation Keys allow activation of a specific number of computers. Each successful activation depletes the activation pool. For example, a MAK key that has 100 activations allows for the activation of 100 computers. The Multiple Activation Key can use the MAK Proxy Activation and the MAK Independent Activation activation methods. MAK Proxy Activation uses a centralized activation request on behalf of multiple products using a single connection to Microsoft's activation servers. MAK Independent Activation requires that each computer activates individually against Microsoft's activation servers.

Key Management Service keys allow for computers to be activated in a managed environment without requiring individual connections to Microsoft. KMS keys enable the Key Management Service on a server and computers in the environment connect to that computer to perform activation. Organizations using KMS should have two KMS servers deployed, one of which will function as a backup host to ensure redundancy. KMS requires at least 25 computers connecting before activation can occur, and activation must be renewed by reconnecting to the KMS server every 180 days.

You can use KMS and MAK in conjunction with one another. The number of computers, how often they connect to the network, and whether there is Internet connectivity determines which solution you should deploy. You should deploy MAK if substantial numbers of computers do not connect to the network for more than 180 days. If there is no Internet connectivity and more than 25 computers, you should deploy KMS. If there is no Internet connectivity and less than 25 computers, you will need to use MAK and activate each system over the telephone.

Rollback Preparation

In the best of all worlds each upgrade works flawlessly, bringing increased functionality, stability, and performance to the computer that has been upgraded. In reality you will find the best approach to take as a systems administrator is to assume that Murphy's Law is always in effect: Anything that can go wrong probably will. Prior to upgrading a computer from Windows Server 2003 to Windows Server 2008, you should have a rollback plan in place in case something goes dramatically wrong.

Rollback is often necessary when a server's functionality is compromised by the upgrade. For example, a custom application may be deployed on a Windows Server 2003 computer that is rendered nonfunctional by upgrading to Windows Server 2008. If the custom application is critical to a business's function, you will need to roll back to Windows Server 2003 so that the application can continue to be used.

During the upgrade process you can roll back to the existing Windows Server 2003 installation. However, after a successful logon has occurred, the upgrade cannot be rolled back. The drawback of this situation is that often you will not be aware of problems with an upgrade until after successful logon occurs. The only way to roll back is to format the hard disk drive and restore the Windows Server 2003 backups that you took prior to attempting the upgrade. An alternative to formatting the hard disk drive and restoring Windows Server 2003 is to deploy Windows Server 2003 through Windows Server 2008's virtualization feature. Virtualization is covered in more detail in Chapter 5, "Terminal Services and Application and Server Virtualization."

Prior to upgrading a computer from Windows Server 2003 to Windows Server 2008, take the following precautions:

- Perform an Automated System Recovery Backup of the Windows Server 2003 computer.
- Perform a full backup of all data, including system state data.
- Have a plan to roll the upgrade back in the event that something goes wrong.

In the event that you need to remove Windows Server 2008 from a computer that has been upgraded from Windows Server 2003, the quickest way to restore the prior functionality is to apply the Windows Server 2003 ASR backup, restore the system state and user data, and then reinstall all extra applications.

Practice: Installing and Configuring the Windows Deployment Services Role

In this set of exercises you will install and configure Windows Deployment Services, import operating system images from the Windows Server 2008 installation media, and configure a multicast transmission to deploy these operating system images to appropriately configured PXE clients.

▶ **Exercise 1: Prepare for the Installation of the Windows Deployment Services Server Role**

In this short exercise you will perform several housekeeping exercises that will prepare the server for the installation of the Windows Deployment Services server role. This includes the installation of the DHCP server service and the creation of a user account that has limited, but not complete, administrative rights. This user account mirrors the IT professionals whose job role intersects with the types of tasks tested on the 70-646 exam. This account has administrative rights, but is not a member of the Schema Admins or Enterprise Admins groups. To complete this exercise, perform the following steps:

1. Log on to the domain controller Glasgow using the Administrator account.

2. Open Active Directory Users And Computers from the Administrative Tools menu.

3. In the Users container, create a new user account called **Kim_Akers**. Assign Kim's user account the password **P@ssw0rd** and set the password to never expire.

NOTE   For Training Kit convenience only

In a real-world environment you should ensure that administrator accounts have the same password expiration policy as all other user accounts.

---

4. Add the Kim Akers user account to the Domain Admins security group. Do not add the Kim Akers user account to any other administrative group at this time.

5. Log off server Glasgow and log back on using the Kim_Akers account.

6. If the Server Manager console does not open automatically, open it using the Quick Launch toolbar or from the Administrative Tools menu.

7. Right-click the Roles node and then click Add Roles. This will launch the Add Roles Wizard.

8. On the Before You Begin page, click Next.

9. On the Select One Server Roles page, select DHCP Server and then click Next.

10. On the Introduction To DHCP Server page, click Next.

11. On the Network Connection Bindings page, accept the interface 10.0.0.11 as the one that will accept DHCP requests and click Next.

12. Verify that the IPv4 DNS Server Settings match those displayed in Figure 1-27 and then click Next.

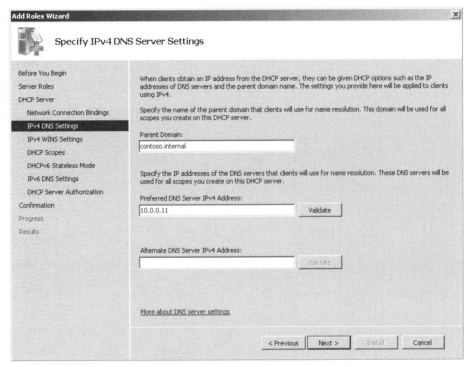

Figure 1-27 DNS settings for DHCP server

13. On the IPv4 WINS Settings page, accept the defaults and click Next.

14. On the DHCP Scopes page, click Add.

15. In the Add Scope dialog box, add entries so that the dialog box appears as shown in Figure 1-28. Click OK and then click Next.

16. Review the default DHCPv6 Stateless Mode settings and then click Next.

17. Review the default DHCP IPv6 DNS Server settings and then click Next.

18. Verify that the Use Current Credentials setting is selected and that the User Name is set to CONTOSO\kim_akers user account. Click Next and then, on the Confirmation page, click Install. The installation of the DHCP Server role will commence.

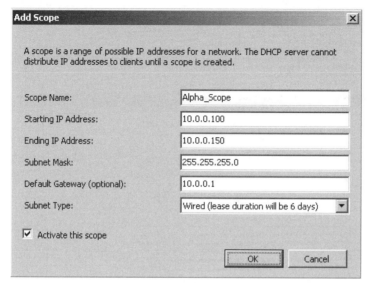

Figure 1-28   DHCP Scope settings

19. When the DHCP Server role has been installed, click Close to dismiss the Add Roles Wizard.

20. Log off the computer.

▶ **Exercise 2: Install the Windows Deployment Services Server Role and add Image Files**

In this exercise you will install the Windows Deployment Services server role and add image files from the Windows Server 2008 installation media. You should ensure that the Windows Server 2008 installation media is located in your computer's DVD-ROM drive. To complete this exercise, perform the following steps:

1. Log on to server Glasgow using the Kim_Akers user account.

2. If the Server Roles console does not automatically open, open it using the shortcut on the Quick Launch toolbar or from the Administrative Tools menu.

3. Right-click the Roles node and then click Add Roles.

4. If you are presented with the Before You Begin page of the Add Roles Wizard, click Next; otherwise, proceed to step 5.

5. On the Select Server Roles page, select the Windows Deployment Services role and then click Next.

6. Review the Things To Note section of the Overview Of Windows Deployment Services page shown in Figure 1-29 and then click Next.

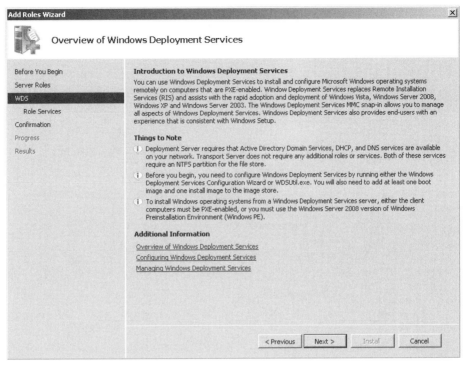

Figure 1-29 WDS overview

7. On the Select Role Services page, ensure that both the Deployment Server and Transport Server role services are selected. Click Next and then click Install. The installation of Windows Deployment Services will commence. When the installation completes, click Close.

8. In the Administrative Tools menu, click Windows Deployment Services. In the User Account Control dialog box, click Continue.

9. On the Windows Deployment Services console, right-click the Servers node and then click Add Server.

10. In the Add Server(s) dialog box, ensure that Local Computer is selected and then click OK.

11. Right-click server Glasgow.contoso.internal and then click Configure Server. This will start the Windows Deployment Services Configuration Wizard. Click Next.

12. Accept the default Remote Installation Folder Location of C:\RemoteInstall and then click Next.

13. On the System Volume Warning, note the recommendation that the remote installation folder should be placed on a volume different than that of the system volume and click Yes.

14. Ensure that the Do Not Listen On Port 67 and Configure DHCP Option 60 To "PXEClient" options are selected, as shown in Figure 1-30, and then click Next.

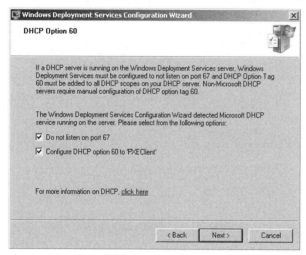

Figure 1-30 DHCP Option 60

15. On the PXE Server Initial Settings page, select the option Respond Only To Known Client Computers and click Finish.

16. On the Configuration Complete page, ensure that the Add Images To The Windows Deployment Server Now option is selected and click Finish.

NOTE Installation media required

Ensure that the Windows Server 2008 installation media is present in the computer's DVD drive prior to attempting step 17. The images will require 1.8 GB of disk space.

---

17. In the Windows Image Files Location dialog box, click Browse, navigate to the Sources directory on the DVD drive, click OK, and then click Next.

18. On the Image Group page, verify that the Create A New Image Group option is selected and that the new image group name will be ImageGroup1. Click Next.

19. In the Review Settings dialog box, verify that 1 boot image and 6 install images will be transferred to the server, as shown in Figure 1-31, and then click Next. Images will now be transferred from the Windows Server 2008 DVD to the c:\RemoteInstall folder.

20. When the images have been transferred to the server, click Finish.

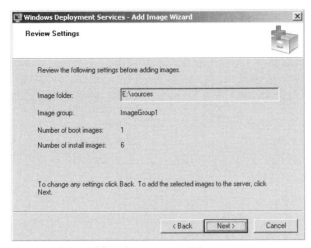

Figure 1-31 Adding images to WDS

21. In the Windows Deployment Services console, right-click the Multicast Transmissions node and then select Create Multicast Transmission.

22. On the Transmission Name page, type **TestAlpha** and click Next.

23. On the Select Image page, verify that ImageGroup1 is selected and then click Next.

24. On the Multicast Type page, shown in Figure 1-32, ensure that Scheduled-Cast is selected. Select the Start Automatically When The Number Of Clients Ready To Receive This Image Is option. Set the threshold value to 10. Click Next and then click Finish.

25. Close the Windows Deployment Services console and then log off.

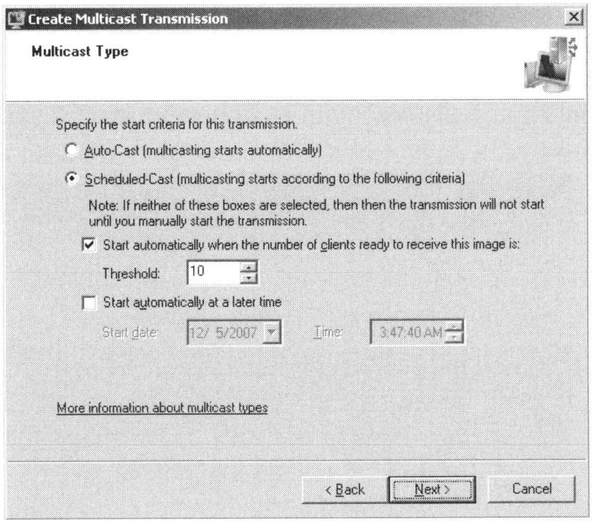

Figure 1-32 Ten clients are required before this multicast starts

Lesson Summary

- A Windows Server 2008 answer file allows an administrator to automate some or all of the installation process by providing information to the setup routine on the components and configuration settings necessary for the installation of Windows Server 2008.

- The answer file, typically called autounattend.xml, is created using the Windows System Image Manager (Windows SIM), a component of the Windows Automated Installation Kit (WAIK). WAIK is a freely available add-on to Windows Server 2008 that can be downloaded from Microsoft's Web site.

- You can store answer files on a removable USB memory device, where they will automatically be detected by the Windows Server 2008 setup routine. Alternatively they can be located on a network share and called if a network setup is started from within Windows PE.

- You can use Windows Deployment Services (WDS) to deploy Windows Server 2008 operating system images to PXE clients using multicast transmissions. The advantage of a multicast transmission is that the image data is transmitted only once over the network, minimizing bandwidth use.

- You can schedule multicast transmissions to occur at particular times, when a particular number of clients have connected to the WDS server, or a combination of both. It is also possible to create an Auto-Cast, which begins automatically.

- If the WDS server also hosts the DHCP Server service, you must configure WDS to listen on a separate port and to configure DHCP option tag 60 for all scopes.

- Volume activation allows for the use of two types of activation keys. The Multiple Activation Key (MAK) is a single key that you can use to activate multiple computers. This can occur on a per-computer basis or through a MAK proxy. The Key Management Service (KMS) key requires a minimum of 25 computers that need to connect to the KMS server every 180 days. KMS is most suitable in environments where there is no Internet connectivity.

Lesson Review

You can use the following questions to test your knowledge of the information in Lesson 2, "Automated Server Deployment." The questions are also available on the companion CD if you prefer to review them in electronic form.

NOTE Answers

Answers to these questions and explanations of why each answer choice is correct or incorrect are located in the "Answers" section at the end of the book.

1. You have just installed Windows Server 2008 on a computer on which you intend to deploy the Windows Deployment Services (WDS) server role. Which of the following requirements must be met prior to installing the WDS server role? (Each correct answer presents part of the solution. Choose three.)

   A. The computer must be made a member of an Active Directory domain.

   B. An authorized DHCP server must be present in the network environment.

   C. A DNS server must be present in the network environment.

   D. The Application Server role must be installed on the Windows Server 2008 computer.

2. Which of the following environments allows you to initiate an unattended installation?

   A. Windows PE 2.0

   B. Windows NT Boot Disk

   C. MS DOS Boot Disk

   D. Windows Server 2008 Installation Media

3. You have just deployed the Windows Deployment Services server role on a computer that functions as a domain controller, DHCP server, and DNS server. When you try to start a server with a PXE network card, you are unable to connect to the PXE server on WDS. Which of the following should you do to try to resolve this issue?

   A. Configure the DHCP settings in the Windows Deployment Services server properties.

   B. Configure DHCP settings on the DHCP Server console.

   C. Configure DNS settings on the DNS Server Console.

   D. Configure the client settings in the Windows Deployment Services server properties.

4. You have configured a multicast transmission in Windows Deployment Services (WDS) to start at 7:00 pm on Friday night as soon as 10 clients are ready to

receive the image. Your WDS server is located in a server room downstairs and the 10 computers on which you are going to install Windows Server 2008 are located in the staging room, next to your fourth-floor office. The server room and the rest of the building are on separate subnets. DNS and DHCP in your environment are hosted on a different server to the WDS server. You have configured the WDS server with an appropriate unattended installation file. You stay at the office to verify that the deployment starts correctly, but find that it does not. Which of the following changes will be necessary before you can get this method of deployment to function?

   A. Update DNS zones to ensure that they are Active Directory Integrated.

   B. Configure a special IPv6 DHCP scope for PXE clients.

   C. Configure a special IPv6 DHCP scope for PXE clients.

   D. Replace the router with one that supports multicast.

5. You have 15 Windows Server 2008 server images to deploy to clients using Windows Deployment Services (WDS). All servers need to be configured in an almost identical manner. None of the servers have floppy disk drives or optical media drives. How can you configure WDS as to minimize the amount of manual intervention required for the installation of these servers?

   A. Place an Unattended XML file on a shared folder.

   B. Configure the properties of the Multicast transmission within WDS.

   C. Configure an Unattended XML file within the WDS server's properties.

   D. Place an Unattended XML file on a removable USB device and connect it to each server.

Chapter Review

To further practice and reinforce the skills you learned in this chapter, you can perform the following tasks:

■ Review the chapter summary.

■ Review the list of key terms introduced in this chapter.

■ Complete the case scenarios. These scenarios set up real-world situations involving the topics of this chapter and ask you to create a solution.

■ Complete the suggested practices.

■ Take a practice test.

Chapter Summary

■ Determining which edition of Windows Server 2008 is appropriate requires understanding needs such as hardware requirements, clustering requirements, and what roles the server will need to provide.

■ Windows Server 2008 is traditionally deployed by using DVD-ROM installation media. You can also use Windows PE to boot into an environment with a network share containing the Windows Server 2008 installation files, although this is generally only done when a PXE network adapter is not available and WDS cannot be used.

■ BitLocker requires a very specific hard disk partitioning scheme to be implemented prior to operating system deployment. If this partitioning scheme is not implemented, you will need to remove any installed operating system and partition the hard disk correctly prior to reinstalling and deploying BitLocker.

■ BitLocker can be deployed without a TPM 1.2 compatible chip as long as the Group Policy that enables the BitLocker key to be stored on a removable USB memory device is enabled and the computer's BIOS supports accessing USB memory devices prior to operating system startup.

■ Windows Server 2008 answer files are usually called autounattended.xml and are generated using the System Image Manager, a tool available in the Windows AIK. You can configure WDS to use autounattended.xml to automate the installation process.

■ Windows Deployment Services allows operating system images to be deployed to multiple computers with PXE network cards using scheduled multicast transmissions. Multicast transmissions minimize the amount of bandwidth used, and scheduling allows for the disruption of operating system image transmission to occur during periods of low network utilization.

Key Terms

Do you know what these key terms mean? You can check your answers by looking up the terms in the glossary at the end of the book.

- Boot partition
- DHCP
- Multicast
- PXE
- System partition
- Windows PE

Case Scenarios

In the following case scenarios, you will apply what you have learned about planning server installs and upgrades. You can find answers to these questions in the "Answers" section at the end of this book.

Case Scenario 1: Contoso's Migration to Windows Server 2008

Contoso is in the process of moving their network infrastructure to Windows Server 2008 from Windows Server 2003 under the direction of Windows Server 2008 Enterprise Administrators. In several of the situations involved in the migration plan the staff at Contoso would welcome your advice on the specifics of implimentation. The situations in which they wish to ask your opinion include:

1. Five of Contoso's branch office servers will be updated so that they are running the Server Core installation option of Windows Server 2008 Standard Edition. These servers are currently running Windows Server 2003 Standard Edition. Each server has a 2GHz Core 2 Duo processor, 4 GB of RAM and 1 TB of free hard disk space. What plans would you make to meet this goal?

2. What plans should be made to prepare for the deployment of BitLocker on five servers that will function as read-only domain controllers?

3. Which edition of Windows Server 2008 would be most appropriate to deploy on the Contoso screened subnet given that the only functionality the server requires is hosting the corporate Web site?

Case Scenario 2: Tailspin Toys Automates Windows Server 2008 Deployment

Tailspin Toys is a toy aircraft manufacturer with an aging network infrastructure. Determined to modernize, Tailspin Toys will be deploying a significant number of Windows Server 2008 computers as a part of a comprehensive IT infrastructure upgrade. You have been brought in as a consultant by Tailspin Toys to assist them with planning the deployment of all of these new server computers.

1. The physical infrastructure of Tailspin Toys network is almost a decade old. Which important part of the infrastructure might have to be upgraded or replaced prior to attempting to deploy Windows Server 2008 using multicast transmissions?

2. If the server that will host the WDS role also hosts the DHCP Server role, what steps need to be taken?

3. You have 10 servers that you want to use WDS to install. You are concerned that the multicast transmission will begin before you have all 10 servers ready and you want to avoid multiple transmissions. What steps can you take to ensure that this does not occur?

Suggested Practices

To help you successfully master the exam objectives presented in this chapter, complete the following tasks.

Plan Server Installations and Upgrades

If you have the available hardware or virtual machine capacity and you want to further investigate automated server deployment, perform the following practice exercises based on what you have learned in this chapter:

- **Practice 1: Install the Evaluation Edition of Windows Server Core** Install the evaluation edition of Windows Server Core.

- **Practice 2: Configure Server Core Server Roles** Add the Windows Server Core computer to the domain created in the practice exercise using the command-line tools discussed in this chapter.

  Add the IIS server role to the Windows Server core computer.

Plan For Automated Server Deployment

If you have the available hardware or virtual machine capacity and you want to further investigate automated server deployment, perform the following practice exercises based on what you have learned in this chapter:

- **Practice 1: Deploy the Windows AIK**   Download and install the Windows Automated Installation Kit from Microsoft's Web site.

- **Practice 2: Create a Custom Image**   Use Windows System Image Manager, a component of the Windows Automated Installation Kit, to create a custom image based on one of the Windows Server 2008 installation images.

- **Practice 3: Create an Unattended Installation File**   Use the Windows System Image Manager, a component of the Windows Automated Installation Kit, to create an answer file for the installation of Windows Server 2008.

Take a Practice Test

The practice tests on this book's companion CD offer many options. For example, you can test yourself on just one exam objective, or you can test yourself on all the 70-646 certification exam content. You can set up the test so that it closely simulates the experience of taking a certification exam, or you can set it up in study mode so that you can look at the correct answers and explanations after you answer each question.

MORE INFO   **Practice tests**

For details about all the practice test options available, see the section "How to Use the Practice Tests" in this book's Introduction.

Chapter 2
Configuring Network Connectivity

Internet Protocol (IP) has been used to successfully implement network connectivity on internal networks and on the Internet for many years. Internet Protocol version 4 (IPv4) was defined in Request For Comment (RFC) 791, published in 1981, and has not changed substantially since. IPv4 is a robust protocol implemented throughout most of the current Internet; the vast majority of workstations and servers have IPv4 addresses, typically provided by Dynamic Host Configuration Protocol (DHCP) servers or Automatic Private IP Addressing (APIPA).

However, the Internet has expanded hugely since 1981, and this has led to the following problems related to the use of IPv4 and specified requirements for its eventual replacement:

- The likely exhaustion of IPv4 address space
- Maintaining large routing tables on Internet backbone routers
- The requirement for simpler and more automatic configuration of IP addresses and other configuration settings that do not rely on DHCP
- The requirement for secure, end-to-end encryption implemented by default
- The requirement for better support for real-time delivery of data

This chapter discusses how IPv6 addresses these problems and meets these requirements. IPv6 was available for previous Windows Server operating systems but needed to be installed. It is available by default on Windows Server 2008 (and also on Windows Vista, where it is used in peer-to-peer networking).

However, IPv4 is not about to disappear in the near future. Most of the Internet still uses IPv4. Therefore, IPv6 must be compatible with IPv4. This chapter discusses IPv4-to-IPv6 transition strategy and how you should plan for IPv4 and IPv6 interoperability. The chapter also looks at the tools you would use to configure IPv6 and debug IPv6 connectivity problems, and goes on to discuss DHCP version 6 (DHCPv6) and Windows Server 2008 enhancements to the Domain Name System (DNS).

Exam objectives in this chapter:

- Plan infrastructure services server roles.

Lessons in this chapter:

Before You Begin

To complete the lesson in this chapter, you must have done the following:

- Installed Windows Server 2008 and configured your test PC as a domain controller (DC) in the Contoso.internal domain as described in the Introduction and Chapter 1, "Installing, Upgrading, and Deploying Windows Server 2008." You also need a client PC running Windows Vista Business, Enterprise, or Ultimate that is a member of the Contoso.internal domain. This can be a separate PC or a virtual machine installed on the same PC as your DC. Although you can carry out most of the practice sessions by using a client PC running Windows XP Professional, you could have problems with some of the practices in Chapter 5, "Terminal Services and Application and Server Virtualization" and in Chapter 4, "Application Servers and Services." Using a Windows XP Professional client is therefore not recommended.

Real World

Ian McLean

Do you remember the millennium bug?

In 1999, the world of networking was supposedly in turmoil, at least according to media reports. It seemed that on the stroke of midnight, as the new millennium began, all computers would explode and airplanes would fly backward. Managers reacted predictably, ordering that everything be switched off five minutes before midnight and switched on again five minutes into the new day.

Networking professionals knew the dreaded bug was about as real as Cinderella's slipper. A few ancient 4-bit processors might be affected, but nothing big was about to happen as 2000 dawned. And we had a bit more to worry about than some fictitious year-end problem. You see, the world of networking was in turmoil.

It had been predicted that by April 2000, no more IPv4 addresses would be available to be allocated. IPv6 and the IPv6 section of the Internet existed. However, the IPv6 Internet was not widely used. Some professional network engineers were displaying signs of a most unprofessional panic. A cynical old author called McLean was negotiating a book about IPv6.

The book was never written, which was just as well because it wouldn't have sold. Suddenly NAT and private networks became popular. Organizations clamoring for hundreds of public addresses found they could cope perfectly well with two. The use of Classless Interdomain Routing (CIDR) enabled the Internet Assigned Numbers Authority (IANA) to wrest back IP addresses from organizations that had been allocated sixty-five thousand of them in a Class B network but had only ever used a thousand. The problem had been solved.

Except that it hadn't. It had been masked, but it is still there. IPv4 address space remains under threat of depletion. IPv4 header structure is still causing problems with Internet routers. APIPA allocates only non-routable internal addresses, and we rely heavily on DHCP. All that has happened is that we have bought some time for the clean, calm transition that's happening now. By default, "Internet Protocol" always meant IPv4. Now it means IPv6. Modern server and client operating systems use IPv6.

Lesson 1: Using IPv6 in Windows Server 2008

IPv4 and IPv6 addresses can be readily distinguished. An IPv4 address uses 32 bits, resulting in an address space of just over 4 billion. An IPv6 address uses 128 bits, resulting in an address space of 2^{128} or 340,282,366,920,938,463,463,374, 607,431,768,211,456–a number too large to comprehend. This represents $6.5*2^{23}$ or 54,525,952 addresses for every square meter of the earth's surface. In practice, the IPv6 address space allows for multiple levels of subnetting and address allocation between the Internet backbone and individual subnets within an organization. IPv6 address space has been described as an "unlimited resource." (Bear in mind that the same description was given to the IPv4 address space in 1981.)

However, the vastly increased address space available allows us to allocate not one but several unique IPv6 addresses to a network entity, with each address being used for a different purpose. This lesson describes IPv6 notation and the various types of IP address, including the IPv6 addresses used for IPv4 compatibility.

After this lesson, you will be able to:

- Explain how IPv6 addresses IPv4 limitations
- Identify the various types of IPv6 addresses and explain their use
- Recommend an appropriate IPv4-to-IPv6 transition strategy
- Identify IPv6 addresses that can be routed on the IPv4 Internet
- Implement IPv4 and IPv6 interoperability
- Use IPv6 tools
- Configure DHCPv6 scopes

Estimated lesson time: 50 minutes

Addressing Problems Caused by IPv4 Limitations

The first IPv4 limitation is the potential exhaustion of IPv4 address space. In retrospect, 32 bits was not sufficient for an addressing structure. IPv6 offers 128 bits. This gives enough addresses for every device that requires one to have a unique public IPv6 address. In addition, the 64-bit host portion (interface ID) of an IPv6 address can be automatically generated from the network adapter hardware.

Automatic Address Configuration

Typically, IPv4 is configured either manually or by using DHCP. Automatic configuration (autoconfiguration) through APIPA is available for isolated subnets that are not routed to other networks. IPv6 deals with the need for simpler and more automatic address configuration by supporting both stateful and stateless address configuration. Stateful configuration uses DHCPv6. If stateless address configuration is used, hosts on a link automatically configure themselves with IPv6 addresses for the link and (optionally) with addresses that are derived from prefixes advertised by local routers. You can also configure stateless DHCPv6 configuration where hosts are autoconfigured but DNS servers (for example) obtain their configuration from DHCPv6.

Quick Check

1. How many bits are in an IPv4 address?
2. How many bits are in an IPv6 address?

Quick Check Answers

1. 32
2. 128

Header Size and Extension Headers

IPv4 and IPv6 headers are not compatible, and a host or router must use both IPv4 and IPv6 implementations to recognize and process both header formats. Therefore, one design aim was to keep the size of the IPv6 header within a reasonable limit. Non-essential and optional fields are moved to extension headers placed after the IPv6 header. As a result, the IPv6 header is only twice as large as the IPv4 header, and the size of IPv6 extension headers is constrained only by the size of the IPv6 packet.

Routing Table Size

The IPv6 global addresses used on the IPv6 section of the Internet are designed to create an efficient, hierarchical, and summarizable routing infrastructure based on the common occurrence of multiple levels of Internet Service Providers (ISPs). On the IPv6 section of the Internet, backbone routers have greatly reduced routing tables that use route aggregation and correspond to the routing infrastructure of top-level aggregators.

Route Aggregation

Route aggregation provides for routing of traffic for networks with smaller prefixes to networks with larger prefixes. In other words, it permits a number of contiguous address blocks to be combined and summarized as a larger address block. Route aggregation reduces the number of advertised routes on large networks. When an ISP breaks its network into smaller subnets to provide service to smaller providers, it needs to advertise the route only to its main supernet for traffic to be sent to smaller providers.

> Route aggregation is used when the large ISP has a continuous range of IP addresses to manage. IP addresses (IPv4 or IPv6) that are capable of summarization are termed *aggregatable addresses*.

Network Level Security

Private communication over the Internet requires encryption to protect data from being viewed or modified in transit. Internet Protocol Security (IPsec) provides this facility, but its use is optional in IPv4. IPv6 makes IPsec mandatory. This provides a standards-based solution for network security needs and improves interoperability among different IPv6 implementations.

Real-Time Data Delivery

Quality of Service (QoS) exists in IPv4, and bandwidth can be guaranteed for real-time traffic (such as video and audio transmissions) over a network. However, IPv4 real-time traffic support relies on the Type of Service (ToS) field and the identification of the payload, typically using a User Datagram Protocol (UDP) or Transmission Control Protocol (TCP) port.

The IPv4 ToS field has limited functionality, and payload identification using a TCP and UDP port is not possible when an IPv4 packet payload is encrypted. Payload identification is included in the Flow Label field of the IPv6 header, so payload encryption does not affect QoS operation.

Removal of Broadcast Traffic

IPv4 relies on Address Resolution Protocol (ARP) broadcasts to resolve IP addresses to the Media Access Control (MAC) addresses of the Network Interface Cards (NICs). Broadcasts increase network traffic and are inefficient because every host processes them.

The Neighbor Discovery (ND) protocol for IPv6 uses a series of Internet Control Message Protocol for IPv6 (ICMPv6) messages that manage the interaction of nodes on the same link (neighboring nodes). ND replaces ARP broadcasts, ICMPv4 Router Discovery, and ICMPv4 Redirect messages with efficient multicast and unicast ND messages.

Analyzing the IPv6 Address Structure

IPv6 provides addresses that are equivalent to IPv4 address types and others that are unique to IPv6. A node can have several IPv6 addresses, each of which has its own unique purpose. This section describes the IPv6 address syntax and the various classes of IPv6 address.

IPv6 Address Syntax

The IPv6 128-bit address is divided at 16-bit boundaries, and each 16-bit block is converted to a 4-digit hexadecimal number. Colons are used as separators. This representation is called *colon-hexadecimal*.

Global unicast IPv6 addresses are described later in this lesson and are equivalent to IPv4 public unicast addresses. To illustrate IPv6 address syntax, consider the following IPv6 global unicast address:

21cd:0053:0000:0000:03ad:003f:af37:8d62

IPv6 representation can be simplified by removing the leading zeros within each 16-bit block. However, each block must have at least a single digit. With leading zero suppression, the address representation becomes:

21cd:53:0:0:3ad:3f:af37:8d62

A contiguous sequence of 16-bit blocks set to 0 in the colon-hexadecimal format can be compressed to ::. Thus, the previous example address could be written:

21cd:53::3ad:3f:af37:8d62

Some types of addresses contain long sequences of zeros and thus provide good examples of when to use this notation. For example, the multicast address ff05:0:0:0:0:0:0:2 can be compressed to ff05::2.

IPv6 Address Prefixes

The prefix is the part of the address that indicates either the bits that have fixed values or the network identifier bits. IPv6 prefixes are expressed in the same way as CIDR IPv4 notation, or *slash notation*. For example, 21cd:53::/64 is the subnet on which the address 21cd:53::23ad:3f:af37:8d62 is located. In this case, the first 64 bits of the address are the network prefix. An IPv6 subnet prefix (or subnet ID) is assigned to a single link. Multiple subnet IDs can be assigned to the same link. This technique is called *multinetting*.

NOTE   IPv6 does not use dotted decimal notation in subnet masks

Only prefix length notation is supported in IPv6. IPv4 dotted decimal subnet mask representation (such as 255.255.255.0) has no direct equivalent.

IPv6 Address Types

The three types of IPv6 address are unicast, multicast, and anycast.

- **Unicast**   Identifies a single interface within the scope of the unicast address type. Packets addressed to a unicast address are delivered to a single interface. RFC 2373 allows multiple interfaces to use the same address, provided that these interfaces appear as a single interface to the IPv6 implementation on the host. This accommodates load-balancing systems.

- **Multicast**   Identifies multiple interfaces. Packets addressed to a multicast address are delivered to all interfaces that are identified by the address.

- **Anycast**   Identifies multiple interfaces. Packets addressed to an anycast address are delivered to the nearest interface identified by the address. The nearest interface is the closest in terms of routing distance, or number of hops. An anycast address is used for one-to-one-of-many communication, with delivery to a single interface.

MORE INFO   IPv6 addressing architecture

For more information about IPv6 address structure and architecture, see RFC 2373 at *http://www.ietf.org/rfc/rfc2373.txt*.

NOTE   Interfaces and nodes

IPv6 addresses identify interfaces rather than nodes. A node is identified by any unicast address that is assigned to one of its interfaces.

IPv6 Unicast Addresses

IPv6 supports the following types of unicast address:

- Global
- Link-local
- Site-local

- Special
- Network Service Access Point (NSAP) and Internetwork Packet Exchange (IPX) mapped addresses

Global Unicast Addresses   Global unicast addresses are the IPv6 equivalent of IPv4 public addresses and are globally routable and reachable on the IPv6 section of the Internet. These addresses can be aggregated to produce an efficient routing infrastructure and are therefore sometimes known as aggregatable global unicast addresses. An aggregatable global unicast address is unique across the entire IPv6 section of the Internet. (The region over which an IP address is unique is called the *scope* of the address.)

The Format Prefix (FP) of a global unicast address is held in the three most significant bits, which are always 001. The next 13 bits are allocated by the Internet Assigned Numbers Authority (IANA) and are known as the Top Level Aggregator (TLA). IANA allocates TLAs to local Internet registries that in turn, allocate individual TLAs to large Internet Service Providers (ISPs). The next 8 bits of the address are reserved for future expansion.

The next 24 bits of the address contain the Next Level Aggregator (NLA). This identifies a specific customer site. The NLA enables an ISP to create multiple levels of addressing hierarchy within a network. The next 16 bits contain the Site Level Aggregator (SLA), which is used to organize addressing and routing for downstream ISPs and to identify sites or subnets within a site.

The next 64 bits identify the interface within a subnet. This is the 64-bit Extended Unique Identifier (EUI-64) address, as defined by the Institute of Electrical and Electronics Engineers (IEEE). EUI-64 addresses are either assigned directly to network adapter cards or derived from the 48-bit MAC address of a network adapter as defined by the IEEE 802 standard. Put simply, the interface identity is provided by the network adapter hardware.

Privacy Extensions for Stateless Address Autoconfiguration in IPv6

Concerns have been expressed that deriving an interface ID directly from computer hardware could enable the itinerary of a laptop and hence that of its owner to be tracked. This raises privacy issues and future systems might allocate interface IDs differently.

RFC 3041 and RFC 4941 address this problem. For more information see *http://www.ietf.org/rfc/rfc3041.txt* and *http://www.ietf.org/rfc/rfc4191.txt.*

To summarize, the FP, TLA, reserved bits, and NLA identify the public topology; the SLA identifies the site topology; and the interface identity (ID) identifies the interface. Figure 2-1 illustrates the structure of an aggregatable global unicast address.

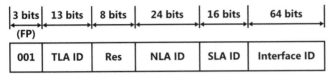

Figure 2-1 Global unicast address structure

MORE INFO Global unicast address format

For more information about aggregatable global unicast addresses, see RFC 2374 at *http://www.ietf.org/rfc/rfc2374.txt*.

Exam Tip You need to know that an aggregatable global unicast address is the IPv6 equivalent of an IPv4 public unicast address. You should be able to identify a global unicast address from the value of its three most significant bits. Knowing the various components of the address helps you understand how IPv6 addressing works, but the 70-646 examination is unlikely to test this knowledge in the depth of detail provided by the RFCs.

Link-Local Addresses Link-local IPv6 addresses are equivalent to IPv4 addresses that are autoconfigured through APIPA and use the 169.254.0.0/16 prefix. You can identify a link-local address by an FP of 1111 1110 10, which is followed by 54 zeros (link-local addresses always begin with fe8). Nodes use link-local addresses when communicating with neighboring nodes on the same link. The scope of a link-local address is the local link. A link-local address is required for ND and is always automatically configured, even if no other unicast address is allocated.

Site-Local Addresses Site-local IPv6 addresses are equivalent to the IPv4 private address space (10.0.0.0/8, 172.16.0.0/12, and 192.168.0.0/16). Private intranets that do not have a direct, routed connection to the IPv6 section of the Internet can use site-local addresses without conflicting with aggregatable global unicast addresses. The scope of a site-local address is the site (or organization internetwork).

Site-local addresses can be allocated by using stateful address configuration, such as from a DHCPv6 scope. A host uses stateful address configuration when it receives router advertisement messages that do not include address prefixes. A host will also use a stateful address configuration protocol when no routers are present on the local link.

Site-local addresses can also be configured through stateless address configuration. This is based on router advertisement messages that include stateless address prefixes and require that hosts do not use a stateful address configuration protocol.

Alternatively, address configuration can use a combination of stateless and stateful configuration. This occurs when router advertisement messages include stateless address prefixes but require that hosts use a stateful address configuration protocol.

MORE INFO   IPv6 address autoconfiguration

For more information about how IPv6 addresses are configured, see *http://www.microsoft.com/ technet/technetmag/issues/2007/08/CableGuy/*. Although the article is titled "IPv6 Autoconfiguration in Windows Vista," it also covers Windows Server 2008 autoconfiguration and describes the differences between autoconfiguration on a client and a server operating system.

Site-local addresses begin with feC0, followed by 32 zeros and then by a 16-bit subnet identifier that you can use to create subnets within your organization. The 64-bit Interface ID field identifies a specific interface on a subnet.

Figure 2-2 shows link-local and site-local addresses (for DNS servers) configured on interfaces on the Windows Server 2008 DC Glasgow. No global addresses exist in the configuration because DCs are never exposed directly to the Internet. The IPv6 addresses on your test computer will probably be different.

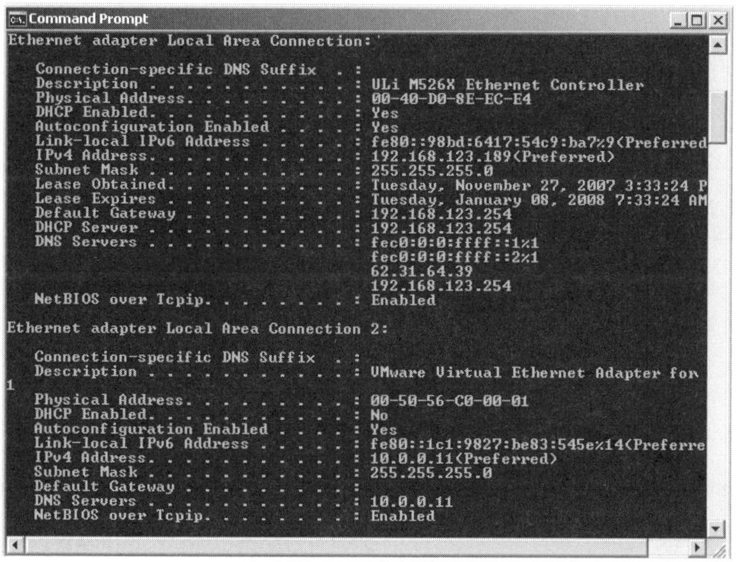

Figure 2-2   IPv6 addresses on computer interfaces

> ## Link-Local and Site-Local Addresses
>
> You can implement IPv6 connectivity between hosts on an isolated subnet by using link-local addresses. However, you cannot assign link-local addresses to router interfaces (default gateways) and you cannot route from one subnet to another if only link-local addresses are used. DNS servers cannot use only link-local addresses. If you use link-local addresses, you need to specify their interface IDs—that is the number after the % symbol at the end of the address, as shown in Figure 2-2. Link-local addresses are not dynamically registered in Windows Server 2008 DNS.
>
> For these reasons, site-local addresses are typically used on the subnets of a private network to implement IPv6 connectivity over the network. If every device on the network has its own global address (a stated aim of IPv6 implementation), global addresses can route between internal subnets, to peripheral zones, and to the Internet.

Special Addresses Two special IPv6 addresses exist—the unspecified address and the loopback address. The unspecified address 0:0:0:0:0:0:0:0 (or ::) is used to indicate the absence of an address and is equivalent to the IPv4 unspecified address 0.0.0.0. It is typically used as a source address for packets attempting to verify whether a tentative address is unique. It is never assigned to an interface or used as a destination address. The loopback address 0:0:0:0:0:0:0:1 (or ::1) is used to identify a loopback interface and is equivalent to the IPv4 loopback address 127.0.0.1.

NSAP and IPX Addresses NSAP addresses are identifying labels for network endpoints used in Open Systems Interconnection (OSI) networking. They are used to specify a piece of equipment connected to an Asynchronous Transfer Mode (ATM) network. IPX is no longer widely used because modern Novell Netware networks support TCP/IP. IPv6 addresses with an FP of 0000001 map to NSAP addresses. IPv6 addresses with an FP of 0000010 map to IPX addresses.

Exam Tip   The 70-646 examination is unlikely to include questions about NSAP or IPX mapping.

IPv6 Multicast Addresses

IPv6 multicast addresses enable an IPv6 packet to be sent to a number of hosts, all of which have the same multicast address. They have an FP of 11111111 (they always start with ff). Subsequent fields specify flags, scope, and group ID, as shown in Figure 2-3.

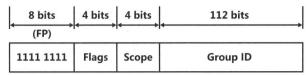

Figure 2-3   Multicast address structure

The flags field holds the flag settings. Currently the only flag defined is the Transient (T) flag that uses the low-order field bit. If this flag is set to 0, the multicast address is well known—in other words, it is permanently assigned and has been allocated by IANA. If the flag is set to 1, the multicast address is transient.

Quick Check

- What type of address is fec0:0:0:eadf::1ff?

Quick Check Answer

- Unicast site-local

The scope field indicates the scope of the IPv6 internetwork for which the multicast traffic is intended. Routers use the multicast scope, together with information provided by multicast routing protocols, to determine whether multicast traffic can be forwarded. For example, traffic with the multicast address ff02::2 has a link-local scope and is never forwarded beyond the local link. Table 2-1 lists the assigned scope field values.

Table 2-1   Scope Field Values

Value	Scope
0	Reserved
1	Node-local scope
2	Link-local scope
5	Site-local scope
8	Organization-local scope
E	Global scope
F	Reserved

The group ID represents the multicast group and is unique within the scope. Permanently assigned group IDs are independent of the scope. Transient group IDs are relevant only to a specific scope. Multicast addresses from ff01:: through ff0f:: are reserved, well-known addresses.

In theory, 2^{112} group IDs are available. In practice, because of the way that IPv6 multicast addresses are mapped to Ethernet multicast MAC addresses, RFC 2373, "IP Version 6 Addressing Architecture," recommends assigning the group ID from the low-order 32 bits of the IPv6 multicast address and setting the remaining original group ID bits to zero. In this way, each group ID maps to a unique Ethernet multicast MAC address.

MORE INFO   Assigning group IDs

For more information about assigning group IDs, see *http://www.ietf.org/rfc/rfc2373.txt*.

The Solicited-Node Multicast Address   The solicited-node multicast address facilitates the querying of network nodes during address resolution. IPv6 uses the ND message to resolve a link-local IPv6 address to a node MAC address. Rather than use the local-link scope all-nodes multicast address (which would be processed by all nodes on the local link) as the neighbor solicitation message destination, IPv6 uses the solicited-node multicast address. This address comprises the prefix ff02::1:ff00:0/ 104 and the last 24 bits of the IPv6 address that is being resolved.

For example, if a node has the link-local address fe80::6b:28c:16d2:c97, the corresponding solicited-node address is ff02::1:ffd2:c97.

The result of using the solicited-node multicast address is that address resolution uses a mechanism that is not processed by all network nodes. Because of the relationship between the MAC address, the Interface ID, and the solicited-node address, the solicited-node address acts as a pseudo-unicast address for efficient address resolution.

IPv6 Anycast Addresses

An anycast address is assigned to multiple interfaces. Packets sent to an anycast address are forwarded by the routing infrastructure to the nearest of these interfaces. The routing infrastructure must be aware of the interfaces that are assigned anycast addresses and their distance in terms of routing metrics. Currently, anycast addresses are used only as destination addresses and are assigned only to routers. Anycast addresses are assigned from the unicast address space, and the scope of an anycast address is the scope of the unicast address type from which the anycast address is assigned.

The Subnet-Router Anycast Address   The Subnet-Router anycast address is created from the subnet prefix for a given interface. In a subnet-router anycast address the bits in the subnet prefix retain their current values and the remaining bits are set to zero.

All router interfaces attached to a subnet are assigned the subnet-router anycast address for that subnet. The subnet-router anycast address is used for communication with one of multiple routers that are attached to a remote subnet.

Quick Check

■ A node has the link-local address fe80::aa:cdfe:aaa4:cab7. What is its corresponding solicited-node address?

Quick Check Answer

■ ff02::1:ffa4:cab7

Planning an IPv4 to IPv6 Transition Strategy

No specific time frame is mandated for IPv4-to-IPv6 transition. As a network manager, one of your decisions is whether to be an early adopter and take advantage of IPv6 enhancements such as addressing and stronger security or wait and take advantage of the experience of others. Both are valid strategies.

However, you do need to find out whether your upstream ISPs support IPv6, and whether the networking hardware in your organization also supports the protocol. The most straightforward transition method, dual stack, requires that both IPv4 and IPv6 be supported. By the same token, do not delay the decision to transition to IPv6 for too long. If you wait until the IPv4 address space is fully depleted, dual stack will no longer be available and you (and the users you support) will find the transition process much more traumatic.

Currently the underlying assumption in transition planning is that an existing IPv4 infrastructure is available and that your most immediate requirement is to transport IPv6 packets over existing IPv4 networks so that isolated IPv6 network islands do not occur. As more networks make the transition, the requirement will change to trans-porting IPv4 packets over IPv6 infrastructures to support legacy IPv4 applications and avoid isolated IPv4 islands.

Several transition strategies and technologies exist, because no single strategy fits all. RFC 4213, "Basic Transition Mechanisms for Hosts and Routers," describes the key elements of these transition technologies, such as dual stack and configured tunneling. The RFC also defines a number of node types based upon their protocol support, including legacy systems that support only IPv4, future systems that will support only IPv6, and the dual node that implements both IPv6 and IPv4.

MORE INFO   **IPv4-to-IPv6 transition**

For more information about basic transition mechanisms, see *http://www.ietf.org/rfc/rfc4213.txt* and download the white paper "IPv6 Transition Technologies" from *http://technet.microsoft.com/en-us/library/bb726951.aspx.*

Dual Stack Transition

Dual stack (also known as a dual IP layer) is arguably the most straightforward approach to transition. It assumes that hosts and routers provide support for both protocols and can send and receive both IPv4 and IPv6 packets. Thus a dual stack node can interoperate with an IPv4 device by using IPv4 packets and interoperate with an IPv6 device by using IPv6 packets. It can also operate in one of the following three modes:

- Only the IPv4 stack enabled
- Only the IPv6 stack enabled
- Both IPv4 and IPv6 stacks enabled

Because a dual stack node supports both protocols, you can configure it with both IPv4 32-bit addresses and IPv6 128-bit addresses. It can use, for example, DHCP to acquire its IPv4 addresses and stateless autoconfiguration or DHCPv6 to acquire its IPv6 addresses. Current IPv6 implementations are typically dual stack. An IPv6-only product would have very few communication partners.

Configured Tunneling Transition

If a configured tunneling transition strategy is employed, the existing IPv4 routing infrastructure remains functional but also carries IPv6 traffic while the IPv6 routing infrastructure is under development. A tunnel is a bidirectional, point-to-point link between two network endpoints. Data passes through a tunnel using encapsulation, in which the IPv6 packet is carried inside an IPv4 packet. The encapsulating IPv4 header is created at the tunnel entry point and removed at the tunnel exit point. The tunnel endpoint addresses are determined from configuration information that is stored at the encapsulating endpoint.

Configured tunnels are also called *explicit tunnels*. You can configure them as router-to-router, host-to-router, host-to-host, or router-to-host, but they are most likely to be used in a router-to-router configuration. The configured tunnel can be managed by a *tunnel broker*. A tunnel broker is a dedicated server that manages tunnel requests coming from end users, as described in RFC 3053, "IPv6 Tunnel Broker."

MORE INFO   Tunnel broker

For more information about tunnel broker, see *http://www.ietf.org/rfc/rfc3053.txt*.

Automatic Tunneling

RFC 2893, "Transition Mechanisms for IPv6 Hosts and Routers," (replaced by RFC 4213) describes automatic tunneling. This allows IPv4/IPv6 nodes to communicate over an IPv4 routing infrastructure without using preconfigured tunnels. The nodes that perform automatic tunneling are assigned a special type of address called an IPv4-compatible address, described later in this lesson, which carries the 32-bit IPv4 address within a 128-bit IPv6 address format. The IPv4 address can be automatically extracted from the IPv6 address.

MORE INFO   Automatic tunneling

For more information about automatic tunneling, see *http://www.ietf.org/rfc/rfc2893.txt*. Be aware, however, that the status of this document is obsolete and RFC 4213 is the current standard.

6to4

RFC 3056, "Connection of IPv6 Domains via IPv4 Clouds," describes the 6to4 tunneling scheme. 6to4 tunneling allows IPv6 sites to communicate with each other via an IPv4 network without using explicit tunnels, and to communicate with native IPv6 domains via relay routers. This strategy treats the IPv4 Internet as a single data link.

MORE INFO   6to4 tunneling

For more information about 6to4 tunneling, see *http://www.ietf.org/rfc/rfc3056.txt*.

Teredo

RFC 4380, "Teredo: Tunneling IPv6 over UDP through Network Address Translations (NATs)," describes Teredo, which is an enhancement to the 6to4 method and is supported by Windows Server 2008. Teredo enables nodes that are located behind an IPv4 NAT device to obtain IPv6 connectivity by using UDP to tunnel packets. Teredo requires the use of server and relay elements to assist with path connectivity.

MORE INFO   Teredo

For more information about Teredo, see *http://www.ietf.org/rfc/rfc4380.txt* and *http:// www.microsoft.com/technet/network/ipv6/teredo.mspx*.

Intra-Site Automatic Tunnel Addressing Protocol

RFC 4214, "Intra-Site Automatic Tunnel Addressing Protocol (ISATAP)," defines ISATAP, which connects IPv6 hosts and routers over an IPv4 network using a process that views the IPv4 network as a link layer for IPv6, and other nodes on the network as potential IPv6 hosts or routers. This creates a host-to-host, host-to-router, or router-to-host automatic tunnel.

MORE INFO   ISATAP

For more information about ISATAP, see *http://www.ietf.org/rfc/rfc4214.txt* and download the white paper "Manageable Transition to IPv6 using ISATAP" from *http://www.microsoft.com/downloads/ details.aspx?FamilyId=B8F50E07-17BF-4B5C-A1F9-5A09E2AF698B&displaylang=en*.

Implementing IPv4-to-IPv6 Compatibility

In addition to the various types of addresses described earlier in this lesson, IPv6 provides the following types of compatibility addresses to aid migration from IPv4 to IPv6 and to implement transition technologies.

IPv4-Compatible Address

The IPv4-compatible address 0:0:0:0:0:0:w.x.y.z (or ::w.x.y.z) is used by dual stack nodes that are communicating with IPv6 over an IPv4 infrastructure. The last four octets (w.x.y.z) represent the dotted decimal representation of an IPv4 address. Dual stack nodes are nodes with both IPv4 and IPv6 protocols. When the IPv4-compatible address is used as an IPv6 destination, the IPv6 traffic is automatically encapsulated with an IPv4 header and sent to the destination using the IPv4 infrastructure.

IPv4-Mapped Address

The IPv4-mapped address 0:0:0:0:0:ffff:w.x.y.z (or ::ffff:w.x.y.z) is used to represent an IPv4-only node to an IPv6 node and hence to map IPv4 devices that are not compatible with IPv6 into the IPv6 address space. The IPv4-mapped address is never used as the source or destination address of an IPv6 packet.

Teredo Address

A Teredo address consists of a 32-bit Teredo prefix. In Windows Server 2008 (and Windows Vista) this is 2001::/32. The prefix is followed by the IPv4 (32-bit) public address of the Teredo server that assisted in the configuration of the address. The next 16 bits are reserved for Teredo flags. Currently only the highest ordered flag bit is defined. This is the cone flag and is set when the NAT connected to the Internet is a cone NAT.

NOTE **Windows XP and Windows Server 2003**

In Windows XP and Windows Server 2003, the Teredo prefix was originally 3ffe:831f::/32. Computers running Windows XP and Windows Server 2003 use the 2001::/32 Teredo prefix when updated with Microsoft Security Bulletin MS06-064.

The next 16 bits store an obscured version of the external UDP port that corresponds to all Teredo traffic for the Teredo client interface. When a Teredo client sends its initial packet to a Teredo server, NAT maps the source UDP port of the packet to a different, external UDP port. All Teredo traffic for the host interface uses the same external, mapped UDP port. The value representing this external port is masked or obscured by exclusive ORing (XORing) it with 0xffff. Obscuring the external port prevents NATs from translating it within the payload of packets that are being forwarded.

The final 32 bits store an obscured version of the external IPv4 address that corresponds to all Teredo traffic for the Teredo client interface. The external address is obscured by XORing the external address with 0xffffffff. As with the UDP port, this prevents NATs from translating the external IPv4 address within the payload of packets that are being forwarded.

The external address is obscured by XORing the external address with 0xffffffff. For example, the obscured version of the public IPv4 address 131.107.0.1 in colon-hexadecimal format is 7c94:fffe. (131.107.0.1 equals 0x836b0001, and 0x836b0001 XOR 0xffffffff equals 0x7c94fffe.) Obscuring the external address prevents NATs from translating it within the payload of the packets that are being forwarded.

For example, Northwind Traders currently implements the following IPv4 private networks at its headquarters and branch offices:

■ Headquarters: 10.0.100.0 /24

■ Branch1: 10.0.0.0 /24

■ Branch2: 10.0.10.0 /24

■ Branch3: 10.0.20.0 /24

The company wants to establish IPv6 communication between Teredo clients and other Teredo clients, and between Teredo clients and IPv6-only hosts. The presence of Teredo servers on the IPv4 Internet enables this communication to take place. A Teredo server is an IPv6/IPv4 node connected to both the IPv4 Internet and the IPv6 Internet that supports a Teredo tunneling interface. The Teredo addresses of the Northwind Traders networks depend on a number of factors such as the port and type of NAT server used, but they could, for example, be the following:

■ Headquarters: 2001::ce49:7601:e866:efff:f5ff:9bfe through 2001::0a0a:64fe:e866:efff: f5ff:9b01

■ Branch 1: 2001:: ce49:7601:e866:efff:f5ff:fffe through 2001::0a0a:0afe:e866:efff: f5ff:ff01

■ Branch 2: 2001:: ce49:7601:e866:efff:f5ff:f5fe through 2001::0a0a:14fe:e866:efff: f5ff:f501

■ Branch 3: 2001:: ce49:7601:e866:efff:f5ff:ebfe through 2001::0a0a:1efe:e866:efff: f5ff:ebfe

Note that, for example, 10.0.100.1 is the equivalent of 0a00:6401, and 0a00:6401 XORed with ffff:ffff is f5ff:9bfe.

Exam Tip   The 70-646 examination is unlikely to ask you to generate a Teredo address. You might, however, be asked to identify such an address and work out its included IPv4 address. Fortunately you have access to a scientific calculator during the examination.

Cone NATs

Cone NATs can be full cone, restricted cone, or port restricted cone. In a full cone NAT, all requests from the same internal IP address and port are mapped to the same external IP address and port and any external host can send a packet to the internal host by sending a packet to the mapped external address.

In a restricted cone NAT, all requests from the same internal IP address and port are mapped to the same external IP address and port but an external host can send a packet to the internal host if the internal host had previously sent a packet to the external host.

In a port-restricted cone NAT, the restriction includes port numbers. An external host with a specified IP address and source port can send a packet to an internal host only if the internal host had previously sent a packet to that IP address and port.

ISATAP Addresses

IPv6 can use an ISATAP address to communicate between two nodes over an IPv4 intranet. An ISATAP address starts with a 64-bit unicast link-local, site-local, global, or 6to4 global prefix. The next 32 bits are the ISATAP identifier 0:5efe. The final 32 bits hold the IPv4 address in either dotted decimal or hexadecimal notation. An ISATAP address can incorporate either a public or a private IPv4 address.

For example, the ISATAP address fe80::5efe:w.x.y.z address has a link-local prefix; the fec0::1111:0:5efe:w.x.y.z address has a site-local prefix; the 3ffe:1a05:510:1111:0:5efe: w.x.y.z address has a global prefix; and the 2002:9d36:1:2:0:5efe:w.x.y.z address has a 6to4 global prefix. In all cases w.x.y.z represents an IPv4 address.

By default Windows Server 2008 automatically configures the ISATAP address fe80::5efe:w.x.y.z for each IPv4 address that is assigned to a node. This link-local ISATAP address allows two hosts to communicate over an IPv4 network by using each other's ISATAP address.

You can implement IPv6 to IPv4 configuration by using the IPv6 tools *netsh interface ipv6 6to4*, *netsh interface ipv6 isatap*, and *netsh interface ipv6 add v6v4tunnel*. For example, to create an IPv6-in-IPv4 tunnel between the local address 10.0.0.11 and the remote address 192.168.123.116 on an interface named *Remote* you would enter *netsh interface ipv6 add v6v4tunnel "Remote" 10.0.0.11 192.168.123.116*.

You can also configure the appropriate compatibility addresses manually by using the *netsh interface ipv6 set address* command or the Internet Protocol Version 6 (TCP/IPv6) Graphical User Interface (GUI) as described in the next section of this lesson.

NOTE 6to4cfg

Windows Server 2008 does not support the 6to4cfg tool.

Using IPv6 Tools

Windows Server 2008 provides tools that let you configure IPv6 interfaces and check IPv6 connectivity and routing. Tools also exist that implement and check IPv4 to IPv6 compatibility. Lesson 2 in this chapter discusses tools that verify DNS name resolution for IPv6 addresses.

In Windows Server 2008 the standard command-line tools such as *ping*, *ipconfig*, *pathping*, *tracert*, *netstat*, and *route* have full IPv6 functionality. For example, Figure 2-4 shows the *ping* command used to check connectivity with a link-local IPv6 address on a test network. The IPv6 addresses on your test network will be different. Note that if you were pinging from one host to another you would also need to include the interface ID, for example *ping fe80::fd64:b38b:cac6:cdd4%15*. Interface IDs are discussed later in this lesson.

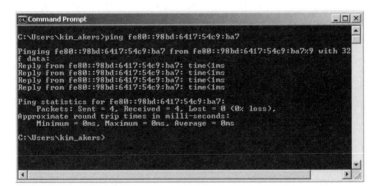

Figure 2-4   Pinging an IPv6 address

NOTE Ping6

The ping6 command-line tool is not supported in Windows Server 2008.

Tools specific to IPv6 are provided in the powerful *netsh* (network shell) command structure. For example the *netsh interface ipv6 show neighbors* command shows the IPv6 interfaces of all hosts on the local subnet. You use this command in the practice session later in this lesson, after you have configured IPv6 connectivity on a subnet.

Verifying IPv6 Configuration and Connectivity

If you are troubleshooting connectivity problems or merely want to check your configuration, arguably the most useful tool—and certainly one of the most used—is *ipconfig*. The *ipconfig /all* tool displays both IPv4 and IPv6 configuration. The output from this tool was shown in Figure 2-2 earlier in this lesson.

If you want to display the configuration of only the IPv6 interfaces on the local computer, you can use the *netsh interface ipv6 show address* command. Figure 2-5 shows the output of this command run on the Glasgow computer. Note the % character followed by a number after each IPv6 address. This is the interface ID, which identifies the interface that is configured with the IPv6 address.

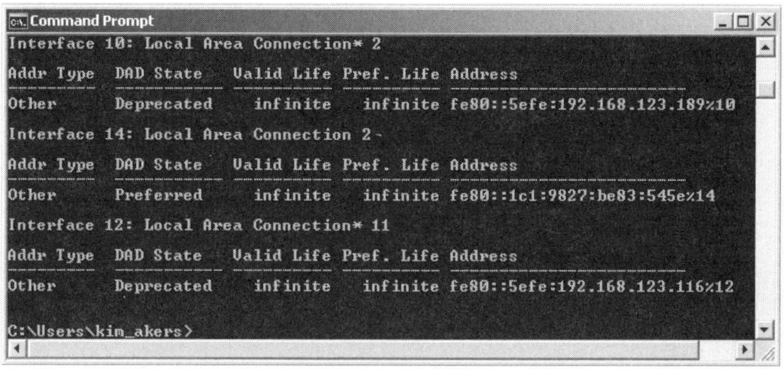

Figure 2-5 Displaying IPv6 addresses and interface IDs

If you are administering an enterprise network with a number of sites, you also need to know site IDs. You can obtain a site ID by using the command *netsh interface ipv6 show address level=verbose*. Part of the output from this command is shown in Figure 2-6.

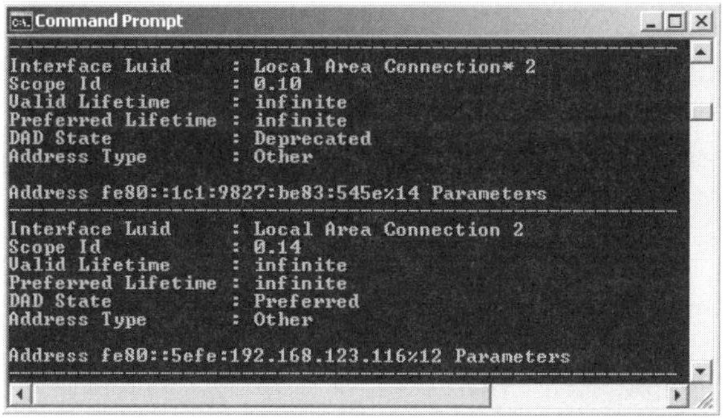

Figure 2-6 Displaying IPv6 addresses and site IDs

Configuring IPv6 Interfaces

Typically, most IPv6 addresses are configured through autoconfiguration or DHCPv6. However, if you need to manually configure IPv6 addresses, you can use the *netsh interface ipv6 set address* command, as in this example: *netsh interface ipv6 set address "local area connection 2" fec0:0:0:fffe::2.* You need to run the Command Console as an administrator to use this command. In Windows Server 2008 (and in Windows Vista) you can also manually configure IPv6 addresses from the properties of the Internet Protocol Version 6 (TCP/IPv6) Graphical User Interface (GUI). Figure 2-7 shows this configuration.

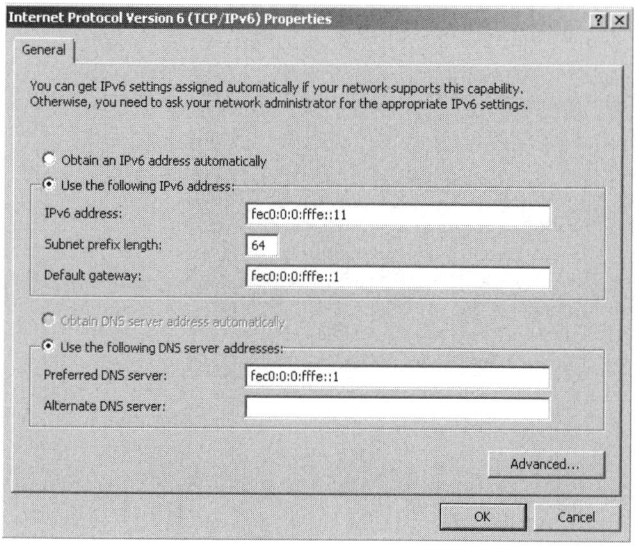

Figure 2-7   Configuring an IPv6 address through a GUI

The advantage of using the TCP/IPv6 GUI is that you can specify the IPv6 addresses of one or more DNS servers in addition to specifying the interface address. If, however, you choose to use Command Line Interface (CLI) commands, the command to add IPv6 addresses of DNS servers is *netsh interface ipv6 add dnsserver*, as in this example: *netsh interface ipv6 add dnsserver "local area connection 2" fec0:0:0:fffe::1.* To change the properties of IPv6 interfaces (but not their configuration), use the *netsh interface ipv6 set interface* command, as in this example: *netsh interface ipv6 set interface "local area connection 2" forwarding=enabled.* You need to run the Command Console as an administrator to use the *netsh interface ipv6 add* and *netsh interface ipv6 set* commands.

> **Quick Check**
>
> ■ What *netsh* command lists site IDs?
>
> **Quick Check Answer**
> ■ *netsh interface ipv6 show address level=verbose*

Verifying IPv6 Connectivity

To verify connectivity on a local network your first step should be to flush the neighbor cache, which stores recently resolved link-layer addresses and might give a false result if you are checking changes that involve address resolution. You can check the contents of the neighbor cache by using the command *netsh interface ipv6 show neighbors*. The command *netsh interface ipv6 delete neighbors* flushes the cache. You need to run the Command Console as an administrator to use the *netsh* tool.

You can test connectivity to a local host on your subnet and to your default gateway by using the *ping* command. You can add the interface ID to the IPv6 interface address to ensure that the address is configured on the correct interface. Figure 2-8 shows a *ping* command using an IPv6 address and an interface ID.

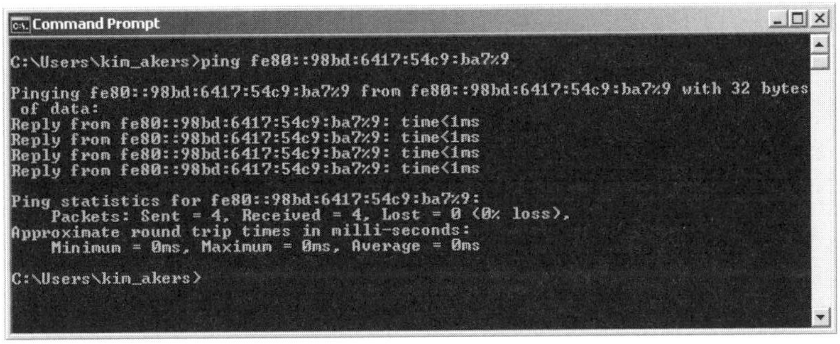

Figure 2-8   Pinging an IPv6 address with an interface ID

To check connectivity to a host on a remote network, your first task should be to check and clear the destination cache, which stores next-hop IPv6 addresses for destinations. You can display the current contents of the destination cache by using the *netsh interface ipv6 show destinationcache* command. To flush the destination cache, use the *netsh interface ipv6 delete destinationcache* command. You need to run the Command Console as an administrator to use this command.

Your next step is to check connectivity to the default router interface on your local subnet. This is your default gateway. You can identify the IPv6 address of your default router interface by using the *ipconfig*, *netsh interface ipv6 show routes*, or *route print* command. You can also specify the zone ID, which is the interface ID for the default gateway on the interface on which you want the ICMPv6 Echo Request messages to be sent. When you have ensured that you can reach the default gateway on your local subnet, ping the remote host by its IPv6 address. Note that you cannot ping a remote host (or a router interface) by its link-local IPv6 address because link-local addresses are not routable.

If you can connect to the default gateway but cannot reach the remote destination address, trace the route to the remote destination by using the *tracert −d* command followed by the destination IPv6 address. The *−d* command-line switch prevents the *tracert* tool from performing a DNS reverse query on router interfaces in the routing path. This speeds up the display of the routing path. If you want more information about the routers in the path, and particularly if you want to verify router reliability, use the *pathping -d* command, again followed by the destination IPv6 address.

Quick Check

- What *netsh* command could you use to identify the IPv6 address of your default router interface?

Quick Check Answer

- *netsh interface ipv6 show route*

Troubleshooting Connectivity

As an experienced administrator, you know that if you cannot connect to a remote host, you first want to check the various hardware connections (wired and wireless) in your organization and ensure that all network devices are up and running. If these basic checks do not find the problem, the Internet Protocol Security (IPsec) configuration might not be properly configured, or firewall problems (such as incorrectly configured packet filters) might exist.

You can use the IP Security Policies Management Microsoft Management Console (MMC) snap-in to check and configure IPsec policies and the Windows Firewall With Advanced Security snap-in to check and configure IPv6-based packet filters. Figures 2-9 and 2-10 show these tools.

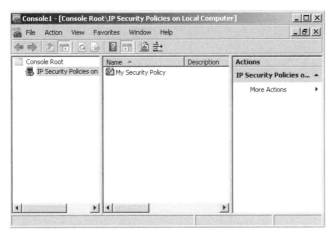

Figure 2-9   The IP Security Policies Management snap-in

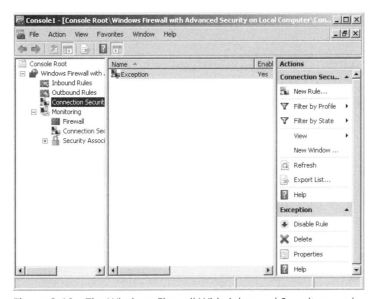

Figure 2-10   The Windows Firewall With Advanced Security snap-in

---

NOTE   IPSec6

The IPSec6 tool is not implemented in Windows Server 2008.

You might be unable to reach a local or remote destination because of incorrect or missing routes in the local IPv6 routing table. You can use the *route print, netstat –r,* or *netsh interface ipv6 show route* command to view the local IPv6 routing table and verify that you have a route corresponding to your local subnet and to your default gateway. Note that the *netstat −r* command displays both IPv4 and IPv6 routing tables.

If you have multiple default routes with the same metric, you might need to modify your IPv6 router configurations so that the default route with the lowest metric uses the interface that connects to the network with the largest number of subnets. You can use the *netsh interface ipv6 set route* command to modify an existing route. To add a route to the IPv6 routing table, use the *netsh interface ipv6 add route* command. The *netsh interface ipv6 delete route* command removes an existing route. You need to run the Command Console as an administrator to use these commands.

If you can access a local or remote host by IPv4 address but not by host name you might have a DNS problem. Tools to configure, check, and debug DNS include *dnscmd, ipconfig, netsh interface ipv6 show dnsservers, netsh interface ipv6 add dnsserver, nslookup,* and the Internet Protocol Version 6 (TCP/IPv6) GUI. Lesson 2 of this chapter discusses DNS.

Verifying IPv6-based TCP Connections

If the telnet client tool is installed, you can verify that a TCP connection can be established to a TCP port by typing **telnet**, followed by the destination IPv6 address and the TCP port number, as in this example: **telnet fec0:0:0:fffe::1 80**. If telnet successfully creates a TCP connection, the telnet> prompt appears and you can type telnet commands. If the tool cannot create a connection, it will return an error message.

MORE INFO   **Installing telnet client**

For more information about telnet, including how to install the telnet client, search Windows Server 2008 Help for "Telnet: frequently asked questions."

Configuring Clients Through DHCPv6

You can choose stateless or stateful configuration when configuring hosts by using DHCPv6. Stateless configuration does not generate a host address—which is instead autoconfigured—but it can, for example, specify the address of a DNS server. Stateful configuration specifies host addresses.

Whether you choose stateful or stateless configuration, you can assign the IPv6 addresses of DNS servers through the DNS Recursive Name Server DHCPv6 option (option 0023). If you choose stateful configuration, the IPv6 addresses of DNS servers can be configured as a scope option, so different scopes could have different DNS servers. Scope options override server options for that scope. This is the preferred method of configuring DNS server IPv6 addresses, which are not configured through router discovery.

With DHCPv6, an IPv6 host can receive subnet prefixes and other configuration parameters. A common use of DHCPv6 for Windows-based IPv6 hosts is to automatically configure the IPv6 addresses of DNS servers.

Currently when you configure an IPv6 scope you specify the 64-bit prefix. By default, DHCPv6 can allocate host addresses from the entire 64-bit range for that prefix. This allows for IPv6 host addresses that are configured through adapter hardware. You can specify exclusion ranges, so if you wanted to allocate only host addresses in the range fec0::0:0:0:1 through fec0::0:0:0:fffe, you would exclude addresses fec0::0:0:1:1 through fec0::ffff:ffff:ffff:fffe.

Several DHCPv6 options exist. Arguably the most useful option specifies the DNS server. Other options are concerned with compatibility with other systems that support IPv6, such as the Unix Network Integration Service (NIS).

DHCPv6 is similar to DHCP in many aspects. For example, scope options override server options, and DHCPv6 requests and acknowledgements can pass through BootP-enabled routers and layer-3 switches (almost all modern routers and switches) so that a DHCPv6 server can configure clients on a remote subnet.

As with DHCP, you can implement the 80:20 rule so that a DHCPv6 server is configured with a scope for its own subnet that contains 80 percent of the available addresses for that subnet, and a second scope for a remote subnet that contains 20 percent of the available addresses for that subnet, A similarly configured DHCPv6 server on the remote subnet provides failover. If either server fails, the hosts on both subnets still receive their configurations.

For example, Tailspin Toy's Melbourne office network has two private VLANS that have been allocated the following site-local networks:

- VLAN1: fec0:0:0:aaaa::1 through fec0:0:0:aaaa::fffe
- VLAN2: fec0:0:0:aaab::1 through fec0:0:0:aaab::fffe

Exceptions are defined so that IPv6 addresses on the VLANS can be statically allocated to servers. In this case you could implement the 80:20 rule by configuring the following DHCPv6 scopes on the DHCP server on VLAN1:

- fec0:0:0:aaaa::1 through fec0:0:0:aaaa::cccb
- fec0:0:0:aaab::cccc through fec0:0:0:aaab::fffe

You would then configure the following DHCPv6 scopes in the DHCP server on VLAN2:

- fec0:0:0:aaab::1 through fec0:0:0:aaab::cccb

- fec0:0:0:aaaa::cccc through fec0:0:0:aaaa::fffe

DHCP servers, and especially DHCP servers that host 20-percent scopes, are excellent candidates for virtualization because they experience only limited I/O activity. Additionally you can deploy this role on Server Core. This technique is particularly applicable to more complex networks.

NOTE   Virtual DNS servers

Like DHCP servers, DNS servers—particularly secondary DNS servers—are good candidates for virtualization.

For example, Trey Research is a single-site organization but has five buildings within its site, connected by fiber-optic links to a layer-3 switch configured to allocate a VLAN to each building. VLAN1, allocated to the main office, supports the majority of the company's computers. VLAN3 supports most of the remainder. VLAN2, VLAN4, and VLAN5 each support only a few computers.

In this case you can configure the DHCP server on VLAN1 to host 80 percent of the VLAN1 address range. You can configure a virtual DHCP server on the same VLAN to host 20 percent of the VLAN2 through VLAN5 address ranges. On VLAN3 you can configure a DHCP server to host the 80-percent ranges for VLAN2 through VLAN5 and a virtual server to host the 20-percent range for VLAN1. If either server fails, hosts on all the VLANs can continue to receive their configurations through DHCP. Chapter 5 discusses virtualization.

NOTE   The 80:20 rule

The 80:20 rule is typically implemented within a site because a WAN link (with routers over which you have no control) might not pass DHCP traffic. In general, if you implement DHCP failover by using the 80:20 rule, you need at least two DHCP servers per site.

Installing the DHCP server role and configuring a DHCPv6 scope are practical procedures and are therefore covered in detail in the practice session later in this lesson.

Planning an IPv6 Network

Configuring IPv6 and implementing IPv6 is relatively straightforward. Planning an IPv6 network is rather more complex. Every scenario has unique features, but in general you might want to deploy IPv6 in conjunction with an existing IPv4 network. You might have applications that require IPv6, although your network is principally IPv4. You might want to design a new network or restructure a current one so it is primarily IPv6. You could be designing a network for a large multinational company with multiple sites and thousands of users, or for a small organization with a head office and a single branch office.

Whatever the scenario, you will need to maintain interoperability with legacy functions and with IPv4. Even in a new IPv6 network, it is (currently) unlikely that you can ignore IPv4 completely.

Analyzing Hardware Requirements

An early step in the design process will be to identify and analyze the required network infrastructure components. Hardware components could include the following:

- Routers
- Layer-3 switches
- Printers
- Faxes
- Firewalls
- Intrusion-detection equipment
- Hardware load balancers
- Load-balancing server clusters
- Virtual Private Network (VPN) entry and exit points
- Servers and services
- Network interconnect hardware
- Intelligent Network Interface Cards (NICs)

This list is not exclusive, and you might need to consider other hardware devices depending upon the scenario. Which of these hardware devices store, display, or allow the input of IP addresses? Can all the necessary hardware be upgraded to work with IPv6? If not, what are the workarounds? If you need to replace hardware, is there a budget and a time frame for hardware refresh?

Analyzing Software and Application Requirements

From the software and applications viewpoint, network management is the area most likely to be affected by the version of IP used, although some LOB applications could also be affected. You might need to consider the IPv6 operation and compatibility of the following components:

- Network infrastructure management, such as WINS
- Network management systems, such as systems based on Simple Network Management Protocol (SNMP)
- Performance management systems
- High-level network management applications (typically third-party applications)
- Configuration management, such as DHCP and DHCPv6
- Security policy management and enforcement
- LOB applications
- Transition tools

Consideration of transition tools implies the requirement—except in a new IPv6 network—of determining the transition strategy you want to deploy. Transition strategies were discussed earlier in this lesson and depend largely on the planned scenario and whether both IPv4 and IPv6 stacks are available. If some legacy components do not support IPv6, you need to consider how to support them while transitioning is in progress and whether you will continue to support them in a dual stack network when transitioning is complete. You need to ensure interoperability between IPv4 and IPv6 components.

Possibly your first step in configuration management is to decide whether to use stateful or stateless configuration. With IPv6 it is possible to have every component on your network configured with its own global unicast address. Security is implemented by firewalls, virus filters, spam filters, IP filtering, and all the standard security methods. IPSec provides end-to-end encryption. You can configure peripheral zones in IPv6 networks as you can in IPv4 networks. DHCPv6 in stateless mode can configure options—for example, DNS servers—that are not configured through router discovery. In either case you need to ensure that your provider is IPv6-compliant and obtain a range of IPv6 addresses.

You may, however, decide that exposing the global unicast addresses of all your components to the IPv6 section of the Internet represents a security risk. This is a matter of debate in the networking community and outside the scope of this book. If you do make that decision, you can choose to implement site-local IPv6 addresses on your internal subnets, assuming your NAT servers support IPv6. You can choose stateful configuration by DHCPv6. Assuming that your routers or layer-3 switches can pass DHCP traffic, you can follow the 80:20 rule across your subnets or virtual local area networks (VLANs) to ensure that configuration still occurs if a DHCP server is down.

When you have made the basic decisions about network infrastructure and transitioning strategy, and have discovered whether you current network (or proposed new network) is capable of supporting IPv6, you then need to address other requirements and considerations. For example, unless you are implementing a new IPv6 network, you need to ensure that IPv4 infrastructure is not disrupted during the transition. With this requirement in mind, it may not be feasible to deploy IPv6 on all parts of your network immediately.

On the other hand, if your only requirement is to deploy a set of specified IPv6 applications (such as peer-to-peer communication), your IPv6 deployment might be limited to the minimum required to operate this set of applications.

Documenting Requirements

Your next step is to determine and document exactly what is required. For example, you might need to address the following questions:

- Is external connectivity (to the IPv6 section of the Internet, for example) required?
- Does the organization have one site or several sites? If the latter, what are the geographical locations of the sites, and how is information currently passed securely between them?
- What is the current IPv4 structure of the internetwork?
- What IPv6 address assignment plan is available from the provider?
- What IPv6 services does the provider offer?
- How should prefix allocation be delegated in the enterprise?
- Are site-external and site-internal IPv6 routing protocols required? If so, which ones?
- Does the enterprise currently use an external data center? (For example, are servers located at the provider?)

- Is IPv6 available using the same access links as IPv4?

- Which applications need to support IPv6 and can they be upgraded to do so? Will these application need to support both IPv4 and IPv6?

- Do the enterprise platforms support both IPv4 and IPv6? Is IPv6 installed by default on server and client platforms?

- Is NAT v4-v6 available, and do the applications have any issues with using it?

- Do the applications need globally routable IP addresses?

- Will multicast and anycast addresses be used?

You also need to analyze and document the working patterns and support structure within the organization. You need to obtain the following information:

- Who takes ownership of the network? For example, is network support in-house or outsourced?

- Does a detailed asset management database exist?

- Does the organization support home workers? If so, how?

- Is IPv6 network mobility used or required for IPv6?

- What is the enterprise's policy for geographical numbering?

- Do separate sites in the enterprise have different providers?

- What is the current IPv4 QoS policy (assuming you are not designing a new IPv6-only network)? Will this change when IPv6 is implemented?

- What proposals are in place for training technical staff in the use of IPv6?

Documenting and analyzing this information will take a lot of time. However, without this documentation you will not know the precise requirements for IPv6 implementation and the project will take much longer and result in a less satisfactory outcome. When you have gathered the information, you can plan the tasks you and your team need to perform and the requirements for each. You will have a better idea of the time and cost of the project, and whether it should be implemented in stages.

Your next step is to draw up and implement a project plan. Project planning is beyond the scope of this book. However, you would be wise to heed a word of warning: Do not ignore what might seem to be peripheral or non-time-critical activities. Training your technical staff is a good example. Every part of the final plan is important, and unless every aspect is implemented the result will be less than optimal. In the worst case, the project can fail completely for the want of an unconsidered component.

MORE INFO   IPv6 network scenarios

For more information about IPv6 planning and specific scenario examples, see RFC 4057, "IPv6 Enterprise Network Scenarios," at *http://www.ietf.org/rfc/rfc4057*.

Practice: Configuring IPv6 Connectivity

In this practice session you will configure site-local IPv6 addresses on the network connections on your server and client computers that connect to your private subnet (the IPv4 10.0.0.0/24 subnet). You use IPv6 tools to test connectivity. You then configure DHCPv6 on your server.

Exercise 2 is optional. You need to install the DHCP Server role on your DC to set up a DHCPv6 scope in Exercise 3. However, if the DHCP Server role is already installed on your server, you do not need to complete (and should not attempt) Exercise 2.

NOTE   Logging on to the client

You can perform the server configurations in this practice session by logging directly on to the server with an administrative-level account. However, in a production network this would be bad practice. Therefore the exercises ask you to log on to your client PC and use Remote Desktop to connect to your server. Other practices in this book involve only the server, and for convenience these practices ask you to log on to the server. Please be aware, however, that in a production network you would normally access a server through Remote Desktop or by running Administrative Tools on a client and specifying the server within the tool.

IMPORTANT   Windows XP Professional clients

If your client computer is running Windows XP Professional (not recommended), install the IPv6 protocol on the appropriate interface before attempting these practices.

▶ **Exercise 1: Configure IPv6**

In this exercise you will configure IPv6 site-local addresses on your client and server computers and test connectivity.

1. Log on to your client PC by using the kim_akers administrative level account.

2. From Control Panel, click Network And Sharing Center. If you are not using Classic View, first click Network and then click Internet. Click Manage Network Connections. On XP Professional clients, open Network Connections.

3. Right-click the interface that connects to your private network and click Properties.

4. If a User Account Control (UAC) box appears, click Continue.

5. Select Internet Protocol Version 6 (TCP/IPv6) and click Properties.

6. Configure a static site-local IPv6 address fec0:0:0:fffe::a.

7. Configure the default gateway address fec0:0:0:fffe::1.

8. Configure a DNS server address fec0:0:0:fffe::1. The Properties dialog box should look similar to Figure 2-11.

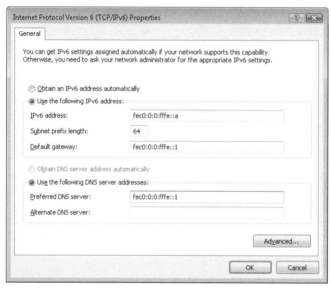

Figure 2-11   IPv6 configuration on the client

9. Click OK. Close the Local Area Connections Properties dialog box.

10. Close the Network And Connections dialog box.

11. Close Network And Sharing Center.

12. Enter **Remote Desktop** in the Search box. (On XP Professional clients, enter **mstsc** in the Run box.)

13. Connect to the Glasgow computer (the domain controller) by using the kim_akers account credentials (contoso\kim_akers).

14. Start Network And Sharing Center from Control Panel. Click Manage Network Connections.

15. If a UAC dialog box appears, click Continue to close it.

16. Right-click the network connection to your private network and click Properties.

17. Select Internet Protocol Version 6 (TCP/IPv6) and click Properties.

18. Configure a static site-local IPv6 address fec0:0:0:fffe::1.

19. Configure a DNS server address fec0:0:0:fffe::1. The Properties dialog box should look similar to Figure 2-12.

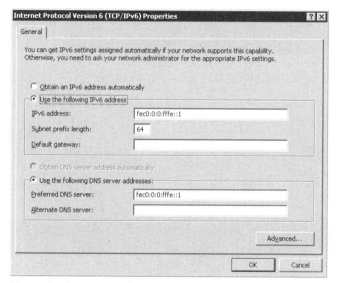

Figure 2-12   IPv6 configuration on the domain controller

20. Click OK. Close the Local Area Connections Properties dialog box.

21. Close the Network And Connections dialog box.

22. Close Network And Sharing Center.

NOTE   **Virtual machines**

If you are using a virtual machine to implement your server and client on the same PC, it is a good idea to close your virtual machine and restart your computer after configuring interfaces.

---

23. Open the Command Console on your domain controller.

24. Enter **ping fec0:0:0:fffe::a**. You should get the response shown in Figure 2-13. Note that if the firewall on your Melbourne computer blocks ICMP traffic, you need to reconfigure it before this command will work.

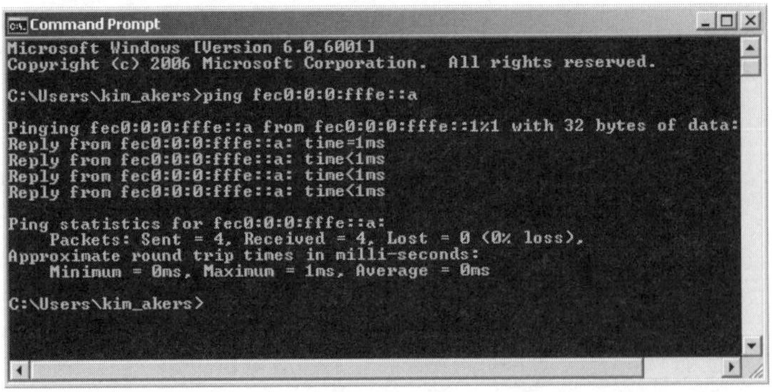

Figure 2-13 Pinging the client from the domain controller

25. Enter **netsh interface ipv6 show neighbors**. Figure 2-14 shows the fec0:0:0:fffe::a interface as a neighbor on the same subnet as the domain controller.

Figure 2-14 Showing the domain controller neighbors

26. Log off to close the Remote Desktop connection to the domain controller.

27. Open the Command Console on the client computer. Enter **ping fec0:0:0:fffe::1**. You should get the response from the domain controller shown in Figure 2-15.

Figure 2-15 Pinging the domain controller from the client

28. Enter **ping glasgow**. Note that the domain controller host name resolves to the IPv6 address.

▶ **Exercise 2: Install the DHCP Server Role (Optional)**

In this exercise you will install the DHCP Server role and specify that DHCPv6 can provide stateful IPv6 configuration. You need to complete this exercise only if this server role is not already installed on your Glasgow server.

1. If necessary, log on to the client with the kim_akers account and use Remote Desktop to connect to the domain controller.

2. If the Initial Configuration Tasks window opens when you log on, click Add Roles. Otherwise, open Server Manager from Administrative Tools, right-click Roles in the left pane, and click Add Roles.

3. The Add Roles Wizard starts. If the Before You Begin page appears, click Next.

4. Select the DHCP Server check box as shown in Figure 2-16 and click Next.

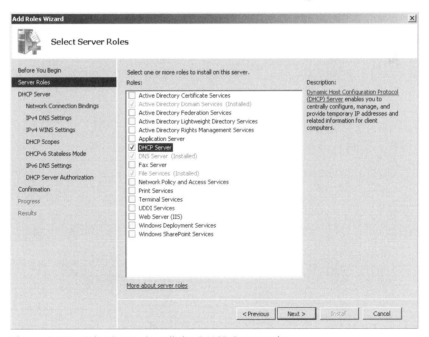

Figure 2-16   Selecting to install the DHCP Server role

5. On the DHCP Server page, select Network Connection Bindings. Ensure that only the 10.0.0.11 IPv4 interface is selected for DHCP.

6. Select IPv4 DNS Settings. Verify that the domain is contoso.internal and the Preferred DNS Server IPv4 Address is 10.0.0.11.

7.   Select IPv4 WINS Settings. Verify that WINS Is Not Required For Applications On This Network is selected.

8.   Select DHCP Scopes. Only IPv4 scopes can be defined on this page, so the scope list should be empty.

9.   Select DHCPv6 Stateless Mode. Select Disable DHCPv6 Stateless Mode For This Server. This lets you use the DHCP Management Console to configure DHCPv6 after the DHCP Server role has been installed. Figure 2-17 shows this setting.

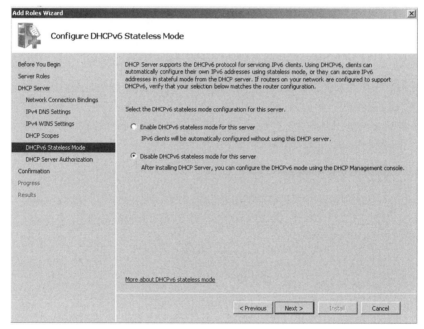

Figure 2-17   Disabling DHCPv6 stateless mode

10.   Select DHCP Server Authorization. Ensure that Use Current Credentials is selected.

11.   Select Confirmation and check your settings.

12.   Click Install. Click Close when installation completes.

13.   Restart the domain controller.

▶ **Exercise 3: Set Up a DHCPv6 Scope**

In this exercise you configure a DHCPv6 scope. You need to complete the first practice in this lesson before you can carry out this one. You also need to have the DHCP Server role installed on your DC. If you did not install this role while studying Chapter 1, you also need to complete the second exercise in this session before attempting this one.

1. If necessary, log on to the client with the kim_akers account and use Remote Desktop to connect to the domain controller.

2. In Administrative Tools, click DHCP.

3. If a UAC dialog box appears, click Continue to close it.

4. Expand glasgow.contoso.internal. Expand IPv6. Ensure that a green arrow appears beside the IPv6 icon. This confirms that the DHCPv6 Server is authorized.

5. Right-click IPv6 and click New Scope. The New Scope wizard opens. Click Next.

6. Give the scope a name (such as **Private Network Scope**) and type a brief description. Click Next.

7. Set Prefix to fec0::fffe. You are configuring only one IPv6 scope on this subnet and do not need to set Preference. Your screen should look similar to Figure 2-18. Click Next.

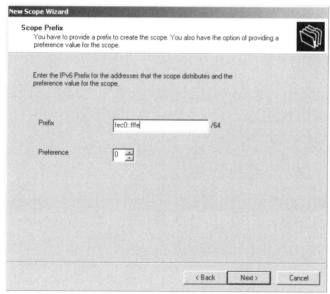

Figure 2-18   Setting a DHCPv6 prefix

8. You want to exclude IPv6 addresses fec0:0:0:fffe::1 through fec0:0:0:fffe::ff from the scope. Specify a Start Address of 0:0:0:1 and an End Address of 0:0:0:ff on the Add Exclusions page and click Add, as shown in Figure 2-19. Click Add.

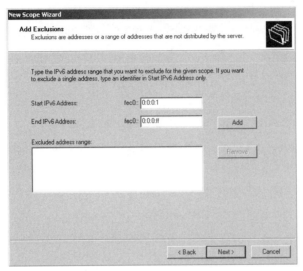

Figure 2-19   Configuring scope exclusions

9. Click Next. You can set the scope lease on the Scope Lease page. For the purposes of this practice the lease periods are acceptable. Click Next. Check the scope summary, ensure that Activate Scope Now is selected, and then click Finish.

10. In the DHCP tool, expand the scope, right-click Scope Options, click Configure Options, and examine the available options. Select Option 0023 DNS Recursive Server IPv6 Address List. Specify fec0:0:0:fffe::1 as the DNS Server IPv6 address, as shown in Figure 2-20.

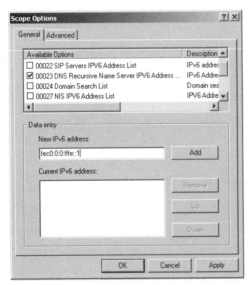

Figure 2-20   Specifying a DNS server for DHCPv6 configuration

11. Click Add and then click OK. Close the DHCP tool.

12. Close the Remote Desktop connection by logging off from the domain controller.

Lesson Summary

- IPv6 is fully supported in Windows Server 2008 and addresses problems such as lack of address space that are associated with IPv4.

- IPv6 supports unicast, multicast, and anycast addresses. Unicast addresses can be global, site-local, link-local, or special. IPX and NSAP mapped addresses are also supported.

- IPv6 is designed to be backward-compatible, and IPv4-compatible addresses can be specified. Transitioning strategies include dual stack, configured tunneling, automatic tunneling, 6to4, Teredo, and ISATAP.

- IPv6 addresses can be configured through stateful (DHCPv6) and stateless (autoconfiguration) methods. DHCPv6 can also be used statelessly to configure (for example) DNS servers while hosts are autoconfigured.

- Tools to configure and troubleshoot IPv6 include *ping*, *ipconfig*, *tracert*, *pathping* and *netsh*. You can also configure IPv6 by using the TCP/IPv6 Properties GUI.

Lesson Review

Use the following questions to test your knowledge of the information in Lesson 1, "Using IPv6 in Windows Server 2008." The questions are also available on the companion CD if you prefer to review them in electronic form.

NOTE Answers

Answers to these questions and explanations of why each answer choice is correct or incorrect are located in the "Answers" section at the end of the book.

---

1. Which protocol uses ICMPv6 messages to manage the interaction of neighboring nodes?

    A. ARP

    B. ND

    C. DHCPv6

    D. EUI-64

2. A node has a link-local IPv6 address fe80::6b:28c:16a7:d43a. What is its corresponding solicited-node address?

   A. ff02::1:ffa7:d43a

   B. ff02::1:ff00:0:16a7:d43a

   C. fec0::1:ff a7:d43a

   D. fec0::1:ff00:0:16a7:d43a

3. What type of IPv6 address is the equivalent to a public unicast IPv4 address?

   A. Site-local

   B. Link-local

   C. Global

   D. Special

4. Which IPv6 to IPv4 transition strategy uses preconfigured tunnels and encapsulates an IPv6 packet within an IPv4 packet?

   A. Configured tunneling

   B. Dual stack

   C. ISATAP

   D. Teredo

5. What command lets you configure an IPv6 address manually on a specified interface?

   A. *netsh interface ipv6 show address*

   B. *netsh interface ipv6 add address*

   C. *netsh interface ipv6 set interface*

   D. *netsh interface ipv6 set address*

6. Trey Research is a well-established, innovative research organization that prides itself on being at the forefront of technology. The company currently has 82 client PCs all running Windows Vista Ultimate edition. All its servers—including its DCs—have recently been upgraded to Windows Server 2008. Trey's site consists of two buildings linked by a fiber-optic cable. Each building has its own VLAN and Trey's peripheral zone is on a separate VLAN. All Trey's clients receive their IPv4 configurations through DHCP, and the 80:20 rule is used to implement failover if a DHCP server goes down. All servers and router interfaces are configured manually, as are the company's network printers and network

projectors. Trey has a Class C public IPv4 allocation and sees no need to implement NAT. It uses a network management system based on SNMP. It uses a number of high-level graphics applications in addition to business software and the 2007 Microsoft Office system. The company wants to introduce IPv6 configuration and access the IPv6 section of the Internet. It has verified that its provider and all its network hardware fully support IPv6. Which of the following are likely to form part of Trey's IPv6 implementation plan? (Choose all that apply.)

   A. Trey is likely to adopt a dual stack transition strategy.

   B. Trey is likely to adopt a configured tunneling transition strategy.

   C. Trey is likely to configure its internal network hosts with site-local unicast addresses.

   D. Trey is likely to configure its internal network hosts with global unicast addresses.

   E. Trey needs to ensure that its servers and clients can support IPv6.

   F. Trey needs to ensure that its network projectors and network printers support IPv6.

   G. Trey needs to ensure that its network management system is compatible with IPv6.

   H. Trey needs to ensure that its graphic applications are compatible with IPv6.

Lesson 2: Configuring DNS

DNS mainly resolves IP host names to IP addresses. It can also resolve IP addresses to host names in Reverse Lookup DNS zones. Name resolution is important for IPv4 because IPv4 addresses are difficult to remember. It is even more important for IPv6 because remembering IPv6 addresses is almost impossible. As an experienced network professional, you are familiar with DNS–the purpose of this lesson is not to teach you the basics of how DNS works. Instead, the lesson covers the enhancements to DNS introduced in Windows Server 2008 and how DNS deals with IPv6 addresses.

After this lesson, you will be able to:

- List and explain the Windows Server 2008 DNS features
- List and explain the Windows Server 2008 enhancements to DNS
- Configure static IPv6 DNS records
- Configure an IPv6 Reverse Lookup Zone
- Administer DNS using the MMC snap-in and command-line tools

Estimated lesson time: 30 minutes

Real World

Ian McLean

Once, not so very long ago, there was a network called the Arpanet. Most of the hosts on this network were controlled by the American military, although some were in universities such as the University of California at Berkeley. Name resolution in this network was implemented with static hosts files that held host names and corresponding network addresses.

When the number of hosts on the network got above 80, hosts files became long and clumsy. So DNS was developed and a computer was configured as a DNS server. That's right, a single DNS server.

How many DNS servers are there in the world today? If anyone ever tells you, say, "No, there are more than that," because by the time the two of you have finished speaking, there will be. Could anyone have predicted back in the days of the Arpanet how big the Internet would become? Was there anyone in the world stupid enough to make that sort of prediction?

There was. I had been working for a commercial distance-learning company and always had an interest in alternative methods of learning and teaching.

I researched open learning, programmed learning, and the excellent work the radio teacher network was doing in Australia.

Even then I was a bit of a computer geek and kept myself informed about network development, including the documentation coming out of Berkeley. I decided to study for a doctorate combining network technology with developing teaching techniques.

I called my idea the Information Highway and postulated a future where a worldwide network would provide information and learning on demand to homes, schools, and colleges. Even more ridiculously, I predicted a future where computers would be so inexpensive and easy to use that every home would have one, schools would have hundreds, and colleges would have thousands.

Unfortunately I had to defend my thesis to a panel of crusty academics who considered chalk and blackboard to be dangerously advanced technology. I don't think they even looked at my references. I was told that doctorates were not given out for science fiction.

The moral of this rather sad story is that it is very difficult to predict just how far and fast technology will develop. In thirty years' time we will look on today's World Wide Web and computer technology as simple and primitive. What will we be using by then? Is anyone in the world stupid enough to make that sort of prediction?

Not me.

Using Windows Server 2008 DNS

The Windows Server 2008 DNS server role is fully compliant with all published standards and is compatible with most DNS systems. It retains the features introduced by Windows Server 2003 DNS, including dynamic configuration and incremental zone transfer, and introduces several new features and significant enhancements.

Windows Server 2008 DNS Compliance and Support

The DNS Server role in Windows Server 2008 complies with all RFCs that define and standardize the DNS protocol. It uses standard DNS data file and resource record formats and can work successfully with most other DNS server implementations, such as DNS implementations that use the Berkeley Internet Name Domain (BIND) software.

Windows Server 2008 DNS in a Windows-based network supports Active Directory Domain Services (AD DS). If you install the AD DS role on a server, and a DNS server that meets AD DS requirements cannot be located, you can automatically install and configure a DNS server. Typically this happens when you are installing the first domain controller in a forest.

A partition is a data container in AD DS that holds data for replication. You can store DNS zone data in either the domain or application directory partition of AD DS. You can specify which partition should store the zone. This in turn defines the set of domain controllers to which that zone's data is replicated. Although other types of DNS server can support AD DS deployment, Microsoft recommends that you use the Windows Server 2008 DNS Server service for this purpose. Partitions help to ensure that only updates to DNS zones are replicated to other DNS servers. Incremental zone transfer is discussed later in this lesson.

NOTE File-backed DNS servers

A file-backed DNS server is a DNS server that is not integrated with AD DS. You can install file-backed DNS servers on any stand-alone computer on your network. Typically, file-backed DNS servers are used in peripheral zones where the use of member servers (and especially domain controllers) could be seen as a security risk.

Windows Server 2008 DNS supports stub zones. A *stub zone* is a copy of a zone that contains only the resource records necessary to identify the authoritative DNS servers for that zone. Using stub zones ensures that the DNS server hosting a parent zone can determine authoritative DNS servers for its child zone, thus helping to maintain efficient DNS name resolution. Figure 2-21 shows a stub zone specified in the New Zone Wizard.

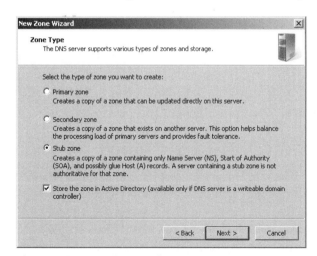

Figure 2-21 Creating a stub zone

You can use stub zones, for example, when name servers in the target zone are often in transition—for example, if part or all of company network is undergoing IP address transition and resolution of names is problematic.

Close integration with other Windows services, including AD DS, WINS (if enabled), and DHCP (including DHCPv6) ensures that Windows 2008 DNS is dynamic and requires little or no manual configuration. Windows 2008 DNS is fully compliant with the dynamic update protocol defined in RFC 2136. Computers running the DNS Client service register their host names and IPv4 and IPv6 addresses (although not link-local IPv6 addresses) dynamically. You can configure the DNS Server and DNS Client services to perform secure dynamic updates. This ensures that only authenticated users with the appropriate rights can update resource records on the DNS server. Figure 2-22 shows a zone being configured to allow only secure dynamic updates.

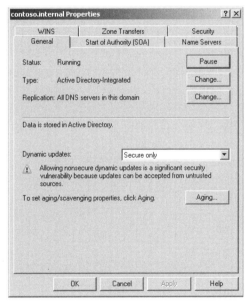

Figure 2-22   Allowing only secure dynamic updates

MORE INFO   **Dynamic update protocol**

For more information about the dynamic update protocol, see *http://www.ietf.org/rfc/rfc2136.txt* and *http://www.ietf.org/rfc/rfc3007*.

NOTE   **Secure dynamic updates**

Secure dynamic updates are only available for zones that are integrated with AD DS.

Zone Replication

For failover, and to improve the efficiency of DNS name resolution, DNS zones are replicated between DNS servers. Zone transfers implement zone replication and synchronization. If you add a new DNS server to the network and configure it as a secondary DNS server for an existing zone, it performs a full zone transfer to obtain a read-only copy of resource records for the zone. Prior to Windows Server 2003, a full zone transfer was required to replicate any changes in the authoritative DNS zone to the secondary DNS server.

Windows Server 2003 introduced incremental zone transfer, which is fully implemented in Windows Server 2008. Incremental transfer enables a secondary server to pull only those zone changes that it needs to synchronize its copy of the zone with its source zone, which can be either a primary or secondary copy of the zone that is maintained by another DNS server.

You can allow zone transfers to any DNS server, to DNS servers listed on the Name Servers tab (any server that has registered an NS record), or only to specified DNS servers. Figure 2-23 shows a DNS zone configured to allow zone transfers only to DNS servers listed on the Name Servers tab.

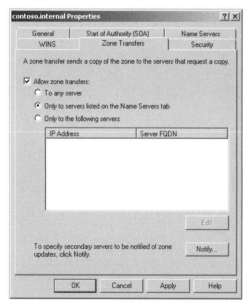

Figure 2-23   Configuring zone transfer

DNS Forwarders

If a DNS server does not have an entry in its database for the remote host specified in a client request, it can respond to the client with the address of a DNS server more likely to have that information, or it can query the other DNS server itself. This process can take place recursively until either the client computer receives the IP address or the DNS server establishes that the queried name cannot be resolved. DNS servers to which other DNS servers forward requests are known as *forwarders*.

The Windows 2008 DNS Server service extends the standard forwarder configuration by using conditional forwarders. A conditional forwarder is a DNS server that forwards DNS queries according to the DNS domain name in the query. For example, you can configure a DNS server to forward all the queries that it receives for names ending with adatum.com to the IP address of one or more specified DNS servers. This feature is particularly useful on extranets, where several organizations and domains access the same private internetwork.

Figure 2-24 shows the dialog box used to create a conditional forwarder. You cannot actually do this on your test network because you have only one DNS server.

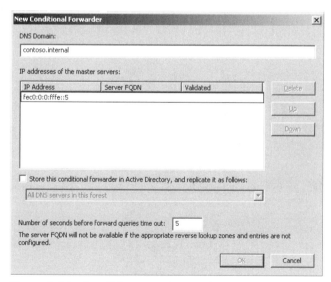

Figure 2-24   Specifying a conditional forwarder

Administering DNS

You can use the DNS Manager MMC snap-in GUI to manage and configure the DNS Server service. Windows Server 2008 also provides configuration wizards for performing common server administration tasks. Figure 2-25 shows this tool and also displays the IPv4 and IPv6 host records dynamically registered in DNS.

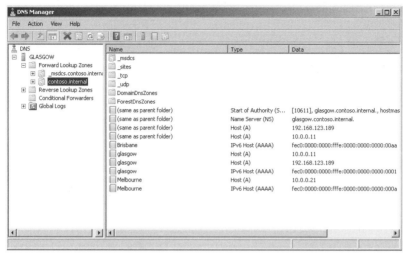

Figure 2-25   DNS Manager

Other tools are provided to help you better manage and support DNS servers and clients on your network. You can use the *dnscmd* tool to configure and administer both IPv4 and IPv6 records. Figure 2-26 shows the command-line switches you can use with this versatile tool. Typically, you need to run the Command Console as an administrator to use the *dnscmd* tool.

```
C:\Users\kim_akers>dnscmd /help

Usage: DnsCmd <ServerName> <Command> [<Command Parameters>]

<ServerName>:
  IP address or host name      -- remote or local DNS server
                               -- DNS server on local machine
<Command>:
  /Info                        -- Get server information
  /Config                      -- Reset server or zone configuration
  /EnumZones                   -- Enumerate zones
  /Statistics                  -- Query/clear server statistics data
  /ClearCache                  -- Clear DNS server cache
  /WriteBackFiles              -- Write back all zone or root-hint datafile(s)
  /StartScavenging             -- Initiates server scavenging
  /IpValidate                  -- Validate remote DNS servers
  /ResetListenAddresses        -- Set server IP address(es) to serve DNS requests
  /ResetForwarders             -- Set DNS servers to forward recursive queries to
  /ZoneInfo                    -- View zone information
  /ZoneAdd                     -- Create a new zone on the DNS server
  /ZoneDelete                  -- Delete a zone from DNS server or DS
  /ZonePause                   -- Pause a zone
  /ZoneResume                  -- Resume a zone
  /ZoneReload                  -- Reload zone from its database (file or DS)
  /ZoneWriteBack               -- Write back zone to file
  /ZoneRefresh                 -- Force refresh of secondary zone from master
  /ZoneUpdateFromDs            -- Update a DS integrated zone by data from DS
  /ZonePrint                   -- Display all records in the zone
  /ZoneResetType               -- Change zone type
  /ZoneResetSecondaries        -- Reset secondary\notify information for a zone
  /ZoneResetScavengeServers    -- Reset scavenging servers for a zone
  /ZoneResetMasters            -- Reset secondary zone's master servers
  /ZoneExport                  -- Export a zone to file
  /ZoneChangeDirectoryPartition -- Move a zone to another directory partition
  /EnumRecords                 -- Enumerate records at a name
  /RecordAdd                   -- Create a record in zone or RootHints
  /RecordDelete                -- Delete a record from zone, RootHints or cache
  /NodeDelete                  -- Delete all records at a name
  /AgeAllRecords               -- Force aging on node(s) in zone
  /EnumDirectoryPartitions     -- Enumerate directory partitions
  /DirectoryPartitionInfo      -- Get info on a directory partition
  /CreateDirectoryPartition    -- Create a directory partition
  /DeleteDirectoryPartition    -- Delete a directory partition
  /EnlistDirectoryPartition    -- Add DNS server to partition replication scope
  /UnenlistDirectoryPartition  -- Remove DNS server from replication scope
  /CreateBuiltinDirectoryPartitions -- Create built-in partitions
  /ExportSettings              -- Output settings to DnsSettings.txt in the DNS se
```

Figure 2-26   The *dnscmd* tool

You can use the *ipconfig* command as described in Lesson 1 of this chapter to view interface adapter configurations. You can also release IPv4 and IPv6 configurations by using *ipconfig /release* and *ipconfig /release6* respectively. Similarly you can renew configurations with *ipconfig /renew* and *ipconfig /renew6*.

If a client sends a request to a DNS server and the remote host name cannot be resolved, the DNS cache on the client stores the information that resolution failed. This is designed to prevent clients from continually accessing DNS servers and attempting to resolve unresolvable host names. However, the disadvantage is that if the remote host name cannot be resolved because of a server problem and that problem is subsequently repaired, the client cannot obtain resolution for that host name until the information that it is not resolvable is cleared from the cache. In this situation you can use *ipconfig /flushdns* on the client to clear the cache immediately.

A new client on a network takes some time to register with dynamic DNS. You can speed up this process by using the *ipconfig /registerdns* command. You can display DNS information by using the *ipconfig /displaydns* command. The *ipconfig* commands that display information can be run without elevated privileges, but the commands that configure interfaces, release configuration, flush the cache, or register the client require you to run the Command Console as an administrator. Figure 2-27 shows the command-line switches available with the *ipconfig* command.

Figure 2-27   The *ipconfig* tool

Quick Check

- What Command Line Interface (CLI) tool can you use to create Reverse Lookup zones?

Quick Check Answer

- *dnscmd*

If a client cannot obtain remote host name resolution from a DNS server, and you have used the *ping* command to ensure that you have network connectivity between the server and the host, you can use *nslookup* to check whether the server is providing a DNS service. From the Melbourne client computer, issue the command **nslookup glasgow**. This demonstrates connectivity to the glasgow.contoso.internal server.

Issue the command **nslookup contoso.internal**. This returns the IPv4 addresses of DNS servers on the contoso.internal domain.

Enter **nslookup**. At the nslookup> prompt, enter **ls –d contoso.internal**. This lists all the DNS records in the contoso.internal domain, as shown in Figure 2-28.

Figure 2-28   DNS records in the contoso.internal domain

NOTE Nslookup ls id <domain>

This command does not work unless you have enabled zone transfer (see Figure 2-23), even if you run it on the server that hosts the domain. If you cannot get this to work, try selecting To Any Server on the Zone Transfers tab, but be aware that doing so compromises your security.

A list of *nslookup* commands is shown in Figure 2-29.

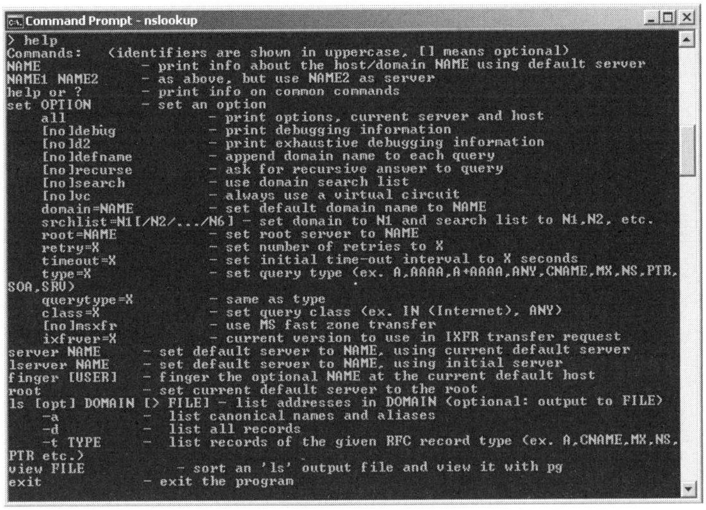

Figure 2-29 *Nslookup* commands

Lesson 1 discussed the *netsh interface ipv6 add dnsserver* command. The *netsh interface ipv6 show dnsservers* command displays IPv6 DNS configurations and also indicates which DNS server addresses are statically configured.

DNS Records

As a network professional you should be familiar with standard DNS record types such as IPv4 host (A), SOA, PTR, CNAME, NS, MX, and so on. Other DNS record types, such as Andrew File System Database (AFSDB) and ATM address, are of interest only if you are configuring compatibility with non-Windows DNS systems. Figure 2-30 shows some of the record types available in Windows 2008 DNS. If you need to create an IPv6 record for a client that cannot register itself with Active Directory, you need to manually create an AAAA record.

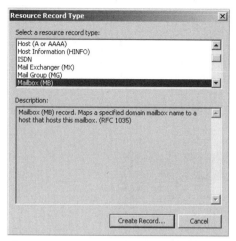

Figure 2-30   DNS record types

Examining New DNS Features and Enhancements

The DNS Server role in Windows Server 2008 provides the following new or enhanced features:

- **Background zone loading**   Loading DNS zone data is a background operation. If you need to restart a DNS server that hosts one or more large DNS zones that are stored in AD DS, the server is able to respond to client queries more quickly because it does not need to wait until all zone data is loaded.

- **Support for read-only domain controllers (RODCs)**   The Windows Server 2008 DNS Server role provides primary read-only zones on RODCs.

- **Global single names**   The GlobalNames DNS zone provides single-label name resolution for large enterprise networks that do not deploy WINS. This zone is used when it is impractical to use DNS name suffixes to provide single-label name resolution.

- **IPv6 support**   The Windows Server 2008 DNS Server role fully supports IPv6 addresses. It implements AAAA and IP6 records and supports IPv6 Reverse Lookup zones.

Background Zone Loading

If you work in a large organization with large Windows Server 2003 (or earlier) zones that store DNS data in AD DS, you will sometimes find that restarting a DNS server can take considerable time. You need to wait while DNS zone data is retrieved from AD DS; the DNS server is unavailable to service client requests while this is happening.

When you upgrade your server operating systems to Windows Server 2008, you will find this situation has been addressed. Windows Server 2008 DNS loads zone data from AD DS in the background while it restarts so that it can respond to requests almost immediately when it restarts, instead of waiting until its zones are fully loaded. Also, because zone data is stored in AD DS rather than in a file, that data can be accessed asynchronously and immediately when a query is received. File-based zone data can be accessed only through a sequential file read and takes longer to access than data in AD DS.

When the DNS server starts, it identifies all zones to be loaded, loads root hints from files or AD DS storage, loads any file-backed zones, and starts to respond to queries and remote procedure calls (RPCs) while using background processes (additional processor threads) to load zones that are stored in AD DS.

If a DNS client requests data for a host in a zone that has already been loaded, the DNS server responds as required. If the request is for information that has not yet been loaded into memory, the DNS server reads the required data from AD DS so that the request can be met.

NOTE Background zone loading in practice

Background zone loading is an enhancement to previous Windows DNS versions, but in practice it would be very unusual for a large organization to have only one DNS server servicing its requests. If a primary server was rebooting, DNS requests would normally be answered by other Active Directory-integrated DNS servers or by secondary servers. The effect of background loading in practice is that a rebooted DNS server comes online more quickly to share the load of satisfying client requests.

Quick Check

■ What DNS record enables a host name to be resolved to an IPv6 address?

Quick Check Answer

■ AAAA

Supporting RODCs

An RODC provides a read-only copy of a domain controller and cannot be directly configured. This makes it less vulnerable to attack. Microsoft advises using RODCs in locations where you cannot guarantee the physical security of a domain controller.

Windows Server 2008 supports primary read-only zones (sometimes called branch office zones). When a Windows Server 2008 server is configured as an RODC it replicates a read-only copy of all Active Directory partitions that DNS uses, including the domain partition, ForestDNSZones, and DomainDNSZones. An administrator can view the contents of a primary read-only zone, but can change the contents only by changing the DNS zone on the master domain controller.

Using the GlobalNames DNS Zone

WINS uses NetBIOS over TCP/IP (NetBT), which Microsoft describes as approaching obsolescence. Nevertheless it provides static, global records with single-label names and is still widely used. Windows Server 2008 DNS introduces the GlobalNames zone to hold single-label names. Typically the replication scope of this zone is the entire forest, which ensures that the zone can provide single-label names that are unique in the forest. The GlobalNames zone also supports single-label name resolution throughout an organization that contains multiple forests—provided that you use Service Location (SRV) resource records to publish the GlobalNames zone location. This enables organizations to disable WINS and NetBT, which will probably not be supported in future Server OS releases.

The GlobalNames zone provides single-label name resolution for a limited set of host names, typically centrally managed corporate servers and Web sites, and is not used for peer-to-peer name resolution. Client workstation name resolution and dynamic updates are not supported. Instead, GlobalNames zone holds CNAME resource records to map a single-label name to a fully qualified domain name (FQDN). In networks that are currently using WINS, the GlobalNames zone usually contains resource records for centrally managed names that are already statically configured on the WINS server.

Microsoft recommends that you integrate the GlobalNames zone with AD DS and that you configure each authoritative DNS server with a local copy of the Global-Names zone. This provides maximum performance and scalability. AD DS integration of the GlobalNames zone is required to support deployment of the GlobalNames zone across multiple forests.

Supporting IPv6 Addresses

Windows Server 2008 DNS supports IPv6 addresses as fully as it supports IPv4 addresses. IPv6 addresses register dynamically and you can create an AAAA (quad-A) host record for any computer on the network whose operating system does not support dynamic registration. You can create IPv6 Reverse Lookup zones. You configure an AAAA record and create an IPv6 Reverse Lookup zone in the practice session later in this lesson.

MORE INFO IPv6 Reverse Lookup

For more information about IPv6 Reverse Lookup zones, and additional information about a wide range of IPv6 topics, see *http://www.microsoft.com/technet/network/ipv6/ipv6faq.mspx.*

The *dnscmd* command-line tool accepts addresses in both IPv4 and IPv6 format. Windows Server 2008 DNS servers can send recursive queries to IPv6-only servers, and a DNS server forwarder list can contain both IPv4 and IPv6 addresses. DHCP clients can register IPv6 addresses in addition to (or instead of) IPv4 addresses. Windows Server 2008 DNS servers support the ip6.arpa domain namespace for reverse mapping.

> ### Quick Check
> - What feature does Windows Server 2008 DNS introduce that will help organizations phase out WINS and NetBT?
>
> ### Quick Check Answer
> - The GlobalNames zone

Planning a DNS Infrastructure

As a network professional you will almost certainly have worked with DNS and know that in a dynamic DNS system most hosts and servers register their host (A) records automatically, and you can configure DHCP to create DNS records when it allocates configurations. In comparison with legacy static DNS, where records needed to be added manually (hence the popularity of WINS), dynamic DNS requires very little manual configuration. You might have created IPv4 Reverse Lookup zones, and in the practice session later in this chapter you will create an IPv6 Reverse Lookup zone.

However, you might not have experience planning a DNS infrastructure. As you advance in your chosen profession you will discover that planning takes up much of your time, and the 70-646 examination guide specifically mentions planning tasks carried out and decisions made by server administrators. You therefore need to consider the process of planning a DNS infrastructure.

Planning a DNS Namespace

Typically, planning and defining a DNS namespace will be a task for an enterprise administrator. Nevertheless you should know the options available so that you can more efficiently plan the implementation of the decisions made at the enterprise level.

If you use a DNS namespace for internal purposes only, the name does not need to conform to the standard defined in RFC 1123, "Requirements for Internet Hosts— Application and Support," RFC 2181, "Clarifications to the DNS Specification," and the character set specified in RFC 2044, "UTF-8, A Transformation Format of Unicode and ISO 10646." The contoso.internal namespace you configured in your test network is an example of this type of namespace.

If, however, you need to specify a corporate namespace to be used on the Internet, it needs to be registered with the appropriate authority and conform to the relevant RFC standards, such as *treyresearch.com* or *tailspintoys.co.uk*. Most organizations have both a private and a public network. You can implement the DNS infrastructure by using one of the following schemes:

- You can use a corporate namespace for both the internal and external (Internet) portions of your network. This is arguably the most straightforward namespace configuration to implement and provides access to both internal and external resources. However, you need to ensure that the appropriate records are being stored on the internal and external DNS servers and that the security of your internal network is protected.

- You can use delegated namespaces to identify your organization's internal network. For example, Trey Research could have the public namespace *treyresearch.com* and the private namespace *intranet.treyresearch.com*. This fits neatly with Active Directory structure and is easily implemented if you use Active Directory–integrated DNS. Internal clients should be able to resolve external namespace addresses, but external clients should not be able to resolve internal namespace addresses. All internal domain data is isolated in the domain tree and requires its own DNS server infrastructure. An internal DNS server will forward requests for an external namespace address to an external DNS server. The disadvantage of namespace delegation is that FQDNs can become quite long. The maximum length of an FQDN is 255 bytes. FQDNs for DCs are limited to 155 bytes.

■ You can use separate namespaces for your external and internal namespaces, such as *tailspintoys.com* and *tailspintoys.private*. This improves security by isolating the two namespaces from each other and preventing internal resources from being exposed directly to the Internet. Zone transfers do not need to be performed between the two namespaces, and the existing DNS namespace remains unchanged.

In Active Directory networks you can gain considerable benefits by specifying Active Directory–integrated DNS. Not least of these benefits is that DNS zone information is automatically replicated through Active Directory replication. You can implement secondary DNS zones on DNS or BIND servers that need not be part of the Active Directory structure. For example, DNS servers on peripheral zones are frequently stand-alone servers. Implementation of Active Directory on your network plays a critical role in determining how domains should be created and nested within each other. You can easily create delegated zones. For example, you could use *engineering.tailspintoys.com* rather than *tailspintoys.com/engineering*.

You can partition your DNS namespace by geographical location, by department, or by both. For example, if Trey Research has several locations but only a single Human Resources department located at central office, you could use the namespace *hr.treyresearch.com*. If Tailspin Toys has a main office in Denver and manufacturing facilities in Boston and Dallas, you could configure namespaces *denver.tailspintoys.com, boston.tailspintoys.com*, and *dallas.tailspintoys.com*. You can combine both systems: *maintenance.dallas.tailspintoys.com*. If you are concerned that the design implements too many hierarchical levels, you can choose instead to use Active Directory organizational units (OUs), such as *dallas.tailspintoys.com/maintenance*.

Planning the Zone Type

Active Directory networks typically use Active Directory–integrated zones for internal name resolution. In this case DNS zone information is held on writable DCs in the domain (usually all the writable DCs). This gives the advantages of Active Directory replication, failover if one DC goes down, and increased availability through a multimaster arrangement. Standard primary zones installed on Windows stand-alone servers can be used where a writable DNS server is required but access to the Active Directory database is seen as a security risk.

Both Active Directory–integrated and standard primary zones can provide zone information to standard secondary DNS zones. In Windows Server 2008 networks, secondary DNS zones (with special features described in Chapter 3, "Active Directory and Group Policy") can be implemented on RODCs. Locating a secondary DNS server at a remote location can significantly improve the speed of name resolution at that location. Secondary zone servers increase redundancy by proving name resolution even if the primary zone server is unresponsive. Secondary zone servers also reduce the load on primary servers by distributing name resolution requests among more DNS servers. A secondary zone server does not need to be part of the Active Directory domain (except in the case of RODCs) and you can install secondary zones on non-Windows servers.

Planning DNS Forwarding

A DNS forwarder accepts forwarded recursive lookups from another DNS server and then resolves the request for that DNS server. For example, a local DNS server can forward DNS queries to a central DNS server that is authoritative for an internal DNS zone. If the forwarding server does not receive a valid resolution from the server to which it forwards the request, it attempts to resolve the request itself, unless it is a subordinate server. Subordinate servers do not try to resolve a resolution request if they do not receive a valid response to a forwarded DNS request. Typically subordinate servers are used in conjunction with secure Internet connections.

Windows Server 2003 introduced conditional forwarding, described earlier in this lesson, and this can be used in Windows Server 2008. You should plan to use conditional forwarders if, for example, you want requests made for internal name resolution to be forwarded to a master DNS server that stores internal DNS zones, and want name resolution requests for Internet domains to be sent to the Internet where they can be satisfied through recursion. You can also use conditional forwarding on an extranet where resolution requests that specify domains in the extranet can be sent to DNS servers authoritative for the DNS zone corresponding to the domain, and requests for the resolution of names external to the extranet can be sent to the Internet for recursive resolution.

Exam Tip   Forwarding DNS requests requires that the DNS server be capable of making recursive queries. Examination answers that suggest that you should configure forwarding and disable recursion can be eliminated as possible correct answers.

A typical DNS forwarding scenario could specify a DNS server that is permitted to forward queries to DNS servers outside the corporate firewall. This implementation allows the firewall to be configured to allow DNS traffic only from this specific DNS server, and to allow only valid replies back to the DNS server to enter the protected network. By using this approach, all other DNS traffic—both inbound and outbound—can be dropped at the firewall. This improves the overall security of the network and the DNS service.

Practice: Configuring DNS

In this practice session you configure a static AAAA record and an IPv6 Reverse Lookup zone.

▶ Exercise 1: Configure an AAAA Record

The stand-alone server Brisbane has an operating system that cannot register in Windows Server 2008 DNS. You therefore need to create a manual AAAA record for this server. Its IPv6 address is fec0:0:0:fffe::aa.

1. Log on to the domain controller with the kim_akers account.

2. In Administrative Tools, open DNS Manager.

3. If a UAC dialog box appears, click Continue.

4. In DNS Manager, expand Forward Lookup zones. Right-click contoso.internal and select New Host (A or AAAA).

5. Enter the server name and IPv6 address as shown in Figure 2-31. Ensure that Create Associated Pointer (PTR) Record is not selected.

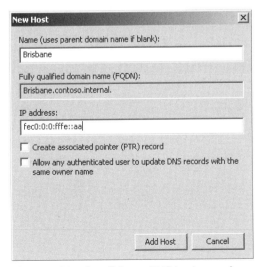

Figure 2-31   Specifying a DNS host record

6. Click Add Host. Click OK to clear the DNS message box.

7. Click Done. Ensure that the new record exists in DNS Manager.

8. Close DNS Manager.

9. Log off of the domain controller.

▶ **Exercise 2: Configure a Reverse Lookup IPv6 Zone**

In the previous exercise you could not create an associated PTR record because a Reverse Lookup zone did not exist. In this exercise you create an IPv6 Reverse Lookup zone for all site-local IPv6 addresses—that is addresses starting with fec0. You then create a PTR record in the zone. Note that in IPv6, Reverse Lookup zone addresses are entered as reverse-order 4-bit nibbles, so fec0 becomes 0.c.e.f.

1. If necessary, log on to the domain controller with the kim_akers account.

2. Click Start. Right-click Command Prompt and select Run As Administrator.

3. If a UAC dialog box appears, click Continue.

4. Enter **dnscmd glasgow /ZoneAdd 0.c.e.f.ip6.arpa /DsPrimary**. Figure 2-32 shows that the zone was created successfully. Close the command console.

Figure 2-32   Creating an IPv6 Reverse Lookup zone

5. Open DNS Manager in Administrative Tools. If a UAC dialog box appears, click Continue.

6. Expand Forward Lookup Zones. Select contoso.internal.

7. Right-click the AAAA record for Glasgow and then click Properties.

8. Select Update Associated Pointer (PTR) Record as shown in Figure 2-33. Click OK.

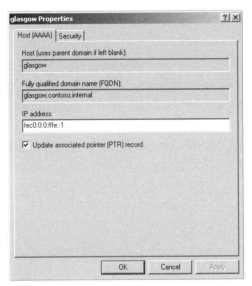

Figure 2-33   Creating a PTR record

9. Expand Reverse Lookup Zones and select 0.c.e.f.ip6.arpa. Ensure that the PTR record for Glasgow exists, as shown in Figure 2-34.

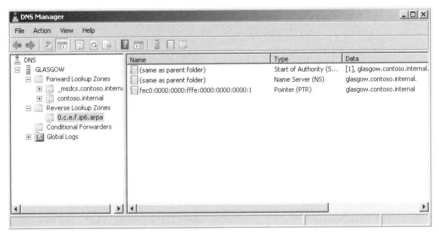

Figure 2-34   The PTR record for Glasgow

10. Log off of the domain controller.

Lesson Summary

- The DNS Server role in Windows Server 2008 complies with all current standards and can work successfully with most other DNS server implementations.

- Windows Server 2008 DNS is dynamic and typically requires very little static configuration. You can use the DNS Manager GUI or CLI tools such as *dnscmd*, *nslookup*, *ipconfig* and *netsh* to configure and manage DNS.

- New Windows Server 2008 DNS functions include background zone loading, support for RODCs, and the GlobalNames DNS zone. Windows Server 2008 DNS fully supports IPv6 Forward Lookup and Reverse Lookup zones.

Lesson Review

Use the following questions to test your knowledge of the information in Lesson 2, "Configuring DNS." The questions are also available on the companion CD if you prefer to review them in electronic form.

NOTE   Answers

Answers to these questions and explanations of why each answer choice is correct or incorrect are located in the "Answers" section at the end of the book.

---

1. You want to create an IPv6 Reverse Lookup zone that holds PTR records for hosts with IPv6 addresses in the fec0::eefd/64 subnet. Your DNS server is called denver and it is also a domain controller. DNS on your domain is AD DS integrated. You use Remote Desktop to connect to denver and run the Command Console as an administrator. What command do you enter to create the Reverse Lookup zone?

   A. *dnscmd denver /ZoneAdd d.f.e.e.0.0.0.0.0.0.0.0.0.0.c.e.f.ip6.arpa /Primary*

   B. *dnscmd denver /ZoneAdd d.f.e.e.0.0.0.0.0.0.0.0.0.0.c.e.f.ip6.arpa /DsPrimary*

   C. *dnscmd denver /ZoneAdd d.f.e.e.0.0.0.0.0.0.0.0.0.0.c.e.f.in-addr.arpa /Primary*

   D. *dnscmd denver /ZoneAdd fec0::eefd/64.ip6.arpa /DsPrimary*

2. You want to list all the DNS records in the adatum.internal domain. You connect to the DNS server Edinburgh.adatum.internal by using Remote Desktop and open the Command Console. You enter **nslookup**. At the nslookup> prompt you enter **ls -d adatum.internal**. An error message tells you that zone data

cannot be loaded to that computer. You know all the DNS records in the domain exist on Edinburgh. Why were they not displayed?

    A. You have not configured the adatum.internal Forward Lookup zone to allow zone transfers.

    B. You need to run the Command Console as an administrator to use *nslookup*.

    C. You should have entered **nslookup ls −d adatum.internal** directly from the command prompt. You cannot use the *ls* function from the nslookup> prompt.

    D. You need to log on to the DNS server interactively to use *nslookup*. You cannot use it over a Remote Desktop connection.

3. A user tries to access the company internal Web site from a client computer but cannot do so because of a network problem. You fix the network problem but the user still cannot reach the Web site, although she can reach other Web sites. Users on other client computers have no problem reaching the internal Web sites. How can you quickly resolve the situation?

    A. Create a static host record for your local Web server in DNS.

    B. Run *ipconfig /flushdns* on the primary DNS server.

    C. Run *ipconfig /registerdns* on the user's computer.

    D. Run *ipconfig /flushdns* on the user's computer.

Chapter Review

To further practice and reinforce the skills you learned in this chapter, you can perform the following tasks:

- Review the chapter summary.
- Review the list of key terms introduced in this chapter.
- Complete the case scenarios. These scenarios set up real-world situations involving the topics in this chapter and ask you to create a solution.
- Complete the suggested practices.
- Take a practice test.

Chapter Summary

- IPv6 is fully supported in Windows Server 2008 and is installed by default. It supports unicast, multicast, and anycast addresses. It is backward-compatible with IPv4 and offers a selection of transitioning strategies.
- IPv6 addresses can be configured through stateful and stateless configuration. Both GUI and CLI tools are available to configure IPv6 and check network connectivity.
- Windows Server 2008 DNS fully supports IPv6, in addition to offering several new and enhanced features. It conforms to all current standards. GUI and CLI tools are available to configure DNS and check DNS functionality.

Key Terms

Do you know what these key terms mean? You can check your answers by looking up the terms in the glossary at the end of the book.

- Address space
- Anycast address
- BootP-enabled
- Forward lookup zone
- Multicast address
- Reverse lookup zone
- Route aggregation

- Scope
- Unicast address

Case Scenarios

In the following case scenarios, you will apply what you have learned about configuring network connectivity. You can find answers to these questions in the "Answers" section at the end of this book.

Case Scenario 1: Implementing Ipv6 Connectivity

You are a senior network administrator at Wingtip Toys. Your company intranetwork consists of two subnets with contiguous private IPv4 networks configured as Virtual Local Area Networks (VLANs) connected to a layer-3 switch. Wingtip Toys accesses its ISP and the Internet through a dual-homed Internet Security and Acceleration (ISA) server that provides NAT and firewall services and connects through a peripheral zone to a hardware firewall and hence to its ISP. The company wants to implement IPv6 connectivity. All of the network hardware supports IPv6, as does the ISP. Answer the following questions:

1. What options are available for the type of unicast address used on the subnets?
2. Given that the Wingtip Toys network can support both IPv4 and IPv6, what is the most straightforward transition strategy?
3. You decide to use stateful configuration to allocate IPv6 configuration on the two subnets. How should you configure your DHCPv6 servers to provide failover protection?

Case Scenario 2: Configuring DNS

You administer the Windows Server 2008 AD DS network at Blue Yonder Airlines. When the company upgraded to Windows Server 2008 it also introduced AD DS-integrated DNS, although two BIND servers are still used as secondary DNS servers. Answer the following questions:

1. Blue Yonder has set up wireless hotspots for the convenience of its customers. However, management is concerned that attackers might attempt to register their computers in the company's DNS. How can you ensure against this?
2. Your boss is aware of the need to replicate DNS zones to the two stand-alone BIND servers. She is concerned that an attacker might attempt to replicate DNS

zone information to an unauthorized server, thus exposing the names and IP addresses of company computers. How do you reassure her?

3. For additional security Blue Yonder uses RODCs at its branch locations. Management is concerned that DNS zone information on these computers is kept up to date. What information can you provide?

4. Blue Yonder wants to use an application that needs to resolve IPv6 addresses to host names. How do you implement this functionality?

Suggested Practices

To help you successfully master the exam objectives presented in this chapter, complete the following tasks.

Configure IPv6 Connectivity

Do Practice 1 and Practice 2. Practice 3 is optional.

- **Practice 1: Investigate Netsh Commands**   The *netsh* command structure provides you with many powerful commands. In particular, use the help function in the Command Console to investigate the *netsh interface ipv6 set*, *netsh interface ipv6 add*, and *netsh interface ipv6 show* commands. Also investigate the *netsh dhcp* commands.

- **Practice 2: Find Out More About DHCPv6 Scope and Server Options**   Use the DHCP administrative tool to list the DHCP scope and server options. Access Windows Server 2008 Help and the Internet to find out more about these options. In the process you should learn something about Network Integration Service (NIS) networks. Although the 70-646 examination objectives do not cover NIS, you should, as a network professional, know what it is.

- **Practice 3: Test DHCPv6 Address Allocation**   If you have access to additional PCs with suitable client operating systems, connect them to your network and configure them to obtain IPv6 configuration automatically. Ensure that the DHCPv6 scope you have configured provides configuration for these computers. Ensure that the host IPv6 addresses configured fall outside the range fec0:0:0:fffe::1 through fec0:0:0:fffe::ff, which includes the IPv6 addresses for the Glasgow and Melbourne computers.

Configure DNS

Do both practices in this section.

- **Practice 1: Use the CLI Tools**   It would take an entire book to do justice to the *nslookup*, *dnscmd*, *ipconfig*, and *netsh* tools. The only way to become familiar with these tools is to use them.

- **Practice 2: Configure IPv6 Reverse Lookup Zones**   This procedure was described earlier in the lesson. Specifying IPv6 Reverse Lookup zones in DNS can be an error-prone procedure because of the way the prefixes are specified. You will become comfortable with this notation only through practice.

Take a Practice Test

The practice tests on this book's companion CD offer many options. For example, you can test yourself on just one exam objective, or you can test yourself on all of the 70-646 certification exam content. You can set up the test so that it closely simulates the experience of taking a certification exam, or you can set it up in study mode so that you can look at the correct answers and explanations after you answer each question.

MORE INFO   Practice tests

For details about all the practice test options available, see the "How to Use the Practice Tests" section in this book's Introduction.

Chapter 3
Active Directory and Group Policy

This chapter looks at Active Directory, and specifically the Active Directory Domain Services (AD DS). It discusses the new features and enhancements introduced by Windows Server 2008 and how Group Policy is implemented in AD DS. The focus of the chapter is planning rather than implementation. You will learn how to use graphical user interface (GUI) and command-line interface (CLI) tools. However, the most important consideration is not how you make configuration changes, but why and when. As you progress in your chosen career, you will spend more and more time planning rather than configuring.

Exam objectives in this chapter:
- Plan infrastructure services server roles.
- Plan and implement group policy strategy.

Lessons in this chapter:

Before You Begin

To complete the lesson in this chapter, you must have done the following:

- Installed Windows Server 2008 and configured your test PC as a domain controller (DC) in the Contoso.internal domain as described in the Introduction and in Chapter 1, "Installing, Upgrading, and Deploying Windows Server 2008." You also need a client PC running Windows Vista Business, Enterprise, or Ultimate that is a member of the Contoso.internal domain. This can be a separate PC or a virtual machine installed on the same PC as your DC.

Real World

Ian McLean

Active Directory has been around for some time. As a network professional you will be familiar with most Active Directory domain administration tasks and with tools such as Active Directory Users And Computers that let you carry them out. Even relatively unsophisticated corporate users might have heard of Active Directory, and they know that if they forget their passwords or need permissions to a folder, an administrator will do something magical in the directory.

However, you might sometimes be called on to explain "this Active Directory thing" to users with little knowledge of, or interest in, the technical aspects of networking. These users are typically managers who can't see why all computers in the organization can't just be linked to each other (some may even have heard of workgroups) and why you need domain controllers and other servers that, as far as they are concerned, don't actually do anything.

I find that a good way to explain a directory structure is to use the analogy of a library. A flat file system, such as that implemented by Windows NT4, is the equivalent of storing all the books in a heap on the floor. If a reader wants to read a particular book, she needs to look at them one at a time until the book is found. A directory structure, on the other hand, is the equivalent of having the books on bookcase shelves, in alphabetical order by author name, and the bookcases themselves located in designated parts of the library.

Thus if I wanted to find a history book I would look in nonfiction, find the history bookcases, and easily locate the volume. In a large library, the bookcases could be further subdivided into (for example) ancient history, American history, European history, and so on.

Even more efficiently, I could consult the library index and find exactly which shelf has a book I'm looking for. I could look at a map of the library layout and determine the physical location of that shelf. This is (approximately) the function of the Active Directory schema. You could extend the analogy to describe rooms in the library that hold specialist materials (organizational units). Specialist researchers would sit in these rooms and read the books located there. You could have access policies for the specialist rooms that differ from those that apply to the main library. You could have a person that controls access to materials within a specific room but has no authority in other rooms or in the main library.

Finally, and most significantly, an ordered library, like an ordered directory structure, can have defined and centrally controlled security policies. In the free-for-all heap of books on the floor, anyone can access any book, write on the flyleaf, and even decide to throw the book away. In a centrally organized system, read, write, and modify rights can be strictly controlled.

Of course the analogy isn't perfect, but I've used it with some success for several years.

Lesson 1: Windows Server 2008 Active Directory

The intention of this lesson is not to describe the basic functions of Active Directory. As an experienced network professional you should know how to add users and groups, assign rights and permissions, and use the AD Find function. If not, these topics are adequately described in the Help files, in white papers, and in many excellent publications. The object of this lesson is to describe the new and enhanced features of Windows Server AD DS and to discuss the planning aspects of AD DS implementation. It is easy enough to raise the domain functional level. Knowing when and whether you should do so is another matter, especially because you cannot reverse the process except by restoring from backup or reinstalling the operating system.

You are unlikely to implement multiple domains on your small test network, and this book does not ask you to do so. You are even less likely to create multiple forests. Nevertheless, planning forest functional levels and forest trusts are tasks that you might be asked to perform when administering a large corporate network. The lesson therefore covers the planning processes involved in inter-forest operations.

After this lesson, you will be able to:

- List and describe the new features and functions in the Windows Server 2008 Active Directory Domain Services (AD DS).
- Plan and configure domain functional levels.
- Plan forest functional levels.
- Plan forest trusts.
- Use the Directory Server.

Estimated lesson time: 55 minutes

Introducing the Windows Server 2008 Directory Server Role

You can use a DC with the Windows Server 2008 AD DS Server role (sometimes known as the Directory Server role) installed to manage users, computers, printers, or applications on a network. AD DS introduces the following features that enable you deploy it more simply and securely and to administer it more efficiently:

- **Read-only domain controllers**   AD DS introduces read-only domain controllers (RODCs) that host read-only partitions of the Active Directory database. You can use RODCs where physical security cannot be guaranteed, such as at branch office locations or where local storage of domain passwords is considered a primary threat (in extranets or in an application-facing role, for example). You can delegate RODC administration to a domain user or security group and can therefore use RODCs in locations where a local administrator is not a member of the Domain Admins group.

- **New and enhanced tools and wizards**   Windows Server 2008 AD DS also introduces an AD DS Installation Wizard and enhances the Microsoft Management Console (MMC) snap-in GUI tools that manage users and resources. For example, the AD DS Installation Wizard lets you specify whether you are installing a writable DC or an RODC. If you are installing the former, you can specify the Password Replication Policy for that DC to determine whether it allows an RODC to pull user credential information.

- **Fine-grained security policies**   Windows Server 2008 AD DS lets you apply different password and account lockout policies to users and global security groups in the same domain, thereby reducing the number of domains you need to manage.

- **Restartable AD DS**   You can stop and restart AD DS. This lets you perform offline operations such as the defragmentation of Active Directory objects without needing to restart a DC in Directory Services Restore Mode.

- **AD DS data mining tool**   You can use the AD DS data mining tool to view AD data stored in snapshots online, compare data in snapshots that are taken at different times, and decide which data to restore without having to restart the DC.

NOTE   Restoring deleted objects and containers

You cannot use the AD DS data mining tool to directly restore deleted objects and containers. You use it to view snapshot data and need to perform data recovery as a subsequent step. However, you no longer need to restore from several backups to find the data you want.

- **Auditing enhancements**   You can use the new Directory Service Changes audit policy subcategory when auditing Windows Server 2008 AD DS. This lets you log old and new values when changes are made to AD DS objects and their attributes. You can also use this new feature when auditing Active Directory Lightweight Directory Services (AD LDS).

MORE INFO   AD LDS

For more information about AD LDS, see *http://technet2.microsoft.com/windowsserver2008/en/ servermanager/activedirectorylightweightdirectoryservices.mspx* and follow the links.

RODCs

In organizations that use Windows Server 2003 (or earlier) domains, users at remote branch locations typically authenticate with a DC at central office through a wide area network (WAN) connection. This is far from ideal and can cause delays. If WAN connectivity is interrupted users are unable to log on.

However, from a security point of view, logging on over a WAN is preferable to having a writable DC at a small location where physical security cannot be guaranteed. Also, it is a poor use of scarce administrative resource to locate a domain administrator at a small branch location, and administering a DC remotely over a WAN can be a time-consuming and frustrating task, particularly if the branch office is connected to a hub site with low network bandwidth.

Windows Server 2008 addresses this problem by introducing the RODC. RODCs offer improved security, faster logon times, and more efficient access to local resources. RODC administration can be delegated to users or groups that do not have administrative rights in the domain.

You might also choose to deploy an RODC if, for example, a line-of-business (LOB) application used at a branch office runs successfully only if it is installed on a domain controller. Alternatively the domain controller might be the only server in the branch office, and might host server applications. In both cases the LOB application owner typically needs to log on to the DC interactively or use Terminal Services to configure and manage the application. This situation creates a security risk to the Active Directory forest. However, the risk is considerably reduced if the LOB application owner (typically not a domain administrator) is granted the right to log on to an RODC.

NOTE   Planning branch offices

In a small branch office where the hardware budget is limited you might need servers that perform a variety of roles, some of which conflict. An RODC can provide part of your solution to this problem, but you should also consider virtualization. Chapter 5, "Terminal Services and Application and Server Virtualization," discusses this in detail.

An RODC receives its configuration from a writable domain controller. Therefore, at least one writable domain controller in the domain must be running Windows Server 2008. In addition, the functional level for the domain and forest must be Windows Server 2003 or higher. Sensitive security information such as user passwords is not replicated to the RODC. The first time a user logs on at the branch office his identity is validated across the WAN. However, the RODC can pull user credentials so that further logons by the same user are validated locally, although you need to specifically permit this in the domain Password Replication Policy with respect to that RODC. You can do this when you create a computer account for the RODC in Active Directory by using Active Directory Users And Computers on a writable DC in the domain.

Quick Check

- You plan to install RODCs in all your company's branch offices. What is the minimum forest functional level that allows you to do this?

Quick Check Answer

- Windows Server 2003.

When an RODC requests credential information from the writable DC, that DC recognizes that the request is coming from an RODC and consults the Password Replication Policy in effect for that RODC. This addresses the security risk of having passwords for every user in a domain stored on a DC at a remote location.

MORE INFO RODC filtered attribute set

For more information about attributes that are filtered out and not replicated to an RODC, see *http://technet2.microsoft.com/windowsserver2008/en/library/0e8e874f-3ef4-43e6-b496-302a47101e611033.mspx?mfr=true.*

RODCs are particularly useful at remote locations that have relatively few users or users with little IT knowledge, inadequate physical security, low network bandwidth, or any combination of these features. They provide a read-only AD DS database, unidirectional replication (from the writable DC to the RODC only), credential caching (to streamline logon) and read-only Domain Name System (DNS) zones.

MORE INFO Deploying an RODC

For more information about the prerequisites for deploying an RODC, see http:// *technet2.microsoft.com/windowsserver2008/en/library/ce82863f-9303-444f-9bb3-ecaf649bd3dd1033.mspx?mfr=true* and *http://technet2.microsoft.com/windowsserver2008/en/library/ea8d253e-0646-490c-93d3-b78c5e1d9db71033.mspx?mfr=true*. For more information about the *adprep /rodcprep* CLI command, see *http://technet2.microsoft.com/windowsserver2008/en/library/aa923ebf-de47-494b-a60a-9fce083d2f691033.mspx?mfr=true.*

You can install the DNS Server service on an RODC, which can then replicate all application directory partitions that DNS uses, including ForestDNSZones and DomainDNSZones. If a DNS server is installed on an RODC, clients can send name resolution queries as they would to any other DNS server.

However, the DNS server on an RODC does not directly support client updates and does not register name server (NS) resource records for any Active Directory–integrated zone that it hosts. When a client attempts to update its DNS records against an RODC, the server returns a referral to a writable DNS server. The RODC then requests the updated DNS record (a single record only) from the writable DNS server. The entire list of changed zone or domain data does not get replicated during this special replicate-single-object request.

Planning RODC Implementation

You can plan to implement RODCs at remote locations either when you roll out a Windows Server 2008 upgrade or if you already have a Windows Server 2008 AD DS domain. You can specify Password Replication Policy for a specific RODC when you create the computer account for the RODC in the domain as the first stage of a two-stage RODC installation as described later in this lesson. Alternatively, you can open Active Directory Users And Computers on an existing writable DC, right-click the account for an RODC in the Domain Controllers container, click Properties, and click the Password Replication Policy tab to permit password caching for that RODC. Figure 3-1 shows the Password Replication Policy tab for an RODC named Edinburgh in the contoso.internal domain.

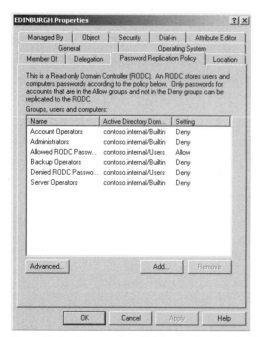

Figure 3-1   Password replication policy for the RODC Edinburgh

For example, Margie's Travel has a number of very small branch offices located in remote rural areas where WAN links can sometimes be slow or unreliable. Because of the size and remote nature of these offices, the hardware budget is limited and servers need to perform several functions. No local domain administrators exist. Central administration from the head office requires that the branch office equipment is part of an Active Directory structure. One of the functions of the servers in the branch offices is currently to act as secondary DNS servers. The remote servers are also file and application servers, and some applications require interactive server logon. Offices at remote locations cannot offer the same level of physical security as can the head office, and logons at remote offices are validated by DCs at the head office. This can result in unacceptable logon delays.

In addition to upgrading the DCs at the main office, a planned Windows Server 2008 upgrade could involve the installation of RODCs at branch offices. You can first create the accounts for these RODCs at the main office, and at that stage you can set the password replication policy for each RODC to allow the remote RODCs to pull account information and cache credentials for users who log on at the branch office. This would speed up logons. At the same time, users or a security group could be granted permission to install RODCs and to log on to these RODCs interactively at the branch office.

Installing DNS on RODCs (the default) implements a secondary DNS server that can replicate all application directory partitions that DNS uses, including ForestDNSZones and DomainDNSZones. Additionally, if a local client record is amended or added, this DNS server can request the appropriate single updated DNS from the writable DNS server without needing to pull the entire list of changed zone or domain data.

You can permit interactive logon if the applications installed on the RODC require it without exposing writable Active Directory data to a user who is not a domain administrator. You should also consider virtualization. File and application servers are seldom virtualized. RODCs and DNS servers can be.

Utilizing Installation Wizard Enhancements

Windows Server 2008 enhances the AD DS Installation Wizard to streamline and simplify AD DS and introduce new features such as the installation of RODCs. Windows Server 2008 also includes changes to the Microsoft Management Console (MMC) snap-in functions that manage AD DS. These changes enable you, for example, to easily locate DCs in a large enterprise network, and to configure the Password Replication Policy for RODCs.

You start the AD DS Installation Wizard by clicking Add Roles in the Initial Configuration Tasks dialog box or in Server Manager, or by running *dcpromo* from a Command prompt or from the Run box. Some of the pages in the wizard appear only if you select Use Advanced Mode Installation on the Welcome page of the wizard. You can also enter **dcpromo /adv** to access advanced mode installation. Figure 3-2 shows how you specify advanced mode installation.

Figure 3-2   Specifying advanced mode installation

Exam Tip   A domain administrator configures the password replication policy for an RODC on a writable DC. You can discard any answer in the 70-646 examination in which a designated user who is not a domain administrator opens Active Directory Users And Computers on the RODC and configures password replication policy.

Advanced mode installation gives you greater control over the installation process. If you do not specify this mode, the wizard uses default options that apply to most configurations. Additional installation options in advanced installation mode include the following:

■ You can select the source DC for the installation. This DC is used to initially replicate domain data to the new DC.

■ You can use backup media from an existing DC in the same domain to reduce network traffic that is associated with initial replication.

- You can create a new domain tree.

- You can change the default NetBIOS name.

- You can set forest and domain functional levels when you create a new forest or a new domain.

- You can configure the Password Replication Policy for an RODC.

You will discover other improvements as you go through the AD DS installation process. For example, if you install an additional DC, you can select the domain name rather than typing it into a dialog box. By default, the new installation wizard uses the credentials of the user who is currently logged on, provided that the user is logged on with a domain account. You can specify other credentials if you need to.

From the wizard's Summary page you can export your settings to an answer file that you can use as a template for subsequent installations or uninstalls. Note that if you specify a value for the Directory Services Restore Mode (DSRM) administrator password in the wizard, and then export the settings to an answer file, the password does not appear in the answer file. If you want this information to be included, you need to manually modify the answer file.

However, the inclusion of clear-text passwords in answer files is not good security practice. For this reason you can omit your administrator password from the answer file. If you type **password=*** in the answer file, the installation wizard prompts you for account credentials. Finally, the installation wizard lets you force the demotion of a domain controller that is started in Directory Services Restore Mode.

Delegating RODC Installation

When planning RODC installation you can choose to implement two-stage installation. Working at the head office, you can delegate the appropriate permissions to a user or a group. At a branch office a user with the delegated permissions can perform the installation, and can subsequently manage the RODC without needing domain administrator rights.

To delegate RODC installation, you first create an RODC account in Active Directory Users And Computers by right-clicking the Domain Controllers container and selecting Pre-Create Read-Only Domain Controller Account. When you create the RODC account, you can delegate the installation and administration of the RODC to a user or a security group, as shown in Figure 3-3.

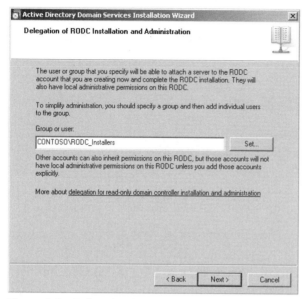

Figure 3-3   Delegating installation and administration of an RODC

A user with delegated installation and administration rights can create a RODC on a designated server by running *dcpromo/UseExistingAccount:Attach*. This user (or all users in a designated security group) can log on to the RODC interactively and administer it without requiring administration rights in the rest of the domain or the forest.

Quick Check

■ You are a domain administrator. You plan to use RODCs at your company's branch offices. Branch office staff who are not administrators will be promoting branch office servers to RODCs. What do you need to do as the first stage of a two-stage RODC installation?

Quick Check Answer

■ You need to create the computer accounts for the RODCs in the domain. You need to give branch office staff (typically one member of staff in each branch office) the appropriate rights to install RODCs.

Utilizing MMC Snap-In Enhancements

Windows Server 2008 enhances the functions of MMC snap-in tools such as Active Directory Users And Computers. The next section of this lesson discusses enhancements to the schema and to Active Directory Users And Computers that provide increased permission granularity and let you plan your permission structure and in some circumstances simplify your domain structure.

The Windows Server 2008 Active Directory Sites And Services snap-in includes a Find command on the toolbar and in the Action menu. This command lets you discover the site in which a DC is placed. This can help you to troubleshoot replication problems. In Windows 2000 Server and Windows Server 2003, Active Directory Sites And Services did not easily provide you with this information.

You saw earlier that when you install a computer account for an RODC, one of the advanced features of the installation wizard provides a Password Replication Policy page that lets you configure settings for that RODC. If you choose not to configure these settings at this stage, you can instead use the Password Replication Policy tab on the RODC's Properties dialog box. This was illustrated in Figure 3-1 earlier in this lesson.

If you click the Advanced button on this tab, you can determine what passwords have been sent to or are stored in the RODC and what accounts have authenticated to the RODC. This lets you discover who is using the RODC. You can use this information when planning your password replication policy. You will not see entries in this dialog box until the RODC has been physically created and has validated logons for local users.

Planning Fine-Grained Password and Account Lockout Policies

In previous Active Directory implementations you could apply only one password and account lockout policy to all users in the domain. If you needed different password and account lockout settings for different sets of users, you needed to create a custom password filter or create multiple domains.

Windows Server 2008 lets you specify fine-grained password policies. You can specify multiple password policies and apply different password restrictions and account lockout policies to different sets of users within a single domain. For example, you might want to increase the minimum password length for administrative-level accounts. This facility also lets you apply a special password policy for accounts whose passwords are synchronized with other data sources.

Windows Server 2008 includes the following two new object classes in the AD DS schema:

- Password Settings Container
- Password Settings

The Password Settings Container (PSC) object class is created by default under the System container in the domain. It stores the Password Settings Objects (PSOs) for that domain. You cannot rename, move, or delete this container. You can create a PSO by saving the parameters (such as password length) in a text file with an .ldf extension and using the *ldifde* command from the Command Console. Alternatively, you can use the ADSI Edit MMC snap-in, as described in the practice section later in this lesson.

MORE INFO   Creating PSOs

For more information about creating and configuring PSOs, see *http://technet2.microsoft.com/ windowsserver2008/en/library/67dc7808-5fb4-42f8-8a48-7452f59672411033.mspx?mfr=true.*

Exam Tip   The 70-646 examination is mainly about planning rather than implementation and is unlikely to ask you to create a PSO under examination conditions, although you might be asked what tools you could use to do it. You are more likely to be asked about the planning considerations for using fine-grained passwords and what advantages they provide.

Before you plan a password policy you need to know what the default settings are. Figure 3-4 shows the default settings for the contoso.internal domain.

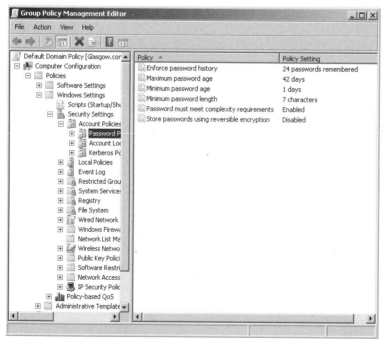

Figure 3-4   Default password settings

As a first step in planning fine-grained password and account lockout policies, you need to decide how many different password policies you need. Typically your policy could include at least three but seldom more than ten PSOs. At a minimum you would probably want to configure the following:

- An administrative-level password policy with strict settings: for example, a minimum password length of 12, a maximum password age of 28 days, and password complexity requirements enabled.

- A user-level password policy with, for example, a minimum password length of 6, a maximum password age of 90 days, and password complexity requirements not enabled.

- A service account password policy with a minimum password length of 32 characters and complexity requirements enabled (service account passwords are seldom typed in). Because of their complexity, service account passwords can typically be set not to expire or have very long password ages.

You also need to look at your existing group structure. If you have existing Administrators and Users groups there is no point creating new ones. Ultimately you need to define a group and Active Directory structure that maps to your fine-grained password and account lockout policies.

You cannot apply PSOs to organizational units (OUs) directly. If your users are organized into OUs, consider creating *shadow groups* for these OUs and then applying the newly defined fine-grained password and account lockout policies to them. A shadow group is a global security group that is logically mapped to an OU to enforce a fine-grained password and account lockout policy. Add OU users as members to the newly created shadow group and then apply the fine-grained password and account lockout policy to this shadow group. If you move a user from one OU to another, you must update user memberships in the corresponding shadow groups.

NOTE   Shadow groups

You will not find a command called Add Shadow Group in Active Directory Users And Computers. A shadow group is simply an ordinary global security group that contains all the user accounts in one or more OUs. When you apply a PSO to a shadow group you are effectively applying it to users in the corresponding OU.

Microsoft applies GPOs to groups rather than OUs because groups offer better flexibility for managing various sets of users. Windows Server 2008 AD DS creates various groups for administrative accounts, including Domain Admins, Enterprise Admins,

Schema Admins, Server Operators, and Backup Operators. You can apply PSOs to these groups or nest them in a single global security group and apply a PSO to that group. Because you use groups rather than OUs you do not need to modify the OU hierarchy to apply fine-grained passwords. Modifying an OU hierarchy requires detailed planning and increases the risk of errors.

If you intend to use fine-grained passwords, you probably need to raise the functional level of your domain. To work properly, fine-grained password settings require a domain functional level of Windows Server 2008. Planning domain and forest functional levels is discussed later in this lesson. Changing functional levels involves irreversible changes. You need to be sure, for example, that you will never want to add a Windows Server 2003 DC to your domain.

By default, only members of the Domain Admins group can create PSOs and apply a PSO to a group or user. You do not, however, need to have permissions on the user object or group object to be able to apply a PSO to it. You can delegate Read Property permissions on the default security descriptor of a PSO object to any other group (such as Help desk personnel). This lets users that are not domain administrators discover the password and account lockout settings applied through a PSO to a security group.

You can apply fine-grained password policies only to user objects and global security groups (or *inetOrgPerson* objects if they are used instead of user objects). If your plan identifies a group of computers that require different password settings, you need to look at techniques such as password filters. Fine-grained password policies cannot be applied to Computer objects.

If you use custom password filters in a domain, fine-grained password policies do not interfere with these filters. If you plan to upgrade Windows 2000 Server or Windows Server 2003 domains that currently deploy custom password filters on DCs, you can continue to use those password filters to enforce additional password restrictions.

If you have assigned a PSO to a global security group, but one user in that group requires special settings, you can assign an exceptional PSO directly to that particular user. For example, the Chief Executive Officer of Northwind Traders is a member of the senior managers group and company policy requires that senior managers use complex passwords. However, the CEO is not willing to do so. In this case you can create an exceptional PSO and apply it directly to the CEO's user account. The exceptional PSO will override the security group PSO when the password settings (msDS-ResultantPSO) for the CEO's user account are determined.

> **Quick Check**
> - By default, members of which group can create PSOs?
>
> **Quick Check Answer**
> - Domain Admins.

Finally, you can plan to delegate management of fine-grained passwords. When you have created the necessary PSOs and the global security groups associated with these PSOs, you can delegate management of the security groups to responsible users or user groups. For example, a Human Resources (HR) group could add user accounts to or remove them from the managers group when staff changes occur. If a PSO specifying fine-grained password policy is associated with the managers group, in effect the HR group is determining to whom these policies are applied.

MORE INFO   **Fine-grained password and account lockout policy configuration**

For more information about fine-grained password and account lockout policies, see *http://technet2.microsoft.com/WindowsServer2008/en/library/2199dcf7-68fd-4315-87cc-ade35f8978ea1033.mspx#BKMK_7.*

Planning the Use of the Data Mining Tool

The data mining tool (*dsamain.exe*) makes it possible for deleted AD DS or AD LDS data to be preserved in the form of snapshots of AD DS taken by the Volume Shadow Copy Service (VSS). You can use a Lightweight Directory Access Protocol (LDAP) tool such as *ldp.exe* to view the read-only data in the snapshots. The data mining tool does not actually recover the deleted objects and containers—you need to perform data recovery as a subsequent step.

When you are planning your strategy for recovering deleted data you need to decide how best to preserve deleted data so that it can be recovered, and recover that data if required. For example, you could schedule a task that regularly runs the *ntdsutil.exe* tool to take snapshots of the volume that contains the AD DS database. You can use the same tool to list the snapshots that are available, and mount the snapshot that you want to view.

The second stage of your strategy involves deciding what snapshot you should restore if data is lost or corrupted. Your plan can involve running *dsamain.exe* to expose the snapshot volume as an LDAP server. As part of the *dsamain* command you specify a port number for the LDAP port. Optionally you can also specify the LDAP-SSL, Global Catalog, and Global Catalog–SSL ports, but if you do not do so the command derives these values from the LDAP port number. You can then run *ldp.exe* and attach to the specified LDAP port. This lets you browse the snapshot just as you would any live DC.

If you know what objects or OUs you need to restore, you can identify them in the snapshots and record their attributes and back-links. You can then reanimate these objects by using the tombstone reanimation feature and manually repopulate them with the stripped attributes and back-links as identified in the snapshots. The data mining tool lets you do this without needing to restart the DC in Directory Services mode.

Your planning process should involve considerations other than when you take snapshots and how you use these snapshots in the data restoration. For example, you also need to take security into account. If an attacker obtains access to an AD DS snapshot, this is as serious as if an AD DS backup were compromised. A malicious user could copy AD DS snapshots from forest A to forest B and use domain or enterprise administrator credentials from forest B to examine the data. You should plan to encrypt AD DS snapshots to help reduce the chance of unauthorized access. As with any data encryption you also need to draw up recovery plans to recover information if the encryption key is lost or corrupted.

Planning AD DS Auditing

In Windows Server 2008, the global audit policy Audit Directory Service Access is enabled by default. This policy controls whether auditing for directory service events is enabled or disabled. If you configure this policy setting by modifying the Default Domain Controllers Policy, you can specify whether to audit successes, audit failures, or not audit at all. You can control what operations to audit by modifying the System Access Control List (SACL) on an object. You can set a SACL on an AD DS object on the Security tab in that object's Properties dialog box.

As an administrator one of your tasks is to configure audit policy. Enabling success or failure auditing is a straightforward procedure. Deciding which objects to audit; whether to audit success, failure or both; and whether to record new and old values if changes are made is much more difficult. Auditing everything is never an option—too much information is as bad as too little. You need to be selective.

In Windows 2000 Server and Windows Server 2003, you could specify only whether DS access was audited. Windows Server 2008 gives you more granular control. You can audit the following:

- DS access
- DS changes (old and new values)
- DS replication

Auditing DS replication is further subdivided so that you can choose two levels of auditing—normal or detailed.

For example, you are a domain administrator at Litware, Inc. Previously you found that the auditing you configured had limitations. You could determine that the attributes of an object in Active Directory had been changed, but not what changes were made. If a change was erroneous you relied on documentation maintained by the domain administration team to reverse or correct the alteration. Such documentation, if it existed at all, was seldom perfect.

Litware has recently upgraded its domain to Windows Server 2008. You can now plan your auditing procedures so that if a change is performed on an object attribute, AD DS logs the previous and current values of the attribute. Only the values that change as a result of the modify operation are logged, so you do not need to search through a long list of attribute values to find the change.

Quick Check

- You are setting up DS replication auditing. What are the two auditing levels from which you can choose?

Quick Check Answer

- Normal or detailed.

If a new object is created, AD DS logs values of the attributes that are configured or added at the time of creation. Attributes that take default values are not logged. If an object is moved within a domain, you can ensure that the previous and new locations are logged. When an object is moved to a different domain, you can access the *Create* event that is generated and logged on the domain controller in the target domain. If an object is undeleted, you can determine the location to which the object is moved. If attributes are added, modified, or deleted during an undelete operation you can determine the values of those attributes from the Security event log.

If Directory Service Changes is enabled, AD DS logs events in the Security event log when changes are made to objects that an administrator has set up for auditing. Table 3-1 lists these events.

Table 3-1   Security Events Related to AD DS Objects

Event ID	Type of event	Event description
5136	*Modify*	A successful modification has been made to an attribute in the directory.
5137	*Create*	A new object has been created in the directory.
5138	*Undelete*	An object has been undeleted in the directory.
5139	*Move*	An object has been moved within the domain.

You need to decide whether to react to such events, and how to do so. By default the events are logged in the Security event log and members of the Domain Admins, Builtin\Administrators, and Enterprise Admins groups can view them by opening Event Viewer. However, you can specify that an event written to the Security event log initiates a task, such as generating an alert or starting an executable program. To do this, select the event in Event Viewer and click Attach Task To This Event on the Action Menu. Figure 3-5 shows this function.

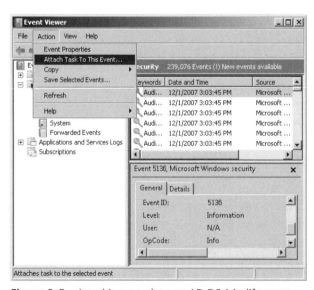

Figure 3-5   Attaching a task to an AD DS *Modify* event

Planning Domain and Forest Functionality

When you upgrade your domains and forests to Windows Server 2008 the temptation is always to raise the domain and forest functional levels. This is very easy to do, and your network will not achieve full functionality until the functional levels are raised. For example, for fine-grained password policy configuration to work properly you need a domain functional level of Windows Server 2008.

Be careful. It is very easy to raise domain and forest functional levels, but almost impossible to lower them. (You need uninstallations and reinstallations, or restores from a backup taken before the functional level was changed.) If you are asked to add Windows Server 2003 DCs to your domain and you have raised the domain functional level to Windows Server 2008, you have a problem. If you have raised your forest functional level to Windows Server 2008 and you find you need to incorporate a Windows Server 2000 domain, you might regret your earlier decision. Planning functional levels is a delicate and difficult balancing act. You need to consider both the additional functionality that raising a functional level provides and the problems it could present.

To plan what functional level you need to set for your domains and forest and when you should raise functional levels, you need to know what DCs each functional level supports and what additional functionality raising the functional level provides. You also need to know the relationship between domain and forest functional levels. For example, if you raise the functional level of your forest to Windows Server 2008, you ensure that the default functional level of all the domains in your forest is Windows Server 2008.

IMPORTANT   Functional levels do not affect member servers

Domain and forest functional levels support DCs. They do not affect member servers. For example, a file server in a Windows Server 2008 domain can have Windows 2000 Server or Windows Server 2003 installed.

Domain Functional Level Considerations

Domain functionality enables features that affect the domain. In Windows Server 2008 AD DS, the following domain functional levels are available:

- Windows 2000 native
- Windows Server 2003
- Windows Server 2008

A default installation of the Windows 2008 AD DS Server role will create a domain with the Windows 2000 native functional level. You raise the functional level of a domain in the practice session later in this lesson. To decide whether you should raise the domain functional level, you first need to know what functional level supports all the DCs that currently exist in your domain, and any that are likely to be added. Table 3-2 lists the domain functional levels and the DCs that each supports.

Table 3-2   Domain Functional Levels and Supported DCs

Domain Functional Level	Supported DCs
Windows 2000 native	Windows 2000 Server
	Windows Server 2003
	Windows Server 2008
Windows Server 2003	Windows Server 2003
	Windows Server 2008
Windows Server 2008	Windows Server 2008

If, for example, you have Windows Server 2003 DCs in your domain, you cannot raise the domain functional level to Windows Server 2008. If all your DCs are Windows Server 2008 but you might need to add a Windows Server 2003 DC at a later date, you would be wise to postpone the decision to raise your domain functional level past Windows Server 2003.

You need to balance these restrictions against the advantages you gain through raising functional levels. For example, fine-grained password policies require a domain functional level of Windows Server 2008 to work properly. To help you make the decision and plan your domain functional levels, Table 3-3 lists the features that each functional level enables.

NOTE   Find out more about the features

Table 3-3 lists the features, but it does not explain them—the table would be far too long. Most of these features are explained elsewhere in this book. If you see a feature you do not recognize, consult this book's index, the Windows Server 2008 Help files, or the Internet (for example, *http://technet2.microsoft.com/windowsserver2008/en/library/2199dcf7-68fd-4315-87cc-ade35f8978ea1033.mspx?mfr=true*).

Table 3-3 **Features Enabled by Domain Functional Levels**

Domain Functional Level	Enabled Features
Windows 2000 native	All default Active Directory features
	Universal distribution and security groups
	Group nesting
	Group conversion
	Security identifier (SID) history
Windows Server 2003	All default Active Directory features
	All Windows 2000 native domain functional level features
	The domain management tool (*netdom.exe*)
	Logon time stamp update
	Setting the *userPassword* attribute as the effective password on the *inetOrgPerson* object and user objects
	Redirecting the Users And Computers containers
	Authorization Manager stores authorization policies in AD DS
	Constrained delegation
	Selective cross-forest authentication
Windows Server 2008	All default Active Directory features
	All Windows Server 2003 domain functional level features
	Distributed File System (DFS) replication support for SYSVOL
	Advanced Encryption Services (AES 128 and 256) support for the Kerberos authentication protocol
	Last Interactive Logon information
	Fine-grained password policies

Forest Function Level Considerations

Forest functionality enables features across all the domains in a forest. In Windows Server 2008 forests the following forest functional levels are available:

- Windows 2000
- Windows Server 2003
- Windows Server 2008

A default installation of the Windows 2008 AD DS Server role that creates a new forest will set the forest functional level to Windows 2000. You can raise the forest functional level to Windows Server 2003 or Windows Server 2008. Forest functional levels are less restrictive than domain functional levels with regard to the DCs that can operate in the forest. However you need to take account of both domain and forest functional levels if you want to determine what DCs can be supported or added. Table 3-4 lists forest functional levels and the DCs each supports. Note that Windows NT4 backup domain controllers (BDCs) can operate in an Active Directory domain.

Table 3-4   Forest Functional Levels and Supported DCs

Forest Functional Level	Supported DCs
Windows 2000	Windows NT 4.0
	Windows 2000 Server
	Windows Server 2003
	Windows Server 2008
Windows Server 2003	Windows Server 2003
	Windows Server 2008
Windows Server 2008	Windows Server 2008

When you raise the forest functional level, domain controllers running earlier operating systems cannot be introduced into the forest. For example, if you raise the forest functional level to Windows Server 2003, domain controllers running Windows 2000 Server cannot be added to the forest. The domain functional level cannot be less than the forest functional level. You cannot, for example, have a Windows 2000 native domain in a Windows Server 2003 forest, but you can have a Windows Server 2008 domain in a Windows 2000 forest.

Raising the functional level of a forest is a decision that requires careful planning. You might be able to guarantee that you will not need to add a Windows Server 2003 DC to a Windows Server 2008 domain, but can you guarantee that you will never be called upon to add a Windows Server 2003 domain to a Windows Server 2008 forest (possibly as part of a company acquisition)?

As with raising the domain functional level, you need to be aware of the advantages of higher functional levels before you can make your final decision. Table 3-5 lists the features enabled by each functional level.

Table 3-5   Features Enabled by Forest Functional Levels

Forest Functional Level	Enabled Features
Windows 2000	All default Active Directory features
Windows Server 2003	All default Active Directory features
	Forest trusts
	Domain renaming
	Linked-value replication
	RODC deployment
	Improved Knowledge Consistency Checker (KCC) algorithms and scalability—such as improved intersite topology generator (ISTG) algorithms
	The ability to create the *dynamicObject* class in a domain directory partition
	The ability to convert an *inetOrgPerson* object instance into a *User* object instance, and vice versa
	The ability to create application basic groups and LDAP query groups to support role-based authorization

The Windows Server 2008 forest functional level does not (currently) support any additional features. However, if you specify this functional level, you ensure that all domains in the forest operate at the Windows Server 2008 domain functional level. You cannot specify the Windows Server 2008 forest functional level unless all DCs in the forest are running Windows Server 2008. You should not do so unless you are sure you will never be asked to add DCs with previous operating systems to your forest.

For example, the partner companies Coho Vineyard and Coho Vineyard and Winery plan to amalgamate their Active Directory structures into a single forest. All of Coho Vineyard's servers have been recently upgraded to Windows Server 2008. Coho Vineyard's management foresees considerable benefits from fine-grained password policies that will enable the company's domain structure to be simplified to a single domain.

Most of Coho Vineyard and Winery's servers, including all their current DCs, run Windows Server 2003. The company does not intend to promote any existing computers running Windows 2000 Server to DCs, but neither does it have any plans to upgrade its servers to Windows Server 2008 in the near future. Coho Vineyard and Winery currently has a single domain structure and has no plans to install multiple domains. Both companies work very closely with Trey Research and plan to implement cross-forest trusts with that company's Windows Server 2003 forest.

In this situation Coho Vineyard's redesigned domain can have a domain functional level of Windows Server 2008. This enables the company to use fine-grained password policy. Coho Vineyard and Winery's domain level can be set to Windows Server 2003 because it does not plan to add any Windows 2000 Server DCs. This in turn allows the forest functional level of the new forest to be raised to Windows Server 2003, enabling cross-forest trusts with Trey Research.

Planning Forest-Level Trusts

A forest trust (or forest-level trust) allows every domain in one forest to trust every domain in a second forest. Forest trusts were introduced in Windows Server 2003 and can be one-way incoming, one-way outgoing, or two-way. For example, you can configure all the domains in Forest A to trust all the domains in Forest B by creating a one-way trust in either Forest B or Forest A. If in addition you want all the domains in Forest B to trust all the domains in Forest A, you need to create a two-way trust.

You can use forest trusts with partner or closely associated organizations. For example, Coho Vineyard and Coho Winery might not choose to amalgamate their Active Directory structures in a single forest, but might instead decide to use a forest trust to give employees of one organization rights and permissions in the other.

Forest trusts can form part of an acquisition or takeover strategy. Northwind Traders has acquired Litware, Inc. The eventual plan is to reorganize the domain structures of both companies into a single forest, but until this process is complete you might plan a forest trust between the organizations.

You can also use forest trusts for Active Directory isolation. You might, for example, want to run Exchange Server 2007 as part of a migration strategy to try out the new features and familiarize your technical staff. However, you do not want to install Exchange 2007 into your production forest because this could affect your current Exchange Server 2003 deployment. You can create a separate forest in which you can run Exchange 2007, but access resources in your production forest while doing so by setting up a forest trust.

Planning Trust Type and Direction

The most common type of trust that operates across forests is the forest trust, and this is the type of trust discussed in this lesson. You should, however, be aware of the other types of trusts that can be set up with entities outside your forest. These include the following:

- **Shortcut trust** A forest trust will enable any domain in one forest to trust any domain in another forest. However, if forests are complex, with several layers of child domains, a client in a child domain might take some time to locate resources in a child domain in another forest, especially when the operation happens over a WAN link. If users in one child domain frequently need to access resources in another child domain in another forest, you might decide to create a shortcut trust between the two domains.

- **External trust** You set up a domain trust when a domain within your forest requires a trust relationship with a domain that does not belong to a forest. Typically, external trusts are used when migrating resources from Windows NT domains (many of which still exist). Windows NT does not use the concept of forests, and a Windows NT domain is a self-contained, autonomous unit. If you plan to migrate resources from a Windows NT domain into an existing Active Directory forest, you can establish an external trust between one of the Active Directory domains and the Windows NT domain.

- **Realm trust** If a UNIX realm uses Kerberos authentication, you can create a realm trust between a Windows domain and a UNIX realm. This is similar to an external trust except that it is between a Windows domain and a UNIX realm.

When you have selected the type of trust you require—typically a forest trust because shortcut, external, and realm trusts are used in specific situations—you then need to decide whether the trust is one-way or two-way and, if the former, what is the trust direction. One-way trusts can be incoming or outgoing.

If users in Forest A require access to resources in Forest B and users in Forest B require access to resources in Forest A, you need to create a two-way trust. Because this is bidirectional you do not need to specify a direction.

If, however, users in Forest A require access to resources in Forest B but users in Forest B do not require access to resources in Forest A, Forest A is the trusted forest and Forest B the trusting or resource forest. Forest B trusts the users in Forest A and allows them to access its resources. If you are creating a one-way forest trust in a resource forest, it is an incoming trust. If you are creating a one-way forest trust in a trusted forest, it is an outgoing trust.

Imagine the trust as an arrow. The resources are at the point of the arrow. The users that are trusted to use these resources are at the other end. Figure 3-6 shows this relationship. The arrow is incoming at the trusting (resource) forest and outgoing at the trusted forest.

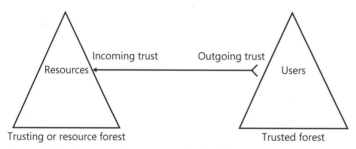

Figure 3-6   One-way forest trust relationship

Creating Forest Trusts

Before you can create a forest trust you need to ensure that the forest functional level of both forests is either Windows Server 2003 or Windows Server 2008. Forest functional levels were discussed earlier in this lesson. Your next step is to ensure that each forest's root domain can access the root domain of the other forest. You need to create the required DNS records and use the *nslookup* tool to ensure that you can resolve domain names in the other forest. You also need to know the user name and password for an enterprise administrator account (an administrator account in the root domain) in each forest, unless you are setting up only one side of the trust and an administrator in the other forest is setting up the other end.

You create forest trusts by opening Active Directory Domains And Trusts from Administrative Tools. You need to connect the tool to a DC in the forest root domain. You then right-click the root domain in the tool's lefthand pane and click Properties. On the Trust tab, click New Trust to launch the New Trust Wizard.

The wizard prompts you to enter the domain, forest, or realm name of the trust. To create a forest trust you enter the domain name of the root domain in the forest with which you want to establish the trust. The wizard asks if you are creating a realm trust or a trust with a Windows domain; select the Windows Domain option. You are then given the choice between creating a forest trust or an external trust. Choose the Forest Trust option and click Next.

At this point the wizard asks you if you want to establish a one-way incoming, one-way outgoing, or two-way trust. If, for example, you are creating a one-way trust in a resource forest, the trust is incoming. (See Figure 3-6.) In practice, however, a two-way trust is typically the most appropriate choice.

The wizard now asks if you want to configure only your own side of the trust or both sides of the trust. An administrative password for both forest root domains is required to establish the trust. If you only have the administrative password for your own domain, choose the This Domain Only option and the administrator of the other forest root domain repeats the procedure at the other end. If you know both passwords, you can configure both sides of the trust at the same time.

Next you need to choose between Forest Wide Authentication and Selective Authentication. Selective Authentication allows you to specify the authentication process in more detail, but it involves a lot more effort. Typically you will choose Forest Wide Authentication.

MORE INFO   Selective authentication

For more information about selective authentication, see *http://technet2.microsoft.com/ windowsserver/en/library/9266b197-7fc9-4bd8-8864-4c119ceecc001033.mspx?mfr=true*. Although this document and linked documents are part of the Windows Server 2003 library, the information they provide is relevant to Windows Server 2008.

The wizard displays a summary of the options you have chosen. Click Next to establish the trust. You can then confirm the link.

NOTE   Confirming a link between forests

In Windows Server 2003 a forest trust could be established and work perfectly well even though the confirmation process failed. Currently it is unclear whether this problem has been fully addressed in Windows Server 2008.

Active Directory Federation Services

You can create forest trusts between two or more Windows Server 2008 forests (or Windows Server 2008 and Windows Server 2003 forests). This provides cross-forest access to resources that are located in disparate business units or organizations. However, forest trusts are sometimes not the best option, such as when access across organizations needs to be limited to a small subset of individuals. Active Directory Federation Services (AD FS) enables organizations to allow limited access to their infrastructure to trusted partners. AD FS acts like a cross-forest trust that operates over the Internet and extends the trust relationship to Web applications (a federated trust). It provides Web single-sign-on (SSO) technologies that can authenticate a user over the life of a single online session. AD FS securely shares digital identity and entitlement rights (known as *claims*) across security and enterprise boundaries.

Windows Server 2003 R2 introduced AD FS and Windows Server 2008 expands it. New AD FS features introduced in Windows Server 2008 include the following:

- **Improved application support**   Windows Server 2008 integrates AD FS with Microsoft Office SharePoint Server 2007 and Active Directory Rights Management Services (AD RMS).

- **Improved installation**   AD FS is implemented in Windows Server 2008 as a server role. The installation wizard includes new server validation checks.

- **Improved trust policy**   Improvements to the trust policy import and export functionality help to minimize configuration issues that are commonly associated with establishing federated trusts.

AD FS extends SSO functionality to Internet-facing applications. Partners experience the same streamlined SSO user experience when they access the organization's Web-based applications as they would when accessing resources through a forest trust. Federation servers can be deployed to facilitate business-to-business (B2B) federated transactions.

AD FS provides a federated identity management solution that interoperates with other security products by conforming to the Web Services Federation (WS-Federation) specification. This specification makes it possible for environments that do not use Windows to federate with Windows environments. It also provides an extensible architecture that supports the Security Assertion Markup Language (SAML) 1.1 token type and Kerberos authentication. AD FS can perform claim mapping—for example, modifying claims using business logic variables in an access request. Organizations can modify AD FS to coexist with their current security infrastructure and business policies.

Finally, AD FS supports distributed authentication and authorization over the Internet. You can integrate it into an organization's existing access management solution to translate the claims that are used in the organization into claims that are agreed on as part of a federation. AD FS can create, secure, and verify claims that move between organizations. It can also audit and monitor the communication activity between organizations and departments to help ensure secure transactions.

MORE INFO   **AD FS server role**

For more information about the AD FS server role in Windows Server 2008, see *http://technet2.microsoft.com/windowsserver2008/en/library/a018ccfe-acb2-41f9-9f0a-102b80a3398c1033.mspx?mfr=true* and follow the links.

Practice: Raising Domain and Forest Functional Levels and Configuring Fine-Grained Password Policy

In this practice session you create and configure a PSO that contains a password policy different than the default policy in the contoso.internal domain. Before you do this, however, you need to raise the functional levels of the domain and forest.

NOTE   **Logging on to the domain controller**

For the sake of brevity and convenience, this practice session (and others in this book) asks you to log on interactively to the DC. You should be aware that in a production domain you probably would not do so. You would instead log on at a workstation and create a Remote Desktop connection to the DC, or you would install Remote Server Administrative Tools (RSAT) on a workstation, open the relevant tool on the workstation, and connect it to the DC.

▶ **Exercise 1: Raise the Domain Functional Level**

In this exercise you raise the domain functional level. You do this first because the forest functional level cannot be higher than the functional level of any domain within the forest.

1. Log on to the DC with the kim_akers account.

2. In the Administrative Tools menu, open Active Directory Domains And Trusts.

3. In the console tree, right-click the contoso.internal domain.

4. The Raise Domain Functional Level control is shown in Figure 3-7. Right-click Raise Domain Functional Level.

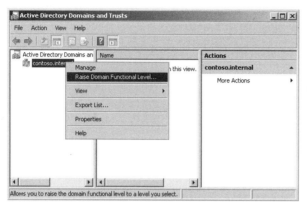

Figure 3-7   The Raise Domain Functional Level control

5. Check the functional level of the domain. If this is already Windows Server 2008, you do not need to carry out the rest of this practice. In this case, click Cancel and then close Active Directory Domains And Trusts and proceed to Practice 2.

6. If the domain functional level is anything but Windows Server 2008, select Windows Server 2008 from the Select An Available Domain Functional Level drop-down box, click Raise, click OK in the Raise Domain Functional Level dialog box, and then click OK again.

7. In the console tree, right-click the contoso.internal domain, click Raise Domain Functional Level. Repeat this process until the domain functional level is Windows Server 2008, as shown in Figure 3-8.

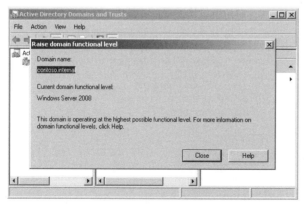

Figure 3-8   A domain functional level of Windows Server 2008

8. Click Close. Close Active Directory Domains And Trusts.

▶ **Exercise 2: Raise the Forest Functional Level**

In this exercise you raise the forest functional level. Do not attempt this exercise until you have completed Exercise 1.

1. If necessary, log on to the DC with the kim_akers account and open Active Directory Domains And Trusts.

2. In the console tree, right-click Active Directory Domains And Trusts.

3. The Raise Forest Functional Level control is shown in Figure 3-9. Right-click Raise Forest Functional Level.

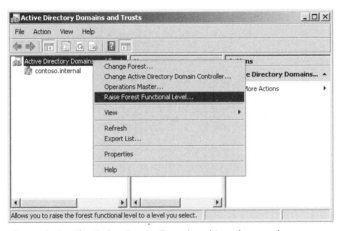

Figure 3-9   The Raise Forest Functional Level control

4. Check the functional level of the forest. If this is already Windows Server 2008, you do not need to finish the rest of this practice. In this case, click Cancel and then close Active Directory Domains And Trusts.

5. If the forest functional level is anything but Windows Server 2008, select Windows Server 2008 from the Select An Available Forest Functional Level drop-down box, click Raise, click OK in the Raise Forest Functional Level dialog box, and then click OK.

6. In the console tree, right-click Active Directory Domains And Trusts, click Raise Forest Functional Level. Repeat this process until the forest functional level is Windows Server 2008, as shown in Figure 3-10.

7. Click OK. Close Active Directory Domains And Trusts.

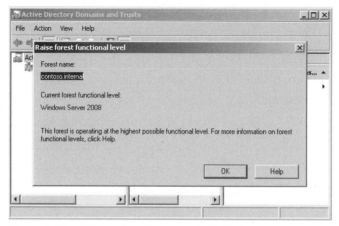

Figure 3-10   A forest functional level of Windows Server 2008

▶ **Exercise 3: Create a PSO**

In this exercise you create a PSO with password policies that are not the same as the default password policies for the contoso.internal domain. You associate this with a global security group called special_password that contains the user don_hall. Do not attempt this exercise until you have completed the previous two exercises.

1. If necessary, log on to the DC with the kim_akers account.

2. Create a user account for don_hall with a password of P@ssw0rd. Create a global security group called special_password. Make don_hall a member of special_password. If you are unsure how to do this consult the Windows Server 2008 Help files.

3. In the Run box, enter **adsiedit.msc**.

4. If this is the first time you have used the ADSI Edit console on your test network, right-click ADSI Edit, and then click Connect To. Type **contoso.internal** in the Name box and then click OK.

5. Double-click contoso.internal.

6. Double-click DC=contoso,DC=internal.

7. Double-click CN=System.

8. Right-click CN=Password Settings Container. Click New. Click Object, as shown in Figure 3-11.

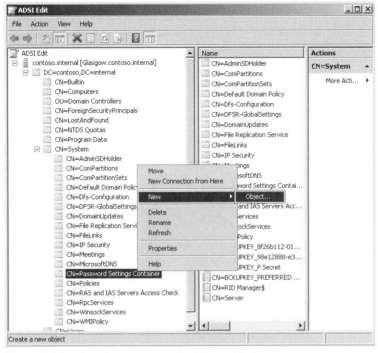

Figure 3-11 Creating a password settings object

9. In the Create Object dialog box, ensure that msDS-PasswordSettings is selected. Click Next.

10. In the CN box, type **PSO1**. Click Next.

11. In the msDS-PasswordSettingsPrecedence box, type **10**. Click Next.

12. In the msDS-PasswordReversibleEncryptionEnabled box, type **FALSE**. Click Next.

13. In the msDS-PasswordHistoryLength box, type **6**. Click Next.

14. In the msDS-PasswordComplexityEnabled box, type **FALSE**. Click Next.

15. In the msDS-MinimumPasswordLength box, type **6**. Click Next.

16. In the msDS-MinimumPasswordAge box, type **1:00:00:00**. Click Next.

17. In the msDS-MaximumPasswordAge box, type **20:00:00:00**. Click Next.

18. In the msDS-LockoutThreshold box, type **2**. Click Next.

19. In the msDS-LockoutObservationWindow box, type **0:00:15:00**. Click Next.

20. In the msDS-LockoutDuration box, type **0:00:15:00**. Click Next.

21. Click Finish.

22. Open Active Directory Users And Computers, click View, and then click Advanced Features.

23. Expand contoso.internal, expand System and then click Password Settings Container.

24. Right-click PSO1. Click Properties.

25. On the Attribute Editor tab, select msDS-PSOAppliesTo, as shown in Figure 3-12.

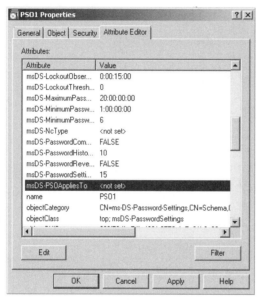

Figure 3-12 Selecting an attribute to edit

26. Click Edit.

27. Click Add Windows Account.

28. Type **special_password** in the Enter The Object Names To Select box. Click Check Names.

29. Click OK. The Multi-Valued Distinguished Name With Security Principal Editor dialog box should look similar to Figure 3-13.

30. Click OK, and then click OK again to close the PSO1 Properties dialog box.

31. Test your settings by changing the password for the don_hall account to a non-complex, six-letter password, such as **simple**.

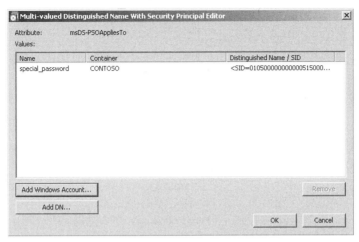

Figure 3-13   Adding the special_password global security group to PSO1

Lesson Summary

- Windows Server 2008 introduces a number of new AD DS features, including RODCs, fine-grained security policies, and the data mining tool.

- RODCs can be installed in branch offices to improve logon and DNS resolution in situations where a writable DC would be a security risk.

- You can configure PSOs that hold password and account lockout policies different from the domain policies. You can associate users or security groups with a PSO.

- The data mining tool makes it possible for deleted AD DS or AD LDS data to be preserved in the form of snapshots of AD DS taken by the VSS.

- Windows Server 2008 introduces enhancements to MMC snap-in tools, including Active Directory Users And Computers and Active Directory Sites And Services.

- Enhancements to AD DS auditing let you determine what AD DS changes have been made and when these changes were made.

- Forest-level trusts allow users in a domain in one forest to access resources in a domain in a second forest.

Lesson Review

You can use the following questions to test your knowledge of the information in Lesson 1, "Windows Server 2008 Active Directory." The questions are also available on the companion CD if you prefer to review them in electronic form.

NOTE   Answers

Answers to these questions and explanations of why each answer choice is correct or incorrect are located in the "Answers" section at the end of the book.

---

1. You have created and configured a PSO that contains non-default account lock-out policies. To which entities can you apply this PSO? (Choose all that apply.)

    A. A global security group

    B. A domain user account

    C. An OU

    D. A global distribution group

    E. A computer account

2. What tool can you use to view Active Directory data stored in snapshots?

    A. SACL

    B. PSC

    C. AD DS data mining tool

    D. AD DS Installation Wizard

3. You plan to migrate resources from a Windows NT4 domain into an existing Active Directory forest. What type of trust do you set up?

    A. forest trust

    B. external trust

    C. realm trust

    D. shortcut trust

4. You are a domain administrator at Litware, Inc. In collaboration with colleagues at branch offices who are not domain administrators you have set up RODCs in all of Litware's branch offices. The Password Replication Policy for one of the Litware RODCs needs to be changed. How should this be done?

    A. Ask your branch office colleague who has the right to log on to the RODC at the relevant branch to open Active Directory Users And Computers and ensure that the tool is connected to her branch RODC. She can then change the settings on the Password Replication Policy tab of the RODC's Properties sheet.

    B. Add the branch office user who has the right to interactively log on to the relevant branch RODC to the Domain Admins group. Ask the user to log on to the RODC and open Server Manager. She can then expand Configuration and access the Password Replication Policy dialog box.

    C. Connect to the relevant RODC by using Remote Desktop. Open Server Manager and expand Configuration. Access the Password Replication Policy dialog box.

    D. Open Active Directory Users And Computers and ensure that the tool is connected to a writable DC at head office. Locate the relevant RODC in the Domain Controllers container and open its Properties dialog box. Make the required change via the Password Replication Policy tab.

5. You are planning to create a two-way forest trust between your company forest and the forest of a recently acquired organization. What minimum forest functional level is required in both organizations?

    A. Windows 2000

    B. Windows 2000 native

    C. Windows Server 2003

    D. Windows Server 2008

6. You plan to use the domain management tool (*netdom.exe*) to rename a domain. All of your DCs currently run either Windows Server 2003 or Windows Server 2008. You do not currently plan to upgrade the Windows Server 2003 DCs. What domain functional level supports this plan?

    A. Windows Server 2008

    B. Windows Server 2003

    C. Windows 2000 native

    D. Windows 2000 mixed

Lesson 2: Group Policy in Windows Server 2008

As an experienced administrator you already know that Group Policy simplifies administration by automating many tasks related to managing users and computers. You should be aware that you can use Group Policy to install permitted applications on clients on demand and to keep applications up to date. Chapter 4, "Application Servers and Services," discusses this aspect in more detail.

This lesson, therefore, does not cover the basic aspects of Group Policy in detail, but rather discusses the enhancements that Windows Server 2008 introduces.

In Windows Server 2008, the Group Policy Management console (GPMC) is built in. You can install GPMC by using the Add Features Wizard in Server Manager. You do this in the practice session later in this lesson. Using GPMC, you can efficiently implement security settings, enforce IT policies, and consistently distribute software across sites, domains, or OUs.

Administrative Template (ADM) files were introduced in Windows NT4 and are used to describe registry-based Group Policy settings. In Windows Sever 2008 (and in Windows Vista), ADM files are replaced by extensible markup language (XML) files known as ADMX files. These new Administrative Template files make it easier to manage registry-based policy settings.

This lesson describes the policy settings introduced by Windows Server 2008 that you can administer by using GPMC. It also discusses ADMX language-neutral and language-specific files.

After this lesson, you will be able to:

- Install GPMC (if necessary) and use the console to administer Group Policy settings.
- List the new Group Policy settings introduced by Windows Server 2008 and explain their functions.
- Write simple ADMX files.
- Discuss the various problems that can occur in Group Policy configuration and how you should troubleshoot them.

Estimated lesson time: 30 minutes

Understanding Group Policy

You already know that Group Policy settings contained in Group Policy objects (GPOs) can be linked to OUs, and that OUs can either inherit settings from parent OUs or block inheritance and obtain their specific settings from their own linked

GPOs. You also know that some policies—specifically, security policies—can be set to "no override" so that they cannot be blocked or overwritten and force child OUs to inherit the settings from their parents.

Windows Server 2008 changes none of this, apart from the introduction of PSOs, described in the previous lesson, that permit some security settings (such as password and account lockout settings) to be configured differently from the domain defaults and applied to security groups.

However, the basic operation of Group Policy as well as its functions remain unchanged. To understand Windows 2008 Group Policy you need to know what new settings Windows Server 2008 introduces.

New Windows Server 2008 Group Policy Settings

The following Group Policy settings have been introduced in Windows Server 2008 (the list is not exclusive):

- **Allow Remote Start Of Unlisted Programs** This computer-based policy setting allows you to specify whether remote users can start any program on the terminal server (TS) when they start a remote session, or whether they can only start programs that are listed in the RemoteApp Programs list. You can use the TS RemoteApp Manager tool to create this list. By default, a user can start only programs in the RemoteApp Programs list during a remote session. Figure 3-14 shows this setting. Figure 3-15 shows the RemoteApp Wizard that opens from the TS RemoteApp Manager and lets you add programs to the RemoteApp Programs list.

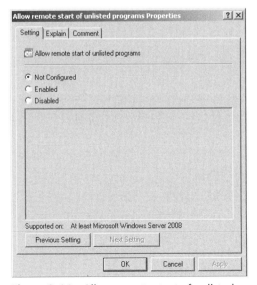

Figure 3-14   Allow remote start of unlisted programs

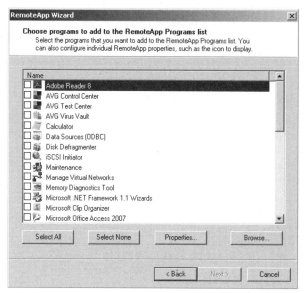

Figure 3-15   The RemoteApp Wizard

MORE INFO   Terminal Services RemoteApp

For more information about Terminal Services RemoteApp, see *http://technet2.microsoft.com/windowsserver2008/en/library/57995ee7-e204-45a4-bcee-5d1f4a51a09f1033.mspx?mfr=true*. For more information about the Terminal Services server role, see Chapter 5 and *http:/technet2.microsoft.com/windowsserver2008/en/library/ddef2b89-73cf-4d74-b13b-47890fd1a6271033.mspx*.

■ **Allow Time Zone Redirection**   This user-based policy setting determines whether the client computer redirects its time zone settings to the Terminal Services session. When you enable this policy setting, clients that are capable of time zone redirection send their time zone information to the server.

■ **Always Show Desktop On Connection**   This user-based policy setting determines whether the desktop is always displayed when a client connects to a remote computer, even if an initial program is already specified in the default user profile, Remote Desktop Connection (RDC), Terminal Services client, or through Group Policy. If an initial program is not specified, the remote desktop is always displayed when the client connects.

■ **Disk Diagnostic: Configure Custom Alert Text**   This computer-based policy setting requires that Desktop Experience is installed on a Windows Server 2008 server. It substitutes custom alert text in the disk diagnostic message shown to users when a disk reports a Self-Monitoring, Analysis, and Reporting Technology (SMART) fault.

NOTE　SMART

Most hard disk manufacturers incorporate SMART logic into their drives. This acts as an early warning system for pending drive problems. For more information, see *http://www.pcguide.com/ref/ hdd/perf/qual/featuresSMART-c.html*. This is not a Microsoft link and the URL might change, in which case you can search the Internet for "Self-Monitoring, Analysis, and Reporting Technology." However, be aware that SMART is not a Microsoft technology and is unlikely to feature in the 70-646 examination.

> ## Desktop Experience
>
> Configuring a Windows Server 2008 server as a terminal server lets you use Remote Desktop Connection 6.0 to connect to a remote computer from your administrator workstation and reproduces on your computer the desktop that exists on the remote computer. When you install Desktop Experience on Windows Server 2008, you can use Windows Vista features such as Windows Media Player, desktop themes, and photo management within the remote connection.
>
> To install Desktop Experience, open Server Manager and click Add Features in the Features Summary section. Select the Desktop Experience check box, click Next, and then click Install.

■ **Disk Diagnostic: Configure Execution Level**　This computer-based policy setting requires that Desktop Experience is installed on your Windows Server 2008 server. It determines the execution level for SMART-based disk diagnostics. The Diagnostic Policy Service (DPS) will detect and log SMART faults to the event log when they occur. If you enable this policy setting, the DPS will also warn users and guide them through backup and recovery to minimize potential data loss.

■ **Do Not Allow Clipboard Redirection**　This user-based policy setting specifies whether to prevent the sharing of clipboard contents (clipboard redirection) between a remote computer and a client computer during a Terminal Services session. By default, Terminal Services allows clipboard redirection. If the policy status is set to Not Configured, clipboard redirection is not specified at the Group Policy level, but an administrator can disable clipboard redirection using the Terminal Services Configuration tool.

- **Do Not Display Initial Configuration Tasks Window Automatically At Logon** This computer-based policy setting allows you to turn off the automatic display of the Initial Configuration Tasks window at logon. If you do not configure this policy setting, the Initial Configuration Tasks window opens when an administrator logs on to the server. However, if the administrator selects the Do Not Show This Window At Logon check box, the window does not open on subsequent logons.

- **Do Not Display Server Manager Page At Logon** This computer-based policy setting allows you to turn off the automatic display of Server Manager at logon. If you enable this policy setting, Server Manager does not open automatically when an administrator logs on to the server. This setting is specific to the server rather than to a particular user account.

- **Enforce Removal Of Remote Desktop Wallpaper** This computer-based policy setting specifies whether desktop wallpaper is displayed on remote clients connecting via Terminal Services. You can use this setting to enforce the removal of wallpaper during a remote session. Windows Server 2003 servers do not by default display wallpaper to remote sessions. If the policy status is set to Enabled, wallpaper never appears to a Terminal Services client. If the status is set to Disabled, wallpaper might appear to a Terminal Services client, depending on the client configuration.

- **Group Policy Management Editor** This user-based policy setting permits or prohibits the use of the Group Policy Management Editor snap-in. If you enable this setting the snap-in is permitted. If this setting is not configured, the Restrict Users To The Explicitly Permitted List Of Snap-Ins setting determines whether this snap-in is permitted or prohibited.

MORE INFO Restrict Users To The Explicitly Permitted List Of Snap-Ins

This policy setting is not new to Windows Server 2008 and therefore is not described in this lesson. If you have never seen this setting and need more information, see *http://www.microsoft.com/technet/prodtechnol/windows2000serv/reskit/gp/251.mspx?mfr=true*.

- **Group Policy Starter GPO Editor** This user-based policy setting permits or prohibits the use of the Group Policy Starter GPO Editor snap-in. If this setting is not configured, the Restrict Users To The Explicitly Permitted List Of Snap-Ins setting determines whether this snap-in is permitted or prohibited.

■ **Redirect Only The Default Client Printer (User)**   This user-based policy setting allows you to specify whether the default client printer is the only printer redirected in Terminal Services sessions.

■ **Redirect Only The Default Client Printer (Computer)**   This computer-based policy setting allows you to specify whether the default client printer is the only printer redirected in Terminal Services sessions. This setting is independent of the logged-on user. Figure 3-16 shows the Properties dialog box that lets you configure this setting.

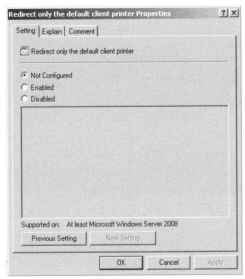

Figure 3-16   Redirect Only The Default Client Printer Properties dialog box

■ **Set The Number Of Retries For Password Sync Servers**   This computer-based policy setting allows you to set the number of retries for synchronization on failure servers. If you enable this policy, all affected Password Sync servers use the number of retries specified by the policy setting. If you disable or do not configure this setting, the user preference will be used for individual Password Sync servers.

■ **Set The Retry Interval For Password Sync Servers**   This computer-based policy setting allows you to set the interval in seconds between retries for synchronization failures. If you disable or do not configure this policy setting, the user preference will be used for individual Password Sync servers.

- **Set Update Interval For NIS Subordinate Servers** This computer-based policy setting allows you to set an update interval for pushing Network Information Service (NIS) maps to NIS subordinate servers. If you enable this policy, the specified update interval is used for all affected Server For NIS (SNIS) DCs. If you disable or do not configure the policy setting, the user preference will be used for individual SNIS DCs.

MORE INFO   Server for NIS

For more information about SNIS and NIS, see *http://technet2.microsoft.com/windowsserver/en/library/d9a0eb27-026f-455b-8d86-fa832b1c2eb31033.mspx?mfr=true.*

- **Use TS Session Broker Load Balancing** This computer-based policy setting allows you to specify whether to use the TS Session Broker load balancing feature to balance the load between servers in a TS farm. If you enable this policy setting, TS Session Broker will redirect users who do not have an existing session to the terminal server in the farm with the fewest sessions.

MORE INFO   TS Session Broker and TS farms

For more information about TS Session Broker and TS farms, see *http://technet2.microsoft.com/windowsserver2008/en/library/4c492494-1a34-4d3e-80b1-4a562b8a0bdc1033.mspx?mfr=true* and follow the links.

- **Turn On Extensive Logging For Password Sync Servers**   This computer-based policy setting allows you to manage the extensive logging feature for Password Sync servers. If you enable this policy, all the affected Password Sync servers log intermediate steps in synchronization attempts.

- **Turn On Extensive Logging For Domain Controllers Running Server For NIS**   This computer-based policy setting allows you to manage the extensive logging feature for SNIS DCs.

- **Turn On The Windows To NIS Password Sync For Migrated Users For Password Sync Servers** This computer-based policy setting allows you to manage the Windows To NIS password sync feature (for UNIX users migrated to Active Directory).

- **Use Terminal Services Easy Print Driver First (User)** This user-based policy setting allows you to specify whether the Terminal Services Easy Print printer driver is used first to install all client printers.

■ **Use Terminal Services Easy Print Driver First (Computer)**   This computer-based policy setting allows you to specify whether the Terminal Services Easy Print printer driver is used first to install all client printers. The computer-based setting is independent of the logged-on user.

Real World

Ian McLean

Books about a major new application version or new operating system tend to cover the new features that are introduced. Fortunately most examinations do the same. Unless they are writing about something completely new, authors tend to move quickly over what has come before. If they didn't, most technical books would be excessively long and very expensive.

However, although examinations and books are mainly about what is new, real life does not reflect this situation. Every day I call on skills and principles that I learned in the days of Windows 2000 Server and even Windows NT4. Nor is there any guarantee that the examination will ask only about new features. If the objectives specify Group Policy, the examiner is entitled to ask anything she likes about Group Policy, whether the feature was introduced in Windows 2000 Server or Windows Server 2008.

I recall coming across a question in an examination a few years ago and thinking it was something I'd learned some time before and hadn't used much since. Fortunately I knew the answer, but it wasn't one I'd have found in any of the books I'd read as preparation. I've sometimes been accosted by colleagues who have read one of my books and told about an examined topic that wasn't included. I smile weakly and tell them it was in a previous book I wrote for a previous examination.

In particular, candidates for the 70-646 examination are expected to be experienced administrators and will be tested as such. I can't put a solid three years' experience in a book plus all the complex new features introduced by Windows Server 2008. I'd need an entire library. The solution is to make sure you have the experience. In the real world you often do the same tasks repeatedly, and let other members of your team take responsibility for other tasks. For your examination preparation, try to get experience in everything. Books are valuable, but there's only one way to get qualifications and to advance your career. Hands on, hands on, and more hands on.

Planning and Managing Group Policy

Planning your Group Policy is in part planning your organizational structure. If you have a huge number of OUs—some inheriting policies, others blocking inheritance, several OUs linking to the same GPO, and several GPOs linking to the same OU—you have a recipe for disaster. While too few OUs and GPOs is also a mistake, most of us err on the side of having too many. Keep your structures simple. Do not link OUs and GPOs across site boundaries. Give your OUs and GPOs meaningful names.

When you are planning Group Policy you need to be aware of the Group Policy settings that are provided with Windows Server 2008. These are numerous and it is not practical to memorize all of them, but you should know what the various categories are. Even if you do not edit any policies, exploring the Group Policy structure in Group Policy Management Editor is worthwhile. You will develop a feel for what is available and whether you need to generate custom policies by creating ADMX files.

You also need a good understanding of how Group Policy is processed at the client. This happens in the following two phases:

- **Core processing**   When a client begins to process Group Policy, it must determine whether it can reach a DC, whether any GPOs have been changed, and what policy settings must be processed. The core Group Policy engine performs the processing of this in the initial phase.

- **Client-side extension (CSE) processing**   In this phase, Group Policy settings are placed in various categories, such as Administrative Templates, Security Settings, Folder Redirection, Disk Quota, and Software Installation. A specific CSE processes the settings in each category, and each CSE has its own rules for processing settings. The core Group Policy engine calls the CSEs that are required to process the settings that apply to the client.

CSEs cannot begin processing until core Group Policy processing is completed. It is therefore important to plan your Group Policy and your domain structure so that this happens as quickly and reliably as possible. The troubleshooting section later in this lesson discusses some of the problems that can delay or prevent core Group Policy processing.

Starter GPOs

Windows Server 2008 Group Policy introduces Starter GPOs. These GPOs let you save baseline templates that you can use when you create new GPOs. You can also export starter GPOs to domains other than those in which they were created.

When you open GPMC in Windows Server 2008 you can locate the Starter GPOs container in the lefthand pane. Until you populate it this container is empty. You create a Starter GPO by right-clicking the Starter GPOs container and selecting New. You can configure GPOs in this container as you would configure any GPO, except that only the Administrative Templates settings are available in both Computer Settings and User Settings.

When you create a new starter GPO you are prompted for a name for the Starter GPO and you can also add a comment. You can edit your starter GPO and set the Administrative templates you require. When you create a Starter GPO you automatically create a new folder on the DC to which GPMC is connected, by default in the C:\Windows\SYSVOL\domain\StarterGPOs path. This is replicated to other DCs as part of SYSVOL replication.

You can create a new (normal) GPO using a Starter GPO as a template by right-clicking the Starter GPO and selecting New GPO From Starter GPO. Alternatively you can right-click the Group Policy Objects container, select New, and then specify a Starter GPO as the Source Starter GPO drop-down list. You can access the same dialog box and specify a Starter GPO if you right-click an OU (or the domain) and select Create A GPO In This Domain, And Link It Here. A Starter GPO lets you easily create multiple GPOs with the same baseline configuration. You only need to configure settings in these GPOs that are not contained in Administrative Templates.

Starter GPOs are not backed up when you click Backup on the GPMC Action menu or right-click the Group Policy Objects container and select Backup All. You need to back up Starter GPOs separately by right-clicking the Starter GPOs container and selecting Back Up All or by right-clicking individual Starter GPOs and selecting Back Up.

MORE INFO **GPO comments and Administrative Template filtering**

The ability to add comments to both Starter GPOs and ordinary GPOs is new in Windows Server 2008. You can enter a comment about the entire GPO and also secondary comments about individual settings. Also new in Windows Server 2008 is the facility to filter a GPO's Administrative Template settings by either setting or comment. For more information, see *http://technet2.microsoft.com/WindowsServer/en/library/e50f1e64-d7e5-4b6d-87ff-adb3cf8743651033.mspx.*

Managing Group Policies by Using ADMX Files

ADMX files, based on XML, are arguably more useful and easier to use than the ADM files they replace. They define registry-based policy settings that are located under the Administrative Templates category in the Group Policy Object Editor. The Group Policy tools such as the Group Policy Object Editor and GPMC remain largely unchanged from Windows Server 2003, except for some additional policy settings that were described in the previous section.

Unlike ADM files, ADMX files are not stored in individual GPOs. You can create a central store location of ADMX files that is accessible by anyone with permission to create or edit GPOs. Group Policy tools continue to recognize ADM files in your existing environment, but will ignore any ADM file that has been superseded by an ADMX file. The Group Policy Object Editor automatically reads and displays Administrative Template policy settings from ADMX files that are stored either locally or in the ADMX central store. All Group Policy settings currently implemented by ADM files in legacy operating systems are available in Windows Server 2008 as ADMX files.

NOTE Windows Vista

Windows Vista also uses ADMX files to implement local policy. If you create a central store on a Windows Server 2008 DC, you can copy ADMX files from a Windows Vista administrative workstation to that store.

Administrative Template files use an XML-based file format that describes registry-based Group Policy. ADMX files are divided into language-neutral resources (.admx files) and language-specific resources (.adml files). This enables Group Policy tools to adjust their user interfaces according to your chosen language. You can add a new language to a set of policy definitions provided that the language-specific resource file is available.

ADMX File Locations

ADMX files on Windows Server 2008 DCs can be held in a central store. This greatly reduces the amount of storage space required to maintain GPOs. In Windows Server 2008, the Group Policy Object Editor does not copy ADMX files to each edited GPO. Instead, it provides the facility to read from a single domain-level location on the DC. If the central store is unavailable, the Group Policy Object Editor will read from the local administrative (Windows Vista) workstation.

The central store is not available by default; you need to create it manually. You do this in the practice session later in this lesson. In addition to storing standard Windows Server 2008 ADMX files in the central store, you can share a custom ADMX file by also copying this file to the central store. This makes it automatically available to all Group Policy administrators in a domain. Table 3-6 shows locations for ADMX files on a DC (assuming a typical Windows 2008 installation and United States English ADMX language-specific files). Microsoft recommends that you manually create the central store on the primary DC on your domain—that is the first Windows 2008 DC that you configured on your domain. This makes it quicker to replicate the files to all other DCs in your domain by using Distributed File System Replication (DFSR). Chapter 6, "File and Print Services," discusses DFSR in detail.

Table 3-6   Locations for ADMX Files on a DC

File Type	File Location
ADMX language neutral (.admx)	C:\Windows\SYSVOL\domain\policies\ PolicyDefinitions
ADMX language specific (.adml)	C:\Windows\SUSVOL\domain\policies\ PolicyDefinitions\en-us

The central store for ADMX files allows all administrators that edit domain-based GPOs to access the same set of ADMX files. After you have created the central store, the Group Policy tools will use the ADMX files only in the central store, ignoring any locally stored versions. To edit GPOs using centrally stored ADMX files you first create the central store, and any subfolders that you need for language-specific files. You can then copy ADMX files from your administrative workstation to the central store. You do this in the practice session later in this lesson.

Creating Custom ADMX files

If the standard Group Policy settings that ship with Windows Server are insufficient for your needs, you might consider creating custom ADMX files. First, a word of warning—ADMX files modify the registry. Be very wary of any registry modification and make sure you double-check your code. Above all, do not install custom ADMX files on a production network before you have tested them on an isolated test network.

Microsoft recommends downloading and installing sample files, and modifying the elements that do not affect the registry until you are confident about using ADMX syntax.

You can download the installation file from *http://www.microsoft.com/downloads/details.aspx?FamilyId=3D7975FF-1242-4C94-93D3-B3091067071A&displaylang=en*.

The ADMX schema defines the syntax for the ADMX files. If you want to view this schema, you can download it from *http://www.microsoft.com/downloads/details.aspx?FamilyId=B4CB0039-E091-4EE8-9EC0-2BBCE56C539E&displaylang=en*. Be aware, however, that the 70-646 examination syllabus does not include schema management.

You can create and edit ADMX files by using an XML editor or a text editor such as Notepad. If you do not want to download sample files you can use Notepad to open any of the ADMX files that you place in the central store in the practice session later in this lesson. Be careful, however, to change the filename before saving any changes you make.

NOTE   Examining ADMX files

ADMX files are quite long, and it is not practical or particularly useful to include one in this book. Instead it is recommended that you open the files in Notepad and examine the contents.

MORE INFO   Custom base ADMX files

If you plan to create a number of ADMX files that display under a single category node in the Group Policy Object Editor, you need to create a custom base file. For more information see *http://technet2.microsoft.com/windowsserver2008/en/library/22f34dbd-1d72-4ddd-9b14-4ba8097827771033.mspx?mfr=true*.

ADMX files are created as one language-neutral file (.admx) and one or more language-specific files (.adml). Note that XML is case sensitive. A language-neutral ADMX file contains the following elements:

- **XML declaration**   This is required for the file to validate as an XML-based file. It contains version and encoding information.

- *PolicyDefinitions* **element**   This contains all other elements for an .admx file.

- *PolicyNamespaces* **element**   This defines the unique namespace for the file. This element also provides a mapping to external file namespaces.

- *Resources* **element**   This specifies the requirements for the language-specific resources, for example the minimum required version of the associated .adml file.

- *SupportedOn* **element**   This specifies references to localized text strings defining the operating systems or applications affected by a specific policy setting.

- *Categories* **element**   This specifies categories under which the policy setting in the file will be displayed in the Group Policy Object Editor. Note that if you specify a category name that already exists in another ADMX file you create a duplicate node.

- *Policies* **element**   This contains the individual policy setting definitions.

A language-specific (or language resource) ADMX file contains the following elements:

- **XML declaration**   This is required for the file to validate as an XML-based file. This element is the same in .admx and .adml files.

- *PolicyDefinitionResources* **element**   This contains all other elements for a language-specific ADMX file.

- *Resources* **element (.adml)**   This contains a *StringTable* element and a *PresentationTable* element for a specified language.

MORE INFO   **ADMX file elements**

For more information, and specifically for examples of each element, see *http://technet2.microsoft.com/windowsserver2008/en/library/22f34dbd-1d72-4ddd-9b14-4ba8097827771033.mspx?mfr=true.* You need to expand ADMX Syntax in the left-hand pane and follow the links.

Exam Tip   The 70-646 examination is most unlikely to ask you to create an ADMX file under examination conditions. However, it might show you a section of XML code and ask you questions about it. Typically the code is not difficult to interpret. For example, a section of code that starts *<policies>* is likely to form part of the *Policies* element.

Troubleshooting Group Policy

Group Policy very seldom "breaks." It is part of AD DS and as such it is sturdy and resilient. What is much more likely to happen is that policies will not be applied the way you or your users expect them to be. For example, a setting in a GPO will be incorrectly configured or, more commonly, policy inheritance and OU structure will not be correctly designed. As a result, users are unable to do things they need to do or (more seriously and more difficult to debug) they can do things they should not be able to do. If you use loopback (machine-based) processing, the computers in the secure room may not be operating as securely as they should be.

Your first step in debugging Group Policy is typically to check that the domain infrastructure has been correctly planned and implemented. You need to ensure that required services and components are running and configured as expected. As with all system debugging, start at the lowest layer and ensure that you have full network connectivity. If a particular client is not working the way it should, verify that it is connected to the network, joined to the domain, and has the correct system time.

No administrator likes exceptions, but we are required to implement them. Typically you might have configured security filtering, Windows Management Instrumentation (WMI) filters, block inheritance settings, no-override settings, loopback processing, and slow-link settings. You need to check that these settings are not affecting normal GPO processing.

Using Group Policy Tools

Group Policy debugging tools are well known, and Windows 2008 does not introduce any significant changes. For example, *GPResult.exe* verifies all policy settings in effect for a specific user or computer. *GPOTool.exe* is a resource kit utility that checks GPOs for consistency on each DC in your domain. The tool also determines whether the policies are valid and displays detailed information about replicated GPOs.

Arguably one of the most useful tools for isolating Group Policy problems is the reporting function in GPMC. You can select a GPO in the lefthand pane of the tool and view the information on the Scope, Details, Settings, and Delegation tabs in the righthand pane. You can also right-click a GPO and select Save Report, as shown in Figure 3-17.

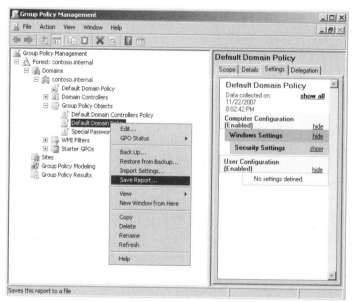

Figure 3-17   Saving a GPMC report

Figure 3-18 shows part of the output from a GPMC report. By default, reports are saved in Hypertext Markup Language (HTML) format and open in Internet Explorer.

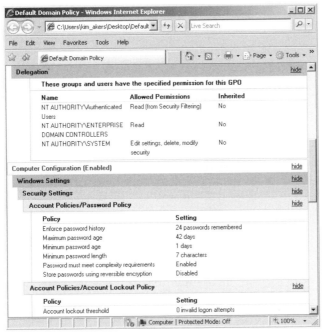

Figure 3-18   GPMC report output

Microsoft recommends that you examine GPMC reports and look for answers to the following questions:

- Does Group Policy Results list the GPO as applied?
- Is the setting listed in Group Policy Results Report?
- Is the GPO listed in the Denied List?

MORE INFO   **Using logs to debug Group Policy**

Event logs can assist you in isolating Group Policy problems, including the Group Policy Operational log. You can access this log by opening Event Viewer, expanding Applications And Services Logs, expanding Microsoft, expanding Windows, and then expanding Group Policy.

Addressing Core Processing Issues

If core processing does not happen quickly and efficiently, CSE processing might not begin and Group Policy will not be applied. A number of factors can affect core processing.

One of the most common causes of a GPO not being applied to a user or computer is that the GPO is not linked to the user or computer's site, domain, or OU. GPOs are delivered to clients based on the site and OU memberships of the computer and the logged-on user.

Quick Check

- What command-line tool verifies all policy settings in effect for a specific user or computer?

Quick Check Answer

- *GPResult.exe.*

Another issue that might cause core processing problems is that replication has not yet occurred. If GPOs are linked across sites (not recommended), this can be especially problematic. When you link a GPO to a site, domain, or OU in the hierarchy, the change must be replicated to the DC from which the client retrieved its GPO. If you add a user or computer to an OU, the GPOs that apply to that OU might not be applied to the client until the change in OU membership has been replicated.

After you make changes to a GPO, these changes need to reach the client. This occurs during Group Policy refresh. Sometimes Group Policy problems can be cured by using the *gpupdate* command.

Network connectivity was mentioned at the start of this section. I make no apology for mentioning it again at the end. You need to ensure that the client computer can connect to the DC. Check that TCP/IP, DNS, and DHCP are configured and running. Make sure a network cable has not fallen out.

Practice: Installing the GPMC and Creating a Central Store for Group Policy Files

In this practice session you install the GPMC, unless it has already been installed when you installed AD DS. You also create and populate a central store for Group Policy (ADMX) definition files.

▶ **Exercise 1: Install the GPMC**

In this exercise you check whether the GPMC is installed. This will depend on how you set up your computer. If the console is not installed, you install it.

1. Log on to the DC by using the kim_akers account.

2. Look under Administrative Tools. If Group Policy Management already exists, you do not need to finish the remainder of this exercise.

3. Under Administrative Tools, open Server Manager.

4. Click Features in the console tree.

5. Click Add Features in the Features pane.

6. In the Add Features Wizard dialog box, select Group Policy Management from the list of available features, as shown in Figure 3-19.

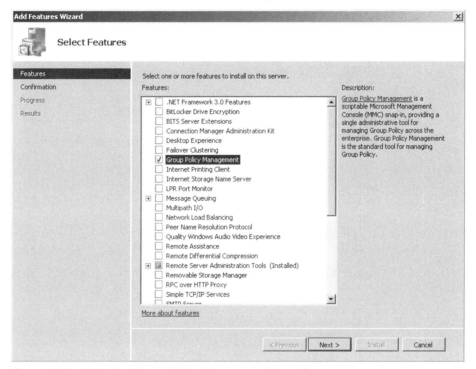

Figure 3-19   Selecting Group Policy Management Console

7. Click Next.

8. Click Install.

9. Close Server Manager when the installation completes.

▶ **Exercise 2: Create a Central Store for ADMX Files**

In this exercise you create a folder that acts as a central store for language-neutral ADMX files. You then create a subfolder to hold language-specific ADMX files. You copy files from your Windows Vista workstation into these folders.

1. If necessary, log on to the DC by using the kim_akers account.

2. Open Windows Explorer and browse to C:\Windows\SYSVOL\domain\policies. Create a subfolder called PolicyDefinitions. You need to click Continue several times in the user access control (UAC) box as you create this folder.

3. Create a subfolder of the Policy definitions folder called en-us. As with the previous step, you will need to clear the UAC dialog box several times. The file structure is shown in Figure 3-20.

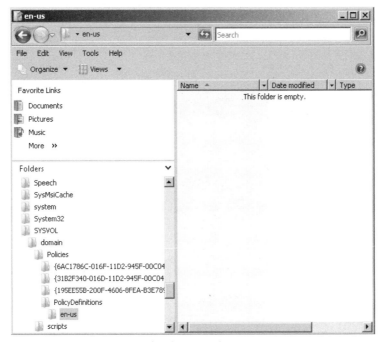

Figure 3-20   File structure for the central store

4. Log on to the client PC or connect to it through Remote Desktop.

5. Locate any files with filetype .admx on the client PC. Copy them into the Policy-Definitions folder on the DC. Click Continue to clear the UAC dialog box as required. Figure 3-21 shows the central store containing ADMX files.

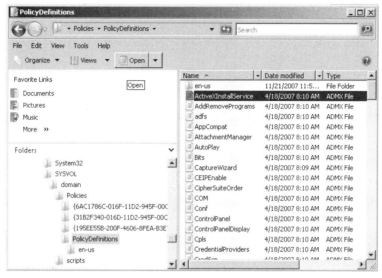

Figure 3-21   ADMX files

6. Locate any files with filetype .adml on the client PC. Copy them into the Policy-Definitions/en-us folder on the DC.

7. Open any ADMX file (.admx or .adml) with Notepad and examine the contents.

Lesson Summary

- GPMC is closely integrated with Windows Server 2008. You can install the tool by using Server Manager.

- Windows Server 2008 introduces a number of new Group Policy settings, in particular settings related to the TS server role.

- ADMX language-neutral and language-specific files define configurable Group Policy settings in Windows 2008 Server domains. You can store these files in a central store on your DCs. You need to create the central store on one DC. DFSR replicates it to other DCs in the domain.

- Various tools exist that help you troubleshoot Group Policy issues. One of the most useful is the ability to save a GPO report by using GPMC.

Lesson Review

You can use the following questions to test your knowledge of the information in Lesson 2, "Group Policy in Windows Server 2008." The questions are also available on the companion CD if you prefer to review them in electronic form.

NOTE   Answers

Answers to these questions and explanations of why each answer choice is correct or incorrect are located in the "Answers" section at the end of the book.

1. Which Group Policy settings require that Desktop Experience be installed on a Windows Server 2008 server? (Choose all that apply.)

    A. Disk Diagnostic: Configure Execution Level

    B. Do Not Allow Clipboard Redirection

    C. Enforce Removal Of Remote Desktop Wallpaper

    D. Set Update Interval To NIS Subordinate Server

    E. Disk Diagnostic: Configure Custom Alert Text

2. Which Group Policy settings are associated with Terminal Services? (Choose all that apply.)

    A. Allow Time Zone Redirection

    B. Disk Diagnostic: Configure Execution Level

    C. Do Not Allow Clipboard Redirection

    D. Enforce Removal Of Remote Desktop Wallpaper

    E. Turn On Extensive Logging For SNIS DCs

3. You are planning your Group Policy structure. Which of the following statements represent good advice? (Choose all that apply.)

    A. Keep the number of GPOs to an absolute minimum by having a lot of configuration settings in any single GPO and by linking GPOs to OUs across site boundaries.

    B. Store your ADMX files in a central store.

    C. Give your OUs and GPOs meaningful names.

    D. Make extensive use of features such as block inheritance, no override, security filtering, and loopback policies.

    E. Ensure that your policy for GPO updates and amendments mandates the use of the *gpupdate* command when reconfiguration is complete.

4. An element of an ADMX language-neutral file contains the following code:

```
<?xml version="1.0" encoding="utf-8"?>
```

What element is this?

   A. The *Policies* element

   B. The *SupportedOn* element

   C. The *PolicyNamespaces* element

   D. The XML declaration

Chapter Review

To further practice and reinforce the skills you learned in this chapter, you can perform the following tasks:

- Review the chapter summary.
- Review the list of key terms introduced in this chapter.
- Complete the case scenarios. These scenarios set up real-world situations involving the topics of this chapter and ask you to create a solution.
- Complete the suggested practices.
- Take a practice test.

Chapter Summary

- New Windows 2003 AD DS features give you more control over security policies, allow you to improve the user experience in branch offices, and help you to locate backed-up information that you need to restore.
- Improvements to GUI tools and auditing enhancements in Windows Server 2008 are designed to make administrative tasks more straightforward and less time-consuming.
- You can raise domain and forest functional levels to support new functionality but you cannot lower them (other than by restore or reinstallation). You can configure trusts between forests.
- Group Policy definition files can be held in a central AD DS store that is replicated between DCs. You can create custom files if required.
- New policy settings introduced in Windows Server 2008 give you additional Group Policy functionality. Troubleshooting tools are available, but (as always) troubleshooting policy and planning is mainly common sense.

Key Terms

Do you know what these key terms mean? You can check your answers by looking up the terms in the glossary at the end of the book.

- Functional levels
- Group Policy Object (GPO)

- Group Policy setting

- Organizational unit (OU)

- Password settings container (PSC)

- Password settings object (PSO)

- Read-only domain controllers (RODC)

- Shadow group

- Two-stage installation

- Volume shadow copy service (VSS)

Case Scenarios

In the following case scenarios, you will apply what you have learned about Active Directory and Group Policy. You can find answers to these questions in the "Answers" section at the end of this book.

Case Scenario 1: Planning a Windows Server 2003 Upgrade

You are a senior domain administrator at Northwind Traders. The company is planning to upgrade its DCs to Windows Server 2008, although some senior managers are still unconvinced. You are currently attending a number of planning meetings. Answer the following questions:

1. Some members of staff (for example, the chief executive officer) want to use non-complex passwords, although the default policy for the northwindtraders.com domain enforces complex passwords. You are asked whether this facility will still be available when you upgrade to Windows Server 2008. What is your reply?

2. The Technical Director is concerned that if you upgrade some of the DCs to Windows Server 2008 and then raise the forest functional level to Windows Server 2008 to take advantage of new features, DCs that still have Windows Server 2003 installed will become inoperable. She is also concerned that the domain currently contains Windows 2000 Server and Windows Server 2003 member servers and the company has no immediate plans to upgrade these computers. What is your response?

3. Currently, users at remote branch offices are reporting that logon is sometimes unacceptably slow. A secondary DNS server is currently installed at each branch office, but DCs are not used at branch offices for security reasons and because

staff at branch offices are not domain administrators. You are asked if upgrading to Windows Server 2008 will help address this problem. What is your reply?

Case Scenario 2: Planning and Documenting Troubleshooting Procedures

You worked on the helpdesk at Litware, Inc for a number of years. One of your tasks was resolving issues related to Group Policy. You have been recently promoted and one of your remits is to create a Procedures and Planning document that will guide less experienced administrators in carrying out troubleshooting tasks efficiently. Answer the following questions.

1. What should the procedure be if a user reports that he does not have access to the same facilities as his colleagues?

2. What should the procedure be if changes in policy settings are not being applied to a particular client computer, but are working on similar computers?

3. Administrators at Litware frequently use the Save Report feature of GPMC to generate GPO reports. What questions should they ask when studying these reports?

Suggested Practices

To help you successfully master the exam objectives presented in this chapter, complete the following tasks.

Configure Windows Server 2008 AD DS

Do all the practices in this section.

- **Practice 1: Configure PSOs**   A PSO can contain a large number of settings, of which you configured only a small subset in the practice session in Lesson 1. Experiment with PSO settings and determine the effects each has on the security policies that affect the users associated with the GPO.

- **Practice 2: Find out more about RODCs**   It is difficult to install and configure an RODC for real on your small test network, although you might consider using a virtual machine. Search the Internet for articles and online discussions that refer to RODCs. This is a new technology and more information should become available on a daily basis.

■ **Practice 3: Configure auditing**   Look at the new features available in Windows Server 2008 for AD DS auditing. Configure auditing to record AD DS changes, make changes, and then examine the security event log.

Configure Group Policy

Do all the practices in this session.

■ **Practice 1: Use GPMC and Group Policy Management Editor**   An administrator typically needs to configure only a few policy settings in the course of her work. A senior administrator, responsible for planning rather than implementation, needs a broader knowledge of what settings are available. Look at GPMC and especially Group Policy Management Editor. Expand the lists of policy settings. Use the *Explain* function to find out what each one does.

■ **Practice 2: Examine ADMX files**   The ability to understand and create code is invaluable if you want to develop your career. Administrators are not software designers, but the ability to generate simple files in (for example) XML is a valuable asset. Examine the standard ADMX files. Install and experiment with the sample ADMX files that Microsoft provides. (The link is given in Lesson 2.)

■ **Practice 3: Examine GPO reports**   Use the *Save Report* function in GPMC to generate and save GPO reports. Examine these reports until you feel comfortable with their structure and know what information they provide.

Take a Practice Test

The practice tests on this book's companion CD offer many options. For example, you can test yourself on just one exam objective, or you can test yourself on all the 70-646 certification exam content. You can set up the test so that it closely simulates the experience of taking a certification exam, or you can set it up in study mode so that you can look at the correct answers and explanations after you answer each question.

MORE INFO   **Practice tests**

For details about all the practice test options available, see the "How to Use the Practice Tests" section in this book's Introduction.

Chapter 4

Application Servers and Services

This chapter discusses the support Windows Server 2008 provides for applications, and in particular server roles, such as the Application Server role, that enhance application availability and accessibility. The chapter also discusses application deployment and resilience and the use of tools such as Microsoft System Center Configuration Manager 2007.

Exam objectives in this chapter:

■ Plan infrastructure services server roles.

■ Plan application servers and services.

■ Provision applications.

Lessons in this chapter:

Before You Begin

To complete the lesson in this chapter, you must have done the following:

■ Installed Windows Server 2008 and configured your test computer as a domain controller (DC) in the Contoso.internal domain as described in the Introduction and Chapter 1, "Installing, Upgrading, and Deploying Windows Server 2008." You also need a client computer running Windows Vista Business, Enterprise, or Ultimate that is a member of the Contoso.internal domain. This can be a separate computer or a virtual machine installed on the same computer as your DC.

■ If you want to complete the optional practice session exercise in Lesson 2, you need to add a Windows Server 2003 server to your test network as a member server in the Contoso.internal domain. This is because at the time of this writing, Microsoft System Center Essentials will not install on a Windows Server 2008 server.

Real World

Ian McLean

It's not pleasant to be made responsible for something you have no control over, although administrators get used to this.

I once worked for an educational organization that had commissioned and purchased (at some considerable cost) a custom software package for timetabling and resource allocation. By the time I came across this software it could certainly be described as legacy. It was 16-bit, although the phrase "two bit" was a better description. The company that supplied it had never fixed its obvious bugs (or so it seemed). They were now out of business.

Because the software had been expensive, management insisted that it be used. It no doubt performed its function after a fashion, although it could be described as "quirky." It supported only one concurrent user, and if that user did not exit gracefully nobody else could access the software until a timeout occurred. I found an update CD still in its wrapping and hoped this would solve some of the problems. However, I was concerned to find that the only update mechanism was to manually uninstall and reinstall the software. There was no way to automatically ensure that the software was up to date—or to update it if it was not.

What finally killed off this software package, however, was that the organization had a good reputation as an equal opportunities employer and this package had no accessibility features. It did not factor in the accessibility features of the operating system and provided no additional features. It was not compatible with any screen-reading software I could find.

Reluctantly, senior management decided to commission another custom package. The reason given was the "technical difficulties" in supporting the current software. I advised that perfectly good commercial software packages were available to do the job for a fraction of the cost, but the organization wanted "its own" software.

I asked to be involved in the talks with the application developers. I wanted the new software properly planned so that it would be available, accessible, and resilient. I was told that this was a business decision and my technical input was not required.

I said I wanted to make sure there would be no technical difficulties in supporting the new software. Sometimes you need to swallow your pride and get the job done.

Lesson 1: Application Servers

Chapter 11, "Clustering and High Availability," discusses high-availability techniques for mission-critical applications. This lesson, therefore, concentrates on the support provided for line-of-business (LOB) applications through the Application Server server role. BackOffice applications such as Microsoft Exchange Server 2007 and Microsoft SQL Server 2008 do not require this role, nor do standard applications such as the Microsoft 2007 Office system. This lesson discusses the specific support that the server role provides.

> **After this lesson, you will be able to:**
> - Plan application availability.
> - Plan and implement application accessibility.
> - Provide for application resilience.
>
> **Estimated lesson time: 50 minutes**

Planning Application Availability

In your initial planning process you need to determine the types of applications your organization is likely to run, currently and in the future. The component that provides support for LOB applications is Application Server, which is installed as a server role in Windows Server 2008. You need to plan ahead and know what applications you are likely to need to support. This in turn determines what components you need to specify when installing this server role.

The Application Server server role provides an environment for deploying and running LOB applications built with the Microsoft .NET Framework version 3.0. When you install this server role, you can select services that support applications that are designed to use COM+, Message Queuing, Web services, and distributed transactions. You install the Application Server server role in the practice session later in this lesson.

The Application Server server role provides the following:

- **Installation Wizard**   The Installation Wizard lets you choose the various role services and features that you need to run applications. The wizard automatically installs the features for a given role service.

- **Core runtime**   This supports the deployment and management of high-performance LOB applications.

- **The .NET Framework**   This is a development environment that delivers an efficient programming and execution model for server-based applications.

- **Web services**   The .NET Framework in turn enables Web services, and integrates new and existing applications with each other and with the server infrastructure.

Application Server is a Windows Server 2008 expanded server role. It simplifies the process of deploying applications that respond to requests sent over the network from remote client computers or from other applications. Typically, applications that are deployed on Application Server take advantage of one or more of the following technologies:

- The Microsoft .NET Framework versions 3.0 and 2.0

- Internet Information Services version 7 (IIS7)

- Message Queuing

- Microsoft Distributed Transaction Coordinator (MS DTC)

- Web services built with Windows Communication Foundation (WCF)

As part of your planning process you need to determine what specific role services a custom application requires. Typically, you need to work with the application developers to understand the application's requirements, such as whether it uses COM+ components or the .NET Framework 3.0.

For example Margie's Travel has commissioned an LOB order processing application that accesses customer records stored in a database through a set of WCF Web services. In this case, because WCF is part of the .NET Framework 3.0, you can use Application Server to deploy and configure WCF on any computer where the company wants the order processing application to run. You can install the database on the same computer or on a different computer. The next section of this lesson discusses WCF in more detail.

The Application Server Foundation (ASF) feature of Application Server is installed by default. You can select others during role installation. The following features are available:

- ASF

- Web server

- COM+ network access

- Windows Process Activation Service (WAS)

- Net.TCP port sharing

- Distributed transactions

Application Server Foundation

ASF is installed by default when you install the Application Server server role. It adds the .NET Framework 3.0 features to the .NET Framework 2.0, which is included in Windows Server 2008 regardless of whether any server role is installed. The Common Language Runtime (CLR) is included in the .NET Framework 2.0 and provides a code-execution environment that promotes safe execution of code, simplified code deployment, support for interoperability of multiple languages, and applications libraries.

The .NET Framework 3.0 consists of the following components:

- The .NET Framework
- WCF
- Windows Presentation Foundation (WPF)
- Windows Workflow Foundation (WF)

MORE INFO **The .NET Framework 3.0 components**

For more information about the .NET Framework, see *http://msdn2.microsoft.com/en-us/netframework/default.aspx*. More information about WCF, WPF, and WF is given later in this lesson.

Web Server

If you select the Web Server option, this installs IIS7 on your Windows Server 2008 server. IIS has been significantly enhanced for Windows Server 2008 and provides improvements in security, performance, reliability, management, supportability, and modularity.

IIS7 enables Application Server to host internal or external Web sites or services with static or dynamic content. It provides support for ASP.NET applications that are accessed from a Web browser and for Web services that are built with WCF or ASP.NET.

MORE INFO **ASP.NET**

For more information about the ASP.NET technology, see *http://asp.net/*.

MORE INFO **IIS7**

For more information about IIS7, see *http://www.iis.net*.

Quick Check

■ Which feature of the Application Server server role is installed by default?

Quick Check Answer

■ ASF

COM+ Network Access

This option adds COM+ Network Access for remote access (or invocation) of application components that are built on and hosted in COM+. These application components are also sometimes called Enterprise Services components.

Windows 2000 Server introduced COM+ Network Access and Windows Server 2008 continues to support it. However, newer applications typically use WCF to support remote invocation because WCF provides loose coupling, which makes integrated systems less dependent on each other and provides interoperability across multiple platforms.

MORE INFO WCF and loose coupling

For more information about WCF programming, including the implementation of loose coupling, go to *http://msdn2.microsoft.com/en-us/library/ms735119.aspx* and follow the links.

Exam Tip The 70-646 examination is likely to test whether you know what WCF is and the facilities it provides. You are not likely to be asked to generate WCF code under examination conditions.

Windows Process Activation Service

This option adds WAS, which is a new process activation mechanism for the Windows Vista and the Windows Server 2008 operating systems. IIS7 uses WAS to implement message-based activation over HTTP. WCF can provide message-based activation by using non-HTTP protocols supported by WAS, such as TCP, Message Queuing, and Named Pipes, in addition to HTTP. This allows applications that use communication protocols to take advantage of IIS features (such as process recycling) that were previously available only to HTTP-based applications.

Quick Check

- What four components does the .NET Framework 3.0 provide in addition to those provided by the .NET Framework 2.0?

Quick Check Answer

- The .NET Framework, WCF, WPF, and WF

Net.TCP Port Sharing

Windows Server 2008 introduces Net.TCP Port Sharing. This option adds the Net.TCP Port Sharing Service, which makes it possible for multiple applications to use a single TCP port for incoming communications. Port sharing, or multiplexing, is typically required when firewall configurations or network restrictions allow only a limited number of open ports or when multiple instances of a WCF application need to run simultaneously.

The Net.TCP Port Sharing service accepts incoming connection requests by using TCP. The service then forwards incoming requests to the various WCF services based on the target addresses of the requests. Port sharing works only when the WCF applications use the Net.TCP protocol for incoming communications.

Distributed Transactions

Microsoft Windows NT Server 4.0 introduced distributed transaction support and this remains supported in Windows Server 2008. Applications that connect to and perform updates on multiple databases or other transactional resources may require that these updates are performed on an all-or-nothing basis, sometimes known as ACID properties (Atomicity, Consistency, Isolation, Durability). These databases and transactional resources may be on a single computer or distributed across a network. MS DTC in Windows Server 2008 provides this functionality.

MORE INFO   **The Application Server server role**

For more information about the Application Server server role, see *http://technet2.microsoft.com/ windowsserver2008/en/servermanager/applicationserver.mspx*.

Application Server Foundation Components

Application Server Foundation was discussed earlier in this lesson. This section gives more details about the Application Server Foundation components: WCF, WF, and WPF. Each component is installed as a set of libraries and .NET assemblies. WCF and WF are primarily used in server-based applications and WPF is primarily used in client-based applications.

WCF

WCF is the Microsoft programming model for building service-oriented applications that use Web services to communicate with each other. Developers use WCF to build secure, reliable, transaction-based applications that can integrate across platforms and interoperate with existing systems and applications.

WF

WF is the Microsoft programming model that enables developers to build workflow-enabled applications on Windows Server 2008. It supports system workflow and human workflow across a variety of scenarios. For example, developers can use WF to implement the following:

- LOB applications
- Business-rule-driven workflow
- Human workflow
- Composite workflow for service-oriented applications
- Document-centric workflow
- User interface (UI) page flow
- Systems management workflow

WPF

WPF is the Microsoft programming model that developers use to build Windows smart-client applications. WPF is installed as a part of Application Server Foundation. However, it is not typically used in server-based applications.

Ensuring Application Availability

Microsoft defines application availability as the readiness of an application (and the service it runs under) to handle customer requests and to return timely and accurate responses. To ensure satisfactory application availability, you need to define availability goals that meet your organization's business needs and set up systems that measure your application availability and let you test that your goals are being met. You also need to be aware—and make your users aware—of the compromises and tradeoffs that might be required. For example, high application availability might come with the cost of lower performance or an easing of network security requirements.

Application Availability Planning

When planning application availability one of the factors you need to consider is the type of applications your organization wants its employees to use. Applications can be server-based or client-based. Server-based applications can be accessed remotely through a client interface or a Web interface (or both). Some LOB applications require the user to connect directly to the server.

Client-based applications, such as the Microsoft Office suite, can be installed on client computers, for example through an imaging process or through Group Policy. Once installed, these applications are available to the user, even when working offline. However, many client-based applications require periodic access to an organizational network so that user files can be synchronized and central patch management can apply updates obtained (for example) through the Windows Server Update Services (WSUS). If service packs or new revisions of the installed software are made available through Group Policy, a domain logon is required. Home workers can connect to the organizational network through a virtual private network (VPN) or by using third-party products such as Citrix MetaFrame. An administrator working remotely can use Terminal Services to create a Remote Desktop (RD) connection to a specific server.

Other applications are server-based, and some LOB applications require either interactive logon or an RD connection to the server that runs the application. BackOffice applications typically have client interfaces to server-based software. For example, Microsoft Outlook, Outlook Express, and Outlook Web Access (OWA) are client interfaces for Microsoft Exchange Server. Many modern applications use a Web browser, typically Internet Explorer version 7, to run Web applications, such as applications developed by using ASP.NET.

Whether applications are client-based or server-based, and whatever interface is used, application availability is largely dependent on network connectivity. If an application is server-based, can the user connect to the server? If the application uses certain ports, do any firewalls between the client and server need to be reconfigured? Does the user understand the requirement for an RD connection, and that this requires a second logon?

Users connecting remotely, such as home workers, bring you different problems, some of them outside your control. How fast and reliable is the user's Internet link? A user might claim to have a fast broadband connection but further investigation shows that this is a 2-Mb link that typically experiences high rates of contention. Some home workers, particularly in remote areas, might still be using dial-up modems. Have you made it clear that connecting to the organizational domain through a VPN over a 56Kb dial-up link requires a degree of patience? Do users understand that the logon password their ISP requires is not in any way related to the password they use to log on to the domain?

When you are planning application availability you need to consider other factors in addition to the applications you intend to install. User induction, particularly for users connecting remotely, is important to your overall strategy. Licensing is also a consideration. If an application is licensed for 25 concurrent users, do users understand that they need to close the application when they finish using it? Some applications require that users log off rather that merely shut down the application. If the application license permits unlimited concurrent use, do users understand that a large number of concurrent users will result in a drop in performance?

Typically, administrators use RD to administer servers. You expect your administrators to know that they need to log off of an RD connection rather than shut it down. Can you expect the same of a user that uses RD to run an LOB application on a server? Do users understand that the maximum number of RD connections a server supports is very limited (typically two)?

Your planning process needs to be technically correct. You need to determine how you will install the applications, where you will install them, and how you will measure performance and availability. As with most aspects of planning, however, planning application availability cannot be done in isolation. You need to discuss the applications with your users and determine an acceptable balance of performance, availability, and security. You need to talk to trainers, not only about how to use the application but also about how to connect to and disconnect from it. A junior administrator can choose to work in isolation behind a shield of technical jargon. As you progress in your chosen profession, however, you need to develop people skills.

Availability of Web-Based Applications

To ensure availability of Web-based applications, you first need to ensure that your network is available and that your Web server is up and running. You need to set availability goals, configure IIS to meet the demands that users are placing on your applications, and test your applications for functional compatibility with IIS7 application pool modes.

Application pools consist of one or more URLs that are served by a worker process or a set of worker processes. They use process boundaries to separate applications. This prevents an application from affecting another application on a Web server, and hence lets you test the availability of a Web application in isolation, without needing to allow for interference from other applications. IIS7 application pools continue to use IIS6 worker process isolation mode, and you can specify Integrated mode or Internet Server Application Programming Interface (ISAPI) mode, commonly known as Classic mode, to determine how IIS7 processes requests that involve managed resources.

MORE INFO **IIS6 worker process isolation mode**

For more information about IIS6 worker process isolation mode, see *http://www.microsoft.com/ technet/prodtechnol/WindowsServer2003/Library/IIS/333f3410-b566-49bc-8399- 57bcc404db8c.mspx?mfr=true.*

When an application pool is in Integrated mode, the application can use the integrated request-processing architecture of IIS and ASP.NET. When a worker process in an application pool receives a request, the request passes through an ordered list of events. Each event calls the necessary modules to process the request and to generate a response. If an application pool runs in Integrated mode the request-processing models of IIS and ASP.NET are integrated into a unified process model. This integrates steps that were previously duplicated in IIS and ASP.NET, such as authentication.

When an application pool is in Classic mode, IIS7 handles requests in the same way as IIS6 worker process isolation mode. ASP.NET requests first go through native processing steps in IIS and are then routed to Aspnet_isapi.dll for processing of managed code. The request is then routed back through IIS, which sends the response.

If you have a Web application that was developed to work with IIS6 (or earlier), you need to test its compatibility in Integrated mode before upgrading to IIS7 in the production environment and assigning the application to an application pool in Integrated mode. You should add an application to an application pool in Classic mode only if the application fails to work in Integrated mode.

To ensure that the level of Web application availability on your Windows Server 2008 server meets the needs of your customers, you must first define availability, service, and request-handling goals that represent customer needs. You then need to create application pools and configure IIS features to isolate applications and to tune and monitor the application pools. Finally, you need to assess the tradeoffs between availability and other aspects of running your applications, such as performance.

Quick Check

1. What is an application pool?

2. In what two modes can an application pool operate in IIS7?

3. Which of these modes handles requests in the same way as IIS6 worker process isolation mode?

Quick Check Answers

1. An application pool is one or more URLs that are served by a worker process or a set of worker processes.

2. Integrated mode and Classic (or ISAPI) mode.

3. Classic mode.

MORE INFO   Managing application pools

For more information about managing application pools in IIS7, see *http://technet2.microsoft.com/ windowsserver2008/en/library/1dbaa793-0a05-4914-a065-4d109db3b9101033.mspx?mfr=true.*

Exam Tip   The 70-646 examination tests planning and administration skills. It does not test your skills as a program developer. You need to know that you can test Web application availability in application pools and that IIS7 provides two application pool modes. You are not expected to be able to develop Web applications.

Implementing Application Accessibility

For application software to be more accessible, it needs to be designed so that the greatest possible number of people can use it without needing special adaptive software or hardware. This is referred to as Direct Accessibility. Software also needs to work with access features built into the operating system, such as the Ease of Access Center provided in Windows Server 2008. An important part of accessibility—one that is too often ignored—is ensuring that documentation, training, and customer support systems are readily accessible.

Physical Disability

People with physical disabilities can have a wide range of abilities and limitations. Some may have very limited range of motion, but have good movement control within that range. Others may suffer from uncontrolled, sporadic movements that accompany their more purposeful actions. Some people, such as arthritis sufferers, find joint movement both physically limited and painful.

Typically a physical disability that places limits on movement does not affect a person's ability to understand information displayed on a computer screen. Access is dependent on the user's ability to manipulate an interface device.

Therefore, implementing accessibility involves avoiding timed responses or allowing response times to be changed, providing keyboard access to all toolbars, menus, and dialog boxes, and using operating system facilities such as StickyKeys, SlowKeys, and Key Repeating.

Hearing Impairment

Users with hearing impairment need to have some method for adjusting volume or for coupling audio output directly to their hearing aids. Profoundly deaf users require a visual display of auditory information. In addition, you should make sure that support is reachable via Text Telephones.

Visual Impairment

Visual impairment can range from color blindness, through low vision, to legal blindness. You can improve accessibility for the color blind user by using means of conveying information that do not involve color coding, ensuring that software can operate in monochrome mode, and using colors that differ in darkness.

Users with low vision might suffer from poor acuity (blurred or fogged vision), loss of central vision (only seeing with edges of their eyes), tunnel vision (like looking through a tube), or loss of vision in different parts of the visual field. Other problems can include sensitivity to glare or night blindness. A common method of improving access to information on the screen is to enlarge or otherwise enhance the current area of focus. You can allow users to adjust fonts, colors, and cursors; use high contrast between text and background; avoid placing text over a patterned background; use a consistent and predictable screen layout; and adjust line widths.

Many people who are legally blind have some residual vision. Some can perceive only light and dark, while others can view things that are magnified. The best design strategy is therefore not to assume any vision but at the same time allow users to make use of whatever residual vision they have.

Access is typically accomplished using special screen-reading software to access and read the contents of the screen. Typically the output is sent to a voice synthesizer or dynamic Braille display. Modern operating systems make extensive use of graphic user interfaces (GUIs). This is good news for most users, but not for the blind. Software designed for accessibility makes text available to screen-reading software even when that text is embedded in an image. It uses consistent and predictable screen and dialog box layouts and presents tools in separate toolbars, palettes, and menus rather than in one large graphic or toolbar.

Pop-up help balloons should not disappear but should remain locked in place until users can access and read them. Controls should have logical names that can be read by screen-reading software even if they do not appear on the screen. Applications should use single-column text wherever possible and should provide keyboard access to all tools, menus, and dialog boxes. They should avoid control schemes that use unlabeled "hot spots" on pictures.

Documents and training materials are more accessible if designed so that they can be understood by reading the text only. Information in pictures and graphics should also be presented as text descriptions. If information is presented as an animated graphic or movie, it should be accompanied by a synchronized audio description.

Language or Cognitive Disabilities

This category includes individuals with general processing difficulties (mental retardation, brain injury, and so on), specific deficits (inability to remember names, poor short-term memory, and so on), learning disabilities, and language delays. The range of impairment can vary from minimal to severe.

Software that is designed to be user-friendly can facilitate access for people with language or cognitive impairments. Messages and alerts should stay on screen until they are dismissed. Language, both on-screen and in documentation, should be as simple and straightforward as possible. Screen layout should be simple and consistent.

Planning Accessibility

All of the information and guidance in this section so far has been general—not specific to Windows Server 2008 and the applications it supports. However, as a senior administrator you will be (and certainly ought to be) consulted when your organization plans to purchase commercial application packages or commission custom applications. One of your planning considerations should be the accessibility features of any software you plan to roll out. If the duties of your team include product and desktop support, you need to be aware of the difficulties that can be experienced by users with disabilities and how best you can support such users.

MORE INFO Accessibility

For more information about accessibility and assistive technology products, see the Microsoft Accessibility Web site at *http://www.microsoft.com/enable/*.

Using the Ease of Access Center

Windows Server 2008 implements the Ease Of Access Center, which provides a centralized location for accessibility settings and programs that used to be found in Accessibility Options. The Ease Of Access Center also features a new questionnaire that you can use to receive suggestions about which accessibility features you might find useful. This questionnaire replaces the Accessibility Wizard provided by previous Windows operating systems. You access the questionnaire by clicking Get Recommendations To Make Your Computer Easier To Use in the Ease Of Access Center.

You can open the Ease Of Access Center from Control Panel or by using the same keyboard shortcut (Windows key + U) that you used to open Utility Manager in previous Windows versions. The Ease Of Access Center replaces Utility Manager. You can add other assistive technology products to your computer if you need more accessibility features. These are available from the Microsoft Accessibility Web site. Figure 4-1 shows the Ease Of Access Center.

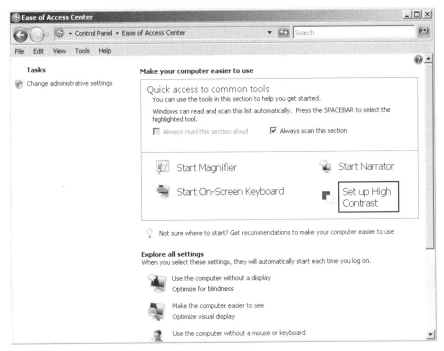

Figure 4-1 The Ease of Access Center

The Ease Of Access Center provides access that lets you configure the following accessibility settings and programs included in Windows Server 2008:

- **Use The Computer Without A Display**   Windows Server 2008 provides a basic screen reader called Narrator that will read text on the screen and provide voice output. You can also configure settings that control audio descriptions of videos and how dialog boxes appear.

NOTE   Additional facilities

Programs and hardware that are compatible with Windows Server 2008, including screen readers, Braille output devices, and so on can be found on the Microsoft Accessibility Web site.

- **Make The Computer Easier To See**   You can configure a number of settings that make the information on the screen easier to see and understand. For example, the screen can be magnified, screen colors can be adjusted, and unnecessary animations and background images can be removed.

- **Use The Computer Without A Mouse Or Keyboard**   Windows Server 2008 provides an on-screen keyboard. You can also configure Speech Recognition to control your computer with voice commands and dictate text entry.

- **Make The Mouse Easier To Use**   You can change the size and color of the mouse pointer. You can also configure the keyboard to control the mouse.

- **Make The Keyboard Easier To Use**   You can configure how Windows Server 2008 responds to mouse or keyboard input so that key combinations are easier to use (keys do not need to be pressed simultaneously), typing is easier, and inadvertent key presses are ignored.

- **Use Text And Visual Alternatives For Sounds**   Windows Server 2008 can replace system sounds with visual alerts and spoken dialog with text captions.

- **Make It Easier To Focus On Tasks**   You can configure a number of settings to make it easier for users to focus on reading and typing. You can use Narrator to read information on the screen, adjust how the keyboard responds to certain predefined keystrokes, and control whether specified visual elements are displayed.

> **Quick Check**
>
> ■ Which Ease Of Access Center setting might assist users with hearing difficulties?
>
> **Quick Check Answer**
>
> ■ Use Text And Visual Alternatives For Sounds

Exam Tip The settings in the Ease Of Access Center are relatively easy to understand and configure, and detailed explanation is not appropriate in a book at this level. Nevertheless you are expected to be familiar with the available features. It is a very good idea to spend some time using the Ease Of Access Center so that you are familiar with the accessibility settings.

Planning Application Resilience

Application resilience means that if an installed application is corrupted or if its executable file is deleted, the application automatically reinstalls. It also means that applications are kept up to date and new updates, service packs, and application revisions are installed as required. Windows Server 2008 server provides a number of tools that maintain application resilience. Typically, the tools used to deploy applications also provide resilience. Lesson 2 of this chapter discusses application deployment.

Providing Resilience Through Windows Installer

Windows Installer 4.0 ships with Windows Server 2008 and provides resiliency features that keep applications stable. It provides the following features (or entry points):

■ **Shortcuts** Windows Installer introduces a special type of shortcut that is transparent to the user and verifies the status of a specified application's installation prior to launching the application.

■ **File Associations** Windows Installer can intercept calls for a user file's associated application so that when a user opens the file, Windows Installer can verify the application before launching it.

■ **COM Advertising** Windows Installer provides a link to the Component Object Model (COM) subsystem so that any application that creates an instance of a COM component installed by Windows Installer receives this instance only after Windows Installer has verified the status of that component's installation.

When planning application resilience—particularly if you need to install custom LOB and third-party applications—you need to meet with the application developers and determine whether Windows Installer entry points are provided when an application is accessed through a shortcut, through invocation, or through COM advertising.

When Windows Installer deploys an application and provides a shortcut on a user's Start menu, it typically configures this shortcut so that it accesses the entry point (or transparent shortcut) that it uses to detect the status of the application and repair it as needed. Windows Installer will replace any missing files and install any required updates. Typically Windows Installer will access the necessary files at the network location from which it originally installed them. Otherwise, the user could be prompted to provide media or a location path. Usually you do not want this to happen, and you need to ensure that network connectivity is maintained and that the installation files are kept up to date.

If a Windows Installer entry point is provided by file invocation, you can examine the registry on the computer on which the application runs and determine the file associations. Figure 4-2 shows the relevant key. The REG_MULTI-SZ value in this key is known as a *Darwin Descriptor*. It is an encoded representation of a specific product, component, and feature. Fortunately you do not need to interpret this value, merely to verify that it is there. If the Darwin Descriptor exists, Windows Installer decodes the data and uses it to perform checks against that product and component.

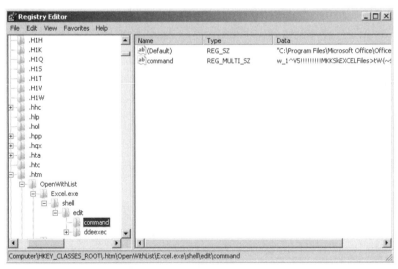

Figure 4-2   Darwin Descriptor for file invocation

A COM component library provides components that several different applications can use. For example, a component vendor might provide a COM-based shared library that provides travel directions when a user specifies a home address and a destination address. This could be used with several applications, but Windows Installer needs to check the status of the component through COM Advertising independent of the application that uses it (and even independent of whether the application was installed using Windows Installer). COM Advertising ensures that the component remains properly installed and registered. When an application creates an instance of this component, Windows Installer links to the process in a similar way as it links to a file association. Figure 4-3 shows the Darwin Descriptor for a COM component, which is stored in the InprocServer32 registry value.

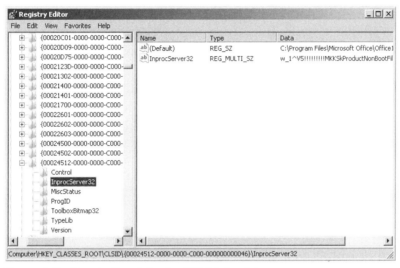

Figure 4-3   Darwin Descriptor for COM Advertising

Sometimes, the built-in resiliency features of Windows Installer might not be able to detect all the problems with an application's configuration, or the application might run in such a way that the required entry points are not being activated. The Windows Installer Application Program Interface (API) provides additional resiliency features in such situations.

For example, an application may use more than one executable file. The first executable could check for and install updates to the second executable, which then provides the main user interface. In this case, the first executable is invoked when the user clicks a shortcut on the Start menu. In this situation it is possible that problems with the main application executable will not be detected by the Windows Installer engine. In this case the application developer needs to utilize Windows Installer's knowledge of the application's configuration that is already defined in the deployment package.

An administrator is not expected to be a software developer. Nevertheless, you will be the first to know if a business-critical application is not updated or repaired. As part of the planning process you need to know which applications might not access the built-in Windows Installer entry points and whether the application developers have implemented resilience through the API. Typically you might need to ensure that resilience has been configured for the following types of application:

- Scheduled tasks
- Applications that run from the command line
- System services
- Applications that initially access the operating system (typically associated with run or run-once registry keys)
- Applications that call other applications

MORE INFO Application resilience

For more information about application resilience, see *http://msdn2.microsoft.com/en-us/library/aa302344.aspx*. This article is written from a developer's viewpoint and is not specific to Windows Server 2008. Treat it as background information.

Implementing Resilience by Using System Center Configuration Manager 2007

Lesson 2 of this chapter discusses Microsoft System Center Configuration Manager 2007 in detail. The purpose of this section is to look at how you use the facilities this software provides to deploy software updates and help ensure application resilience.

System Center Configuration Manager 2007 replaces Microsoft System Management Server (SMS) 2003 and makes it easier for you to track and apply software updates throughout your organization. It provides an integrated solution that deploys software (and hardware) updates across physical and virtual clients, servers, and mobile devices, independent of location. You can use it to distribute both security and non-security related updates of Microsoft products, third-party applications, and custom LOB applications.

System Center Configuration Manager's software update management is built on Windows Server Update Services (WSUS). This improves the speed and efficiency of updates, helps limit vulnerabilities, and provides scheduled updates.

MORE INFO **WSUS**

For more information about WSUS, see *http://technet.microsoft.com/en-us/wsus/default.aspx.*

System Center Configuration Manager 2007 supports custom software update catalogs for third-party and custom LOB software. These catalogs enable in-house software development teams or third-party software vendors to create custom update definitions and publish them to WSUS. Custom software update catalogs built by Microsoft partners such as Citrix and Adobe are included with System Center Configuration Manager 2007.

Software update catalogs are relative easy to write (at least compared to writing software packages). As a result, System Center Configuration Manager 2007 provides a single, integrated solution that allows administrators to manage the distribution of updates of Microsoft products and other software across their organization.

System Center Configuration Manager 2007 provides the following features:

- **Granular control** You can use System Center Configuration Manager 2007 to deploy updates seamlessly across your organization. The package provides granular control over when updates are applied and software is repaired. You can specify an allowed period of time during which System Center Configuration Manager 2007 can perform updates to a managed collection of computers. You can coordinate the frequency and duration of these maintenance windows with the service level agreements (SLAs) currently in force in your organization.

- **Automated vulnerability assessment** System Center Configuration Manager 2007 also provides automated vulnerability assessment that discovers missing updates on devices across your network and generates recommendations. This can often enable you to solve problems before they occur, or at least before your users notice them. In addition to implementing application resilience, the package lets you add updates (such as security updates) to operating system images so that any new computers you deploy are up to date and secure.

- **Internet-based client management** Ensuring application resilience for software installed on clients used by mobile and home workers that rarely attach to your corporate network generates an additional layer of complexity. Such client computers are particularly vulnerable because they frequently integrate with public-facing networks outside your corporate firewall. This makes keeping applications resilient and, in particular, applying security updates even more important. System Center Configuration Manager 2007 offers Internet-based client management and can deliver updates to both internal and Internet-based clients. This enables timely software updates to occur regardless of how often a client computer is attached to the internal network. Because managing client computers on a public network requires higher security, Internet-based client management requires mutual authentication using public key infrastructure (PKI)-based certificates, and data to and from these clients is encrypted using Secure Sockets Layer (SSL).

- **Wake On LAN**   System Center Configuration Manager 2007 provides Wake On LAN, which enables updates to occur after business hours. Wake On LAN sends wake-up packets to computers that require software updates. This means that you do not need to leave computers turned on to provide maintenance outside of regular business hours. It also eases your scheduling constraints and minimizes network disruption.

- **Integration with network access protection (NAP)**   System Center Configuration Manager 2007 lets your organization enforce compliance of software updates on client computers. This helps protect the integrity of the corporate network through integration with the Microsoft Windows Server 2008 NAP policy enforcement platform. NAP policies enable you to define which software updates to include in your system health requirements. If a client computer attempts to access your network, NAP and System Center Configuration Manager 2007 work together to determine the client's health state compliance and determine whether the client is granted full or restricted network access. If the client is noncompliant, System Center Configuration Manager 2007 can deliver the necessary software updates so that the client can meet system health requirements and be granted full network access.

MORE INFO   NAP

Although Windows Server Update Services 3.0, System Center Configuration Manager 2007, and System Center Essentials 2007 (described later in this chapter) can all be utilized as a part of the NAP client remediation process, they are not essential to the system health validation process. For more information about NAP for Windows Server 2008, see *http://www.microsoft.com/windowsserver2008/network-access-protection.mspx*.

■ **Flexible reporting**   System Center Configuration Manager 2007 provides a wide variety of reports that show the status of software updates across your corporate network. These reports let you view (for example) deployment status and compliance statistics. You can group multiple reports to make it easier to view and compare results.

MORE INFO   **System Center Configuration Manager 2007**

For more information about System Center Configuration Manager 2007, see *http://www.microsoft.com/systemcenter/configmgr*. You can download a trial version of this software from *http://technet.microsoft.com/en-us/configmgr/default.aspx*.

NOTE   **System Center Essentials 2007**

System Center Essentials is a unified tool that provides similar facilities to System Center Configuration Manager, including application update and resilience. System Center Essentials is designed for medium-sized networks and is limited to 30 servers and 500 clients. Lesson 2 of this chapter describes the tool in detail.

Using WSUS

WSUS version 3.0 (WSUS 3.0) lets you deploy Microsoft product updates to computers running Microsoft Windows Server 2008 and to client operating systems on your organizational network. The WSUS management infrastructure consists of the Microsoft Update Web site (*http://update.microsoft.com*) and WSUS server installed on a Windows Server 2008 computer. WSUS server enables you to manage and distribute updates by using the WSUS 3.0 Administration Console (Update Services), shown in Figure 4-4, which you can install on an administrative workstation to manage the WSUS 3.0 server remotely.

In addition, a Windows Server 2008 server running WSUS server can act as an upstream server—an update source for other WSUS servers within your organization. At least one WSUS server in your network must connect to the Microsoft Update Web site to get available update information. How many other servers connect directly to Microsoft Update is something you need to determine as part of your planning process, and depends upon network configuration and security requirements.

The Automatic Updates client component built into your client and server operating systems enables computers on your network to receive updates directly from Microsoft Update or from a server running WSUS. In a managed corporate network, updates are typically controlled using WSUS in combination with SMS or System

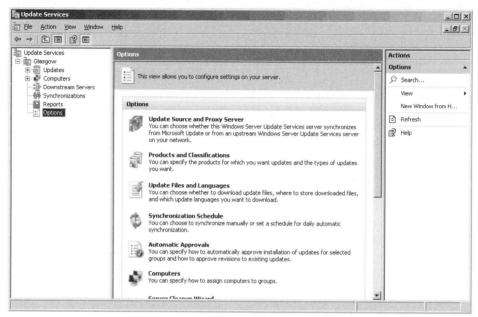

Figure 4-4   Update Services

Center Configuration Manager. This lets you test updates before rolling them out to computers on your production network. It also enables you to schedule updates so that they occur during periods of low network usage—for example, during the night.

WSUS has been around for some time, and as an experienced administrator you are probably familiar with it. If not, go to the WSUS home page at *http://technet.microsoft .com/en-us/wsus/default.aspx* and follow the links. This book discusses the enhancements to WSUS provided by version 3.0. WSUS 3.0 provides improvements in the following areas:

- Enhanced deployment
- Usability
- Performance and bandwidth optimization
- Support for complex server hierarchies
- Improved APIs

Enhanced Deployment   WSUS 3.0 lets you configure your WSUS server to synchronize updates automatically as often as once per hour (WSUS 2.0 let you synchronize once per day). You can obtain and replicate critical updates more quickly, although it is a judgment call whether you should do so, and how long you should take to test (for example) a security update marked as urgent or critical before deploying it. WSUS 3.0 lets you specify multiple auto-approval rules so that different products and update classifications might or might not be automatically approved. Auto-approval rules are applied to all updates that are currently on a WSUS 3.0 server.

WSUS 3.0 provides a WSUS Reporters security group. Members of this group have read-only access to the WSUS server. They can generate reports but cannot approve updates or configure the server.

Usability   The WSUS 3.0 administration console is now an MMC snap-in. This interface (shown previously in Figure 4-4) provides home pages at each node containing an overview of the tasks associated with the node. It offers advanced filtering features and the ability to sort updates according to Microsoft Security Response Center (MSRC) number, MSRC severity, Knowledge Base (KB) article, and installation status. The console provides shortcut menus and lets you integrate your reports with update views. It also provides custom views of WSUS information.

The WSUS 3.0 administration console provides access to a configuration wizard that steps through the process of post-setup server configuration. You can generate reports directly from the update view. You can report on update subsets, such as security updates not yet approved for installation. You can save these reports in Microsoft Office Excel or PDF format.

WSUS 3.0 logs detailed server health information in the event log. You can use System Center Operations Manager to monitor events generated by the WSUS server. The server can notify you about new updates through e-mail. WSUS 3.0 provides a cleanup to remove obsolete computer records, updates, and update files from your server.

You can upgrade WSUS 2.0 to WSUS 3.0. This preserves previous settings and approvals. However, upgrading from WSUS 2.0 to WSUS 3.0 is a one-way process. Reverting to WSUS 2.0 requires that you first remove WSUS 3.0 and then reinstall WSUS 2.0.

Performance and Bandwidth Optimization   Microsoft estimates that WSUS 3.0 provides a 50 percent performance improvement compared to WSUS 2.0. In addition, WSUS 3.0 comes with native x64 support to improve performance and scalability on 64-bit hardware.

Branch offices with slow WAN connections to the central server but broadband connections to the Internet can be configured to get metadata from the central server and update content from the Microsoft Update Web site.

You can configure a branch office to download updates in fewer languages than the central server. For example, you could configure the central server to download updates in all languages and a branch office to download updates in U.S. English only.

Supporting Complex Server Hierarchies   The WSUS 3.0 administration console enables you to inspect and manage all the WSUS servers in your hierarchy, and you can create update reports for all the computers updated through WSUS. You can cluster WSUS 3.0 servers for fault tolerance.

You can move a child server between replica mode and autonomous mode without needing to reinstall WSUS 3.0. In replica mode, an upstream WSUS server shares updates, computer groups, and approval status with its downstream replica servers, which inherit update approvals and cannot be administered apart from their upstream server. In autonomous mode, an upstream WSUS server shares updates with its downstream servers during synchronization, but not update approval status or computer group information. Downstream WSUS servers must be administered separately in this mode.

WSUS 3.0 permits a computer to belong to multiple target groups. You can also create hierarchical groups and specify approvals for the parent target group that are automatically inherited by computers in the child groups.

Improved APIs   The WSUS 3.0 API is based on the .NET Framework 2.0. Microsoft has created additional APIs for advanced management tools (such as System Center Configuration Manager). However, these APIs are not available from the WSUS administration console and are beyond the scope of this chapter.

The WSUS 3.0 API lets you create approvals for optional installation. This makes the update available for installation from Programs And Features in Control Panel, but not via Automatic Updates. Finally, the WSUS 3.0 API lets you publish applications and third-party updates.

Implementing Resilience by Using Group Policy

Windows 2000 Server introduced Group Policy software installation as an extension of the Group Policy Object Editor MMC snap-in. In production networks you typically use methods of providing software installation and resilience that you can schedule and control. Nevertheless, Group Policy remains a valid method of assigning or publishing applications and implementing updates, particularly in a small network.

You can publish software to users, assign software to users, or assign software to computers. You can use a combination of these methods to ensure that software is available to the users who need it, and to ensure that software is resilient and updates and new revisions are installed as appropriate.

When you publish a software installation (.msi) package to users in a site, domain, or OU, the users can use Programs And Features in Control Panel to install the software. It is important to remember that non-administrative users cannot by default install software on client computers through Programs And Features unless that software has previously been published by an administrator.

If you publish an application in a new GPO, you must link the GPO to a site, domain, or OU and refresh Group Policy before the application appears in Programs And Features. If you select Auto-Install when you publish software, you can install the application by opening an associated document. This is known as *document invocation*.

Publishing software installation packages enables users to choose whether to install a new version or apply updates. A user can use Add Or Remove Programs to install the software, or to remove it and later reinstall it. This method of implementing resilience is typically employed when users are relatively sophisticated. Organizations with users who are less computer-aware typically use Group Policy to block user access to Control Panel, in which case publishing software installation packages is not appropriate.

You can assign software to users on demand, assign it to users upon logon, or assign it to computers. If you assign software on demand, the software is advertised on the desktop. The user installs the software by clicking the desktop shortcut, by accessing the software through the Start menu, or by document invocation. If Control Panel is available, the user can also install the software through Programs And Features.

You can also assign software to users so that it installs the next time a user logs off (or reboots the computer) and logs on again. Even if the user removes the software, it becomes available again at logon. Updates and new versions are automatically installed on logon.

If you assign software to users in an OU and users in different OUs use the same computer, the software might be available to one user and not to another. If you want the software to be available to all users of a computer or group of computers, you can assign software to computers. The software is installed when the computer turns on, and any updates or new revisions are installed on reboot. If you assign software to a computer, the computer user cannot remove it. Only a local or domain administrator can remove the software, although a user can repair it.

MORE INFO Publishing and assigning software

For more information about publishing and assigning software, and a step-by-step illustration, see *http://technet2.microsoft.com/WindowsServer/en/library/d3d52f5d-45ab-4be9-a040-28ffe09bc8f81033 .mspx?mfr=true*. Although this is a Windows Server 2003 article, it is also relevant to Windows Server 2008.

Quick Check

- Which software package can you use to install software applications and maintain application resilience, and also supports custom software update catalogs for third-party and custom LOB software?

Quick Check Answer

- System Center Configuration Manager 2007

Practice: Installing the Application Server Server Role

In this practice session you install the Application Server server role. You install all features included in this role except COM+ network access, so the installation takes some time. You then make sure that installing the Web server service has installed IIS7.

▶ **Exercise 1: Install the Application Server Server Role**

In this exercise, you install the Application Server server role. You install all features of this role except COM+ network access. To complete this exercise, perform the following steps:

1. Log on to the DC with the kim_akers account.
2. Click Start, point to Administrative Tools, and then click Server Manager.
3. When the UAC dialog box appears, click Continue.
4. On the Action menu, click Add Roles.
5. The Add Roles Wizard appears. Click Next.
6. On the Select Server Roles page, select the Application Server check box.
7. In the Add Features Required For Application Server dialog box, shown in Figure 4-5, click Add Required Features.

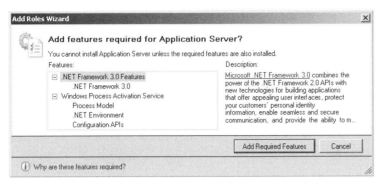

Figure 4-5 Adding the features required for the Application Server server role

8. In the Select Server Roles page of the Add Roles Wizard, Application Server is now selected, as shown in Figure 4-6. Click Next.

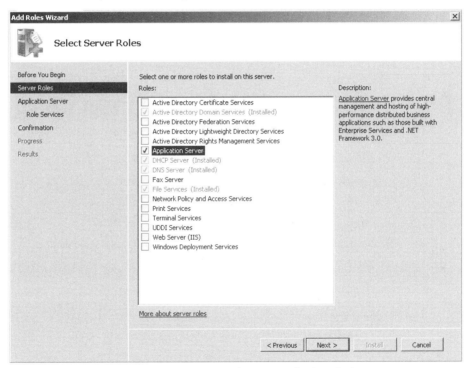

Figure 4-6 The Application Server server role can now be installed

9. Information about the Application Server role appears as shown in Figure 4-7. Read this information and then click Next.

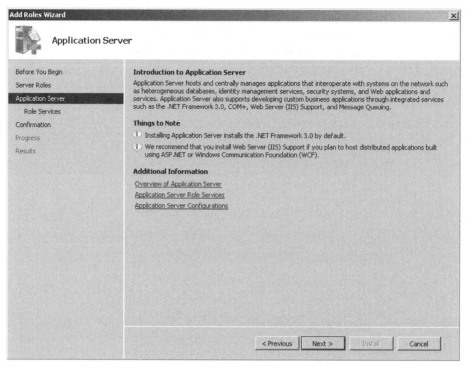

Figure 4-7   Information about the Application Server server role

10. On the Select Role Services page, select Web Server (IIS) Support.

11. In the Add Services And Features Required For Web Server (IIS) Support dialog box, click Add Required Role Services.

12. Select the TCP Port Sharing check box.

13. Select the Windows Process Activation Service Support check box.

14. In the Add Role Services And Features Required For Windows Process Activation Service Support dialog box, click Add Required Role Services.

15. Select the Distributed Transactions check box. The Select Role Services page of the Add Roles Wizard should appear as shown in Figure 4-8. Click Next.

16. On the Choose A Server Authentication Certificate For SSL Encryption page, select Choose A Certificate For SSL Encryption Later, as shown in Figure 4-9. Click Next.

17. Information about Web Server (IIS) appears. Read this information and click Next.

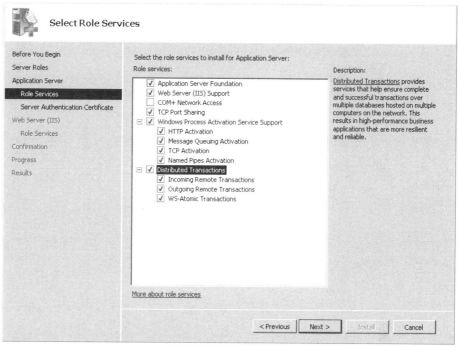

Figure 4-8 Role services selected

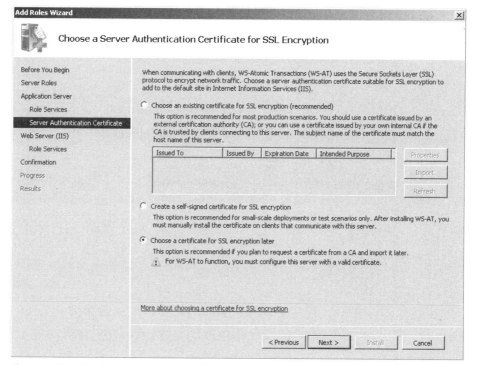

Figure 4-9 Electing to choose a certificate for SSL encryption later

18. A Select Role Services page for Web Server (IIS) appears. Select the ASP check box, as shown in Figure 4-10. Click Next.

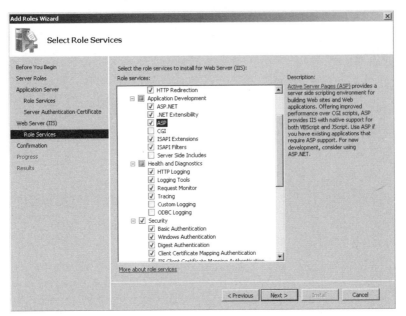

Figure 4-10   Selecting Web Server role services

19. Read the information on the Confirm Installation Selections page, as shown in Figure 4-11. If you are satisfied with the installation options selected, click Install.

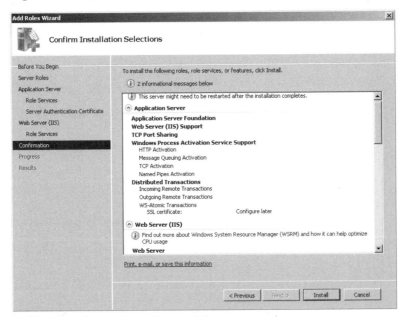

Figure 4-11   Selected installation options

20. When the installation process is finished, the status of the installation appears on the Installation Results page, as shown in Figure 4-12. Click Close.

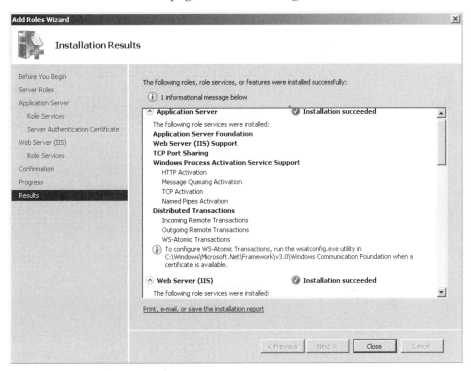

Figure 4-12   Installation Results page

21. Close Server Manager.

▶ **Exercise 2: Verify That IIS7 Is Installed**

IIS7 is installed when you install the Application Server server role and select Web Server (IIS) Support Role Service. In this exercise, you verify IIS7 installation. Do not attempt Exercise 2 until you have completed Exercise 1. To complete this exercise, perform the following steps:

1. If necessary, log on to the DC with the kim_akers account.

2. Click Start, point to Administrative Tools, and then click Internet Information Services (IIS) Manager.

3. When the UAC dialog box appears, click Continue. IIS Manager opens, as shown in Figure 4-13.

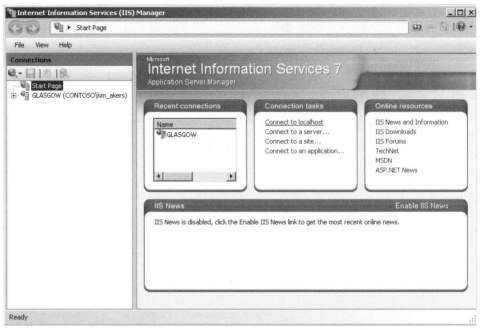

Figure 4-13 Internet Information Services (IIS) manager

4. Click Connect To Localhost. IIS information for the Glasgow DC is displayed, as shown in Figure 4-14.

Figure 4-14 Internet Information Services (IIS) manager points to Glasgow server

5. Expand GLASGOW (CONTOSO\kim_akers), expand Sites, and then click Default Web Site. Scroll to IIS and click Default Document, as shown in Figure 4-15.

Figure 4-15   Selecting the default document on the default Web site

6. Right-click Default Document and then click Open Feature. The file default.htm should be at the top of the list of default documents, as shown in Figure 4-16.

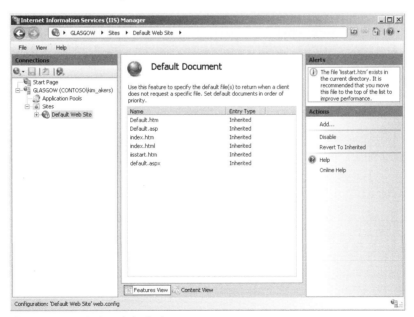

Figure 4-16   Listing default documents

7. Click iisstart.htm, and then click Move Up on the Actions pane. Click Yes to clear the Default Document dialog box.

8. Continue to click Move Up until iisstart.htm is at the top of the list of default documents.

9. Open Internet Explorer.

10. Type **localhost** in the address box and press the Enter key. Verify that you access iisstart.htm, as shown in Figure 4-17.

Figure 4-17   Accessing the iisstart display

11. Close Internet Explorer and then close Internet Information Services (IIS) Manager.

Lesson Summary

■ The Application Server server role provides an environment for deploying and running LOB applications built with the Microsoft .NET Framework version 3.0. The role provides an installation wizard, core runtime support, and support for the .NET Framework, which in turn enables Web services.

- ASF is installed by default when you install the Application Server server role. It adds the .NET Framework 3.0 features—including WCF, WF, and WPF—to the .NET Framework 2.0, which is included in Windows Server 2008 regardless of whether any server role is installed.

- You can use application pools to test the availability of Web-based applications in isolation so that they are not affected by interference from other applications.

- The Windows Server 2008 Ease Of Access Center provides access to the accessibility features of Windows Server 2008. Applications that run on Windows Server 2008 servers should at a minimum provide access to these accessibility features. Some applications provide additional accessibility features.

- You can implement application resilience on a Windows Server 2008 network by using Windows Installer, System Center Configuration Manager, System Center Essentials, and Group Policy. System Center Configuration Manager and System Center Essentials use WSUS to obtain and deploy Microsoft product updates. They also require access to a SQL database.

Lesson Review

You can use the following questions to test your knowledge of the information in Lesson 1, "Application Servers and Services." The questions are also available on the companion CD if you prefer to review them in electronic form.

NOTE Answers

Answers to these questions and explanations of why each answer choice is correct or incorrect are located in the "Answers" section at the end of the book.

---

1. Which feature of the Application Server server role does IIS7 use to implement message-based activation over HTTP?

    A. ASF

    B. WAS

    C. Net.TCP port sharing

    D. Distributed transactions

2. Which of the following are .NET Framework 3.0 components? (Choose all that apply.)

    A. WCF

    B. WPF

    C. WF

    D. WAS

    E. MS DTC

3. What configuration tool does Windows Server 2008 provide to let you configure accessibility features?

    A. Accessibility Wizard

    B. Utility Center

    C. Accessibility Options

    D. Ease Of Access Center

4. Although Windows Server 2008 continues to support COM+ Network Access, newer applications typically use which ASF component to support remote invocation?

    A. WCF

    B. WF

    C. WAS

    D. WPF

5. You want to use Group Policy to install a software package on all the client computers in an OU. You want Group Policy to install the software and any updates or new revisions when a client computer turns on. You want all the users who log on at any of the computers to have access to the software. How do you configure the software installation package in Group Policy?

    A. Assign the software at logon to all users in the OU.

    B. Publish the software to all users in the OU.

    C. Assign the software to all computers in the OU.

    D. Publish the software to all computers in the OU.

Lesson 2: Application Deployment

Deploying applications in a production network can be complex and requires careful planning, particularly in a large organization. Your plans need to recognize business requirements and you also need to take account of costs, such as the cost of individual and multiple-user licenses. Different considerations apply for server-based and client-based applications. You need to ensure that applications are available to users who require them while not wasting time and money by deploying applications to users who will never use them. This lesson looks at the planning process, and at the facilities provided by System Center Configuration Manager 2007, which is the deployment tool Microsoft recommends for large Windows Server 2008 networks, and at System Center Essentials 2007, which is used for deployment in medium-sized enterprises with fewer than 30 servers and 500 clients.

After this lesson, you will be able to:
- Plan application deployment.
- Deploy applications.
- Use System Center Configuration Manager.

Estimated lesson time: 35 minutes

Planning Application Deployment

In modern business organizations you rarely see administrators going from computer to computer installing software from optical media. Instead they employ solutions such as System Center Configuration Manager 2007 that use the facilities provided by Windows Installer 4.0 to implement comprehensive solutions for planning, testing, deploying, analyzing, and optimizing software applications. You need to plan solutions that help enable the seamless deployment of business applications to all computers, from servers to client computers to handheld devices.

Arguably the first thing you need to know when planning the deployment of new applications is the status of your organization's current hardware and software assets. You need to determine compatibility and understand how these assets are currently used. Both SMS 2003 and its replacement, System Center Configuration Manager 2007, provide hardware and software inventory features with integrated Web-based reporting, as does System Center Essentials 2007. You can use this asset information to step through the deployment process in a test environment that is based on the actual systems configurations. You can group systems with the same configurations (collections) together (such as for a System Center Configuration Manager 2007 site) and plan departmental rollouts. If the applications need to be deployed to a certain subset of business users or client computers, you can use information embedded in Active Directory user and computer accounts during the deployment process.

Both System Center Essentials 2007 and System Center Configuration Manager 2007 use Windows Installer 4.0. This allows self-healing or resilient software packages to be created directly from a Windows Installer (.msi) file. Lesson 1 in this chapter discussed application resilience. Your plan should also address bandwidth and security implications. Application deployment should have little or no impact upon normal business operations and needs to be highly secure. An invader who hijacks your software installation traffic could do considerable damage.

Real World

Ian McLean

It started with Microsoft Operations Monitor (MOM).

Some time ago I was advising an organization that wanted to monitor operations on its servers, in particular its e-mail servers. They'd been doing some investigation before asking for my advice, and had identified MOM as a solution to their requirements, which indeed it was.

However, I had to point out that their current database management system (DBMS) was not SQL Server. MOM required access to a SQL Server database. Management was less than happy about purchasing a SQL Server license and configuring a server, although I did point out that the organization could use a virtual machine.

Eventually the organization decided to redesign its DBMS, which was experiencing problems in any case. SQL Server was introduced and MOM was used for monitoring. However, I have remained careful when investigating solutions to any given problem to find out what the prerequisites of a particular software package are. It can be very easy to miss a single line in a requirements specification and cause yourself considerable embarrassment.

System Center Essentials 2007 and System Center Configuration Manager 2007 require access to a SQL Server database. Both tools also use WSUS 3.0, but WSUS 3.0 doesn't need SQL Server and is a solution for software deployment and resilience if SQL Server is not used in an organization.

> However, it seems to be more and more the case that SQL Server is a prerequisite, and it is becoming an almost essential part of Windows network infrastructure. Always check the prerequisites carefully.

Deploying Applications Using System Center Essentials

You can use Microsoft System Center Essentials 2007 to manage your software deployment. The tool provides a wide range of additional facilities and features, including troubleshooting end user problems, automating management tasks, managing multiple systems, and diagnosing and resolving IT problems. System Center Essentials 2007 is seen as a solution for medium-sized organizations. If your organization has or is likely to have more than 30 servers or 500 clients, you should use System Center Configuration Manager 2007 instead.

System Center Essentials 2007 provides a single solution with a single console for managing your servers, clients, hardware, software, and IT services for a more unified experience. The tool is built on WSUS 3.0 and requires access to a SQL Server database. However, if a SQL Server database does not exist in your organization and cannot be specified, installing System Center Essentials 2007 installs SQL Server 2005 Express with reporting by default.

NOTE **Organizational policy precludes the use of SQL Server**

If your organization's policy precludes the use of SQL Server, you should not install System Center Essentials 2007, but should instead use WSUS, which System Center Essentials 2007 is based on. However, be aware that WSUS does not offer the range of reporting and other facilities provided by the System Center packages and can install and update only the software that Microsoft provides on the Microsoft Update Web site.

System Center Essentials Reporting

System Center Essentials 2007 provides unified reporting based on the SQL Server reporting engine. You can review, save, or print information about the status of your IT environment, and you can e-mail this information to other IT professionals in your team. The reporting feature provides you with preconfigured reports to meet your reporting needs. These reports cover, for example, asset inventory, IT environment status, capacity planning, software deployment, and update compliance. You can configure System Center Essentials 2007 to e-mail you or your colleagues a comprehensive daily status report at a scheduled time of day.

The reports provided by System Center Essentials 2007 include support and diagnostic information for Windows Server and Client operating systems, Active Directory, Microsoft Office, Exchange, SQL Server, SharePoint Server, and IIS. The tool provides a unified console, shown in Figure 4-18, from which you can view and manage servers, clients, hardware, software, and IT services

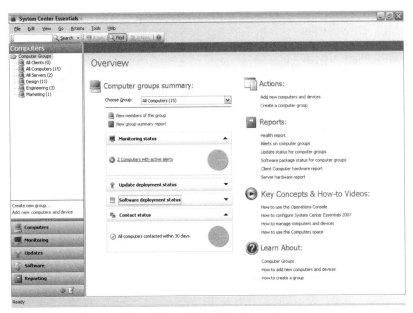

Figure 4-18   System Center Essentials unified console

Distributing Applications and Updates

You can use the System Center Essentials 2007 unified console to assess, configure, and distribute updates and to deploy software to targeted groups and computers. System Center Essentials 2007 provides an update configuration wizard that enables you to set update behavior for your network clients and servers. You specify update parameters, such as which products to update and what types of update to push out or install on demand. The wizard prompts you for the following information:

- Proxy information, such as port 80
- Applications and versions you want to update, such as Exchange Server 2007, the 2007 Office system, and so on
- Your update language or languages
- Types of updates you want to install, such as critical and security updates
- Your download, install, and approval preferences

When you have specified your update settings you can deploy updates for Microsoft operating systems, hardware updates, third-party updates, drivers, and Microsoft and non-Microsoft software applications manually or automatically. System Center Essentials 2007 automatically checks for new updates available and applicable to your IT environment and provides notification and access reports on update deployment progress to help you troubleshoot any update deployment issues.

System Center Essentials 2007 simplifies the task of deploying operating system upgrades or installing application suites (such as the 2007 Office system) by providing a wizard that walks you through the process of deploying software by creating a package and targeting installation on clients and servers in your network. You can deploy Microsoft Software Installation (MSI) and non-MSI applications, drivers, and Microsoft and non-Microsoft quick fix engineering (QFE) releases. You can target software installations by grouping computers and defining command-line configurations.

Installation settings default to silent installation. However, you can use the command-line functionality in the wizard to enable special configuration scenarios. When you use the wizard, you can browse to .msi or .exe packages and walk through a short process to deploy them to your clients and servers. The wizard completes the installation process while allowing you to specify where the software is installed, set an installation deadline, track installation progress, and troubleshoot the installation. Figure 4-19 shows the software package installation screen that lets you approve groups for deployment.

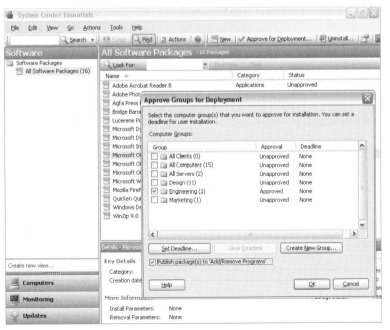

Figure 4-19 Approving groups for deployment

Troubleshooting and Asset Inventory

System Center Essentials 2007 notifies you as soon as a problem occurs and helps you to proactively diagnose and fix it. It also provides health status information, performance information, key events, and a network topology view of simple network management protocol (SNMP)-capable network devices such as routers, switches, and wireless access points (WAPs). The tool ships with and installs management packs that provide expert knowledge to enable you to receive notification of any problems and troubleshoot more efficiently and effectively.

The tool also automates software and hardware inventory, which lets you review assets and optimize configuration and compliance. You can perform searches, define filters, and generate reports that include up-to-date lists of all installed software applications and installed hardware. This is useful if you want to generate hardware readiness reports for the deployment of major applications or new operating systems.

MORE INFO   System Center Essentials 2007

For more information and a link to download trial software, see *http://www.microsoft.com/ systemcenter/essentials/default.mspx*.

Using System Center Configuration Manager 2007

System Center Configuration Manager 2007 is seen as an update of SMS 2003. It performs similar functions to System Manager Essentials 2007, although it is more fully featured. The distinction between the two packages is that System Management Essentials 2007 is designed for medium-sized organizations and has limits of 30 servers or 500 clients, while System Center Configuration Manager 2007 is designed for large organizations and has no such limits. Both packages rely on WSUS 3.0 Server and use SQL Server databases to store critical configuration information.

System Center Configuration Manager 2007 enables you to deploy server and client operating systems, applications, and updates. It lets you measure software usage and remotely administer computers. The tool works with the Windows Server 2008 Network Policy Server to restrict network access to computers that do not meet specified requirements, such as having required security updates installed.

You need to plan the deployment of System Center Configuration Manager 2007 with considerable care. The tool has the potential to affect every computer in your organization. If you deploy and manage with it careful planning and consideration of your business needs, you can reduce your administrative overhead and total cost of ownership (TCO). If you deploy System Center Configuration Manager 2007 without sufficient planning, your entire network may be disrupted.

After it is installed and configured, System Center Configuration Manager 2007 can assist your deployment planning by providing you with a hardware and software inventory and an assessment of the variances between your current configuration and predefined desired or recommended configurations.

System Center Configuration Manager 2007 collects information in a SQL Server database. This allows you to consolidate information throughout your organization through SQL Server queries and reports. If you want to look at the tool in a test environment, the disadvantage is that you need to install SQL Server in that environment as a prerequisite. However, this is not typically a problem in production networks, which usually support SQL Server. Unlike System Center Essentials 2007, System Center Configuration Manager 2007 does not provide the option of installing SQL Server Express 2005 during its installation. It requires that SQL Server already exists on the network.

Exam Tip   If you see the words "unified solution" in a question, accompanied by "configuration management," "client management," "update," "installation," "inventory," or "report," the answer is probably System Center Configuration Manager 2007, System Center Essentials 2007, or both.

System Center Configuration Manager 2007 Prerequisites

You can install System Center Configuration Manager 2007 on a server with a minimum processor speed of 233 MHz. Microsoft recommends a 300 MHz or faster Intel Pentium/Celeron family or comparable processor. A minimum of 128 MB RAM is required, although less than 256 MB is not recommended and a minimum of 384 MB is required if you want to use the tool to deploy operating systems. In theory you need 350 MB minimum free disk space for a new installation. In practice you should have at least 5 GB to spare, because client installation creates a temporary program download folder that will automatically increase to 5 GB if necessary. Although the resources available on a modern server computer are typically well in excess of these minimum requirements, you might need to keep them in mind if you want to use a virtual server.

Given that your server hardware meets the installation requirements, your network must support the following conditions:

- Servers that host System Center Configuration Manager 2007 must be member servers in a Windows 2000 or Windows 2003 Active Directory domain. Currently the prerequisites do not specify a Windows Server 2008 Active Directory domain.

- IIS 6.0 or later must be installed on your network. Although System Center Configuration Manager 2007 will install if IIS is not available, its functionality will be severely reduced—see the IIS sidebar later in this section.

- Background Intelligent Transfer Service (BITS) 2.0 or later is required if Configuration Manager distribution point systems that use BITS bandwidth throttling are configured.

- Internet Explorer (IE) 5.0 or later must be installed on all network servers.

- Microsoft Management Console (MMC) 3.0 must be installed on the server or administrative workstation that will manage System Center Configuration Manager 2007.

- The .NET Framework 2.0 must be installed on the server that hosts System Center Configuration Manager 2007.

- Currently SQL Server 2005 SP2 is the only version of SQL Server supported for hosting the System Center Configuration Manager 2007 database. SQL Server 2008 is not specified in the prerequisites. The SQL database service is the only SQL Server component you need to install to host the database.

IIS

IIS (6.0 or later) is required to support the following System Center Configuration Manager 2007 functions:

- A BITS-enabled distribution point. This functionality requires BITS server extensions and Web Distributed Authoring And Versioning (WebDAV) extensions.

- A management point. This requires BITS server IIS extensions and WebDAV IIS extensions.

- A reporting point. This requires Active Server pages.

- A software update point.

- A server locator point.

Because the functionality of System Center Configuration Manager 2007 would be severely limited without these features, IIS is generally considered to be a prerequisite, even though System Center Configuration Manager 2007 will still install if it is not available.

NOTE Secondary site prerequisites

System Center Configuration Manager 2007 is typically installed on a per-site basis. System Center Configuration Manager 2007 sites can be the same as Active Directory sites or can be independent of the Active Directory structure. A *site* is a collection of computers that have the same or similar configuration requirements. The first site on which System Center Configuration Manager is installed is the Primary site. If you are installing the tool on a Windows Server 2003 server in a Secondary site, you might need to apply the updates available at *http://support.microsoft.com/default.aspx?scid=kb;en-us;906570* and *http://support.microsoft.com/kb/914389/en-us*.

Quick Check

- What is the Microsoft recommendation for the processor on a server on which you intend installing System Center Configuration Management 2007?

Quick Check Answer

- Microsoft recommends a 300 MHz or faster Intel Pentium/Celeron family or comparable processor.

System Center Configuration Manager 2007 Client Deployment

You can use a number of methods to deploy the System Center Configuration Manager 2007 client on computer systems on your network. Table 4-1 lists and briefly describes these methods.

Table 4-1   Methods of Deploying System Center Configuration Manager 2007 Client

Installation Method	Description
Client push installation	Targets the client to assigned resources
Software update point installation	Installs the client by using the System Center Configuration Manager 2007 software updates feature
Group Policy installation	Installs the client by using Group Policy
Logon script installation	Installs the client by means of a logon script
Manual installation	Installs the client manually

Table 4-1 Methods of Deploying System Center Configuration Manager 2007 Client

Installation Method	Description
Upgrade installation	Installs upgrades to the client software by using the software distribution feature in System Center Configuration Manager 2007
Client imaging	Pre-stages the client installation in an operating system image

MORE INFO Client deployment

For more information about the System Center Configuration Manager 2007 client installation methods listed in Table 4-1, go to *http://technet.microsoft.com/en-us/library/bb632762.aspx* and follow the links.

Planning System Center Configuration Manager 2007 Deployment

You need to plan your implementation of System Center Configuration Manager 2007 carefully. You must thoroughly research, document, and test your plan before you deploy the software. The planning process can be divided into the following stages:

- **Preplanning** This involves examining and documenting the current computing environment, determining your organizational objectives, analyzing risk, creating project plan documentation, setting up a test network to pilot the project, and learning as much as you can about the System Center Configuration Manager 2007 tool.

- **Planning** In this stage, you complete your project plan documents. You need to document your planned System Center Configuration Manager 2007 hierarchy, the requirements for your pilot project, how you plan to deploy the tool, how you will use its features, and your security and recovery plans.

- **Deployment** In this stage, you first deploy the tool on your test network and validate your design. You then deploy System Center Configuration Manager 2007 to your Primary site, configure security and site settings, build your site hierarchy, and (if necessary) deploy the tool to additional sites. You also carry out a phased deployment of System Center Configuration Manager 2007 client software.

The planning process also requires that you create checklists. You need a checklist for planning the implementation of System Center Configuration Manager 2007—a deployment checklist. You also need to create administrator workflows for software distribution, software updates, and (if necessary) operating system deployment.

MORE INFO **Administrator workflows**

For more information about administrator workflows, see *http://technet.microsoft.com/en-us/library/ bb632865.aspx*, *http://technet.microsoft.com/en-us/library/bb680675.aspx*, and *http://technet .microsoft.com/en-us/library/bb694121.aspx*.

Quick Check

■ What installation method installs the System Center Configuration Manager 2007 client by using the tool's software updates feature?

Quick Check Answer

■ Software update point installation.

System Center Configuration Manager 2007 Features

System Center Configuration Manager 2007 provides a single tool for change and configuration management. Its function is to enable you to provide relevant software and updates to users quickly, cost-effectively, and from a single MMC snap-in. The tool provides the following functions:

■ Hardware and software inventory

■ Distributing and installing software applications

■ Distributing and installing software updates, such as security fixes

■ Deploying operating systems

■ Specifying a desired client configuration and monitoring adherence to that configuration

■ Restricting network access if a computer does not adhere to configuration requirements

■ Metering software usage

■ Remotely controlling computers to provide troubleshooting support

Figure 4-20 shows the System Center Configuration Manager 2007 console and the various options available.

The prerequisites for installing System Center Configuration Manager 2007 server were discussed earlier in this lesson. You can install System Center Configuration Manager 2007 client software on client computers, servers, portable computers, mobile devices running Windows Mobile or Windows CE, and devices running Windows XP Embedded (such as automated teller machines).

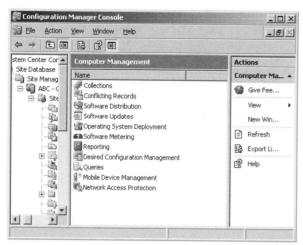

Figure 4-20   The System Center Configuration Manager 2007 console

System Center Configuration Manager 2007 is site-based. This provides a method of grouping clients into manageable units with similar requirements for feature sets, bandwidth, connectivity, language, and security. System Center Configuration Manager 2007 sites can match Active Directory sites or can be totally independent of them. Clients can move between sites or be managed remotely.

The System Center Configuration Manager 2007 tool offers many features to manage your client computers and mobile devices. After you have installed and configured the tool and installed client software on your network computers, you can perform the following common tasks:

- **Collect hardware and software information**   You can use System Center Configuration Manager 2007 to collect hardware and software inventory from your network clients. Hardware and software client inventory agents are enabled on a site-wide basis. When the hardware inventory client agent is enabled you can collect hardware inventory data. This provides system information, for example available disk space, processor type, and operating system for each client computer. When the software inventory client agent is enabled you can collect software inventory data. This gives you information about the installed applications and file properties on client systems.

- **Manage clients over the Internet**   Internet-based client management lets you manage clients that are not connected to your organizational network but have an Internet connection. You do not need to use virtual private networks (VPNs) and you can deploy scheduled software updates. For the purposes of security and mutual authentication, Internet-based client management requires that the site is in native mode. If you manage clients over the Internet, features that rely on Active Directory or are not appropriate for a public network are unavailable. For example, you cannot target software distribution to users, use branch distribution points, deploy System Center Configuration Manager 2007 client, automatically assign a site, use Network Access Protection (NAP), implement Wake On LAN, use remote control, or deploy operating systems.

MORE INFO   Site modes

For more information about mixed and native System Center Configuration Manager 2007 site modes, see *http://technet.microsoft.com/en-us/library/bb680658.aspx*.

■ **Distribute software**   Software distribution enables you to push applications and updates to client computers. It uses packages (for example, MSI packages) to deploy software applications. Within those packages, commands known as programs tell the client what executable file to run. A single package can contain multiple programs. Packages can also contain command lines to run files already present on the client. Advertisements are used to specify which clients receive the program and the package. Distributing applications using System Center Configuration Manager 2007 involves creating the software distribution package, creating programs to be included in the package, selecting package distribution points, and then creating an advertisement for a program. Note that System Center Configuration Manager 2007 does not create the packages; it merely distributes them to clients.

NOTE   Assignment schedule

If the advertisement is mandatory, you also need to specify an assignment schedule.

■ **Deploy updates**   The System Center Configuration Manager 2007 software updates feature provides a set of tools and resources to help you manage the complex task of tracking and applying software updates (such as security updates) to client computers on your network. Software updates are composed of metadata and an update file. Metadata is information about the software update and is stored in the site server database. The update file is what client computers download and run to install the software update. During the synchronization phase, the software update metadata is synchronized from the upstream WSUS 3.0 server (or, less typically, from Microsoft Update) and inserted into the site server database. During the compliance assessment phase, client computers scan for software update compliance and report their compliance state for synchronized software updates. During the deployment phase, software updates you select for deployment and updates selected through the software updates policy are sent to client computers. The software update files are downloaded to and installed on the clients.

■ **Deploy operating systems** System Center Configuration Manager 2007 provides an operating system deployment feature that enables you to create images that can be deployed to computers managed by System Center Configuration Manager 2007. You can also deploy operating system images to unmanaged computers by using bootable media such as a CD set or a DVD. The image, in a WIM format file, contains the required Microsoft Windows operating system and can also include any LOB applications that need to be installed. The operating system deployment feature captures and deploys images, provides user state migration by using the User State Migration Tool (USMT) 3.0, and lets you control the task sequences required for operating system image deployment.

NOTE Third-party operating systems

System Center Configuration Manager 2007 can deploy third-party client operating systems provided that partner organizations supply the relevant code for operating system deployment.

MORE INFO UserState Migration Tool

For more information about USMT 3.0, see *http://technet2.microsoft.com/WindowsVista/en/library/91f62fc4-621f-4537-b311-1307df0105611033.mspx?mfr=true*.

■ **Manage mobile devices** System Center Configuration Manager 2007 mobile device management lets you manage mobile devices, including Smartphones and Pocket PCs, in much the same way as desktop computers. By default, mobile device clients use HTTP to communicate with the device management points. Mobile device clients poll the device management point at configurable intervals to report discovery data and receive policy advertisements. You can specify the polling interval in the System Center Configuration Manager 2007 Administrator console.

■ **Manage desired configurations** System Center Configuration Manager 2007 desired configuration management allows you to assess the compliance of client computers with respect to various configuration settings, such as operating system version and settings, and installed applications and application configuration. You can also check for compliance with software updates and security settings. Compliance is evaluated against a configuration baseline. This contains the configuration items you want to monitor and rules that define the required compliance. This configuration data can be imported from the Web in System Center Configuration Manager 2007 Configuration Packs as best practices defined by Microsoft and other vendors. You can also define configuration data within System Center Configuration Manager 2007, or define it externally and then import it into the tool.

NOTE   **Web-based configuration data**

You can download configuration data published by Microsoft and other software vendors and solution providers from the System Center Configuration Manager 2007 Configuration Packs Web page at *https://www.microsoft.com/technet/prodtechnol/scp/configmgr07.aspx.*

- **Meter software usage**   System Center Configuration Manager 2007 software metering allows you to collect software usage data from System Center Configuration Manager 2007 clients. Software metering can tell you which applications are actively being used (as opposed to software inventory that tells you what is installed). Software metering allows you to acquire or renew licenses for applications that are actually being used, rather than purchasing licenses for applications that lie dormant on client computers. The System Center Configuration Manager 2007 reporting feature can present summary data gathered by the software metering feature.

- **Perform remote administration**   To remotely administer computers by using System Center Configuration Manager 2007, you need to install and enable the remote tools client agent. The remote tools feature enables permitted viewers to access any client computer in the System Center Configuration Manager 2007 site that has the remote tools client agent components installed. Remote control is a feature of the remote tools application that you can use to view or operate a computer anywhere in the site hierarchy. You can use remote control to troubleshoot hardware and software configuration problems on remote clients and to provide remote help desk support when you need access to the client computer.

MORE INFO   **Integration with Remote Desktop**

Remote administration provides the ability to integrate System Center Configuration Manager 2007 with Remote Desktop. For more information about Remote Desktop, refer to Chapter 5, "Terminal Services and Application and Server Virtualization."

- **Restrict network access**   System Center Configuration Manager 2007 NAP enables you to include software updates in your system health requirements. NAP policies define which software updates need to be included, and the System Center Configuration Manager 2007 System Health Validator point passes the client's compliant or noncompliant health state to the Network Policy Server, which determines whether to grant the client full or restricted network access. Noncompliant clients can be automatically brought into compliance through remediation. This requires the System Center Configuration Manager 2007 software updates feature to be configured and operational.

- **Wake up clients from sleep mode**   You can configure scheduled System Center Configuration Manager 2007 activities to take place outside business hours by using the Wake On LAN feature. Wake On LAN can send a wake-up transmission prior to the configured deadline for a software update deployment. Wake-up packets are sent only to computers that require the software updates. In addition, Wake On LAN can send a wake-up transmission prior to the configured schedule of a mandatory advertisement. This can be for software distribution or a task sequence.

MORE INFO   Wake On LAN

For System Center Configuration Manager 2007 to use Wake On LAN, the System Configuration Manager 2007 client software must be installed on the computer, the client network card must support magic packet format, and the client BIOS must be configured for wake-up packets on the network card.

For more information and example scenarios, see *http://technet.microsoft.com/en-gb/library/bb932183.aspx*.

MORE INFO   Troubleshooting System Center Configuration Manager 2007

For troubleshooting information, go to *http://technet.microsoft.com/en-gb/library/bb932183.aspx* and follow the links.

System Center Configuration Manager Client Reports

System Center Configuration Manager 2007 client reports help you manage and troubleshoot clients. You can use reports to gather, organize, and present information about users, hardware and software inventory, software updates, site status, and other System Center Configuration Manager 2007 operations. The tool provides a number of predefined reports. If necessary, you can modify predefined reports or create custom reports to meet your needs. This section lists only a subset of the many reports available in System Center Configuration Manager 2007. For a complete list, click Reports in the Configuration Manager console, as shown in Figure 4-21.

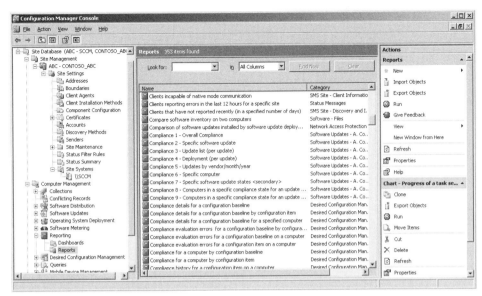

Figure 4-21 Available reports

Quick Check

1. What System Center Configuration Manager 2007 feature lets you install updates at night when network traffic is low and most client computers are in sleep mode?

2. What System Center Configuration Manager 2007 feature tells you whether an application installed on a client is actually used?

Quick Check Answers

1. Wake On LAN

2. Software metering

The following client deployment and assignment reports, which do not require that clients are assigned a fallback status point, help you track and monitor client deployment for both System Center Configuration Manager 2007 clients and SMS 2003 clients:

- Computers assigned but not installed for a particular site

- Computers with a specific SMS client version

- Count clients assigned and installed for each site

- Count clients for each site

- Count SMS client versions

The following client deployment and assignment reports, which require that clients are assigned a fallback status point, help you track and monitor client deployment for Configuration Manager 2007 clients only:

- Client Assignment Detailed Status Report
- Client Assignment Failure Details
- Client Assignment Status Details
- Client Assignment Success Details
- Client Deployment Failure Report
- Client Deployment Status Details
- Client Deployment Success Report

The following client communication reports, which apply to Configuration Manager 2007 clients only and require that these clients are assigned a fallback status point, help you to identify client communication problems:

- Issues by incidence detail report for a specific collection
- Issues by incidence summary report for a specific collection
- Issues by incidence detail report for a specific site
- Issues by incidence summary report

Client mode reports help you to manage clients when sites are configured for native mode, which requires public key infrastructure (PKI) certificates for all clients, and specific site systems. You can use the Summary Information Of Clients In Native Mode report when you are migrating sites from mixed mode to native mode. This report identifies the clients that have successfully switched their site mode configuration.

The following client mode reports help you to determine whether clients are ready to be migrated to native mode, but require that the Configuration Manager Native Mode Readiness Tool is first run on System Center Configuration Manager 2007 clients:

- Clients incapable of native mode
- Summary information of clients capable of native mode

MORE INFO   **Migrating clients to native mode**

For more information about migrating clients to native mode, see *http://technet.microsoft.com/ en-us/library/bb680986.aspx* and *http://technet.microsoft.com/en-us/library/bb632727.aspx.*

Exam Tip   Examiners often ask you to identify the appropriate tool to perform a specified job. Tools with similar sounding names are listed as incorrect answers. Remember that both System Center Configuration Manager 2007 and System Center Essentials 2007 provide unified solutions that provide inventories and reports and permit you to install applications and updates and perform patch management. Both tools use WSUS 3.0 Server and require a SQL Server database. System Center Configuration Manager 2007 is used in large organizations. System Center Essentials 2007 is limited to 30 servers or 500 clients.

If SQL Server cannot be used in an organization, WSUS can be used for deploying updates. However, WSUS can deploy only Microsoft operating system and application updates published on the Microsoft Update Web site. System Center Operations Manager 2007 cannot be used as an update deployment tool. It is primarily a monitoring tool that provides information about a server's current state and functionality. System Center Virtual Machine Manager 2007 performs centralized management of a virtual machine infrastructure and is not used for application deployment or patch management.

MORE INFO   **Operations Manager and Virtual Machine Manager**

For more information about System Center Operations Manager 2007 and System Center Virtual Machine Manager 2007, see http://*www.microsoft.com/systemcenter/opsmgr/default.mspx* and *http:// technet.microsoft.com/en-us/scvmm/bb871026.aspx*.

Practice: Installing System Center Essentials 2007 (Optional)

In this exercise, you install System Center Essentials 2007. However, at the time of this writing you need to have a computer running Windows Server 2003 Standard or Enterprise Edition on your network, because System Center Essentials 2007 requires WSUS 3.0, which is incompatible with Windows Server 2008. If a software update becomes available to solve this incompatibility, you can then install System Center Essentials 2007 on your Windows Server 2008 server.

▶ **Exercise : Install System Center Essentials 2007**

In this exercise you install System Center Essentials 2007 on a Windows Server 2003 server in your test network. This installs SQL Server 2005 Express with reporting on the same computer. In a production network you would probably choose the option of installing System Center Essentials 2007 on one server and SQL Server on another. To complete the exercise, perform the following steps:

1. If necessary, log on to the domain at your Windows Server 2003 server by using the kim_akers account.

2. Browse to the Internet link that lets you download the trial System Center Essentials 2007 software. Currently this is *http://technet.microsoft.com/en-us/ bb738028.aspx*.

3. If you are prompted to install Microsoft Silverlight, click Click To Install and then click Run. Microsoft Silverlight then installs.

4. On the Evaluate System Center Essentials 2007 Today Web page, select your installation language, which is typically English (United States).

5. Click the button marked ">" to the right of the language selection box.

6. If necessary, click the information bar and select Display Blocked Content.

7. Sign in using your Windows Live ID (for example, your Microsoft Passport account). If you do not have a Windows Live ID, click Sign Up Now and follow the prompts.

8. Verify and, if necessary, update your personal details. Click Continue.

9. Read the information on the Download Center Web page shown in Figure 4-22. Click Continue.

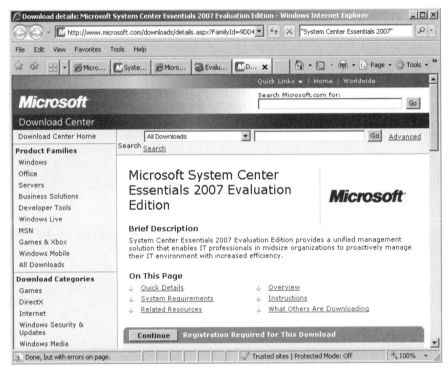

Figure 4-22   Download Center Web page

10. If prompted, re-enter your Windows Live ID password and click Sign In.

11. If a dialog box appears asking if you want to try the new Silverlight-powered Download Center, click No.

12. On the Download Center Web page, click Download Files Below.

13. Click the Download button beside SCE2007RTMEval.exe, as shown in Figure 4-23.

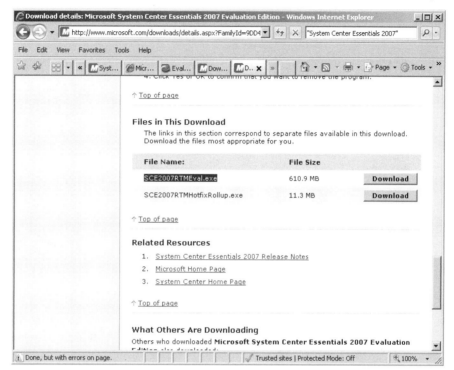

Figure 4-23   Selecting a file to download

14. In the File Download–Security warning dialog box, click Run and then select Close This Dialog Box When Download Completes.

15. The installation file downloads. Click Run and then click OK.

16. Do not change the default unzip folder. Click Unzip.

17. Click OK in the Files Unzipped Successfully dialog box.

18. On the System Center Essentials 2007 Setup page shown in Figure 4-24, click Full Setup under Install.

19. The System Center Essentials 2007 Setup Wizard opens. Click Next.

20. The wizard checks the installation prerequisites. Click Next.

21. Follow the steps in the installation wizard. You will need to agree to the licensing terms, register your installation, specify an installation location or accept the default, and specify a SQL database (or choose to install SQL Server 2005 Express). Typically you will accept the default administration account and error and usage reports. You will be presented with a summary. If this is acceptable, click Install.

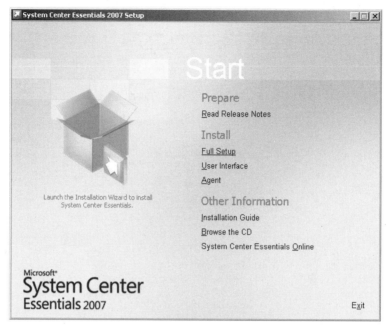

Figure 4-24   The System Center Essentials 2007 Setup page

22. Microsoft Update checks whether any online updates are available and installs them as required. Your installation is confirmed.

23. Open System Center Essentials 2007. You should see a screen similar to that shown in Figure 4-18 earlier in this lesson.

Lesson Summary

- System Center Essentials 2007 is a unified client management tool that can deploy applications and operating systems and distribute updates. It can also compile hardware and software inventories and generate reports. The tool is designed for medium-sized organizations with fewer than 30 servers or 500 clients.

- System Center Configuration Manager 2007 is a unified client management tool that can deploy applications and operating systems and distribute updates. It can also compile hardware and software inventories, generate reports, check compliance with optimal configuration, and restrict network access to clients that do not meet compliance standards. The tool can provide software metering and Wake On LAN and you can also use it to manage remote computers over the Internet and to manage handheld devices.

- Both System Center Essentials 2007 and System Center Configuration Manager 2007 are based on WSUS 3.0 server and require access to a SQL database. System

Center Configuration Manager 2007 requires that this database already exists, but System Center Essentials 2007 will install SQL Server Express 2005 if SQL Server is unavailable on a network.

Lesson Review

You can use the following questions to test your knowledge of the information in Lesson 2, "Application Deployment." The questions are also available on the companion CD if you prefer to review them in electronic form.

NOTE Answers

Answers to these questions and explanations of why each answer choice is correct or incorrect are located in the "Answers" section at the end of the book.

---

1. You are using the System Center Essentials 2007 update configuration wizard to set update behavior for your network clients and servers. For which of the following does the wizard prompt you? (Choose all that apply.)

   A. Applications and versions you want to update

   B. The location of your image file

   C. Your update language

   D. Types of updates you want to install

   E. Your installation settings

2. You are using System Center Configuration Manager 2007 to manage clients over the Internet. Which of the following are you unable to do? (Choose all that apply.)

   A. Set the System Center Configuration Manager 2007 site to native mode.

   B. Target software distribution to users.

   C. Distribute security updates.

   D. Use NAP.

   E. Implement Wake On LAN.

   F. Create a software inventory.

3. Which of the following are necessary client computer conditions for System Center Configuration Manager 2007 to use Wake On LAN? (Choose all that apply.)

   A. System Center Configuration Manager 2007 must be installed on a server running Windows Server 2003 SP1 or later.

    B. At least one Windows Server 2008 server must exist on the network and must be configured with the Network Policy Server role.

    C. USMT 3.0 must be installed and running on the System Center Configuration Manager 2007 server.

    D. System Configuration Manager 2007 client software must be installed on the computer.

    E. The client network card must support magic packet format.

    F. The client BIOS must be configured for wake-up packets on the network card.

4. You are migrating System Center Configuration Manager 2007 sites from mixed mode to native mode. Which report identifies clients that have successfully switched their site mode configuration?

    A. Summary Information Of Clients In Native Mode

    B. Client Assignment Failure Details

    C. Summary Information Of Clients Capable Of Native Mode

    D. Clients Incapable Of Native Mode

Chapter Review

To further practice and reinforce the skills you learned in this chapter, you can perform the following tasks:

- Review the chapter summary.
- Review the list of key terms introduced in this chapter.
- Complete the case scenarios. These scenarios set up real-world situations involving the topics of this chapter and ask you to create a solution.
- Complete the suggested practices.
- Take a practice test.

Chapter Summary

- You install the Application Server server role on a Windows Server 2008 server to provide an environment for deploying and running LOB applications. The role provides an installation wizard, core runtime support, and support for the .NET Framework 3.0. It also helps implement application availability.
- The Windows Server 2008 Ease Of Access Center provides access to the accessibility features of Windows Server 2008. You can provide application resilience by using Windows Installer, Group Policy, System Center Essentials 2007, and System Center Configuration Manager 2007.
- System Center Essentials 2007 and System Center Configuration Manager 2007 are unified client management tools that can deploy applications and operating systems and distribute updates, compile hardware and software inventories, and generate reports. System Center Configuration Manager 2007 is used in large networks and provides additional features such as software metering, NAP, and Wake On LAN. Both packages utilize WSUS 3.0 and require access to a SQL Server database.

Key Terms

Do you know what these key terms mean? You can check your answers by looking up the terms in the glossary at the end of the book.

- The .NET framework
- ACID properties
- Application accessibility
- Application availability

- Application resilience
- ASP.NET
- Component object model (COM)
- Line-of-business (LOB) application
- Network access protection (NAP)
- Remediation
- Wake on LAN

Case Scenarios

In the following case scenarios, you will apply what you have learned about application servers and services. You can find answers to these questions in the "Answers" section at the end of this book.

Case Scenario 1: Planning LOB Application Resilience

You are a senior network administrator at Blue Sky Airlines. You are currently liaising with a software company that is developing a suite of LOB applications for Blue Sky. You want the new applications to be resilient, you want new versions and updates to install automatically, and you want missing and corrupted files to be replaced. Answer the following questions:

1. Application resilience will be supported by Windows Installer. What assurances do you require from the software developers?

2. The developers intend to use a COM component library to provide components that can be used by several different applications in the suite. What does Windows Installer check in the registry of the computer on which a component runs and in which registry value is this stored?

3. You are satisfied that the LOB applications that are implemented by a single file are designed to be resilient. However, you need to ensure that applications that use several files also provide resilience through Windows Installer. What types of application should you be concerned about?

Case Scenario 2: Managing Clients and Deploying Software

You have recently been employed as a senior domain administrator at Trey Research, a medium-sized but rapidly expanding organization. Trey's single-site network currently has 25 server and 450 client computers. Some of the clients are laptops used by sales personnel and home workers. Managers are issued Pocket PCs in addition to their desktop clients. Trey currently uses WSUS to distribute Microsoft updates and a WSUS 3.0 server is installed on the network. The company makes extensive use of SQL Server and a server cluster currently runs SQL Server 2005 SP2.The company Web site runs on an IIS7 server. Trey has upgraded all its DCs to Windows Server 2008 but its member servers still run Windows Server 2003. Answer the following questions:

1. Management asks you to recommend a unified single tool that will manage clients; create hardware and software inventories; install operating systems, applications, and updates; and create reports. What do you recommend and why?

2. The Financial Director is concerned about the cost of software licenses. She believes that some software packages installed on all clients are often used by only a small percentage of the workforce. Software inventories only identify the software installed on computers, not whether it is used. What do you suggest as a solution to this problem?

3. The Technical Director is concerned that salespersons and home workers sometimes bring laptop computers into the office that have been connected to other networks or have been turned off when security updates were distributed. He is worried that such computers might pose a security risk if given full network access. What do you tell him?

Suggested Practices

To help you successfully master the exam objectives presented in this chapter, complete the following tasks.

Use the Application Server Server Role, IIS, and WSUS

Do all the practices listed in this section.

■ **Practice 1: Investigate the Application Server server role**   In Lesson 1 you installed the Application Server Server Role. Experiment with the new features this added to your server. In addition to the information provided in this chapter about this server role, search the Help files, Microsoft TechNet, and the Internet for more information.

■ **Practice 2: Revise IIS**   As an experienced network administrator you have probably already used IIS. Revise what you know. If you have not previously used version 7, find out what new features it provides. Make the default internal Web site on your Glasgow server more interesting.

- **Practice 3: Revise WSUS** As an experienced network administrator you have probably already used WSUS. Revise what you know. If you have not previously used WSUS 3.0 Server, find out what new features it provides.

Use the Unified Client Management Tools

Do Practice 2 in this section. The other practices are optional.

- **Practice 1: Investigate System Center Essentials 2007** If you installed System Center Essentials 2007 in Lesson 2, investigate the features provided by this tool. Read the Help files and experiment with the procedures they describe.

- **Practice 2: Use Technet Resources to Investigate System Center Essentials 2007 and System Center Configuration Manager 2007** Explore TechNet and look for virtual labs, the Virtual Hard Disk (VHD) program facilities that let you investigate System Center Essentials 2007, and System Center Configuration Manager 2007. Both types of resource are free. Currently these tools are based on Windows Server 2003, but the concepts and procedures for using the tools are unchanged.

- **Practice 3: Install and Investigate System Center Configuration Manager 2007** You will probably need additional hardware to carry out this practice, unless your test computer is sufficiently powerful to support at least one and possibly two additional virtual servers. You will need to install an evaluation version of SQL Server and other software (such as WSUS 3.0 Server) to meet the prerequisites. You can then search for and install an evaluation version of System Center Configuration Manager 2007. This is not an easy installation, but you will learn a lot by carrying it out. When System Center Configuration Manager 2007 is installed, experiment with its many features.

Take a Practice Test

The practice tests on this book's companion CD offer many options. For example, you can test yourself on just one exam objective, or you can test yourself on all the 70-646 certification exam content. You can set up the test so that it closely simulates the experience of taking a certification exam, or you can set it up in study mode so that you can look at the correct answers and explanations after you answer each question.

MORE INFO Practice tests

For details about all the practice test options available, see the "How to Use the Practice Tests" section in this book's Introduction.

Chapter 5

Terminal Services and Application and Server Virtualization

Windows Server 2008 introduces many new technologies, though few of these technologies will impact the way you plan your network deployment as much as those covered in this chapter. Although virtualization products have existed on the Windows Server platform for some time, Hyper-V—formerly known as Windows Server Virtualization—ties virtualization directly into the operating system. In this chapter you will learn about Hyper-V functionality and how this technology will influence the decisions you make with respect to deploying Windows Server 2008. Terminal Services—a technology that allows a relatively low-powered client to run high-powered applications on a remote server as though they were on the local computer—also includes some significant improvements in this latest server operating system release. The Terminal Services Session Broker (TS Session Broker) service simplifies the process of setting up a group of load-balanced Terminal Servers; the Terminal Services Gateway (TS Gateway) service allows authorized users to connect to Terminal Servers over the Internet without requiring you to configure a VPN server; and RemoteApp allows you to deploy specific applications—rather than entire remote desktops—to the clients on your network. In this chapter you will learn about all these technologies and how to plan their deployment to maximize the benefits to your organization.

Exam objectives in this chapter:
- Plan application servers and services.
- Provision applications.

Lessons in this chapter:

Before You Begin

To complete the lessons in this chapter, you must have done the following:

■ Have installed and configured the evaluation edition of Windows Server 2008 Enterprise Edition in accordance with the instructions listed in the first practice exercise of Lesson 1 in Chapter 1, "Installing, Upgrading, and Deploying Windows Server 2008." The practice exercises require that the client computers are running either Windows XP Service Pack 3 or Windows Vista Service Pack 1.

No additional configuration is required for this chapter.

Real World

Orin Thomas

The first Terminal Server I ever deployed was as an experimental solution to help out some of the accountants at the company I worked for. The accountants had been running a custom application on a single Windows NT 4.0 server that interfaced with SQL Server 7. The setup was such that only one person could work on the application at a time, which caused a bottleneck because time with the server would have to be scheduled in advance. The application itself wasn't network-aware and had to be installed and used on the same server that hosted the database. Eventually a new server was purchased because the original server performed poorly as a result of inadequate hardware. Although the easiest course of action would have been to simply install NT4 on the new hardware and to continue as before, Windows 2000 had just been released and I was itching to see whether I could use Terminal Services as a solution. After we ascertained that the application ran without problems on Windows 2000, we uninstalled it, reconfigured the server to run Terminal Services, reinstalled the application, and began a trial with multiple users. It worked like a charm, which left us with one last problem: licensing. We contacted the local company who had written the custom application. They'd never heard of anyone trying to get their application working with Terminal Services, so they came out to have a look at the server. They didn't have any rules about licensing this sort of setup, but they were quite impressed with how multiple users were able to interact with their non-network-aware application at once. Because they were going to start recommending the configuration to other customers, they decided that we were still in compliance and everyone ended up happy.

Lesson 1: Terminal Services

This lesson will teach you about the factors you should consider in planning the deployment of the Windows Server 2008 Terminal Services role in your organization's environment. You will learn what to take into consideration when planning a licensing strategy for Terminal Server clients, and what impact new technologies such as the TS Session Broker service will have on the deployment of Terminal Server at headquarters and branch office sites.

After this lesson, you will be able to:

■ Plan Terminal Services infrastructure.

■ Plan Terminal Services licensing.

■ Configure and monitor Terminal Services.

■ Configure Terminal Services Session Broker.

■ Plan the deployment of Terminal Services gateway servers.

Estimated lesson time: 40 minutes

Planning Terminal Server Infrastructure

A Terminal Server provides a remotely accessible desktop to clients. A computer only needs to have a compatible Remote Desktop Protocol (RDP) client and it will be able to connect to a Terminal Server that hosts everything else. Many organizations save money by providing cheap client hardware and having their users connect to a Terminal Server session to run more powerful applications, such as word processors, Internet browsers, and e-mail clients. The benefits to implementing this configuration include:

■ User workstations run a minimal amount of software and need little direct attention. If a problem occurs with a user workstation, the user's desktop environment exists on the Terminal Server, so the failed workstation can be swapped out without requiring any data to be migrated to the replacement.

■ User data is always stored in a central location rather than on user workstations, simplifying the data backup and recovery process.

■ Anti-spyware and antivirus software is installed and updated on the Terminal Server, ensuring that all definition files are up to date.

■ Rather than updating each application installed on a user's workstation, applications are updated centrally.

When used in a sustained manner, remote desktop connections to a Terminal Server require high bandwidth and low latency. This is because users expect a certain level of responsiveness from the applications they use on a daily basis. Although it is possible to optimize the remote desktop experience for low-bandwidth connections, the better the bandwidth between your clients and the Terminal Server, the happier those users are going to be. This means that you need to consider deploying a Terminal Server to each branch office site. You also need to consider the necessity of balancing the number of clients that will connect to the Terminal Server with the cost of deploying the Terminal Server to that location. For example, if you only have three users at your organization's Yarragon branch office that need access to the same applications you deploy using a Terminal Server farm to your Melbourne head office, it might be easier to directly install the applications on each user's computer or optimize the RDP connection to use the WAN link from Melbourne to Yarragon. Unless a really good business case can be made, most organizations are going to be reluctant to deploy server-class hardware to meet the occasional needs of only three users!

Planning Terminal Server Hardware

Terminal Servers need powerful processors and lots of RAM. Every client session needs to utilize the Terminal Server's hardware and resources. For this reason you should consider deploying the x64 versions of Windows Server 2008 Enterprise or Datacenter Edition as Terminal Servers in your environment. These versions of the operating system support the most RAM and the highest number of CPUs. If a Terminal Server's hardware becomes overburdened, you can add more RAM and CPUs before you have to consider adding a second Terminal Server and starting a Terminal Server farm. Terminal Server farms will be covered in "Terminal Server Session Broker" later in this chapter.

Although in general you should avoid virtualizing a Terminal Server, deploying this type of solution might make sense when you are confronted with situations such as the three users at the Yarragon branch office mentioned earlier. A small number of users will not have such a significant impact on the performance of the virtual server host, and Terminal Servers with a small number of users and a small performance footprint make good candidates for virtualization. Hyper-V is covered in more detail in Lesson 2, "Server and Application Virtualization."

You can use tools such as the Windows System Resource Manager and Performance Monitor to determine memory and processor usage of Terminal Services clients. Once you understand how the Terminal Server's resources are used, you can determine the necessary hardware resources and make a good estimate as to the Terminal Server's overall client capacity. Terminal Server capacity directly influences your deployment plans: A server that has a capacity of 100 clients is not going to perform well when more than 250 clients attempt to connect. Monitoring tools are covered in more detail in "Monitoring Terminal Services" later in this lesson.

Planning Terminal Server Software

Software that is going to be used by clients connecting to a Terminal Server must be installed after the Terminal Server role is deployed. Many applications perform a check during installation to determine whether the target of the installation is a Terminal Server. In some cases, different executable files will be installed when the installation target is a Terminal Server as opposed to a normal, stand-alone computer. Alternatively, some applications will generate a pop-up dialog box informing you that installing the application on a Terminal Server is not recommended and that the vendor does not support this deployment configuration.

Applications that are deployed on a Terminal Server might conflict with one another. Prior to deploying a new Terminal Server configuration in a production environment, you should plan a testing period. During this testing period you should organize a small group of users and get them to use the Terminal Server as a part of their day-to-day activities. If you follow this procedure, you will become aware of any possible problems and conflicts prior to deploying the Terminal Server more widely in your organization's production environment. The section "Microsoft Application Virtualization" in Lesson 2 has more information on how to deploy applications that conflict or are incompatible with a default Terminal Services deployment.

Terminal Services Licensing

All clients that connect to a Terminal Server require a special license called a Terminal Services client access license (TS CAL). This license is not included with Windows Vista and is not a part of the standard CALs that you use when licensing a server. These licenses are managed by a TS license server, which is a role service component that can be installed as a part of a Terminal Server deployment.

You need to make several decisions when planning a TS license server deployment. The most important of these decisions revolve around the following questions:

- What is the scope of the license server?
- How will the license server be activated?
- How many license servers are required?
- What type of licenses will be deployed?

License Server Scope

The license server's discovery scope determines which Terminal Servers and clients can automatically detect the license server. The license server scope is configured during the installation of the TS License Server role service, as shown in Figure 5-1. You can change the scope once it is set. The three possible discovery scopes are This Workgroup, This Domain, and The Forest.

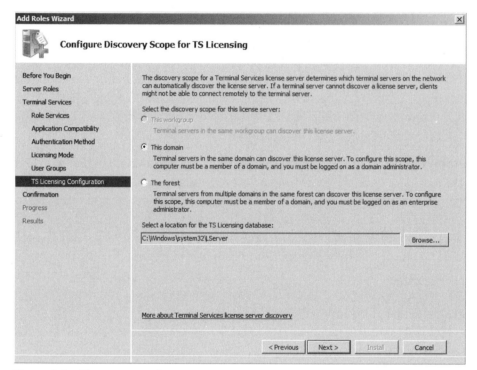

Figure 5-1   License server discovery scope

- **This Workgroup**   This scope is not available if the computer is joined to an Active Directory domain. This discovery scope is most often installed on the same computer as the Terminal Services role. Terminal servers and clients in the same workgroup can automatically discover this license server.

- **This Domain**   The domain discovery scope allows Terminal Servers and clients that are members of the same domain to automatically acquire TS CALs. This scope is most useful if TS CALs are going to be purchased on a per-domain basis.

- **This Forest**   The forest discovery scope allows Terminal Servers and clients located anywhere in the same Active Directory forest to automatically acquire TS CALs.

A drawback to this scope is that in large forests with many domains, TS CALs can be acquired rapidly.

Exam Tip   If an exam question mentions that TS CALs are going to be managed and purchased locally, this should lead you towards answers that suggest the discovery scope.

License Server Activation

Before a TS license server can issue CALs, it must be activated with Microsoft in a procedure similar to Windows Product Activation. During the activation process a Microsoft-issued digital certificate used to validate both server ownership and identity is installed on the TS license server. This certificate will be used in transactions with Microsoft for the acquisition and installation of further licenses. As shown in Figure 5-2, a license server can be activated through three methods.

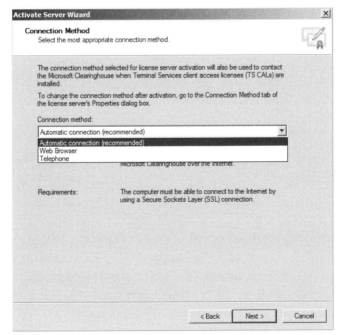

Figure 5-2   Three methods of activating a TS license server

The first method occurs transparently through a wizard, like Windows Product Activation. This method requires the server be able to directly connect to the Internet using an SSL connection, which means that it will not work with certain firewall configurations.

The second method involves navigating to a Web page. This method can be used on a computer other than the license server and is appropriate in environments where the network infrastructure does not support a direct SSL connection from the internal network to an Internet host.

The third method involves placing a telephone call to a Microsoft Clearinghouse operator. This is a toll-free call from most locations. The method used for activation will also be used to validate TS CALs that are purchased at a later state, though you can change this method by editing the TS license server's properties. If a license server is not activated, it can only issue temporary CALs. These CALs are valid for 90 days.

If the certificate acquired during the activation process expires or becomes corrupted, you might need to deactivate the license server. A deactivated license server cannot issue permanent TS Per Device CALs, though it can still issue TS Per User CALs and temporary TS Per Device CALs. You can deactivate TS license servers using the automatic method or over the telephone, but you cannot deactivate them using a Web browser on another computer.

Terminal Services Client Access Licenses

A Windows Server 2008 TS license server can issue two types of CAL: the Per Device CAL and the Per User CAL. The differences between these licenses are as follows:

- **TS Per Device CAL**   The TS Per Device CAL gives a specific computer or device the ability to connect to a Terminal Server. TS Per Device CALs are automatically reclaimed by the TS license server after a random period between 52 and 89 days. This will not impact clients that regularly use these CALs because any available CAL will simply be reissued the next time the device reconnects. In the event that you run out of available CALs, 20 percent of issued TS Per Device CALs for a specific operating system can be revoked using the TS Licensing Manager console on the license server. For example, 20 percent of issued Windows Vista TS Per Device CALs can be revoked or 20 percent of issued Windows Server 2003 Per Device CALs can be revoked at any one time. Revocation is not a substitute for ensuring that your organization has purchased the requisite number of TS Per Device CALs for your environment.

- **TS Per User CAL**   A TS Per User CAL gives a specific user account the ability to access any Terminal Server in an organization from any computer or device. TS Per User CALs are not enforced by TS Licensing, and it is possible to have more client connections occurring in an organization than actual TS Per User CALs installed on the license server. Failure to have the appropriate number of TS Per User CALs is a violation of license terms. You can determine the number of TS

Per User CALs by using the TS Licensing Manager console on the license server. You can either examine the Reports node or use the console to create a Per User CAL Usage report.

You can purchase TS CALs automatically if the Terminal Server is capable of making a direct SSL connection to the Internet. Alternatively, just as when you activate the Terminal Server, you can use a separate computer that is connected to the Internet to purchase TS CALs by navigating to a Web site or calling the Microsoft Clearinghouse directly.

MORE INFO   More on TS CALs

To learn more about Terminal Services client access licenses, see the following TechNet Web site: *http://technet2.microsoft.com/windowsserver2008/en/library/aa57d355-5b86-4229-9296-a7fcce77dea71033.mspx?mfr=true.*

Backing Up and Restoring a License Server

To back up a TS license server you need to back up the System State data and the folder where the TS Licensing database is installed. You can use Review Configuration, shown in Figure 5-3, to determine the location of the TS Licensing database. To restore the license server, rebuild the server and reinstall the TS Licensing Server role, restore the System State data, and then restore the TS Licensing database. When restored to a different computer, unissued licenses will not be restored and you will need to contact the Microsoft Clearinghouse to get the licenses reissued.

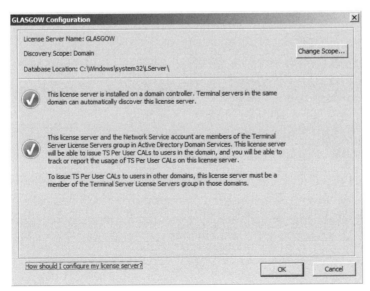

Figure 5-3   Reviewing the configuration

License Server Deployment

When planning the deployment of Windows Server 2008 Terminal Servers in an environment with Terminal Services running on earlier versions of Microsoft's server operating system, consider the fact that Windows Server 2003 TS license servers and Windows 2000 Server TS license servers cannot issue licenses to Windows Server 2008 Terminal Servers. Windows Server 2008 Terminal Servers, however, support earlier versions of Terminal Services. If your organization is going to have a period where Windows Server 2003 Terminal Servers will coexist with Windows Server 2008 Terminal Servers, you should first upgrade your organization's license servers to Windows Server 2008 so that they can support both the new and existing Terminal Servers.

Quick Check

1. Which type of TS CAL can be revoked?
2. At what point should you install the applications that are going to be used by Terminal Services clients on the Terminal Server?

Quick Check Answers

1. Per-device client access licenses can be revoked.
2. After the Terminal Server role has been installed on the server.

Configuring Terminal Servers

When planning the deployment of Terminal Servers, you should be aware of what configuration settings can be applied at the Terminal Server and the protocol level. Primarily you will be interested in configuration settings at the protocol level. You can edit settings at the protocol level by opening the Terminal Services Configuration console—located in the Terminal Services folder of the Administrative Tools menu—right-clicking the RDP-Tcp item in the Connections area, and clicking Properties. This will bring up the RDP-Tcp Properties dialog box.

The General tab of this dialog box, shown in Figure 5-4, allows the administrator to configure the Security Layer, Encryption Level, and other connection security settings. The default setting for the Security layer security level is negotiated; the default for the Encryption level is Client Compatible. By default an attempt will be made to negotiate the strongest security layer and encryption, but administrators can set a specific level. Clients that cannot meet this level will be unable to establish a connection to a Terminal Server. Windows Vista and Windows XP Service Pack 2 clients can make traditional Terminal Services connections when the security settings are set to their strongest level, though this rule does not apply to RemoteApp connections made through TS Web Access, which are covered in more detail in the section on Remote-App in Lesson 2 of this chapter.

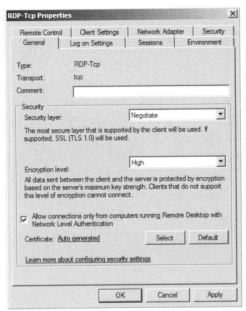

Figure 5-4   The General tab of the RDP-Tcp Properties dialog box

The Security Layer settings are used to configure server authentication, which is how the server verifies its identity to the client. This allows an SSL certificate issued by a trusted certificate authority to be installed as a method of verifying the Terminal Server's identity to a connecting client. Use this setting when clients are connecting to a Terminal Server from untrusted networks such as the Internet. Verification of a Terminal Server's identity reduces the risk that a user in your organization will provide their authentication credentials to a rogue Terminal Server. Although it is possible to use a self-signed certificate generated by the Terminal Server, this can lead to problems if clients are not properly configured to trust the server's SSL certificate.

The Encryption Level is used to protect the contents of the Terminal Server from interception by third parties. The four settings have the following properties:

- **High**   This level of encryption uses a 128-bit key and is supported by RDP 5.2 clients (Windows XP SP2+, Windows Server 2003 SP1+, and Windows Vista).

■ **FIPS**   Traffic is encrypted using Federal Information Process Standard (FIPS) 140-1 validated encryption methods. This is primarily used by government organizations.

■ **Client Compatible**   This method negotiates a maximum key length based on what the client supports.

■ **Low**   Data sent from the client to the server is encrypted using a 56-bit key. Data sent from the server to the client remains unencrypted.

The Security tab of the RDP-Tcp properties dialog box allows you to specify which groups of users can access the Terminal Server and what level of control they have. With the Sessions tab, shown in Figure 5-5, you can specify how long a Terminal Server allows active connections to last and how to treat idle and disconnected sessions. In environments where every extra session places resource pressure on a Terminal Server to the point where sessions are limited, ensuring that idle and disconnected sessions are ejected can be an excellent way of managing a Terminal Server resource.

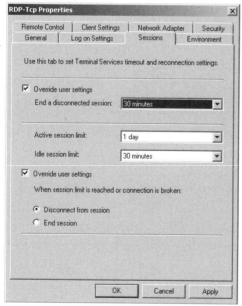

Figure 5-5   The Sessions tab of the RDP-Tcp Properties dialog box

The Remote Control tab of the RDP-Tcp Properties dialog box allows you to specify what level of control an administrator has over connected sessions. You can ensure that remote control sessions—which are primarily used by support staff—can only be enacted if the connected user provides permission for support personnel to connect in a similar manner to the remote assistance functionality that ships with Windows Vista. The Network Adapter tab, shown in Figure 5-6, allows administrators to limit the number of active connections to the Terminal Server and to specify which Network Adapter clients will use to connect. This setting is important on Terminal Servers where the number of clients connecting can exhaust hardware resources and a limit needs to be put in place to ensure that server functionality does not diminish to the point of user frustration.

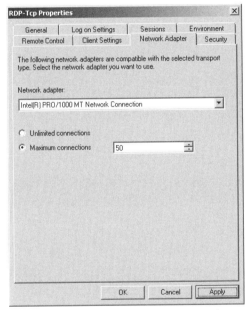

Figure 5-6   Network Adapter settings

Server Properties

In addition to the RDP connection properties covered earlier, the properties of each Terminal Server also impact on the client experience. As shown in Figure 5-7, you can configure each Terminal Server to use temporary folders for each session and have those folders deleted when the session completes. You can also restrict a user to a single session on a Terminal Server. This setting is important because if the RDP connection settings are not set to disconnect idle sessions, a user could be responsible for multiple idle sessions on a server. You should use the User Logon Mode settings when you need to take a Terminal Server offline for maintenance. For example, if you set the User Logon Mode to Allow Reconnections, But Prevent New Logons Until The

Server Is Restarted, you can monitor the number of active connections and then shut down the server and perform maintenance tasks without interrupting users's work.

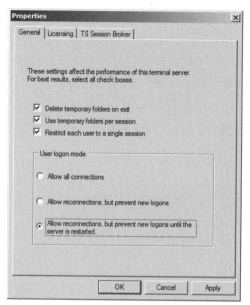

Figure 5-7   Terminal Server properties

Configuring Terminal Services with Group Policy

In large Terminal Server deployments, you will not configure the RDP-Tcp connection settings and Terminal Server properties on a per-Terminal Server basis. You would apply these settings through Active Directory. The Computer Configuration\Policies\ Administrative Templates\Windows Components\Terminal Services\Terminal Server Node of Group Policy contains several nodes of policies whose functionality mirrors the settings that can be applied on the server. Because of the vast number of policies, they are only covered briefly here.

- **Connections**   The Connections node contains the following policies: Automatic Reconnection, Allow Users To Connect Remotely Using Terminal Services, Deny Logoff Of An Administrator Logged In To The Console Session, Configure Keep-Alive Connection Interval, Limit Number Of Connections, Set Rules For Remote Control Of Terminal Services User Sessions, Allow Reconnection From Original Client Only, Restrict Terminal Services Users To A Single Remote Session, and Allow Remote Start Of Unlisted Programs.

- **Device and Resource Redirection**   The Device And Resource Redirection node contains the following policies: Allow Audio Redirection, Do Not Allow Clipboard Redirection, Do Not Allow COM Port Redirection, Do Not Allow Drive Redirection, Do Not Allow LPT Port Redirection, Do Not Allow Supported Plug And Play Device Redirection, Do Not Allow Smart Card Device Redirection, and Allow Time Zone Redirection.

- **Licensing**   The Licensing node contains the following policies: Use The Specified Terminal Services License Servers, Hide Notifications About TS Licensing Problems That Affect The Terminal Server, and Set The Terminal Services Licensing Mode.

- **Printer Redirection**   The Printer Redirection node contains the following policies: Do Not Set Default Client Printer To Be Default Printer In A Session, Do Not Allow Client Printer Redirection, Specify Terminal Server Fallback Printer Driver Behavior, Use Terminal Services Easy Print Printer Driver First, and Redirect Only The Default Client Printer.

- **Profiles**   The Profiles node contains the following policies: Set TS User Home Directory, Use Mandatory Profiles On The Terminal Server, and Set Path For TS Roaming User Profile.

- **Remote Session Environment**   The Remote Session Environment node contains the following policies: Limit Maximum Color Depth, Enforce Removal Of Remote Desktop Wallpaper, Remove Disconnect Option From Shut Down Dialog Box, Remove Windows Security Item From Start Menu, Set Compression Algorithm For RDP Data, Start A Program On Connection, and Always Show Desktop On Connection.

- **Security**   The Security node contains the following policies: Server Authentication Certificate Template, Set Client Connection Encryption Level, Always Prompt For Password Upon Connection, Require Secure RPC Communication, Require Use Of Specific Security Layer For Remote (RDP) Connections, Do Not Allow Local Administrators To Customize Permissions, and Require User Authentication For Remote Connections By Using Network Level Authentication.

- **Session Time Limits**   The Session Time Limits node contains the following policies: Set Time Limit For Disconnected Sessions, Set Time Limit For Active But Idle Terminal Services Sessions, Set Time Limit for Active Terminal Services Sessions, Terminate Session When Time Limits Are Reached, and Set Time Limit For Logoff Of RemoteApp Sessions.

- **Temporary Folders** The Temporary Folders node contains the following policies: Do Not Delete Temp Folder Upon Exit, and Do Not Use Temporary Folders Per Session.

- **TS Session Broker** The policies in this folder are covered in detail in "Terminal Services Session Broker" later in this lesson.

Although this list may seem daunting at first, it is reproduced here to give you an idea of how you can configure Terminal Services to best meet the requirements of your organization, not because you will be expected to recite it by rote on the exam. You should read through the list and consider how each policy might impact on the number of clients that can be serviced as well as how each policy might influence the number of Terminal Servers that need to be deployed. Some policies will be irrelevant to your pursuit of these objectives and other policies will be critical.

From the perspective of an administrator who needs to plan the deployment of Terminal Services, the most important policy groups are located in the *Connections* and *Session Time Limits* nodes. With these nodes you control how many clients are connected to each Terminal Server and how long they remain connected, both of which directly affect the Terminal Server's capacity. If you allow lots of idle sessions to take up memory in the Terminal Services environment, you will need to plan the deployment of more Terminal Servers because the existing ones will reach their natural capacity quickly. If you limit idle sessions to a specified period of time, you will ensure that capacity is not wasted, but you might also disrupt the way that people in your organization actually work. As with everything else related to deployment and planning, getting the settings right is a matter of finding your organization's unique balance point.

TS Web Access

Terminal Services Web Access (TS Web Access) allows clients to connect to a Terminal Server through a Web page link rather than by entering the Terminal Server address in the Remote Desktop Connection client software. Unlike the similar functionality that was available in Windows Server 2003, TS Web Access in Windows Server 2008 does not rely on an ActiveX control to provide the RDC connection, but instead uses the RDC client software that is installed on client computers. This means that to use TS Web Access, client computers need to be running either Windows XP SP2, Windows Vista, Windows Server 2003 SP1, or Windows Server 2008. TS Web Access must be installed on the Terminal Server that it is providing access to. To deploy TS Web Access, you must not only install the TS Web Access server role, but also the Web Server (IIS) role and a feature called Windows Process Activation Service. TS Web Access is installed in the third practice exercise, "Installing TS Web Access," at the end of this lesson.

Terminal Server Session Broker

A single Terminal Server can only support a limited number of clients before it begins to run out of resources and the client experience begins to deteriorate. The precise number will depend on what applications and tasks the clients are performing as well as the specific hardware configuration of the Terminal Server itself. Eventually, as the number of clients grow, you will need to add a second Terminal Server to your environment to take some load off the first. From a planning perspective this is fairly obvious, but gives rise to the question "How do I ensure that clients are distributed equally between the new and the old terminal server?" If everyone jumps on the new server, it will soon have the same resource pressure problem that the old server had! The Terminal Server Session Broker (TS Session Broker) role service simplifies the process of adding capacity, allowing the load balancing of Terminal Servers in a group and the reconnection of clients to existing sessions within that group. In TS Session Broker terminology, a group of Terminal Servers is called a farm.

The TS Session Broker service consists of a database that keeps track of Terminal Server sessions. TS Session Broker can work with DNS Round Robin or with Network Load Balancing to distribute clients to Terminal Servers. When configured with load balancing, the TS Session Broker service monitors all Terminal Servers in the group and allocates new clients to the Terminal Servers that have the largest amount of free resources. When used with DNS Round Robin, clients are still distributed; the main benefit is that the TS Session Broker remembers where a client is connected. Thus a disconnected session is reconnected appropriately rather than a new session being created on a different Terminal Server. The limitation of the TS Load Balancing service is that it can only be used with Windows Server 2008 Terminal Servers. Windows Server 2003 Terminal Servers cannot participate in a TS Session Broker farm.

To deploy TS Session Broker Load Balancing in your organization, you must ensure that clients support RDP 5.2 or later. TS Session Broker also supports the User Logon Mode settings, discussed earlier in "Configuring and Monitoring Terminal Server." These settings allow you to stop new connections being made to an individual server in the farm until you have completed pending maintenance tasks.

You can join a Terminal Server to a farm using the Terminal Services configuration MMC, available from the Terminal Services folder of the Administrative Tools menu.

As shown in Figure 5-8, joining a farm is a matter of specifying the address of a TS Session Broker Server, a farm name, that the server should participate in Session Broker Load-Balancing, and the relative weight of the server—based on its capacity—in the farm. You should configure more powerful servers with higher weight values than those that you configure for less powerful servers. You should only clear the IP Address Redirection option in the event that your load-balancing solution uses TS Session Broker Routing Tokens, which are used by hardware load-balancing solutions and which mean that the load balancing is not handled by the TS Session Broker Server. As discussed earlier, you can also apply these configuration settings through Group Policy, with the relevant policies located under the Computer Configuration\Policies\Administrative Templates\Windows Components\Terminal Services\Terminal Server\TS Session Broker node of a Windows Server 2008 GPO.

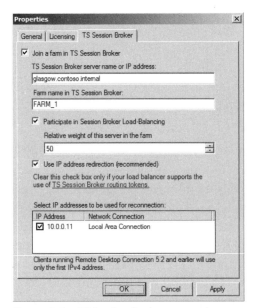

Figure 5-8   TS Session Broker properties

In conjunction with these configuration settings, you must add the Terminal Server's Active Directory computer account to the Session Directory Computers local group on the computer hosting the TS Session Broker service. After you complete these tasks, you then need to configure the load-balancing feature on each of the computers in the farm. You will learn more about the Network Load Balancing feature and DNS Round Robin in Chapter 11, "Clustering and High Availability."

MORE INFO   **More on configuring TS Session Broker**

To learn more about configuring the TS Session Broker, see *http://technet2.microsoft.com/ windowsserver2008/en/library/f9fe9c74-77f5-4bba-a6b9-433d823bbfbd1033.mspx?mfr=true.*

> ## Quick Check
> - Which group does a Terminal Server's computer account have to be added to on the computer hosting the Terminal Services Session Broker role before it can become a member of a farm?
>
> ## Quick Check Answer
> - Session Directory Computers local group

Monitoring Terminal Services

You need to regularly monitor Terminal Servers to ensure that the user experience is still acceptable and that the Terminal Server still has adequate hardware resources with which to perform its role. Hardware bottlenecks on Terminal Servers primarily occur around the processor and memory resources. These are the resources that you need to be most careful in monitoring because although you can make estimates about a server's capacity, until clients are actually performing day-to-day tasks, you will not really know how much load the server can take before the user experience begins to deteriorate. You will use two specific tools to manage and monitor Terminal Server resources: System Monitor and the Windows System Resource Manager.

Using System Monitor to Monitor Terminal Services

In addition to the typical Windows Server 2008 monitoring tools that you will be familiar with, System Monitor contains Terminal Server-specific performance counters that help you determine what level of use the current client sessions are having on the server that hosts them. The two broad categories of counters are those located under the Terminal Services category and those located under the Terminal Services Sessions category. The Terminal Services category tracks the number of active, inactive, and total sessions. The Terminal Services Sessions category breaks down resource usage into detail. You can use this category to track memory and processor usage as well as receive detailed troubleshooting information such as the number of frame errors and protocol cache hits.

Windows System Resource Manager

Windows System Resource Manager (WSRM) is a feature that you can install on a Windows Server 2008 computer that controls how resources are allocated. The WSRM console, shown in Figure 5-9, allows an administrator to apply WSRM policies. WSRM includes four default policies and also allows administrators to create their own. The two policies that will most interest you as someone responsible for planning and deploying Terminal Services infrastructure are Equal_Per_User and Equal_Per_Session.

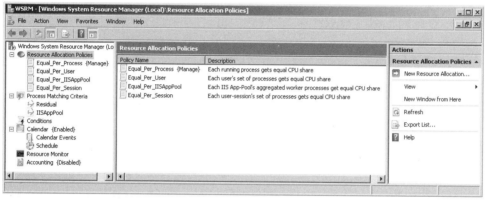

Figure 5-9   The WSRM console

The Equal_Per_User WSRM policy ensures that each user is allocated resources equally, even when one user has more sessions connected to the Terminal Server than other users. Apply this policy when you allow users to have multiple sessions to the Terminal Server—it stops any one user from monopolizing hardware resources by opening multiple sessions. The Equal_Per_Session policy ensures that each session is allocated resources equally. If applied on a Terminal Server where users are allowed to connect with multiple sessions, this policy can allow those users to gain access to a disproportionate amount of system resources in comparison to users with single sessions.

MORE INFO   Terminal Services and WSRM

To learn more about using Terminal Services with Windows System Resource Manager, see the following TechNet article: *http://technet2.microsoft.com/windowsserver2008/en/library/a25ed552-a42d-4107-b225-fcb40efa8e3c1033.mspx?mfr=true*.

Terminal Services Gateway

TS Gateway allows Internet clients secure, encrypted access to Terminal Servers behind your organization's firewall without having to deploy a Virtual Private Network (VPN) solution. This means that you can have users interacting with their corporate desktop or applications from the comfort of their homes without the problems that occur when VPNs are configured to run over multiple Network Address Translation (NAT) gateways and the firewalls of multiple vendors.

TS Gateway works using RDP over Secure Hypertext Transfer Protocol (HTTPS), which is the same protocol used by Microsoft Office Outlook 2007 to access corporate Exchange Server 2007 Client Access Servers over the Internet. TS Gateway Servers can be configured with connection authorization policies and resource authorization policies as a way of differentiating access to Terminal Servers and network resources. Connection authorization policies allow access based on a set of conditions specified by the administrator; resource authorization policies grant access to specific Terminal Server resources based on user account properties.

What makes connection authorization policies different is that TS Gateway Servers can be configured to use Network Access Protection (NAP). NAP performs a client health check. This means you can disallow a user access if the client with which the user is trying to access the Terminal Server does not pass a series of health tests, such as proving that antivirus and anti-spyware software is up to date and the most recent set of updates and service packs from Microsoft update are applied. Client health checks are important—you want to ensure that any clients that connect to a Terminal Server hosting important business resources are not infested with spyware, viruses, and Trojans that might otherwise be transmitted to your organization's network infrastructure. You will learn more about how to implement NAP and more on TS Gateway Server policies in Chapter 9, "Remote Access and Network Access Protection."

MORE INFO   More on TS Gateway Services

To learn more about TS Gateway Servers, see the following TechNet site: *http:// technet2.microsoft.com/windowsserver2008/en/library/9da3742f-699d-4476-b050- c50aa14aaf081033.mspx?mfr=true.*

Practice: Deploying Terminal Services

In this set of practices you will install and configure Terminal Services. This process will include the initial setup, configuration adjustments, and deployment of the TS Web Access role service. These practice exercises require that your client computer have RDC 6.0 or later software installed. This software is available by default with Windows Vista, but requires an extra component be downloaded and installed for Windows XP.

MORE INFO   Getting RDC 6.0

You can obtain RDC version 6.0 for Windows Server 2003 or Windows XP from the following site: *http://support.microsoft.com/?kbid=925876.*

▶ **Exercise 1: Install the Terminal Services Role**

In this exercise, you will install the Terminal Services role on the computer Glasgow. To complete this exercise, perform the following steps:

1. Log on to server Glasgow using the Kim_Akers user account.

2. Open the Server Manager console from Quick Launch or the Administrative Tools menu if it does not open automatically.

3. Click the Roles node and then click the Add Roles item in the Roles Summary section of the Server Manager console. This will start the Add Roles Wizard. Click Next on the Before You Begin page.

4. On the Server Roles page, select Terminal Services and then click Next.

5. On the Terminal Services page, review the information and then click Next.

6. On the Select Role Services page, select Terminal Server. When you select Terminal Server you will be presented with a warning that Installing Terminal Server with Active Directory Domain Services is not recommended. Because this is a practice exercise to demonstrate the technology, and not a real-world deployment, click Install Terminal Server Anyway (Not Recommended). Click Next.

7. On the Uninstall And Reinstall Applications For Compatibility page, review the information and then click Next. Deploying applications through Terminal Services is covered in detail in Lesson 2, "Server and Application Virtualization."

8. On the Specify Authentication Method For Terminal Server page, select Require Network Level Authentication as shown in Figure 5-10 and then click Next.

9. On the Specify Licensing Mode page, select Per User and then click Next.

10. On the Select User Groups Allowed Access To This Terminal Server page, verify that the Administrators group is selected and then click Next.

11. Review the summary information on the Confirm Installation Selections page and then click Install. The Terminal Services role will now be installed on the server Glasgow.

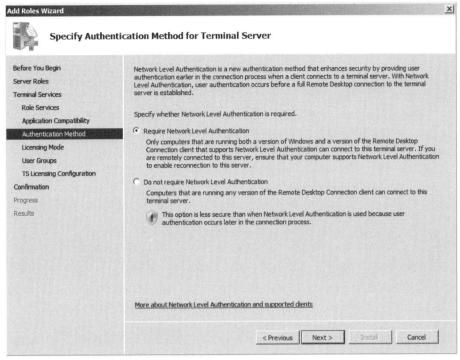

Figure 5-10   Specify the authentication method

12. You need to restart the server to complete the role installation process. On the Installation Results page, click Close. In the Add Roles Wizard dialog box, click Yes when asked if you want to restart the server now.

13. When the server restarts, log on using the Kim_Akers user account. After the logon process has completed, the Resume Configuration Wizard will automatically start and complete the installation of the Terminal Services role. When the wizard completes, click Close.

NOTE   120 days

You may receive a warning at the end of the installation process informing you that Terminal Services will stop working in 120 days. Dismiss this warning; you will configure the license server in the next practice exercise.

---

14. Open Active Directory Users And Computers. In the Users container, create a user account with the user name **Sam_Abolrous.** Assign the password **P@ssw0rd** and select the Password Never Expires option. Add the Sam_Abolrous user to the Remote Desktop Users group.

15. From the Start Menu, click Run and then type **gpedit.msc.** This will open the local Group Policy Editor.

16. Navigate to the Computer Configuration\Windows Settings\Security Settings\ Local Policies\User Rights Assignment node and open the Allow Log On Through Terminal Services policy.

17. Click Add User Or Group and add the Remote Desktop Users Group. Click OK and then run gpupdate.exe from an elevated command prompt.

NOTE   Terminal Services and domain controllers

By default, only members of the Administrators group can log on to a domain controller through Terminal Services. By modifying this policy, you can allow other groups to log on to the domain controller using Terminal Services, though it is important to note that for security reasons you would avoid this in a real-world deployment.

---

18. Log on to the client computer Melbourne using the Sam_Abolrous user account. Open Remote Desktop Connection and connect to the server named Glasgow. Ensure that you provide the credentials shown in Figure 5-11.

Figure 5-11   Authentication credentials

19. After you verify that the connection works, close the remote desktop session and log off of the client computer Melbourne.

▶ **Exercise 2: Configure Terminal Services**

In this exercise, you will configure some of the common Terminal Server settings that allow you to manage how connections are made to the server. To complete this exercise, perform the following steps:

1. Ensure that you are logged on to the server Glasgow with the Kim_Akers user account.

2. Click Start, click Administrative Tools, click Terminal Services, and then click Terminal Services Configuration.

3. In the User Account Control dialog box, click Continue. You will now be presented with the Terminal Services Configuration Console shown in Figure 5-12.

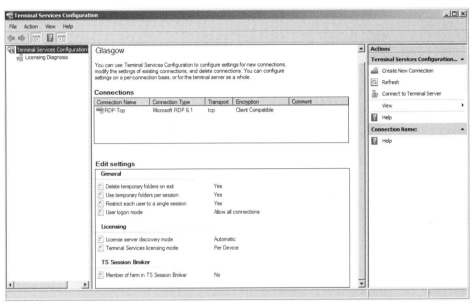

Figure 5-12   The Terminal Services Configuration console

4. Right click RDP-Tcp in the Connections area and select Properties.

5. On the General tab of the RDP-Tcp Properties dialog box, set the Encryption Level to High and then click Apply.

6. Click the Remote Control tab. Select Use Remote Control With The Following Settings. Verify that the Require User's Permission option is selected and that in the Level Of Control section the View The Session is selected, as shown in Figure 5-13. Click Apply.

7. Click the Network Adapters tab. Select the Maximum Connections option and then set the value of the option to 15. Click Apply and then click OK to close the dialog box. Click OK to dismiss the warning informing you that current sessions will not be influenced by the changes made.

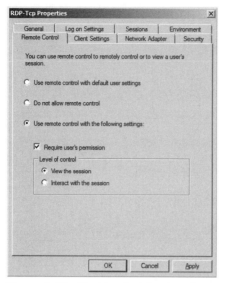

Figure 5-13   The Terminal Services Remote Control settings

8. In the Edit Settings section, double-click the Terminal Services Licensing Mode setting. This will open the Licensing tab of the Terminal Servers properties.

9. Change the Terminal Services Licensing mode to Per Device. In the Specify The License Server Discovery mode, select Use The Specified License Servers and type **glasgow.contoso.internal** as shown in Figure 5-14.

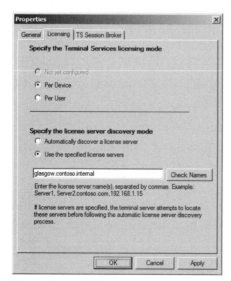

Figure 5-14   TS license server settings

10. Click Apply and then click OK. Click OK to dismiss the warning informing you that current sessions will not be influenced by the changes made.

11. Close the Terminal Services Configuration Manager console.

NOTE   No license server at glasgow.contoso.internal

In this set of practices a license server was not set up because it would require activation. The aim of step 9 is to show you how to override the automatic license server discovery process.

▶ **Exercise 3: Install TS Web Access**

In this exercise, you will install and configure the TS Web Access server role. You will then connect with a client to verify that the server role has installed correctly. To complete this exercise, perform the following steps:

1. Ensure that you are logged on to the server Glasgow with the Kim_Akers user account.

2. If the Server Manager console does not open automatically, click the shortcut located on the Quick Launch toolbar or open the Server Manager console from the Administrative Tools menu. Click Continue if presented with a User Account Control dialog box.

3. Click the Roles node. In the Roles pane, scroll down to the Terminal Services role and then click Add Role Services. This will launch the Add Role Services Wizard.

4. On the Select Role Services page, select the TS Web Access role service and then click Next.

5. In the Add Role Services And Features Required For TS Web Access dialog box, click Add Required Role Services. Click Next.

6. Click Next until you reach the Confirm Installation Selection page of the Add Role Services Wizard. Click Install. When the installation process completes, click Close.

7. Log on to the client computer using the sam_abolrous@contoso.internal user account.

8. Open Internet Explorer, navigate to *http://glasgow.contoso.internal/ts* and when prompted authenticate using the sam_abolrous@contoso.internal user account.

9. Dismiss any warnings presented and install the Terminal Services ActiveX Client. Click the Remote Desktop item on the TS Web Access Web Page.

NOTE   Trusted sites

To successfully make connections, you need to configure the TS Web Access Site as an Intranet Site in Internet Explorer.

---

10. In the Connect To dialog box, type the address **glasgow.contoso.internal** and then click Options, as shown in Figure 5-15. Click Connect.

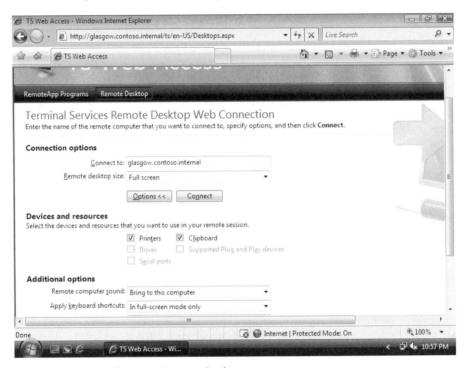

Figure 5-15   TS Web Access Remote Desktop

11. If presented with a Trust warning, click Yes. If presented with the Internet Explorer Security warning, shown in Figure 5-16, click Allow.

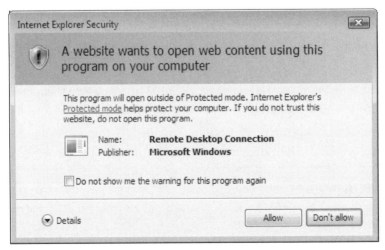

Figure 5-16   Connection warning

12. In the Windows Security dialog box, enter the credentials for the sam_abolrous @contoso.internal user account.

13. In the Do You Trust The Computer You Are Connecting To dialog box, shown in Figure 5-17, click Yes. The Terminal Services session will now be initiated.

Figure 5-17   Terminal Server trust query

14. After you verify that the TS Web Access Remote Desktop page has correctly initiated a connection to the Terminal Server at glasgow.contoso.internal, log off to terminate the connection.

Lesson Summary

- Terminal Server License Servers must be activated before it is possible to install TS CALs. The discovery scope of a license server determines which clients and TS servers can automatically detect the server.

- TS Session Broker allows you to create a Terminal Services farm. TS Session Broker can be paired with DNS Round Robin or Network Load Balancing and ensures that disconnected clients are always reconnected to the correct session on the appropriate server.

- TS Web Access allows clients to connect to a Terminal Server using a browser shortcut, but still requires that the latest RDC software be installed.

- TS Gateway Servers can allow clients from the Internet to connect to Terminal Servers behind the firewall without having to implement a VPN solution.

Lesson Review

You can use the following questions to test your knowledge of the information in Lesson 1, "Terminal Services." The questions are also available on the companion CD if you prefer to review them in electronic form.

NOTE Answers

Answers to these questions and explanations of why each answer choice is correct or incorrect are located in the "Answers" section at the end of the book.

---

1. Your organization has a single Terminal Server. Users are allowed to connect to the Terminal Server with up to two concurrent sessions. You want to ensure that users who are connected to two sessions do not use more resources on the Terminal Server than a user connected with a single session. Which of the following strategies should you pursue?

    A. Apply the Equal_Per_User WSRM policy.

    B. Apply the Equal_Per_Session WSRM policy.

    C. Configure the server's properties in Terminal Server Management console.

    D. Configure RDP-Tcp properties.

2. Your organization has two offices, one located in Sydney and one located in Melbourne. A data center in Canberra hosts infrastructure servers. Both the Melbourne and Sydney offices have their own Terminal Server farms. The offices are connected by a high-speed WAN link. Each office has its own Active Directory domain, which are both a part of the same forest. The forest root domain is located in the Canberra data center and does not contain standard user or computer accounts. For operational reasons, you want to ensure that CALs purchased and installed at each location are only allocated to devices at that location. Which of the following license server deployment plans should you implement?

    A. Deploy a license server to each location and set the discovery scope of each license server to Domain.

    B. Deploy a license server to each location and set the discovery scope of each license server to Forest.

    C. Deploy a license server to the Canberra data center and set the discovery scope of the license server to Forest.

    D. Deploy a license server to the Canberra data center and set the discovery scope of the license server to Domain.

3. Which of the following steps do you need to take prior to installing CALs on a TS license server? (Each correct answer presents a complete solution. Choose two.)

   A. Select license server scope.

   B. Set the domain level to Windows Server 2008 functional level.

   C. Activate the license server.

   D. Select the license type.

   E. Install Internet Information Services (IIS).

4. The organization that you work for is going through a period of growth. Users access business applications from client terminals. You are concerned that the growth in users will outstrip the processing capacity of the host Terminal Server. Which of the following solutions allows you to increase the client capacity without requiring client reconfiguration?

   A. Use WSRM to ensure that all users are able to access resources equally.

   B. Install Hyper-V on a computer running Windows Server 2008 Enterprise Edition and add virtualized servers as required.

   C. Add Terminal Servers as required and reconfigure clients to use specific Terminal Servers.

   D. Create a Terminal Server farm and add Terminal Servers as required.

5. You need to ensure that clients connecting to your Terminal Servers have passed a health check. Which of the following deployments should you implement?

   A. Install OneCare Live on the Terminal Servers.

   B. Implement TS Session Broker.

   C. Mediate access using a TS Gateway Server.

   D. Mediate access using ISA Server 2006.

Lesson 2: Server and Application Virtualization

This lesson looks at two different types of virtualization technology: server virtualization and application virtualization. When configured for virtualization, either entire computer or individual applications are run in their own separate environments. This ensures that no conflicts occur as each operating system or application is located in the equivalent of its own sealed environment. In this lesson, you will learn about the Hyper-V feature of Windows Server 2008. You will learn about RemoteApp, which allows you to run Terminal Services applications without having to run it in a normal Terminal Services window. You will also learn about Microsoft Application Virtualization, formerly known as SoftGrid, a technology available from Microsoft that allows applications that would otherwise conflict or not run on a Terminal Server to be virtualized and served to client computers over the network.

After this lesson, you will be able to:

- Plan the deployment of Hyper-V.
- Plan the deployment of TS RemoteApp.
- Plan the deployment of application virtualization.

Estimated lesson time: 40 minutes

Real World

Orin Thomas

One of the most challenging environments that I've worked in as a systems administrator is one where developers were working and updating applications on a server that I was responsible for managing. Like most systems administrators, I prefer to keep the configuration of servers I manage as static as possible. Once I've got a server functioning properly I tend to not want anyone to change the configuration, which can lead to instability and thus lead to more work for me! During the application development process a lot of configuration changes can be made to a server that later have to be undone. Depending on how invasive the application's installation procedure is, it can often be easier to wipe and reinstall rather than attempt to remove an application's previous build so that you can test and deploy the new one. This is why I love *snapshots*. Snapshots are a functionality of Hyper-V that allows you to save a computer's configuration at a point in time. Prior to installing a new build of an application, or even applying a new set of updates, I create a snapshot. This allows me to quickly roll back to a known good configuration if the change to the server made by the update makes the whole system unstable. If you are working in an environment with developers, I recommend you corral them into virtualized servers. That way when they inevitably break something, it is simply a matter of rolling back to a known snapshot rather than having to reinstall the operating system from scratch.

Hyper-V

Hyper-V is a Windows Server 2008 feature that allows you to run virtualized computers under x64 versions of Windows Server 2008. Hyper-V has many similarities to Virtual Server 2005 R2 in terms of functionality, though unlike Virtual Server 2005 R2, Hyper-V is built directly into the operating system as a role and does not sit above the operating system as an application. Hyper-V also allows you to run 64-bit virtual machines, which is not possible under Virtual Server 2005 R2.

Virtualization through Hyper-V on Windows Server 2008 provides the following benefits over traditional installations:

- **More efficient use of hardware resources**   Services such as DHCP and DNS, while vital to network infrastructure, are unlikely to push the limits of your server's processor and RAM. Although it is possible to co-locate the DNS and DHCP roles on the one Windows Server 2008 computer, the strategy of separating network roles onto separate partitions allows you to relocate those partitions to other host computers if the circumstances and usage of those roles change in future.

- **Improved availability**   Consolidating these services onto a single hardware platform can reduce costs and maintenance expenses. Although moving from many platforms to one might look like it would lead to a single point of failure, implementing redundancy technologies (clustering and hot-swappable hardware such as processors, RAM, power supplies, and hard disk drives) provides a greater level of reliability for lower cost. Consider the following situation: Four Windows Server 2008 computers are each running a separate application provided to users on your network. If a hardware component fails on one of those servers, the application that the server provides to users of the network is unavailable until the component is replaced. Building one server with redundant components is cheaper than building four servers with redundant components. In the event that a component fails, the built-in redundancy allows all server roles to remain available.

■ **Services only need to be intermittently available**   Some servers only need to be available on an intermittent basis. For example, as stated in Chapter 10, "Certificate Services and Storage," the best practice with an Enterprise Root CA is to use subordinate CAs to issue certificates and to keep the Root CA offline. With virtualization, you could keep the entire virtualized server on a removable USB hard disk drive in a safe, only turning it on when necessary and thereby ensuring the security of your certificate infrastructure. This frees up existing hardware that is rarely used—or means that it never need be purchased.

■ **Role sandboxing**   Sandboxing is a term used to describe the partitioning of server resources so that an application or service does not influence other components on the server. Without sandboxing, a failing server application or role has the capacity to bring down an entire server. Just as Web application pools in IIS sandbox Web applications so that the failure of one application will not bring all of them down, running server applications and roles in their own separate virtualized environment ensures that one errant process does not bring down everything else.

■ **Greater capacity**   Adding significant hardware capacity to a single server is cheaper than adding incremental hardware upgrades to many servers. Capacity can be increased by adding processors and RAM to the host server and then allocating those resources to a virtual server as the need arises.

■ **Greater portability**   Once a server has been virtualized, moving it to another host if the original host's resources become overwhelmed is a relatively simple process. For example, suppose that the disks on a Windows Server 2008 Enterprise Edition computer hosting 10 virtualized servers are reaching their I/O capacity. Moving some of the virtualized servers to another host is a simpler process than migrating or upgrading a server. Tools such as System Center Virtual Machine Manager, covered later in the chapter, make the process even simpler.

■ **Easier back up and restore**   Tools such as volume shadow copy allow you to back up an entire server's image while the server is still operational. In the event that a host computer fails, the images can be rapidly restored on another host computer. Rather than backing up individual files and folders, you can back up the entire virtualized computer in one operation. System Center Virtual Machine manager allows you to move virtual machines back and forth to the Storage Area Network (SAN) and even migrate virtual machines between hosts.

Creating Virtual Machines

Creating a virtual machine is a relatively simple process and involves running the New Virtual Machine Wizard from the Virtualization Management Console. To create the virtual machine, perform the following steps:

1. Specify a name and location for the virtual machine. Placing a virtual machine on a RAID-5 volume—or even better a RAID 0+1 or RAID 1+0 volume—ensures redundancy. You should avoid placing virtual machines on the same volume as the host operating system. The name of the virtual machine does not need to be simply the computer's name, but can include other information about the virtual machine's functionality.

2. Specify memory allocation. The maximum amount of memory depends on the amount of RAM installed on the host computer. Remember that each active virtual machine must be allocated RAM and that the total amount of allocated RAM for all active virtual machines and the host operating system cannot exceed the amount installed on the host computer.

3. Specify networking settings. Specify which of the network cards installed on the host will be used by the virtual machine. Where you expect high network throughput, you might add an extra network card and allocate it solely to a hosted virtual machine.

4. Specify virtual hard disk. Virtual machines use flat files to store hard disk data. These files are mounted by Hyper-V and appear to the virtual machine as a normal hard disk drive that can even be formatted and partitioned. When creating a virtual hard disk, you should specify enough space for the operating system to grow, but do not allocate all available space if you intend to add other virtual machines later.

5. Specify operating system installation settings. In the final stage of setting up a virtual machine, you specify how you will install the operating system, either from an image file such as an .ISO, optical media such as a DVD-ROM, or a network-based installation server such as WDS, which was covered in Lesson 2, "Automated Server Deployment," in Chapter 1.

From this point you can turn on the virtual machine and then begin the installation process using the method that you selected in step 5.

Virtualization Candidates

When you are considering server deployment options, it will be advantageous in some situations to deploy a virtualized server rather than the real thing. One factor is cost: As mentioned in Chapter 1, a Windows Server 2008 Enterprise Edition license includes the licenses for four hosted virtual instances. Although you need to consider many other costs when making a comparison, from a licensing perspective one enterprise edition license will cost less than five standard edition licenses. Also remember that server-grade hardware will always cost significantly more than a Windows Server 2008 Enterprise Edition license, especially if your organization has a licensing agreement with Microsoft.

Although each situation will be different, in certain archetypical situations you would plan a virtualized server rather than a traditional installation, including the following:

- You want to use Windows Deployment Services at a branch office location for a rollout that will last several days, but you do not have the resources to deploy extra hardware to that location. In this case you could virtualize a WDS server and only turn on the virtual machine when it was needed. In the event that more operating systems need to be rolled out at a later stage, the virtual machine could be turned on.

- You have two applications hosted on the same server that conflict with each other. Because custom applications do not always play well together, sometimes you need to place each application in its own virtual machine. Applications hosted on separate computers are unlikely to conflict with each other! Another solution is to virtualize the application itself. Virtualizing applications is covered later in this lesson.

- You are working with developers who need to test an application. If you have worked as a systems administrator in an environment with developers, you know that some projects are not stable until they are nearly complete, and until that time they have a nasty habit of crashing the server. Giving developers their own virtual machine to work with allows them to crash a server as often as they like without you worrying about the impact on anyone outside the development group.

Some server deployments make poor candidates for virtualization. Servers that have high I/O requirements or high CPU requirements make poor candidates. A server that monopolizes CPU, memory, and disk resources on a single computer will require the same level of resources when virtualized, and a traditional server installation will provide better performance than running that same server virtualized on the same hardware. In general, you are reasonably safe in deciding to deploy virtual servers if the server does not have a large performance footprint. When a server is expected to have a significant performance footprint, you will need to develop further metrics to decide whether virtualization offers any advantage.

TIP   Remember that Windows Server 2008 Datacenter Edition (x64) has unlimited licenses for virtual hosts and that Windows Server 2008 Enterprise Edition (x64) has only four.

Virtualizing Existing Servers

When you plan the deployment of Windows Server 2008 at a particular site that has an existing Windows server infrastructure, you will be making an assessment about which of the existing servers can be virtualized, which need to be migrated, and which need to be upgraded. When you have determined the need to virtualize a server, the next step is to move that server from its existing hardware to a virtualized partition running under Windows Server 2008. You can use two tools to virtualize a server installed on traditional hardware: the Virtual Server Migration Toolkit (VSMT) and System Center Virtual Machine Manager. Both tools are compatible not only with Hyper-V but also with Virtual Server 2005 R2.

VSMT is the best tool to use when you have a small number of servers that need to be virtualized. The tool is command-line-based and uses XML files to store configuration data that is used during the migration process. You cannot use the VSMT tool to manage virtualized servers—it is purely a tool for migrating existing servers to a virtualized environment.

MORE INFO   **More on VSMT**

To find out more about how you can use VSMT to virtualize servers, see the following TechNet article: *http://www.microsoft.com/technet/virtualserver/evaluation/vsmtfaq.mspx*.

Use System Center Virtual Machine Manager when you have a large number of virtual machines to manage in a single location. System Center Virtual Machine Manager requires a significant infrastructure investment and is primarily designed to manage large virtual server deployments rather than just migrating a couple of branch office servers into a virtual environment. If you are planning to virtualize a large number of servers, you will find the extra functionality of System Center Virtual Machine Manager valuable. Unlike the Virtual Server Migration Toolkit, System Center Virtual Machine Manager is fully integrated with Windows PowerShell, providing you with a greater degree of flexibility in migrating servers from physical to virtualized environments.

You should note that deployment of System Center Virtual Machine Manager requires a connection to a SQL Server database. System Center Virtual Machine Manager uses this database to store virtual machine configuration information. This should remind you that deploying this product is not to be undertaken lightly and should only be done after ensuring that the product actually solves the sorts of problems that your organization is likely to experience. In addition to virtualizing traditional server installations, you can use System Center Virtual Machine Manager to:

- Monitor all of the virtualized servers in your environment.
- Monitor all Hyper-V hosts in your environment.
- When connected to a Fibre Channel SAN environment, move virtualized servers from one Hyper-V host to another.
- Move virtualized servers to and from libraries.
- Delegate permissions so that users with non-administrative privileges are able to create and manage their own virtual machines.

MORE INFO   **More on System Center Virtual Machine Manager**

To learn more about System Center Virtual Machine Manager, see the following TechNet link: *http://technet.microsoft.com/en-us/scvmm/default.aspx*.

Managing Virtualized Servers

Hyper-V is managed through the Hyper-V Manager Console, shown in Figure 5-18. You can use this console to manage virtual networks, edit and inspect disks, take snapshots, revert to snapshots, and delete snapshots, as well as to edit the settings for individual virtual machines. You can also mount virtual hard disks as volumes on the host server should the need arise.

Snapshots

Snapshots are similar to a point-in-time backup of a virtualized machine. The great benefit of snapshots is that they allow you to roll back to an earlier instance of an operating system far more quickly than any other technology would. For example, assume that your organization hosts its intranet Web server as a virtual machine under Hyper-V. A snapshot of the intranet Web server is taken every day. Because of an unforeseen problem with the custom content management system, the most recent set of updates to the intranet site have wiped the server completely. In the past, as an administrator, you would have to go to your backup tapes and restore the files. With Hyper-V, you can just roll back to the previous snapshot and everything will be in the state it was when the snapshot was taken.

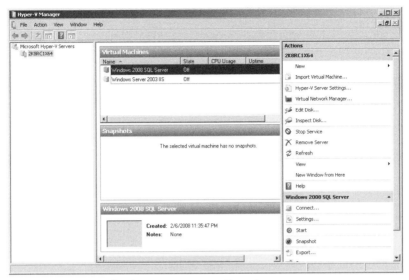

Figure 5-18   Virtualization Management Console

Licensing

All operating systems that run in a virtualized environment need to be licensed. Products such as Windows Server 2008 Enterprise and Datacenter Editions allow a certain number of virtual instances to be run without incurring extra license costs because the licenses for these editions include the virtualized component. The applications that run on the virtualized servers also need licenses. As with all licensing queries, in more complicated situations you should check with your Microsoft representative if you are unsure whether you are in compliance.

MORE INFO   More on licensing virtual machines

To learn more about what you need to consider when licensing a virtual machine, see *http://download.microsoft.com/download/6/8/9/68964284-864d-4a6d-aed9-f2c1f8f23e14/ virtualization_brief.doc.*

Modifying Hardware Settings

You can edit virtual machine settings. This allows you to add resources such as virtual hard disks and more RAM, and to configure other settings such as the Snapshot File Location. Figure 5-19 shows the Integration Services for a specific virtual machine. Integration Services allow information and data to be directly exchanged between host and virtual machine. To function, these services must be installed on the guest operating system. This task is performed after the guest operating system is set up. Some settings, such as the optical drive settings, can be edited while the virtual machine is running. Other settings, such as assigning and removing processors from a virtual machine, require the virtual machine to be turned off.

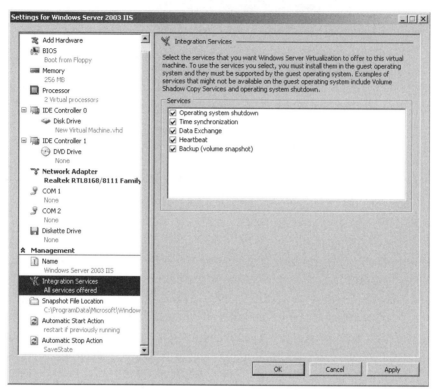

Figure 5-19   Modifying the settings of a virtual machine

Not only can you assign processors to virtual machines, but you can also limit the amount of processor usage by a particular virtual machine. You do this with the Virtual Processor settings shown in Figure 5-20. This way you can stop one virtual machine that has relatively high processing needs from monopolizing the host server's hardware. You can also use the Virtual Processor settings to assign a relative weight to a hosted virtual machine. Rather than specifying a percentage of system resources to which the virtual machine is entitled, you can use ratios to weight virtual machine access to system resources. The benefit of using relative weight is that it means you do not have to recalculate percentages each time you add or remove virtual machines from a host. You simply add the new host, assign a relative weight, and let Hyper-V work out the specific percentage of system resources that the virtual machine is entitled to.

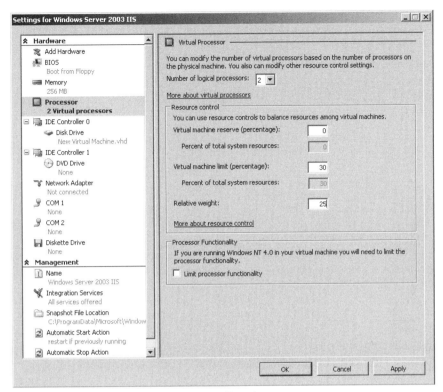

Figure 5-20   Virtual machine processor allocation

Quick Check

1. Which versions of Windows Server 2008 can you install the Hyper-V role on?

2. Which performance characteristics indicate that an existing Windows Server 2008 computer would be a poor candidate for virtualization?

Quick Check Answers

1. You can install the Hyper-V role on the 64-bit editions of the Standard, Enterprise, and Datacenter editions of Windows Server 2008 in both the standard and server-core modes.

2. Computers that have high CPU, hard disk, or RAM utilization make poor candidates for virtualization.

Terminal Services RemoteApp

RemoteApp differs from a normal Terminal Server session in that instead of connecting to a window that displays a remote computer's desktop, an application being executed on the Terminal Server appears as if its being executed on the local computer. For example, Figure 5-21 shows WordPad running locally and as a TS RemoteApp on the same Windows Vista computer. The visible difference between these two is that one does not have the Windows Vista borders and retains the Windows Server 2008 appearance.

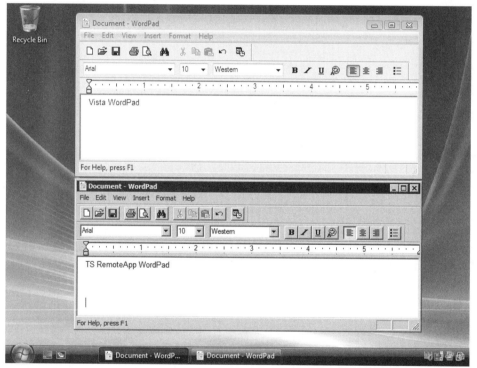

Figure 5-21   Two different instances of WordPad

A benefit of this technology is that all of the memory, disk, and processor resources required by the application are provided by the Terminal Server hosting the application rather than the client computer. This allows applications that require significant amounts of RAM and CPU resources to run quickly on computers that do not have sufficient resources for a traditional installation and application execution.

When multiple applications are invoked from the same host server, the applications are transmitted to the client using the same session. This means that if you have configured a Terminal Server to allow a maximum of 20 simultaneous sessions, a user having three separate RemoteApp applications open will only account for one open session instead of three.

RemoteApp includes the following benefits:

■ Easier to deploy application updates. Updates only need to be applied on the Terminal Server rather than having to be deployed to client computers.

■ Simpler application upgrade path. As with the application of updates, it is only necessary to upgrade the application on the Terminal Server to a newer version. The client computer does not need to be upgraded.

You can use three methods to deploy a TS RemoteApp to the clients in your organization:

■ Create a RDP shortcut file and distribute this file to client computers. You can do this by placing the RDP shortcut on a shared folder.

■ Create and distribute a Windows Installer package. The deployment of Windows Installer packages was covered in Lesson 2, "Application Deployment," in Chapter 4, "Application Servers and Services."

■ Get clients to connect to the TS Web Access Web site and launch the RemoteApp application from a link on the page.

The primary drawback of using TS Web Access to deploy RemoteApp applications is that the TS Web Access Web site must be deployed on the Terminal Server hosting the application that the Web site provides the connection to. Although this works well when only one server is used to remotely deploy applications, it is not compatible with Terminal Server farms managed by the TS Session Broker. As with full remote desktop sessions, TS Web Access is best suited to single Terminal Server deployments rather than groups of load-balanced Terminal Servers.

RemoteApp users still need to be a members of the Remote Desktop Users group on the Terminal Server. If you are in the situation in which RemoteApps are being deployed from a computer that is also functioning as a domain controller, you will need to modify the Allow Log On Through Terminal Services policy to enable RemoteApp access.

To calculate the memory footprint of a RemoteApp application on a Terminal Server, examine Task Manager and locate a user with an open RemoteApp. As shown in Figure 5-22, you will be able to see how much memory the specific application is using as well as how much memory the processes associated with RemoteApp are using. Multiplying the memory footprint of applications by the number of users should give a good estimate of the RAM required for RemoteApp. Remember only to use this number as an estimate—only monitoring the Terminal Server will allow you to determine the actual capacity of the server in your organization's environment.

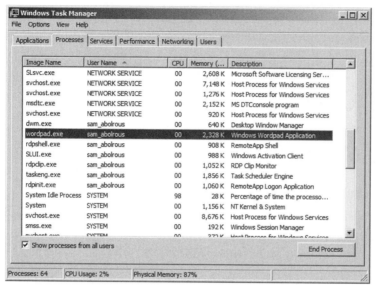

Figure 5-22   Assessing a RemoteApp application's memory requirements

---

MORE INFO   Drill down on TS RemoteApp

To learn more about TS RemoteApp, see *http://technet2.microsoft.com/windowsserver2008/en/library/57995ee7-e204-45a4-bcee-5d1f4a51a09f1033.mspx?mfr=true.*

Microsoft Application Virtualization

Hyper-V creates a separate partitioned space for an entire operating system and any applications and services that it hosts. Application virtualization goes further than this. Instead of creating a separate partitioned space for the entire operating system, it creates a separate partitioned space for a specific application. This technology is called Microsoft Application Virtualization, formerly SoftGrid, an additional product that you can purchase and install on a Windows Server 2008 computer.

Although from the client perspective Microsoft Application Virtualization might appear superficially similar to RemoteApp, the two application deployment technologies are significantly different. The primary difference is that a virtualized application executes on the client computer. It does so in a special virtualized space called a *silo* that separates it from applications executed locally. RemoteApp has the application execute on the host Terminal Server and uses remote desktop technology to display the application on the local computer.

MORE INFO Terminal Services and Microsoft Application Virtualization

To learn more about how Microsoft Application Virtualization works with Terminal Services, see *http://www.microsoft.com/systemcenter/softgrid/evaluation/softgrid-ts.mspx.*

Microsoft Application Virtualization also differs from running a program from a network share in that it streams across the network only the parts of the application that are actually being utilized by the client. Because the application is virtualized in a silo, Microsoft Application Virtualization allows you to do the following:

- Deploy multiple versions of the same application from the same server. It is even possible to run multiple versions of the same application on a local client as the silos, ensuring that the two applications will not conflict. This is especially useful in application development environments where different versions of the same application need to be tested simultaneously.

- Deploy applications that would normally conflict with each other from the same server. When deploying applications using RemoteApp, you can only install applications that do not conflict with one another on the same Terminal Server.

- Deploy applications that are not compatible with Terminal Server. Because of conflicts with the Terminal Server architecture, not all applications work with Terminal Server. Microsoft Application Virtualization allows these applications to be deployed to clients in a manner similar to that of Terminal Server.

MORE INFO Microsoft Application Virtualization TechCenter

You can learn more about Microsoft Application Virtualization and how you can plan for the deployment of this technology in your environment at *http://technet.microsoft.com/en-us/softgrid/default.aspx.*

Practice: Configuring and Deploying RemoteApp

In this set of exercises, you will use two different methods to deploy applications using RemoteApp to clients on the network. The first will be to configure an RDP shortcut and place it in a shared folder accessible to clients. The second method will be to set up a TS Web Access site and open the deployed application using its link on the TS Web Access Web site. These exercises require that the client computer Melbourne either be running Windows Vista or, if Windows XP is being used, that you install RDC version 6.0.

NOTE   Obtaining RDC 6.0

You can obtain RDC version 6.0 for Windows Server 2003 or Windows XP from the following site: *http://support.microsoft.com/?kbid=925876* .

▶ **Exercise 1: Deploy WordPad using RemoteApp and an RDP Shortcut**

In this exercise, you will configure TS RemoteApp so that clients can run WordPad without the accompanying remote desktop from an RDP shortcut located on a shared folder. To complete this exercise, perform the following steps:

1. Ensure that you are logged on to the server Glasgow with the Kim_Akers user account.

2. Click Start, click Administrative Tools, click the Terminal Services folder and then click TS RemoteApp Manager. In the User Account Control dialog box, click Continue. The TS RemoteApp Manager console will open.

3. In the Actions pane of the TS RemoteApp Manager console (Figure 5-23), click Add RemoteApp Programs. This will launch the RemoteApp Wizard.

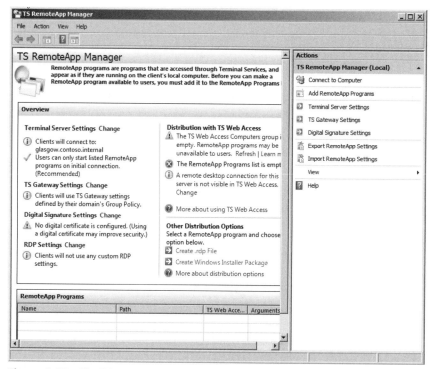

Figure 5-23   The TS RemoteApp Manager console

4. On the RemoteApp Wizard Welcome page, click Next.

5. On the Choose Programs To Add To The RemoteApp Programs List page, select WordPad, as shown in Figure 5-24. Click Next.

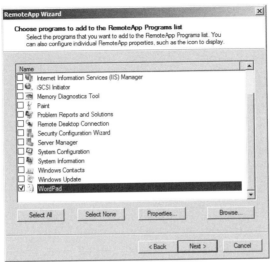

Figure 5-24   Adding a program to the TS RemoteApp programs list

6. On the Review Settings page, click Finish.

7. Create a shared folder named **RemoteAppDist** on Volume C.

8. On the TS RemoteApp Manager Console, click WordPad and then click Create .RDP File in the Actions pane. This will launch the RemoteApp Wizard. Click Next on the Welcome page.

9. On the Specify Package Settings page shown in Figure 5-25, specify the location of the shared folder that you created in step 7 and then click Next.

10. On the Review Settings page, click Finish.

11. Log on to the client computer using the sam_abolrous@contoso.internal user account.

12. Open the shared folder \\glasgow\RemoteAppDist and then double-click the WordPad remote desktop connection item.

13. In the Enter Your Credentials dialog box, enter the password for the sam_abolrous user account.

14. In the Do You Trust The Computer You Are Connecting To dialog box, review the defaults and then click Yes. The RemoteApp WordPad will now start.

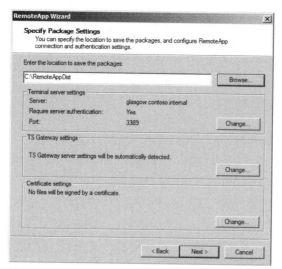

Figure 5-25   RemoteApp shortcut distribution

15. Verify that the WordPad RemoteApp functions correctly by saving a document containing the words **The Quick Brown Fox Jumped Over The Lazy Dog** to the desktop of the client computer.

16. Close the RemoteApp application.

▶ **Exercise 2: Deploy Microsoft Paint using RemoteApp and Terminal Services Web Access**

In this exercise, you will set up Microsoft Paint as an available application shortcut on the RemoteApp Programs page of Terminal Services Web Access.

NOTE   Service packs required

This exercise requires Windows Vista Service Pack 1 or Windows XP Service Pack 3 to be installed on the computer functioning as the client. For more information about the software necessary to use TS Web Access with TS RemoteApp, see *http://go.microsoft.com/fwlink/?LinkID=56287*.

To complete this exercise, perform the following steps:

1. Ensure that you are logged on to the server Glasgow with the Kim_Akers user account.

2. Click Start, click Administrative Tools, click the Terminal Services folder and then click TS RemoteApp Manager. In the User Account Control dialog box, click Continue. The TS RemoteApp Manager console will open.

3. In the Actions pane of the TS RemoteApp Manager console, click Add Remote-App Programs. This will launch the RemoteApp Wizard.

4. On the RemoteApp Wizard Welcome page, click Next.

5. On the Choose Programs To Add To The RemoteApp Programs List page, select Paint, then click Next and click Finish on the Review Settings page.

6. Log on to the client computer as sam_abolrous@contoso.internal and open the Web site *http://glasgow.contoso.internal/ts*. When prompted for credentials, authenticate using the sam_abolrous@contoso.internal user account. This will bring up the TS Web Access RemoteApp Programs Web page shown in Figure 5-26.

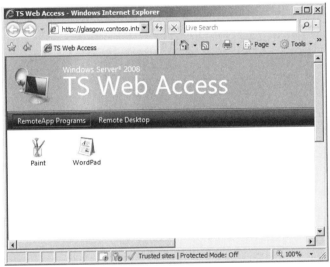

Figure 5-26 RemoteApp programs available through TS Web Access

7. On the TS Web Access RemoteApp Programs Web page, click Paint.

8. Review the warning shown in Figure 5-27. Verify that the correct user account is being used for authentication and that the remote computer is glasgow.contoso.internal. Click Connect.

9. Using the Microsoft Paint tools, create an image using the RemoteApp application and then save it to the local computer.

10. Close the application and then log off the client computer.

11. Log off the server Glasgow.

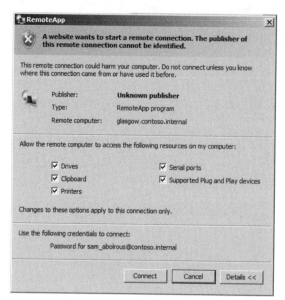

Figure 5-27 TS Web Access RemoteApp warning

Lesson Summary

- Hyper-V is an add-on role for 64-bit versions of Windows Server 2008 that you can use to host and manage virtualized operating systems.

- Snapshots allow the state of a server to be taken at a point in time, such as prior to the deployment of an update, so that the server can be rolled back to that state at some point in the future.

- The best candidates for virtualization are servers that do not intensively use processor, RAM, and disk resources.

- The Virtual Server Migration Toolkit provides tools you can use to virtualize existing servers. The toolkit uses XML-based files to assist in the transition from a traditional to a virtualized installation. Use this option if you have a small number of existing servers to virtualize.

- System Center Virtual Machine Manager allows you to manage many virtual machines at once. It includes tools that allow you to move virtual machines between hosts, allow non-privileged users to create and manage their own virtual machines, and perform bulk virtualizations of servers installed on traditional hardware. Only use System Center Virtual Machine Manager with large virtual machine deployments.

- TS RemoteApp allows Terminal Server applications to be presented straight to a client desktop without requiring that a normal Terminal Services session be established.

- Microsoft Application Virtualization allows applications to be virtualized. This has the advantage of allowing applications that might conflict with each other to be run concurrently. Microsoft Application Virtualization differs from Terminal Services in that applications execute on the client rather than on the server.

Lesson Review

You can use the following questions to test your knowledge of the information in Lesson 2, "Server and Application Virtualization." The questions are also available on the companion CD if you prefer to review them in electronic form.

NOTE Answers

Answers to these questions and explanations of why each answer choice is correct or incorrect are located in the "Answers" section at the end of the book.

---

1. Which of the following scenarios provides the most compelling case for the planned deployment of System Center Virtual Machine Manager 2007?

    A. You need to virtualize four Windows Server 2000 computers.

    B. You want to be able to move virtualized servers between hosts on your Fibre Channel SAN.

    C. You are responsible for managing 10 virtualized Windows Server 2008 servers at your head office location.

    D. You need to automate the deployment of five Windows Server 2008 Enterprise Edition computers with the Hyper-V role installed.

2. Which of the following platforms can you install Hyper-V on?

    A. A Server Core installation of the x64 version of Windows Server 2008 Enterprise Edition

    B. A Server Core installation of the x86 version of Windows Server 2008 Datacenter Edition

    C. A standard installation of the x86 version of Windows Server 2008 Enterprise Edition

    D. A standard installation of the x86 version of Windows Server 2008 Datacenter Edition

3. Which of the following methods can you use to deploy a TS RemoteApp application to users in your organization? (Each correct answer presents a complete solution. Choose all that apply.)

   A. Bookmark to TS Web Access deployed through Group Policy.

   B. Windows Installer Package deployed through Group Policy.

   C. RDP shortcut on an accessible shared folder.

   D. Install the application on an accessible shared folder.

4. You work as a systems administrator for a software development company. During the application development phase it is necessary to deploy several versions of the same software from the same Terminal Server. When you attempt to install the applications side by side it causes a conflict. Which of the following solutions should you plan to use?

   A. Deploy the applications using TS RemoteApp.

   B. Deploy a TS Gateway Server.

   C. Deploy Microsoft Application Virtualization.

   D. Deploy the applications using TS Web Access.

5. Windows XP clients in your organization are unable to connect using the TS Web Access Web page to RemoteApp applications. Windows Vista clients are able to connect without any problems. Which of the following steps should you take to resolve this problem?

   A. Install Internet Explorer 6.0 on the Windows XP Clients.

   B. Disable the Windows XP firewall.

   C. Upgrade the Windows XP computers to Service Pack 3.

   D. Install Windows Defender on the Windows XP Clients.

Chapter Review

To further practice and reinforce the skills you learned in this chapter, you can perform the following tasks:

- Review the chapter summary.
- Review the list of key terms introduced in this chapter.
- Complete the case scenarios. These scenarios set up real-world situations involving the topics of this chapter and ask you to create a solution.
- Complete the suggested practices.
- Take a practice test.

Chapter Summary

- Servers that do not have large hardware footprints can be virtualized and hosted on a Windows Server 2008 64-bit computer running the Hyper-V role.
- System Center Virtual Machine Manager should be deployed when an administrator must manage large numbers of virtual machines.
- Terminal Servers require significant amounts of RAM and CPU capacity if they are to host many client sessions.
- TS license servers must be activated before they can have TS Per-Device and TS Per-User CALs installed.
- TS RemoteApp allows just the application, rather than the entire remote desktop, to be displayed on the Terminal Services client.
- TS Gateway Servers allow clients on the Internet to connect to protected Terminal Servers without requiring the setup of a VPN.
- TS Session Broker allows the creation of Terminal Server farms and ensures that clients are connected to the correct session if they become disconnected.
- Microsoft Application Virtualization allows applications that could not otherwise be installed on a Terminal Server, or coexist on a Terminal Server, to be streamed to clients. This is achieved through application virtualization.

Key Terms

Do you know what these key terms mean? You can check your answers by looking up the terms in the glossary at the end of the book.

- Hyper-V
- Silo
- Softgrid
- Virtualized

Case Scenarios

In the following case scenarios, you will apply what you have learned about Terminal Services and application and server virtualization. You can find answers to these questions in the "Answers" section at the end of this book.

Case Scenario 1: Tailspin Toys Server Consolidation

Tailspin Toys has an aging deployment of computers running Windows 2000 Server. Management has decided to transition to a Windows Server 2008 infrastructure. One goal of the transition project is to reduce the number of physical servers and to retire all existing server hardware, which is now more than five years old. You have been brought in as a consultant to assist in the development of plans for server consolidation at a Tailspin Toys branch office. Each site has a unique set of needs and applications. The characteristics of each site are as follows:

1. The Wangaratta site currently hosts a Windows 2000 domain controller that also hosts the DHCP and DNS services. A Windows 2000 computer hosts a SQL Server 2000 database and two other servers, each of which host custom business applications. These applications cannot be co-located with each other or with the SQL Server 2000 database. How could you minimize the number of physical servers using virtualization and what would the configuration of these servers be?

2. The Yarragon site currently hosts six Terminal Servers, each of which hosts a separate business application. One of these applications uses a SQL Server 2005 database. These applications cannot be co-located without causing problems on the host Terminal Servers. Because the Yarragon site has only a small number of users, the hardware resources of the Terminal Servers are underutilized. How can you minimize the number of Terminal Servers required to support the staff at the Yarragon site?

Case Scenario 2: Planning a Terminal Services Strategy for Wingtip Toys

You are planning the deployment of Terminal Services for the company Wingtip Toys. Wingtip Toys has an office in each state of Australia. Because of the decentralized nature of the Wingtip Toys organization, each state office has its own domain in the Wingtiptoys.internal forest. All clients in the organization are using Windows Vista without any service packs applied. Taking this into consideration, how will you resolve the following design challenges?

1. Each state office should be responsible for the purchase and management of TS CALs. What plans should be made for TS license server deployment?

2. The Terminal Server in the Queensland office is reaching capacity and cannot be upgraded further. How can you continue to service clients in the Queensland office and ensure that interrupted sessions are reconnected?

3. What steps need to be taken to ensure that Windows Vista clients can access RemoteApp applications through TS Web Access?

Suggested Practices

To help you successfully master the exam objectives presented in this chapter, complete the following tasks.

Provision Applications

Do all the practices in this section.

- **Practice 1: Create a Windows Installer Package for Notepad**   Using TS RemoteApp manager, create a Windows Installer Package for the Notepad application.

- **Practice 2: Install and Activate TS license server**   Install the TS License Server role service on the Glasgow computer. Activate the computer using the Web page method using another computer that is connected to the Internet.

Plan Application Servers and Services

Do all the practices in this section.

- **Practice 1: Install Hyper-V**   Obtain a 64-bit evaluation version of Windows Server 2008 from the Microsoft Web site. Install this operating system on a computer with a 64-bit processor. Configure the server as a stand-alone computer and do not join it to any domain. Download and install Hyper-V from the Microsoft Web site.

NOTE Obtaining evaluation software

You will be able to obtain the necessary software from *http://www.microsoft.com/ windowsserver2008*.

■ **Practice 2: Virtualize Windows Server 2008**   After you configure Windows Server 2008 with the Hyper-V role, install the Server Core version of Windows Server 2008 as a child virtual machine on the computer.

Take a Practice Test

The practice tests on this book's companion CD offer many options. For example, you can test yourself on just one exam objective, or you can test yourself on all the 70-646 certification exam content. You can set up the test so that it closely simulates the experience of taking a certification exam, or you can set it up in study mode so that you can look at the correct answers and explanations after you answer each question.

MORE INFO   Practice tests

For details about all the practice test options available, see "How to Use the Practice Tests" in this book's Introduction.

Chapter 6

File and Print Servers

This chapter looks at the File Server and Print Server server roles and describes how you can plan to meet your organization's printing, file storage, and access security needs. It also discusses how to provision organizational data by sharing resources, configuring offline access, designing and implementing a replication structure, configuring indexing, and planning data availability.

Exam objectives in this chapter:
- Plan file and print server roles.
- Provision data.

Lessons in this chapter:

Before You Begin

To complete the lesson in this chapter, you must have done the following:

- Installed Windows Server 2008 and configured your test PC as a domain controller (DC) in the Contoso.internal domain as described in the Introduction and Chapter 1, "Installing, Upgrading, and Deploying Windows Server 2008." You also need a client computer running Windows Vista Business, Enterprise, or Ultimate that is a member of the Contoso.internal domain. This can be a separate computer or a virtual machine installed on the same computer as your DC.

Real World

Ian McLean

In July 1993, Microsoft introduced the new technology file system (NTFS). Whether it can still be called "new" is debatable, but it was a remarkable development in its time. Folders and files could now be protected from interactive as well as network users, and protection could be implemented at file level rather than

---

folder level. I won't go into the many other developments that NTFS enabled—this isn't a history book—but I know that I have lost data on NTFS disks far less often than on FAT disks.

However, NTFS was not unalloyed good news, particularly for a network engineer (me) who was studying for his first MCSE at the time. NTFS introduced a level of complexity in calculating user permissions that almost guaranteed examination failure to those who couldn't quite understand how permissions interacted, particularly when the old No-Access permission was replaced by the more granular Deny.

Software was developed for determining resultant user permissions, but you can't take that into the examination room. My solution was much simpler. I drew three rectangular boxes next to each other. I marked the right-hand box "File," the middle box "Folder," and the left-hand box "Share."

Then I wrote in the NTFS permissions a user had on a file, and the permissions the same user had on the folder that contained the file. File overrides folder. So I had my resultant NTFS permissions. If a user was logged on locally, that was his permissions on the folder. I wrote the shared folder permission into the Share box. If a user was accessing remotely, I took the more restrictive between share and resultant NTFS. I had worked out the user permission.

I used this technique in exams and in my profession. When I became an MCT I taught it to my students, and whiteboards blossomed with rectangular boxes throughout the land. It's a simple technique. Some have even called it dumb.

It works. Try it.

Lesson 1: Managing File and Print Servers

As far as the users in your organization are concerned, two of the major functions they require from a computer network are the ability to create files and save them where they can easily be retrieved, and the ability to print files easily and without fuss.

From your point of view, you need to ensure that users cannot read confidential files unless they are allowed to. You need to control usage so that users cannot clog the network with high numbers of large files. You need to publish printers so that your users can print to them, while at the same time controlling the use of expensive printing assets. This lesson looks at the Print Services and File Services server roles and how you configure quotas and publish printers.

After this lesson, you will be able to:

- Use the Share And Storage Management tool to provision shared folders and disk storage.
- Plan the role services that you need to add to the File Services server role.
- Install the Print Services server role and install and manage printers and print drivers.
- Configure quotas and quota templates.
- Access the tools that enable you to configure file screens and storage reports.

Estimated lesson time: 45 minutes

Planning the File Services Server Role

A file server provides a central network location where users can store files and share them with other users on the network. If a user requires a file that is typically accessed by many users, such as a company policy document, she should be able to access the file remotely. For the purposes of centralized administration, backup and restore, and the implementation of shadow copies, you need to store user files on a file server rather than on individual computers, although users typically also need to have the facility of working with their files offline.

You configure a Windows Server 2008 server as a file server by adding the File Services role. This role consists of a number of role services. The File Server role service is installed by default. Figure 6-1 shows the role services you can install as part of the File Services server role.

As part of your planning process you need to decide what role services you require and how these should be configured. The temptation is to install everything just in case you need it. Resist this temptation. The more services you install on a server the more pressure you put on limited resources, and the larger the footprint for attack.

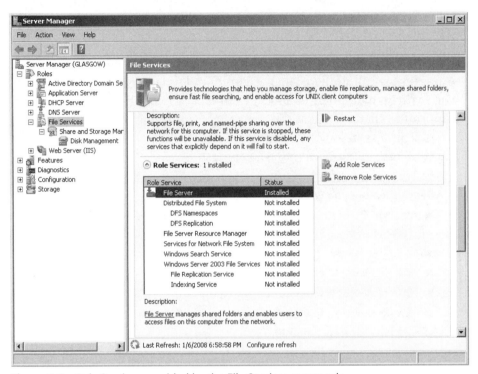

Figure 6-1   Role Services provided by the File Services server role

The Role Services server role provides the following role services:

- Share And Storage Management (provided by File Services)
- Distributed File System (DFS)
- File Server Resource Manager (FSRM)
- Services For Network File System (NFS)
- Windows Search Service
- Windows Server 2003 File Services

NOTE   Optional features

Often the Windows Server Backup, Storage Manager for storage area networks (SANs), Failover Clustering, and Multipath input/output (I/O) features are installed at the same time as the role services provided by the File Services server role. Chapter 12, "Backup and Recovery," and Chapter 10, "Certificate Services and Storage," discuss these features.

Share And Storage Management

Share And Storage Management is installed by default with the File Server role service. You can access the Share And Storage Management console through Server Manager or directly from Administrative Tools. It uses the Microsoft Service Message Block (SMB) 2.0 protocol to share the content of folders and to manage shared folders. Figure 6-2 shows the shared folders on the Glasgow server. Your server might have additional shares if you created them when you were experimenting with your network.

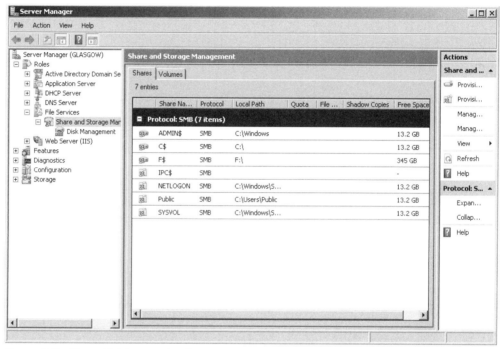

Figure 6-2   Shared folders on the Glasgow server

MORE INFO   Microsoft SMB protocol

If you want to learn more about this protocol, sometimes known as the Common Internet File System (CIFS) protocol, see *http://msdn2.microsoft.com/en-us/library/aa365233.aspx*. However, the 70-646 examination is unlikely to ask you detailed questions about this protocol.

You can manage volumes and disks by using the Share And Storage Management tool. Figure 6-3 shows this tool accessed from Administrative Tools rather than from Server Manager. Again, the volumes on your Glasgow server might differ from those shown in the figure.

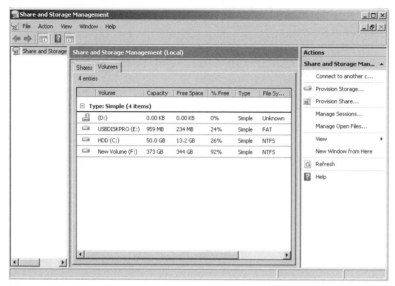

Figure 6-3 Managing volumes

If you access Share And Storage Management from Server Manager, you can access the Disk Management console shown in Figure 6-4. The disks in your Glasgow server might again differ from those shown in the figure.

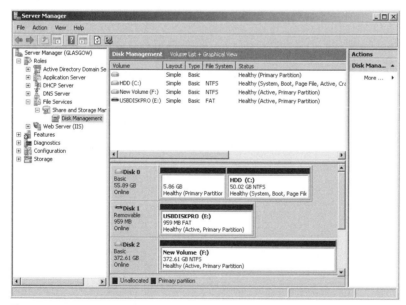

Figure 6-4 Managing disks

You can share the content of folders and volumes on a Windows Server 2008 server over the network by using the Provision A Shared Folder Wizard, which you can access from the Actions pane in the Share And Storage Management console. Figure 6-5 shows this wizard, which guides you through the steps required to share a folder or volume and configure its properties.

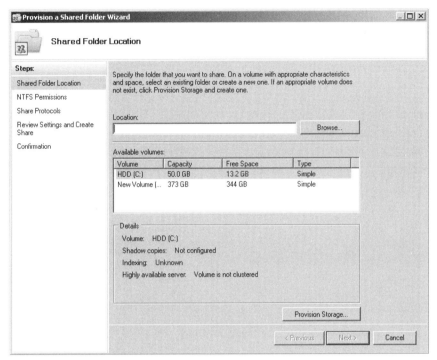

Figure 6-5   The Provision A Shared Folder Wizard

You can use the Provision A Shared Folder Wizard to do the following:

- Specify a folder or volume to share, or create a new folder to share.
- Specify the network sharing protocol used to access the shared resource.
- Change the local NTFS permissions for the folder or volume you are sharing.
- Configure the share access permissions, user limits, and offline access to files in the shared resource.
- Publish the shared resource to a Distributed File System (DFS) namespace.

If you have installed the Services For Network File System (NFS) role service, you can specify NFS-based access permissions for the shared resource. If you have installed the File Server Resource Manager role service, you can apply storage quotas to the new shared resource and limit the type of files that can be stored in it.

You can use Share And Storage Management to stop sharing a resource by selecting it on the Shares tab (shown previously in Figure 6-2) and clicking Stop Sharing in the Actions pane. If a folder or volume is shared for access by both the SMB and the NFS protocols, you need to stop sharing for each protocol individually. Before you stop sharing a folder or volume you need to ensure that it is not in use by using the Manage Sessions and Manage Open Files features of Share And Storage Management. These features are described later in this section.

You can also use Share And Storage Management to view and modify the properties of a shared folder or volume, including the local NTFS permissions and the network access permissions for that shared resource. To do this you again select the shared resource on the Shares tab and select Properties in the Actions pane. Figure 6-6 shows the Properties dialog box for the share folder Public. The Permissions tab lets you specify share and NTFS permissions. Clicking Advanced lets you configure user limits and caching and disable or enable access-based enumeration (ABE). ABE is enabled by default and lets you hide files and folders from users who do not have access to them.

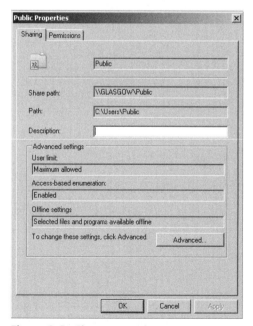

Figure 6-6   Share properties

NOTE Administrative shares

You cannot modify the access permissions of folders or volumes shared for administrative purposes, such as C$ and ADMIN$.

If you want to view and close open sessions and open files—for example, if you intended to stop sharing a resource—you can click Manage Sessions and Manage Open Files in the Share And Storage Management Actions pane. Figures 6-7 and 6-8 show the resulting dialog boxes.

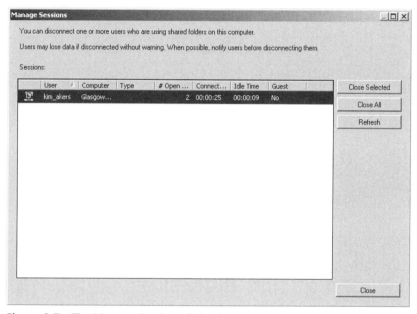

Figure 6-7 The Manage Sessions dialog box

Share And Storage Management enables you to provision storage on disks on your Windows Server 2008 server or on storage subsystems that support Virtual Disk Service (VDS). The Provision Storage Wizard guides you through the process of creating a volume on an existing disk or on a storage subsystem (such as a SAN) attached to your server. If you create a volume on a storage subsystem, the wizard enables you to create a logical unit number (LUN) to host that volume. You can also use the wizard to create a LUN, and use the Disk Management console (shown previously in Figure 6-4) to create the volume later. Chapter 12 discusses LUNs and storage systems in more detail.

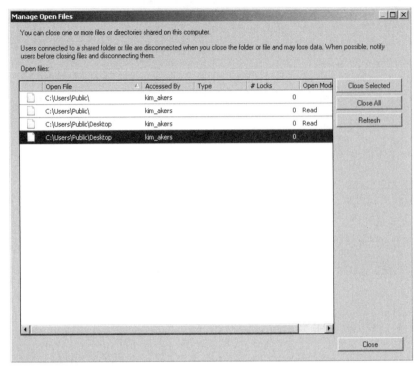

Figure 6-8 The Manage Open Files dialog box

NOTE Provisioning storage

You can run the Provision Storage Wizard only if your server can access disks with unallocated space or storage subsystems with available storage for which a VDS hardware provider is installed. Also, you can only create a volume on a disk that is online.

Provided that you have the available disk or storage subsystem resources, the Provision Storage Wizard can perform the following functions:

- Choose the disk on which the volume is created.
- Specify the volume size.
- Assign a drive letter or a mount point.
- Format the volume. (You can also do this from the Disk Management console.)

You can use Share And Storage Management to monitor and manage volumes on your server. The tool enables you to perform the following operations:

- Extend the size of a volume.
- Format a volume.

- Delete a volume.

- Change volume properties, including compression, security, offline availability, and indexing.

- Access disk tools for error checking, defragmentation, and backup.

LUNs

A LUN refers to a portion of a storage subsystem. A LUN can include a disk, a section of a disk, a whole disk array, or a section of a disk array. LUNs simplify storage management by providing logical identifiers through which you can assign access and control privileges.

You can use the Provision Storage Wizard in Share And Storage Management to create LUNs on Fibre Channel and iSCSI disk drive subsystems connected to your server. You can then assign the LUN to your server or to other servers on the network. While creating the LUN, you can also create a volume on that LUN and format it. Alternatively, you can create the LUN first and the volume later.

If you want to create a LUN on a disk storage subsystem, you need to ensure that all the following requirements are met:

- The storage subsystem supports VDS.

- The VDS hardware provider for the storage subsystem is installed on the server.

- Storage space is available on the subsystem.

- The storage subsystem is attached directly to the server or is accessible over the network.

If you want to assign a LUN to a server or cluster other than the server on which you run the Provision Storage Wizard, you need to configure the server connections by using Storage Manager for SANs. (See Chapter 10.) If you want to assign the LUN to a cluster, ensure that each server in the cluster is a member of only one cluster and has been configured by installing Failover Clustering. Also, if you enable multiple Fibre Channel ports or iSCSI initiator adapters for LUN access, make sure that the server supports Multipath I/O (MPIO).

NOTE Storage Manager For SANs

Storage Manager For SANs is not installed by default. You can install it by clicking Add Features in the Features node in Server Manager. Chapter 10 gives more details.

MORE INFO   iSCSI

For more information about iSCSI, see *http://www.microsoft.com/WindowsServer2003/technologies/storage/iscsi/default.mspx.*

MORE INFO   MPIO

For more information about MPIO, see *http://technet2.microsoft.com/windowsserver2008/en/library/1b48614a-9f2c-4293-bf2b-ffa9b17e15401033.mspx?mfr=true.*

MORE INFO   Share and storage management

For more information open the Command Console (or Command Prompt window) and type **hh storagemgmt.chm**.

Distributed File System (DFS)

DFS is considerably enhanced in Windows Server 2008. It consists of two technologies, DFS Namespaces and DFS Replication, that you can use (together or independently) to provide fault-tolerant and flexible file sharing and replication services.

DFS Namespaces lets you group shared folders on different servers (and in multiple sites) into one or more logically structured namespaces. Users view each namespace as a single shared folder with a series of subfolders. The underlying shared folders structure is hidden from users, and this structure provides fault tolerance and the ability to automatically connect users to local shared folders, when available, instead of routing them over wide area network (WAN) connections.

DFS Replication provides a multimaster replication engine that lets you synchronize folders on multiple servers across local or WAN connections. It uses the Remote Differential Compression (RDC) protocol to update only those files that have changed since the last replication. You can use DFS Replication in conjunction with DFS Namespaces or by itself.

This lesson summarizes DFS only very briefly as part of your planning considerations. Lesson 2 of this chapter discusses the topic in much more depth.

Exam Tip   Previous Windows Server examinations have contained a high proportion of DFS questions. There is no reason to believe 70-646 will be any different.

File Server Resource Manager (FSRM)

FSRM includes tools that enable you to understand, control, and manage the quantity and type of data stored on your servers. You can use FSRM to place quotas on folders and volumes, actively screen files, and generate storage reports. Details of the facilities available from FSRM console are given later in this lesson.

Services for Network File System (NFS)

NFS provides a file sharing solution for organizations with a mixed Windows and UNIX environment. Services for NFS lets you transfer files between computers running Windows Server 2008 and UNIX operating systems by using the NFS protocol. The Windows Server 2008 version of Services for NFS supports the following enhancements:

- **Active Directory lookup**   Identity management for the UNIX extension of the Active Directory schema includes the UNIX user identifier (UID) and group identifier (GID) fields. This enables Server for NFS and Client for NFS to refer to Windows-to-UNIX user account mappings directly from Active Directory Domain Services (AD DS). Identity management for UNIX simplifies mapping user accounts from Windows to UNIX in AD DS.

- **64-bit support**   You can install Services for NFS on all editions of Windows Server 2008, including 64-bit editions.

- **Enhanced server performance**   Services for NFS includes a file filter driver. This significantly reduces server file access latencies.

- **UNIX special device support**   Services for NFS provides support for UNIX special devices based on the *mknod* (make a directory, a special file, or a regular file) function.

MORE INFO   Mknod

For more information on the *mknod* function, see *http://www.opengroup.org/onlinepubs/009695399/ functions/mknod.html*. However, the 70-646 examination is unlikely to ask about UNIX functions.

- **Enhanced UNIX support**   Services for NFS supports the following UNIX versions: Sun Microsystems Solaris version 9, Red Hat Linux version 9, IBM AIX version 5L 5.2, and Hewlett Packard HP-UX version 11i.

MORE INFO Services for NFS

For more information open the Command Console (Command Prompt window) and type **hh nfs__lh.chm**.

Windows Search Service

Windows Search Service enables you to perform fast file searches on a server from client computers that are compatible with Windows Search. It creates an index of the most common file and non-file data types on your server, such as e-mail, contacts, calendar appointments, documents, photographs, and multimedia. Indexing files and data types enables you to perform fast file searches on your Windows Server 2008 server from client computers running Windows Vista or from Windows XP clients with Windows Desktop Search installed.

Windows Search Service replaces the Indexing Service that was provided in Windows Server 2003 server. Although you have the option of installing Windows Server 2003 File Services—including the Indexing Service—on a Windows Server 2008 server as part of the File Services server role, you cannot install Indexing Services if you choose to install Windows Search Service.

When you install Windows Search Service you are given the option to select the volumes or folders that you want to index. Microsoft recommends that you select a volume rather than a folder only if that volume is used exclusively for hosting shared folders.

Windows Server 2003 File Services

The File Services role in Windows Server 2008 includes the following role services that are compatible with Windows Server 2003:

- **File Replication Service (FRS)**   The File Replication Service (FRS) enables you to synchronize folders with file servers that use FRS. Where possible you should use the DFS Replication (DFSR) service. You should install FRS only if your Windows Server 2008 server needs to synchronize folders with servers that use FRS with the Windows Server 2003 or Windows 2000 Server implementations of DFS.

MORE INFO FRS

For more information on FRS, see *http://technet2.microsoft.com/WindowsServer/en/library/965a9e1a-8223-4d3e-8e5d-39aeb70ec5d91033.mspx?mfr=true.*

- **Indexing Service**   The Indexing Service catalogs contents and properties of files on local and remote computers. If you install the Windows Search Service you cannot install the Indexing Service.

Optional Features

Optionally, you can install the following additional features to complement the role services in the File Services role:

- **Windows Server Backup**   Windows Server Backup provides a reliable method of backing up and recovering the operating system, certain applications, and files and folders stored on your server. This feature replaces the previous backup feature that was available with earlier versions of Windows.

MORE INFO   **Windows Server Backup**

For more information open the Command Console (Command Prompt window) and type **hh backup.chm**.

- **Storage Manager for SANs**   Storage Manager For SANs lets you provision storage on one or more Fibre Channel or iSCSI storage subsystems on a SAN.

MORE INFO   **Storage Manager for SANs**

For more information open the Command Console (Command Prompt window) and type **hh sanmgr.chm**.

- **Failover clustering**   The Failover Clustering feature enables multiple servers to work together to increase the availability of services and applications. If one of the clustered servers (or nodes) fails, another node provides the required service through failover.

MORE INFO   **Failover clustering**

For more information on failover clustering, see *http://technet2.microsoft.com/windowsserver2008/en/ library/13c0a922-6097-4f34-ac64-18820094128b1033.mspx?mfr=true*.

- **MPIO**   MPIO provides support for multiple data paths between a file server and a storage device (known as *multipathing*). You can use MPIO to increase data availability by providing redundant connections to storage subsystems. Multipathing can also load-balance I/O traffic and improve system and application performance.

Managing Access Control

Access control is the process of permitting users, groups, and computers to access objects on the network or on a computer. It involves permissions, permission inheritance, object ownership, user rights, and auditing.

Permissions define the type of access granted to a user or group for an object. When a folder or volume is shared over a network and users access its contents remotely (as is the case with files on a file server), share or shared folder permissions apply to these users. A folder or file on an NTFS volume also has NTFS permissions, which apply whether it is accessed locally or across the network. Access permissions to files on a file server are typically a combination of NTFS permissions and the shared folder permissions set on the folder or folder hierarchy that contains the files. Printer objects have associated print permissions.

Every container and object on a network has associated (or attached) access control information defined within a security descriptor. This controls the type of access allowed to users and security groups. Permissions defined within an object's security descriptor are associated with, or assigned to, specific users and security groups. Each assignment of permissions to a user or group is represented in the system as an access control entry (ACE). The entire set of permission entries in a security descriptor is known as a permission set, or access control list (ACL).

You can set NTFS permissions for objects such as files, Active Directory objects, registry objects, or system objects such as processes. You set NTFS permissions on the Security tab of the object's Properties dialog box, sometimes known as the Access Control User Interface. Permissions can be granted to individual users, security groups, computers, and other objects with security identifiers in the domain. It is a good practice to assign permissions to security groups rather than to individual users.

The permissions attached to an object depend on the type of object. For example, the permissions that can be attached to a file are different from those that can be attached to a printer or to a registry key. When you set permissions, you specify the level of access for groups and users. For example, you can let one user read the contents of a file, let another user make changes to the file, and prevent all other users from accessing the file.

Microsoft states that permission inheritance allows administrators to easily assign and manage permissions and ensures consistency of permissions among all objects within a given container. Inheritance automatically causes objects within a container to inherit all the inheritable permissions of that container. For example, child folders by default inherit the permissions of their parent, and files within a folder have their permissions automatically set depending upon folder permissions.

Undoubtedly, inheritance is convenient when configuring permissions. You can block folder inheritance and assign explicit rather than inherited permissions to child objects. You can change file permissions so that some files in a folder can have different access permissions than others. This gives you a lot of flexibility but can lead to complexity, so inheritance can make permissions more difficult to manage rather than easier. As with all administrator tasks, the key is to plan carefully to avoid exceptions. You should also limit the use of explicit Deny permissions. If a user is a member of a group that has a Deny permission, or has been explicitly denied a permission, that user will be denied that permission no matter what other groups he is a member of.

An owner is assigned to an object when that object is created—typically an object is owned by the user that creates it, so files saved in a My Documents folder in a user profile are owned by that user. The owner of the object can always change the permissions on an object.

MORE INFO Object ownership

For more information on object ownership, see *http://technet2.microsoft.com/windowsserver2008/en/ library/cb906e8c-9c49-4cd7-ac44-e7d91d1572511033.mspx?mfr=true.*

User rights grant specific privileges and logon rights to users and security groups. You can assign specific rights to group accounts or to individual user accounts. These rights authorize users to perform specific actions, such as logging on to a system interactively or backing up files and directories.

User rights are different from permissions because user rights apply to user accounts, and permissions are attached to objects. Although you can apply user rights to individual user accounts, it is good practice to apply them to security groups rather than to individual users. You can administer user rights through the Local Security Settings MMC snap-in.

You can audit successful or failed access to objects on a per-user basis. You select which object's access to audit by using the Access Control User Interface, but first you must enable the Audit Policy by selecting Audit Object Access under Local Policies in the Local Security Settings snap-in. You can then view these security-related events in the Security log in Event Viewer.

MORE INFO Security auditing

For more information on security auditing, see *http://technet2.microsoft.com/windowsserver2008/en/ library/cb906e8c-9c49-4cd7-ac44-e7d91d1572511033.mspx?mfr=true.*

Configuring Access Permissions

By default, File Sharing and Public Folder Sharing are enabled on a Windows Server 2008 server. You can enable and disable these features in the Network And Sharing Center, which you can access through Control Panel. You can also open the Microsoft Management Console (MMC) and add the Shared Folders snap-in. If you then right-click Shares and select New Share, the Create A Shared Folder Wizard starts. This wizard lets you specify the path to a folder you want to share, the name of the share, and the shared folder access permissions.

You can specify standard shared folder permissions—users have Read permission and administrators have Full Control, for example—or you can set custom permissions. Figure 6-9 shows the Customize Permissions dialog box. The wizard also lets you configure offline settings. You can share a folder or a volume.

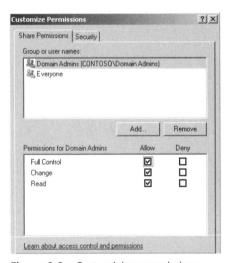

Figure 6-9 Customizing permissions

If you choose to customize permissions, you can also access a Security tab that lets you set NTFS permissions. For users who access folders on a server over a network (the vast majority of users), access permissions are a combination of shared folder and NTFS permissions.

You can also use the Provision A Shared Folder Wizard to share a folder or volume and configure access permissions. As described earlier in this lesson, you access this wizard from the Share And Storage Management console. This wizard lets you specify the path to the folder you want to share. You then have the option of configuring NTFS permissions, as shown in Figure 6-10.

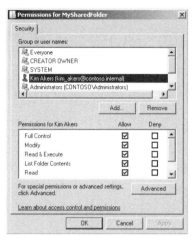

Figure 6-10   Configuring NTFS permissions

You can then select the protocol over which users can access the shared folder—SMB, NFS, or both. Note that you can specify NFS only if you have installed the Services for NFS role service. You then have the option of setting a user limit, disabling user-based enumeration, and reconfiguring offline settings. You can either choose one of three standard shared folder permission configurations or to customize these permissions, as shown in Figure 6-11. If you choose to customize shared folder permissions, the wizard presents you with a dialog box very similar to the Customize Permissions dialog box in the Create A Shared Folder Wizard shown earlier in Figure 6-9.

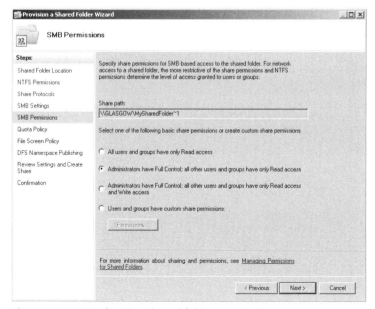

Figure 6-11   Configuring shared folder permissions

The wizard then prompts you to create a quota policy and a file screen policy, and gives you the option to publish the share to a DFS namespace. Quotas and file screen policies are discussed later in this lesson. DFS namespaces are discussed in Lesson 2. Finally, the wizard summarizes your settings, and you click Create to create the share.

You can also share a folder manually and set shared folder and NTFS permissions by right-clicking a folder or volume in Windows Explorer or My Computer and clicking Properties. If you choose to share a folder by this method, you will see a dialog box similar to that shown in Figure 6-12. The permission levels are classified in a different fashion than that used by the wizards: They are Owner, Co-Owner, Contributor, and Reader. If you click the Security tab, you get an NTFS permissions dialog box similar to that shown previously in Figure 6-10.

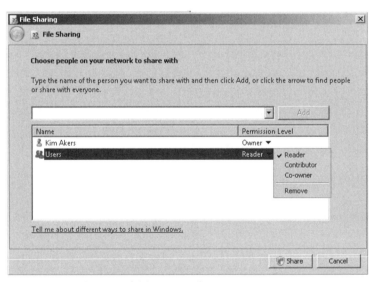

Figure 6-12 Sharing a folder manually

Combining Share and NTFS Permissions

Files, folders, and other objects are typically accessed across a network, such as when they are held on a file server. Access control entries (ACEs), however, are applied at both the share level (share permissions) and at the file system level (NTFS permissions). This means you need to remember to change permissions in two different places.

For example, if you want members of the Managers security group to be able to add, edit, and delete files in a folder called Reports, when previously they could only view them, you would change the NTFS permission for the security group to Modify. If, however, the share permission of the folder is Read and you forget to change this, group members will still only be able to view the contents of the files.

One solution to this problem is to grant everyone full access at the share level and to assign restrictive NTFS permissions. The NTFS permissions are then the effective permissions because they are the more restrictive. However, many administrators are not happy about assigning non-restrictive share permissions. The security best practice in this situation is to use (at most) the Change share permission.

To figure out what permissions a security group has on a file, you first figure out the effective NTFS permissions, remembering that any explicit permissions set at file level override the folder permissions. You then compare share and NTFS permissions; the effective permissions are the more restrictive of the two. This process becomes even more complex when you want to figure out access permissions for a user that might be a member of several security groups.

You can figure out a user's effective permissions manually. This is a tedious process, but it gets easier with practice. Currently no Windows Server 2008 tool exists to automate the process, but you should consider downloading Server Share Check from the Windows Server 2003 Resource Kit. This tool runs on Windows Server 2008 servers. You can download the Resource Kit at *http://www.microsoft.com/downloads/details .aspx?familyid=9d467a69-57ff-4ae7-96ee-b18c4790cffd&displaylang=en.*

MORE INFO **Server Share Check**

For more information on Server Share Check, see *http://searchwindowssecurity.techtarget.com/tip/ 0,289483,sid45_gci1194946,00.html.* This is not a Microsoft TechNet link and the URL might change. If you cannot access it, search the Internet for "Server Share Check."

Using FSRM to Configure Quotas and File Screen Policy

Windows Server 2008 offers enhanced quota management. You can apply quotas to folders as well as volumes, and you have a set of quota templates that you can use to create quotas quickly and easily. You can create a custom quota or derive a quota from an existing template.

Microsoft recommends deriving quotas from templates. This simplifies the management of quotas because you can automatically update all quotas that are based on a specific template by editing that template. You then have the option of updating the settings of any quotas you created by using the template. You can also exclude specified quotas from this update. For example, if you created a quota from a template and then manually changed some of its settings, you might not want to update that quota when you change the template because you could lose these settings.

You can create an auto-apply quota and assign a quota template to a parent volume or folder. Quotas based on that template are then automatically generated and applied to each of the existing subfolders and to any subfolders you create in the future.

Creating Quotas

If the FSRM File Services server role is installed, you can use FSRM to create quotas. The Create Quota dialog box is shown in Figure 6-13. Note that you will be unable to access this box if you have not installed the appropriate server role, which you will do in the practice session later in this lesson.

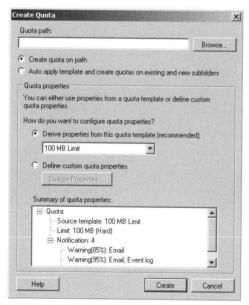

Figure 6-13   The Create Quota dialog box

You specify a path to the volume or folder for which you want to create the quota and then specify whether you want to create a quota only on that path or whether a template-based quota will be automatically generated and applied to existing and new subfolders on the path of the parent volume or folder. To specify the latter action, select Auto Apply Template And Create Quotas On Existing And New Subfolders.

Typically you would select Derive Properties From This Quota Template (Recommended) and select a template. You can, if you want, define custom quota properties, but this is not recommended. You can select templates that specify the quota size that is allocated to each user and whether the quota is hard or soft. A hard quota cannot be exceeded. A user can exceed a soft quota, but typically exceeding the quota limit generates a report in addition to sending an e-mail notification and logging the event. Soft quotas are used for monitoring. Quota templates include the following:

- **100 MB Limit**   This is a hard quota. It e-mails the user and specified administrators if the 100 percent quota limit has been reached and writes an event to the event log.

- **200 MB Limit Reports to User**   This is a hard quota. It generates a report, sends e-mails, and writes an event to the event log if the 100 percent quota limit has been reached.

- **200 MB Limit with 50 MB Extension**   Technically this is a hard quota because it performs an action when the user attempts to exceed the limit, rather than merely monitoring the exceeded limit. The action is to run a program that applies the 250 MB Extended Limit template and effectively gives the user an additional 50 MB. E-mails are sent and the event is logged when the limit is extended.

- **250 MB Extended Limit**   The 250 MB limit cannot be exceeded. E-mails are sent and the event is logged when the limit is reached.

- **Monitor 200 GB Volume Usage**   This is a soft quota that can be applied only to volumes. It is used for monitoring.

- **Monitor 50 MB Share Usage**   This is a soft quota that can be applied only to shares. It is used for monitoring.

You can also configure templates to send e-mails and write to the event log if a defined percentage of the quota is reached. Figure 6-14 shows the properties of the 200 MB Limit Reports To User template.

When you have created a quota or an auto-apply quota you can edit it. Figure 6-15 shows a Quota Properties box. You can change the Quota Template, Space Limit, and Notifications Thresholds and add a label. You can add new Notification Thresholds and specify what action should be taken if a threshold is reached. For example, you can specify whether an e-mail is sent to the user and to one or more specified administrators. You can also specify a command, generate a report, and specify whether the event is to be logged. If you edit quota settings or create a custom quota, you can use the quota to create a new template.

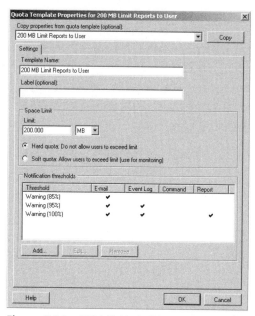

Figure 6-14   200 MB Limit Reports To User template properties

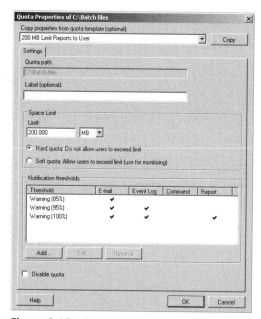

Figure 6-15   Quota properties

Creating Templates

If none of the supplied templates is suitable for your purposes, you can create a new template. You can optionally copy settings from an existing template and edit them, or you can specify new settings. Figure 6-16 shows the Create Quota Template dialog box. Many of the settings are similar to those you can configure when editing a quota.

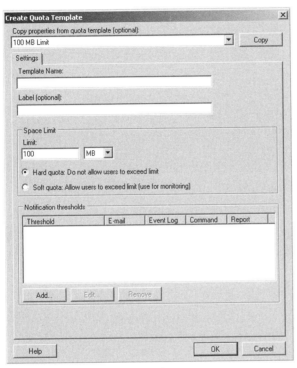

Figure 6-16 Creating a template

Managing File Screens

You can use FSRM to create and manage file screens that control the types of files that users can save, and generate notifications when users attempt to save unauthorized files. You can also define file screening templates that you can apply to new volumes or folders and use across your organization.

FSRM also enables you to create file screening exceptions that extend the flexibility of the file screening rules. You could, for example, ensure that users do not store music files in personal folders, but you could allow storage of specific types of media files, such as training files that comply with company policy. You could also create an exception that allows members of the senior management group to save any type of file they want to (provided they comply with legal restrictions).

You can also configure your screening process to notify you by e-mail when an executable file is stored on a shared folder. This notification can include information about the user who stored the file and the file's exact location.

Exam Tip File screens are not specifically included on the objectives for the 70-646 examination. You should know what they are, what they do, and that you can manage them from FSRM. You probably will not come across detailed questions about file screen configuration.

Managing Storage Reports

FSRM provides a Storage Reports Management node. This enables you to generate storage-related reports, such as reports about duplicate files, the largest files, which files are accessed most frequently, and which files are seldom accessed. It also lets you schedule periodic storage reports, which help you identify trends in disk usage, and monitor attempts to save unauthorized files.

For example, you could schedule a report to run at midnight every Sunday and provide you with information about the most recently accessed files from the previous two days. This lets you monitor weekend storage activity and plan server down time so that it has a minimum impact on users who connect from home over the weekend.

You could use the information in a report that identifies duplicate files so that you can reclaim disk space without losing data, and you could create other reports that enable you to analyze how individual users are using shared storage resources.

MORE INFO   FSRM

For more information open the Command Console (or Command Prompt window) and type **hh fsrm.chm**.

Planning the Print Services Server Role

As an experienced administrator you will almost certainly be familiar with administrating printers and print devices. Please treat most of this section as revision. What is new in Windows Server 2008 is that Print Services is a server role that you need to install on a server to create a print server. You install this role in the practice session later in this lesson. Windows Server 2008 also introduces the Print Management console.

The Print Services server role lets you manage print servers and printers. If you configure a Windows Server 2008 server as a print server, you reduce administrative and management workload by centralizing printer management tasks through the Print Management console.

By default, installing the Print Services server role installs the Print Server role service, which lets you share printers on a network and publish them to Active Directory. Optionally, you can install the Line Printer Daemon (LPD), which lets you print to printers connected to a UNIX server, and Internet Print, which lets you use a Web interface to connect to and manage printers.

NOTE Printers and print devices

A print device is a physical device that prints hard copy. A printer controls a print device. You can install several printers connected to a single print device and set different access permissions and schedules for different users. For example, if you have an expensive color print device, you might want to allow access to ordinary users outside of normal working hours, but allow access at any time to the Managers security group. You can do this by creating two printers, both connected to the print device.

Planning the Print Services server role involves analyzing current and required printing needs within an organization and configuring printer scheduling and access permissions. Do you have a department that sends very large but non-urgent jobs to a print device? In this case you need to configure a printer that sends such jobs to a print device outside of office hours.

Does everyone in your organization need to print in color? If you give them the opportunity, they are likely to do so, whether they need to or not. You cannot prevent users from habitually clicking Print several times whenever they want to print a document, or from printing out all their e-mail messages. You can, however, set up auditing to detect high printer usage and identify those users with bad printing habits. As this book states in several places, an administrator needs to be able to solve people problems as well as technical problems.

Some of your planning decisions will be practical and pragmatic. It might be a good idea to have a print device with multiple input trays for special paper types, but it is probably a bad idea to use this for general-purpose printing. A print device that stops and flashes an error message whenever a user specifies the wrong size of paper is also a bad choice for general printing needs. You should consider using a printer pool—where a single printer controls several print devices—if you need to provide high availability of print devices.

Managing Printer Entities

If the Print Services server role is installed on your server, you can manage the following entities:

- **Print queue**   A print queue is a representation of a print device. Opening a print queue displays the active print jobs and their status. If a print job at the head of the queue is not being processed, possibly because an incorrect paper size is specified, you can delete this job and allow the remainder of jobs in the queue to be processed.

- **Print spooler service**   A print server has a single print spooler service. This manages all the print jobs and print queues on that server. Typically the print spooler service starts automatically. If, however, the service has stopped for any reason, you need to restart it. A symptom of this is a print job at the head of a queue that is not being processed but cannot be deleted.

- **Printer driver**   A print queue requires a printer driver to print to a print device. You need to ensure that the print driver exists on your print server, is working correctly, and is up to date.

- **Network printer port**   A printer driver uses a network printer port to communicate with a physical device across a network. These ports may, for example, be TCP/IP printer ports, Line Printer Remote (LPR) ports, or standard COM and LPT ports.

- **Print server cluster**   Printing is typically a mission-critical operation and you might choose to cluster your print servers to ensure high availability and failover support. Chapter 11, "Clustering and High Availability," discusses cluster administration.

Publishing a Printer

If you share a printer on a network but do not publish it in Active Directory, users then need to know its network path to use it. If you do publish the printer in Active Directory, it is easier to locate. If you decide to move a printer to another print server, you do not need to change the settings on client computers—you only need to change its record in Active Directory.

If a printer is shared but not published, you can publish it by selecting the List In The Directory check box on the Sharing tab of the printer's Properties dialog box. If you add a printer on a Windows Server 2008 print server and share it, the printer is automatically published provided that the Group Policy settings Automatically Publish New Printers In Active Directory and Allow Printers To Be Published are enabled, which they are by default. A published printer needs to be shared. If you stop sharing the printer it is no longer published.

Managing Printers with the Print Management Console

The Windows Server 2008 Print Management console is installed as part of the Print Services server role. You can also install it by opening Server Manager, clicking Features in the console tree and then clicking Add Features. You then expand Remote Server Administration Tools, expand Role Administration Tools and select the Print Services Tools check box. Click Next, and then click Install. Click Close when the tool is installed.

The Print Management console is a remote server administration tool that lets you implement single-seat administration in a large organization that has a number (typically a large number) of print servers. When you have installed the Print Management console, you can open it from the Administration Tools menu or from within Server Manager. When you have installed Print Management console you need to configure it to identify the printers and print servers you want to manage. You can add printers manually, or you can scan the network to automatically identify printers. Figure 6-17 shows the Print Management console. Note that you cannot access this tool unless you have installed it as a Remote Administration Tool or have installed the Print Services server role. You install the Print Services server role in the practice session later in this lesson.

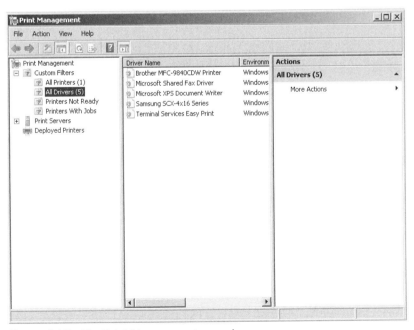

Figure 6-17   The Print Management console

You can add a print server to the Print Management console by right-clicking Print Servers and selecting Add/Remove Servers. You can add new printers to a Windows Server 2008 network by using the Add Printer Wizard that was available in previous Windows versions. The Print Management console gives you the option of running this wizard on a remote print server; previously you needed to run it locally. To start the Add Printer Wizard within the Print Management console, expand Print Servers and right-click the print server that you want to host the printer. Then click Add Printer, as shown in Figure 6-18 and follow the steps of the Add Printer Wizard. The Print Management console lets you run this wizard on a remote print server.

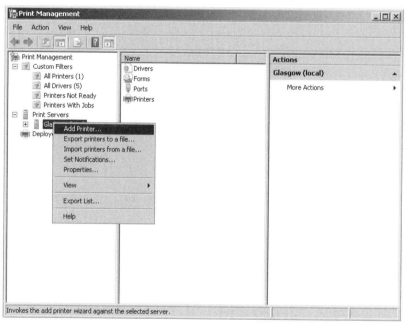

Figure 6-18   Adding a printer through the Print Management console

When you have added remote print servers to the Print Management console and configured printers on these servers, you can centrally view, manage, and administer these printers and print servers. Some of the tasks you perform from the Print Management console you previously carried out locally on the print server, such as changing printer ports, adding or modifying forms, and viewing the status of printers. Other tasks are new to the Print Management console, including creating custom printer filters that allow you and other administrators to view and manage selected printers based on their site, rights, and roles.

If you right-click Custom Filters you can access the Add New Printer Filter Wizard that steps you through this task. You can create custom printer filters that filter by manufacturer or by printer type (such as laser, color laser, and plotter). This lets you view assets by make, model, or configuration.

You can expand any of the print servers listed in the console tree and manage drivers, ports, forms, or printers. If you right-click Forms and select Manage Forms you can create and delete new forms to support different size paper or to specify a custom letterhead paper form. For any listed print server you can also change a printer port, define log settings, and enable notifications. Figure 6-19 shows the Advanced tab of the Print Server Properties dialog box that you can access from the Print Management console to configure logs and notifications.

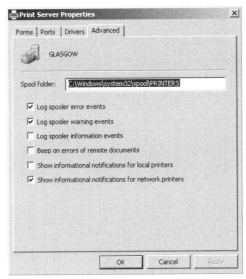

Figure 6-19   Configuring logs and notifications

Practice: Adding Role Services to the File Services Server Role and Adding the Print Services Server Role

In this practice session you add selected role services to the File Services server role and add the Print Services server role on your domain controller (DC).

NOTE   Using a DC to host other server roles

In your small test network, you log on interactively to your DC and add server roles and role services. You should be aware that in a production domain you probably would not add additional roles to a DC, nor would you log on interactively to a DC or any other important server.

▶ **Exercise 1: Add Role Services to the File Services Server Role**

In this exercise you open Server Manager and add selected role services to the File Services server role. You do not add any of the optional features associated with this server role. To complete the exercise, follow these steps:

1. Log on to the DC with the kim_akers account.

2. In the Administrative Tools menu, open Server Manager (unless it opens automatically on logon). If a UAC dialog box appears, click Continue to close it.

3. Expand Roles and click File Services. In the right-hand pane, locate the list of Role Services shown in Figure 6-20.

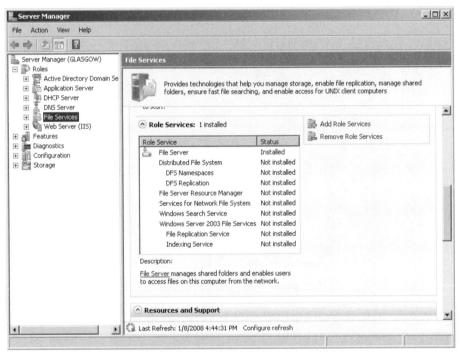

Figure 6-20 Role services that you can add

4. Click Add Role Services.

5. In the Select Role Services dialog box, select all uninstalled role services except the Windows Server 2003 File Services, as shown in Figure 6-21.

6. Click Next.

7. Call the DFS namespace **MyNameSpace** as shown in Figure 6-22. Click Next.

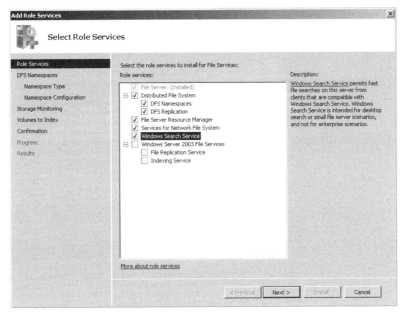

Figure 6-21 Selecting role services

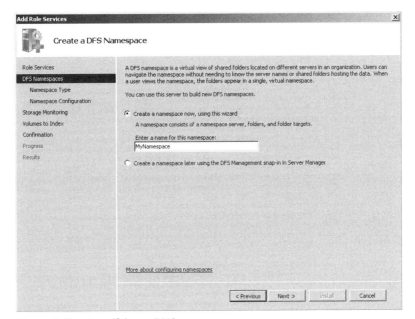

Figure 6-22 Specifying a DNS namespace

8. Specify a domain-based namespace (the default) as shown in Figure 6-23. Click Next.

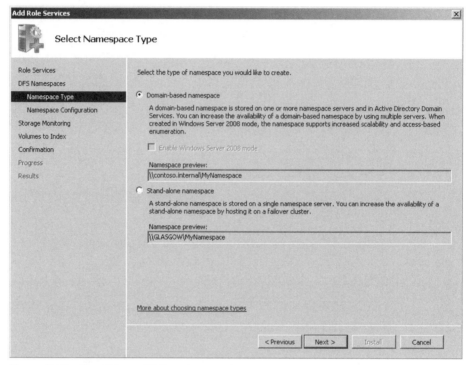

Figure 6-23 Specifying a DNS namespace type

NOTE Domain-based and stand-alone namespaces

Lesson 2 of this chapter discusses domain-based and stand-alone namespaces.

---

9. In the Configure Namespace dialog box, click Add. Click Browse in the Add Folder To Namespace dialog box.

10. In the Browse For Shared Folders, dialog box click Show Shared Folders. As shown in Figure 6-24, Public is selected by default. Click OK.

11. By default the corresponding folder in your namespace takes the same name as the shared folder you selected. Click OK to accept this default.

12. Your Configure Namespace dialog box should look similar to Figure 6-25. Click Next.

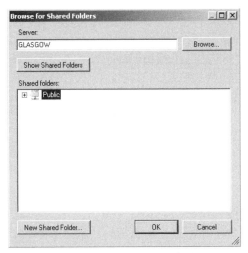

Figure 6-24   Selecting a shared folder

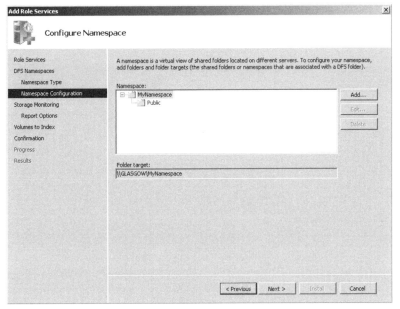

Figure 6-25   Configuring a namespace

13. In the Configure Storage Usage Monitoring page, select your C: volume, as shown in Figure 6-26. Your volume size and usage will probably differ from what is shown in the figure. Do not change the default options. Click Next.

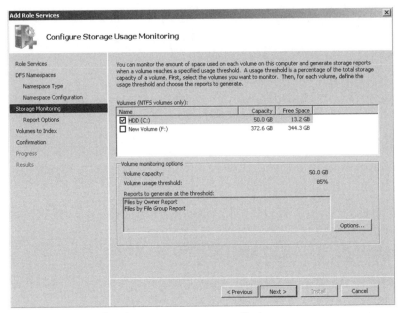

Figure 6-26   Configuring storage usage monitoring

14. Accept the defaults in the Set Report Options dialog box as shown in Figure 6-27. Click Next.

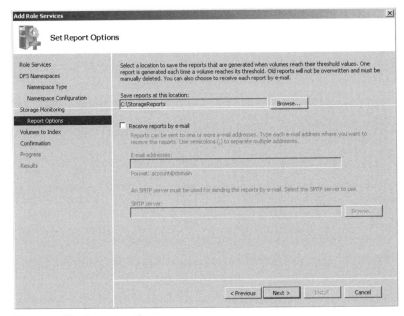

Figure 6-27   Report options

15. Choose to index a volume that does not contain your operating system. If the only volume on your server is C: do not index any volumes. Click Next.

16. Check your installation selections. If you are satisfied with them, click Install.

17. When installation completes, click Close.

▶ **Exercise 2: Install the Print Services Server Role**

In this exercise you install the Print Services server role. This lets you share (or publish) printers on a network. To complete the exercise, follow these steps:

1. If necessary, log on to the DC with the kim_akers account and open Server Manager. If a UAC dialog box appears, click Continue to close it.

2. In the console tree, click Server Manager. Locate the Roles Summary in the right-hand pane, as shown in Figure 6-28.

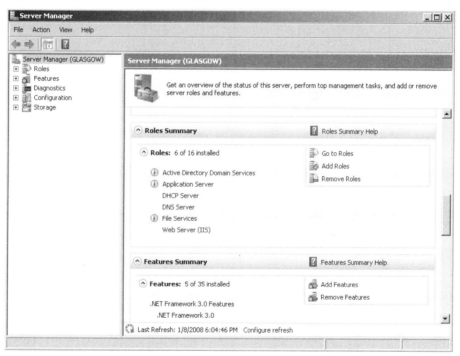

Figure 6-28   Roles summary

3. Click Add Roles. The Add Roles Wizard starts. If the Before You Begin page appears, click Next.

4. Select Print Services as shown in Figure 6-29. Click Next.

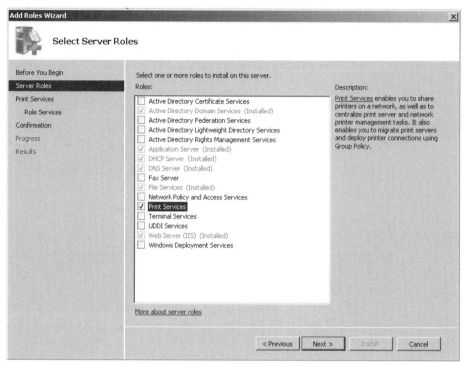

Figure 6-29   Selecting to install Print Services

5. Read the Print Services summary. If you want, you can also click the links to the Help files. Click Next.

6. On the Select Role Services page, Print Server should be selected by default. Select Internet Printing. If the Add Role Services Required For Internet Printing dialog box appears, click Add Required Role Services. Click Next on the Select Role Services page.

7. If the Web Server (IIS) page appears, read the information and then click Next.

8. The Web Service server role was installed with the Application Server server role in Chapter 4, "Application Servers and Services." If you did not complete the practice sessions in Chapter 4, you need to select the Web Server role services on the Select Role Services page. Click Next.

9. Read the information on the Confirm Installation Selections page, which should be similar to Figure 6-30. Note that you might need to reboot your server when installation is complete. Click Install.

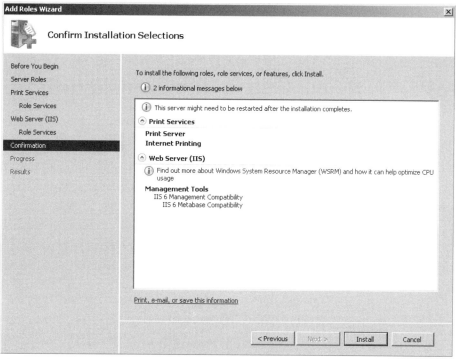

Figure 6-30   The Confirm Installation Selections page

10. Click Close when installation completes.

11. Save any unsaved files, close all open windows, and reboot your DC. It is a good idea to do this after installing a server role even if you are not prompted to do so.

Lesson Summary

- The File Server role service in the File Services server role is installed by default and allows access to the Share And Storage Management console. This console in turn provides access to the Provision Storage Wizard and the Provision A Stored Folder Wizard and lets you configure access control and manage shared folders, volumes, open sessions, and open files.

- Optionally, you can install the Distributed File System (DFS), File Server Resource Manager (FSRM), Services for Network File System (NFS), and Windows Search Service role services. DFS Management includes DFS Namespaces and DFS Replication. You can also install the Windows Server 2003 File Services server role for compatibility with earlier versions of Windows.

- The FSRM console lets you configure quotas and file screens and generate storage reports. You can set quotas on shared folders as well as volumes.

- If you install the Print Services server role, you can install and manage printers and print drivers. The Print Management console provides single-seat management of printers on remote print servers on your network.

Lesson Review

You can use the following questions to test your knowledge of the information in Lesson 1, "Managing File and Print Servers." The questions are also available on the companion CD if you prefer to review them in electronic form.

NOTE   Answers

Answers to these questions and explanations of why each answer choice is correct or incorrect are located in the "Answers" section at the end of the book.

---

1. Which of the following wizards can you access from the Share And Storage Management console? (Choose all that apply.)

   A. Provision A Shared Folder Wizard

   B. New Namespace Wizard

   C. Provision Storage Wizard

   D. Create Quota Wizard

   E. Create File Screen Wizard

2. You have not installed any role services for the File Services server role and only the default File Server role service is installed. You start the Provision A Shared Folder Wizard. All your volumes are formatted with NTFS. Which of the following tasks can you carry out by using the wizard? (Choose all that apply.)

   A. Specify a folder to share.

   B. Create a new folder to share.

   C. Specify the network sharing protocol used to access the shared resource.

   D. Change the local NTFS permissions for the folder or volume you are sharing.

   E. Publish the shared resource to a DFS namespace.

3. When you install the Print Services server role you can use the Print Management console to remotely carry out a number of jobs that previously you needed to do locally on the print server that held the printer. The console also introduces features that were not available in previous Windows versions. Which of the following tasks is new to the Print Management console?

   A. Changing printer ports

   B. Viewing the printer status

   C. Adding or modifying forms

   D. Creating custom printer filters

4. Which of the following quota templates, available by default, creates a soft quota that can be applied only to volumes?

   A. 100 MB Limit

   B. 200 MB Limit Reports To User

   C. Monitor 200 GB Volume Usage

   D. Monitor 50 MB Share Usage

Lesson 2: Provisioning Data

Lesson 1 in this chapter introduced the Share And Storage Management tool, which gives you access to the Provision Storage Wizard and the Provision A Shared Folder Wizard. These tools allow you to configure storage on the volumes accessed by your server and to set up shares. When you add the Distributed File System (DFS) role service to the File Services server role you can create a DFS Namespace and go on to configure DFSR. Provisioning data ensures that user files are available and remain available even if a server fails or a WAN link goes down. Provisioning data also ensures that users can work on important files when they are not connected to the corporate network.

In a well-designed data provisioning scheme, users should not need to know the network path to their files, or from which server they are downloading them. Even large files should typically download quickly—files should not be downloaded or saved across a WAN link when they are available from a local server. You need to configure indexing so that users can find information quickly and easily. Offline files need to be synchronized quickly and efficiently, and whenever possible without user intervention. A user should always be working with the most up-to-date information (except when a shadow copy is specified) and fast and efficient replication should ensure that where several copies of a file exist on a network they contain the same information and latency is minimized.

You have several tools that you use to configure shares and offline files, configure storage, audit file access, prevent inappropriate access, prevent users from using excessive disk resource, and implement disaster recovery. However, the main tool for provisioning storage and implementing a shared folder structure is DFS Management, specifically DFS Namespaces. The main tool for implementing shared folder replication in a Windows Server 2008 network is DFS Replication.

After this lesson, you will be able to:

- Configure a DFS Namespace.
- Configure DFSR.
- Configure files for offline usage.
- Configure indexing.

Estimated lesson time: 50 minutes

Real World

Ian McLean

Well-designed data provisioning, like a good administrator, should mostly be invisible.

Users want to be able to access, update, save, and print their work efficiently and easily. They are not interested in which of the strange-looking pieces of equipment in what is normally called the communication room stores their files, or even if any of them do. Servers don't usually resemble what an ordinary user would understand by the term *computer*, and most users wouldn't know a server from a firewall or a switch.

What users want—and this is hardly unreasonable—is to get on with their jobs. They want to access their files in the same way each day, and they want the files to be there. They don't want to know that a server has gone down or there's been a network glitch. They want their files. If a user works at home in the evening, she does not want to see the results of her work disappear when she connects to the corporate network. If a file gets lost or corrupted, a user might accept the loss of a few hours of work, but not the loss of several months of effort. A well-designed share structure and data provisioning system will provide this stability and reliability, with replication, indexing, synchronization, and file-path switching all going on in the background, invisible to the user.

Unfortunately, not all users are susceptible to reason. I once had a user bring me her laptop first thing in the morning. Apparently she had dropped it and a truck had run over it—a very heavy truck by the look of it.

"I had months of work on it," she moaned.

I explained that if she sat at one of the spare desktop computers and logged on with her name and password, her files would still all be there. She was skeptical at first, then relieved, then annoyed.

"I spent hours last night updating that spreadsheet," she complained, "but I don't see any of the changes." I explained, as simply as I could, that the changes had been made on the now-defunct laptop and not on the file on the corporate network, and were now unfortunately lost.

"Well, find them," she said.

Using DFS Namespace to Plan and Implement a Shared Folder Structure and Enhance Data Availability

When you add the DFS Management role service to the Windows Server 2008 File Services Server role, the DFS Management console is available from the Administrative Tools menu or from within Server Manager. This console provides the DFS Namespaces and DFS Replication tools as shown in Figure 6-31

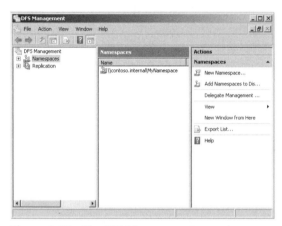

Figure 6-31   The DFS Management console

DFS Namespaces lets you group shared folders that are located on different servers into one or more logically structured namespaces. Each namespace appears to users as a single shared folder with a series of subfolders.

This structure increases availability. You can use the efficient, multiple-master replication engine provided by DFSR to replicate a DFS Namespace within a site and across WAN links. A user connecting to files within the shared folder structures contained in the DFS Namespace will automatically connect to shared folders in the same AD DS site (when available) rather than across a WAN. You can have several DFS Namespace servers in a site and spread over several sites, so if one server goes down, a user can still access files within the shared folder structure.

Because DFSR is multimaster, a change to a file in the DFS Namespace on any DFS Namespace server is quickly and efficiently replicated to all other DFS Namespace servers that hold that namespace. Note that DFSR replaces the File Replication Service (FRS) as the replication engine for DFS Namespaces, as well as for replicating the AD DS SYSVOL folder in domains that use the Windows Server 2008 domain functional level. You can install FRS Replication as part of the Windows Server 2003 File Services role service, but you should use it only if you need to synchronize with servers that use FRS with the Windows Server 2003 or Windows 2000 Server implementations of DFS.

Creating a DFS Namespace

You can (optionally) create a namespace when you install the DFS Management role service. You can add additional namespaces by right-clicking DFS Namespaces in the DFS Management console and selecting New Namespace. You can create namespaces on a Windows Server 2008 member server or DC. However, you cannot create more than one namespace on a Windows Server 2008 Standard server. You can create multiple namespaces on Windows Server 2008 Enterprise and Datacenter.

A namespace is a virtual view of shared folders in an organization and it has a path similar to a Universal Naming Convention (UNC) path to a shared folder. You can create two types of namespaces. A *domain namespace* uses a domain as its namespace root, such as *Contoso.internal\MyNameSpace*. A *stand-alone namespace* uses a namespace server as its namespace root, such as *Glasgow\MyNameSpace*. A domain-based namespace can be hosted on multiple namespace servers to increase its availability and its metadata is stored in AD DS.

A namespace contains folders, which define the structure and hierarchy to the namespace. Folders in a namespace provide shortcuts to folder targets, which store data and content. For example, in the namespace you created in the practice session in Lesson 1, the folder Public points to the folder target *Glasgow\Public*. If you had also associated the namespace folder Public with a folder called Public on the server Brisbane, a user who browsed to *Contoso.internal\MyNameSpace\Public* would be directed to either *Glasgow\Public* or *Brisbane\Public*. Figure 6-32 shows the folder and folder target for *Contoso.internal\MyNameSpace*.

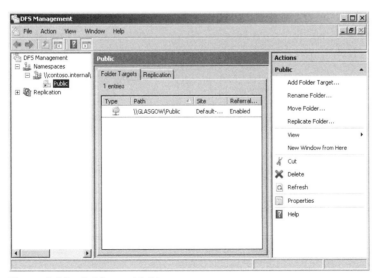

Figure 6-32   Folder and folder target

If the Glasgow and Brisbane servers were in different sites, a user in the same site as the Brisbane server would be automatically directed to the *Brisbane**Public* folder target. If that folder target was unavailable (for example, if the Brisbane server was offline) the user would be redirected to the *Glasgow**Public* target folder. Multimaster DFSR ensures that the same versions of files are available on the two target folders.

MORE INFO **Client failback**

If a server is offline and a client is redirected to a folder target on another server, possibly in another site, client failback ensures that when the preferred server becomes available again, referrals should be made to that server. Some client operating systems support client failback; others do not. For more information, search for "Review DFS Namespaces Client Requirements" in the Windows Server 2008 Help files.

You can add folders to a namespace and add folder targets to folders in a namespace. Folders can contain folder targets or other DFS folders, but not both at the same level in the folder hierarchy. You can use the DFS Namespaces tool to configure a namespace so that a folder is hosted by multiple servers. This increases data availability and distributes the client load across servers. You can use the DFS Replication tool to ensure that each target folder contains up-to-date data.

Exam Tip   DFS Namespaces distributes a namespace across several servers. DFSR ensures that data in the relevant target folders is consistent and up to date. You cannot use DFSR to distribute a namespace.

Stand-Alone Namespaces

Stand-alone namespaces can be created on a single server that contains an NTFS volume to host the namespace. Although the namespace is not domain-based, the server still needs to be a member server or a DC. The advantage of a stand-alone namespace is that it can be hosted by a failover cluster to increase its availability. Provided that it is created on a Windows Server 2008 server, a stand-alone namespace can support access-based enumeration, which is discussed later in this lesson.

You would choose a stand-alone namespace if your organization does not use AD DS, if you needed to create a single namespace with more than 5,000 DFS folders but your organization did not support Windows Server 2008 domain functional mode, or if you wanted to use a failover cluster to increase availability.

Domain-Based Namespaces

You can create domain-based namespaces on one or more member servers or DCs in the same domain. Metadata for a domain-based namespaces is stored by AD DS. Each server must contain an NTFS volume to host the namespace. Multiple namespace servers increase the availability of the namespace and ensure failover protection. A domain-based namespace cannot be a clustered resource in a failover cluster. However, you can locate the namespace on a server that is also a node in a failover cluster provided that you configure the namespace to use only local resources on that server. A domain-based namespace in Windows Server 2008 mode supports access-based enumeration. Windows Server 2008 mode is discussed later in this lesson.

You choose a domain-based namespace if you want to use multiple namespace servers to ensure the availability of the namespace, or if you want to make the name of the namespace server invisible to users. When users do not need to know the UNC path to a namespace folder it is easier to replace the namespace server or migrate the namespace to another server.

If, for example, a stand-alone namespace called *Glasgow**Books* needed to be transferred to a server called Brisbane, it would become *Brisbane**Books*. However, if it were a domain-based namespace (assuming Brisbane and Glasgow are both in the Contoso.internal domain), it would be *Contoso.internal**Books* no matter which server hosted it, and it coud be transferred from one server to the other without this transfer being apparent to the user, who would continue to use *Contoso.internal**Books* to access it.

Namespace Modes

If you choose a domain-based namespace, you can use the Windows 2000 Server mode or the Windows Server 2008 mode. The Windows Server 2008 mode includes support for access-based enumeration and provides increased scalability (more than 5,000 DFS folders). Whenever possible, Microsoft recommends that you choose the Windows Server 2008 mode. To use this mode the domain needs to be at the Windows Server 2008 domain functional level and all namespace servers must be running Windows Server 2008. If you want to use multiple namespaces, your servers must also be running Enterprise or Datacenter Editions.

If your environment does not support domain-based namespaces in Windows Server 2008 mode, you need to use Windows 2000 Server mode for the namespace. The following servers can host multiple namespaces in Windows 2000 Server mode:

- Windows Server 2008 Enterprise
- Windows Server 2008 Datacenter
- Windows Server 2003 R2, Enterprise Edition
- Windows Server 2003 R2, Datacenter Edition

- Windows Server 2003, Enterprise Edition
- Windows Server 2003, Datacenter Edition

The following servers can host only a single namespace, although you can apply a hotfix that lets you create multiple domain-based namespaces on a server running Windows Server 2003, Standard Edition (see *http://support.microsoft.com/default.aspx?scid=kb; en-us;903651*):

- Windows Server 2008 Standard
- Windows Server 2003 R2, Standard Edition
- Windows Server 2003, Web Edition
- Windows Server 2003, Standard Edition
- Any version of Windows 2000 Server

Table 6-1 summarizes namespace characteristics and their dependencies on namespace type and mode.

Table 6-1 Namespace Characteristics

Characteristic	Stand-Alone Namespace	Domain-Based Namespace Windows 2000 Server Mode	Domain-Based Namespace Windows Server 2008 Mode
Namespace path	*ServerName* *RootName*	*NetBIOS DomainName*\ *RootName*	*NetBIOSDomainName*\ *RootName*
Metadata storage	In the registry and in a memory cache on the server	In AD DS and in a memory cache on each server	In AD DS and in a memory cache on each server
Scalability	More than 5,000 folders with targets	The size of the namespace object in AD DS should be less than 5 MB (approximately 5,000 folders with targets)	More than 5,000 folders with targets

Table 6-1 Namespace Characteristics

Characteristic	Stand-Alone Namespace	Domain-Based Namespace Windows 2000 Server Mode	Domain-Based Namespace Windows Server 2008 Mode
Minimum AD DS domain functional level	AD DS not required	Windows 2000 mixed	Windows Server 2008
Minimum supported namespace servers	Windows 2000 Server	Windows 2000 Server	Windows Server 2008
DFSR supported	Yes (if joined to AD DS domain)	Yes	Yes
Availability	Failover cluster	Multiple servers (in same domain)	Multiple servers (in same domain)
Support for access-based enumeration	Yes (requires Windows Server 2008 server)	No	Yes

Tuning DFS Namespaces

You can tune and optimize how DFS Namespaces handles referrals and polls AD DS for updated namespace data. For example, if you know that a server is undergoing maintenance, you can disable referrals to folder targets on that server by clicking the DFS folder that refers to that target in the DFS Management console tree, clicking the folder target on the Folder Targets tab, and selecting Disable Folder Target in the Actions pane.

You can search for folders or folder targets by selecting a namespace, clicking the Search tab, specifying a search string in the text box, and then clicking Search. Figure 6-33 shows search results.

You can right-click a namespace in DFS Management and select Properties. This enables you to determine the size of the namespace on the General tab. This tab lets you determine the namespace mode, but you cannot change it in this dialog box.

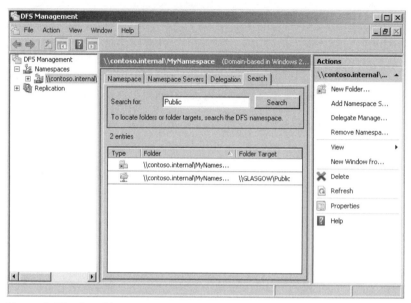

Figure 6-33   Searching a namespace

The Referrals tab lets you set how long a client caches referrals. You can also set the ordering method, which determines the order in which a client attempts to access folder targets outside its site. You can specify Random Order, Lowest Cost, or Exclude Targets Outside Of The Clients Site.

If a client accesses a non-preferred folder target because the preferred target is disabled, you can specify whether referral will failback to the preferred folder target when it becomes available (provided that the client operating system supports failback). You do this by selecting or clearing the Clients Fail Back To Preferred Targets check box. You can set this in the Namespace Properties dialog box for all folders in the namespace or in the Properties dialog box of an individual folder.

On the Advanced tab of the Namespace Properties dialog box, you can optimize namespace polling for domain-based namespaces. Namespace servers periodically poll AD DS to obtain the most current namespace data and maintain a consistent domain-based namespace. You should select Optimize For Consistency if 16 or fewer namespace servers are hosting the namespace. If there are more than 16 servers, you should choose Optimize For Scalability, which reduces the load on the Primary Domain Controller (PDC) Emulator. However, you should be aware that this setting increases latency—the time it takes for changes to the namespace to replicate to all namespace servers—and therefore increases the likelihood of users having an inconsistent view of the namespace.

Setting Target Priority to Override Referral Ordering

A referral is an ordered list of targets that a client receives from a DC or namespace server when a user accesses a namespace root or a folder that has folder targets in the namespace. Each folder target in a referral is ordered according to the method defined for the namespace root or folder—for example, Random Order or Lowest Cost. You can refine how targets are ordered by setting a priority on individual targets. For example, you can specify that the target is first among all targets, last among all targets, or first (or last) among all targets of equal cost.

To set target priority on a root target for a domain-based namespace, you expand the namespace in the DFS Management console, click the relevant folder, right-click the folder target, and click Properties. On the Advanced tab, shown in Figure 6-34, you can select the Override Referral Ordering check box and specify one of the following options:

- **First Among All Targets**   Users are always referred to this target if it is available.

- **Last Among All Targets**   Users are never referred to this target unless all other targets are unavailable.

- **First Among Targets Of Equal Cost**   Users are referred to this target before other targets of equal cost (typically in the same site).

- **Last Among Targets Of Equal Cost**   Users are never referred to this target if other targets of equal cost are available (typically in the same site).

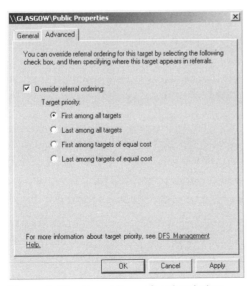

Figure 6-34   Overriding referral ordering

NOTE **Administering namespaces**

You can administer namespaces by using DFS Management, the *dfsutil* command-line utility, or scripts that call Windows Management Instrumentation (WMI) procedures.

Access-Based Enumeration

Access-based enumeration is a new feature in Windows Server 2008 DFS that allows users to see only files and folders on a file server that they have permission to access. This feature is not enabled by default for namespaces. However, it is enabled by default on newly created shared folders in Windows Server 2008. It is only supported in a DFS namespace when the namespace is a stand-alone namespace hosted on a computer running Windows Server 2008 or a domain-based namespace in Windows Server 2008 mode. To enable access-based enumeration in a namespace, you enter a command-line command with the following syntax:

```
dfsutil property abde enable \\<namespace_root>
```

Windows Server 2008 enhances the features of the *dfsutil* utility and introduces the *dfsdiag* utility. For more information open the Command Console (or Command Prompt window) and type **dfsutil /?** and **dfsdiag /?**.

Configuring a DFSR Structure

DFSR provides a multimaster replication engine that replicates data between multiple servers over LAN and WAN network connections. It replaces the FRS as the replication engine for DFS Namespaces, as well as for replicating the AD DS SYSVOL folder in domains that use the Windows Server 2008 domain functional level. DFSR uses the remote differential compression (RDC) compression algorithm that detects changes to the data in a file and enables DFSR to replicate only the changed file blocks instead of the entire file.

If you want to use DFSR, you need to create replication groups and add replicated folders to these groups. A replication group is a set of servers known as members. The group participates in the replication of one or more replicated folders, which are synchronized on each member. The connections between the members form the replication topology.

When you create multiple replicated folders in a single replication group, the process of deploying replicated folders is simplified because the topology, schedule, and bandwidth throttling for the replication group are applied to each replicated folder. Because each replicated folder has unique settings, you can filter out different files and subfolders for each replicated folder.

If you want to deploy additional replicated folders, you can use the New Replication Group Wizard from the DFS Management console or the *dfsradmin* command-line utility to define the local path and permissions for the new replicated folder. You specify the servers (two or more) that are included in the replication group and the topology, which can be hub or spoke, mesh, or no topology. Figure 6-35 shows the Topology Selection page of the New Replication Group Wizard.

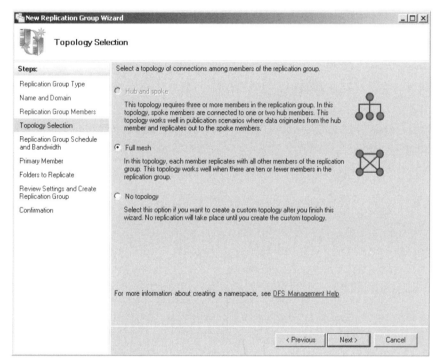

Figure 6-35   Selecting a replication topology

The replicated folders stored on each member can be located on different volumes and the replicated folders do not need to be shared folders or part of a namespace. However, you can use the DFS Management console to share replicated folders and (optionally) publish them in an existing namespace.

You can use the New Replication Group Wizard to set up a replication group for data collection (not only for DFS namespace replication). This sets up a two-way replication between two servers, such as a branch and hub server. This enables administrators at the hub office to back up data on the branch server from the hub server and removes the necessity of performing backups at branch offices where the required expertise might not be available. If you use DFSR in this manner, ensure that you set up permissions so that replication is from hub to branch (this is typically what is required) and not the other way.

Deploying DFSR

Deploying DFSR requires that you perform the following tasks (at a minimum):

- Review requirements for DFSR.
- Create a replication group.
- Add a replicated folder to a replication group.
- Add a member to a replication group.
- Create a connection.
- Delegate the ability to perform DFSR tasks.

Before you can deploy DFSR, you need to ensure that the AD DS schema has been extended to include the required schema additions. You can use the *adprep* command-line utility to include schema additions. You need to verify that all members of the replication group are running Windows Server 2008 or Windows Server 2003 R2. You need to install the DFSR role service on all servers that will act as members of a replication group.

Not all virus protection software is compatible with DFSR. Before deploying DFSR, you need to contact your antivirus software vendor. You need to ensure that the folders you want to replicate are held on NTFS volumes. If folders you want to replicate are on failover clusters, you need to locate them on a specific node. The DFSR service does not coordinate with cluster components, and the service will not fail over to another node.

Servers in your replication group must be located in the same forest. You cannot enable DFSR across servers in different forests. If you need to replicate data across forests, you should investigate other methods, such as the Robust File Copy (*robocopy*) utility that is currently available in the Windows Server 2003 Resource Kit (see *http:// www.microsoft.com/downloads/details.aspx?familyid=9d467a69-57ff-4ae7-96ee-b18c4790cffd&displaylang=en*).

You can use the New Replication Group Wizard in the DFS Management console to create a replication group and the New Member Wizard adds a member. The New Replicated Folders Wizard in the same tool adds a replicated folder to a replication group. Note that when you add a new replicated folder it is not replicated immediately. DFSR settings must first be replicated to all DCs, and each member in the replication group needs to poll its closest DC to obtain the new settings. The amount of time this takes depends on AD DS replication latency and the long polling interval (typically 60 minutes) on each member.

To create a connection, right-click the replication group in which you want to create a new connection and then click New Connection. You then specify the sending and receiving members and specify the schedule to use for the connection. At this point, replication is one-way and you need to select Create A Second Connection In The Opposite Direction to implement two-way replication.

CAUTION One-way replication

Although it is possible to create a one-way replication connection, doing so can cause (for example) health-check topology errors, staging issues, and issues with the DFSR database.

You can delegate the ability to perform DFSR tasks. For example, you can right-click the Replication node in the DFS Management console and then click Delegate Management Permissions. This lets you delegate the tasks of creating a replication group, administering a replication group, or enabling DFSR on a folder that has folder targets. To add a server to a replication group, a user must be a local administrator on the server or a member of the Domain Admins security group.

Initial Replication

When you set up replication, you choose a primary member. Typically you would choose the member that has the most up-to-date files because the primary member's content is considered authoritative. During initial replication, the primary member's files will always win the conflict resolution that occurs when the receiving members have files that are older or newer than the associated files on the primary member.

Initial replication always occurs between the primary member and its receiving replication partners. After a partner has received all files from the primary member, it will in turn replicate files to its receiving partners. Thus replication for a new replicated folder starts from the primary member and then propagates to the other members of the replication group.

If a file on a replication partner is identical to a file on the primary member, the file is not replicated. If the version of a file on the receiving member is different from the primary member's version, the receiving member's version is moved to the Conflict And Deleted folder and RDC is used to download only the changed blocks. To determine whether files on the primary member and a receiving member are identical, DFSR compares the files by using a hash algorithm. If the files are identical, only minimal metadata is transferred.

When all existing files in a replicated folder are added to the DFSR database, the primary member designation is removed. The member that was the primary member is then treated like any other member. Any member that has completed initial replication is considered authoritative over members that have not completed initial replication.

Managing DFSR

You can manage DFSR by using DFS Management, the *dfsradmin* and *dfsrdiag* command-line utilities, or by using scripts that call WMI classes. Managing DFSR requires that you perform the following tasks (at a minimum):

- Edit replication schedules or manually force replication.
- Enable or disable replication.
- Enable or disable replication on a specific member of a replication group.
- Change the size of staging folders or Conflict And Deleted folders.
- Specify the file types to be replicated.
- Share a replicated folder on a network or add the folder to a DFS namespace.
- Specify and if necessary change the topology of a replication group.

To edit the replication schedule for a replication group or to force replication with a specific member of a replication group, right-click the replication group with the schedule that you want to edit and then click Edit Replication Group Schedule. To force replication immediately, select the appropriate replication group, click the Connections tab, and right-click the member you want to use to replicate. Then click Replicate Now.

To enable or disable replication for a specific connection, click the replication group that contains the connection you want to edit, click the Connections tab in the Details pane, right-click the connection, and click Enable or Disable as appropriate.

You can enable or disable replication with specific members of a replication group in the DFS Management console. However, after you have enabled a disabled member the member must complete an initial replication of the replicated folder. Initial replication will cause about 1 KB of data to be transferred for each file or folder in the replicated folder and any updated or new files present on the member will be moved to the *DfsrPrivate\PreExisting* folder on the member and be replaced with authoritative files from another member.

If all members are disabled for a replicated folder, the first member that you enable is automatically the primary member. If the discretionary access control list (DACL) on the local path for this member contains any inherited ACEs, they are converted to explicit ACEs with the same permissions so that all members will have the same DACL on the replicated folder root.

To enable or disable replicating a replicated folder to a specific member, click the replication group that contains the membership you want to enable or disable and select the replicated folder on the specific member. Right-click the replicated folder and click Enable or Disable as appropriate. Membership changes are not applied immediately. They must be replicated to all DCs and the member must poll its closest DC to obtain the changes. The amount of time this takes depends on AD DS replication latency and the short polling interval (typically 5 minutes) on the member.

DFSR uses staging folders for each replicated folder. These act as caches for new and changed files that are ready to be replicated from sending members to receiving members. These files are stored in the DfsrPrivate\Staging folder in the local path of the replicated folder. When a file is modified on two or more members before the changes can be replicated, the most recently updated file is chosen for replication and the remaining file or files are copied to the Conflict And Deleted folder (*DfsrPrivate\ConflictandDeleted*). The Conflict And Deleted folder also stores files that are deleted from replicated folders.

By default, the quota size of each staging folder is 4,096 MB, and the quota size of each Conflict And Deleted folder is 660 MB. The size of each folder on a member is cumulative. If multiple replicated folders exist on a member, DFSR creates multiple staging and Conflict And Deleted folders, each with its own quota.

You can change the quota size of staging folders or Conflict And Deleted folders on a per-replicated-folder, per-member basis. To do this in the DFS Management console, click the replication group that contains the replicated folder with the quotas that you want to edit. On the Memberships tab in the details pane, right-click the replicated folder on the member with the quota that you want to edit, and then click Properties. On the Advanced tab, edit the quotas as required.

NOTE **The staging quota for DFSR**

Unlike the staging quota for FRS, the staging quota for DFSR is not a hard limit, and can grow larger than its configured size. When the quota is reached, DFSR deletes old files from the staging folder to reduce the disk usage. The staging folder does not reserve hard disk space, and it only consumes as much disk space as is currently needed.

You can configure file and subfolder filters that specify file types and folders to be replicated or, to be accurate, what file types and which folders you do not want to replicate. Both types of filter are specified on a per-replicated-folder basis. You can exclude subfolders by specifying their names or by using the wildcard character (*). You can exclude files by specifying their names or by using the wildcard character to specify filenames and extensions.

By default, no subfolders are excluded from replication and the following files are excluded:

■ Filenames starting with a tilde (~) character

■ Files with .bak or .tmp extensions

Regardless of how you specify your filters, the following types of files are always excluded from replication:

■ NTFS volume mount points

■ Files that are encrypted by using the encrypting file system (EFS)

■ Any reparse points except those associated with DFS Namespaces

■ Files on which the temporary attribute has been set

To edit the replication filters for a replicated folder, click the replication group that contains the replicated folder with the filters that you want to edit. In the Details pane, on the Replicated Folders tab, right-click a replicated folder, and then click Properties. On the General tab, edit the existing filters or add new filters. Note that you cannot create file or subfolder filters by specifying a full path, such as C:\Replicatedfolder\Temp or C:\Replicatedfolder\file.dat. Also, you cannot use a comma in a filter because commas are used as delimiters.

When a member detects a new filter it scans its database and removes the file records of files that match the filter. Because the files are no longer listed in the database, future changes to the files are ignored. When a member detects that a filter has been removed it scans the file system, adds records for all files that match the removed filter, and replicates the files.

You can enable file sharing on a replicated folder and specify whether to add (publish) the folder to a DFS namespace. In the DFS Management console, click the replication group that contains the replicated folder you want to share. In the Details pane, on the Replicated Folders tab, right-click the replicated folder that you want to share, and then click Share And Publish In Namespace. In the Share And Publish Replicated

Folder Wizard, click Share The Replicated Folder and follow the steps in the Share And Publish Replicated Folder Wizard, specifying whether to publish the folder when you are prompted for that setting. If you do not have an existing namespace, you can create one on the Namespace Path page in the wizard. To do so, click Browse on the Namespace Path page and then click New Namespace.

Specifying the Replication Topology

The replication topology defines the logical connections that DFSR uses to replicate files among servers. When choosing or changing a topology, remember that that two one-way connections are created between the members you choose, thus allowing data to flow in both directions. To create or change a replication topology in the DFS Management console, right-click the replication group for which you want to define a new topology and then click New Topology. The New Topology Wizard lets you choose one of the following options:

- **Hub And Spoke** This topology requires three or more members. For each spoke member, you should choose a required hub member and an optional second hub member for redundancy. This optional hub ensures that a spoke member can still replicate if one of the hub members is unavailable. If you specify more than one hub member, the hub members will have a full-mesh topology between them.

- **Full Mesh** In this topology, every member replicates with all the other members of the replication group. This topology works well when 10 or fewer members are in the replication group.

New Functionality Provided by DFSR

Provided that all members of the replication group are running the new operating system, Windows Server 2008 DFSR provides the following enhancements:

- **Content freshness** This prevents a server that was offline for a long time from overwriting fresh data when it comes back online with out-of-date data.

- **Improvements for handling unexpected shutdowns** Windows Server 2008 DFSR provides quicker recovery from unexpected shutdowns, including unexpected DFSR shutdown caused by insufficient resources, computer crashes, or disk problems. In such situations, Windows Server 2008 (unlike Windows Server 2003 R2) usually does not need to rebuild the database and thus recovers more quickly.

- **Performance improvements**   Replication is faster for both for small and large files, initial synchronization completes sooner, and network bandwidth utilization is improved both on LANs and high-latency networks such as WANs.

- **Technical enhancements**   Windows Server 2008 uses Remote Procedure Call (RPC) Async Pipes when replicating with other servers running Windows Server 2008. It makes use of asynchronous, unbuffered, low-priority I/Os, thereby reducing the load on the system as a result of replication.

- **Concurrent file downloads**   Windows Server 2008 DFSR permits 16 concurrent file downloads. Windows Server 2003 R2 permitted only four.

- **Propagation report**   The Windows Server 2008 DFS Management console provides access to a new type of diagnostic report called a propagation report, which displays the replication progress for the test file created during a propagation test.

- **Immediate replication**   You can force replication to occur immediately, temporarily ignoring the replication schedule. This procedure was described earlier in this lesson.

- **Support for Read-Only Domain Controllers (RODCs)**   Windows Server 2008 DFSR supports RODCs, which were discussed in Chapter 3, "Active Directory and Group Policy." However, DFSR does not support read-only replication groups and only supports RODCs in leaf nodes.

- **SYSVOL replication**   DFSR replaces FRS as the replication engine for replicating the AD DS SYSVOL folder in domains that use the Windows Server 2008 domain functional level.

MORE INFO   DFS management

For more information, open the Command console (Command Prompt window) and type **hh dfs2.chm**.

Configuring Offline Data Access

You can use the Share And Storage Management console to configure how (and whether) files and programs in a shared folder or volume on your Windows Server 2008 server are made available offline. Users, in turn, need to set the Offline Files feature on their client computers.

Typically, when users are online they will download and edit data files (such as Microsoft Office Word documents or Microsoft Office Excel spreadsheets) stored on a server, and will save their updated files to the server. If an executable file (for example a .exe or .dll file) has been downloaded to the client, the local file will usually run on the client when required.

User files marked for offline access can be configured so that they are downloaded to the client whenever the user logs off or initiates an orderly shutdown. The user can then work with these files offline. When the user logs on to the network, any amended files on the client are uploaded to the server. This process is known as *synchronization*, and only files that have been opened since the last synchronization or new files that have been created are synchronized.

You can configure server shares that contain high-security files (such as encrypted files) so that these files are not synchronized. The Offline Files feature on client computers stores offline files in a reserved portion of the client's disk known as the local cache.

Configuring Offline Settings

In the Share And Storage Management console you can access a shared folder on the Shares tab and click Properties. You then click Advanced on the Sharing tab of the share's Properties dialog box. This enables you to access the settings on the Caching tab of the Advanced dialog box as shown in Figure 6-36.

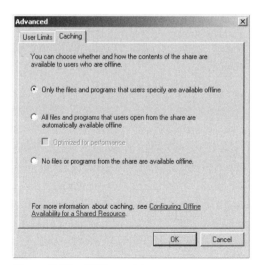

Figure 6-36 Offline settings

You can choose an offline availability option for the shared resource. If you want, you can configure each shared resource on your server with the offline setting you choose. The following settings are available:

- **Only The Files And Programs That Users Specify Are Available Offline**   This is the default option. With this option, no user or program files are available offline unless the user specifies that they should be. The user chooses the files that are synchronized and available offline. You would use this option if your users are relatively sophisticated and can sensibly choose the files they want to work with.

- **All Files And Programs That Users Open From The Share Are Automatically Available Offline**   Whenever a user accesses the shared folder or volume and opens a user or program file, that file or program is automatically made available offline to that user. Files and programs that are not opened are not available offline. This has the advantage that users do not need to choose the files that are synchronized. Any file a user opens during working hours is available on that user's laptop at home. The setting has the disadvantage that if the user opens a lot of files, or some very large files (or both) it might take quite a long time for him to log off in the evening because the files need to be transferred from the client to the server. The Optimized For Performance option (discussed later in this section) can alleviate (but not remove) this problem.

- **No Files Or Programs From The Share Are Available Offline**   This option blocks the Offline Files feature on the client from making copies of the files and programs on the shared resource. Typically you would select this option to prevent secure shared resources from being stored offline on non-secure computers. If company policy prevents you from selecting this option, ensure that you set share and NTFS to configure the appropriate level of access control.

Optimizing for Performance

If you select All Files And Programs That Users Open From The Share Are Automatically Available Offline, you can optionally select the Optimized For Performance check box. If you do so, executable files that a client runs from the shared resource are automatically cached on that client. The next time the client computer needs to run one of those executable files, it will access its local cache instead of the shared resource on the server. You should configure this setting on file servers that host applications, because this reduces network traffic and improves server scalability. Note, however, that the Optimized For Performance server setting does not alter the caching behavior of Windows Vista clients.

Exam Tip The Offline Files feature must be enabled on the client for files and programs to be automatically cached, no matter which settings you configure on Windows Server 2008 servers.

Configuring Indexing in the Windows Search Service

Windows Server 2008 provides the Windows Search Service as a role service in the File Services server role . The service provides an indexing solution that creates an index of the most common file and non-file data types on the server. When you index files and data types, this enables you to perform fast file searches on your server from clients running Windows Vista or running Windows XP or Windows Server 2003 with Windows Desktop Search installed.

You can instead install the legacy Indexing service that was used in previous versions of Windows as part of the Windows Server 2003 role service. However, you should do this only if you have a customized or non-Microsoft application that requires you to run this service on your server. You cannot install the Windows Search Service and the Indexing Service on the same computer, and Microsoft recommends that you upgrade any applications that require the Indexing service to be compatible with Windows Search Service, which offers several enhancements, especially in the areas of extensibility, usability, and performance.

Selecting Volumes and Folders to Index

You are given the option to select volumes to index when you add the Windows Search Service role service. You should always index shared resources only. The Windows Search Service enables you to search for files on your server from a client computer and there is little point in indexing folders that cannot be accessed over the network.

Microsoft recommends that you select a volume that is used exclusively for hosting shared folders. You are not required to specify a volume to install the role service and you can add individual shared folders after the service is installed. When you install Windows Search Service, default indexing locations are selected, even if you do not select a volume to index. You can review the default locations by opening Indexing Options in Control Panel as shown in Figure 6-37. In this figure the F: volume was specified when the role service was installed. The User and Start Menu folders are default locations.

Figure 6-37   The Indexing Options dialog box

Configuring Indexing

When you click Modify in the Indexing Options dialog box shown previously in Figure 6-37, click Show All Locations in the Indexed Locations dialog box, and clear the UAC dialog box to populate the Indexed Locations dialog box, you obtain a list of indexed locations that you can edit, as shown in Figure 6-38. Figure 6-39 shows the shared folder C:\Books being added to the list of locations.

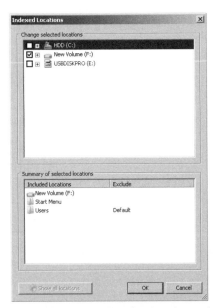

Figure 6-38   Populated Indexed Locations dialog box

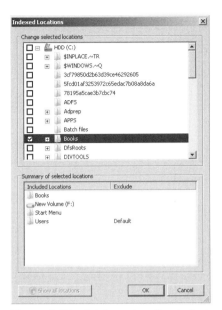

Figure 6-39   Adding a location to index

When you add a new location indexing will begin. You can click Pause if you need to pause indexing to do something else. As previously, you need to clear the UAC dialog box. You can also click Advanced in the Indexing Options dialog box (again you need to clear the UAC dialog box). This lets you access the Advanced Options dialog box. The Index Settings tab of this dialog box is shown in Figure 6-40.

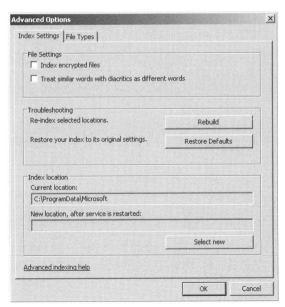

Figure 6-40   The Index Settings tab of the Advanced Options dialog box

On the Index Settings tab you can choose to index encrypted files and to treat similar words with diacritics as different words. Diacritics are marks above, through, or below letters (such as accents). You can also choose to rebuild your index or re-index selected locations and to change the location of your index. If you change the index location you need to stop and restart the service.

On the File Types tab of the same dialog box you can add or remove file types that you want to index and specify whether to index by properties only or by properties and content. You can also specify a file extension that is not on the list and click Add New Extension.

Practice: Migrating a Namespace to Windows Server 2008 Mode

When you created the domain-based namespace *contoso.internal**MyNameSpace* in the practice session in Lesson 1, you created it in Windows 2000 Server mode (assuming you carried out the instructions as written). In this practice session you migrate the namespace to Windows Server 2008 mode.

▶ **Exercise: Migrate a Namespace**

In this exercise you use both the DFS Management console and the *dsfutil* command-line utility. You first confirm that the namespace you created is in Windows 2000 Server mode. You then export the namespace to a file, delete the namespace, recreate it in Windows Server 2008 mode, and then import the namespace settings from the file you created. You need to have completed the exercises in Lesson 1 before you carry out this exercise. To complete the exercises, follow these steps:

1. Log on to the DC using the kim_akers account.

2. Open the DFS Management console from the Administrative Tools menu. Click Continue to close the UAC dialog box.

3. Expand Namespaces. Right-click \\contoso.internal\MyNameSpace and click Properties.

4. On the General tab shown in Figure 6-41, confirm that the namespace is in Windows 2000 Server mode. If the namespace is in Windows Server 2008 mode you do not need to carry out the rest of this exercise.

5. Click Cancel to close the Properties dialog box. Close the DFS Management console.

6. Open the Command Console (sometimes known as the Command Prompt window) in elevated mode (Run as Administrator). Click Continue to clear the UAC dialog box.

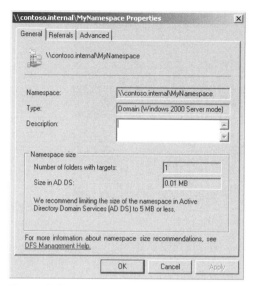

Figure 6-41 Namespace in Windows 2000 Server mode

7. Type **dfsutil root export \\contoso.internal\MyNameSpace C:\MyNameSpace.xml** as shown in Figure 6-42.

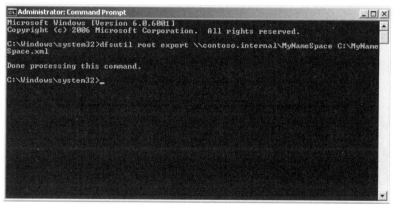

Figure 6-42 Exporting the namespace properties

8. To delete the namespace, enter the command **dfsutil root remove \\contoso .internal\MyNameSpace**.

9. To re-create the namespace in Windows Server 2008 mode, enter the command **dfsutil root adddom \\Glasgow\MyNameSpace**. Your Command Console should look similar to Figure 6-43.

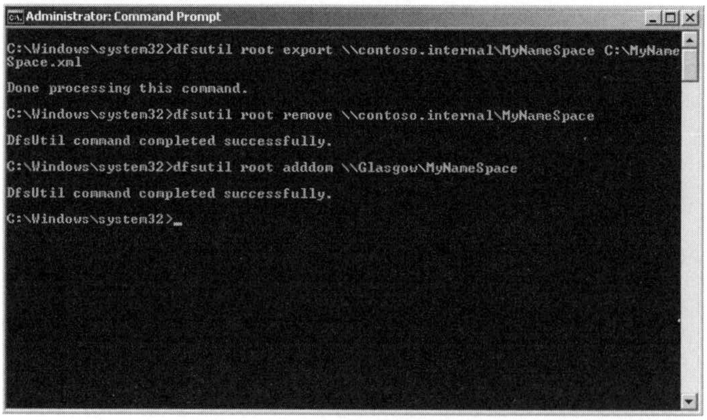

Figure 6-43   Deleting and re-creating a namespace

NOTE   **Adddom**

The *adddom* parameter in the command ensures that the namespace is domain-based. You need to specify a server. If your namespace is distributed over several servers this configuration is restored when you merge the settings from the namespace you deleted. You do not need to add V2 to the command because Windows Server 2008 mode is the default.

---

10.   Now import the namespace settings from the export file you created earlier. Enter the command **dfsutil root import merge C:\MyNameSpace.xml \\contoso .internal\MyNameSpace**. The output of this command is shown in Figure 6-44. If you were migrating a namespace with more configuration settings, your update statistics, links, targets, and roots would show different values.

Figure 6-44   Importing namespace settings

11.   Open the DFS Management console from the Administrative Tools menu. Click Continue to close the UAC dialog box.

12. Expand Namespaces. Right-click \\contoso.internal\MyNameSpace and then click Properties.

13. On the General tab shown in Figure 6-45, confirm that the namespace is in Windows Server 2008 mode.

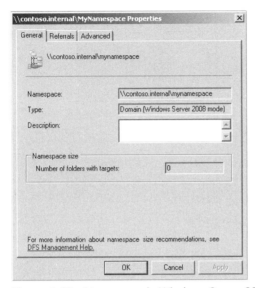

Figure 6-45   Namespace in Windows Server 2008 mode

Lesson Summary

■ The DFS Namespaces tool in the DFS Management console lets you group shared folders at different locations into logically structured namespaces so that users can view each namespace as a single shared folder with a series of subfolders. This structure provides fault tolerance and the ability to automatically connect users to local shared folders when available.

■ The DFS Replication tool in the DFS Management console lets you manage DFSR, which provides a multimaster replication engine that lets you synchronize folders on servers across local or WAN connections. It updates only those files that have changed since the last replication. You can use DFSR in conjunction with DFS Namespaces or by itself.

■ You can use the Share And Storage Management console to configure how files and programs in a shared folder or volume on your Windows Server 2008 server are made available offline.

■ The Windows Search Service role service indexes files, folders, and volumes to enable fast searches of server files to be implemented from a client computer. You can configure indexing settings from the Indexing Options tool in Control Panel.

Lesson Review

You can use the following questions to test your knowledge of the information in Lesson 2, "Provisioning Data." The questions are also available on the companion CD if you prefer to review them in electronic form.

NOTE   Answers

Answers to these questions and explanations of why each answer choice is correct or incorrect are located in the "Answers" section at the end of the book.

---

1. Which of the following servers can support multiple DFS namespaces in Windows Server 2008 mode? (Choose all that apply.)

   A. Windows Server 2008 Standard

   B. Windows Server 2008 Enterprise

   C. Windows Server 2008 Datacenter

   D. Windows Server 2003 R2, Datacenter Edition

   E. Windows Server 2003 R2, Enterprise Edition

2. Which of the following DFS namespaces can support more than 5000 DFS folders? (Choose all that apply.)

   A. Stand-alone namespace on a Windows Server 2008 server

   B. Stand-alone namespace on a Windows Server 2003 R2 server

   C. Domain-based namespace in Windows 2000 Server mode

   D. Domain-based namespace in Windows Server 2008 mode

3. What new feature in Windows Server 2008 DFS allows users to see only files and folders on a file server that they have permission to access?

   A. File screen

   B. Access-based enumeration

   C. Soft quota

   D. Folder target

4. DFSR uses staging folders for each replicated folder. These act as caches for new and changed files that are ready to be replicated from sending members to receiving members. By default, what storage quota is set on a staging folder and what happens when the quota is exceeded?

    A. 4,096 MB. When this limit is reached no additional files are stored in the staging folder.

    B. 660 MB. When this limit is reached no additional files are stored in the staging folder.

    C. 4,096 MB. When this limit is reached DFSR deletes old files from the staging folder to reduce the disk usage.

    D. 660 MB. When this limit is reached DFSR deletes old files from the staging folder to reduce the disk usage.

5. You are configuring offline access on a Windows Server 2008 server. Users in your organization's domain use Windows XP Professional clients, all of which are configured to use the Offline Files feature. You want to ensure that executable files that a client runs from the shared resource are automatically cached on that client, and that the next time the client needs to run one of those executable files, it will access its local cache instead of the shared resource on the server. In the Share And Storage Management console you access the Offline tab of the Advanced dialog box for the shared folder that stores the files to be synchronized and used offline. What settings do you configure?

    A. Select Only The Files And Programs That Users Specify Are Available Offline. Clear the Optimize For Performance check box.

    B. Select Only The Files And Programs That Users Specify Are Available Offline. Select the Optimize For Performance check box.

    C. Select All Files And Programs That Users Open From The Share Are Automatically Available Offline. Clear the Optimize For Performance check box.

    D. Select All Files And Programs That Users Open From The Share Are Automatically Available Offline. Select the Optimize For Performance check box.

Chapter Review

To further practice and reinforce the skills you learned in this chapter, you can perform the following tasks:

- Review the chapter summary.
- Review the list of key terms introduced in this chapter.
- Complete the case scenarios. These scenarios set up real-world situations involving the topics of this chapter and ask you to create a solution.
- Complete the suggested practices.
- Take a practice test.

Chapter Summary

- The role services in the File Services server role let you configure access control; manage shared folders, volumes, open sessions, and open files; manage DFS namespaces and DFSR; configure quotas and file screens; generate storage reports; configure offline files settings; and configure indexing.
- The Print Services server role lets you manage printers, print drivers, print queues, and printer permissions both on locally installed printers and on printers installed on other print servers on your network.
- DFSR replaces FRS, which was used in earlier versions of Windows to copy AD DS SYSVOL information. Windows Server 2008 DFSR provides fast, efficient, multimaster replication of distributed DFS namespace data. Domain-level DFS namespaces in Windows Server 2008 mode and stand-alone DFS namespaces on Windows Server 2008 servers provide many enhancements, including access-based enumeration.
- The Windows Search Service replaces the Indexing service used in previous versions of Windows. Quotas can be set on shared folders as well as volumes and a wide variety of storage reports can be generated. File screens let you prevent users from saving inappropriate file types.

Key Terms

Do you know what these key terms mean? You can check your answers by looking up the terms in the glossary at the end of the book.

- Access control

- Access control entry (ACE)

- Access control list (ACL)

- DFS namespace

- DFS replication (DFSR)

- DFS root

- Distributed file system (DFS)

- Indexing

- Offline file

- Quota

Case Scenario

In the following case scenario, you will apply what you have learned about File and Print Servers. You can find answers to these questions in the "Answers" section at the end of this book.

Case Scenario: Planning a Windows Server 2003 Upgrade

You are a senior domain administrator at Blue Yonder Airlines. The company has recently upgraded its DCs to Windows Server 2008 Enterprise. Its member servers run Windows Server 2003 R2 and Blue Yonder has no immediate plans to upgrade. Answer the following questions.

1. The Technical Director has Microsoft qualifications and retains a keen interest in new developments. She is eager to make use of the facilities offered by multiple domain-based DFS namespaces in Windows Server 2008 mode. What do you tell her?

2. The Financial Director is concerned that if a server goes down, data might not be available. He is also worried that if a server is replaced or a new server is introduced, the UNC paths to folder shares on all the company's client computers would need to be updated. How do you reassure him?

3. The Chief Executive Officer is concerned that some employees habitually store music and video files in shared folders on servers. She wants to know if this can be prevented. The training manager, however, is concerned that company-approved training video files should remain on the system and that new training files can

be saved to folders as required. How do you respond to these apparently contra-dictory requirements?

Suggested Practices

To help you successfully master the exam objectives presented in this chapter, complete the following tasks.

File and Print Servers

Do practices 1 through 4 in this section. Practices 5 and 6 are optional.

■ **Practice 1: Use the Share And Storage Management console**   You can become famil-iar with a tool only through practice. This chapter does not have sufficient space to fully describe every feature and setting that this tool offers. Use all the features of the tool and the wizards it provides.

■ **Practice 2: Create quotas and generate reports**   Create quotas and define interme-diate limits that will write to the Event Log and generate reports. Set the quota limits low so that you can easily reach them. Investigate the types of report that can be generated and what information each report type contains.

■ **Practice 3: Investigate DFS namespaces**   Add additional domain-based DFS namespaces to your domain on the Glasgow server. Add DFS folders and link them to folder targets. Look at all the settings and wizards provided by DFS Namespaces in the DFS Management tool.

■ **Practice 4: Investigate indexing**   Investigate indexing with the Windows Search Service. Become familiar with the settings available in the Indexing Options tool.

■ **Practice 5: Use files offline (optional)**   If you want to complete this practice con-vincingly, your Melbourne client needs to be a separate computer rather than a virtual machine. Configure your client and server so that you can access files when the client is offline and synchronize with the server at logon and logoff.

■ **Practice 6: Investigate DFSR**   You need an additional Windows Server 2008 server for this practice. If your computer has sufficient resources, this can be a virtual machine. Set up DFSR between the two servers. Look at the available settings.

Take a Practice Test

The practice tests on this book's companion CD offer many options. For example, you can test yourself on just one exam objective, or you can test yourself on all the 70-646 certification exam content. You can set up the test so that it closely simulates the experience of taking a certification exam, or you can set it up in study mode so that you can look at the correct answers and explanations after you answer each question.

MORE INFO   **Practice tests**

For details about all the practice test options available, see the "How to Use the Practice Tests" section in this book's Introduction.

Chapter 7

Windows Server 2008 Management, Monitoring, and Delegation

Planning how servers will be managed is as important as planning their deployment. If you, as the systems administrator, do not put enough care into determining the method by which servers will be managed,your job becomes much more difficult. And just as it is important to plan the management of servers, it is also important to plan how you will monitor the servers on an organization-wide basis. Without a set of coherent procedures, you are less likely to become aware of server performance degradation over time, only noticing it when it begins to inconvenience users. Finally, as a system administrator your time is important. In a large organization, you do not have enough time to deal with every small problem that comes across your desk. You should consider delegating minor administrative tasks to trusted users so that you can focus your attention on more complicated matters. This chapter explains how you can deal with all of these issues, from the excellent remote management technology in Windows Server 2008 to specific tools that allow you to optimize a server's performance to produce the best possible result for your organization.

Exam objectives in this chapter:
- Plan server management strategies.
- Plan for delegated administration.
- Monitoring servers for performance evaluation and optimization.

Lessons in this chapter:

Before You Begin

To complete the lessons in this chapter, you must have done the following:

■ Installed and configured the evaluation edition of Windows Server 2008 Enterprise Edition in accordance with the instructions listed in the first practice exercise of Lesson 1 in Chapter 1, "Installing, Upgrading, and Deploying Windows Server 2008."

No additional configuration is required for this chapter.

Real World

Orin Thomas

I used to have one of the world's longest telecommutes. For a couple of years I used remote desktop technology to perform daily management tasks on a server hosted in a Minneapolis, Minnesota data center from where I live in Melbourne, Australia. Rather a long drive to work if I had ever needed to manually change a backup tape! Today, in the age of offshoring and outsourcing, such an arrangement is less likely to raise an eyebrow. Back in 2000 it was dizzying stuff! Remote management technology is a boon and a bane to systems administrators: a boon because it lets you manage a server from anywhere in the world; a bane because you are expected to be able to manage a server from anywhere in the world. When you have a laptop and a 3G modem, you can find yourself on the Trans-Siberian railway restoring data on a server out at Puckapunyal. Sure, the people you work for know that you are on holiday, but when no one else knows how to do the job, that laptop and 3G modem are what can save the day.

Lesson 1: Server Management Strategies

In this lesson, you will learn several methods of remotely administering Windows Server 2008. When you understand the technologies through which you can remotely manage Windows Server 2008, you can apply this knowledge to planning how to manage and monitor servers on an organization-wide basis. The key to applying this knowledge is understanding the difference between the functionality of a particular technology when you use it directly in the server room and applying that technology to managing servers in another state or even on another continent.

After this lesson, you will be able to:
- Plan for the local and remote administration of Windows Server 2008.
- Determine which server management technology to deploy for a given situation.

Estimated lesson time: 40 minutes

Tools for the Administration of Windows Server 2008

In many cases the tools that you decide to use to manage the servers on your organization's Windows Server 2008 network will be more a matter of personal preference than technical necessity. You have a great deal of flexibility in how you can manage servers, but as a systems administrator you will be called upon to advise people in your organization on the best way to manage servers in a given set of circumstances. Throughout this lesson you will learn about different Windows Server 2008 management technologies and situations in which you might choose to use one technology over another to achieve the most efficient server management outcome.

Server Manager Console

The Server Manager console, shown in Figure 7-1, is an expanded Microsoft Management Console that allows you to manage all aspects of a Windows Server 2008 computer. The Server Manager console contains the most commonly used tools that an administrator will need. As you add or remove roles and features, the relevant components are added or removed from the Server Manager console. The Server Manager console is not available on Windows Server core installations.

The server that you are logged on to locally, or through Remote Desktop, is the only server that you can directly manage with this console. Managing other servers using Microsoft Management Consoles is covered in "Microsoft Management Consoles" later in this lesson.

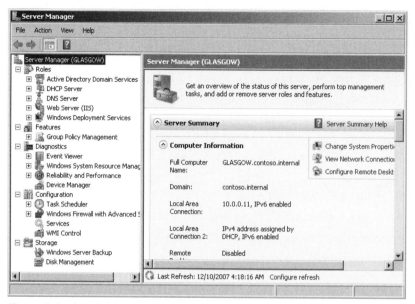

Figure 7-1   Server Manager console

MORE INFO   Server Manager console

To learn more about the Server Manager console, consult the following TechNet article: *http://technet2.microsoft.com/windowsserver2008/en/library/b3274a34-7574-4ea6-aec0-e05ba297481e1033.mspx?mfr=true.*

Servermanagercmd.exe is a command-line utility that can be run from an elevated console on Windows Server 2008 standard installations to add and remove server roles and features. Executing the command *servermanagercmd.exe –query* will display a list of all roles, role services, and features available to a Windows Server 2008 computer and whether they are installed on the computer. On a computer installed with the Server Core installation option, the oclist.exe and ocsetup.exe commands provide the same functionality.

Microsoft Management Consoles

Although a default set of consoles is available in the Administrative tools menu, the snap-ins that you can use to create a custom console allow for greater functionality and customization. A custom console allows you to quickly access a common toolset. You can also copy the console to other computers such as a management workstation so that you have the same toolkit available regardless of where you are logged on.

With some snap-ins you can specify a set of credentials when running the snap-in against a remote computer. Creating a custom console is straightforward. To do this, perform the following steps:

1. From the Start menu, type **mmc** in the Run dialog box. This will open a blank MMC console.

2. From the File menu, click Add/Remove Snap-in. This will open the Add Or Remote Snap-ins dialog box, shown in Figure 7-2. Add the snap-ins that you want to use with the console and then click OK.

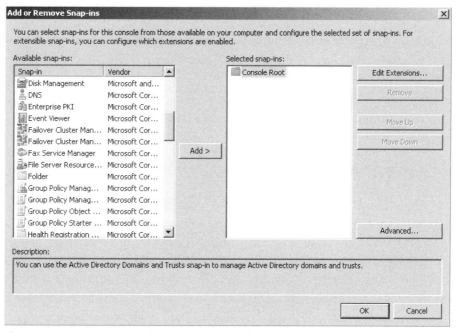

Figure 7-2   Snap-ins extend the functionality of a console

3. If asked which computer to focus the MMC on, select that computer and then click OK.

4. From the File menu, save the console.

Although snap-ins for all roles and features present on the server will be available, some snap-ins are for services and features that are not installed. These extra snap-ins will not be available unless you install the appropriate Remote Server Administration Tools (RSAT) feature. The RSAT tools are covered in "Remote Server Administration Tools" later in this lesson.

Windows PowerShell

Windows PowerShell is a scripting and command-line shell language specifically designed for systems administration tasks. Although Windows PowerShell can look daunting to systems administrators who are not used to performing a significant amount of their duties from the command prompt, after a few hours spent using Windows PowerShell to accomplish day-to-day server management tasks you might be reluctant to go back to GUI-based system administration utilities.

The Windows PowerShell feature is not enabled by default. When planning to use Windows PowerShell as a server administration technology in your environment, you need to ensure that you deploy Windows Server 2008 computers with the Windows PowerShell feature enabled. You can achieve this during the deployment process by ensuring that you add the required feature to the WDS operating system images. WDS was covered in Lesson 2 of Chapter 1.

NOTE Windows PowerShell and Windows Server 2003

Windows PowerShell is also available as an add-on component to Windows Server 2003, meaning that Windows PowerShell commands that you use to manage Windows Server 2008 can also be used to manage Windows Server 2003.

From the perspective of planning Windows Server 2008 management strategies, you can use Windows PowerShell scripts to automate almost all complex systems administration tasks. You can call Windows PowerShell scripts from the Task Scheduler, allowing you to automate many daily systems administration tasks. Because Windows PowerShell is also a scripting language, you can build conditional logic into your scripts, allowing automated tasks to execute in a certain manner depending on the conditions that exist when the script is run. Windows PowerShell scripts work best for planned tasks where you know exactly what needs to be done. Windows Power-Shell scripts do not work as well when you are performing tasks that require you to make a significant number of on-the-spot decisions about which way to proceed.

MORE INFO Windows PowerShell and Windows Server 2008

Windows PowerShell is a deep topic that cannot be done justice in a few pages. Several good books are available from Microsoft Press that will teach you about how to best use Windows PowerShell in your environment. To get started, consult the Windows PowerShell and Windows Server 2008 page on the Microsoft Web site at *http://www.microsoft.com/windowsserver2008/ powershell.mspx*.

Scripting and Command-Line Tools

Command-line tools and scripts are available for all of the server roles and features that you can install on Windows Server 2008. Although the command-line tools are not as straightforward to use as the GUI-based utilities, with a little effort you can use them to perform all of the tasks that you can complete with the GUI tools. An advantage of the command-line tools is that you can use them in scripts that you create. If you can create a script that automates a complicated administrative task that works on one Windows Server 2008 computer, you can then copy that script to use on other Windows Server 2008 computers.

Traditional scripting using Windows Scripting Host as an administrative tool in Windows Server 2008 has been deprecated in favor of Windows PowerShell. That does not mean that you cannot use existing management scripts with Windows Server 2008; it simply means that Microsoft recommends that you use Windows PowerShell, which was specifically designed as a scripting and command-line shell for systems administration in a way that Windows Scripting Host scripts are not. In some circumstances—especially in terms of the script-based management of computers running in the Server Core configuration—you will not have any choice but to use traditional scripts because Windows PowerShell is not fully compatible with Windows Server Core.

Scripting Versus GUI-Based Administration

To the uninitiated who are only comfortable with GUI-based tools, Windows PowerShell looks horribly complex. Why would anyone choose to use a script when perfectly good, GUI-based tools are available? The answer is repetition. Creating 10 users using the Active Directory Users And Computers interface is a relatively straightforward task. Creating 1000 users using the same process is repetitive. Repetition is not only tedious, but it also leads to mistakes. The primary benefit of scripting is that you can speed up a long, repetitive task by automating it. You get more accurate results and your task is completed more quickly. If you remain unconvinced, think of it this way: Imagine that you have a task that takes you three minutes to complete with the GUI-based tools that are included with Windows Server 2008. You have to perform this task 80 times. Let us assume that you can teach yourself how to script the same task in two hours. Because running scripts only takes a couple of seconds, you would save two hours by writing the script instead of performing the same task with the GUI. So although scripting might seem horribly complex, learning how to effectively

> script with tools such as Windows PowerShell will save you hours of tedium when it comes to the repetitive tasks that take up a significant portion of a systems administrator's day.

EMS

Emergency Management Services (EMS) allows a server to be controlled when it is in a minimally functional state, such as the network card and display adapter being non-functional. EMS allows an out-of-band connection, generally through a serial port using an application such as Telnet. With the appropriate hardware, you can also perform almost all normal server management tasks through EMS, although you must complete all of these tasks from the command line.

An advantage to EMS is that it is accessible when other methods of administration are not. You can access EMS when the computer is in the process of starting up or shutting down. For example, EMS allows access to a server if it has frozen during shutdown or in some cases even when a STOP error has occurred. You can also use EMS when a server is not responsive to traditional input methods because of a runaway process. For example: In your experience as a systems administrator you might have encountered a server that appears to have frozen and you are unable to log on. In this situation, you might be able to use EMS to manage the server and even shut down the errant process. This will not always be the case—sometimes you cannot do much with a frozen server other than manually turn it off, but EMS provides you with a final fallback position for working with a server before that last resort.

EMS must be enabled on a server. How you enable it depends on the type of hardware configuration that a Windows Server 2008 computer has. For example, the method of enabling and configuring EMS on a computer with Extensible Firmware Interface (EFI) firmware is different from the method of enabling and configuring EMS on a computer that has an Advance Configuration and Power Interface (ACPI) Serial Port Console Redirection (SPCR) table. Enabling requires you to use the *bcdedit* command to edit Windows Server 2008's boot settings, but the exact syntax is dependent on a server's hardware configuration. From a planning perspective, you should enable EMS on servers prior to deployment. That way, if you do encounter a situation in which the tools might be useful, they will be available to you.

MORE INFO   More on EMS configuration

To learn more about the specifics of enabling EMS on Windows Server 2008, consult the following MSDN article: *http://msdn2.microsoft.com/en-us/library/ms791506.aspx*.

Although you can use EMS to perform almost all management tasks on a server through a command-prompt interface, most organizations primarily use EMS to manage a server that is not responding to normal management technologies. The Special Administration console is an EMS-specific tool, but it is only available if Windows is functioning normally. The !SAC console is available when the operating system is not operating normally and the SAC console has failed to load and has ceased to operate. Typing **help** or **?** at either the SAC or !SAC prompt brings up a list of commands that you can use with EMS at its current level of functionality.

MORE INFO   Using EMS

For more information on the specifics of how to use EMS to perform server management tasks, including a complete list of SAC and !SAC commands, consult the following TechNet document: *http://technet2.microsoft.com/windowsserver/en/library/ed1f3d57-e3a3-4ef6-857a-adbff20302701033.mspx?mfr=true.*

Remote Administration Technologies

You are not limited to choosing one or the other when considering which remote administration technology to deploy to manage the servers in your organization's environment. Each technology has its benefits and drawbacks. It will make sense to perform some management tasks using a remote desktop connection while in other situations you might be better served by connecting to a server using a Telnet application when you need to execute a script. The next part of this lesson covers remote administration using Remote Desktop, the Remote Systems Administration Tools, and Telnet.

Remote Desktop

Remote Desktop is likely to be the most commonly used remote administration technology deployed in your Windows Server 2008 environment because it most closely simulates the experience of being directly in front of a server. Administrators connect to servers using the Remote Desktop Client software that is included with Windows operating systems, although as you learned in Chapter 5, "Terminal Services and Application and Server Virtualization," the more stringent security settings require the Remote Desktop Connection client that ships with Windows Server 2003 Service Pack 2, Windows XP Service Pack 3, or Windows Vista Service Pack 1.

After you enable Remote Desktop on a Windows Server 2008 computer, members of the local Administrators group and Remote Desktop Users group are automatically able to connect. It is important to note that on domain controllers, just being a member of the Remote Desktop Users group does not confer the right to log on using Remote Desktop.

You can change this by editing the Computer Configuration\Policies\Windows Settings\Security Settings\Local Policies\User Rights Assignment\Allow Log On Through Terminal Services policy.

Remote Desktop allows two administrators to make simultaneous remote connections to a Windows Server 2008 computer. This limit is important because by default there are no active or idle session limits. This means that a forgetful administrator who is disconnected from a server she is in the process of managing might find that she is unable to reconnect to a server because the existing administration session is still active. As Figure 7-3 shows, you can resolve this by configuring RDP-Tcp properties to end disconnected and idle sessions after a reasonable amount of time has passed. If a connection is being made to a server that also hosts the Terminal Services role, rather than using up a Terminal Services client access license (TS CAL), you can ensure that a connection is made to one of the two available sessions reserved for administrator use by using the *mstsc /admin* command from the Run dialog box.

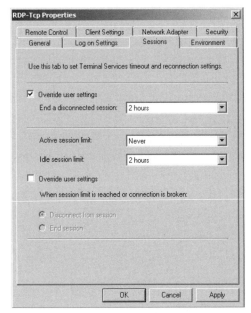

Figure 7-3   Session limits ensure that administrators can always connect

As shown in Figure 7-4, the Remote Desktop firewall exception is automatically enabled when you enable Remote Desktop for administration on a Windows Server 2008 computer. Although Windows Firewall is automatically configured to allow remote desktop traffic, other firewalls might exist between the client computer and the server you want to manage. If you encounter this situation, you must ensure that you configure the firewalls to allow traffic on TCP port 3389.

Figure 7-4   The firewall is automatically configured when you enable Remote Desktop.

In certain situations, you will need to perform administrative tasks on servers located on private networks at organizations that you can only connect to using the Internet. These servers are likely to be protected by firewalls and will also not be directly addressable by Internet hosts. For example, you cannot make a direct connection to a Windows Server 2008 computer that is using IP address 192.168.15.100 on a remote organization's network if the only way that you can connect to that network is through the Internet.

In the event that you do need to perform regular administrative duties on servers on private networks that you do not have a direct connection to, you have two options:

- You can configure a VPN server on the remote screened subnet. After a VPN connection is established from your workstation to the remote private network, you can make an administrative connection to the server you want to manage.

- You can install a Terminal Services Gateway on the remote screened subnet. You can then make an RDP connection through this gateway to any server located on the remote organization's private network.

Although configuring a VPN server on the remote organization's screened subnet is an option in many circumstances, setting up a VPN server does involve a significant amount of effort. If you only need to make RDP connections to remote servers, installing a TS Gateway Server is a simpler process.

Terminal Services Gateway (TS Gateway) is a service new to Windows Server 2008 that allows users on the Internet to connect to Terminal Servers on a protected network through a TS Gateway Server hosted behind a firewall on a screened subnet. TS Gateway Servers were discussed briefly in Chapter 5. TS Gateway works using RDP over HTTPS, which means that external firewalls only need to have Port 443 open rather than opening up the Remote Desktop port. A direct connection is made from the Internet host through the firewall to the TS Gateway Server, and that gateway server then forwards authorized traffic to servers located on a protected private network. Although primarily used to allow normal users to access terminal server applications when connecting from clients on the Internet, TS Gateway also can be used to assist in the remote administration of servers on a protected network.

MORE INFO More on TS Gateway

For more information on TS Gateway and how to use it with Remote Desktop, consult the following TechNet article: *http://technet2.microsoft.com/windowsserver2008/en/library/9da3742f-699d-4476-b050-c50aa14aaf081033.mspx?mfr=true.*

RSAT Tools

By default, only the administration tools for the services and features installed on a Windows Server 2008 computer are available on that computer. Therefore, if you wanted to manage a remote server running Active Directory Rights Management Server, you would not be able to add that snap-in or access the tool from the Administrative Tools menu unless you had installed the RSAT tools or the specific ADRMS component of the RSAT tools.

The RSAT tools are available for Windows Vista SP1 Business, Enterprise, and Ultimate Editions as an additional download. In earlier versions of Windows Server, the tools were called the Windows Server 2003 Administrator Tools pack, which was shortened by most administrators to AdminPak.msi, after the filename from which the tools are installed. The RSAT tools contain all necessary management consoles for the administration of the roles or features that ship with Windows Server 2008.

Remote Administration Tools for Non-Administrator Users

In Lesson 3, "Delegated Administration," you will learn techniques for delegating administrative privileges to non-administrator users. Before non-administrator users can perform the tasks that they have been delegated, they need to have access to the tools that allow them to perform those tasks.

One method that you can use to provide them with those tools is to create and distribute custom Microsoft Management Consoles. You simply add the console related to the delegated task to the custom console, save that console, and deploy it to the user. Although you could install the RSAT tools on the workstation of a staff member with non-administrative privileges, having 30 consoles available when the staff member only needs one to perform her job function may prove confusing.

Although you might be tempted to, you should not give normal users access to a server through remote desktop. In general, when planning for remote administration, you should limit the number of people who are able to directly access a server. Users that have been delegated limited administrative responsibilities can almost always complete their tasks by using tools installed on their workstations

Using Telnet for Remote Administration

A final method of performing Remote Administration on Windows Server 2008 computers is by connecting through Telnet. Telnet allows you to make a text-based connection over the network to a Windows Server 2008 computer to a command console. You can run any text-based commands remotely that you would normally be able to run locally on a command prompt. The advantage of Telnet as a remote administration technology is that you can use it over extremely low bandwidth connections, such as those that are below normal 56K dialup speeds and might not be able to support Remote Desktop.

After the Telnet Server feature is installed, you can configure options by running the *tlntadmn.exe* command from an elevated command prompt. Options that you can configure include the idle session timeout, the maximum number of supported Telnet connections, the port that Telnet operates on, and the maximum number of failed login attempts. The default authentication mechanism for the Telnet server is NTLM. Because Telnet is not an encrypted protocol, you should secure connections to a Telnet Server using IPsec if possible.

Quick Check

1. Which console automatically adds and removes components as you add and remove roles and features?
2. Which port are EMS connections to a server usually made through?

Quick Check Answers

1. Server Manager Console.
2. EMS connections are almost always made through a serial port.

Exam Tip Consider the complexity of the tasks that you need to perform and then consider which tool is best for the job.

Managing Windows Server 2008 Event Logs

A significant component of planning for the management and monitoring of Windows Server 2008 is determining how to deal with Event Logs. The core problem with event logging is ensuring that you are aware that something important has happened by ensuring that you not only have logged the relevant event, but that you can also actually find it. The problem that you face in doing this is twofold:

- If you log everything, how do you ensure that you do not miss that one important event in the tens of thousands that are recorded?

- If you restrict the amount of data that you log, how can you be sure that you are not missing something vitally important because you have chosen to record only a select number of events?

When you have to manage tens or even hundreds of servers, you can be quickly flooded with data. In the following section, you will learn how to use the Event Viewer that ships with Windows Server 2008 to make event log data more manageable.

By default, Windows Server 2008 has the following logs available under the *Windows Logs* node in the Event Viewer:

- **Application** The application log stores data generated by applications that are installed on the Windows Server 2008 computer. This includes applications such as the Certificate Services client, Desktop Windows Manager, and other applications such as Notepad. With the application log, you must remember that there is also a node in the event viewer called *Applications And Service Logs* that also stores application and server role log data. In general, you should check under the *Applications And Service Logs* node first for application-related information before you check the application log itself. Alternatively, you can set up a filter. You will learn how to set up filters later in this lesson.

- **Security** The security log contains audited security events, such as logons or accessing of audited objects such as files. What is important to remember about this log is that you must configure auditing to ensure that the events you want logged actually are. You will not be able to determine who has attempted to access a specific file unless you have configured auditing for that file. If you have configured auditing, the related events are written to the security log file.

- **Setup**   The setup log contains events related to the setup of applications on the server.

- **System**   The system log stores events logged by system components, including events such as the failure of a device driver or the failure of a service.

- **Forwarded Events**   This event log stores events collected from other computers. This log is very useful for administrators who want to view important log data in a single location rather than by checking the individual logs of each server that they manage. You can only collect events from other computers using subscriptions, which are covered in "Configuring Log Subscriptions" later in this lesson.

Another important planning decision related to Event Logs is deciding how large the logs can be and what to do when the log file reaches the maximum specified log size. This is often described as setting a log retention policy. As you can see in Figure 7-5, the options are to Overwrite Events As Needed, Archive The Log When Full, and Do Not Overwrite Events (Clear Log Manually). If you set this final policy security log remember that depending on how you configure Group Policy, a server could become unavailable until the appropriate log file is manually cleared. As you will learn in Chapter 8, "Security Policies," Microsoft recommends that you configure log retention policies so that security log events are never overwritten.

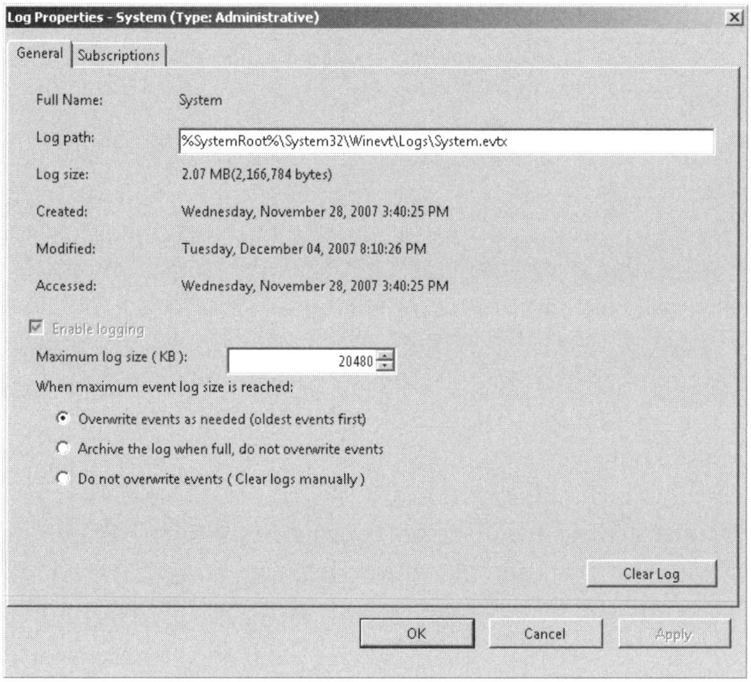

Figure 7-5   Log file properties

Filters

Filters are a way of reducing the number of events displayed in a log to those that are pertinent to your interests. For example, the filter shown in Figure 7-6 will only display Critical, Warning, and Error events in the System Log that were recorded between 7:36 P.M. and 8:36 P.M. on December 4, 2007. To use a filter you need to know something about the type of the event you are looking for. The higher the number of conditions that you place on the filter, the fewer the events that will be displayed. Unlike custom views, you cannot save filters—they must be generated each time you want to use them.

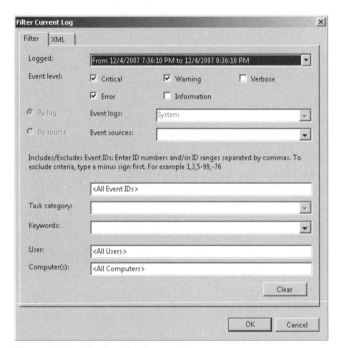

Figure 7-6   Filtering the System Log

Custom Views

You can think of a custom view, shown in Figure 7-7, as a special filter that can be saved. You can also apply a custom filter to multiple logs rather than to a single log. Rather than having to create the filter, you can create a custom view and select that view each time you enter the Event Viewer console. You can also import and export custom views if you want to use them on other Windows Server 2008 computers. You will create a custom view in the second practice exercise at the end of this lesson.

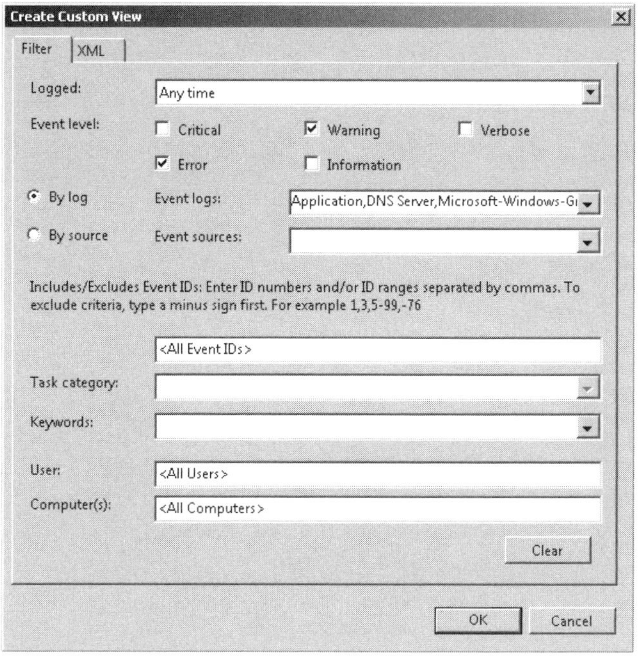

Figure 7-7   Creating a custom view

Attaching Tasks To Events

As shown in Figure 7-8, attaching a task to an event allows you to either start a program, send an e-mail, or display a message each time a specific event is written to a particular event log. Attaching tasks to events allows you to be more proactive about the management of important events. Rather than only finding out about the event when you examine the log files after the event occurs, you can be informed immediately that the event has occurred, which allows you to take direct action. As with any direct notification, you should avoid setting up too many direct notifications. If you set up too many direct notifications, you may start to feel flooded by tasks that might not require your immediate attention. Only organize for a direct notification for the kind of event that you would need to respond urgently to. Tasks that are attached to event logs are stored in Task Scheduler. If you want to remove an attached task, you must do this from Task Scheduler rather than from Event Viewer.

The limitations of attaching tasks to events are that the event must already exist within the log file, you cannot attach tasks to events in analytic or debug logs, and you cannot assign a task to an event stored in a saved log file. You cannot use this functionality to run a task to an event if the event has not occurred, although you can

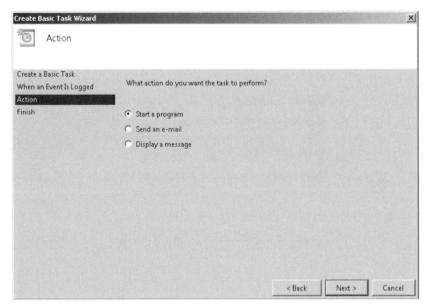

Figure 7-8   Creating a basic task

mimic such functionality by creating a Windows PowerShell script that runs on a scheduled basis. Using Windows PowerShell with log files is covered in more detail later in this lesson. You will attach a task to an event in the practice exercises at the end of this lesson.

Configuring Log Subscriptions

Log subscriptions are a form of centralized log management. Rather than having to check the logs of each server that you are responsible for, you can use log subscriptions to centralize all important events that occur across the organization in a single place. Then, by applying custom views, you can quickly single out specific events of interest.

You can configure two types of subscriptions. In a collector initiated subscription, the computer that will store the collected events (the collector) retrieves them from the computer that generates the event. In a source computer initiated subscription, the computers that generate the events forward the events to the collector computer.

To set up a collector initiated subscription, perform the following steps:

1. On each source computer, open an elevated command prompt and issue the command *winrm quickconfig*. You will also need to accept the request to create a firewall exception.

2. On each source computer, add the computer account of the collector computer to the local Administrators group.

3. On the computer that will function as the collector, open an elevated command prompt and issue the command *wecutil qc*. This will start the Windows Event Collector service and configure it to start automatically with a delayed start.

4. Open Event Viewer on the collector computer and click the Subscriptions item. In the Actions pane, click Create Subscription. This will open the Subscription Properties dialog box shown in Figure 7-9.

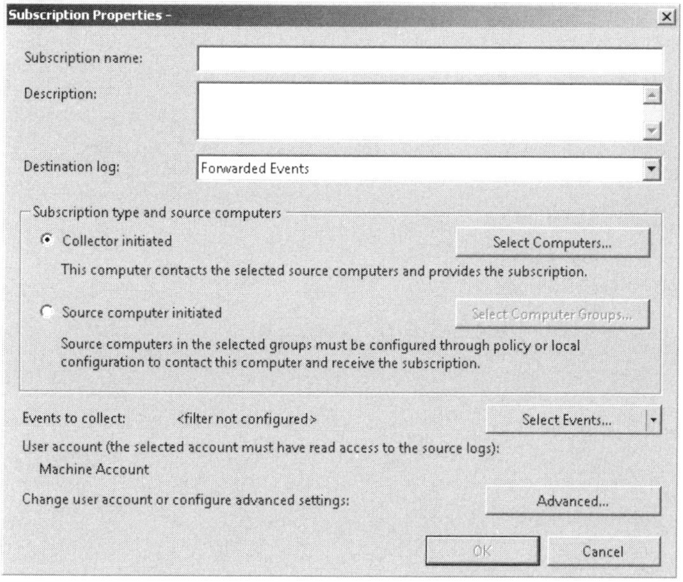

Figure 7-9   Configuring a subscription

5. Click Select Computers to select the source computers.

6. When all source computers are selected, click Select Events to configure a filter for the type of events that you want the collector computer to gather.

7. When you have completed the creation of the filter, click OK twice to activate the subscription.

The configuration of a subscription filter is more like the configuration of a custom view in that you are able to specify multiple event log sources, rather than just a single Event Log source. In addition, the subscription will be saved whereas you need to re-create a filter each time you use one. By default, all collected Event Log data will be written to the Forwarded Event Event Log. You can forward data to other logs by configuring the properties of the subscription. Even though you use a filter to retrieve only specific events from source computers and place them in the destination log, you can still create and apply a custom view to data that is located in the destination log. You could create a custom view for each source computer, which would allow you to quickly limit events to that computer rather than viewing data from all source computers at the same time.

You configure collector initiated subscriptions through the application of Group Policy. To do this you must configure the collector computer in the same manner as you did in the previous steps. When configuring the subscription type, select Source Computer Initiated rather than Collector Initiated. To set up the source computers, apply a GPO where you have configured the Computer Configuration\Policies\Administrative Templates\Windows Components\Event Forwarding node and configure the Server Address, Refresh Interval, And Issuer Certificate policy with the details of the collector computer, as shown in Figure 7-10.

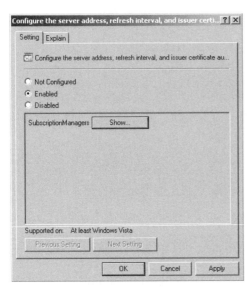

Figure 7-10   Event forwarding policy

MORE INFO   **Source initiated subscription**

For more details on setting up a source initiated subscription, consult the following MSDN link: *http://msdn2.microsoft.com/en-us/library/bb870973.aspx.*

Applications and Service Logs

When you install an application or role on a Windows Server 2008 computer, it will most likely add a new log under the *Applications And Services* log node of the Event

Viewer. Application And Service Logs is a new category of event logs introduced with Windows Server 2008. Because this category of event log is new, applications produced prior to the release of Windows Server 2008 might still write events to the traditional application log, covered earlier in this lesson. As Figure 7-11 shows, you can also view the analytic and debug logs of a server under this node. These logs are viewable only if you select the Show Analytic And Debug logs option under the View menu in the Event Viewer console.

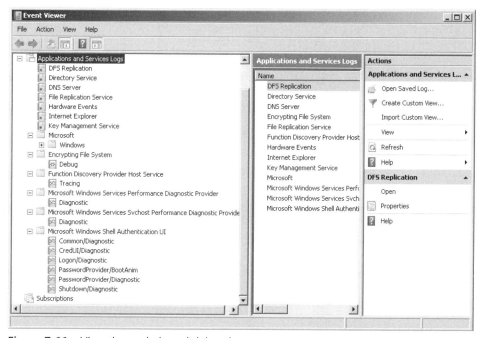

Figure 7-11   View the analytic and debug logs

Application And Service Logs can be defined by four broad categories:

- **Admin**   Admin logs will describe a problem and suggest a solution that an administrator can implement. Messages in admin logs almost always tell an administrator how to rectify a problem.

- **Operational**   Operational events provide information to assist in the analysis and diagnosis of problems. Although these events will not provide information on how to resolve the problem that generated the event, you can use these events as a task trigger to alert an administrator that this event has just occurred.

- **Analytic**   Only viewable when enabled, analytic events are written in high volume and indicate problems that generally cannot be resolved easily.

■ **Debug** Debug logs are used by developers who are troubleshooting applications that they have created.

Using Event Viewer on a Remote Computer

Just as you can with other management consoles, you can use the event viewer console to connect to remote Windows Server 2008 computers. To do this, select the Connect To Another Computer option on the Action menu of the console. To view Event Logs remotely on a computer that has Windows Firewall enabled, you must enable the Remote Event Log Management exception.

When you connect to another computer remotely using the event viewer, the custom views that you can access are those stored on the local computer. Custom views stored on the remote computer will be unavailable. When you run a local custom view when connected to a remote computer, the custom view will be run against the remote event logs rather than the local ones. For example, if you have a custom view that only shows Error events from the System log, when connected to a remote computer your custom view will only show Error events from the remote computer's System log.

Because you are likely to use subscriptions to forward event data to a centralized location for analysis, from a planning perspective you are only likely to make remote connections with Event Viewer when you have found an event worthy of your attention and you want to dig deeper by looking at other events on that original computer. Forwarding everything that is interesting to a centralized location and allowing a local follow-up provides a good balance between storing details and displaying what is probably important.

Archiving Event Logs

When planning the management of Event Log data in an organization, be sure to consider your Event Log storage policies. You will need to create a policy that specifies how long Event Log data has to be retained. For example, if an employee is caught accessing confidential data, evidence of this activity might exist in security logs that were taken over the last several months. If logs are automatically overwritten when they reach a particular size, or simply deleted after a cursory examination, information pertinent to an investigation might be lost. The simplest way to manage the archiving of an organization's server event logs is to implement Event Log forwarding and then to export the collected Event Log data to files that can be backed up separately and stored securely for the required period. You can save log files by clicking Save Log File As in the Action menu. You can select from the following formats:

- Event Files (*.evtx)
- XML (*.xml)
- Text (tab-delimited) (*.txt)
- CSV (comma-separated) (*.csv)

When you save log files using the Event Viewer Save Log File function, you are prompted about whether you want to save display information. If you do not include this information with the saved log file, the log file may not display properly when imported to other computers. You can also save log files when you apply filters or custom views. This can reduce the size of saved log files, though you might fail to save an event that later turns out to be important when you are performing an investigation. Although the other file types can be useful in specific circumstances, only files stored in Event Viewer format can be reopened in the Event Viewer on another computer.

Managing Event Logs with Wevtutil and Windows PowerShell

Wevtutil has much of the same functionality as the Event Viewer GUI. It allows administrators to view, filter, and manage event log data directly from a command line. For example, to use wevtutil to export a log to a file, use the following command:

```
wevtutil epl Logname Filename.evtx
```

Given this information, it is a relatively simple exercise for most administrators to create a script based on wevtutil to perform a daily export of all log files to a shared directory. The Event Viewer console does not allow for this type of automation. Automating the backup of log file data is useful when you are considering the management of event logs on an organization-wide basis.

MORE INFO More on wevtutil

You can find out more about wevtutil by consulting the following in-depth Technet article: *http://technet2.microsoft.com/windowsserver2008/en/library/d4c791e0-7e59-45c5-aa55-0223b77a48221033.mspx?mfr=true.*

Although wevtutil does provide the ability to analyze event log data, the tool provides only simple event management functionality and is not as extensible as Windows PowerShell, which provides another method of monitoring and managing event logs through the Get-Eventlog cmdlet. The advantage of using Windows PowerShell is that you can create more complicated scripts than you can with wevtutil. All data analysis and manipulation occurs within the Windows PowerShell script, whereas with wevtutil your script will call an outside application and then attempt to deal with that outside application's output. Put another way, Windows PowerShell components are designed to interact with one another, and this makes writing and managing Windows PowerShell scripts a simpler task for you as a systems administrator.

You can use a Windows PowerShell command to list all instances of an event in a specified log. For example, to find all events with event ID 1000 in the System log, you would enter the following PowerShell command:

```
Get-Eventlog System | where {$_.EventID -eq 1000}
```

MORE INFO   **More on Get-Eventlog**

To find out more about how you can leverage the Get-EventLog cmdlet, consult the following TechNet article: *http://www.microsoft.com/technet/scriptcenter/topics/msh/cmdlets/get-eventlog.mspx.*

As a programming and scripting language, PowerShell allows you to quickly build complicated commands for analyzing Windows event log data. From a planning perspective, you should consider Windows PowerShell scripts for the management of event logs when built-in tools such as custom views, filters, and attaching tasks to specific events are not providing you with enough control to meet your needs. The functionality built into the Event Viewer is likely to meet the majority of your needs, but if you need to go further, using Windows PowerShell will help you achieve your goals.

MORE INFO   **Microsoft's Log Parser tool**

Log Parser is a wonderful Microsoft tool that allows you to use SQL queries against Windows Event Logs to extract data. Although Log Parser is not likely to be mentioned on the 70-646 exam, it is a log management tool worth testing in your environment. You can find out more about Log Parser at *http://www.microsoft.com/technet/scriptcenter/tools/logparser/default.mspx.*

Microsoft System Center Operations Manager 2007

When planning the centralized monitoring and management of large numbers of Windows Server 2008 computers, you should consider implementing Microsoft System Center Operations Manager 2007. System Center Operations Manager 2007 was touched on briefly during Chapter 4, "Application Servers and Services." Microsoft System Center Operations Manager 2007 allows you to centrally manage and monitor thousands of servers and applications and provides a complete overview of the health of your network environment. System Center Operations Manager 2007 is the most recent version of Microsoft Operations Manager 2005 (MOM). System Center Operations Manager 2007 provides the following features:

- Proactive alerts that recognize conditions that are likely to lead to failure of critical services, applications, and servers in the future

- The ability to configure tasks to automatically execute to resolve problems when given events occur

- The collection of long-term trend data from all servers and applications across the organization with the ability to generate comparison reports against current performance

- Correlation of auditing data generated across the organization, allowing the detection of trends that might not be apparent when examining server auditing data in isolation

In addition to the monitoring components that are part of a default Operations Manager 2007 installation, you can use management packs, which are add-on components that extend Operations Manager 2007 monitoring capability. Microsoft provides more than 60 different management packs that you can use with Operations Manager 2007, covering everything from Exchange Server 2007 and SQL Server 2005 to Windows Server Update Services 3.0. You can use a management pack to determine whether a particular technology is configured according to best practice. You can also use management packs can to analyze the performance of a technology and make recommendations on what configuration changes should be made to best suit the way that the technology is being used. This is similar to using a Best Practices Analyzer, but instead of being limited to analyzing one computer at a time, you can examine a specific technology's deployment across the organization.

Like other enterprise-wide monitoring and management solutions, such as System Center Virtual Machine Manager 2007, Microsoft System Center Operations Manager 2007 requires access to a SQL Server 2005 SP1 or later or SQL Server 2008 database to store data. Because SQL Server instances are able to host multiple databases, a single SQL Server can host configuration databases for System Center Virtual Machine Manager 2007, System Center Operations Manager 2007, and services such as Microsoft Virtual Application Server 2007. Even if an organization does not require a database server as an application server, in enterprise environments, SQL Server increasingly finds a place as a core component of network infrastructure.

MORE INFO   **More on System Center Operations Manager 2007**

You can find out more about System Center Operations Manager 2007 and download a 180-day evaluation version of the software from the following Microsoft Web site: *http://www.microsoft.com/ systemcenter/opsmgr/default.mspx.*

Practice: Remotely Managing Windows Server 2008

In this set of exercises, you will install the Remote System Administration tools, configure a server to accept remote desktop connections, and configure event viewer custom views and tasks.

▶ **Exercise 1: RSAT Tools and Remote Desktop Configuration**

In this exercise, you will install all available remote administration tools on server Glasgow and configure the server to be managed using Remote Desktop. To complete this exercise, perform the following steps:

1. Log on to server Glasgow using the Kim_Akers user account.

2. Click Start, right-click Computer and then click Properties. This will open the System Control Panel.

3. In the Tasks pane, click Remote Settings and then click Continue when prompted by the UAC dialog box.

4. On the Remote tab of the System Properties dialog box, ensure that Allow Remote Connections Only From Computers Running Remote Desktop With Network Level Authentication (More Secure) is selected, as shown in Figure 7-12.

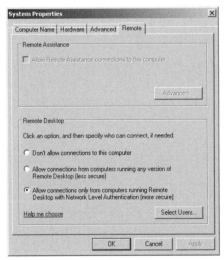

Figure 7-12   Configuring Remote Desktop properties

5. Click Select Users. This will open the Remote Desktop Users dialog box. Verify that no users are selected and then click Cancel twice. If any users are present, remove them from this group.

6. Open the Server Manager console, right-click the *Features* node and then click Add Features. When presented with the UAC prompt, click Continue.

7. On the Select Features page of the Add Features Wizard, click the plus sign (+) next to Remote Server Administration Tools to expand this item.

8. Expand and select all items under Role Administration Tools and Feature Administration tools as shown in Figure 7-13. Depending on the configuration of your server, it may be necessary to add IIS 6 Management Components at this point.

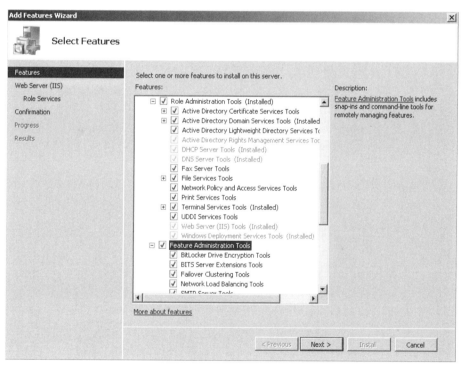

Figure 7-13   Installing Role Administration Tools and Feature Tools

9. When all components are selected, click Next and then click Install.

10. Click Close and then, if necessary allow the server to restart. The installation will complete after the server has restarted.

▶ **Exercise 2: Use Event Viewer to Configure a Custom View and to Attach a Task to an Event**

In this exercise, you will configure a custom view that will display any error messages that have occurred in the last 24 hours from all logs. You will also attach a task to a specific event. To complete this exercise, perform the following steps:

1. While logged on to server Glasgow with the Kim_Akers user account, open the Event Viewer from the Administrative Tools menu. Click Continue when presented with the User Account Control dialog box.

2. In the Actions menu of the Event View console, click Create Custom View.

3. In the Create Custom View dialog box, click the Logged drop-down menu and select Last 24 Hours.

4. In the Event Level category, select only the Error option.

5. Click the Event Logs drop-down menu and select both the Windows Event Logs and the Applications And Service Logs check boxes.

6. Verify that the Create Custom View dialog box now matches Figure 7-14 and then click OK. When presented with the warning, click Yes.

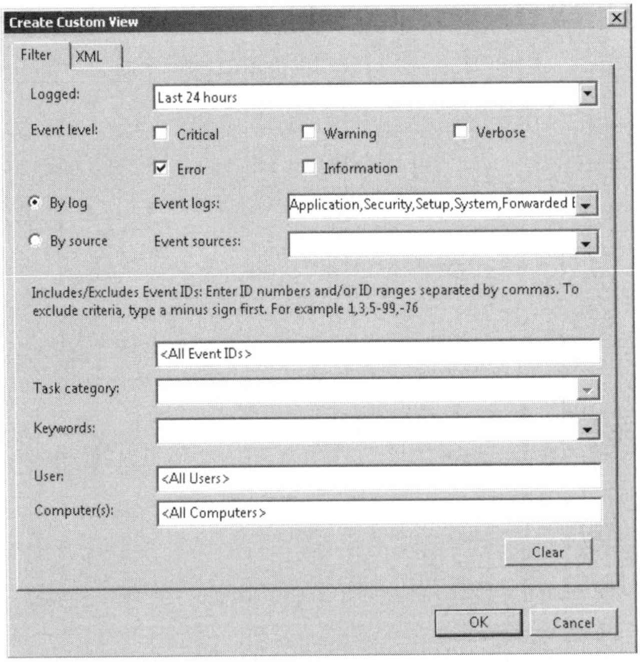

Figure 7-14   Creating a custom view

7. In the Save Filter To Custom View dialog box, type the view name as **Errors Last 24 Hours** and then click OK. The custom view has now been created.

8. View the results of the filter.

9. Expand the *Windows Log* node and then select the System log.

10. Locate any error or warning events in the log and click it. If there are no error or warning events, randomly select an information event.

11. Right-click the event and click Attach Task To This Event. This will start the Create A Basic Task Wizard. Click Next twice.

12. On the Action page of the Create A Basic Task Wizard, select Display A Message and then click Next.

13. On the Display A Message page, set the title to **Event Log Message** and set the message to **This is the task based message that I created.** Click Next and then click Finish.

14. Click OK to dismiss the informational message.

Lesson Summary

- You must enable Remote Desktop on Windows Server 2008 before you can make connections to the server. By default, members of the local Administrators and Remote Desktop Users group can log on to a server using Remote Desktop. This does not apply to domain controllers, where only members of the Administrators group can log on.

- Emergency Management Service allows you to manage a computer that has become nonfunctional.

- The RSAT tools include consoles for administering all of the roles and features that ship with Windows Server 2008. The RSAT tools are included as an installable feature on Windows Server 2008 and can be downloaded and installed onto computers running Windows Vista SP1.

- Filters allow you to limit the display of a single event log to a specific set of events. You cannot save filters, although custom views allow you to apply a saved filter to multiple event logs.

- You can attach tasks to specific logs or events. When the event occurs, the task is triggered. You can edit or delete existing Event Log-based tasks in Task Scheduler.

Lesson Review

You can use the following questions to test your knowledge of the information in Lesson 1, "Server Management Strategies." The questions are also available on the companion CD if you prefer to review them in electronic form.

NOTE Answers

Answers to these questions and explanations of why each answer choice is correct or incorrect are located in the "Answers" section at the end of the book.

---

1. At the time of Windows Server 2008's release, on which of the following computers would you be able to install the Remote System Administration Tools (RSAT)? (Each correct answer presents a complete solution. Choose two.)

   A. Windows Vista Enterprise SP 1

   B. Windows XP SP 2

   C. Windows Server 2003 Enterprise Edition R2

   D. Windows Vista Home Basic SP 1

   E. Windows Server 2008 Enterprise Edition

2. By default, members of which of the following groups are able to connect via Remote Desktop to a stand-alone Windows Server 2008 computer? (Each correct answer presents a complete solution. Choose two.)

   A. Administrators

   B. Remote Desktop Users

   C. Power Users

   D. Print Operators

   E. Backup Operators

3. Which of the following technologies can you use to cleanly shut down a Windows Server 2008 server that continues to function after an electrical surge that has burned out its graphics and network adapters?

   A. Remote Desktop

   B. Telnet

   C. EMS

   D. MMC

4. It will be necessary in the coming months for you to perform regular administrative tasks on several Windows Server 2008 computers hosted at a subsidiary company's office. Because this is a subsidiary of your company, there is no direct WAN link to their office location from your company's head office. However both the subsidiary company and yours have a direct connection to the Internet and the third-party firewall is configured to allow port 443 traffic through if the source address is within your company's head office public IP address range. Which of the following solutions should you plan to implement to allow for the remote administration of these Windows Server 2008 computers from your head office location?

   A. Configure a Terminal Services Gateway Server and place it at the subsidiary office.

   B. Configure a Terminal Services Gateway Server and place it at your company's head office.

   C. Configure the subsidiary office's firewall to allow port 25 traffic if the source IP address is within your company's head office public IP address range.

   D. Configure the subsidiary office's firewall to allow port 25 traffic if the source IP address is within your company's head office private IP address range.

5. You have configured a collector computer to collect event log data from 50 different Windows Server 2008 computers that are scattered across your organization. When you open the Forwarded Events log in the Event Viewer you are overwhelmed with data. Each time you open the Event Viewer you want to be able to quickly ascertain whether any critical events are located that have occurred within the last 24 hours. Which of the following solutions should you implement?

   A. Create a custom filter.

   B. Create a custom view.

   C. Create a subscription.

   D. Configure a WSRM policy.

Lesson 2: Monitoring and Optimizing Performance

In this lesson, you will learn about the technologies included with Windows Server 2008 that allow you to monitor and optimize server performance. Once you understand the technologies through which it is possible to monitor and enhance the performance of a single Windows Server 2008 server, you can apply this knowledge to planning how servers can be monitored and their performance enhanced on an organization-wide basis.

After this lesson, you will be able to:

- Create a performance baseline for Windows Server 2008.
- Monitor Key Performance Indicators.
- Optimize the performance of Windows Server 2008.
- Manage Event Logs.

Estimated lesson time: 40 minutes

Reliability and Performance

The *Reliability And Performance* node is located under the diagnostics node of the Server Management Console. Reliability And Performance Monitor can also be added as a snap-in to a custom MMC. The advantage of the Reliability And Performance Monitor console over previously available tools is that it collects the functionality of System Monitor, Performance Logs And Alerts, and Server Performance Advisor into a single interface with a common method of configuring which data will be collected. The default view of the Reliability And Performance Monitor console is the Resource Overview. The Resource Overview, shown in Figure 7-15, displays graphical data about real-time CPU, hard disk drive, memory, and network performance.

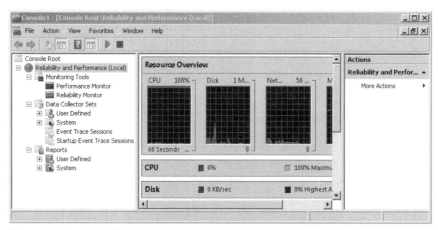

Figure 7-15   Reliability And Performance console snap-in

Although superficially similar to the output shown in Task Manager's Performance tab, the benefit of using Resource Overview is that it allows you to quickly list which processes and applications are consuming the bulk of a specific resource. If a server that you are managing has become unresponsive to client requests, examining the Resource Overview will allow you to quickly ascertain which specific application or service is monopolizing a hardware resource. The drawback of the Resource Overview is that it is a reactive tool. It gives you a point-in-time view of server performance. You cannot use the Resource Overview to track long-term trends or to forward an alert in the event that a particular threshold is exceeded. You are most likely to find the Resource Overview useful when you are aware that a problem exists with a server and are trying to diagnose a cause.

Reliability Monitor

The Reliability Monitor, shown in Figure 7-16, provides a quick graphical overview of a server's stability over the last few weeks. The Reliability Monitor records failures of hardware components, applications, and services. The Reliability Monitor also records configuration changes such as the installation of new software updates and applications. The benefit to you as an administrator is that you can quickly determine whether a configuration change made to a server has caused a decrease in that server's stability. From a planning perspective, creating a console that connects to the Reliability Monitor on multiple servers allows a quick, high-level overview of the reliability of all servers. In the event that you locate a server whose reliability graph shows a steep decline, you can then start digging deeper to determine exactly why the server is experiencing problems.

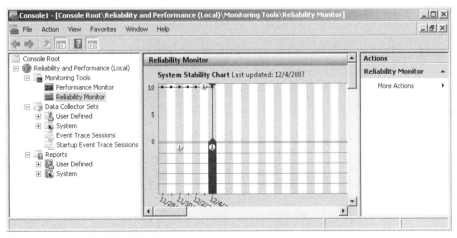

Figure 7-16 Reliability Monitor

Performance Monitor

Performance Monitor allows you to display performance counters either in real time or by loading historical data. Performance counters can be added individually or by creating what is known as a Data Collector Set. Data Collector Sets contain performance counters, event trace data, and system configuration information. Data Collector Sets are explained in more detail in "Data Collector Sets" later in this lesson.

When evaluating the performance of servers by looking at performance counters, it is necessary to look at averages over time rather than point-in-time figures, which can vary significantly from the average and do not give a good indication of how servers are functioning under load. The following list of performance statistics, if taken over a period of average server usage, should be followed up on by a systems administrator:

- Disk Queue Length averages over time should be at or below four requests per physical disk.

- Memory Pages/Sec should have an average value lower than 50.

- Processor % Processor Time should not exceed 85 percent.

- Network Total Bytes/Sec should not exceed 90 percent of line capacity.

Data Collector Sets

Data Collector Sets organize multiple data collection points into a single component that you can use to assess the performance of a computer running Windows Server 2008. Data Collector Sets include performance counters, event trace data, and system configuration information (such as the values for specific registry keys). Data Collector Sets are a key tool in evaluating and optimizing the performance of Windows Server 2008. You can create Data Collector Sets using two methods:

- **Creating a Data Collector Set from Performance Monitor**   When you have added a set of Performance Monitor counters that you want to watch, you can use them to create a new Data Collector Set by clicking New in the Actions pane and then selecting Data Collector Set. This will start the New Data Collector Set Wizard.

- **Creating a Data Collector Set manually**   You can run the Data Collector Set Wizard manually by expanding the *Data Collector Sets* node of the Reliability And Performance Monitor, right-clicking the *User Defined* node and then clicking New Data Collector Set. As Figure 7-17 shows, the wizard provides you with the ability to select performance counter, event trace data, and system configuration information data to include in the Data Collector Set.

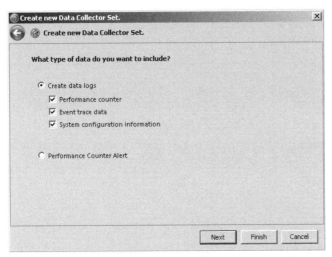

Figure 7-17   Creating a new Data Collector Set manually

The other option, when creating a Data Collector Set manually, is to create a Performance Counter Alert, which allows you to configure a task to occur when a particular performance counter threshold is met. Possible tasks include writing a log entry to the application event log, starting an existing Data Collector Set, or executing an application. The ability to start a Data Collector Set allows you to record very detailed information about the status of the Windows Server 2008 computer in the period immediately after the Performance Counter Alert threshold has been triggered. You will create a Performance Counter Alert in the practice exercises at the end of this lesson.

You can import and export Data Collector Sets through the use of templates. As shown in Figure 7-18, four default templates match the existing Data Collector Sets available under the *System* node of the *Data Collector Sets* node. You can also browse for customized templates. You can use customized Data Collector Set Templates as a method of ensuring that the same performance data is being recorded on each server that you manage.

Creating Baselines

A *baseline* is a set of average Performance Monitor counter statistics taken during a normal period of server utilization. Baseline figures allow you to understand how a server performed at a specific point in time so that you can use this as a point of comparison for future server performance. When generating baseline figures, it is important to choose a period of normal server use and to take the statistics over a reasonable amount of time. Collecting the data over a period of time ensures that any unusual peaks and dips in the figures are evened out. Collecting data during periods of normal use also allows you to understand how the server performs generally, rather than under unusually high or unusually low loads.

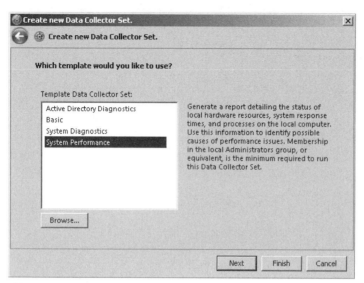

Figure 7-18   Data Collector Set Templates

Keeping Track of Trends

You should regularly gather and retain performance data on mission-critical servers. This allows you to monitor trends in server performance. Many systems administrators find trend data particularly useful when they must present a case to financial decision makers about upgrading or replacing existing servers. If you can go into a meeting proving that server utilization has steadily grown over the last year and that the server's hardware has nearly reached capacity, your argument will be more persuasive than if you simply present the most recent set of statistics. Decision makers are almost always more swayed by data indicating an obvious trend than they are by a claim that after the most recent examination, the server appears to be approaching the limits of its capacities.

Creating and Scheduling Logs from Data Collector Sets

Running a Data Collector Set generates data logs. You can configure the storage options for each Data Collector Set by editing the Data Collector Set properties. You can include information about the log in the filename, whether data is overwritten or appended, and the file size limit for each log file. Data Collector Sets run as the System user by default.

Performance monitoring is performed in many organizations by users who are not granted administrative rights. These users are generally members of the Performance Log Users group. For these users to be able to initiate data logging or to edit Data Collector Sets using the Event Viewer in Windows Server 2008, you must assign the Performance Log Users group the Log On As A Batch Job user right.

To begin logging, right-click the Data Collector Set and then click Start. To stop logging, right-click the Data Collector Set and click Stop. In most instances you will want to schedule the execution of Data Collector Sets, which you can do by right-clicking the Data Collector Set, clicking Properties and then clicking the Scheduling tab. From here you can add starting times to a schedule, as shown in Figure 7-19. Clicking the Stop Condition tab allows you to set the conditions under which the collection will stop. The stop condition can either be expressed as a period of time or a predetermined size in megabytes.

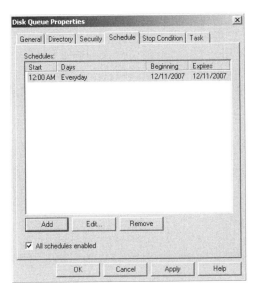

Figure 7-19   Data Collector Set schedule

Reports

Reports are automatically generated from Data Collector Set log data. You can create a report by right-clicking one of the built-in Data Collector Sets and starting it. It will run for a preconfigured amount of time before finishing its execution. When execution has completed, a report based on the Data Collector Set's log data will be present under the node. Clicking this report allows you to view its contents. Figure 7-20 shows an example performance report taken over the default System Performance Data Collector Set interval.

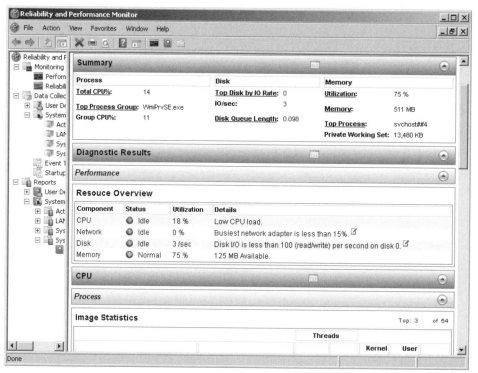

Figure 7-20 Example performance report

Scheduling the System Performance Data Collector Set to run during a server's normal periods of operation, and then comparing the data generated to previously run reports, allows you to view existing trends of server performance. By default, the System Performance Data Collector Set only executes for a minute. If you are interested in creating more robust sets of trend data for periods of peak operation, you should create a User Defined Data Collector Set based on the System Performance template and increase this interval to a figure greater than 20 minutes. You cannot edit the length of time that the default Data Collector Sets execute. You can, however, create a user-defined set based on the default templates and make the modification to the newly created set.

Task Manager and Tasklist

The Task Manager Performance tab provides a graphical overview of CPU usage and has been long used by administrators to quickly determine a server's CPU load. You can also use Task Manager to sort processes according to CPU or memory usage. Similar functionality exists with the Tasklist.exe command-line utility. These tools remain available in Windows Server 2008 even though their functionality is superseded by the functionality of the Reliability And Performance console.

As someone responsible for planning the management of Windows Server 2008 in a production environment, you should consider that although these tools both work well on single servers, they do not scale out well when it comes to managing more than a small number of Windows Server 2008 computers. If you are planning to monitor the performance of more than 10 Windows Server 2008 computers, you are better served by using the Reliability And Performance console than you are by traditional tools such as Task Manager and the tasklist.exe command-line utility.

MORE INFO   **Performance and Reliability Monitoring Step-by-Step Guide**

To learn more about the Performance And Reliability Monitoring enhancements that ship with Windows Server 2008, consult the Performance and Reliability Monitoring Step-by-Step Guide available at *http://technet2.microsoft.com/windowsserver2008/en/library/e571af05-3003-45ae-962c-e5acfaf4958e1033.mspx?mfr=true*.

Quick Check

1. Which tool would allow you to quickly determine the specific application or service that is monopolizing a Windows Server 2008 computer's RAM?
2. What information can be included in a Data Collector Set?

Quick Check Answers

1. Reliability and Performance Monitor give graphical information and provides data sorted in order of resource utilization, for CPU, disk, network, and memory usage.
2. Data Collector Sets can include performance counters, event trace data, and system configuration information.

Optimizing Windows Server 2008 Performance

Windows Server 2008 is designed to perform well right from installation for most customer deployments. Microsoft has spent significant effort creating a dynamically tuned network subsystem and improved file sharing system that should perform in the best possible manner without requiring intervention from an administrator. For specific circumstances, however, an administrator can make changes to the configuration of Windows Server 2008 outside those found in a typical deployment. These changes can enhance performance beyond what the default configuration provides.

The first thing that administrators should note is that Windows Server 2008 registry settings and tuning parameters are significantly different from those in Windows Server 2003. If you plan to implement precisely the same performance tuning procedures on your organizations Windows Server 2008 servers that brought improvements in Windows Server 2003, you are likely to encounter unexpected results. It is also important to remember to perform a system state backup prior to making registry modifications so that if unexpected results do arise, you have a pre-existing configuration that you can fall back to.

Interrupt-Affinity Policy Tool

The default behavior of Windows Server 2008 on multiprocessor systems with eight or fewer logical processors is to forward device interrupts to any available processor. The Interrupt-Affinity Policy Tool, shown in Figure 7-21, allows administrators to alter that default behavior and bind the interrupts from a specific device to a specific processor. Because the Interrupt-Affinity Policy Tool allows you to set up any configuration, including configurations that are detrimental to server performance, you need to ensure that you have good performance baselines against which to compare a newly modified configuration. You can only use the tool on devices that have interrupt resources and are not shared with other devices. Some hardware devices also request processor affinity during the boot process, and these hardware-generated requests override settings applied using the Interrupt-Affinity Policy Tool.

MORE INFO   Getting the Interrupt-Affinity Policy Tool

You can download the Interrupt-Affinity Policy Tool and find out more about how to use it on multiprocessor Windows Server 2008 computers on the following page at the Microsoft Web site: *http://www.microsoft.com/whdc/system/sysperf/IntPolicy.mspx.*

Figure 7-21   Interrupt-Affinity Policy Tool

The primary method of improving performance on any server is to reduce the number of active services and applications. The only applications and services that should be running are those that directly support the server's functionality. The added benefit of shutting down unnecessary services is that not only will it improve performance, it will also make the server more secure by reducing its attack profile.

MORE INFO   Performance tuning guidelines

For more information about performance tuning, consult the document titled "Performance Tuning Guidelines for Windows Server 2008" at *http://www.microsoft.com/whdc/system/sysperf/ Perf_tun_srv.mspx*.

Windows System Resource Manager

Windows System Resource Manager (WSRM), shown in Figure 7-22, is a performance optimization feature that you can install on Windows Server 2008 from the Server Manager console. You can use WSRM to manage processor and memory usage through the application of resource policies. Through WSRM policies, you can ensure that each service is allocated resources on an equal basis or that specific applications, services, or users are apportioned greater amounts of a server's resources. WSRM was briefly mentioned in Lesson 1 of Chapter 5.

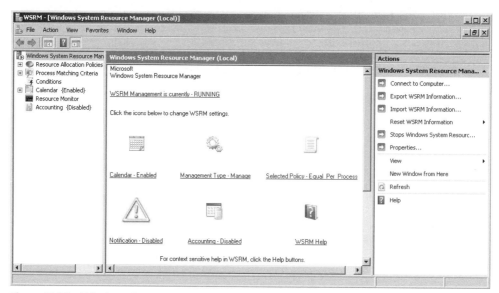

Figure 7-22 Windows System Resource Manager

You can use Windows System Resource Manager to meet the following Windows Server 2008 performance goals:

- Allocate resources on a per-process, per-user, or per-IIS application pool basis.

- Vary how servers allocate resources over time by using the WSRM calendar feature to apply different policies according to a schedule.

- Change which resource policy is applied based on server properties and events.

- Collect resource usage data either in the Windows Internal Database or to a custom SQL Server database.

WSRM ships with the following four resource management policies:

- **Equal Per Session** This policy is designed to be used on a Terminal Server. When the Equal Per Session policy is applied, each TS session that connects to the server is allocated resources equally, regardless of whether the same user is logged on using multiple sessions.

- **Equal Per User** This policy allocates resource on the basis of the user account that is running the process. This policy is primarily applied to application servers. A user who is running four processes will be allocated the same system resources as those allocated to a user running one process. If a user is allocated more resources than he is actually using, WSRM will temporarily allocate those resources to other users who could benefit from them until the original user requires more resources. For example, if four users are connected to an application server and one user is only using 10 percent of the resources, the other three will be allocated 30 percent of available resources until that one user requires more, at which point all users will be limited to 25 percent of the available resources.

- **Equal Per Process**   This policy allocates server resources equally across processes. If a process is not fully using the resources allocated to it by WSRM, WSRM will allocate those unused resources to other processes until such time that the original process's need for resources increases to the allocated limit.

- **Equal Per IIS Application Pool**   This policy assigns resources equally on the basis of an IIS application pool. An IIS application pool is a collection of Web applications hosted on a Windows Server 2008 computer with the Web Server role installed. Applications that are not assigned to application pools will only be able to use resources not being consumed by existing application pools.

As discussed in the policy section earlier, WSRM policies only come into effect when there is contention for resources. If no contention for resources exists, resources will be allocated as needed. In some instances you will want to plan WSRM policies that do not allocate resources on an equitable basis, but allocate more resources to one group of users or processes than to every other user or process, such as the policy displayed in Figure 7-23. Just as you can use per-user, per-process, per-session, and per-application pool processes, you can also create WSRM policies for specific users, specific sessions, specific processes, and specific application pools.

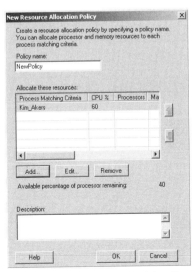

Figure 7-23   Custom WSRM policy

WSRM has some limitations, including being unable to function properly if a computer is being managed by another resource manager. You also should not use WSRM to manage applications that either have built-in resource management or applications that use job objects. In the event that a computer on which you want to use WSRM does have either type of application, you can continue to use WSRM as long as you add these specific applications to the user-defined exception list. For these applications, resource allocation will not be managed by WSRM, but they will also not conflict with WSRM. Finally, you should note that WSRM does not manage processor and memory resources used directly by Windows Server 2008. For example, imagine you apply an equal per user WSRM policy. Four users are running applications on the server and Windows Server 2008 is using 20 percent of the available CPU resources. Each user would be limited to 20 percent of the CPU's capacity because only the 80 percent of CPU capacity not used by Windows Server 2008 is available for allocation through WSRM. WSRM will be explored in more detail in the practice exercise "Applying a Windows System Resource Manager Policy" at the end of this lesson.

Practice: Data Collector Sets, Reports, and WSRM Policies

In this set of exercises, you will create a Data Collector Set, schedule its execution, create a performance alert, view a report generated from a Data Collector Set, and then create and apply a Windows System Resource Manager policy.

▶ **Exercise 1: Create a Windows Server 2008 Data Collector Set and Schedule Its Execution**

In this exercise, you will create a Data Collector Set that monitors several important performance counters. After you create the Data Collection Set, you will create a schedule for its execution. To complete this exercise, perform the following steps:

1. Log on to server Glasgow using the Kim_Akers user account and open the Reliability And Performance Monitor console from the Administrative Tools menu. Click Continue when presented with the User Account Control dialog box.

2. Expand the *Data Collector Sets* node. Right-click the *User Defined* node, click New, and then click Data Collector Set. This will start the Create A New Data Collector Set Wizard. In the Name box type **My System Set**.

3. Ensure that Create From A Template is selected and then click Next.

4. On the Which Template Would You Like To Use page, ensure that System Performance is selected and then click Next.

5. Accept the default location for the data from the Data Collector Set to be saved and then click Next.

6. On the Create A New Data Collector Set page, select the Open Properties For This Data Collector Set option and click Finish. This will open the dialog box shown in Figure 7-24.

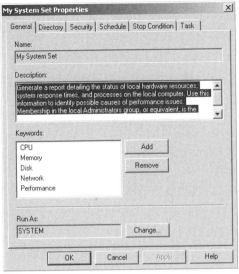

Figure 7-24   Creating a Data Collector Set

7. Click the Schedule tab and then click Add. Set the Start time to 9:30 A.M. and then click OK.

8. Click the Stop Condition tab. Change Overall Duration to 10 minutes and then click OK.

9. Right-click the My System Set Data Collector and click Start. The Data Collector will spend the next 10 minutes collecting information while you start on the next practice exercise.

▶ **Exercise 2: Create Performance Alerts and View Reports**

In this exercise, you will create a performance alert and then view the report generated by the Data Collector Set that you created and executed in the previous exercise. To complete this exercise, perform the following steps:

1. In the Reliability And Performance Monitor, right-click the *User Defined* node, click New, and then click Data Collector Set.

2. On the Create A New Data Collector Set page, type the name **My Disk Queue Alert,** select the Create Manually (Advanced) option and then click Next.

3. On the Create A New Data Collector Set page, select the Performance Counter Alert option and then click Next.

4. On the Which Performance Counters Would You Like To Monitor page, click Add.

5. From the list of available performance counters, add the Logical Disk\Current Disk Queue Length counter as shown in Figure 7-25, click Add and then click OK.

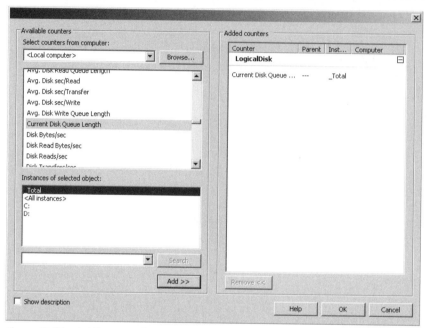

Figure 7-25   Adding a performance counter

6. Set the Alert When Above figure to **50** and then click Next.

7. On the Create The Data Collector Set page, select the Open Properties For This Data Collector Set option and then click Finish. This will open the Data Collector Set Properties dialog box.

8. In the My Disk Queue Alert Properties dialog box, click the Task tab. Because no scheduled tasks have been created, click OK to close this dialog box.

9. Verify that the My System Set Data Collector Set is in the Stopped state and then click the *User Defined* node under the *Reports* node.

10. Double-click My System Set and then double-click the green report item that will have today's date. This will bring up a System Performance Report similar to that shown in Figure 7-26.

Figure 7-26   System Performance Report

▶ **Exercise 3: Create and Apply a Windows System Resource Manager Policy**

In this exercise, you will install Windows System Resource Manager on server Glasgow and then create and apply a custom WSRM policy according to a specific schedule. To complete this exercise, perform the following steps:

1. Log on to server Glasgow using the Kim_Akers user account.

2. Open the Server Manager console if it does not open automatically either from the Quick Launch toolbar or from the Administrative Tools menu.

3. Right-click the *Features* node and then click Add Features. This will start the Add Features Wizard. On the Select Features page, scroll down through the list and select Windows System Resource Manager.

4. When presented with the dialog box that informs you that the Windows Internal Database feature is required, shown in Figure 7-27, click Add Required Features and then click Next.

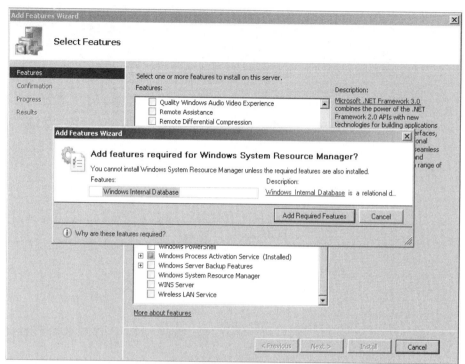

Figure 7-27   Add feature that WSRM depends on

5. On the Confirm Installation Selections page, click Install. When the installation of the new features completes, click Close.

6. In the Administrative Tools menu, click Windows System Resource Manager. Click Continue when prompted by the User Account Control dialog box.

7. When prompted by the Connect To Computer dialog box, ensure that This Computer is selected and then click Connect.

8. Click the *Resource Allocation Policies* node on the left side of the console, and then click New Resource Allocation Policy in the Actions pane. This will launch the New Resource Allocation Policy dialog box, shown in Figure 7-28.

9. In the New Resource Allocation Policy dialog box, type the name **NewPolicy** in the Policy Name box and then click Add.

10. Click Process Matching Criteria and then click New.

11. In the Criteria Name box type the name **AdminResources** and click Add.

12. In the Add Rule dialog box, click the Users Or Groups tab and then click Add.

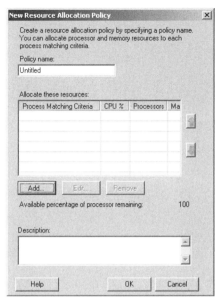

Figure 7-28   New Resource Allocation Policy dialog box

13. In the Select Users Or Groups dialog box, type **Domain Admins** and then click OK.

14. Click OK again. Verify that the New Process Matching Criteria dialog box matches Figure 7-29 and then click OK.

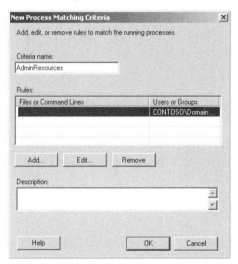

Figure 7-29   New Process Matching Criteria dialog box

15. Set the Percentage Of Processor Allocated For This Resource figure to **30** and then click OK.

16. Set the Policy Name to **AdminResources** and then click OK.

17. Click the newly created AdminResources policy in the list of Resource Allocation Policies and then click Set As Managing Policy in the Actions pane.

18. A warning will appear, informing you that the calendar will be disabled. Click OK.

19. Click the *Windows System Resource Manager (Local)* node in the left pane and verify that the Selected Policy is AdminResources, as shown in Figure 7-30.

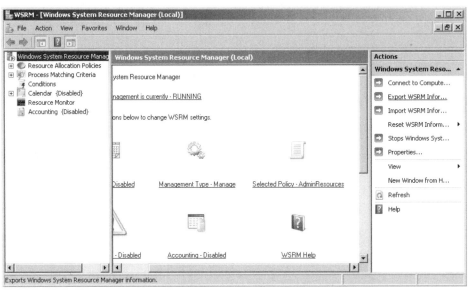

Figure 7-30   Enforcing the new policy

20. In the Actions pane, click Stops Windows System Resource Manager management to disable Windows System Resource Manager.

Lesson Summary

■ A baseline is a set of performance data that represents how the server functioned under normal load, usually when the server was first deployed. How a server is currently performing is often compared to its baseline performance.

■ Data Collector Sets include performance counter data, event trace data, and configuration information. When you execute a Data Collector Set, it generates log data that is then used to generate reports.

- Performance Alerts are Data Collector Sets that execute a task when a particular performance threshold is reached.

- Reports provide easy-to-understand summaries of Data Collector Set log information. Reports are automatically generated after a Data Collector Set has ceased execution.

- Windows System Resource Manager (WSRM) policies allow administrators to set policies that grant applications or users priority access to system resources.

Lesson Review

You can use the following questions to test your knowledge of the information in Lesson 2, "Monitoring and Optimizing Performance." The questions are also available on the companion CD if you prefer to review them in electronic form.

NOTE Answers

Answers to these questions and explanations of why each answer choice is correct or incorrect are located in the "Answers" section at the end of the book.

1. Which of the following tools should you plan to use if you want to bind a network adapter's device interrupts to a particular processor on a Windows Server 2008 computer that has multiple processors?

   A. Microsoft System Center Operations Manager 2007

   B. Windows System Resource Manager

   C. Interrupt-Affinity Policy Tool

   D. Device Manager

2. You need to ensure that for the last week of every month, applications run by members of the Accounting group are given resource priority on three Windows Server 2008 computers that you manage. Which of the following methods should you use to implement this goal?

   A. Configure a WSRM policy that is applied manually.

   B. Configure a WSRM policy that is applied using the Calendar.

   C. Configure an Interrupt-Affinity policy that is applied manually.

   D. Configure an Interrupt-Affinity policy that is applied using Scheduled Tasks.

3. Which of the following Performance Monitor figures should cause you concern if they were found to be the average over the course of a normal period of server load?

    A. An average logical disk queue length of 1

    B. Memory Pages/Sec of 75

    C. Processor % Processor Time of 65%

    D. Network Total Bytes/Sec of 2048 on a 1 GBit network

4. You are concerned that the System Performance Data Collector Set, which you have scheduled to run at 9:00 A.M. every day, is not collecting enough data to give you an accurate picture of how a server performs under normal load. The System Performance Data Collector Set is running according to its default configuration. Which of the following changes could you make to remedy this situation?

    A. Configure the schedule to run at 10:00 A.M. every day.

    B. Create a User Defined Data Collection Set based on the System Performance Data Collector Set template that has a duration of 30 minutes.

    C. Create a User Defined Data Collection Set based on the System Diagnostics Data Collector Set template that has a duration of 30 minutes.

    D. Configure the existing schedule not to expire.

Lesson 3: Delegating Authority

As a systems administrator you often have the privileges to do everything. As a valuable asset to your organization, you should minimize time spent attending to trivial tasks so that your abilities can be deployed against the more complex ones. Delegation of authority is a technology that allows non-privileged users to perform a limited and highly specific set of simple administrative tasks. In this lesson, you will learn how you can plan the delegation of authority to make the management of your organization's Windows Server 2008 network more efficient.

After this lesson, you will be able to:

- Plan delegation policies and procedures.
- Delegate authority.
- Delegate the management of applications.

Estimated lesson time: 40 minutes

Delegation Policies

Human Resources staff is rarely knowledgeable about the capabilities of Active Directory. Delegation of authority is an area that combines both the technical aspects of what can be accomplished through the application of a system administrator's knowledge and the legal and policy framework that must be interpreted and implemented by the Human Resources department. Systems administrators are trusted with critical information by the organizations that they work for. If a system administrator is the only one who can perform a particular task, such as user account creation, permissions modification, or resetting a CEO's password, someone is clearly to blame if something goes wrong. As you will learn in this lesson, systems administrators have the ability to delegate their powers. Delegation of privilege should be done only in situations covered by existing policy, not only because it is the ethical thing to do, but also because there needs to be a clear chain of responsibility.

Delegation Procedures

You can delegate authority by configuring the security settings of objects within Active Directory. Figure 7-31 shows the advanced security settings for an OU where the Kim Akers user account has been delegated permissions. The drawback of performing a manual edit is that it requires far more precision than using the Delegation Of Control Wizard, which performs the configuration automatically. You can also perform delegations by using the dsacls.exe command. Similar to using the GUI, the dsacls.exe command requires that you use precise syntax to set permissions on Active Directory objects. You can learn more about the syntax of the dsacls.exe command by issuing the *dsacls.exe/?* command from an elevated command prompt on a computer running Windows Server 2008. You can also create Windows PowerShell scripts to modify the permissions assigned to an OU as a method of delegation. Because the dsacls.exe command-line utility is specifically designed for the task of modifying the permissions of directory objects, it offers a more direct route for this task than a Windows PowerShell script that achieves the same results for simple delegation tasks.

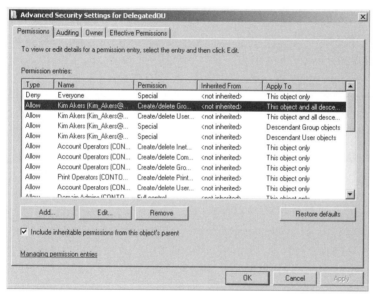

Figure 7-31   Editing permissions for delegation

When planning delegations for your environment, the Delegation Of Control Wizard is the best tool to use for a small number of delegations because it reduces the likelihood of errors and is relatively straightforward to use. When you need to perform a large number of complex delegations, getting a script that uses dsacls.exe or Windows PowerShell functioning is worth the time investment. When you are deciding between using dsacls.exe and Windows PowerShell, you need to assess the complexity of the delegation. You can perform a large number of relatively simple delegations using dsacls.exe. A large number of complex delegations might be better performed using a Windows PowerShell script, because then you can more easily add other components, such as having the script extract data from a database or spreadsheet that describes which delegations need to be performed. In summary, use the following criteria to make your decision:

- If you have a small number of delegations, use the Delegation Of Control Wizard.
- If you have a large number of simple delegations, use the dsacls.exe command-line utility.
- If you have a large number of complex delegations involving components such as CSV files, use a Windows PowerShell script.

Delegation of Administrative Privileges

As mentioned earlier in the lesson, the primary tool for performing delegations is the Delegation Of Control Wizard, shown in Figure 7-32. You can use the wizard at the domain level, although in most organizations delegations will occur at the Organizational Unit level.

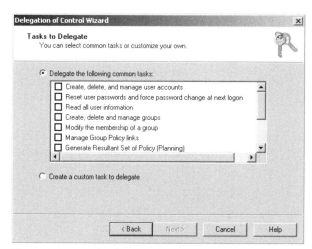

Figure 7-32   Tasks that can be delegated

You can delegate the following common tasks:

- Create, Delete, And Manage User Accounts
- Reset User Passwords And Force Password Change At Next Logon
- Read All User Information
- Create, Delete, And Manage Groups
- Modify The Membership Of A Group

- Manage Group Policy Links
- Generate Resultant Set Of Policy (Planning)
- Generate Resultant Set Of Policy (Logging)
- Create, Delete, And Manage InetOrgPerson Accounts
- Reset InetOrgPerson Passwords And Force Password Change At Next Logon
- Read All InetOrgPerson Information

You can use the Delegation Of Control Wizard to delegate one, some, or all of these tasks to users or groups. You can also, when using the Delegation Of Control Wizard, create a custom task to delegate. When creating a custom task to delegate, you can delegate control of the folder, existing objects of the container, and the creation of new objects in the container, or specific objects. You can delegate control over more than 100 different objects. Figure 7-33 shows some of these objects in the Delegation Of Control Wizard.

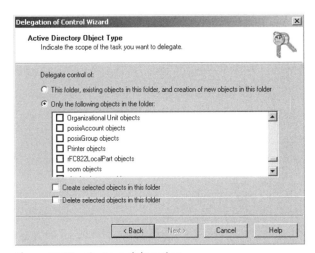

Figure 7-33   Custom delegation

The main reason to plan the delegation of control is that you want to give limited administrator rights to users. This is very important in environments where IT support is centralized and many branch offices are without a member of the IT support staff. It is important because security risks are involved in having some important administrative tasks, such as password resets, performed by someone in a remote headquarters office. For example, an attacker could phone the help desk pretending to be a particular user to get that user's user account password changed. If your organization has robust policies, you need something more than a declaration of "I am

Rooslan" before Rooslan's password is changed. In many organizations, this involves a visit to the help desk and presentation of some form of identification, such as a driver's license. Identity verification becomes more difficult when someone at a branch office forgets her password and no local IT person is available to verify identity or reset the password.

Using the Delegation Of Control Wizard, you can plan policies that allow a trusted person at a branch office site the ability to reset passwords. Because only that particular right is delegated, the trusted person does not have any other administrative rights. When someone at the branch office needs a password changed, he can verify his identity directly with the trusted delegate. The trusted delegate then performs the password reset.

Removing Existing Delegations

Although it is possible, by viewing the Advanced Security Settings for Delegation Properties, to figure out which user accounts have been delegated administrative permissions, it can sometimes be difficult to work out exactly which rights have been delegated, especially if the custom delegation options are used. In a situation in which you are unsure of what has happened previously in terms of delegation and no written records exist, you would be prudent to reset settings to their default configuration. The next time a delegation is requested, you can make sure that a paper trail exists to explain why (and for whom) the delegation was performed.

The Restore Defaults button in the Advanced Security Settings for Delegation dialog box—which you can locate by clicking Advanced from the OU properties Security tab—allows you to reset the OU to a default non-delegated state. You can also reset existing delegations using the dsacls.exe command-line utility. For example, to reset the OU named Delegation in the contoso.internal domain, you would issue the following command:

```
Dsacls "OU=Delegation,DC=contoso,DC=internal" /resetDefaultDACL
```

Delegating the Management of a Group

You can delegate control over the membership of a group through specifying a manager with the Managed By tab of a user account's properties. The user account specified as the manager can edit the membership of the group, adding and removing users as necessary. Figure 7-34 shows that Kim Akers' user account has been given the ability to update the membership list of the group named ExampleGroup. The manager can either be a user account or a group that exists within Active Directory.

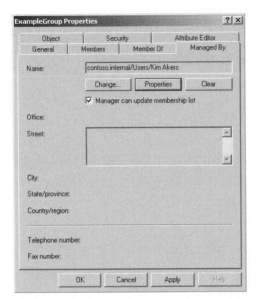

Figure 7-34 Group Manager settings as delegation

Credential Delegation

Credential delegation is an automatic process that is different from delegation of control. Delegation of control allows someone with a large set of rights to grant a subset of those rights to another user. Credential delegation, also known as delegated authentication, allows a computer to impersonate a user for the purposes of gaining access to resources that the user would normally have access to.

When the domain and forest functional level are set to Windows Server 2008, the Delegation tab, shown in Figure 7-35, becomes available on the computer account's properties dialog box in Active Directory Users And Computers.

You can confugure the following delegation settings by editing the properties of a computer account:

- Do Not Trust This Computer For Delegation
- Trust This Computer For Delegation To Any Service (Kerberos Only)
- Trust This Computer For Delegation To Specified Services Only

In terms of planning, you should deny computers that are not physically secure the ability to participate in delegated authentication. In the event that this is not practical, you can plan to use constrained delegation. Constrained delegation allows you to select specific services that can be requested through delegation by a computer that you trust for delegation. For example, in Figure 7-36 the computer account for the computer named Adelaide is configured so that it can only be used to present delegated credentials to the DNS service on computer GLASGOW.contoso.internal.

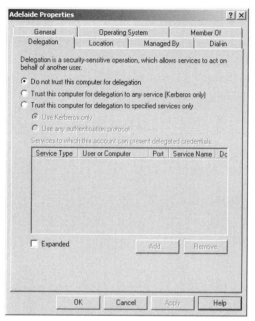

Figure 7-35   Computer account delegation settings

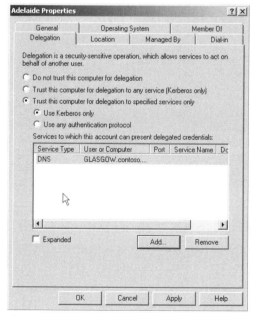

Figure 7-36   Limiting delegation

You can block important user accounts from participating in delegation. On the Account tab of a user account's properties in Active Directory User And Computers, under Account Options you will find the option to set an account as sensitive and cannot be delegated, as shown in Figure 7-37. Delegated authentication allows a network service to assume a user's identity when connecting to a second network service. For example, if Encrypting File System (EFS) is utilized in an organization, delegated authentication allows for the storage of encrypted files on file servers because the file server needs to assume the user's identity to obtain the necessary certificates to encrypt the file. Although this is acceptable for normal user accounts, Microsoft recommends that all domain-level administrator accounts should be marked as sensitive and prohibited from delegation. That way there is no chance that administrative rights will be hijacked by a sophisticated attack that uses delegation and impersonation.

Figure 7-37 Stopping the delegation of a sensitive user account

Quick Check

1. Why does Human Resources staff need the input of systems administrators when generating organizational policy regarding privilege delegation?

2. Which types of user accounts should be marked as sensitive and prohibited from participating in credential delegation?

> **Quick Check Answers**
> 1. In most cases Human Resources staff is unlikely to be aware of what is and what is not technically possible with respect to privilege delegation.
> 2. Administrator accounts, specifically domain- and enterprise-level administrator accounts, should be marked as sensitive and be prohibited from participating in credential delegation.

NOTE Auditing delegation activity

Just as you should keep a record of the use of administrative permissions, you should also configure auditing so that there are records of the activities of the user that you have delegated privileges to.

Delegating the Management of Applications

In many large organizations, different people are responsible for different administrative tasks. Often the person who installs the application is not the person who is responsible for maintaining that application. An example of this might be Microsoft Exchange Server 2007, where the person who is responsible for the network overall and who has administrative privileges over all Windows Server 2008 computers is not actually responsible for managing the Exchange Server 2007 infrastructure. Figure 7-38 provides an example of Exchange Server 2007 security groups that are used to assign roles to Exchange administrators. In Exchange Server 2007, delegation of privileges can be achieved by adding user accounts to special groups that themselves have been granted privileges across an Exchange organization.

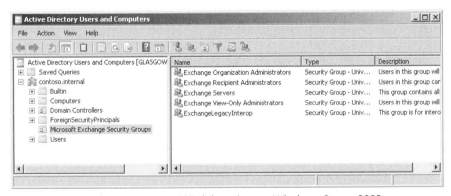

Figure 7-38 Exchange Server 2007 delegation on Windows Server 2003

Role-Based Delegation

Almost all Microsoft server products, such as Exchange 2007, SQL Server 2008, and System Center Operations Manager 2007 use this method of role-based delegation, where users are assigned particular administrative roles. In almost all cases, users that are delegated administrative roles for a particular application require no separate administrative rights on the server that hosts that application.

Just as Windows Server 2008 has the RSAT tools, most application servers come with a set of administration tools that you can install on a client operating system such as Windows Vista. This allows for the remote management of the application without requiring direct access to the server that hosts that application. The guiding principle behind planning the administration of application servers installed on Windows Server 2008 hosts is attempting to minimize the amount of direct interaction that application administrators have with the actual server that hosts that application.

IIS Configuration Delegation

IIS 7.0 configuration delegation, a feature new to IIS 7.0, allows administrators of computers hosting the Web Server role to delegate Web site configuration tasks. This means that rather than requiring the administrator of the Windows Server 2008 computer to configure settings such as a Web site's default document or SSL settings, these configuration tasks can be delegated to Web site owners or users without server level administrative rights on a per-Web site basis. To perform feature delegation it is necessary to be logged on, or invoke, the built-in Administrator account. You cannot perform feature delegation with an account that is a member of the local Administrators group on the computer hosting IIS 7 because of the security architecture of Windows Server 2008.

MORE INFO   **IIS configuration delegation**

For more information on configuration delegation, consult the following link written by Microsoft's IIS team: *http://www.iis.net/articles/view.aspx/IIS7/Managing-IIS7/Delegation-in-IIS7/Delegating-Permission-in-Config/How-to-Use-Configuration-Delegation-in-IIS7.*

Practice: Delegating Administrative Permissions in Windows Server 2008

In this set of exercises, you will perform the types of delegation tasks that you are likely to encounter in the day-to-day management of a Windows Server 2008 environment.

In the first exercise, you will delegate the management of user account passwords to a trusted user. In the second exercise, you will rescind this delegation.

▶ **Exercise 1: Delegate the Management of User Passwords for All User Accounts in an Organizational Unit**

In this exercise, you will delegate the ability to manage user passwords for a specific OU to a specified user account. This procedure is likely where you have planned to allow a designated person at a branch office location to to reset passwords, but where you do not want to allow that person the ability to perform tasks such as create user accounts or manage groups. To complete this exercise, perform the following steps:

1. Log on to DC Glasgow with the Kim_Akers user account.

2. In the Administrative Tools menu, click Active Directory Users And Computers.

3. In Active Directory Users And Computers, create an account for **Andy_Jacobs** in the Users container. Assign the password **P@ssword.**

4. In Active Directory Users And Computers, create a new Organizational Unit called Delegation under the contoso.internal domain.

5. Right-click the Delegation OU and then click Delegate Control. This will start the Delegation Of Control Wizard. Click Next.

6. On the Selected Users And Groups page, click Add, then add **andy_jacobs@ contoso.internal** and click OK. The Delegation Of Control Wizard should resemble Figure 7-39. Click OK and then click Next.

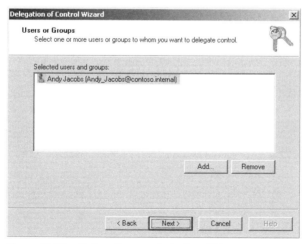

Figure 7-39 Delegating control of an OU

7. On the Tasks To Delegate page, ensure that the Delegate The Following Common Tasks option is selected and then select the Reset User Passwords And Force Password Change At Next Logon option, as shown in Figure 7-40. Click Next.

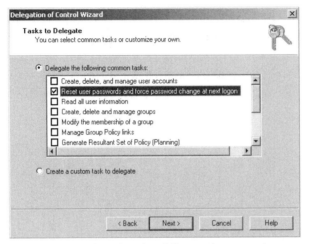

Figure 7-40 Delegating the ability to change and reset passwords

8. Click Finish to close the Delegation Of Control Wizard.

▶ **Exercise 2: Reset a Delegation Using the DSACLS Command**

In this exercise, you will undo the delegation that you performed in Exercise 1. You can achieve this goal by several methods. You will examine the first method and then perform the second. To complete this exercise, perform the following steps:

1. Log on to DC Glasgow with the Kim_Akers user account.

2. In the Administrative Tools menu, click Active Directory Users And Computers.

3. Click View and then click Advanced Features. This will display extended properties for Active Directory objects.

4. Right-click the Delegation OU, click Properties and then click the Security tab. Click Advanced. You should be able to see that the Andy Jacobs user account has been assigned the permissions shown in Figure 7-41. Note the Restore Defaults button on this dialog box. You can also use this button to reset a delegated OU to its initial configuration.

5. Click Cancel twice to close the permissions and OU properties dialog boxes.

6. Open an Administrative command prompt by right-clicking Command Prompt in the Start menu and then clicking Run As Administrator.

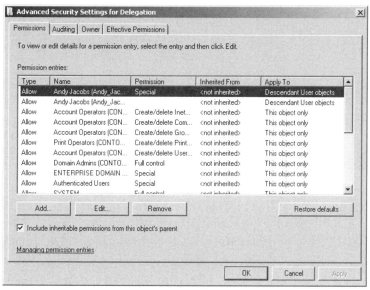

Figure 7-41   Advanced Security Settings

7. When the command prompt opens, issue the following command:

   ```
   dsacls "OU=Delegation,DC=contoso,DC=internal" /resetDefaultDACL
   ```

8. When you receive the message The Command Completed Successfully, close the command prompt.

9. View the Advanced Security Settings dialog box for the Delegation OU using the procedure outlined in step 4. Verify that the Andy Jacobs user account no longer has any permissions to the Delegation OU.

Lesson Summary

- You should consult with the Human Resources department and develop written delegation policies before proceeding with an actual delegation.

- Delegation is usually performed using the Delegation Of Control Wizard. You can also perform delegation using the dsacls.exe command. It is also possible to reset delegation settings back to their defaults using the dsacls.exe command.

- Domain Administrator accounts should be marked as sensitive and prohibited from participating in delegation.

- Application delegation usually involves adding users to special groups that are added to the domain by an application's installation routine.

Lesson Review

You can use the following questions to test your knowledge of the information in Lesson 3, "Delegating Authority." The questions are also available on the companion CD if you prefer to review them in electronic form.

NOTE Answers

Answers to these questions and explanations of why each answer choice is correct or incorrect are located in the "Answers" section at the end of the book.

---

1. You have just logged on to a Windows Server 2008 computer that hosts the Web Server role using Remote Desktop. The server is a member of your organization's domain. You are in the process of configuring the server to host Web sites for several different departments in your company. You want to delegate authority in such a way that each department can manage its own Web site. When you attempt this, you are unable to perform the feature delegation. Which of the following strategies should you pursue to accomplish this goal?

   A. Log on using the built-in Administrator account.

   B. Add your domain account to the local Administrators group.

   C. Add your domain account to the Domain Admins group.

   D. Add your local account to the local Administrators group.

2. You are planning a Windows Server 2008 network for your organization. Your organization has a head office location and five branch office locations scattered around the country. IT personnel will only be located in the head office location. You want to avoid having branch office users contact the head office when they need a password changed, but do not want to grant non-IT staff unnecessary privileges. Which of the following plans would meet these goals?

   A. Plan to delegate the Create, Delete, And Manage Groups task to a trusted user at each branch office using the Delegation Of Control Wizard.

   B. Plan to delegate the Create, Delete, And Manage User Accounts task to a trusted user at each branch office using the Delegation Of Control Wizard.

   C. Plan to delegate the Read All User Information task to a trusted user at each branch office using the Delegation Of Control Wizard.

   D. Plan to delegate the Reset User Passwords And Force Password Change At Next Logon task to a trusted user at each branch office using the Delegation Of Control Wizard.

3. You want give Sam Abolrous the ability to change the membership of the Interns universal security group. The group is located in the Contractors OU. This OU hosts the user accounts and security groups related to temporary workers at your organization. Which of the following steps should you take to accomplish this goal?

   A. Use the Delegation Of Control Wizard to grant Sam's user account the Modify The Membership Of A Group right on the Contractors OU.

   B. Use the Delegation Of Control Wizard on the Interns security group. Grant the Modify The Membership Of A Group right to Sam's user account.

   C. Use the Delegation Of Control Wizard on the Interns security group. Grant the Create, Delete And Manage Groups right to Sam's user account.

   D. Set the Interns security group to be managed by Sam's user account. Ensure that Sam has the ability to update the membership list.

4. The Students OU contains 300 user accounts and 40 groups. Your assistant reports that she made an error when using the Delegation Of Control Wizard and she is not precisely sure which rights she may have delegated away. Which of the following actions could you take to return the Students OU to the state it existed in prior to delegation occurring? (Each correct answer presents a complete solution. Choose two.)

   A. Use the dsacls command with the /resetDefaultDACL option.

   B. Use the Restore Defaults button on the OU's Advanced Security Settings for Delegation dialog box.

   C. Use the Clear button on the Managed By tab of the OU properties.

   D. Use the Change button on the Managed By tab of the OU properties.

   E. Use the dsquery command.

Chapter Review

To further practice and reinforce the skills you learned in this chapter, you can perform the following tasks:

- Review the chapter summary.
- Review the list of key terms introduced in this chapter.
- Complete the case scenarios. These scenarios set up real-world situations involving the topics of this chapter and ask you to create a solution.
- Complete the suggested practices.
- Take a practice test.

Chapter Summary

- Remote Desktop is commonly used for the remote administration of Windows Server 2008 computers. The RSAT tools allow the roles and features of a Windows Server 2008 computer to be managed from a client workstation. Windows PowerShell is a powerful administrative scripting language that allows administrators to automate repetitive and complex systems administration tasks.
- Event Log subscriptions allow all of an organization's events to be forwarded to a single collector computer for analysis. Custom views are persistent filters that allow an administrator to quickly locate important Event Log data.
- Performance Monitor Data Collector Sets allow performance and configuration data to be captured and then summarized in reports. Data Collector Sets are excellent tools for generating baseline data about computer performance.
- Windows System Resource Manager allows you to apply resource policies on a per-user, per-group or per-application basis.
- The Delegation Of Control Wizard can be used to delegate the ability to perform administrative duties to non-administrative users.

Key Terms

Do you know what these key terms mean? You can check your answers by looking up the terms in the glossary at the end of the book.

- Collector computer
- Data collector set

- Delegation
- Privilege
- Reliability

Case Scenarios

In the following case scenarios, you will apply what you have learned about Windows Server 2008 management, monitoring, and delegation. You can find answers to these questions in the "Answers" section at the end of this book.

Case Scenario 1: Fabrikam Event Management

One of the members of the Systems Administration team at Fabrikam is retiring in the new year and, rather than replace that member of staff, management has offered you a deal in which they will increase your salary if you can implement more efficient server management technologies. One of the most time-consuming tasks has been the management of Event Log data on the company's many servers. You have decided to implement some of the new log management functionality that ships with Windows Server 2008 as a way of becoming more efficient. To do this you need to find answers to the following questions:

1. What steps need to be taken to configure a single Windows Server 2008 computer as a log collector?

2. There are 30 servers, all located within an OU named AppServers. How can you ensure that the events written to the event logs from these 30 servers are forwarded to the computer configured as a collector?

3. You want to be notified by an SMS sent to your cellular phone when particular error events occur. You have written a Windows PowerShell script that generates the SMS based on the event data, but you need some way to trigger this script when the event occurs. What steps do you need to take to implement this?

Case Scenario 2: Server Performance Monitoring at Blue Yonder Airlines

Blue Yonder Airlines is just about to take delivery of 20 new computers that will have the Windows Server 2008 Enterprise Edition operating system installed on them. Your manager wants to keep performance data on these servers so that she can report how well they function with their assigned load. She also wants to store data so that over time performance trends can be accounted for and new equipment requisitioned during future budget meetings. With this in mind, you need to complete several tasks and consider several questions. For example:

1. You want to create a Data Collector Set that records processor usage, the amount of available RAM, and the load on the disk subsystem. Which counters should you include?

2. What should you keep in mind when generating a baseline report using the Reports functionality of the Reliability And Performance MMC Snap-in?

3. What method would you use to prove that new server hardware might be required because the current server hardware is inadequate?

Case Scenario 3: Delegating Rights to Trusted Users at Wingtip Toys

You are helping to plan administrative procedures and policy for a new Windows Server 2008 environment to be implemented in the medium-sized business Wingtip Toys. Wingtip Toys has approximately 500 staff members spread across one office and two factory locations. Wingtip Toys wants to minimize the number of staff members who have a direct IT responsibility and wants to delegate specific IT-related tasks to trusted users throughout the organization. For example, departmental administrative assistants should be able to reset the passwords of members of their departments and team leaders should be able to add and remove user accounts from security groups that correspond to their teams. Team leaders should not be able to modify the membership of other team leaders' security groups. All user accounts are currently stored in the Users container and each department is represented by a security group. Given this information:

1. What steps must you take to implement the plan to allow departmental administrative assistants to reset passwords of the user accounts of staff within their respective departments?

2. What steps must you take to implement the plan to allow team leaders to add and remove user accounts from security groups that correspond to their teams?

Suggested Practices

To help you successfully master the exam objectives presented in this chapter, complete the following tasks.

Plan Server Management Strategies

Do all the practices in this section.

- **Practice 1: Command-Line Tools and Scripts**   Create a comma-delimited file with the details of five users. Create a Windows PowerShell script to import these users into Active Directory.

  Create a second comma-delimited file with the details of five more users. Do not use the user names that you configured for the first part of this practice. Use the traditional csvde.exe command-line utility to import the second set of five users into Active Directory.

- **Practice 2: Creating a Custom View**   Create a custom view that displays all events from the DiskQuota event source.

  Create a custom view that displays all Warning, Critical, and Error events from the Forwarded Events log only.

Plan for Delegated Administration

Do all the practices in this section.

- **Practice 1: Perform a Custom Delegation**   Create a new OU called **CompanyContacts**. Create a new security group named **ContactAdmins**. Delegate the ability to create and delete Contact objects in the CompanyContacts OU to members of the ContactAdmins security group.

- **Practice 2: Virtual Host Delegation**   In IIS, create a new virtual host called **cohovineyard.com**. Create a new security group named **CohoAdmins**.

  Delegate control of the newly created Web site to the Cohoadmins group.

Monitor Servers for Performance Evaluation and Optimization

Do all the practices in this section.

- **Practice 1: Data Collector Set**   Create a Data Collector Set using Performance Monitor, focusing specifically on counters related to disk queue length.

  Create a report using the disk queue length-based Data Collector Set that spans a period of five minutes.

- **Practice 2: Windows System Resource Manager**   Create a security group named **ResourceHogs**. Create a Windows System Resource Manager policy that allows members of the ResourceHogs security group to use up to 80 percent of CPU resources.

Take a Practice Test

The practice tests on this book's companion CD offer many options. For example, you can test yourself on just one exam objective, or you can test yourself on all the 70-646 certification exam content. You can set up the test so that it closely simulates the experience of taking a certification exam, or you can set it up in study mode so that you can look at the correct answers and explanations after you answer each question.

MORE INFO   Practice tests

For details about all the practice test options available, see the "How to Use the Practice Tests" section in this book's Introduction.

Chapter 8
Patch Management and Security

This chapter examines several themes that fall under the broad category of security. The first part of this chapter examines the centralized deployment of updates through Windows Server Update Services. The chapter moves on to cover how you can ensure that centralized patch deployment is actually working through reports. From there you will learn how to use different auditing policies to track sensitive items and data within your organization. The chapter ends with a discussion on how to use Windows Firewall with Advanced Security to secure domain communication so that only authorized computers are able to communicate with each other.

Exam objectives in this chapter:
- Implement patch management strategy.
- Monitor and maintain security and policies.

Lessons in this chapter:

Before You Begin

To complete the lesson in this chapter, you must have done the following:

- Installed and configured the evaluation edition of Windows Server 2008 Enterprise Edition in accordance with the instructions listed in the first practice exercise of Lesson 1 in Chapter 1, "Installing, Upgrading, and Deploying Windows Server 2008."

No additional configuration is required for this chapter.

Real World

Orin Thomas

A willful and stubborn user can undo the most elegantly designed security solution. The most rigorous password policy in the world is useless if it is so onerous that users scribble their passwords on bits of notepaper and paste them to their monitors. A NAP policy can't be considered a success if users simply stop trying to connect their laptops to the corporate VPN to access Microsoft Exchange and start exclusively using a free webmail account for work-related e-mail. As an administrator, you need to take a holistic approach to securing Windows Server 2008. This involves more than just configuring elegant security policies: You must also inform the people that use the servers that you manage on a day-to-day basis why certain security policies have been enforced and the steps that they can take to resolve problems caused by security policies when they inevitably arise. Always remember that securing servers is more than the technical process of configuring server security—it also involves educating and informing users how they can continue to do their job with those security settings in place.

Lesson 1: Windows Server 2008 Patch Management Strategies

Windows Server Update Services (WSUS) is a freely available add-on component for Windows Server 2008 that functions as a Microsoft Update server in your environment. Rather than having every computer in your organization download megabytes worth of updates over the Internet, you can configure a WSUS server to be the only computer that downloads updates, and then you configure every other computer in your organization to use the WSUS server as the source of update files. In this lesson, you will learn how to configure and use WSUS as the primary method of managing updates in your Windows Server 2008 environment. You will also learn about advanced software solutions, such as Microsoft System Center Essentials 2007 and Microsoft System Center Configuration Manager 2007, which you can use to ensure that the computers in your environment are fully updated and compliant with relevant rules and regulations.

> **After this lesson, you will be able to:**
> - Manage operating system patch level maintenance.
> - Manage Windows Server Update Services.
> - Manage application patch level maintenance.
>
> **Estimated lesson time: 40 minutes**

Deploying Updates with WSUS

The first step in deploying WSUS 3.0 SP1 on a Windows Server 2008 computer in your organization is downloading the WSUS 3.0 SP1 software from Microsoft's Web site. WSUS 3.0 SP1 is not included as a role or feature in Windows Server 2008, though the software itself is freely available and can be installed on licensed Windows Server 2008 computers. WSUS 3.0 SP1 cannot be installed on computers running Windows Server Core, though this functionality may be available in later versions of the update server software.

MORE INFO   **Obtaining WSUS**

You can download the latest version of WSUS from the following Web page: *http://technet.microsoft.com/en-us/wsus/default.aspx*.

WSUS 3.0 SP1 is the first version of WSUS that you can install and run on a Windows Server 2008 computer. You can, of course, run earlier versions of WSUS on a Windows Server 2003 virtual machine on a Windows Server 2008 host, but because the 70-646 exam is focused on Windows Server 2008, discussion will be limited to running WSUS 3.0 SP1 on that operating system.

You can only install WSUS 3.0 SP1 if the following Windows Server 2008 components are enabled:

- Windows Authentication
- Static Content
- ASP.NET
- IIS 6.0 Management Compatibility
- IIS 6.0 Metabase Compatibility

The final necessary component is the Microsoft Report Viewer, version 2005 or later, which is not available as an add-on role or feature. This software must be downloaded from Microsoft's Web site. After these components are enabled and Report Viewer is installed, you can install WSUS 3.0 SP1.

NOTE Download Microsoft Report Viewer

Download Microsoft Report Viewer from the following address: *http://www.microsoft.com/Downloads/details.aspx?familyid=8A166CAC-758D-45C8-B637-DD7726E61367&displaylang=en.*

The installation of WSUS 3.0 SP1 on a Windows Server 2008 computer generates the following two local groups, which function as WSUS administrative roles. You can assign roles to users by adding their user accounts to the relevant groups.

- **WSUS Administrators** Users who have accounts that are members of this local group are able to administer the WSUS server. This includes WSUS administration tasks, from approving updates and configuring computer groups to configuring automatic approvals and the WSUS server's update source. A user that is a member of this group can use the Update Services console to connect remotely to manage WSUS.

- **WSUS Reporters** Users who have accounts that are members of this local group are able to create reports on the WSUS server. A user that is a member of this group can connect remotely to the WSUS server using the Update Services console to run these reports.

Although the default is to use its own database, installed during the WSUS installation process, it is also possible to use a SQL Server 2005 SP1 or later database to store WSUS configuration and reporting information. Organizations that want to generate customized reports use this option, writing their own applications to interact with the SQL Server database rather than relying upon the default reporting options available from the Update Services console. For example, developers in your organization could write a database application that extracts data from the database and forwards it to administrators on a daily basis through e-mail. Organizations considering this type of deployment might also consider using System Center Essentials 2007 as an update management solution because it includes more detailed reporting functionality. System Center Essentials 2007 is covered later in this lesson.

Deployment Scenarios

How WSUS is deployed in your organization depends on your organization's network architecture. The following section details four common WSUS deployment configurations and the network environments they best suit.

Single WSUS server deployment   In a single WSUS server deployment, a single WSUS server is deployed in a protected environment and synchronizes content directly with Microsoft Update. Updates are distributed to clients as shown in Figure 8-1. This type of deployment is the most common, and a single WSUS 3.0 SP1 server can serve as the update server for up to 25,000 WSUS clients.

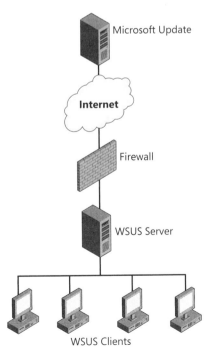

Figure 8-1   Single WSUS server deployment

Multiple independent WSUS servers The multiple independent WSUS deployment is common in organizations that have branch offices in disparate locations. Each WSUS server functions as a stand-alone server. Configuration and approval data is managed on a per-WSUS server basis, usually by onsite administrators. Figure 8-2 shows a multiple independent WSUS server deployment.

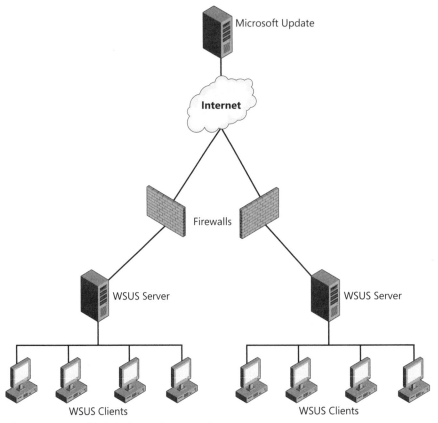

Figure 8-2 Multiple independent WSUS servers

Multiple internally synchronized WSUS servers In this deployment model, the WSUS server that receives updates from the Microsoft Update server is designated as the upstream server. A WSUS server that retrieves updates from another WSUS server is designated as a downstream server. This type of deployment is becoming less common because WSUS 3.0 supports up to 25,000 clients and Background Intelligent Transfer service (BITs) peer-caching. BITs peer-caching is a Windows Vista and Windows Server 2008 technology that allows updates to be shared in a peer-to-peer manner among clients on the LAN. BITs peer-caching allows one computer on a local subnet to download an update from a WSUS server and then share it with other compatible clients on the same subnet. When studied on Microsoft's network, BITS peer-caching reduced the load on the WSUS servers so much that it was determined that 70 percent of updates were retrieved from other computers on the same LAN rather than being downloaded directly from the WSUS server. This means that except for the purposes of redundancy, a single WSUS server can provide updates to all but the largest sites. The multiple internally synchronized deployment model is shown in Figure 8-3.

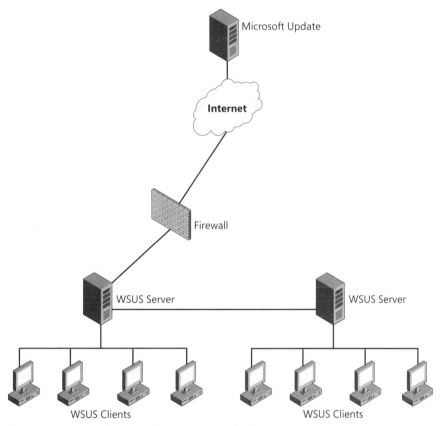

Figure 8-3 Multiple Internally Synchronized WSUS Servers

Disconnected WSUS servers In the disconnected model, one server retrieves updates from the Internet and then those updates are transferred using other media—either writable DVD-ROM or removable USB hard disk drive—and transferred to other servers, which deploy them to clients. Many administrators use a variant of this model when dealing with remote branch offices. Rather than transfer gigabytes of existing updates across slow WAN or Internet links to the new WSUS server at the remote office, the data is physically transported and added to a new WSUS server. Figure 8-4 shows the disconnected WSUS server deployment model.

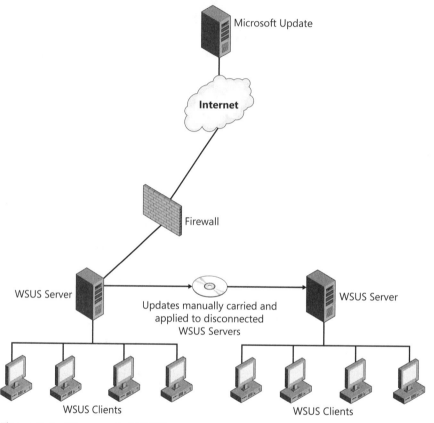

Figure 8-4   Disconnected WSUS servers

MORE INFO   More on WSUS deployment

For detailed information on WSUS deployment, consult the WSUS deployment guide at: *http://www.microsoft.com/downloads/details.aspx?FamilyID=208e93d1-e1cd-4f38-ad1e-d993e05657c9&DisplayLang=en.*

Replica Mode and Autonomous Mode

You have two options when configuring the administration model for your organization's downstream WSUS servers. The first option, shown in Figure 8-5, is to configure the downstream WSUS server as a replica of the upstream server. When you configure a WSUS server as a replica, all approvals, settings, computers, and groups from the upstream server are used on the downstream server. The downstream server cannot be used to approve updates when configured in replica mode, though you can change a replica server to the second mode—called autonomous mode—if an update urgently needs to be deployed.

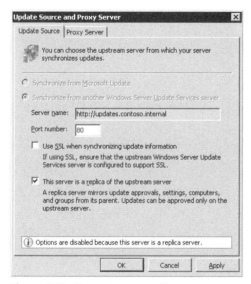

Figure 8-5   Downstream replica server

Autonomous mode allows for a local WSUS administrator to configure separate update approval settings, but still retrieves updates from the upstream WSUS server. Autonomous mode conserves bandwidth for the organization by ensuring that updates are downloaded only once from the Internet, but retains the benefit of allowing local administrators discretion with regard to the approval of updates.

Using Computer Groups

In the most basic form of WSUS deployment, every computer that is a client of the WSUS server receives approved updates at the same time. Although this method works well for many organizations, other organizations prefer to perform staggered rollouts of updates. Groups allow the staggered and targeted deployment of updates. Microsoft does everything possible to ensure that the updates it releases do not cause problems with other software, but if your organization deploys custom applications, a conflict may arise between a newly released update and your organization's important custom business application. By creating a test group, you can deploy newly released updates to a subset of the computers in your organization. This gives you a chance to verify that new updates do not conflict with existing deployed configurations before rolling out the update to everyone in your organization.

WSUS computer groups have the following properties:

- The two default computers are All Computers and Unassigned Computers. Unless a client computer is already assigned to a group, when it contacts the WSUS server for the first time, it will be added to the Unassigned Computers group.

- Groups can be organized in a hierarchy. An update added to a group at the top of the hierarchy will also be deployed to computers that are in groups lower in the hierarchy. The Unassigned Computers group is a part of the All Computers hierarchy.

- Computers can be assigned to multiple groups.

As Figure 8-6 shows, administrators can use two methods to assign computer accounts to WSUS groups. The first method is known as server-side targeting. To use this method, choose the Use The Update Services Console option under the Computers item in the Options section of the Update Services console. When a computer contacts the WSUS server for the first time, it is placed in the Unassigned Computers group. A user with WSUS Administrator privileges then manually assigns the computer to a Computers group using the WSUS console.

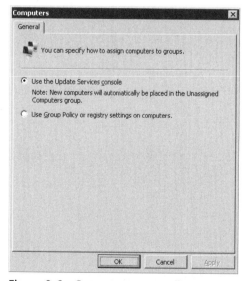

Figure 8-6   Computer group option

The other method of assigning computers to groups is to use Group Policy or registry settings on clients of the WSUS server. This method, known as client-side targeting, is less onerous in large environments and simplifies the group assignment process. Regardless of which method you use to assign computers to groups, you must first create the groups using the WSUS console. To configure a Group Policy object (GPO) to support client-side targeting, perform the following steps:

1. Open the GPO that you will use to assign the computer group.

2. In Computer Configuration\Policies\Administrative Templates\Windows Components\Windows Update, open the Enable Client-Side Targeting Policy item.

3. Select the Enabled option and then specify a computer in the Target Group Name For This Computer box, as shown in Figure 8-7.

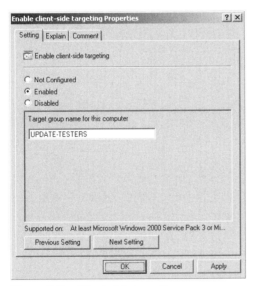

Figure 8-7   Client-side targeting

WSUS Client Configuration

Although WSUS clients can be configured manually using the registry, in most enterprise environments WSUS clients will be configured using Group Policy. The policies related to WSUS are located in the Computer Configuration\Policies\Administrative Templates\Windows Components\Windows Update node and are shown in Figure 8-8. It is important to remember that if you want a Windows Server 2008 computer hosting WSUS to receive updates, you must configure it like you would any other client computer.

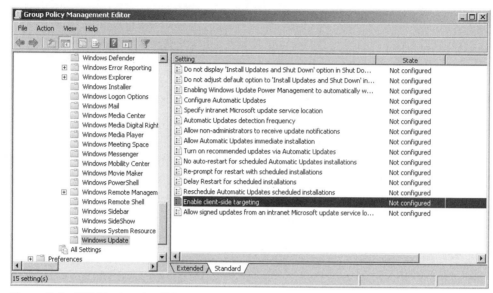

Figure 8-8   WSUS-related policies

Update Installation Behavior

Other than the policies that determine the assignment of computers to WSUS groups and the location of the local WSUS server, the most important WSUS-related policies relate to how and when WSUS updates are downloaded and installed. As an administrator you want to avoid the situation of updates never being installed—either because a user intervenes to cancel update installation or the updates are always scheduled to be installed when the computer turns off. Stopping user intervention must be balanced with interrupting a user's work. No one will be particularly happy to lose several hours of work on an important spreadsheet because you have configured the update settings to install and reboot the computer without giving the user a chance to do anything about it.

When planning the scheduling of update deployments, you should take the following policy items into account:

- **Enabling Windows Update Power Management To Automatically Wake Up The System To Install Scheduled Updates**   This policy only works with Windows Vista that has compatible hardware and an appropriately configured BIOS. Rather than worrying about whether users will be interrupted by reboots during the update deployment process, use this policy to allow computers to be woken in the middle of the night, have the relevant updates deployed, and then returned to sleep.

■ **Configure Automatic Updates** The Configure Automatic Updates policy allows you to specify whether updates are automatically downloaded and scheduled for installation or whether the user is simply notified that updates (either already downloaded or on the WSUS server) are available.

■ **Automatic Updates Detection Frequency** If this policy is not enabled, the default detection frequency is 22 hours. If you want to configure a more frequent interval, use this policy to do so.

■ **Allow Automatic Updates Immediate Installation** When enabled, this policy automatically installs all updates that do not require a service interruption or for Windows to restart.

■ **No Auto-Restart For Scheduled Automatic Updates Installations** When this policy is enabled, the computer will not automatically restart, but will wait for the user to restart the computer on her own time. The user will be notified that the computer needs to be restarted before the installation of updates is completed. If this policy is not enabled, the computer will automatically restart five minutes after the updates are installed to complete update installation.

■ **Delay Restart For Scheduled Installations** This policy enables you to vary the automatic restart period. As mentioned previously, the default period is five minutes. This policy allows you to set a delay period of up to 30 minutes.

■ **Reschedule Automatic Updates Scheduled Installations** This policy ensures that a scheduled installation that did not occur—perhaps because the computer was switched off or disconnected from the network—will occur the specified number of minutes after the computer is next started. If this policy is disabled, a missed scheduled installation will occur with the next scheduled installation.

WSUS Support for Roaming Clients

Many organizations have staff who regularly move between locations. These staff are often assigned laptop computers. In terms of the deployment of updates, this means that unless a technology like Network Access Protection (NAP) is installed, these computers might not receive updates until the staff member who uses them logs on back at their home office. (For more details on NAP, see Chapter 9, "Remote Access and Network Access Protection.")

The way to ensure that roaming clients can access updates on any WSUS server in your organization is to configure all update clients to point to the same WSUS server name through Group Policy and then configure DNS so that the FQDN resolves to the local IP address in each subnet. To do this, configure DNS Round Robin with netmask ordering as shown in Figure 8-9. When you configure DNS Round Robin with netmask ordering, the DNS server will return the host record that is located on the querying computer's subnet. For example, the FQDN for wsus.contoso.internal will resolve to 10.10.10.100 when DNS is queried at the Sydney branch office and 10.10.20.100 when DNS is queried at the Melbourne branch office.

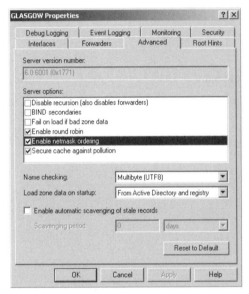

Figure 8-9   Enabling netmask ordering

Updates and Synchronization Strategies

When updates are downloaded to a WSUS server, either from Microsoft Update or an upstream server, the metadata and the update files are stored in separate locations. The update metadata is stored in the WSUS database. Depending on the configuration of WSUS, the actual update files themselves are stored on the WSUS server or on the Microsoft Update servers. This configuration setting is determined during the installation of WSUS. When updates are stored on the Microsoft Update servers, approved updates are downloaded by clients directly from Microsoft's servers rather than from the WSUS server.

Automatic approval rules allow you to approve specific categories of updates automatically. You can configure updates for a specific classification, for specific products, and to apply to specific WSUS computer groups. The available classifications are Critical Updates, Definition Updates, Drivers, Feature Packs, Security Updates, Service Packs,

Tools, Update Rollups, and Updates. The product category includes almost all current Microsoft products and is too numerous to list here. You can have multiple automatic approvals rules and can enable and disable them as necessary. Automatic approval rules are configured through the Automatic Approvals dialog box shown in Figure 8-10, which is available under Options in the Update Services console. By default, no updates are automatically approved for distribution by WSUS 3.0 SP1.

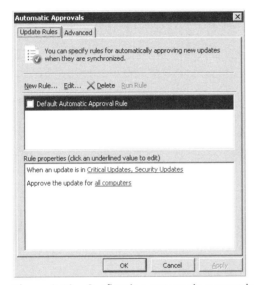

Figure 8-10   Configuring automatic approvals

To approve an update, you need to perform the following steps:

1. Open the Update Services console. Under the Updates node, click All Updates.

2. Choose Unapproved from the Approval drop-down list and choose Any from the Status drop-down list.

3. Right-click an update and then click Approve. This will bring up the Approve Updates dialog box.

4. Click the icon next to All Computers and then click Approved For Install.

5. Right-click the newly approved update in the All Computers Group, click Deadline, and then click 2 Weeks. The approved update will now be deployed with the set deadline.

NOTE   Forcing updates

If you want an update to be immediately deployed, set the Update Deadline to a date in the past.

Quick Check

1. What mode should you deploy a downstream WSUS 3.0 SP1 server in if you want it to use the approvals and computer group configuration of the designated upstream server?

2. Aside from the WSUS 3.0 SP1 software, what other software must be downloaded from Microsoft's Web site prior to the installation of WSUS?

Quick Check Answers

1. You should put the downstream WSUS server into replica mode if you want it to use the approvals and computer group configuration of the designated upstream server.

2. It is necessary to download and install Report Viewer 2005 or later before you can install WSUS 3.0 SP1.

Update Management and Compliance

Compliance means ensuring that a computer is configured in a mandated way. This involves not only having a specific set of updates installed, but also ensuring that other configuration settings, such as a strong password policy, strong firewall configuration, and anti-spyware software are correctly set up.

WSUS Reporting

WSUS 3.0 SP1 offers basic reporting functionality. The reports are based on information communicated with WSUS. WSUS does not scan computers to determine whether updates are missing, but instead records whether updates have been downloaded to target computers and whether the target computers have reported back to the WSUS server that the update has been successfully installed. You can access WSUS reporting by clicking the Reports node on the Update Services console, as shown in Figure 8-11.

WSUS reports can be printed or exported to Microsoft Office Excel or PDF format. If WSUS data is written to a SQL Server database, you have the ability to perform your own separate analyses using your own set of database queries. You can generate the following reports using WSUS 3.0 SP1 if your user account is a member of the WSUS Reporters or WSUS Administrators groups:

- **Update Status Summary Report** This report contains basic information about update deployment including the number of computers the update is installed on, is needed on, failed to install on, and for which WSUS has no data. One page is available per update. An Update Status Summary Report is shown in Figure 8-12.

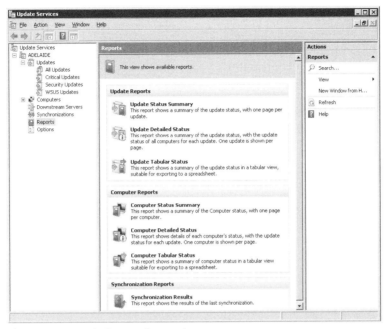

Figure 8-11   WSUS reporting options

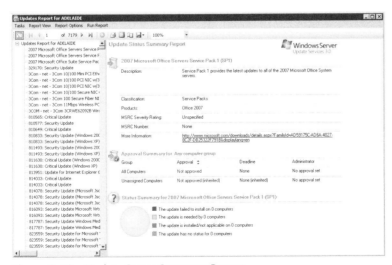

Figure 8-12   Update Status Summary Report

- **Update Detailed Status** This report offers significantly more information about the deployment of updates, providing a list of computers and their update status on an update-per-page basis. When you run a detailed update, you can view the report in summary or tabular format.

- **Update Tabular Status** This report format provides data in a table on a per-update basis. After this report is generated you can switch the report to summary or update detailed status. This form of report is the best to export to Office Excel because it is already in tabular format, as shown in Figure 8-13.

Updates Report for ADELAIDE

Tasks   Report View   Report Options   Run Report

|◀ ◀ 1   of 1 ▶ ▶| ◎ | 🖨 🗔 🕮 🖫 ▾ | 100%   ▾

Update Tabular Status Report

Windows Server
Update Services 3.0

Title ↕	Needed ↕	Installed/Not Applicable ↕	Failed ↕	No Status ↕
Windows XP Update Package, October 25, 2001	0	0	0	0
Critical Update, November 19, 2001	0	0	0	0
Remote Assistance Connection	0	0	0	0
Security Update, December 17, 2001	0	0	0	0
Critical Update, February 10, 2002	0	0	0	0
Security Update, February 12, 2002	0	0	0	0
System Recovered Error Message Update	0	0	0	0
Q311967: Security Update	0	0	0	0
Windows XP Application Compatibility Update, April 2002	0	0	0	0
Security Update, February 13, 2002 (MSXML 4.0)	0	0	0	0
Q318138: Security Update (Windows XP)	0	0	0	0
Q320206: Security Update	0	0	0	0
Q329048: Security Update	0	0	0	0

Figure 8-13 Update status table report

- **Computer Status Summary** Similar to the update detailed status report, this report provides update information on a per-computer rather than per-update basis. Data is presented in summary form.

- **Computer Detailed Status** This report format provides detail about the status of specific updates for a particular computer. After this report is generated, you can switch the report to summary or tabular form.

- **Computer Tabular Status** This report provides a table of update status information, with individual computers as rows. After this report is generated, you can switch the report to summary or tabular form.

- **Synchronization Results** This report shows the result of the WSUS server's last synchronization.

Enabling the Reporting Rollup For Downstream WSUS servers option allows update, computer, and synchronization data for replica downstream servers to be included in reports generated on the upstream WSUS server.

Other Patch Management Tools

Although WSUS is the primary patch management tool covered by the 70-646 Windows Server 2008 Server Administrator exam, you should be aware of some other patch management tools. These include, but are not limited to, the Microsoft Baseline Security Analyzer, System Center Essentials 2007, and System Center Configuration Manager 2007.

Microsoft Baseline Security Analyzer

The Microsoft Baseline Security Analyzer (MBSA) tool is not used for deploying updates, but instead allows systems administrators to scan the network to determine which computers are missing updates or are incorrectly configured. The MBSA tool can integrate with WSUS, so rather than scanning target systems to see whether any updates are missing from the entire catalog of updates, the MBSA tool will just check whether approved updates are missing from a target computer.

System Center Essentials 2007

System Center Essentials 2007 is the next step up from WSUS 3.0 SP1 in terms of patch management in a Windows Server 2008 environment. Limited to managing 500 client computers and 30 servers, System Center Essentials 2007 provides significantly more detailed patch deployment reporting functionality than WSUS. You can also use System Center Essentials 2007 to deploy software updates to non-Microsoft products, and it provides advanced update distribution control and scheduling flexibility. System Center Essentials 2007 also provides basic compliance checking functionality and inventory management. Unlike WSUS 3.0 SP1, which is provided to license holders of Microsoft Windows Server 2008, System Center Essentials 2007 requires you to purchase an additional license. System Center Essentials 2007 also requires access to a SQL Server 2005 SP1 database that also must be properly licensed. Alternatively, it is possible to use the SQL Server Express database included in the System Center Essentials installation files.

MORE INFO   More on System Center Essentials

To learn more about System Center Essentials 2007, consult the product homepage at: *http:// www.microsoft.com/systemcenter/essentials/default.mspx.*

System Center Configuration Manager 2007

System Center Configuration Manager 2007 is the next iteration of the Systems Management Server product line. This product provides more detailed functionality than System Center Essentials 2007 and can be used to monitor almost all aspects of a network environment. System Center Configuration Manager 2007, which provides advanced compliance reporting, is designed for very large environments such as those that exceed the 500-client, 30-server capacity of System Center Essentials 2007.

MORE INFO   Comparing solutions

To see a comparison between WSUS, MBSA, System Center Essentials 2007, and Systems Management Server 2003 (the predecessor of System Center Configuration Manager 2007), consult the following TechNet Link: *http://technet.microsoft.com/en-au/wsus/bb466194.aspx*.

Practice: WSUS Server Deployment

Windows Server Update Services functions as a Microsoft Update server on the Local Area Network. It is available as a free download from Microsoft's Web site and can be installed on a standard installation of a Windows Server 2008 computer.

▶ **Exercise 1: Install WSUS 3.0 SP1 on Windows Server 2008**

In this exercise, you will install WSUS 3.0 SP1 on Windows Server 2008. This installation will be configured so that updates are stored on the Microsoft Update servers. This exercise should be considered optional because it requires Internet access. You can configure server Glasgow to access the Internet by adding a second network card or by adding a virtual network card and configuring virtual machine network settings appropriately. This exercise also assumes that you have not installed IIS on server Glasgow. If IIS has been installed, use the Add Role Services functionality to add additional required components listed in step 7 of the following steps instead of performing steps 5 and 6.

MORE INFO   Download locations

You can download WSUS 3.0 SP1 or later from *http://www.microsoft.com/wsus*.

You can download Report Viewer 2005 from *http://www.microsoft.com/Downloads/details.aspx?familyid=8A166CAC-758D-45C8-B637-DD7726E61367&displaylang=en*.

To complete this practice, perform the following steps:

1. Log on to server Glasgow using the Kim_Akers user account.
2. Download the WSUS 3.0 SP1 installer and the ReportViewer installer to the c:\temp folder.

3. Double-click the ReportViewer installer to start the installation of Report Viewer on server Glasgow. Click Continue when prompted by the User Account Control dialog box.

4. Click Next. Accept the terms of the License Agreement and then click Install. Click Finish when the installation process completes.

5. Open the Server Manager console from the Administrative Tools menu. Click Continue to dismiss the User Account Control dialog box, and then right-click the Roles node. Click Add Roles. Click Next.

6. On the Server Roles page of the Add Roles Wizard, select the Web Server (IIS) role. When prompted by the Add Features Required For Web Server (IIS) page, click Add Required Features. Click Next twice.

7. On the Select Role Services page, select ASP.NET. This will bring up a dialog box asking you to add further role services. Click Add Required Role Services. Under Security, select Windows Authentication. Under Management Tools, select IIS 6 Metabase Compatibility. Click Next.

8. Verify that the features listed on the Confirm Installation Selections dialog box match those shown in Figure 8-14 and then click Install.

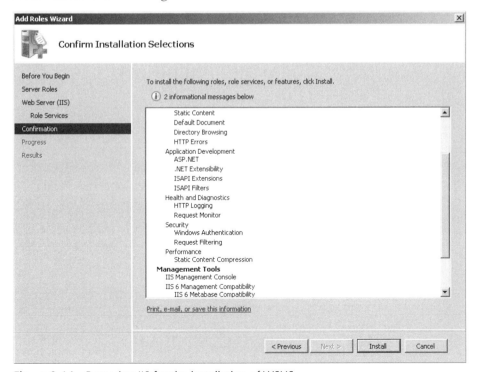

Figure 8-14 Preparing IIS for the installation of WSUS

9. When the installation process completes, click Close.

10. Double-click WSUSSetup.exe to start the WSUS 3.0 SP1 setup process. Click Continue to dismiss the User Account Control dialog box.

11. On the Welcome To Windows Server Update Services 3.0 SP1 Setup Wizard page, shown in Figure 8-15, click Next.

Figure 8-15 Starting WSUS setup

12. On the Installation Mode Selection page, select Full Server Installation Including Administration Console and then click Next.

13. On the License Agreement page, select I Accept The Terms Of The License Agreement and then click Next.

14. On the Select Update Source page, clear the Store Updates Locally option and then click Next.

15. On the Database Options page, select Install Windows Internal Database On This Computer as shown in Figure 8-16 and then click Next.

16. On the Web Site Selection page, select Use The Existing IIS Default Web Site (Recommended) and then click Next. Click Next again to begin the installation process. Click Finish when you are informed that WSUS 3.0 SP1 has been successfully installed.

17. The Windows Software Update Services Configuration Wizard will automatically start when the installation of WSUS 3.0 SP1 is complete. If your Windows Server 2008 computer does not have a connection to the Internet, you should click Cancel at this point. Otherwise, click Next twice.

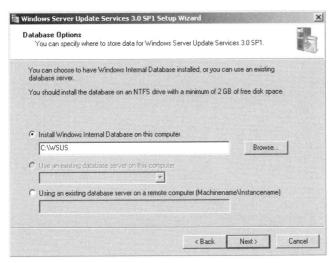

Figure 8-16 Configuring WSUS database options

18. On the Choose Upstream Server page, shown in Figure 8-17, select Synchronize From Microsoft Update and then click Next.

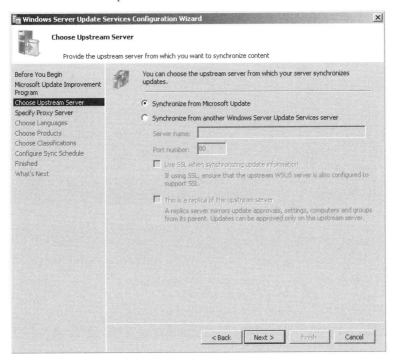

Figure 8-17 Configuring synchronization options

19. Unless your organization uses a proxy server that requires authentication, click Next on the Specify Proxy Server page. If your organization does use a proxy server to access the Internet, fill in the relevant details on this page and click Next.

20. On the Connect To Upstream Server page, click Start Connecting. The server will now contact Microsoft Update to determine the type of updates available, the products that can be updated, and the available languages. When the connection routine completes, click Next.

21. On the Choose Products page shown in Figure 8-18, select All Products and then click Next.

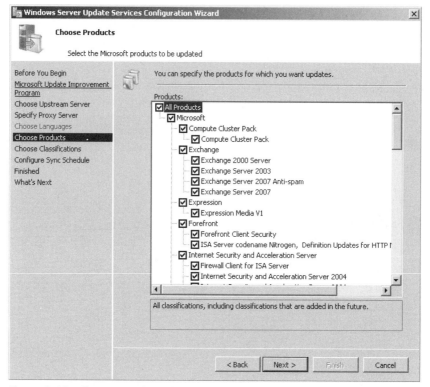

Figure 8-18 Choose products that WSUS can update

22. On the Choose Classifications page, select All Classifications and then click Next.

23. On the Set Sync Schedule page, select Synchronize Manually and then click Next.

24. Ensure that Launch The Windows Server Update Services Administration Console and Begin Initial Synchronization are not selected and then click Finish.

Lesson Summary

- WSUS replicas are downstream servers that inherit the configuration of their upstream server.

- Autonomous-mode WSUS servers are downstream servers that retrieve updates from an upstream server, but their approvals and computer groups are configured by a local administrator.

- Server-side targeting assigns computers to WSUS groups using the WSUS administration console.

- Client-side targeting assigns computers to WSUS groups using Group Policy or by editing the client computer's registry.

- Deploying updates in a staggered manner or to a test environment allows you to test whether a particular update has an adverse impact on client computers.

- System Center Essentials 2007 provides greater functionality than WSUS, but also requires access to a SQL Server 2005 SP1 or later database.

- System Center Configuration Manager 2007 has advanced reporting functionality that you can use to verify that computers meet compliance requirements.

Lesson Review

You can use the following questions to test your knowledge of the information in Lesson 1, "Windows Server 2008 Patch Management Strategies." The questions are also available on the companion CD if you prefer to review them in electronic form.

NOTE Answers

Answers to these questions and explanations of why each answer choice is correct or incorrect are located in the "Answers" section at the end of the book.

---

1. Thirty percent of your organization's workforce uses laptop computers. Most of these employees visit different branch offices each week. Your organization has 30 branch offices spread out across Australia. After doing some compliance reporting, you have determined that these laptop computers are only being updated when they connect to the branch office that they were originally deployed from. How can you ensure that these laptop computers always receive updates from the local branch office WSUS server, no matter which branch office they are connecting to? (Each correct answer presents part of the solution. Choose two.)

   A. Configure Network Load Balancing on each site's WSUS server.

   B. Configure DNS Round Robin and netmask ordering on each DNS server in your organization.

    C. Configure each WSUS server in your organization to use the same Fully Qualified Domain Name (FQDN).

    D. Configure BIND secondaries on each DNS server in your organization.

    E. Configure the hosts file on each client computer with the host name and IP address of all WSUS servers in the organization.

2. You are in the process of planning the deployment of WSUS at a university. The university is made up of five faculties, each of which has its own IT staff. You want to minimize the amount of data downloaded from the Microsoft Update servers, but each faculty's IT staff should have responsibility to approve updates. Which of the following WSUS deployments should you implement?

    A. Configure one upstream server. Configure five downstream servers as replicas of the upstream server.

    B. Configure five replica servers.

    C. Configure one upstream server. Configure five downstream servers as autonomous servers.

    D. Configure five autonomous servers.

3. You want to stagger the rollout of updates from your organization's WSUS 3.0 SP1 server on a departmental basis. The computer accounts for the computers in each department are located in departmental OUs. Which of the following should you do? (Each correct answer presents part of the solution. Choose two.)

    A. Create WSUS computer groups for each department.

    B. Create GPOs and link them to the domain. In each GPO, specify the name of a departmental WSUS computer group.

    C. Create GPOs and link them to each OU. In each GPO, specify the name of a departmental WSUS computer group.

    D. Create separate security groups for all of the computer accounts in each departmental OU.

    E. Create separate security groups for all of the user accounts in each departmental OU.

4. What method can you use to ensure that all security and critical updates are deployed to computers in the PatchTest computer group?

    A. Create a scheduled task.

    B. Create an Automatic Approval rule that uses the All Computers group as a target.

    C. Create an Automatic Approval rule that uses the PatchTest WSUS computer group as a target.

    D. Create an Automatic Approval rule that uses the PatchTest security group as a target.

5. You need a list of computers that a recent update did not install on so that you can send a technician to investigate further. Which of the following reports should you generate to be able to quickly locate this information?

    A. Update Status Summary

    B. Computer Status Summary

    C. Update Detailed Status

    D. Computer Detailed Status

Lesson 2: Monitor and Maintain Server Security

Security is an ongoing process. After you configure Windows Firewall and Connection Security policies, you need to keep an eye on things to ensure that this protective shield you have placed around the server effectively keeps the server secured. Perhaps the biggest problem in securing any environment is the complacency of the person that put the security in place. Not only must you build the fence, but you must also monitor the fence to ensure that it is working as you intended. In this lesson, you will learn about several different layers that you can apply to Windows Server Security. Specifically, you will learn about configuring the Windows Firewall with Advanced Security, Connection Security Policies, data security, and auditing.

After this lesson, you will be able to:

- Monitor server security.
- Monitor authentication and authorization.
- Configure auditing.
- Monitor data security.
- Configure firewall rules and policies.

Estimated lesson time: 40 minutes

Monitoring Server Security

Auditing is the primary method through which you monitor the security of a Windows Server 2008 computer. In the first part of this lesson, you will learn about the different auditing categories that you can apply to Windows Server 2008 computers. You will also learn about the types of situations that you would use each auditing policy to monitor.

Monitoring Security Log

Auditing events are written to the security log in Event Viewer. Managing Event Viewer was covered in Chapter 7, "Managing Windows Server 2008." Techniques covered in that chapter, such as attaching tasks to specific events, are also applicable when it comes to monitoring server security. Using the attached task functionality allows you to be alerted in the event that a particular security event occurs. You can also configure attached tasks to start more detailed logging by triggering Data Collector Sets. With appropriate configuration, Data Collector Sets can allow you to collect detailed data about events on a Windows Server 2008 computer, such as the particular applications that have been opened, processes that are executing, and other diagnostic information. The 70-646 Windows Server 2008 Server Administrator exam does not go into this level of detail, but for those interested in securing Windows Server 2008, combining auditing, attached tasks, and Data Collector Sets is worth further investigation.

Another technique covered in Chapter 7 was event forwarding and subscriptions. When you are tracking user logon information—especially when users might authenticate against any one of multiple domain controllers at a site—you can see the advantage of configuring event log subscriptions so that event data flows to a centralized location from which you can view it. The specifics of this configuration are covered back in Chapter 7. Just make sure that the server that is configured as the collector has enough disk space to store the large log files that will be generated when you forward security events from all of your organization's Windows Server 2008 computers to a centralized location!

Finally, you should return to Chapter 7 to refresh your memory about the creation of custom views. When you implement auditing in a Windows Server 2008 environment, you are likely to be flooded with data. Creating a set of custom views allows you to focus on a set of events that you have already defined as interesting. Going through the security event log line by line can quickly lead to boredom and distraction. If you are distracted, you might miss something. When you discover an interesting event, consider creating a custom view so that you can easily find similar events the next time you examine the security event log.

Auditing Account Logon and Logon Events

There are two types of logon event auditing. Even experienced systems administrators get confused and have to check documentation to be sure that they are using the correct auditing category. These two logon-related auditing policies are:

- Audit Account Logon Events
- Audit Logon Events

Account Logon Events are generated when a domain user account authenticates against a domain controller. Events are written to the logs on the domain controller, and it is on the domain controller that you should configure event forwarding if you want to centralize auditing of domain logons and logoffs. If you do not use event forwarding, you must check the logs of each domain controller at a site, because any domain controller in a site can authenticate account logon events.

Audit Logon Events records local logons. If both Audit Account Logon Events and Audit Logon Events are enabled for successful events, a user logging on to a member server in a domain will generate a Logon Event in the member server's event logs and an Account Logon Event in the domain controller's event logs.

Auditing Account Management

When the Auditing Account Management policy is enabled, events related to account management (on a domain controller or a local computer) will be written to the event log. Account management events include:

- Creation, deletion, or modification of user accounts
- Creation, deletion, or modification of security or distribution groups
- Changed user passwords

This auditing policy is most often used to keep an independent record of the activities of helpdesk and HR staff when it comes to performing the management of user accounts. Rigorous auditing of account management events allows you to answer questions about whether a user account has been modified without permission, such as when a member of the helpdesk staff changes the CEO's password after hours to gain access to sensitive data on a file server.

Auditing Directory Service Access

Directory Service Access auditing allows you to record access to objects within Active Directory that have been configured with System Access Control Lists. This auditing policy is useful in situations where you need to track whether changes have been made to critical objects in Active Directory, such as OUs.

Auditing Object Access

This policy is used for auditing access to all objects except those stored within Active Directory. You can use this policy to record access to specific files, folders, registry keys, and printers. When securing sensitive data, you should configure this policy so that it is possible to audit access attempts to that data. Not only should you record which user accounts successfully access the data, but you should also record which user accounts have unsuccessfully attempted to access the data. This way you can determine whether someone who should not be able to access the data actually can access the data, and you will also be able to determine whether someone is trying to access the data when he should not be.

Auditing Policy Change

The Auditing Policy Change policy is used to audit changes to users rights, audit policies, or trust policies. This policy is often used to track modifications to accounts used by IT staff. In environments with rigorous security policies, it is necessary to keep track of which user accounts have been delegated specific rights. As Chapter 7 discussed, keeping track of which rights have been delegated to a specific account or group can be difficult. Auditing this type of activity allows you to ensure that accounts are not delegated undue rights. You do not want to go on vacation for a week and come back to find that one of your helpdesk staff has managed to delegate himself the privileges of an Enterprise Administrator without adding his user account to that group!

Auditing Privilege Use

When enabled, this policy allows you to track the use of user rights. In high-security environments, this policy is useful for recording how administrator-level accounts are used. You can use this policy to ensure that administrators do not exceed their authority by making unauthorized changes because their accounts have administrative-level privileges.

Auditing System Events and Process Tracking

The Audit System Events and Audit Process Tracking policies monitor computer-related events rather than user-specific events. Process tracking can be used to audit when programs activate, how programs access objects, and when applications terminate. Auditing system events records information about the startup or shutdown of a computer. It can also be used to record data when an event occurs that changes the security log.

MORE INFO   **More on auditing**

To learn more about auditing Active Directory in Windows Server 2008, consult the following TechNet link: *http://technet2.microsoft.com/windowsserver2008/en/library/a9c25483-89e2-4202-881c-ea8e02b4b2a51033.mspx?mfr=true.*

Encrypting File System

Encrypting File System (EFS) is another method through which you can ensure the integrity of data. Unlike BitLocker, which encrypts all data on a volume using a single encryption key that is tied to the computer, EFS allows for the encryption of individual files and folders using a public encryption key tied to a specific user account. The encrypted file can only be decrypted using a private encryption key that is accessible only to the user. It is also possible to encrypt documents to other user's public EFS certificates. A document encrypted to another user's public EFS certificate can only be decrypted by that user's private certificate.

Security Groups cannot hold encryption certificates, so the number of users that can access an encrypted document is always limited to the individual EFS certificates that have been assigned to the document. Only a user that originally encrypts the file or a user whose certificate is already assigned to the file can add another user's certificate to that file. With EFS there is no chance that an encrypted file on a departmental shared folder might be accessed by someone who should not have access because of incorrectly configured NTFS or Shared Folder permissions. As many administrators know, teaching regular staff to configure NTFS permissions can be challenging. The situation gets even more complicated when you take into account Shared Folder permissions. Teaching staff to use EFS to limit access to documents is significantly simpler than explaining NTFS ACLs.

If you are considering deployment of EFS throughout your organization, you should remember that the default configuration of EFS uses self-signed certificates. These are certificates generated by the user's computer rather than a Certificate Authority and can cause problems with sharing documents because they are not necessarily accessible from other computers where the user has not encrypted documents. A more robust solution is to modify the default EFS Certificate Template that is provided with a Windows Server 2008 Enterprise Certificate Authority to enable autoenrollment. EFS certificates automatically issued by an Enterprise CA can be stored in Active Directory and applied to files that need to be shared between multiple users. Another EFS deployment option involves smart cards. In organizations where users authenticate using smart cards, their private EFS certificates can be stored on a smart card and their public certificates stored within Active Directory. You can learn more about configuring templates for autoenrollment in Chapter 10, "Certificate Services and Storage Area Networks."

MORE INFO   **More on EFS**

For more information on Encrypting File System in Windows Server 2008, consult the following TechNet article: *http://technet2.microsoft.com/windowsserver2008/en/library/f843023b-bedd-40dd-9e5b-f1619eebf7821033.mspx?mfr=true.*

Quick Check

1. From a normal user's perspective, in terms of encryption functionality, how does EFS differ from BitLocker?

2. What type of auditing policy should you implement to track access to sensitive files?

Quick Check Answers

1. BitLocker works on entire volumes and is transparent to the user. EFS works on individual files and folders and be configured by the user.

2. Auditing Object Access.

Windows Firewall with Advanced Security

The simplest method of enforcing a standardized firewall configuration across an organization is to use Group Policy. You can configure inbound and outbound rules as well as enable and disable Windows Firewall with Advanced Security for specific profiles through the Computer Configuration\Policies\Windows Settings\Windows Firewall With Advance Security node of Group Policy as shown in Figure 8-19.

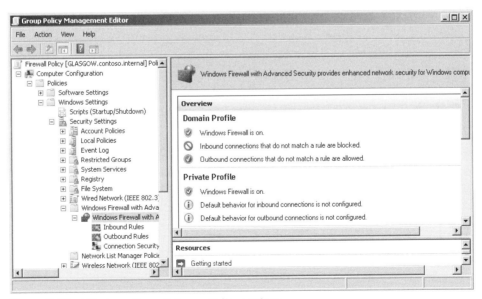

Figure 8-19 Windows Firewall Group Policy settings

You can configure new rules based on a specific program, port, or predefined rule. Rules can be applied to inbound and outbound traffic. In many domain environments, administrators use outbound rules as a way of blocking the use of specific programs, such as file sharing or instant messaging programs. Although the best way to block this sort of traffic is to stop the software from being installed in the first place, many domain environments have users with laptop computers that are taken on and off the network. In some cases, laptop users are given local administrative control over their computers. Applying firewall rules to each computer through Group Policy allows administrators to block programs that may use SSL tunnels to get around perimeter firewall configuration.

MORE INFO **More on Windows Firewall with Advanced Security**

To learn more about deploying Windows Firewall with Advanced Security through Group Policy, consult the following TechNet article: *http://technet2.microsoft.com/windowsserver2008/en/library/ 626058b7-54b4-4fc9-bbdf-7a427bedf4671033.mspx?mfr=true*.

Domain Isolation

Windows Firewall with Advanced Security can be used with Windows Vista and Windows Server 2008 hosts to create connection security rules that secure traffic by using IPsec. Domain isolation uses an Active Directory domain, domain membership, and Windows Firewall with Advanced Security Group Policy settings to enforce a policy that forces domain member computers to only accept incoming communication requests from other computers that are members of the same domain. When enforced, computers that are members of the domain are isolated from computers that are not members of the domain. It is important to remember that in domain isolation scenarios, isolated computers can initiate communication with hosts outside the domain, such as Web servers on the Internet. However, they will not respond when network communication is initiated from a host outside the domain.

Domain isolation policies are applied through the Computer Configuration\ Policies\Windows Settings\Security Settings\Windows Firewall with Advanced Security node of a GPO by accessing the Connection Security Rules item.

MORE INFO **Domain isolation**

To learn more about domain isolation, consult the following TechNet article: *http://technet2 .microsoft.com/windowsserver/en/library/69cf3159-77ea-4a56-9808-a3f35d2ccc3f1033.mspx?mfr=true*.

Configuring Server Isolation

Server isolation works in a similar way to domain isolation except that instead of applying to all computers within a domain, a server isolation policy is applied only to a specific set of servers in a domain. This is usually done by placing the computer accounts of the servers that will be isolated in a specific OU and then applying a GPO that has an appropriately configured connection security rule to that OU. When enforced, only computers that are members of the domain are able to communicate with the isolated servers. This can be an effective way of protecting servers when you must grant network access to third-party computers. The third-party computers are able to access some network resources such as intranet Web and DNS servers, but you can isolate specific network resources, such as file servers and databases, by configuring server isolation policies. You will configure a server isolation policy through a connection security rule in the practice exercise at the end of this lesson.

MORE INFO   Server isolation

To learn more about server isolation, consult the following TechNet article: *http://technet2.microsoft .com/windowsserver/en/library/3b828c92-93a7-40b3-b468-59e7e84c45611033.mspx?mfr=true*.

Practice: Server Isolation Policies

Server isolation policies are IPsec policies that allow administrators to restrict the incoming network traffic to which servers will respond. When applied in domain environments, this technology can ensure that the only hosts a server will respond to are those that have authorized computer accounts in the same Active Directory environment.

▶ **Exercise 1: Configuring a Server Isolation Policy with Connection Security Rules**

In this exercise, you will configure a server isolation policy using connection security rules through Group Policy for an organizational unit called Secure_Servers. In a real-world situation you would be able to apply this connection security rule by placing the computer accounts of servers that you wish to apply the rule to into this OU. To complete this exercise, perform the following steps:

1. Log on to server Glasgow using the Kim_Akers user account.

2. From the Administrative Tools menu, open Active Directory Users And Computers. Click Continue to dismiss the User Account Control dialog box.

3. Right-click contoso.internal, click New, and then click Organizational Unit. In the New Object – Organizational Unit dialog box, type **Secure_Servers** and click OK.

4. From the Administrative Tools menu, open the Group Policy Management Console. Navigate to Forest: Contoso.internal\Domains\contoso.internal. Right-click Group Policy Objects and then click New. In the New GPO dialog box, type the name **Connection_Security** and click OK.

5. Right-click the new Connection_Security GPO and click Edit. This will open the Group Policy Management Editor.

6. Expand the Computer Configuration\Policies\Windows Settings\Security Settings\ Windows Firewall With Advanced Security node and locate the Connection Security Rules object.

7. Right-click Connection Security Rules and select New Rule. This will start the New Connection Security Rule Wizard, shown in Figure 8-20.

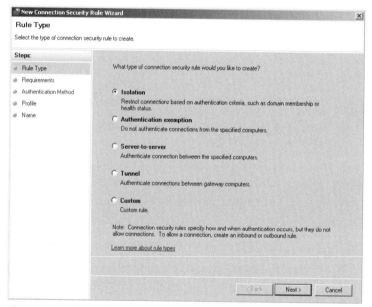

Figure 8-20   The New Connection Security Rule Wizard

8. On the What Type Of Connection Security Rule Would You Like To Create page, select Isolation and click Next.

9. On the Requirements page, select Require Authentication For Inbound And Outbound Connections and click Next.

10. On the Authentication Method page, select Computer (Kerberos V5) as shown in Figure 8-21 and then click Next.

11. On the Profile page, ensure that Domain, Private, and Public are selected and click Next.

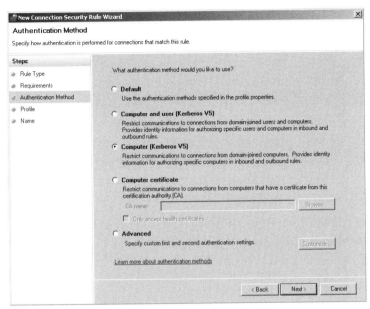

Figure 8-21   Selecting an authentication method

12. On the Name page, type the name **Secure_Servers** and then click Finish.

13. Close the Group Policy Management Editor.

14. In the Group Policy Management Console, right-click the Secure Servers OU and then click Link An Existing GPO.

15. In the Select GPO dialog box, shown in Figure 8-22, select Connection_Security and then click OK.

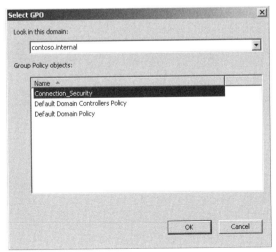

Figure 8-22   Linking a GPO to an OU to apply policy

Lesson Summary

- Account Logon Events are events recorded by a domain controller where the domain controller has authenticated domain logon activity.

- Domain isolation policies stop computers in the domain from accepting communication initiated by computers outside the domain. Computers in the domain can still initiate communication with hosts ouside the domain.

- Server isolation policies are similar to domain isolation policies except they are limited to a set of servers rather than the entire domain.

Lesson Review

You can use the following questions to test your knowledge of the information in Lesson 2, "Monitor and Maintain Server Security." The questions are also available on the companion CD if you prefer to review them in electronic form.

NOTE Answers

Answers to these questions and explanations of why each answer choice is correct or incorrect are located in the "Answers" section at the end of the book.

---

1. Your organization's headquarters site has three domain controllers. You want to configure a member server named Records so that it has a record of all domain logon and logoff activity that occurs at the headquarters site. Which of the following actions should you take?

    A. Configure event forwarding on the domain controllers. Forward events generated by the Audit Account Logon Events policy to server Records.

    B. Configure event forwarding on the domain controllers. Forward events generated by the Audit Account Management policy to server Records.

    C. Configure event forwarding on the domain controllers. Forward events generated by the Audit Logon Events policy to server Records.

    D. Configure event forwarding on the domain controllers. Forward events generated by the Audit Directory Service Access policy to server Records.

2. Five accountants want to use the Accounting shared folder to temporarily share confidential client information with each other. Thirty accountants have access to this folder and past experience has shown that file and folder permissions are almost always incorrectly applied by non-technical users. Which of the following

methods could these five accountants use to secure this confidential data while it is being hosted on the Accounting shared folder?

A. Use BitLocker to encrypt the confidential data.

B. Use EFS to encrypt the confidential data using a special group account.

C. Use EFS to encrypt the confidential data to each of the five accountant's EFS certificates.

D. Use BitLocker to encrypt the confidential data to each of the five accountant's encryption certificates.

3. As a security measure, you want to ensure that computers that are members of the Fabrikam.internal domain are able to communicate with each other and are not accessible to any other host. Which of the following should you do?

A. Implement domain isolation.

B. Configure a VPN.

C. Configure EFS.

D. Configure Network Access Protection.

4. Your organization has a small group of contractors that work onsite. Different contractors work at your company each week. These contractors need network access to services such as DNS, DHCP, the intranet Web server, and Internet access through ISA Server on the network perimeter. You want to ensure that these contractors have no access to your organization's Exchange Server 2007 computers or to any file servers. The contractors all use Windows Vista laptop computers that are not members of your Active Directory domain. Which of the following strategies can you pursue to ensure that the contractors are unable to access these important infrastructure servers?

A. Place the Exchange Server 2007 servers and the file servers on the perimeter network.

B. Configure a domain isolation policy.

C. Configure a Windows Firewall Outbound Rule on the Exchange Server 2007 servers and file servers.

D. Configure a server isolation policy.

Chapter Review

To further practice and reinforce the skills you learned in this chapter, you can perform the following tasks:

- Review the chapter summary.
- Review the list of key terms introduced in this chapter.
- Complete the case scenarios. These scenarios set up real-world situations involving the topics of this chapter and ask you to create a solution.
- Complete the suggested practices.
- Take a practice test.

Chapter Summary

- WSUS server can be used to centralize the deployment of updates in a Windows Server 2008 environment.
- System Center Configuration Manager 2007 has advanced reporting functionality that can be used to verify that computers meet compliance requirements.
- Auditing can be used to record events that are of interest to administrators, from access of sensitive files and folders to domain logon events.
- Windows Firewall with Advanced Security policies can be used to apply firewall rules through Group Policy to Windows Server 2008 and Windows Vista clients.
- Connection security rules can be used to enforce domain and server isolation policies.

Key Terms

Do you know what these key terms mean? You can check your answers by looking up the terms in the glossary at the end of the book.

- Autonomous mode
- Domain isolation policy
- Downstream server
- EFS
- Replica mode

Case Scenario

In the following case scenarios, you will apply what you have learned about patch management and security. You can find answers to these questions in the "Answers" section at the end of this book.

Case Scenario: Deploying WSUS 3.0 SP1 at Fabrikam

After using an ad-hoc approach to patch management over the last few years, the CIO at Fabrikam has decided that during the project to upgrade all existing Windows 2000 Servers to Windows Server 2008, WSUS 3.0 SP1 should also be deployed. Fabrikam is located in the state of Victoria, Australia. The head office is located in the Melbourne Central Business District (CBD) and suburban satellite offices are located in Moonee Ponds, Cheltenham, Endeavour Hills, and Glen Waverley.

The current plan is for a WSUS 3.0 SP1 server to be installed on a Windows Server 2008 host at the head office and then for a phased rollout of WSUS servers at the suburban satellite offices. As all the IT staff work in the Melbourne CBD office, the servers at the satellite offices should use the computer group configuration and the update approvals that are configured on the head office server.

One reason for the ad-hoc approach in the past has been that Fabrikam uses custom software that sometimes conflicts with updates, causing the installation of those updates to fail. The CIO wants to be able to run reports on updates from her desktop computer to determine when these events occur. The CIO does not require administrative access to the server and never performs hands-on administrative tasks, always delegating this to the systems administrators in her team.

With this information in mind, answer the following questions:

1. To which local group on the Windows Server 2008 computer hosting WSUS should you add the CIO's user account?

2. How should you configure the update source of downstream WSUS servers at the Fabrikam satellite offices?

3. Which type of report should you instruct the CIO to generate to gain detailed information about the specific computers where a particular update's installation has failed?

Suggested Practices

To help you successfully master the exam objectives presented in this chapter, complete the following tasks.

Implement a Patch Management Strategy

Complete the following practice exercise:

- **Practice: Configure a WSUS Replica**

   1. Synchronize the WSUS server that you configured in the practice exercise at the end of the first lesson with Microsoft update.

   2. Install WSUS 3.0 SP1 on a second computer.

   3. Configure the second Windows Server 2008 computer as a downstream replica of the WSUS 3.0 SP1 server that you configured in the practice exercise at the end of the first lesson.

   4. Synchronize the downstream WSUS server with the upstream server.

Monitor Server Security

Complete the following practice exercise:

- **Practice: Configure Auditing**

   1. Configure auditing of privilege use.

   2. Configure auditing of Account Logon Events and verify that these events are being logged on server Glasgow.

Take a Practice Test

The practice tests on this book's companion CD offer many options. For example, you can test yourself on just one exam objective, or you can test yourself on all the 70-646 certification exam content. You can set up the test so that it closely simulates the experience of taking a certification exam, or you can set it up in study mode so that you can look at the correct answers and explanations after you answer each question.

MORE INFO   Practice tests

For details about all the practice test options available, see the "How to Use the Practice Tests" section in this book's Introduction.

Chapter 9

Remote Access and Network Access Protection

VPNs can be used to allow remote users to connect to your organization's internal network resources from a hotel wireless hotspot in Gundagai or from a broadband connection in Yarragon. Planning VPN access requires taking into consideration a host of factors. You need to know how the firewall will be configured, what clients are going to connect, and the types of resources that they need to access. In this chapter, you will learn how to plan and deploy a VPN server and you will learn about the new technologies available in Windows Server 2008 to simplify this process.

Network Access Protection is another feature new to Windows Server 2008 that is likely to be addressed by the 70-646 exam. This feature allows you to restrict network access on the basis of client computer health. Put simply, if the client computer is not up to date with patches and antivirus definitions, it does not get full access to the network. If the client computer is up to date, full access is granted. In this chapter, you will learn how to configure and deploy Network Access Protection and the various methods that are available to deal with noncompliant computers.

Exam objectives in this chapter:
- Monitor and maintain security and policies.
- Plan infrastructure services server roles.

Lessons in this chapter:

Before You Begin

To complete the lessons in this chapter, you must have done the following:

- Installed and configured the evaluation edition of Windows Server 2008 Enterprise Edition in accordance with the instructions listed in the first practice exercise of Lesson 1 in Chapter 1, "Installing, Upgrading, and Deploying Windows Server 2008."

■   The practice exercises in this chapter require that you perform a default installation of a second Windows Server 2008 member server and join it to the Contoso .internal domain. It is possible to install this member server using the same installation media that you used to install server Glasgow.contoso.internal. This member server should only be used for the practice exercises and you should not complete the Windows product activation process for this computer. This computer should have two network adapters: one that is connected to the 10.0.0.x /24 network and a second that has the statically assigned IP address of 1.2.3.4 /24. You should name this computer Hobart.

No additional configuration is required for this chapter.

Lesson 1: Managing Remote Access

If your organization is going to allow workers to telecommute, you need to provide them with some way to access resources on your organization's internal network. In this lesson, you will learn how to plan the deployment of VPN servers to allow remote access to your internal network from locations that are external to your organization's network.

After this lesson, you will be able to:

- Plan remote access infrastructure server roles.
- Monitor and maintain remote access security policies.
- Monitor and maintain network access.

Estimated lesson time: 40 minutes

You should deploy the Windows Server 2008 Routing And Remote Access Services Remote Access Server Role Service when you want to provide either of the following resources to your network environment:

- VPN remote access server
- Dial-up remote access server

In this lesson, you will learn specifically how to configure and monitor a Windows Server 2008 VPN remote access server. To install the Routing And Remote Access Services (RRAS) role service, use the Add Roles function and then select Network Policy And Access Services. Routing And Remote Access Services is a role service within this role. To configure Windows Server 2008 to accept incoming VPN and dial-up traffic, select the Remote Access Service role, as shown in Figure 9-1.

The Remote Access Service must be manually enabled after installation. Only members of the local Administrators group are able to enable the Remote Access Service. In domain environments, you should perform this action using a user account that is a member of the Domain Admins group. If your user account is not a member of the Domain Admins security group, organize a domain admin to manually add the RAS server computer account to the RAS and IAS Servers domain security group. It is not necessary to add the RAS server to this group if the Remote Access Server will be using local authentication or authenticating against a Remote Authentication Dial In User Service (RADIUS) server.

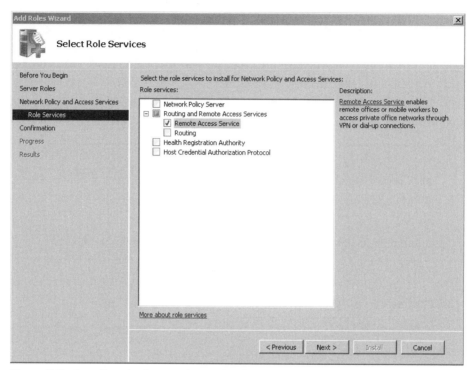

Figure 9-1   Installing the Remote Access Service

To enable Remote Access, open the Routing and Remote Access console from the Administrative Tools menu, right-click the Windows Server 2008 computer that you want to host this role, and then click Configure And Enable Routing And Remote Access. Performing this action starts the Routing And Remote Access Server Setup Wizard. The configuration page of this wizard, shown in Figure 9-2, allows you to select the combination of services that this particular server will provide. The Remote Access (dial-up or VPN) option is selected when you want to provide either or both remote access options to clients external to your organization.

If you have chosen to install a VPN server, you will be presented with the VPN Connection page shown in Figure 9-3. This page requires that you specify the network interface on the computer that connects to the Internet. This will be the interface that has the public IP address rather than the interface that has the private IP address. If additional network adapters are installed on the server that hosts the RAS role after the RAS server is deployed, these can be configured for use with RAS using the RRAS console. If your Windows Server 2008 computer has fewer than two network adapters, you will not be able to perform a standard VPN server setup and will need to perform a custom configuration instead.

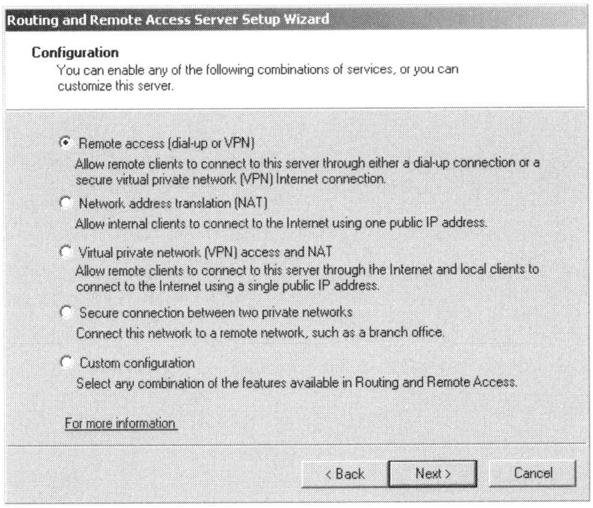

Figure 9-2   Remote Access setup

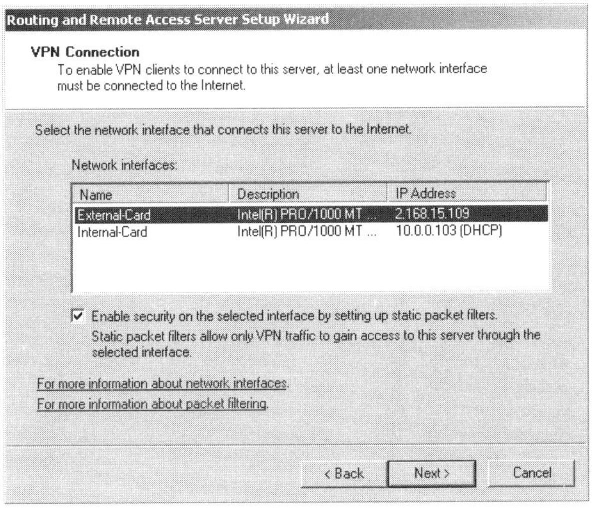

Figure 9-3   Installing the Remote Access Service

Packet filters that only allow VPN protocols are configured and applied to the Internet interface. This means that the server is limited to providing VPN access. In the event that you have deployed other services on the server that will host the RAS role, you will need to configure new packet filters to allow this traffic to the server. As a deployment strategy, you should strongly consider keeping the RAS server separate from other services.

After the external interface is identified, the next step in configuring the RAS role is specifying how IP addresses will be assigned to clients. Client addresses can be leased from a DHCP server within the organization, the RAS server can generate the addresses itself, or you can specify a range of addresses to assign to connecting clients. When using your organization's DHCP infrastructure, the RAS server will lease blocks of 10 addresses, requesting new blocks if previously requested blocks are all currently in use.

Windows Server 2008 DHCP servers have a predefined user class, known as the Default Routing And Remote Access Class, that allows administrators to assign specific options only to Routing And Remote Access clients. This class is configured through the Advanced tab of DHCP Server Options as shown in Figure 9-4.

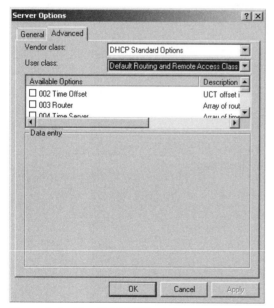

Figure 9-4   The RRAS DHCP class

The next step in configuring a RAS server is determining how authentication will occur. You can configure the RAS server to perform authentication against Active Directory (or the local account database) or you can configure the RAS server as a RADIUS client and allow the RADIUS server to perform the authentication and authorization of client connection requests. RADIUS options are covered in more detail later in this lesson. After you have performed these steps, the RAS server will be functional.

VPN Protocols and Authentication

Virtual Private Networks are an extension of a private network that encompasses encapsulated, encrypted, and authenticated links across shared or public networks. A client computer connects to a public network, such as the Internet, and initiates a VPN connection to a remote server. This remote server is usually located on the screened subnet of the organization that the client wishes to connect to. After the connection is made, an encrypted tunnel forms between the client and the VPN server. This encrypted tunnel carries local area network traffic between the client and the remote network that the client is connected to. Clients are connected to the network in the same way that they would be if they were in the office. Instead of a CAT-5 drop cable connecting them to a switch somewhere in the office, a virtual cable in the form of a VPN tunnel connects them to their organization's network infrastructure.

Understanding Authentication Protocols

The following authentication protocols can be used by a Windows Server 2008 server to authenticate incoming VPN connections. These protocols are listed in order from most secure to least secure:

- **Extensible Authentication Protocol-Transport Level Security (EAP-TLS)**   This is the protocol that you deploy when your VPN clients are able to authenticate using smart cards or digital certificates. EAP-TLS is not supported on stand-alone servers and can only be implemented when the server hosting the Remote Access Service role service is a member of an Active Directory Domain.

- **Microsoft Challenge Handshake Authentication Protocol (MS-CHAPv2)**   This protocol provides mutual authentication and allows for the encryption of both authentication data and connection data. MS-CHAPv2 is enabled by default in Windows Server 2008.

- **Challenge Handshake Authentication Protocol (CHAP)**   An older authentication method that encrypts authentication data using MD5 hashing. CHAP does not support the encryption of data and is most often used to provide compatibility with older, non-Microsoft clients.

- **Extensible Authentication Protocol-Message Digest 5 Challenge Handshake Authentication Protocol (EAP-MD5 CHAP)**   A version of CHAP that has been ported to the EAP framework. This authentication protocol supports encryption of authentication data through MD5 hashing and is generally used to provide compatibility with non-Microsoft clients.

- **Shiva Password Authentication Protocol (SPAP)**   A weakly encrypted authentication protocol that does not support the encryption of connection data.

- **Password Authentication Protocol (PAP)**   When this protocol is used, authentication data is not encrypted, but is passed across the network in plaintext. PAP does not support the encryption of protection data.

The authentication process always attempts to negotiate the use of the most secure authentication protocol. The default authentication protocol used for VPN clients connecting to a Windows Server 2008 VPN is MS-CHAPv2.

Windows Server 2008 VPN Protocols

Windows Server 2008 supports three different VPN protocols: Tunneling Protocol (PPTP), Layer Two Tunneling Protocol over IPsec (L2TP/IPsec), and Secure Socket Tunneling Protocol (SSTP). The factors that will influence the protocol you choose to deploy in your own network environment include client operating system, certificate infrastructure, and how your organization's firewall is deployed.

- **PPTP**   PPTP connections can only be authenticated using MS-CHAP, MS-CHAPv2, EAP, and PEAP. PPTP connections use MPPE to encrypt PPTP data. PPTP connections provide data confidentiality but do not provide data integrity or data origin authentication. It is possible to use PPTP with certificates if EAP-TLS is selected as the authentication protocol, although the advantage of PPTP over the other VPN protocols supported by Windows Server 2008 is that it does not require certificates be installed on the client computer making the connection. With PPTP, you do not need to be concerned about shared secrets or computer certificates or ensuring that the appropriate SSL CA is trusted. PPTP is often used with non-Microsoft operating systems.

MORE INFO   **More on PPTP**

For more information on this older VPN protocol, consult the following MSDN article: *http://msdn2 .microsoft.com/en-us/library/ms811078.aspx.*

- **L2TP/IPsec**   L2TP connections use encryption provided by IPsec. L2TP/IPsec is the protocol that you need to deploy if you are supporting Windows XP remote access clients, because these clients cannot use SSTP. L2TP/IPsec provides per-packet data origin authentication, data integrity, replay protection, and data confidentiality.

L2TP/IPsec connections use two levels of authentication. Computer-level authentication occurs either using digital certificates issued by a CA trusted by the client and VPN server or through the deployment of pre-shared keys. PPP authentication protocols are then used for user-level authentication. L2TP/IPsec supports all of the VPN authentication protocols available on Windows Server 2008.

MORE INFO   **More on L2TP/IPsec**

To learn more about L2TP/IPsec, consult the following Microsoft TechNet link: *http://technet .microsoft.com/en-us/library/bb742553.aspx.*

- **SSTP**   Secure Socket Tunneling Protocol (SSTP) is a VPN technology that makes its debut with Windows Server 2008. SSTP VPN tunnels allow traffic to pass across firewalls that block traditional PPTP or L2TP/IPsec VPN traffic. SSTP works by encapsulating Point-to-Point Protocol (PPP) traffic over the Secure Sockets Layer (SSL) channel of the Secure Hypertext Transfer Protocol (HTTPS) protocol. Expressed more directly, SSTP piggybacks PPP over HTTPS. This means that SSTP traffic passes across TCP port 443, which is almost certain to be open on any firewall between the Internet and a public-facing Web server on an organization's screened subnet.

The PPP of SSTP allows for the deployment of advanced authentication methods such as EAP-TLS, which is most commonly used with smart cards. The SSL component of SSTP provides the VPN tunnel with encryption, enhanced key negotiation, and integrity checking. This means data transferred using this method is encoded and that it is possible to detect whether someone has attempted to intercept the contents of the tunnel between the source and destination points.

When planning for the deployment of SSTP, you need to take into account the following considerations:

- SSTP is only supported with Windows Server 2008 and Windows Vista with Service Pack 1.

- SSTP requires that the client trust the CA that issues the VPN server's SSL certificate.

- The SSL certificate must be installed on the server that will function as the VPN server prior to the installation of Routing and Remote Access; otherwise, SSTP will not be available.

- The SSL certificate subject name and the host name that external clients use to connect to the VPN server must match, and the client Windows Vista SP1 computer must trust the issuing CA.

- SSTP does not support tunneling through Web proxies that require authentication.

- SSTP does not support site-to-site tunnels. (PPTP and L2TP do.)

MORE INFO **More on SSTP**

To learn more about SSTP, see the following SSTP deployment walkthrough document at *http://download.microsoft.com/download/b/1/0/b106fc39-936c-4857-a6ea-3fb9d1f37063/ Deploying%20SSTP %20Remote%20Access%20Step%20by%20Step%20Guide.doc.*

Network Policy Server

Network Policy Servers are deployed on Windows Server 2008 networks to enforce uniform network access policies across the entire organization. Network Policy Server (NPS) is a core component in Network Access Protection, which is the subject of the next lesson in this chapter. This coverage in this lesson concentrates on using NPS either as a RADIUS server or as a RADIUS client, also known as a RADIUS proxy. The same server can function as both a RADIUS server and a RADIUS proxy.

NPS as a RADIUS Server

When an organization has more than one remote access server, an administrator can configure a server that has NPS installed as a RADIUS server and then configure all remote access servers as RADIUS clients. The benefit of doing this is that network policy management is centralized, rather than requiring management on a per-remote-access-server basis.

When RADIUS is used as an authentication provider for RAS servers, the connection request is sent in a RADIUS request message format to a RADIUS server. The RADIUS server performs the authentication and authorization and then passes this information back to the RAS server. The RADIUS server must be a member of an Active Directory domain, but the RAS VPN server passing authentication requests to the RADIUS server can be a stand-alone computer.

NPS and RADIUS clients

RADIUS clients are network access servers such as VPN servers, wireless access points, and 802.1x authenticating switches. Although the computers that access these network access servers are called remote access clients, they are not considered RADIUS clients. RADIUS clients provide network access to other hosts.

To configure a RADIUS client using NPS, open the Network Policy Server Console from the Administrative Tools menu. Right-click Radius Clients and then click New RADIUS Client. This will bring up the dialog box shown in Figure 9-5. Configuration involves providing the following information:

- Friendly Name
- Address (IP or DNS)
- Vendor Name (More than 20 separate vendors are available in this drop-down menu.)
- Shared Secret (configured using the NPS snap-in on the RADIUS client)

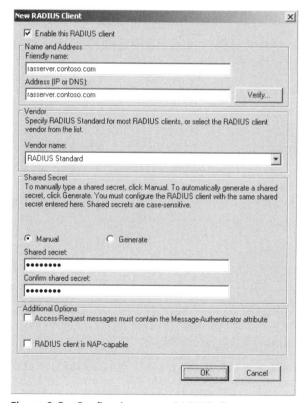

Figure 9-5   Configuring a new RADIUS client

MORE INFO   More on NPS and RADIUS clients

For more information on configuring RADIUS clients, consult the following TechNet link: *http://technet2.microsoft.com/windowsserver2008/en/library/5ba4dfa8-674d-43fe-9196-93fc599ee94d1033.mspx?mfr=true*.

NPS as a RADIUS Proxy

RADIUS proxies route RADIUS messages between remote access servers configured as RADIUS clients and the RADIUS servers that perform authentication, authorization, and accounting. When configured as a RADIUS proxy, an NPS will record information in the accounting log about the messages that it passes on from RAS clients to the RADIUS servers. NPS functions as a RADIUS client when it is configured as a RADIUS proxy.

You should deploy NPS as a RADIUS proxy when you need to provide authentication and authorization for accounts from other Active Directory forests. The NPS RADIUS proxy uses the realm name (the name that identifies the location of the user account) portion of a user name to forward the request to a RADIUS server in the target forest. This allows connection attempts for user accounts in one forest to be authenticated for network access server in another forest. Using a RADIUS proxy for inter-forest authentication is not necessary when both forests are running at the Windows Server 2003 functional level and a forest trust exists.

You should also deploy NPS as a RADIUS proxy when you need authentication and authorization to occur against a database other than the Windows account database. Connection requests that match a specific realm name are forwarded to a RADIUS server, often running on a platform other than Windows, that accesses a separate database of user accounts and authorization data. Hence you would deploy NPS as a RADIUS proxy when authentication and authorization have to occur against a RADIUS server that uses Novell Directory Services or one that runs on UNIX.

A final reason to consider the deployment of NPS as a RADIUS proxy server is when you need to process a large number of connection requests between RAS RADIUS clients and RADIUS servers. An NPS RADIUS proxy can load-balance traffic across multiple RADIUS servers—something that is difficult to configure when dealing with just RADIUS clients and RADIUS Servers.

MORE INFO   More on NPS as a RADIUS proxy

To learn more about configuring NPS as a RADIUS proxy, consult the following link on TechNet: *http://technet2.microsoft.com/windowsserver2008/en/library/94c797c3-1efa-4a62-946b-a6923e0ee0 361033.mspx?mfr=true.*

> ### Quick Check
> 1. Which VPN protocol requires an SSL certificate?
> 2. Which authentication protocol supports smart cards?

> **Quick Check Answers**
> 1. SSTP uses HTTPS and hence requires an SSL certificate.
> 2. EAP-TLS.

Remote Access Accounting

Network Policy Servers can be configured to perform RADIUS accounting. RADIUS accounting allows you to keep track of who is connecting and who has failed to connect. You can use NPS accounting to specifically monitor the following information:

- User authentication requests
- Access-Accept messages
- Access-Reject messages
- Accounting requests and responses
- Periodic Status updates

As Figure 9-6 shows, you have two separate ways of recording log data. Logs can be stored locally or written to SQL Server 2005 SP1 database. Locally written logs are suitable if you have a small number of remote access clients. If you have a significant number of remote access clients, writing data to a SQL Server database will provide you with a much better way of managing what is likely to be a mountain of information.

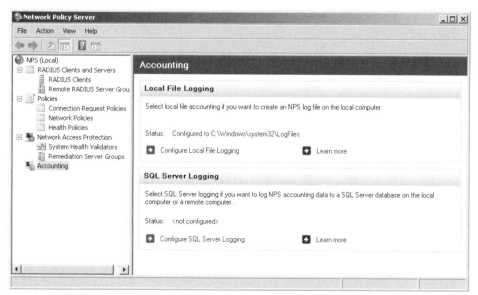

Figure 9-6   Accounting node of the Network Policy Server console

Local File Logging

NPS log files can be written in two formats: IAS and database-compatible. The default format is database-compatible. The frequency at which new log files are created should be tuned to your organization's needs. The benefit of having a single file of unlimited size is that locating a specific event is simpler, because you have to search for only one log file. The drawback of larger log files is that on systems where a log of NPS accounting data is logged, the log files can become huge, making the process of opening them and searching them difficult.

Although logs are written by default to the %Systemroot%\System32\LogFiles folder, Microsoft recommends that you keep log files on a partition separate from the operating system and application or file share data. Log files, unless strictly monitored, have a way of filling all available disk space. If this happens on a critical partition, the server could become unavailable. It is very important to note that NPS accounting data logs are not automatically deleted. You can configure the log retention policy to ensure that older log files are automatically deleted when the disk is full. This works best when log files are written to an isolated partition so that the only impact of a disk full of NPS log files is on the storage of existing NPS log files. If NPS log files must be stored on a partition with other data, or the operating system, you should consider writing a script that auto-matically removes logs when they reach a certain age.

Log files can be written to remote shares. This is done by specifying the UNC path of the share. If you configure this option, it will be necessary to ensure that the share per-missions are configured to allow the account that writes the logs to write data to the shared folder. The Log File tab of the Local File Logging properties dialog box is shown in Figure 9-7.

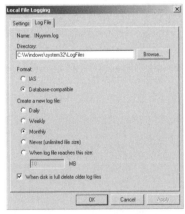

Figure 9-7   Configuring local NPS logging

Configure SQL Server Logging

The alternative to logging NPS accounting data locally is to have it written to a SQL Server computer that is either installed locally or on the local network. NPS sends data to the *report_event* stored procedure on the target SQL Server computer. This stored procedure is available on Microsoft SQL Server 2000, 2005, and 2008.

You can configure which NPS accounting data is sent to the SQL Server computer by selecting options in the SQL Server Logging properties dialog box shown in Figure 9-8. Clicking Configure in this dialog box allows you to specify the properties of the data link to the SQL Server computer. When configuring the Data Link Properties for the SQL Server connection, you must provide the server name, the method of authentication that will be used with the SQL Server computer, and the database on the SQL Server computer that you will use to store the accounting data. Just as it is a good idea to have a separate partition on a computer to store NPS accounting data, it is a good idea to have a separate database that stores NPS accounting data.

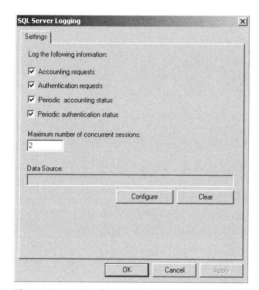

Figure 9-8   Configuring NPS logging to SQL Server

Terminal Services Gateway Servers

Terminal Services Gateway Servers (TS Gateway) allow Remote Desktop Protocol (RDP) over HTTPS connections to RDP servers located on protected internal networks to clients on the Internet. This functionality allows clients on the Internet to access TS-RemoteApp applications, standard Terminal Server sessions, and remote desktop sessions to appropriately configured client computers.

An advantage of TS Gateway is that you do not need to set up RAS VPNs to grant access to resources. Instead of having to deploy client connection kits to everyone in the organization that needs to be able to access resources from the Internet side of the firewall, you can e-mail them a RDP shortcut file and allow them to connect with their Windows XP SP2 or Windows Vista client computers. TS Gateway is essentially SSL VPN that is restricted to RDP. With a regular VPN connection, you can theoretically directly access all resources once connected. So a VPN can be used to connect to internal file shares and shared printers. With TS Gateway you can access a Terminal Server or remote desktop session and through that access resources such as shared drives and printers.

Follow these steps to configure a TS Gateway Server:

1. Install the TS Gateway Role Service on a Windows Server 2008 computer that is located on a screened subnet. The perimeter firewall should be configured so that the TS Gateway Server is accessible on port 443.

2. Obtain an SSL certificate. The certificate name must match the name that clients use to connect to the server. Install the certificate on the server and then use the TS Gateway Manager console to map the server certificate. It is important that you only use TS Gateway Manager to map the SSL certificate. If you use another method, the TS Gateway Server will not function properly.

3. Configure Terminal Services connection authorization policies (TS CAPs) and Terminal Services resource authorization policies (TS RAPs). (These are covered in the next section.)

MORE INFO   Detailed TS Gateway configuration instructions

For detailed information about the preceding steps, consult the TS Gateway Core Scenario document at *http://technet2.microsoft.com/windowsserver2008/en/library/5fdeb161-31c7-41b2-aaa3-7a4d5f5e3cda1033.mspx?mfr=true*.

Connection Authorization Policies

Terminal Services connection authorization policies (TS-CAPs) specify which users are allowed to connect through the TS Gateway Server to resources located on your organization's internal network. This is usually done by specifying a local group on the TS Gateway Server or a group within Active Directory. Groups can include user or computer accounts. You can also use TS-CAPs to specify whether remote clients use password or smart-card authentication to access internal network resources through the TS Gateway Server. You can use TS-CAPs in conjunction with NAP; this scenario is covered in more detail by the next lesson.

Resource Authorization Policies

Terminal Services resource authorization policies (TS-RAPs) are used to determine the specific resources on an organization's network that an incoming TS Gateway client can connect to. When you create a TS-RAP you specify a group of computers that you want to grant access to and the group of users that you will allow this access to. For example, you could create a group of computers called AccountsComputers that will be accessible to members of the Accountants user group. To be granted access to internal resources, a remote user must meet the conditions of at least one TS-CAP and at least one TS-RAP.

Practice: Installing and Configuring Remote Access

In this exercise, you will install and configure a Remote Access Server that will support PPTP VPNs. PPTP is a VPN protocol that is generally used by older clients and clients that do not use Microsoft operating systems.

▶ **Exercise 1: Remote Access Configuration**

As mentioned at the beginning of this chapter, you should have installed a Windows Server 2008 member server named Hobart and joined it to the Contoso.internal domain. This server should have two network adapters, one of which is configured with the static IP address 1.2.3.4. This adapter will simulate an adapter connection to the Internet.

To complete this exercise, perform the following steps:

1. Log on to server Hobart with the Kim_Akers user account.

2. When the Server Manager console opens, right-click Roles and then click Add Roles.

3. On the Before You Begin page, click Next. Select the Network Policy And Access Services item and click Next.

4. On the Introduction To Network Policy And Access Services page, click Next.

5. On the Select Role Services page, select the Remote Access Service option and click Next.

6. On the Confirmation page, click Install. When the installation completes, click Close to close the Add Roles Wizard.

7. From the Administrative Tools menu, open the Routing And Remote Access console. Click Continue to close the User Account Control dialog box.

8. Right-click server Hobart in the Routing And Remote Access console and then click Configure And Enable Routing And Remote Access as shown in Figure 9-9. This will start the Routing And Remote Access Server Setup Wizard. Click Next.

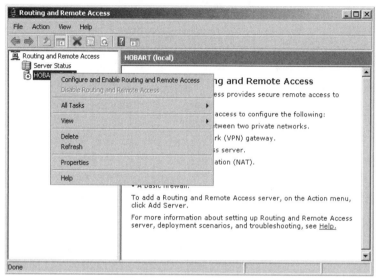

Figure 9-9   Configuring Routing and Remote Access

9. On the Configuration page, select the Remote Access (Dial-Up Or VPN) option.

10. On the Remote Access page, select VPN, as shown in Figure 9-10, and then click Next.

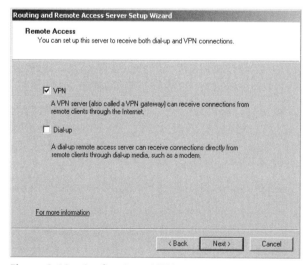

Figure 9-10   Configuring a VPN server

11. On the VPN Connection page, select the external network adapter that you have configured with the IP address 1.2.3.4. Ensure that the Enable Security On The Selected Interface By Setting Up Static Packet Filters option is selected and then click Next.

12. On the IP Address Assignment page ensure that the From A Specified Range Of Addresses option is selected and then click Next.

13. On the Address Range Assignment page, click New. This will open the New IPv4 Address Range. Enter the start IP address as **10.0.0.200** and the end IP address range as **10.0.0.220** and then click OK. Verify that the Address Range Assignment page matches Figure 9-11 and then click Next.

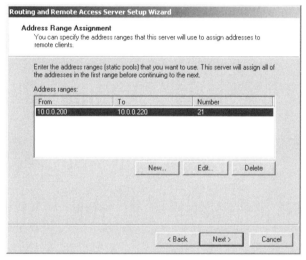

Figure 9-11   Configuring a range of addresses for VPN clients

14. On the Managing Multiple Remote Access Servers page, select No, Use Routing And Remote Access To Authenticate Connection Requests, click Next, and then click Finish.

15. The Routing And Remote Access server will finalize configuration and then start.

16. Close the Routing And Remote Access console.

Lesson Summary

■ SSTP piggybacks PPP over HTTPS. The SSL certificate installed on the RAS server must match the host name that the SSTP client is connecting to. SSTP can only be used by Windows Vista SP1 and Windows Server 2008 clients. SSTP cannot be used for site-to-site tunnels.

- NPS Servers can be configured to write accounting data to local log files or to SQL Server computers that have the *report_event* stored procedure available.

- RADIUS proxies are a useful way of load-balancing requests from RAS servers to RADIUS servers.

- TS Gateway Servers provide another method of remote access, allowing Windows Vista clients to connect to RDP servers using port 443.

Lesson Review

You can use the following questions to test your knowledge of the information in Lesson 1, "Managing Remote Access." The questions are also available on the companion CD if you prefer to review them in electronic form.

NOTE   Answers

Answers to these questions and explanations of why each answer choice is correct or incorrect are located in the "Answers" section at the end of the book.

---

1. Which of the following VPN protocols would you deploy if your firewall blocked all traffic from the Internet except traffic on TCP ports 25, 80, and 443?

    A. L2TP/IPsec

    B. SSTP

    C. PPTP

    D. SLIP

2. VPN clients connecting to your organization's Windows Server 2008 RAS server are assigned IP addresses from a Windows Server 2008 DHCP server. You want to configure a separate set of DHCP options for these clients. Which of the following steps should you take?

    A. Configure a DHCP reservation.

    B. Configure a DHCP exclusion.

    C. Configure the Default User Class on the DHCP server.

    D. Configure the Default Routing And Remote Access Class on the DHCP server.

3. Which of the following clients can connect to your organization's Windows Server 2008 VPN server if the only ports that are available for VPN connections are ports 25, 80, and 443?

    A. Windows 2000 Professional with Service Pack 4

    B. Windows XP Professional with Service Pack 2

    C. Windows Vista RTM

    D. Windows Vista with Service Pack 1

4. Servers VPN1, VPN2, and VPN3 host the RAS server role and accept incoming VPN connections from clients on the Internet. Server NPS1 is configured as a RADIUS server using Network Policy Server server role. Servers VPN1, VPN2, and VPN3 use NPS1 to authenticate incoming connections. Server SQL1 is a Windows Server 2003 computer that has SQL Server 2005 Service Pack 2 installed. You want to improve your ability to search through RADIUS accounting data. Which of the following strategies should you pursue?

    A. Configure VPN1, VPN2, and VPN3 so that NPS accounting data is forwarded to SQL1.

    B. Configure VPN1, VPN2, and VPN3 so that NPS accounting data is forwarded to NPS1.

    C. Configure SQL1 so that NPS accounting data is forwarded to server NPS1.

    D. Configure NPS1 so that NPS accounting data is forwarded to server SQL1.

5. You want to ensure that users connecting over the Internet to your organization's Terminal Servers are only able to access a specific set of Terminal Servers. Which of the following actions should you take?

    A. Install a TS Gateway Server on the screened subnet and configure a RAP.

    B. Install a TS Gateway Server on the screened subnet and configure a CAP.

    C. Install a TS Session Directory server and configure NLB.

    D. Install a TS Session Directory server and configure DNS Round Robin.

Lesson 2: Network Access Protection

You deploy Network Access Protection on your network as a method of ensuring that computers accessing important resources meet certain client health benchmarks. These benchmarks include (but are not limited to) having the most recent updates applied, having antivirus and anti-spyware software up to date, and having important security technologies such as Windows Firewall configured and functional. In this lesson, you will learn how to plan and deploy an appropriate network access protection infrastructure and enforcement method for your organization.

After this lesson, you will be able to:

- Plan Network Access Protection server roles.
- Monitor and maintain Network Access Protection policies.

Estimated lesson time: 40 minutes

System Health Agents and Validators

System Health Agents (SHA) and System Health Validators (SHV) are the components that validate a computer's health against a configured set of benchmarks. The SHV specifies which benchmarks the client must meet. The SHA is the component against which those benchmarks are tested. The Windows Vista and Windows XP SHVs can be configured through the System Health Validators node under Network Access Protection in the Network Policy Server. Figure 9-12 shows the settings that you can configure for the Windows Vista SHV.

Third-party organizations can provide SHAs and SHVs that you can use with their own products and NAP. Deploying third-party SHAs and SHVs involves installing the SHA components on all clients and the SHV on the Windows Server 2008 computer that hosts the Network Policy Server server role. Once installed, you create a new health policy that uses the new SHV as a compliance benchmark. A health policy can call on multiple SHVs. For example, you might create a health policy that requires all conditions on the Windows Vista SHV and the Fabrikam SHV be met before a client is granted access to all network resources.

MORE INFO   More on Windows System Health Agents

To learn more about System Health Agents, consult the following TechNet Web Page: *http://technet2.microsoft.com/windowsserver2008/en/library/ab8507c4-af62-4334-beca-b1cb0c687b011033 .mspx?mfr=true.*

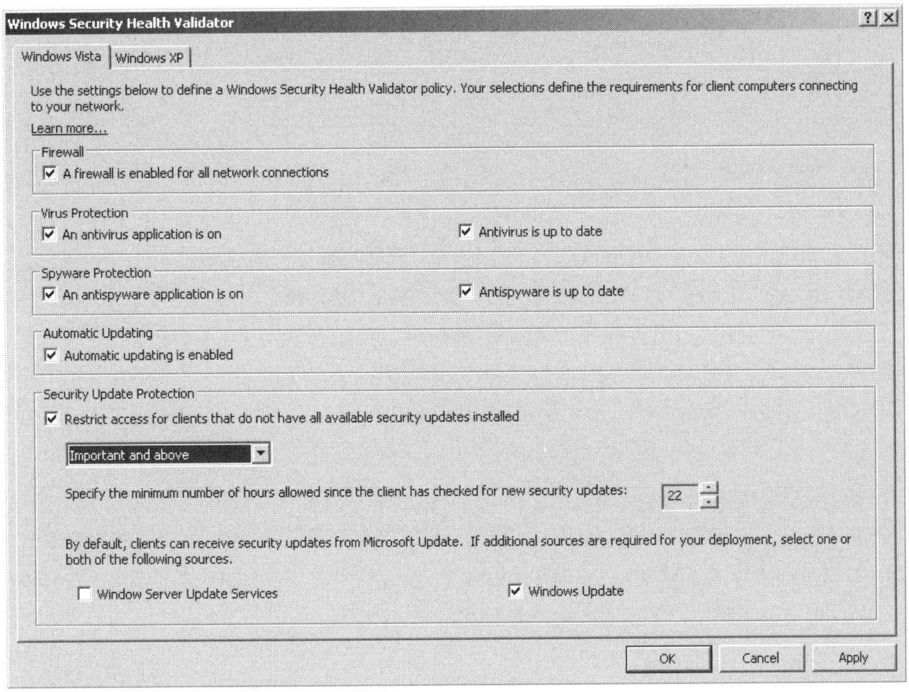

Figure 9-12   Windows Vista SHV

NAP Enforcement Methods

When a computer is found to be noncompliant with the enforced health policy, NAP enforces limited network access. This is done through an Enforcement Client (EC). Windows Vista, Windows XP Service Pack 3, and Windows Server 2008 include NAP EC support for IPsec, IEEE 802.1X, Remote Access VPN, and DHCP enforcement methods. Windows Vista and Windows Server 2008 also support NAP enforcement for Terminal Server Gateway connections.

NAP enforcement methods can either be used individually or can be used in conjunction with each other to limit the network access of computers that are found not to be in compliance with configured health policies. Hence you can apply the remote access VPN and IPsec enforcement methods to ensure that internal clients and clients coming in from the Internet are only granted access to resources if they meet the appropriate client health benchmarks.

IPsec NAP Enforcement

IPsec enforcement works by applying IPsec rules. Only computers that meet health compliance requirements are able to communicate with each other. IPsec enforcement can be applied on a per-IP address, per-TCP port number, or per-UDP port number basis. For example: You can use IPsec enforcement to block RDP access to a Web server so that only computers that are healthy can connect to manage that server, but allow clients that do not meet health requirements to connect to view Web pages hosted by the same Web server.

IPsec enforcement applies after computers have received a valid IP address, either from DHCP or through static configuration. IPsec is the strongest method of limiting network access communication through NAP. Where it might be possible to subvert other methods by applying static addresses or switching ports, the IPsec certificate used for encryption can only be obtained by a host when it passes the health check. No IPsec certificate means communication with other hosts that encrypt their communication using a certificate issued from the same CA is impossible.

To deploy IPsec enforcement a network environment must have a Windows Server 2008 Health Registration Authority and a Windows Server 2008 CA. Clients must be running Windows Vista, Windows Server 2008, or Windows XP Service Pack 3, all of which include the IPsec Enforcement Client (EC).

MORE INFO   IPsec enforcement step-by-step

For more detailed information on implementing IPsec NAP enforcement, consult the following Step-by-Step guide on TechNet: *http://go.microsoft.com/fwlink/?LinkId=85894.*

802.1X NAP Enforcement

802.1X enforcement makes use of authenticating Ethernet switches or IEEE 802.11 Wireless Access Points. These compliant switches and access points only grant unlimited network access to computers that meet the compliance requirement. Computers that do not meet the compliance requirement are limited in their communication by a restricted access profile. Restricted access profiles work by applying IP packet filters or VLAN (Virtual Local Area Network) identifiers. This means that hosts that have the restricted access profile are allowed only limited network communication. This limited network communication generally allows access to remediation servers. You will learn more about remediation servers later in this lesson.

An advantage of 802.1X enforcement is that the health status of clients is constantly assessed. Connected clients that become noncompliant will automatically be placed under the restricted access profile. Clients under the restricted access profile that become compliant will have that profile removed and will be able to communicate with other hosts on the network in an unrestricted manner. For example, suppose that a new antivirus update comes out. Clients that have not installed the update are put under a restricted access profile until the new update is installed. Once the new update is installed, the clients are returned to full network access.

A Windows Server 2008 computer with the Network Policy Server role is necessary to support 802.1X NAP enforcement. It is also necessary to have switch and/or wireless access point hardware that is 801.1x-compliant. Client computers must be running Windows Vista, Windows Server 2008, or Windows XP Service Pack 3 because these operating systems include the EAPHost EC.

MORE INFO   **802.1X enforcement step-by-step**

For more detailed information on implementing 802.1X NAP enforcement, consult the following Step-by-Step guide on TechNet: *http://go.microsoft.com/fwlink/?LinkId=86036*.

VPN NAP Enforcement

VPN enforcement is used on connecting VPN clients as a method of ensuring that clients granted access to the internal network meet system health compliance requirements. VPN enforcement works by restricting network access to non-compliant clients through the use of packet filters. Rather than being able to access the entire network, incoming VPN clients that are noncompliant only have access to the remediation server group.

As is the case with 802.1X enforcement, the health status of a connected client is continuously monitored. If a client becomes noncompliant, packet filters restricting network access will be applied. If a noncompliant client becomes compliant, packet filters restricting network access will be removed. VPN enforcement requires an existing remote access infrastructure and a Network Policy Server. The enforcement method uses the VPN EC, which is included with Windows Vista, Windows Server 2008, and Windows XP Service Pack 3.

MORE INFO   **VPN enforcement step-by-step**

For more detailed information on implementing VPN NAP enforcement, consult the following Step-by-Step guide on TechNet: *http://go.microsoft.com/fwlink/?LinkId=85896*.

DHCP NAP Enforcement

DHCP NAP enforcement works by providing unlimited-access IPv4 address information to compliant computers and limited-access IPv4 address information to noncompliant computers. Unlike VPN and 802.1X enforcement methods, DHCP NAP enforcement is only applied when a client lease is obtained or renewed. Organizations using this method of NAP enforcement should avoid configuring long DHCP leases because this will reduce the frequency at which compliance checks are made.

To deploy DHCP NAP enforcement, you must use a Windows Server 2008 DHCP server because this includes the DHCP Enforcement Service (ES). The DHCP EC is included in the DHCP Client service on Windows Vista, Windows Server 2008, and Windows XP Service Pack 3.

The drawback of DHCP NAP enforcement is that you can get around it by statically configuring a client's IP address. Only users with local administrator access can configure a manual IP, but if your organization gives users local administrator access, DHCP NAP enforcement may not be the most effective method of keeping these computers off the network until they are compliant.

MORE INFO   DHCP enforcement step-by-step

For more detailed information on implementing DHCP NAP enforcement, consult the following Step-by-Step guide on TechNet: *http://go.microsoft.com/fwlink/?LinkId=85897*.

> ## Quick Check
>
> 1. Which NAP enforcement method uses VLANs?
> 2. Which NAP enforcement methods can you get around by configuring a static IP address?
>
> ### Quick Check Answers
>
> 1. The 802.1X NAP enforcement method uses VLANs.
> 2. You can get around the DHCP NAP enforcement method by configuring a static IP address.

Terminal Services Gateway NAP Enforcement

TS Gateway NAP enforcement ensures that Windows Vista and Windows Server 2008 clients located on the Internet that are connecting to a TS Gateway meet health compliance requirements before the TS Gateway allows connections to RDP servers on the internal network. To configure TS Gateway for NAP, you must perform the following basic steps:

1. Enable NAP health policy checking on the TS Gateway Server by configuring the TS Gateway Server to request clients send a statement of health.
2. Remove any existing TS-CAPs. It is not necessary to remove existing TS-RAPs.

3. Configure a Windows Security Health Validator on the TS Gateway Server by editing the properties of the Windows Security Health Validator in the Network Policy Server console on the TS Gateway Server.

4. Create NAP Policies on the TS Gateway server using the Configure NAP Wizard. You will need to create two health policies (one for compliant and one for noncompliant computers), a connection request policy, and three network policies (compliant, noncompliant, and non-NAP-capable).

MORE INFO   **NAP and TS Gateway**

To find out the detailed steps for configuring NAP for TS Gateway, consult the following link: *http://technet2.microsoft.com/windowsserver2008/en/library/b3c07483-a9e1-4dc6-8465-0a7900900 a551033.mspx?mfr=true.*

Remediation Servers

Remediation servers generally host software updates and antivirus and anti-spyware definition files and are used to bring a client that has not passed a health check up to date. Remediation servers are accessible from the restricted networks that noncompliant clients are relegated to when they do not pass system health checks. Remediation servers allow these clients to be brought into compliance so that they can have unrestricted access to the network. Remediation Server Groups are added through the Remediation Server Group node of the Network Policy Server console, as shown in Figure 9-13.

Figure 9-13   Configuring a Remediation Server Group

NOTE   Monitoring-only mode

When NAP is configured to operate in monitoring-only configuration, noncompliant clients are granted unrestricted access to the network, but detailed data about compliance problems is reported in log files. Monitoring-only mode is useful to use prior to a full deployment of NAP, so that you can identify and fix client computers that may suffer disruptive problems when NAP is fully enforced.

MORE INFO   Health Credential Authorization Protocol

Health Credential Authorization Protocol (HCAP) is used to integrate NAP with Cisco Network Admission Control (NAC). You can find out more about this interoperability technology by consulting the following document: *http://www.microsoft.com/presspass/events/ssc/docs/ CiscoMSNACWP.pdf.*

Practice: Configuring NAP with DHCP Enforcement

DHCP NAP enforcement works by providing unlimited-access IPv4 address information to compliant computers and limited-access IPv4 address information to noncompliant computers.

▶ **Exercise 1: Network Policy Server Configuration**

In this exercise, you will install Network Policy Server on Server Glasgow and configure NAP with DHCP enforcement. To complete this exercise, perform the following steps:

1. Log on to server Glasgow with the Kim_Akers user account.

2. If the Server Manager console does not open automatically, open it by clicking the Server Manager Quick Launch item.

3. Right-click the Roles node and then click Add Roles. Click Next to move to the Select Server Roles page.

4. Click the Network Policy And Access Services node and then click Next. On the Network Policy And Access Services page, click Next.

5. On the Role Services page, select only Network Policy Server and then click Next. On the Confirmation page, click Install. When the Network Policy Server role service has installed, click Close to dismiss the Add Roles Wizard.

6. From the Administrative Tools menu, click DHCP. Click Continue in the User Account Control dialog box. The DHCP console will open.

7. Select and right-click the IPv4 node under Glasgow.contoso.internal and then click New Scope. This will launch the New Scope Wizard. Click Next.

8. On the Scope Name page, type the scope name **NAP_Scope.** Click Next.

9. Set the start IP address as **10.100.0.1** and the end IP address as **10.100.0.254.** Set the Subnet Mask Length at **24.** Click Next three times.

10. On the Configure DHCP Options page, select No, I Will Configure These Options Later and then click Next. Click Finish.

11. From the Administrative Tools menu, click Network Policy Server. Click Continue to close the UAC dialog box. The Network Policy Server console will open.

12. On the Getting Started page, shown in Figure 9-14, click Configure NAP.

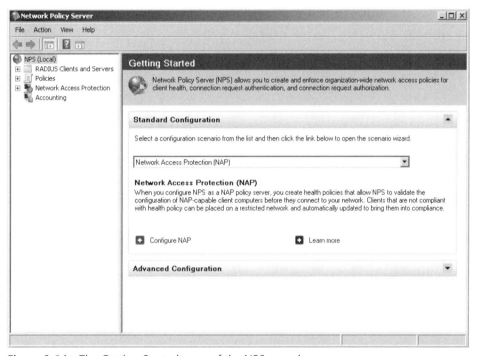

Figure 9-14   The Getting Started page of the NPS console

13. On the Select Network Connection Method For Use With NAP page, use the drop-down menu to select Dynamic Host Configuration Protocol (DHCP) and then click Next.

14. On the RADIUS Clients page, click Next.

15. On the DHCP Scopes page, click Add. In the Specify The Profile Name That Identifies Your DHCP Scope box, type **NAP_Scope** and click OK. Click Next.

16. On the Configure User Groups And Machine Groups page, click Next.

17. On the Specify A NAP Remediation Server Group And URL page, click Next.

18. On the Define NAP Health Policy page, clear the Enable Auto-Remediation Of Client Computers option and select Allow Full Network Access To NAP-ineligible Client Computers, as shown in Figure 9-15. Click Next and then click Finish.

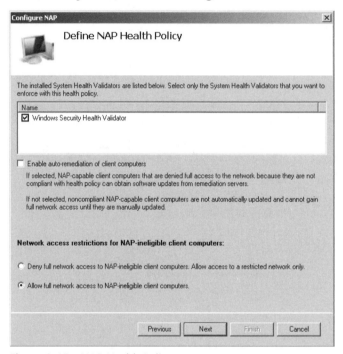

Figure 9-15   NAP Health Policy

Lesson Summary

- A System Health Validator is a set of conditions that a computer must meet to be considered healthy. A System Health Agent is what the Network Policy Server checks with to determine whether a connecting client meets all of the conditions of the System Health Validator.

- The four methods of NAP enforcement that can be applied to Windows Server 2008, Windows Vista, and Windows XP SP3 clients are IPsec, DHCP, VPN, and 802.1X enforcement. TS Gateway NAP can only be used with Windows Vista and Windows Server 2008.

- Network Policy Servers are installed as a part of the Network Policy and Access Server Roles. These servers are where you configure health policies and SHVs that dictate the health compliance benchmark.

Lesson Review

You can use the following questions to test your knowledge of the information in Lesson 2, "Network Access Protection." The questions are also available on the companion CD if you prefer to review them in electronic form.

NOTE Answers

Answers to these questions and explanations of why each answer choice is correct or incorrect are located in the "Answers" section at the end of the book.

---

1. You only want healthy computers on your network to be able to connect to a Windows Server 2008 computer used as an intranet Web server role for management tasks, but you want to allow all clients, healthy or unhealthy, to be able to access Web pages on the same servers. Which of the following NAP enforcement methods should you implement without having to configure the firewall or IP address restrictions on the Windows Server 2008 intranet server?

   A. IPsec

   B. 802.1X

   C. DHCP

   D. VPN

2. Your network contains a mixture of Windows Vista SP1 and Windows XP SP3 clients. You want to enable NAP enforcements for the Windows Vista SP1 clients. Windows XP SP3 clients should not be subjected to NAP enforcement. Which of the following strategies should you pursue? (Each correct answer presents part of the solution. Choose two.)

   A. Create a network policy that specifies the operating system as a condition.

   B. Create a VLAN for all Windows XP clients.

   C. Configure the network policy to allow Windows Vista computers to bypass the health check.

   D. Configure the network policy to allow Windows XP computers to bypass the health check.

   E. Create a VLAN for all Windows Vista clients.

3. Your organization has one Windows Server 2003 domain controller and one Windows Server 2008 domain controller. They are named 2K3DC and 2K8DC respectively. The domain functional level is Windows Server 2003. DNS is installed on a Windows Server 2003 R2 stand-alone computer named DNS1.

DHCP is installed on a Windows Server 2003 R2 stand-alone computer named DHCP1. NPS is installed on a Windows Server 2008 computer named NPS1. Which of the following computers must you upgrade if you want to use DHCP NAP enforcement?

- **A.** 2K3DC
- **B.** DNS1
- **C.** DHCP1
- **D.** NPS1

4. Which of the following server roles must be available on your network if you plan to configure IPsec rules so that only healthy computers can connect to each other? (Each correct answer presents part of the solution. Choose two.)

- **A.** Health Registration Authority
- **B.** Windows Server 2008 Certificate Authority
- **C.** Windows Server 2008 DHCP Server
- **D.** Health Credential Authorization Protocol (HCAP) Server
- **E.** NPS Server configured as a RADIUS proxy

5. Other than 802.1X-compatible switches, which of the following components must be deployed in your network environment to support 802.1X NAP enforcement? (Each correct answer presents a complete solution. Choose two.)

- **A.** NPS Server role on a Windows Server 2008 computer
- **B.** RADIUS proxy server
- **C.** EAPHost EC on clients
- **D.** HCAP Server Role on a Windows Server 2008 computer
- **E.** DHCP Server

Chapter Review

To further practice and reinforce the skills you learned in this chapter, you can perform the following tasks:

- Review the chapter summary.
- Review the list of key terms introduced in this chapter.
- Complete the case scenario. This scenario sets up a real-world situation involving the topics of this chapter and asks you to create a solution.
- Complete the suggested practices.
- Take a practice test.

Chapter Summary

- Windows Server 2008 Remote Access
- Network Access Protection is a method of mediating access—either to the LAN or through remote access servers—to your organization's core network.
- The aspects of NAP are health state validation, health policy compliance, access restriction, and remediation.
- NAP supports the following types of network access or communication: IPsec, IEEE 802.1X switches, VPN connections, and DHCP configurations.

Key Terms

Do you know what these key terms mean? You can check your answers by looking up the terms in the glossary at the end of the book.

- EAP-TLS
- L2TP/IPsec
- PPP
- PPTP
- RADIUS
- SSTP
- VPN

Case Scenario

In the following case scenario, you will apply what you have learned about Remote Access and Network Access Protection. You can find answers to these questions in the "Answers" section at the end of this book.

Case Scenario: Remote Access at Wingtip Toys

Wingtip Toys has branch office locations in Sydney and Melbourne, Australia. The branch office firewalls are configured only to let traffic from the Internet through to hosts on the screened subnet on TCP ports 25, 80, and 443. A TS Gateway Server has been installed on the screened subnet at the Sydney location. A multi-homed Windows Server 2008 computer with the Remote Access will be deployed on the Melbourne screened subnet next week. Given this information, provide answers to the following questions:

1. What type of policy should you configure to limit access at the Sydney location to a list of authorized users?

2. When the Melbourne server is deployed, what VPN protocol would you use to provide access if you are not able to modify the existing firewall rules?

3. What sort of NAP enforcement should you use in the Melbourne location?

Suggested Practices

To help you successfully master the exam objectives presented in this chapter, complete the following tasks.

Configure Remote Access

Do the practice in this section.

- **Practice: Configure a TS Gateway Server**   Configure a TS Gateway Server on a stand-alone Windows Server 2008 computer that has two network cards, one of which is connected to a simulated public network.

  Configure a Resource Authorization Policy and a Connection Authorization Policy.

Configure Network Access Protection

Do the practice in this section.

- **Practice: Configure IPsec NAP Enforcement**   Configure IPsec enforcement so that only healthy clients on the network are able to communicate with each other.

Take a Practice Test

The practice tests on this book's companion CD offer many options. For example, you can test yourself on just one exam objective, or you can test yourself on all the 70-646 certification exam content. You can set up the test so that it closely simulates the experience of taking a certification exam, or you can set it up in study mode so that you can look at the correct answers and explanations after you answer each question.

MORE INFO   Practice tests

For details about all the practice test options available, see the "How to Use the Practice Tests" section in this book's Introduction.

Chapter 10

Certificate Services and Storage Area Networks

As the privacy and security of data becomes an increasingly important concern to those that pay the wages of systems administrators, the deployment of Certificate Services in corporate network environments has become more prevalent. Planning the deployment of Certificate Servers includes not only the deployment of the servers themselves, but the deployment of additional supporting technologies such as Web enrollment, autoenrollment, certificate revocation lists, and Online Responders. In this chapter, you will learn about these technologies and how to apply them to meet your organization's certificate needs.

The second part of this chapter deals with storage area network devices, which, like Certificate Services, form an integral part of a large organization's network infrastructure deployment. The growth in the amount of data that organizations have to deal with is also a challenge to systems administrators. Rather than adding extra hard disks to servers in a piecemeal fashion as they run out of storage space, Storage Area Network (SAN) arrays allow you to configure a centralized storage area network. You can provision the extra storage to servers on an as-needed basis. In this chapter, you will learn how to configure SAN arrays to support Windows Server 2008 computers.

Exam objectives in this chapter:
- Plan infrastructure services server roles.
- Plan storage.

Lessons in this chapter:

Before You Begin

To complete the lesson in this chapter, you must have done the following:

■ Installed and configured the evaluation edition of Windows Server 2008 Enterprise Edition in accordance with the instructions listed in the first practice exercise of Lesson 1 in Chapter 1, "Installing, Upgrading, and Deploying Windows Server 2008."

No additional configuration is required for this chapter.

Lesson 1: Configuring Active Directory Certificate Services

Certificate Authorities are becoming as integral to an organization's network infrastructure as domain controllers, DNS, and DHCP servers. You should spend at least as much time planning the deployment of Certificate Services in your organization's Active Directory environment as you spend planning the deployment of these other infrastructure servers. In this lesson, you will learn how certificate templates impact the issuance of digital certificates, how to configure certificates to be automatically assigned to users, and how to configure supporting technologies such as Online Responders and credential roaming. Learning how to use these technologies will smooth the integration of certificates into your organization's Windows Server 2008 environment.

After this lesson, you will be able to:

- Install and manage Active Directory Certificate Services.
- Configure autoenrollment for certificates.
- Configure credential roaming.
- Configure an Online Responder for Certificate Services.

Estimated lesson time: 40 minutes

Types of Certificate Authority

When planning the deployment of Certificate Services in your network environment, you must decide which type of Certificate Authority best meets your organizational requirements. There are four types of Certificate Authority (CA):

- Enterprise Root
- Enterprise Subordinate
- Standalone Root
- Standalone Subordinate

The type of CA you deploy depends on how certificates will be used in your environment and the state of the existing environment. You have to choose between an Enterprise or a Standalone CA during the installation of the Certificate Services role, as shown in Figure 10-1. You cannot switch between any of the CA types after the CA has been deployed.

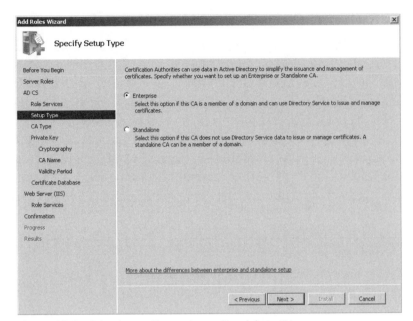

Figure 10-1 Selecting an Enterprise or Standalone CA

Enterprise CAs require access to Active Directory. This type of CA uses Group Policy to propagate the certificate trust lists to users and computers throughout the domain and publish certificate revocation lists to Active Directory. Enterprise CAs issue certificates from certificate templates, which allow the following functionality:

- Enterprise CAs enforce credential checks on users during the certificate enrollment process. Each certificate template has a set of security permissions that determine whether a particular user is authorized to receive certificates generated from that template.

- Certificate names are automatically generated from information stored within Active Directory. The method by which this is done is determined by certificate template configuration.

- Autoenrollment can be used to issue certificates from Enterprise CAs, vastly simplifying the certificate distribution process. Autoenrollment is configured through applying certificate template permissions.

In essence, Enterprise CAs are fully integrated into a Windows Server 2008 environment. This type of CA makes the issuing and management of certificates for Active Directory clients as simple as possible.

Standalone CAs do not require Active Directory. When certificate requests are submitted to Standalone CAs, the requestor must provide all relevant identifying information and manually specify the type of certificate needed. This process occurs automatically with an Enterprise CA. By default, Standalone CA requests require administrator approval. Administrator intervention is necessary because there is no automated method of verifying a requestor's credentials. Standalone CAs do not use certificate templates, limiting the ability for administrators to customize certificates for specific organizational needs.

You can deploy Standalone CAs on computers that are members of the domain. When installed by a user that is a member of the Domain Admins group, or one who has been delegated similar rights, the Standalone CA's information will be added to the Trusted Root Certificate Authorities certificate store for all users and computers in the domain. The CA will also be able to publish its certificate revocation list to Active Directory.

Whether you install a Root or Subordinate CA depends on whether there is an existing certificate infrastructure. Root CAs are the most trusted type of CA in an organization's public key infrastructure (PKI) hierarchy. Root CAs sit at the top of the hierarchy as the ultimate point of trust and hence must be as secure as possible. In many environments, a Root CA is only used to issue signing certificates to Subordinate CAs. When not used for this purpose, Root CAs are kept offline in secure environments as a method of reducing the chance that they might be compromised.

If a Root CA is compromised, all certificates within an organization's PKI infrastructure should be considered compromised. Digital certificates are ultimately statements of trust. If you cannot trust the ultimate authority from which that trust is derived, it follows that you should not trust any of the certificates downstream from that ultimate authority.

Subordinate CAs are the network infrastructure servers that you should deploy to issue the everyday certificates needed by computers, users, and services. An organization can have many Subordinate CAs, each of which is issued a signing certificate by the Root CA. In the event that one Subordinate CA is compromised, trust of that CA can be revoked from the Root CA. Only the certificates that were issued by that CA will be considered untrustworthy. You can replace the compromised Subordinate CA without having to replace the entire organization's certificate infrastructure. Subordinate CAs can be replaced, but a compromised Enterprise Root CA usually means you have to redeploy the Active Directory forest from scratch. If a Standalone Root CA is compromised, it also necessitates the replacement of an organization's PKI infrastructure.

MORE INFO   **Certificate Services overview**

For a more detailed overview of Active Directory Certificate Services in Windows Server 2008, consult the following Microsoft TechNet link: *http://technet2.microsoft.com/windowsserver2008/ en/library/ee335ea9-e1d1-4f85-b9a4-ab0a8e75a7d21033.mspx?mfr=true.*

Certificate Services Role-Based Administration

Given the integral nature of Certificate Services to an organization's security infrastructure, many organizations use different staff members to manage different aspects of Certificate Services. Staff is usually separated into the people responsible for managing the CA itself and the people responsible for managing the certificates that are issued by the CA. This separation is implemented through the assigning of Certificate Services roles.

The two critical roles are the CA Administrator and the Certificate Manager. Roles are designated by assigning permissions using the Security tab of the Certificate Server's properties. You assign the CA Administrator role by granting the Manage CA permission to a user or group. You assign the Certificate Manager role by granting the Issue And Manage Certificates permission to a user or group. By default, the Domain Admins, Enterprise Admins, and local Administrators groups can assign these roles. Figure 10-2 shows that the Alpha group holds the Certificate Manager roles because the group is assigned the Issue And Manage Certificates permission.

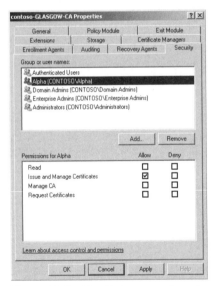

Figure 10-2   The Alpha group is assigned the Certificates Manager role.

These roles have the following properties:

- **CA Administrator**   This role should be assigned to staff who need to configure and maintain the Certificate Authority itself. Users assigned this role can start and stop the certificate server, configure extensions, assign roles, renew CA keys, define key recovery agents, and configure certificate manager restrictions.

■ **Certificate Manager**   This role should be assigned to staff who are responsible for approving certificate enrollment and revocation requests. You can restrict certificate managers to specific groups or specific templates. Hence, you can configure one group with the permission to approve certificates issued from one template and configure another group with separate permission to approve certificates issued from a different template. You configure these restrictions on the Certificate Managers tab, shown in Figure 10-3.

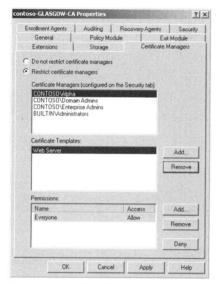

Figure 10-3   The Alpha user group can manage Web Server certificates.

MORE INFO   **More on Role-Based Administration**

For more information on Certificate Services Role-Based Administration, consult the following TechNet Link:

http://technet2.microsoft.com/windowsserver2008/en/library/c651f8cf-5c84-42c0-9a61-37e0000e69891 033.mspx?mfr=true.

Configuring Credential Roaming

Credential roaming allows for the storage of certificates and private keys within Active Directory. For example, a user's encrypting file system certificate can be stored in Active Directory and provided to the user when she logs on to different computers within the domain. The same EFS certificate will always be used to encrypt files. This means that the user can encrypt files on an NTFS-formatted USB storage device on one computer and then decrypt them on another, because the EFS certificate will be transferred to the second computer's certificate store during the logon process. Credential roaming also allows for all of a user's certificates and keys to be removed when he logs off of the computer.

Credential roaming is enabled through the Certificate Services Client policy, located under User Configuration\Policies\Windows Settings\Security Settings\Public Key Policies and shown in Figure 10-4.

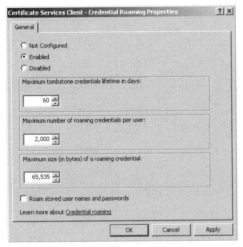

Figure 10-4   Credential Roaming Policy

Credential roaming works in the following manner. When a user logs on to a client computer in a domain where the Credential Roaming Policy has been enabled, the certificates in the user's store on the client computer are compared to certificates stored for the user within Active Directory.

- If the certificates in the user's certificate store are up to date, no further action is taken.
- If more recent certificates for the user are stored in Active Directory, these credentials are copied to the client computer.
- If more recent certificates are located in the user's store, the certificates stored in Active Directory are updated.

Credential roaming synchronizes and resolves any conflicts between certificates and private keys from any number of client computers that a user logs on to, as well as certificates and private keys stored within Active Directory. Credential roaming is triggered whenever a private key or certificate in the local certificate store changes, whenever the user locks or unlocks a computer, and whenever Group Policy refreshes. Credential roaming is supported on Windows Vista, Windows Server 2008, Windows XP SP2, and Windows Server 2003 SP1.

MORE INFO   **More on credential roaming**

For more information on configuring credential roaming, consult the following TechNet link: *http://technet2.microsoft.com/windowsserver2008/en/library/fabc1c44-f2a2-43e1-b52e-9b12a1f19a331 033.mspx?mfr=true.*

Configuring Autoenrollment

Autoenrollment allows certificates to be distributed to clients without direct client intervention. Autoenrollment allows the automatic enrollment of subjects for specific certificates. It also allows for the retrieval of issued certificates and for the automatic renewal of expiring certificates without the need for subject or administrator intervention. In most cases, autoenrollment occurs without the user being aware of it, although you can configure certificate templates in such a way that they do interact with the subjects.

Configuring a Template for Autoenrollment

Before a certificate can be automatically enrolled, it is necessary to configure several aspects of the certificate template. Certificate templates are modified using the Certificate Templates snap-in, which you will need to add to a custom MMC. Only users with the Certificate Manager role's permissions are able to create and modify certificate templates.

When using the Certificate Templates console, note that you cannot configure the autoenrollment permission for a level 1 certificate template. Level 1 certificates have Windows 2000 as their minimum supported CA. Level 2 certificate templates have Windows Server 2003 as a minimum supported CA. Level 2 certificate templates are also the minimum level of certificate template that supports autoenrollment. Level 3 certificates templates are supported only by client computers running Windows Server 2008 or Windows Vista. Level 3 certificate templates allow administrators to configure advanced Suite B cryptographic settings. These settings are not required to allow certificate autoenrollment and most administrators find level 2 certificate templates are adequate for their organizational needs.

If you do create a new certificate template based on an existing one, you should configure the template you copied as a superseded template. This allows certificates that are configured using previous settings to be updated to the new settings. You will also need to configure the CA to publish this new template through the Certification Authority console. To configure automatic certificate enrollment for a specific template, follow these steps:

1. Open the Certificate Templates snap-in.

2. Right-click the Certificate Template that you want to modify and then click Properties.

3. Configure the General, Request Handling, and Issuance Requirements as necessary for the purposes of the certificate. This step is not necessary for autoenrollment, but you should review these settings because they allow you to better tune the automatic issuing of certificates.

4. On the Certificate Template's Security tab, select the group that you will allow to automatically enroll certificates and the select the Allow box next to the Autoenroll permission. Figure 10-5 shows autoenrollment configured for the Authenticated Users group.

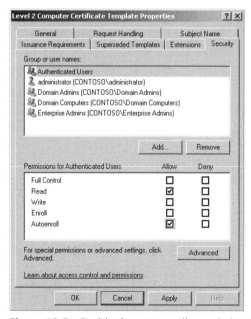

Figure 10-5   Enable the autoenroll permission to allow automatic enrollment

Configuring Group Policy for Autoenrollment

After you have set up the permissions on certificate templates, the next step to deploying autoenrollment of certificates throughout your organization is to configure the default domain policy to support autoenrollment. To configure Group Policy for autoenrollment, perform the following steps:

1. Edit the Default Domain Policy GPO using the Group Policy Management Console feature located in Server Manager.

2. Under User Configuration\Policies\Windows Settings\Security Settings\Public Key Policies, double-click Certificate Services Client – Auto-Enrollment. This will open the Certificate Services Client – Auto-Enrollment Properties policy dialog box, shown in Figure 10-6.

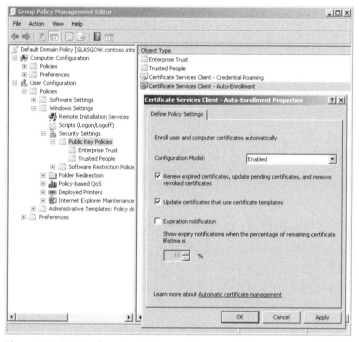

Figure 10-6   Configuring Autoenrollment policies

3. Choose Enabled from the Configuration Model drop-down list and then configure the expiration and update settings.

After you enable the Certificate Services autoenrollment policy, those certificates that have templates configured for autoenrollment will automatically be deployed. You can also enable the following policy options as a part of the autoenrollment policy:

- **Renew Expired Certificates, Update Pending Certificates, And Remove Revoked Certificates**   This policy primarily relates to certificate management. If you have enabled autoenrollment, you will probably want to ensure that expired certificates are automatically renewed, revoked certificates are removed, and pending certificates updated. Enabling this option vastly reduces the workload of certificate administrators.

- **Update Certificates That Use Certificate Templates** When this policy is enabled and the template that the certificate was issued from is revised or replaced, the issued certificate will be updated.

- **Expiration Notification** This policy is less necessary when you configure expired certificates to automatically renew, but can be useful when certificates templates are configured so that automatic renewal (rather than automatic enrollment) does not occur.

MORE INFO More on configuring autoenrollment

To learn more about configuring autoenrollment, consult the following TechNet page: *http://technet2.microsoft.com/windowsserver2008/en/library/a24a23a7-b723-42fc-8295-2641e6fc5de 31033.mspx*.

Quick Check

1. What sort of CA should you install as the first CA in your environment if you want to integrate certificates with Active Directory?

2. Which clients and CAs support level 3 templates?

Quick Check Answers

1. Enterprise Root CA.

2. Windows Vista and Windows Server 2008 support level 3 templates.

Configuring Web Enrollment Support

Web enrollment allows users of Internet Explorer version 6.x or later to submit certificate requests to a CA directly through a Web application. You can use Web enrollment to:

- Request certificates and review existing certificate requests.

- Access certificate revocation lists.

- Perform smart card enrollment.

Web enrollment is primary deployed to provide an enrollment mechanism for organizations that need to issue and renew certificates for users and computers that are not joined to an Active Directory domain or who are using non-Microsoft operating systems. Users of browsers other than Internet Explorer version 6.x and later are able to submit enrollment requests using the Web enrollment application, but they must first create a PKCS #10 request before submitting it through the Web enrollment pages. Once the request is successfully made, users can reconnect to the Web enrollment application and are able to download and install their requested certificates.

To configure a server to support Web enrollment, the Certification Authority Web Enrollment role service needs to be added to the server role. When the Certification Authority Web Enrollment role service is installed on a computer that is operating as a CA, no future configuration steps are required. If the Certification Authority Web Enrollment service is installed on a separate computer from the CA, the CA needs to be specified during the Certification Authority Web Enrollment role service installation process.

Web enrollment has the following limitations:

- Web enrollment cannot be used with version 3 certificate templates. Only version 1 and 2 certificate templates are supported by Web enrollment.

- Computer certificates cannot be requested using Web enrollment from a Windows Server 2008 CA.

- If IIS is installed on a 64-bit version of Windows Server 2008, 32-bit Web applications, such as WSUS, cannot be installed because this will force IIS to run in 32-bit mode. The Web enrollment role service will attempt to install as a 64-bit Web application and the installation will fail. This does not apply to 32-bit versions of Windows Server 2008.

MORE INFO   **Setting up Web enrollment**

For more information on setting up Web enrollment support, consult the following TechNet link: *http://technet2.microsoft.com/windowsserver2008/en/library/d6e60022-fcad-4192-b038-be51c15b8f 6a1033.mspx?mfr=true.*

Configuring Certificate Revocation Lists

Certificate Services do more than issue certificates. Certificates are tokens of trust and in certain cases those tokens of trust need to be revoked. This process is called *certificate revocation*. The most common method of publishing information about which certificates issued by a CA are no longer valid is the certificate revocation list (CRL). Certificate revocation lists are lists of certificate serial numbers for certificates that have either been revoked or are placed on hold. CRLs are issued by the CA that issues the corresponding certificate, rather than an upstream or a downstream CA. When a certificate is to be used, a check against the issuing CA's CRL needs to be made. The location of the CRL is included with the certificate so that the client knows where on the network to look to verify that the certificate that it is about to accept is still actually valid.

Specifying a CRL Distribution Point

The Extensions tab on a Certificate Server's properties, shown in Figure 10-7, allows you to add, remove, or modify CRL distribution points. When you make a modification to the list of distribution points, you should be aware that this will only apply to certificates issued from that point on and does not apply retroactively. Your user account must have been assigned the Certificate Manager role to modify CRL distribution point configuration information. CRL URLs can use HTTP, FTP, LDAP, or FILE addresses.

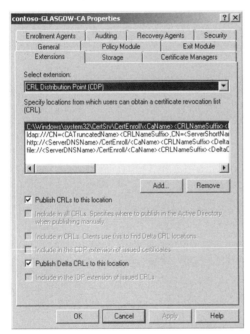

Figure 10-7   Configuring a CRL distribution point

Configuring CRL and Delta CRL Publication

Because CRLs can become very large, you can publish a smaller type of CRL called a delta CRL at a more frequent interval. A delta CRL contains only data about certificates that have been revoked since the publication of the last full CRL. This allows clients to retrieve the small delta CRL and add it to a cached copy of the full CRL to build a complete list of revoked certificates. Delta CRLs allow for revocation data to be published more frequently, which makes the deployment of Certificate Services more secure. An outdated CRL cannot be used to inform clients of the most recent revocations because these revocations will not be published until the next time the full CRL is published.

The CRL and delta CRL publication intervals are configured by modifying the properties of the Revoked Certificates node on a CA from the Certificate Authority console, as shown in Figure 10-8. The default CRL publication interval is once a week and the default delta CRL publication interval is once a day.

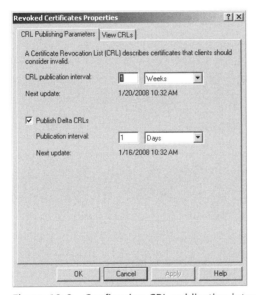

Figure 10-8   Configuring CRL publication interval

MORE INFO   **More on revocation**

For more information on configuring certificate revocation, consult the following TechNet article: *http://technet2.microsoft.com/windowsserver2008/en/library/336d3a6a-33c6-4083-8606-c0a4fdca9 a251033.mspx?mfr=true*.

Configuring an Online Responder for Certificate Services

The problem with CRL publication is that significant delays occur during periods of peak activity, such as when large numbers of users log on using smart cards, encrypt files, or use digital signatures. This is because the entire CRL has to be checked and, as mentioned earlier in the lesson, CRLs can become very large. CRL checks cannot be load-balanced to another CA if the issuing CA is experiencing a traffic spike. Attempts have been made to solve this problem using solutions such as partitioned CRLs, delta CRLs, and indirect CRLs. All of these prior solutions ended up increasing the complexity of CA implementation without significantly reducing the problem of traffic spikes. This is where Online Certificate Status Protocol (OCSP) comes in.

An Online Responder receives and responds only to requests about the status of individual certificates. For example, rather than having to download the CA's entire CRL to see whether the signing certificate issued to Rooslan is valid, the client queries the Online Responder to see if Rooslan's signing certificate is valid and receives a response that only provides information about Rooslan's signing certificate. This significantly reduces the load on the issuing CA and also reduces network traffic. CRLs can get very large, and distributing a CRL to each of 100 clients can use a lot of bandwidth. Depending on the size of the CRL, providing revocation information about 100 different specific certificates may use less bandwidth than forwarding the current CRL to a single client.

The Windows Server 2008 OCSP feature includes the following features:

- **Web proxy caching**   The Online Responder Web proxy cache is the interface that clients connect with to access Online Responder data. It is implemented as an ISAPI extension hosted by IIS.

- **Support for nonce and no-nonce requests**   You can set nonce and no-nonce request configuration options to prevent replay attacks on Online Responders. Replay attacks work by either repeating or delaying the transmission of legitimate data. A replay attack could be used to indicate that a revoked certificate is still valid.

- **Advanced cryptography support**   You can configure OCSP to use elliptic curve and SHA-256 cryptography.

- **Kerberos protocol integration**   OCSP requests and responses can be processed with Kerberos password authentication, allowing for the validation of server certificates during the logon process.

- **Single point or responder array**   A single computer can function as an Online Responder, or multiple linked computers can host Online Responders, allowing for certificate validity checks to be balanced across multiple hosts.

You can install the Online Responder service on a CA, but Microsoft recommends deploying the Online Responder service on a separate computer. A single computer with the Online Responder service deployed can provide revocation status data for certificates issued by a single or multiple CAs. As mentioned earlier, a single CA's revocation data can be distributed across multiple Online Responders.

The Online Responder service is installed on Windows Server 2008 computers. You should deploy Online Responders after the deployment of Certificate Authorities but prior to the issuance of client certificates. To deploy the Online Responder service to a Windows Server 2008 computer, the following conditions must be met:

- IIS must already be installed on the computer that will host the Online Responder service.

- An OCSP Response Signing certificate template must be configured on the CA and autoenrollment must be used to issue an OCSP Response Signing certificate to the computer that will host the Online Responder service. An Online Responder cannot provide status information for a certificate issued from a CA higher in the CA chain than the one that issued its signing certificate.

- The URL for the Online Responder must be included in the Authority Information Access (AIA) extension of certificates issued by the CA. This URL will be used by clients to locate the Online Responder so that certificate validation can occur.

The Online Responder service is managed through the Online Responder Management console, shown in Figure 10-9. After you have deployed the Online Responder, you must

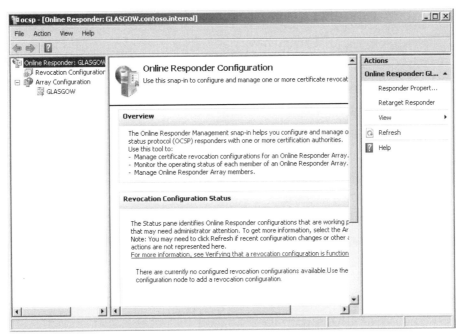

Figure 10-9 Online Responder console

create a revocation configuration for each CA and CA certificate that will be serviced by the Online Responder. Revocation configurations include all settings required to reply to client status requests with respect to certificates issued using a specific CA key. These settings include the CA certificate, signing certificate for the Online Responder, and the revocation provider that provides revocation data used by the revocation configuration. When configuring a single Online Responder for multiple CAs, ensure that the Online Responder has a key and signing certificate for each CA that it supports. In the practice exercise at the end of this lesson, you will configure an Online Responder.

Configuring Responder Arrays

In the event that the Online Responder that you have deployed in your network environment is unable to cope with projected traffic, you can deploy an array of computers functioning as Online Responders. As mentioned earlier in this lesson, an array of Online Responders can handle the revocation traffic of one or more issuing CAs. Online Responder Arrays are also often deployed for fault tolerance purposes. Nodes in Online Responder Arrays can also be deployed at branch or satellite office locations that have only intermittent network connectivity to the site that hosts the issuing CA.

Online Responder Arrays have one member of the array configured as the Array controller and the rest as array members. Although each Online Responder in an array can be managed and configured separately, when conflicts arise, the configuration settings for the Array controller override configuration settings for array members.

To create an Online Responder Array you need to perform the following general steps:

1. Configure the CAs in your organization that are used to issue certificates to support Online Responders.

2. Add the Online Responder service to all servers that will participate in the planned array.

3. Add the Online Responders to the array by opening the Online Responder console, selecting the Array Configuration Members node, and using the Add Array Members item in the Actions pane.

OCSP Group Policy Settings

Windows Server 2008 includes several Group Policy settings that enhance the management of OCSP and CRL data use. These policies are located on the Revocation tab of the properties of the Computer Configuration\Policies\Windows Settings\Security Settings\Public Key Policies\Certificate Path Validation Settings node, which is shown in Figure 10-10. One of the reasons for these policies is that CRLs have expiration dates and if the expiration date passes prior to the update becoming available, the certificate chain validation might fail, even with an Online Responder deployed. Problems can occur when an Online Responder is forced to rely upon an expired CRL. By selecting Allow CRL And OCSP Responses To Be Valid Longer Than Their Lifetime, you can effectively issue an extension to CRLs in the event that they are not updated in a timely manner.

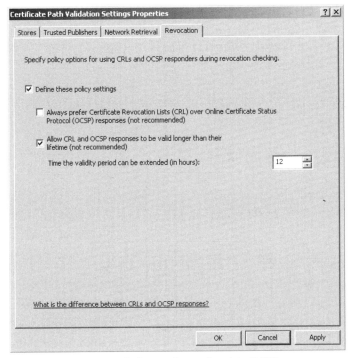

Figure 10-10   Group Policy options related to OCSP

MORE INFO   **More on OCSP support**

For more information on the support for OCSP in Windows Server 2008, consult the following TechNet link: *http://technet2.microsoft.com/windowsserver2008/en/library/99d1f392-6bcd-4ccf-94ee-640fc100ba5f1033.mspx?mfr=true*.

Network Device Enrollment Service

The Network Device Enrollment Service allows a Windows Server 2008 CA to issue and manage certificates for routers and other network devices that do not have accounts within the Active Directory database. The Network Device Enrollment Service allows network devices to obtain certificates based on the Simple Certificate Enrollment Protocol (SCEP). The Network Device Enrollment Service provides the following functionality to a network environment:

■ Generates and provides one-time enrollment passwords to administrators of network devices

■ Submits SCEP enrollment requests on behalf of network devices to a Windows Server 2008 CA

■ Retrieves issued certificates from the CA and directs them to the network device

By default, the Network Device Enrollment Service can only cache five passwords at a time. This limits the number of network devices that can participate in the enrollment process to five. It is possible to flush stored passwords from the cache by restarting IIS, and it is also possible to configure the Network Device Enrollment Service to cache more than five passwords at a time.

MORE INFO   **More on enrolling network devices**

To learn more about using the Network Device Enrollment Service to enroll devices, consult the following TechNet article: *http://technet2.microsoft.com/windowsserver2008/en/library/f3911350-ab45-494d-a07e-d0b9696a651e1033.mspx?mfr=true.*

Using Enterprise PKI to Monitor CA Health

You can add the Enterprise PKI snap-in to a custom console (shown in Figure 10-11) to monitor the health of all CAs within a public key infrastructure (PKI). The Enterprise PKI tool allows you to view the status of all of your organization's PKI environment. In an organization that has multiple levels of issuing CAs, having an at-a-glance view of all certificate servers allows administrators to manage the CA hierarchy and troubleshoot CA errors easily and effectively. The Enterprise PKI tool provides data on the validity or accessibility of Authority Information Access (AIA) locations and CRL distribution points.

Enterprise PKI works on both Windows Server 2008 and Windows Server 2003 Enterprise CAs. The Enterprise PKI tool provides the following status information about each CA in the PKI hierarchy:

■ Question Mark: Health status is being evaluated.

■ Green Indicator: CA is problem-free.

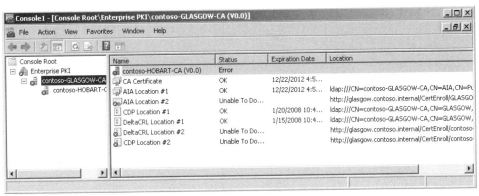

Figure 10-11   Enterprise PKI indicating configuration errors

- Yellow Indicator: CA has a non-critical problem.
- Red Indicator: CA has a critical problem.
- Red Cross Over CA Icon: CA is offline.

The most common configuration problems are likely to be the second AIA location, the second delta CRL location, and the CDP location. When confronted with CA configuration issues, you should use the following strategies in an attempt to resolve the issue:

- If the issue is CA-related, such as problems connecting to a current CRL, use the Certification Authority console to manage the problem by connecting to the CA experiencing the problem.
- If the issue relates to the Online Responder, use the Online Responder Management console to resolve the issue.
- If the Enterprise PKI console reports that CA certificates are about to expire, you should use the Certificates snap-in of a custom console to renew these certificates.
- It is possible to enable CryptoAPI 2.0 diagnostics to obtain detailed information about PKI-related issues. This is done by enabling the Operational log under Applications And Service Logs\Microsoft\Windows\CAPI2 log in Event Viewer, shown in Figure 10-12.

MORE INFO   More on Enterprise PKI

For more information about Enterprise PKI, consult the following article on TechNet: *http://technet2.microsoft.com/windowsserver2008/en/library/bf9c7dca-26d7-4de5-890d-47e30308690e1033.mspx.*

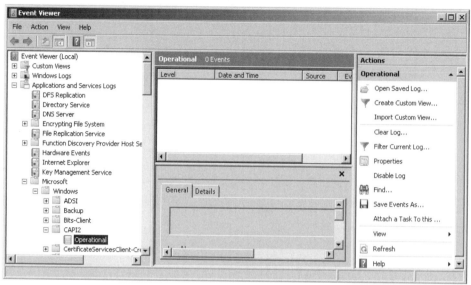

Figure 10-12   Use the operational log for CryptoAPI 2.0 diagnostics

Practice: Deploying Active Directory Certificate Services and an Online Responder

An Enterprise Root CA forms the core of a Windows Server 2008 PKI deployment. In smaller environments an Enterprise Root CA will be kept offline and an Enterprise Subordinate CA will be used to issue certificates for day-to-day use.

▶ **Exercise 1: Install AD CS and Configure an Online Responder**

In this exercise, you will deploy Active Directory Certificate Services. Once Active Directory Certificate Services is deployed, you will then deploy and configure an Online Responder. To complete this practice exercise, perform the following steps:

1. Log on to server Glasgow using the Kim_Akers user account. When the Server Manager console opens, from within the Roles Summary section, click the Add Roles item. If the Server Manager console does not open automatically, open it from the Administrative Tools menu.

2. On the Select Server Roles page, select Active Directory Certificate Service and click Next twice.

3. On the Select Role Services page, verify that Certification Authority and Certification Authority Web Enrollment are selected. If you are prompted to install additional role services and features for the Web Server (IIS) and Windows Process Activation Service, click Add Required Role Services. Click Next.

4. On the Specify Setup Type page, ensure that Enterprise is selected and then click Next.

5. On the Specify CA Type page, ensure that Root CA is selected as shown in Figure 10-13 and then click Next.

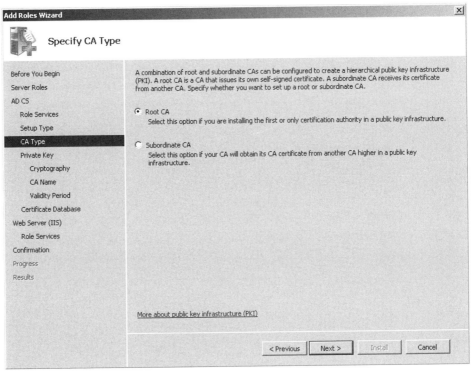

Figure 10-13   Selecting a Root or Subordinate CA

6. On the Set Up Private Key page, ensure that Create A New Private Key is selected and then click Next.

7. On the Configure Cryptography for CA page, verify that the RSA#Microsoft Software Key Storage Provider CSP is selected, a Key Character Length of 2048 is selected, and the hash algorithm is set to SHA1. Click Next.

8. Verify that the Common Name For This CA is set to Contoso-GLASGOW-CA and then click Next.

9. Accept the default validity period of 5 years and then click Next until you reach the Confirm Installation Selections page, shown in Figure 10-14. Click Install. When the installation process completes, click Close.

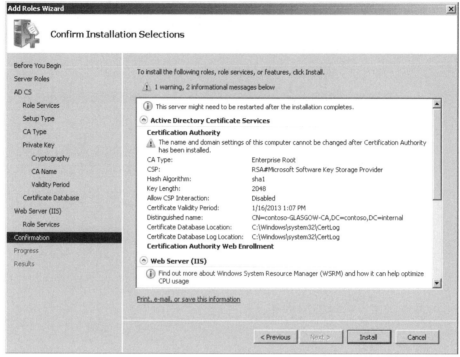

Figure 10-14 Confirming settings

10. From the Administrative Tools menu, open the Certification Authority console. Click Continue when prompted by the UAC dialog box. Verify that Contoso-GLASGOW-CA has a green check mark icon next to it.

11. Select the Certificate Templates node. Verify that the list of certificate templates match those in Figure 10-15.

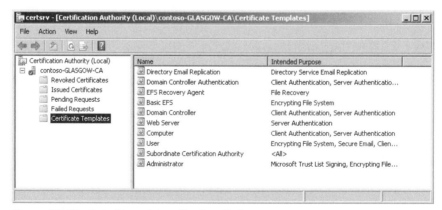

Figure 10-15 Set of templates after installation

12. Close the Certification Authority Console.

13. Open the Server Manager Console. Under the Roles node, select Active Directory Certificate Services. In the Role Services section, click the Add Role Services item.

14. On the Select Role Services page, select Online Responder and click Next. Click Install to install the Online Responder service. Click Close when the installation process completes.

15. Click Start, click Run, and type **MMC** to open a Microsoft Management Console. Click Continue to dismiss the User Account Control dialog box. From the File menu, click Add/Remove Snap-in. Add the Certificate Templates Snap-in as shown in Figure 10-16 and then click OK.

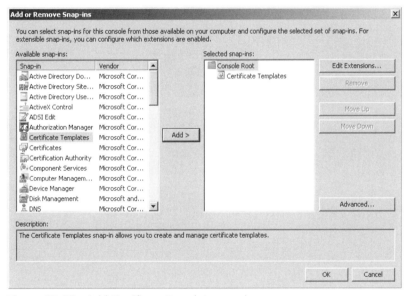

Figure 10-16   Add Certificate Template snap-in

16. Expand the Certificate Templates snap-in. Right-click the OCSP Response Signing template and then click Properties.

17. Click the Security tab and then click Add. Click Object Types and ensure that the Computers object type is selected. Click OK to close the Object Types dialog box. Under Enter The Object Names To Select, type **Glasgow** and then click OK.

18. When the Glasgow object is selected, set the Read, Enroll, and Autoenroll permissions to Allow, as shown in Figure 10-17. Click OK.

19. Close the custom console. Open the Certification Authority console from the Administrative Tools menu.

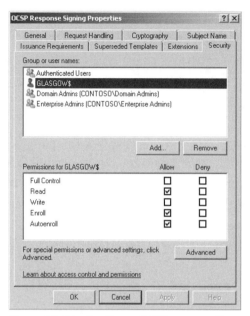

Figure 10-17   Configure OCSP autoenrollment

20. Right-click Contoso-GLASGOW-CA and then click Properties. Click the Extensions tab. Select Authority Information Access (AIA) from the Select Extension drop-down list.

21. Click Add. This will open the Add Location dialog box. Type **http://glasgow. contoso.internal/ocsp** and then click OK.

22. Select Include In The AIA Extension Of Issued Certificates and Include In The Online Certificate Status Protocol (OCSP) Extension, as shown in Figure 10-18 and then click OK.

23. You will be informed that it is necessary to restart Active Directory Certificate Services for the changes to take effect. Click Yes to restart the service.

24. In the Certificate Authority console, right-click the Certificate Templates node and then click New, Certificate Template To Issue. Select the OCSP Response Signing template and then click OK.

25. Review the list of Certificate Templates under the Certificate Template node and verify that the OCSP Response Signing template is listed.

26. Minimize the Certification Authority console.

27. From the Features node of Server Manager, select the Group Policy Management Console.

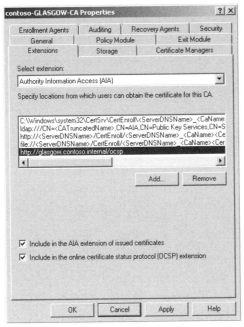

Figure 10-18 Configuring CA OCSP extensions

28. Edit the Default Domain Group Policy object. Enable the Autoenrollment policy located under User Configuration\Policies\Windows Settings\Security Settings\ Public Key Policies. Do the same for the Autoenrollment settings under the Computer Configuration section.

29. Close the GPO editor and restart server Glasgow.

Lesson Summary

- Enterprise CAs are used to support Active Directory. Enterprise CAs are automatically added to domain user's trusted certificates stores. Most Certificate Services deployments in Windows Server 2008 network environments use Enterprise CAs.

- Standalone CAs do not require the deployment of Active Directory and cannot be configured to use certificate templates.

- Online Responders process requests for CRL data more efficiently than traditional CRL publishing methods.

- Credential roaming ensures that users' certificates are up to date by frequently comparing local certificates with certificates stored in Active Directory.

- Autoenrollment allows certificates to be automatically deployed to eligible clients without user or administrator intervention. Autoenrollment has to be enabled within a Certificate Template and within Group Policy.

Lesson Review

You can use the following questions to test your knowledge of the information in Lesson 1, "Configuring Active Directory Certificate Services." The questions are also available on the companion CD if you prefer to review them in electronic form.

NOTE Answers

Answers to these questions and explanations of why each answer choice is correct or incorrect are located in the "Answers" section at the end of the book.

1. Digital certificates distributed through autoenrollment are widely used at a company's head office location. Which of the following CA types would you deploy to a regional branch office to issue certificates in support of autoenrollment policies configured within the default domain GPO?

   A. Enterprise Root CA

   B. Enterprise Subordinate CA

   C. Standalone Root CA

   D. Standalone Subordinate CA

2. Which of the following steps must you take before deploying autoenrollment? (Each correct answer presents part of the solution. Choose two.)

   A. Configure Group Policy to support autoenrollment.

   B. Configure autoenrollment permissions on certificate templates.

   C. Modify CRL publication settings.

   D. Configure an Online Responder.

   E. Configure Web enrollment.

3. You want to configure server ocsp.contoso.internal as an Online Responder for ca1.contoso.internal. Server ocsp.contoso.internal has IIS installed. Which of the following steps will you need to take as a part of this process? (Each correct answer presents part of a solution. Choose three.)

   A. Install an OCSP Response Signing certificate on ca1.contoso.internal.

   B. Configure an OCSP Response Signing certificate template on ca1.contoso. internal.

    C. Install an OCSP Response Signing certificate on ocsp.contoso.internal.

    D. Configure the AIA extension with the URL ocsp.contoso.internal.

    E. Configure the AIA extension with the URL ca1.contoso.internal.

4. Your organization's Queensland branch office makes extensive use of digital certificates. Queensland satellite offices have similar usage patterns. The Queensland branch office has a single Enterprise Root CA from which all certificates in Queensland are issued. Because of low-bandwidth WAN links, it sometimes takes a long time for clients in branch office locations to validate the authenticity of certificates that have already been issued. Which of the following steps can you take to improve certificate validation times for clients in satellite offices?

    A. Deploy an Enterprise Subordinate CA at the branch office.

    B. Deploy an Enterprise Subordinate CA at each satellite office.

    C. Deploy a Standalone Subordinate CA at the branch office.

    D. Place an Online Responder at each satellite office. Configure an Online Responder Array.

5. Which of the following tools can you use to view the health of multiple CAs in your organization's PKI environment?

    A. Certification Authority console

    B. Online Responder Management console

    C. Enterprise PKI

    D. Certificates MMC snap-in

Lesson 2: Planning the Deployment of Storage Area Networks

In this lesson, you will learn about LUNs, SANs, iSCSI, MPIO, VDS, and Fibre Channel. As intimidating as these acronyms can be, by the end of this lesson you will understand how the concepts that they represent fit together so that you can plan the deployment of storage area networks in your Windows Server 2008 environment.

After this lesson, you will be able to:

- Plan the assignment of LUNs.
- Plan the deployment of iSCSI SANs.
- Plan the deployment of Fibre Channel SANs.
- Plan Multipath I/O.
- Plan the deployment of VDS.

Estimated lesson time: 40 minutes

Logical Unit Numbers

A Logical Unit Number (LUN) is a logical reference to a portion of a storage subsystem. A LUN can represent a disk, a section of a disk, an entire disk array, or a section of a disk array in the storage subsystem. When a LUN is assigned to a server it acts as a physical disk drive that the server is able to perform read and write operations on. LUNs are used to simplify storage resource management on SANs.

You can use any LUN type that is supported by the storage subsystem that you are deploying. The different LUN types are:

- **Simple**   A simple LUN uses either an entire physical drive or a portion of that drive. The failure of a disk in a simple LUN means that all data stored on the LUN is lost.

- **Spanned**   A spanned LUN is a simple LUN that spans multiple physical drives. The failure of any one disk in a spanned LUN means that all data stored on the LUN is lost.

- **Striped**   Data is written across multiple physical disks. This type of LUN, also known as RAID-0 has improved I/O performance because data can be read and written to multiple disks simultaneously, but like a spanned LUN, all data will be lost in the event that one disk in the array fails.

- **Mirrored**   This LUN type, also known as RAID-1, is fault tolerant. Identical copies of the LUN are created on two physical drives. All read and write operations occur concurrently on both drives. If one disk fails, the LUN continues to be available on the unaffected disk.

- **Striped with Parity**   This LUN type, also known as RAID-5, offers fault tolerance and improved read performance, although write performance is hampered by parity calculation. This type requires a minimum of three disks and the equivalent of one disk's worth of storage is lost to the storage of parity information across the disk set. This LUN type will retain data if one disk is lost, but all data will be lost if two disks in the array fail at the same time. In the event that one disk fails, it should be replaced as quickly as possible.

You may have noticed that LUN types almost directly correspond to the volume deployment options that are available in Windows Server 2008. You can learn more about the configuration of local volumes for high availability in Chapter 11, "Clustering and High Availability."

Creating a LUN

The Provision Storage Wizard, which is accessible from Storage Manager For SANs, allows you to create a LUN on a Fibre Channel or iSCSI disk storage subsystem. Prior to attempting to create a LUN, you should verify that the following requirements have been met:

- The storage subsystem supports Virtual Disk Service (VDS).

- The VDS hardware provider for the storage subsystem is already installed.

- Storage space is available on the storage subsystem.

- If you are assigning the LUN to a cluster, Failover Clustering has been installed.

- If you are assigning the LUN to a server, ensure that server connections have been configured. How to configure server connections is covered in more detail in the sections on iSCSI and Fibre Channel later in this chapter.

After a LUN has been assigned to a server or cluster, it will be listed as a disk on that server and you will be able to create a volume on the disk. The performance and reliability characteristics of volumes created on the disk are determined by the LUN type.

Managing LUNs

You can extend a LUN if storage space is available in the subsystem where the LUN was created. Extending a LUN will not extend its file system partition. You must use the Disk Management console or a similar tool to extend the file system partition from the server that has access to the LUN after the LUN has been extended using Storage Manager for SANS.

Deleting a LUN will remove all data on all volumes on the LUN. This operation is irreversible. A LUN can only be deleted if all applications that access the LUN have been shut down. An alternative to deleting a LUN is to unassign it. When you unassign a LUN you make the LUN invisible to the server or cluster but retain the data stored in the LUN. The LUN can be reassigned at a later point in time. LUNs are deleted using Storage Manager For SANs. Select the target LUN under the LUN Management node and, from the Actions pane, click Delete LUN. To unassign a LUN, perform the same actions except click Unassign LUN instead of Delete LUN.

Virtual Disk Service (VDS)

Virtual Disk Service (VDS) provides a standard set of application programming interfaces (APIs) that provide a single interface through which disks can be managed. VDS provides a complete solution for managing storage hardware and disks and enables you to create volumes on those disks. This means that you can use a single tool to manage devices in a mixed storage environment rather than tools provided by different hardware vendors. Before you can manage a LUN using Storage Manager For SANs, you must install its VDS hardware provider. This will usually be provided by the hardware vendor. Prior to purchasing a storage device to be used on your organization's SAN, you should verify that a compatible VDS hardware provider exists.

VDS defines a software and a hardware provider interface. Each of these providers implements a different portion of the VDS API. The software provider is a program that runs on the host and is supported by a kernel-mode driver. Software providers operate on volumes, disks, and partitions. The hardware provider manages the actual storage subsystem. Hardware providers are usually disk array or adapter cards that enable the creation of logical disks for each LUN type. The LUN type that can be configured will depend on the options allowed by the VDS hardware provider. For example, some VDS hardware providers will allow the RAID-5 (Striped with Parity) LUN type to be implemented, while others might be limited to providing the Mirrored or Spanned LUN types.

MORE INFO   More on VDS

For more information on the functionality of VDS, consult the following TechNet article: *http://technet2.microsoft.com/windowsserver/en/library/dc77e7c7-ae44-4483-878b-6bc3819e64dc1033.mspx?mfr=true.*

Quick Check

1. Your storage subsystem consists of 5 1-terabyte drives. Which LUN type will allow you to create a volume of approximately 5 terabytes?

2. You have just extended a LUN using Storage Manager For SANs. Which tool should you use to extend the file system partition on this LUN?

Quick Check Answers

1. Spanned LUN type.

2. The Disk Management console or an equivalent tool. You cannot use Storage Manager For SANS to increase the size of the file system, only the size of the LUN.

Storage Manager For SANs

You can use the Storage Manager For SANs console to create LUNs on Fibre Channel and iSCSI storage arrays. You install Storage Manager For SANs as a Windows Server 2008 feature. To use Storage Manager For SANs to manage LUNs, the following criteria must be met:

- The storage subsystems that you are going to manage must support VDS.

- The VDS hardware provider for each subsystem must already be installed on the Windows Server 2008 computer.

When you open Storage Manager For SANs from the Administrative Tools menu, you are presented with three main nodes, which have the following functionality:

- **LUN Management** This node lists all of the LUNs created with Storage Manager For SANs. From this node you can create new LUNs, extend the size of existing LUNs, assign and unassign LUNs, and delete LUNs. You can also use this node to configure the Fibre Channel and iSCSI connections that servers use to access LUNs.

- **Subsystems** This node lists all of the storage subsystems currently discovered within the SAN environment. You can rename subsystems using this node.

- **Drives** This node lists all of the drives in the storage subsystems discovered in the SAN. You can identify drives that you are working with by making the drive light blink from this node.

Managing Fibre Channel LUNs

In a Fibre Channel environment, LUNs created on a Fibre Channel disk storage subsystem are assigned directly to a server or cluster. Servers access the LUN through one or more Fibre Channel host bus adapter (HBA) ports. Using Storage Manager For

SANs you can identify the server that will access the LUN and then specify which HBA ports will be used for LUN traffic. You can add ports manually by specifying their World Wide Name. You can also view detailed information about Fibre Channel HBAs for servers in your SAN by using the Storage Explorer console. Storage Explorer is covered in more detail later in this lesson.

Managing iSCSI LUNs

iSCSI is a SAN protocol that uses traditional network technologies—rather than the special cabling used by Fibre Channel—to send SCSI commands from initiators installed on servers to SCSI-based storage devices located on the network. Unlike Fibre Channel, iSCSI LUNs are not assigned directly to a server or cluster, but are assigned to logical entities called targets. These targets manage the connections between the iSCSI hardware and the servers that access it. A target includes the IP address, or *portal*, of the iSCSI device as well as the device's security settings—usually whatever credentials the server needs to provide to authenticate with the device. The specifics of the credentials vary from vendor to vendor.

To connect to a target, a server uses an iSCSI initiator. An iSCSI initiator is a logical entity that allows communication with the target from the server. The Windows Server 2008 iSCSI initiator is located in Control Panel. The iSCSI initiator logs on to the target and, when granted access, allows the server to read and write to all LUNs assigned to that target. Each iSCSI initiator can communicate through one or more network adapters. The Windows Server 2008 iSCSI initiator is shown in Figure 10-19.

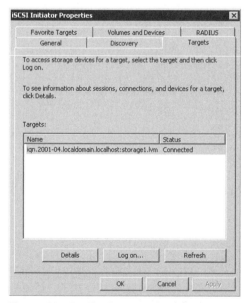

Figure 10-19 The Targets tab of the iSCSI initiator

MORE INFO More on Storage Manager For SANs

To learn more about Storage Manager For SANs on Windows Server 2008, consult the following TechNet article: *http://technet2.microsoft.com/windowsserver2008/en/library/6ebeae3b-da04-4cb4-96e0-ff5cf95580d11033.mspx?mfr=true.*

Multipath I/O

Multipath I/O (MPIO) is a feature of Windows Server 2008 that allows a server to use multiple data paths to a storage device. This increases the availability of storage resources because it provides alternate paths from a server or cluster to a storage subsystem in the event of path failure. MPIO uses redundant physical path components (adapters, switches, cabling) to create separate paths between the server or cluster and the storage device. If one of the devices in these separate paths fails, an alternate path to the SAN device will be used, ensuring that the server is still able to access critical data. You configure failover times through the Microsoft iSCSI Software initiator driver or by modifying the Fibre Channel HBA driver parameter settings, depending on the SAN technology deployed in your environment.

If the server will access a LUN through multiple Fibre Channel ports or multiple iSCSI initiator adapters, you must install MPIO on servers. You should verify that a server supports MPIO prior to enabling multiple iSCSI initiator adapters or multiple Fibre Channel ports for LUN access. If you do not do this, data loss is likely to occur. In the event that you are unsure whether a server supports MPIO, only enable a single iSCSI initiator adapter or Fibre Channel port on the server.

Windows Server 2008 MPIO supports iSCSI, Fibre Channel, and Serially Attached Storage (SAS) SAN connectivity by establishing multiple connections or sessions to the storage device. The Windows Server 2008 MPIO implementation includes a Device Specific Module (DSM) that works with storage devices that support the asymmetric logical unit access (ALUA) controller model as well as storage devices that use the Active/Active controller model. MPIO also supports the following load-balancing policies:

- **Failover** When this policy is implemented no load balancing is performed. The application specifies a primary path and a group of standby paths. The primary path is used for all device requests. The standby paths are only used in the event that the primary path fails. Standby paths are listed from most preferred path to least preferred path.

- **Failback** When this policy is configured, I/O is limited to a preferred path while that path is functioning. If the preferred path fails, I/O is directed to an alternate path. I/O will automatically switch back to the preferred path when that path returns to full functionality.

- **Round-robin** All available paths are used for I/O in a balanced fashion. If a path fails, I/O is redistributed among the remaining paths.

- **Round-robin with a subset of paths** When this policy is configured, a set of preferred paths is specified for I/O and a set of standby paths is specified for failover. The set of preferred paths will be used until all paths fail, at which point failover will occur to the standby path set. The preferred paths are used in a round-robin fashion.

- **Dynamic least queue depth** I/O is directed to the path with the least number of outstanding requests.

- **Weighted path** Each path is assigned a weight. The path with the least weight is chosen for I/O.

Load-balancing policies are dependent on the controller model (ALUA or true Active/Active) of the storage array attached to the Windows Server 2008 computer. MPIO is added to a Windows Server 2008 computer by using the Add Features item in the Features area of Server Manager.

MORE INFO   More on MPIO

To learn more about Multipath I/O, consult the following TechCenter article:
http://www.microsoft.com/WindowsServer2003/technologies/storage/mpio/default.mspx.

Storage Explorer

Storage Explorer, shown in Figure 10-20 and available in the Administrative Tools menu, is used to manage Fibre Channel and iSCSI fabrics on the SAN. A *fabric* is a network topology where storage devices are interconnected through one or more data paths. In a Fibre Channel fabric, this network will include multiple Fibre Channel switches that are used to connect servers and storage devices to each other through virtual point-to-point connections. In iSCSI fabrics the network will include multiple Internet Storage Name Service (iSNS) servers that allow for the discovery and partitioning of resources.

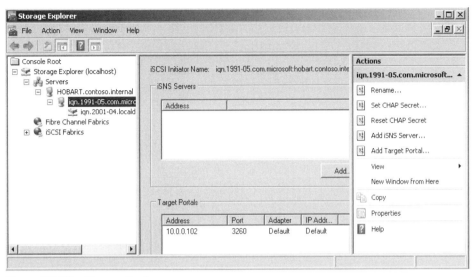

Figure 10-20   Storage Explorer

The Storage Explorer console can display detailed information about servers that are connected to the SAN as well as data about fabric components such as host bus adapters, Fibre Channel switches, iSCSI initiators, and iSCSI targets. Storage Explorer can be used to configure iSCSI security, configure iSCSI target portals, add iSNS servers, and manage Discovery Domains and Discovery Domain Sets. To view and manage an iSCSI fabric, you must enable the WMI exception in Windows Firewall on each server running Windows Server 2008 that is a part of the fabric. Many of the iSCSI-related management tasks that you can perform using Storage Explorer can also be performed using the Microsoft iSCSI Initiator (located in Control Panel) or from the Microsoft iSNS Server.

MORE INFO   **More on Storage Explorer**

For more information on Storage Explorer, consult the following TechNet article: *http://technet2.microsoft.com/windowsserver2008/en/library/aed88bb0-d9e0-4c5e-8e90-c398547f379e1033.mspx?mfr=true.*

Lesson Summary

- A Logical Unit Number (LUN) is a logical reference to a portion of a storage subsystem. A LUN can represent a disk, a section of a disk, an entire disk array, or a section of a disk array in the storage subsystem.

- Multipath I/O (MPIO) supports multiple data paths to storage devices. MPIO must be installed on a server if a LUN will be accessed through multiple Fibre Channel HBA ports or multiple iSCSI initiators.

- Servers and clusters connect to Fibre Channel arrays using host bus adapter (HBA) ports. Servers and clusters use iSCSI initiators to connect to iSCSI targets, which manage iSCSI arrays.

- Storage Manager For SANS is used to create and manage LUNs on iSCSI and Fibre Channel devices. Storage Explorer is used to manage iSCSI and Fibre Channel fabrics.

Lesson Review

You can use the following questions to test your knowledge of the information in Lesson 2, "Planning the Deployment of Storage Area Networks." The questions are also available on the companion CD if you prefer to review them in electronic form.

NOTE Answers

Answers to these questions and explanations of why each answer choice is correct or incorrect are located in the "Answers" section at the end of the book.

---

1. Which of the following Windows Server 2008 features should you install prior to enabling access to a LUN through multiple Fibre Channel ports?

   A. Remote Differential Compression

   B. UDDI

   C. MPIO

   D. RPC over HTTP Proxy

2. Assuming that your iSCSI storage device supports all LUN types, which LUN type would you select when you want to maximize I/O performance but retain fault tolerance?

   A. Spanned

   B. Striped

   C. Simple

   D. Striped with Parity

3. Which of the following MPIO policies should you choose to ensure that a server that is configured with four paths between the server and the SAN array directs traffic equally to all paths during normal operation?

   A. Failback

   B. Round-robin

   C. Weighted Path

   D. Dynamic Least Queue Depth

4. Which of the following Windows Server 2008 tools would you use to create LUNs on a Fibre Channel storage array?

   A. Storage Manager For SANs

   B. Storage Explorer

   C. Device Manager

   D. Disk Management

Chapter Review

To further practice and reinforce the skills you learned in this chapter, you can perform the following tasks:

- Review the chapter summary.
- Review the list of key terms introduced in this chapter.
- Complete the case scenarios. These scenarios set up real-world situations involving the topics of this chapter and ask you to create a solution.
- Complete the suggested practices.
- Take a practice test.

Chapter Summary

- Enterprise Certificate Authorities are used to issue digital certificates to Active Directory user and computer accounts.
- The processes of autoenrollment and credential roaming can reduce the administrative burden of certificate deployment in Windows Server 2008 environments.
- Online Responders and Online Responder Arrays reduce the bandwidth impact of CRL checks. A single Online Responder or Online Responder Array can provide CRL information for one or more Certificate Authorities.
- A LUN is a logical reference point to a portion of a storage subsystem, ranging from a partition on a disk to an entire storage array.
- MPIO is used to provide fault-tolerant paths from servers to SAN arrays.

Key Terms

Do you know what these key terms mean? You can check your answers by looking up the terms in the glossary at the end of the book.

- Autoenrollment
- CA
- CRL
- LUN

Case Scenario

In the following case scenarios, you will apply what you have learned about Certificate Services and Storage Area Networks. You can find answers to these questions in the "Answers" section at the end of this book.

Case Scenario: Deploying Certificate Services and a SAN Array at Coho Vineyard and Winery

Coho Vineyard and Winery has recently installed a Windows Server 2008 network in all of its offices across the Yarra Valley winemaking region of Australia. They have approached you for assistance with several network configuration issues that they hope you will be able to resolve. The first issue is that management feels that network communication across the Coho WAN and LAN should be better protected. They want to implement IPsec and use certificate-based authentication for the process. The WAN links between the head office and the satellite offices are already choked with traffic. You have been asked to develop some method by which the impact of CRL checks on WAN bandwidth is minimized. Finally, during the original deployment phase, several iSCSI arrays that supports all LUN types were purchased. These arrays are intended for use as SAN devices by the Coho Vineyard and Winery Windows Server 2008 file servers. This hardware has now arrived and management would like your assistance to deploy it. With these facts in mind, answer the following questions:

1. What steps can be taken to ensure that IPsec certificates are deployed to all computers that are members of the domain?

2. What steps need to be taken to ensure that revocation checks occur with a minimum use of bandwidth?

3. What LUN type should you configure for the SAN array to ensure the best mix of performance and fault tolerance?

Suggested Practices

To help you successfully master the exam objectives presented in this chapter, complete the following tasks.

Plan Infrastructure Services Server Roles

Do the practice in this section.

- **Practice: Configure Web Enrollment**   Configure Web enrollment on server Glasgow.

  Use a client computer to request a Web Server certificate using the Web enrollment interface. Approve the request using the Certification Authority console and then download the Web Server certificate from the Web enrollment pages.

Configure Storage

Do the practice in this section if you have access to the appropriate SAN array hardware.

- **Practice: Create a LUN**   Configure a LUN of the RAID-5 type on SAN hardware that you have access to (either iSCSI or Fibre Channel).

  Assign this LUN to a Windows Server 2008 computer.

Take a Practice Test

The practice tests on this book's companion CD offer many options. For example, you can test yourself on just one exam objective, or you can test yourself on all the 70-646 certification exam content. You can set up the test so that it closely simulates the experience of taking a certification exam, or you can set it up in study mode so that you can look at the correct answers and explanations after you answer each question.

MORE INFO   **Practice tests**

For details about all the practice test options available, see the "How to Use the Practice Tests" section in this book's Introduction.

Chapter 11

Clustering and High Availability

Today's business environment demands 24/7, always-on access to critical applications. Databases, Web applications, e-mail and communication systems, and Internet access are just some of the critical applications that must always be available. Business requirements dictate which applications are deemed critical and just how much downtime is acceptable for these applications.

When looking at availability of an application, you must consider areas outside of the server that could fail and cause downtime for the end users of the application. These areas include network connections, data security, and environmental factors such as building security. When an application has been deemed business-critical, the role of a server administrator is to ensure that the application remains online using the tools available. Windows Server 2008 builds upon the high-availability framework of Windows Server 2003 and provides tools to ensure availability of the server and the business-critical applications running on it.

This chapter concentrates on the tools that provide high-availability solutions with Windows Server 2008. Windows Server 2008 supports two primary methods for clustering: Network Load Balancing (NLB) and server clustering. A third method, DNS Round Robin, can provide additional availability through the use of DNS records. You can combine all three of these methods to create highly available, highly scalable solutions. Within this chapter, you will learn about the different technologies for providing high availability in Windows Server 2008 environments. This includes choosing a methodology (DNS Round Robin or NLB) and implementing NLB. You will also learn about Failover Clustering, including how to validate a cluster and how to configure Failover Clustering and related parameters such as Quorum Models.

Exam objectives in this chapter:
- Plan high availability.

Lessons in this chapter:

Before You Begin

To complete the lessons in this chapter, you must have done the following:

- Installed Windows Server 2008 and configured your test PC as a domain controller (DC) in the Contoso.internal domain as described in the Introduction and Chapter 1, "Installing, Upgrading, and Deploying Windows Server 2008." You also need to install the DNS Server role as described in Chapter 2, "Configuring Network Connectivity."

- If you want to carry out the practice exercises in this chapter and cluster servers you need to create at least one additional member server. This can be a virtual machine if the resources on your computer are sufficient to support it. The server should be on your internal network. For the practice sessions to work as written, name the server Perth and give it the IPv4 address 192.168.1.50 and subnet mask 255.255.255.0.

IMPORTANT   Private IPv4 network

This chapter has been written for a 192.168.1.0/24 private network. This allows connection to most cable modems or wireless access points (WAPs). However, the practice exercises do not require Internet access and, if you prefer, you can use the 10.0.0.0/24 network that was set up in Chapter 1 and used in Chapter 2. In this case, the IPv4 address for Perth is 10.0.0.50. The only differences will be in the figures that show the network address.

Lesson 1: Understanding DNS Round Robin and Load Balancing

This lesson looks at DNS Round Robin and NLB as techniques for sharing application load across multiple servers and providing availability. You will learn the difference between DNS Round Robin and NLB and when each is appropriate in a given environment.

After this lesson, you will be able to:
- Understand DNS Round Robin.
- Understand Network Load Balancing.
- Implement DNS Round Robin.
- Configure Network Load Balancing.

Estimated lesson time: 35 minutes

Real World

Steve Suehring

Regardless of the availability strategy you choose, a failure elsewhere within the network—between the end user and the servers—will result in the application being unavailable. For this reason, it's important to consider all of the places where a failure could occur between the end users and the servers. These include everything from switches and routers to facility power, security, and environmental factors such as fire and flood. No amount of load balancing or clustering will help if the servers involved are in the same rack in the same building that just lost power and has no generator.

Reducing single points of failure is key to availability, but this comes at a cost. Providing redundant routers and switches is relatively inexpensive, but costs quickly rise when the requirements include providing redundant *hot sites*, or physical locations with redundant data stores.

Use of dedicated WAN links is common to provide enough bandwidth between the main site and the hot site so that data can be replicated in real time. Testing the backup and redundancy strategies through the use of scheduled (and unscheduled) disaster exercises helps teams build confidence and find previously unseen areas that need redundancy.

> Creating step-by-step disaster recovery plans is also key to identifying possible failure areas. Ultimately, the organization must decide how much to invest in providing redundancy and reducing the single points of failure within the network.

Plan Availability Strategies

DNS Round Robin and NLB are two techniques for ensuring application availability. These have remained unchanged since Windows Server 2003 and so will be familiar to any administrator who used them in the previous version of Windows. When requests are dispersed across multiple servers, the load on any individual server is reduced. Like Windows Server 2003, Windows Server 2008 supports DNS Round Robin and NLB as availability strategies.

Both DNS Round Robin and NLB are used for applications that have their own data store. Each server—also referred to as a *host*—within this type of cluster uses its own set of data. Contrast this with Failover Clustering, in which a shared data store can be used. Applications such as Internet Information Services (IIS) and proxy servers are candidates for both DNS Round Robin and NLB because they frequently service one-time requests rather than requests that must be handled by the same server throughout the session.

Contrast DNS Round Robin and NLB with Failover Clustering, another availability technology in Windows Server 2008. Formerly known as server clustering, Failover Clustering creates a group of computers that all have access to the same data store or disk resource or network share. The applications running on a Failover Cluster must be cluster-aware. Failover Clustering has had some changes since Windows Server 2003. Lesson 2 will cover these changes.

DNS Round Robin

DNS Round Robin works by providing different IP responses from a DNS server to requests for the same host name. For example, assume that the DNS record for www.contoso.internal is associated with two servers located at 192.168.1.1 and 192.168.2.1. When a client requests a resource from www.contoso.internal, the client would first perform a DNS lookup to obtain the IP address associated with www.contoso.com. The first client to request the IP address of the DNS server that hosts contoso.com will be provided with the IP address 192.168.1.1. The next client to request the IP address from the same DNS server will instead be forwarded the IP address 192.168.2.1. Through this method of providing alternating results to the query for www.contoso.com's IP address, client load is spread across multiple hosts. The number of IP addresses that you can associate with a particular host name is unlimited. For example, you could associate 20 different IP addresses with a host name. When you enable DNS Round Robin on the DNS server, the DNS server works through the list, returning a different address to each querying client until all 20 addresses have been provided and the process starts again.

Figure 11-1 shows the *nslookup* utility being used to query the nameserver on the local computer for the www.contoso.internal record. Notice that in the initial query, the first address in the list is 192.168.1.1, while in the second query 192.168.2.1 appears first.

Figure 11-1   A DNS Round Robin configuration with two host records returned

An additional DNS Round Robin technology, known as netmask ordering, takes into account the IP address of the querying client. When netmask ordering is enabled, the DNS server will attempt to return a host IP address that is on the same subnet as the querying client. For example, if DNS Round Robin was configured as discussed earlier (with the IP addresses 192.168.1.1 and 192.168.2.1 for the two www.contoso.com host records), and netmask ordering was enabled, a client on subnet 192.168.1.x /24 would always be returned the 192.168.1.1 when querying for www.contoso.com because the DNS server would recognize that both hosts are on the same subnet. If a host on 192.168.100.1 made a query, it would receive a Round Robin result because the querying host is not on the same subnet as any of the www.contoso.com hosts. To enable DNS Round Robin and netmask ordering, open the DNS Manager console from the Administrative Tools menu, edit the DNS server properties, and click the Advanced tab. Ensure that Enable Round Robin and Enable Netmask Ordering are selected, as shown in Figure 11-2.

Figure 11-2 Enabling DNS Round Robin and netmask ordering

Using the DNS Manager to Create a DNS Round Robin Configuration

The DNS Manager console is the primary tool for day-to-day DNS management in Windows Server 2008. The DNS Manager is an MMC snap-in and can also be found by clicking DNS from the Administrative Tools menu. The DNS Manager is shown in Figure 11-3.

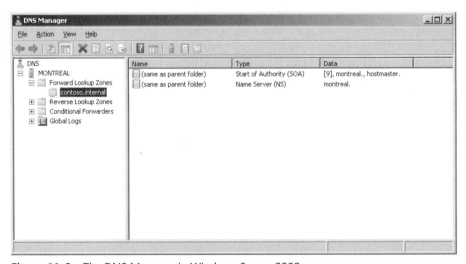

Figure 11-3 The DNS Manager in Windows Server 2008

Figure 11-3 shows the Forward Lookup Zones on this computer, with the contoso .internal domain selected. The records within the zone are shown and currently include only the default Start of Authority (SOA) and Name Server (NS) records for the domain.

Creation of a DNS Round Robin entails creating two or more records, typically A records, with the same host name. Do this by right-clicking the zone or selecting New Host (A Or AAAA) from the Action menu. Within the New Host dialog box, enter the host name **www** along with one of the IP addresses for this Round Robin, 192.168.1.1, as illustrated in Figure 11-4.

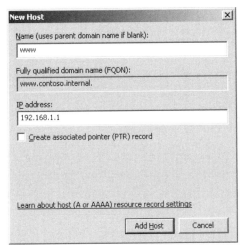

Figure 11-4   Adding a new host record as part of a Round Robin configuration

The next host is added in the same fashion though using a different IP address. This continues until all hosts that will serve in the Round Robin group are added. The final result is shown through DNS Manager in Figure 11-5.

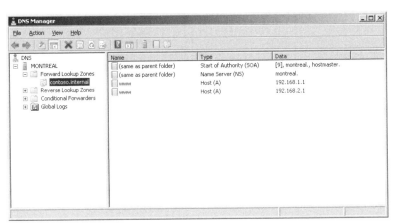

Figure 11-5   A DNS Round Robin with two hosts as seen through DNS Manager

Configuring Windows Network Load Balancing

While DNS Round Robin is a simple way of distributing requests, Windows Server 2008 NLB is a much more robust form of providing high availability to applications. Using NLB, an administrator can configure multiple servers to operate as a single cluster and control the usage of the cluster in near real-time.

NLB operates differently than DNS Round Robin in that NLB uses a virtual network adapter on each host. This virtual network adapter gets a single IP and media access control (MAC) address, which is shared among the hosts participating in the load-balancing cluster. Clients requesting services from an NLB cluster have their requests sent to the IP address of the virtual adapter, at which point it can be handled by any of the servers in the cluster.

NLB automatically reconfigures as nodes are added and removed from the cluster. An administrator can add and remove nodes through the NLB Manager interface or the command line. For example, an administrator might remove each node in turn to perform maintenance on the nodes individually and cause no disruption in service to the end user.

Servers within NLB clusters are in constant communication with each other, determining which servers are available with a process known as heartbeats and convergence. The heartbeat consists of a server participating in an NLB cluster that sends out a message each second to its NLB-participating counterparts. When five (by default) consecutive heartbeats are missed, convergence begins. Convergence is the process by which the remaining hosts determine the state of the cluster.

During convergence, the remaining hosts listen for heartbeats from the other servers to determine the host with the highest priority, which is then selected as the default host for the NLB cluster. Generally, two scenarios can trigger convergence. The first is the missed heartbeat scenario mentioned earlier; the second is removal or addition of a server to the cluster by an administrator. The heartbeat is reduced by one half during convergence. A less common reason for convergence is a change in the host configuration, such as a host priority.

Adding Hosts to an NLB Cluster

NLB is configured within the Network Load Balancing Manager MMC snap-in shown in Figure 11-6. The Network Load Balancing Manager is installed by using Add Features within Server Manager.

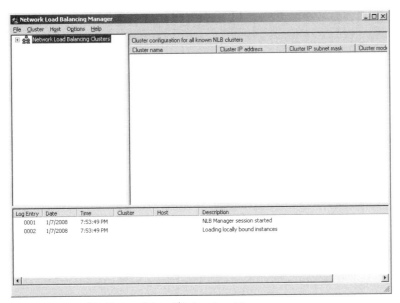

Figure 11-6   The Network Load Balancing Manager

You can add hosts to an NLB cluster through the Network Load Balancing Manager. It is important to ensure that the cluster information is refreshed each time the NLB Manager is used to manage a cluster. This is because the information about a given cluster is cached from the last time that the NLB Manager connected to the cluster and that information could be outdated. When a new host is added to the cluster, the host comes online within the cluster only after the new configuration information has had a chance to propagate throughout the other cluster hosts.

To add a host, follow these steps:

1. Right-click the cluster where you want to add the new host and then select Add Host To Cluster.

2. Enter the computer name of the host you want to add and click Connect.

3. Select the network adapter you want to use for this host and configure the remaining host parameters as needed or accept the defaults.

MORE INFO   **More on adding hosts**

For more information on adding hosts to NLB clusters, consult the TechNet document at *http://technet2.microsoft.com/windowsserver2008/en/library/46d9994c-0af3-43b0-a8ca-7f1be65fd5331033.mspx?mfr=true.*

Managing NLB Clusters

Managing NLB clusters includes actions such as altering the port rules and parameters under which the cluster operates. When you manage NLB clusters—including adding hosts—you must be a member of the Administrators group or have been granted the appropriate authority on the cluster.

You connect to an NLB cluster by connecting to a single host or by using a host list. To connect using a single host, from within NLB Manager right-click NLB Clusters and select Connect To Existing. Enter the name of the cluster host you want to connect to and click Connect. The available cluster names will appear. Click the name of the cluster to manage and then click Finish.

Some conditions, such as setting up two hosts with the same priority, might prevent you from being able to connect using NLB Manager. In such cases, you can attempt to connect using a Host List. A Host List is a plain text file containing a list of cluster hosts, each on its own line. For example, a Host List of three hosts called MONTREAL, GLASGOW, and PERTH would look like this:

```
MONTREAL
GLASGOW
PERTH
```

To use a Host List from within NLB Manager, select Load Host List from the File menu, locate the text file, and select Open.

To remove hosts from NLB clusters through the NLB Manager, simply right-click the host you want to remove and select Delete Host. You can remove the entire cluster by right-clicking the cluster and selecting Delete Cluster. Be aware that all connections to the cluster will be immediately dropped.

MORE INFO   **More on managing NLB clusters**

See *http://technet2.microsoft.com/windowsserver2008/en/library/5a49da8e-c157-4024-9305-5207f910cf481033.mspx?mfr=true* for more information on managing NLB in Windows Server 2008.

Setting NLB Parameters

NLB clusters operate with several parameters that control their operation. In this section, you will see how to set cluster parameters, how to set the cluster operation mode, and how to configure port rules.

Cluster parameters include the cluster IP address, subnet mask, its Internet Name, and Operation Mode. You configure all of these properties from within the NLB Manager by right-clicking the cluster and selecting Cluster Properties. This opens the Properties dialog box shown in Figure 11-7.

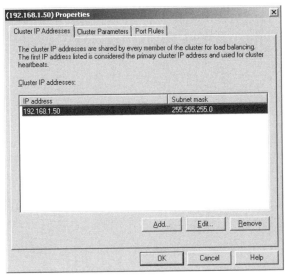

Figure 11-7   Use the Cluster Properties dialog box to set the cluster's parameters

The cluster parameters, including IP address, subnet mask, Internet name, and operating mode, are configured on the Cluster Parameters tab. You only need to change these parameters on one host. The changes are then propagated to other hosts within the NLB cluster.

Cluster Operation Mode   NLB has two modes of operation: unicast and multicast. All servers within a cluster must operate in one mode or the other—the two operational modes cannot be mixed within an NLB cluster. These operational modes function as follows:

- **Unicast Mode**   The MAC address created for the virtual network adapter is shared among the participants within the cluster. On single-homed servers (servers with a single network card), the cluster's virutal MAC address logically replaces the physical MAC address for that network card. The server will still retain its original IP, but it too will resolve to the MAC address of the new virtual network adapter. In effect, this means that only computers within the same subnet as a given server will be able to communicate with that server but other servers within the cluster will not. To resolve this you can use unicast mode with two network cards installed on a host. The first network card participates in the cluster while the other is used for management and inter-server communication.

- **Multicast Mode**   In NLB multicast mode, the server retains its original MAC address with its original IP address in addition to the virtual MAC and IP created for the cluster. Communication to the original server can then take place as normal, and multicast is used for cluster communication. However, network devices, such as switch infrastructure, must support multicast MAC addressing for multicast mode to be an option for NLB.

- **IGMP Multicast Mode**   In IGMP Multicast Mode, the Internet Group Management Protocol is used. IGMP multicast enhances network performance and allows for multicast clients to register with an IGMP Multicast server. When this happens, the multicast traffic is only forwarded on switch ports or trunks that connect to other multicast clients, which improves network traffic performance. IGMP multicast ensures that a switch is not flooded with traffic.

Quick Check

- Name a primary difference between the operational modes of NLB.

Quick Check Answer

- A primary difference between the two modes, unicast and multicast, is that all network devices must support multicast MAC addressing to use multicast mode. Other differences include the server retaining its original IP and MAC address with multicast mode, and the servers being unable to communicate directly with each other in unicast mode.

NLB Port Rules   Port rules are also set from within the Cluster Properties dialog box, specifically on the Port Rules tab shown in Figure 11-8. Port rules are used to control

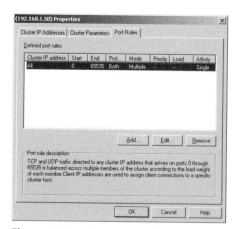

Figure 11-8   The Port Rules tab in the Cluster Properties dialog box

how traffic on a given port is handled for the cluster. For example, an NLB cluster for Terminal Services might use a port rule for port 3389 alone, rather than the entire range of ports 0 through 65535, which is the default. Port rules must match for each host within the NLB cluster. Normally the NLB Manager will take care of this task. However, if a node attempts to join a cluster and has a different set of rules, the node will not be able to join.

When creating an NLB cluster port rule, you must configure the appropriate filtering mode. Configuring the mode allows you to specify whether only a single node, some nodes, or all nodes in the cluster respond to requests from a single client during the session. This is important for some applications, such as e-commerce Web sites, that require all session traffic to occur only between a single host and the client. The following three filtering modes are used:

- **Single Host**   When you configure the single host filtering mode, all traffic sent to the cluster IP address that matches a port rule is handled by a single node within the cluster.

- **Disable Port Range**   This port range is used to tell the cluster not to respond to traffic on these ports. Traffic sent by clients on these ports to the cluster will automatically be discarded.

- **Multiple Host Filtering**   Multiple host filtering allows all nodes in the cluster to handle traffic sent to the cluster. Multiple Host Filtering takes into account affinity settings. You can configure three affinity settings:

  - ❑ **None** All requests are distributed equally across the cluster, even if a client has an established session.

  - ❑ **Network** This is similar to netmask ordering and directs clients to the closest node on the basis of subnet.

  - ❑ **Single** After a client makes a request, all subsequent requests in the session will be directed to the same node in the cluster. This allows sessions that require stateful data, such as SSL Web applications or Terminal Server sessions. This is the default filtering mode on port rules.

MORE INFO   Configuring NLB parameters

More information on configuring NLB parameters can be found at *http://technet2.microsoft.com/ windowsserver2008/en/library/a49ce864-eeaa-4d5b-b56a-71286177207e1033.mspx?mfr=true*.

Comparing DNS Round Robin and Network Load Balancing

DNS Round Robin has the following drawbacks when compared to Network Load Balancing.

- **No control over the distribution of the load**   Because you cannot control how a client will use a DNS lookup, you have no way to effectively balance the load between the servers using DNS Round Robin. A client might perform a DNS lookup and then never use the application, or the client might only use the application for a short time. The next client might use an application for an extended period. This can result in an unbalanced load, with more clients using one server and fewer using another.

- **Possible downtime because of DNS Time-to-Live (TTL)**   Client computers and client's downstream DNS servers will cache the DNS record using the Time-to-Live (TTL) value configured by the domain administrator for the given DNS record. This means that until the TTL has expired, a client may continue to send requests to a server that is no longer available at the IP address.

- **DNS Round Robin is not fault tolerant**   DNS Round Robin does not automatically compensate for the loss of a Round Robin host. If a host fails, clients will still be directed to that host until the host's record is removed from DNS.

- **DNS Round Robin is not session-friendly**   The DNS TTL may expire while a client is actively using an application. When this occurs, the client will query for the server's address. With Round Robin, you have no way to control which address the client will receive, meaning that the client's next request could be sent to a different server that does not have session information for that client. This usually does not present a problem for most applications because most users complete their transactions well within the DNS TTL period. DNS Round Robin is appropriate for stateless applications that do not require a session to be established. Static Web sites are good candidates, along with FTP sites that serve single files through a single session.

Using Both DNS Round Robin and Network Load Balancing

DNS Round Robin and NLB are not mutually exclusive—you can use DNS Round Robin and NLB together to create an additional level of redundancy. For example, you might configure two servers at two different sites to be load-balanced with NLB and then another two servers at those same sites in another load-balanced configuration.

You then use DNS Round Robin to rotate requests between the two Network Load Balanced configurations. In this way, if one server fails, the application will still continue to serve requests, and even if one site goes offline, the application will still work because of the load balancing between sites. This is helpful for large implementations where several NLB clusters can be used and DNS Round Robin can be combined to make a large set of redundant clusters.

Spreading the load over multiple NLB clusters located at multiple data centers in various geographical locations is one way to reduce single points of failure for the application being served by the cluster. In this way, even a large-scale natural disaster affecting an entire geographical region would not affect the availability of the application. However, users of the application located within that affected region may have difficulty using the application if the basic necessities such as power and a viable Internet connection are unavailable.

Practice: Configuring Network Load Balancing

In this exercise, you will install the Network Load Balancing Manager and test its configuration. You need to carry out the exercises logged on at a member server (for example, Perth) with the Kim_Akers account. If you cannot add a member server to your network, treat this practice session as optional.

IMPORTANT Do not use your domain controller

Do not attempt to carry out this exercise on your domain controller (Glasgow). If you do not have an additional member server do not attempt the exercise.

▶ **Exercise 1: Install the Network Load Balancing Manager**

In this exercise, you will install the Network Load Balancing Manager. This application is used to manage NLB clusters on the local server and on other servers as well.

1. Open Server Manager (unless it was already opened at logon) by clicking Administrative Tools from the Start menu and selecting Server Manager.

2. Within Server Manager, scroll down to find the Features Summary section, shown in Figure 11-9, and select Add Features.

3. The Add Features Wizard will open. Select Network Load Balancing from the list of available features and click Next, as shown in Figure 11-10.

4. Click Install to start the installation process.

Figure 11-9 Server Manager

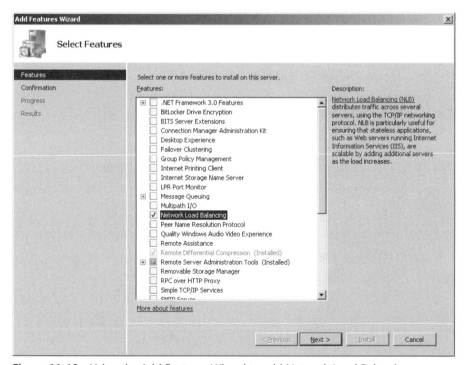

Figure 11-10 Using the Add Features Wizard to add Network Load Balancing

5. When installation is complete, the Installation Results dialog box opens. Click Close to complete the wizard and close the dialog box.

6. Close Server Manager if it is still open.

▶ **Exercise 2: Create a Network Load Balance Configuration**

This exercise will walk you through the steps involved in creating a Network Load Balancing cluster. As before, you need to be logged on at a member server with the Kim_Akers account.

1. Open the Network Load Balancing Manager by clicking Start, pointing to Administrative Tools, and clicking Network Load Balancing Manager.

2. Within the Network Load Balancing Manager, click Cluster and then select New. This will open the New Cluster: Connect dialog box.

3. Within the New Cluster: Connect dialog box, enter the host name of the server from which you are running the cluster. You could also enter the IP address instead. In this example, the host name Perth is entered into the Host text box. Click Connect to initiate the connection and populate the interfaces, as shown in Figure 11-11. Click Next.

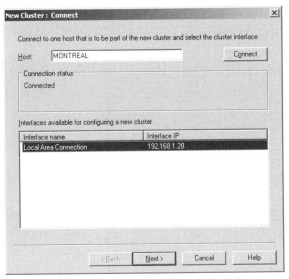

Figure 11-11   The New Cluster: Connect dialog box

4. The New Cluster: Host Parameters dialog box opens next, as shown in Figure 11-12. You do not need to change anything in this dialog box. Click Next.

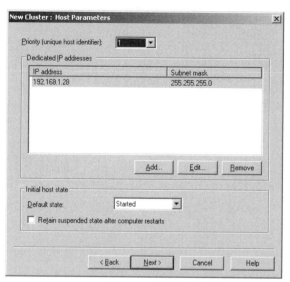

Figure 11-12 The New Cluster: Host Parameters dialog box

5. The New Cluster: Cluster IP Addresses dialog box opens. This is the dialog box where you will choose the virtual IP address for the cluster. Click Add to open the Add IP Address dialog box shown in Figure 11-13.

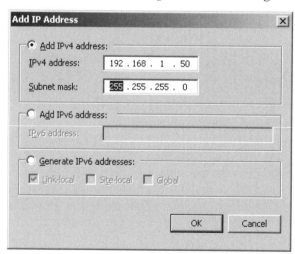

Figure 11-13 The Add IP Address dialog box

6. Within the Add IP Address dialog box, type **192.168.1.50** (or another IP address that is in use in your private network—for example, 10.0.0.50 if you are using the 10.0.0.0/24 network) with a netmask of **255.255.255.0**. Click OK to add the IP address and click Next.

7. The New Cluster: Cluster Parameters dialog box opens. Click Next.

8. The New Cluster: Port Rules dialog box opens. Click Finish.

Though it contains only one host, the newly created NLB cluster will be shown in the Network Load Balancing Manager interface. You will now also be able to ping the virtual IP address 192.168.1.50 (or 10.0.0.50 if you are using the 10.0.0.0/24 network).

Lesson Summary

- Windows Server 2008 provides tools for high availability and redundancy including Failover Clustering and Network Load Balancing. Additionally, DNS Round Robin is another approach that you can use in conjunction with other availability strategies.

- DNS Round Robin does not require any special software, but instead relies simply on the configuration of DNS records to provide a level of availability.

- DNS Round Robin is less configurable and less controllable than NLB but can be combined with NLB to provide additional availability.

- NLB creates a virtual network adapter among one or more servers. Clients then send their requests to that virtual network adapter.

Lesson Review

The following questions test your knowledge of the information in Lesson 1, "Round Robin and Network Load Balancing." The questions are also available on the companion CD if you prefer to review them in electronic form.

NOTE Answers

Answers to these questions and explanations of why each answer choice is correct or incorrect are located in the "Answers" section at the end of the book.

1. Assuming that the Windows Server 2008 server is authoritative for a domain, which console or tool do you use to create the DNS Round Robin configuration?

   A. Network Load Balancing Manager

   B. DNS Manager

   C. nslookup

   D. Server Manager

2. Which of the following are disadvantages of DNS Round Robin? (Choose all that apply.)

   A. DNS Round Robin cannot be used for Internet-facing applications.

   B. The DNS administrator has no control over the Time-to-Live (TTL) for the records.

   C. DNS Round Robin does not work well with stateful applications.

   D. The administrator has no control over the strategy for load balancing with Round Robin.

3. NLB creates a virtual network adapter and shares which of the following among cluster participants?

   A. A MAC address and an IP address

   B. An IP address

   C. A MAC address

   D. A routing table

4. By default, members within a Network Load Balanced cluster will listen for how many missed heartbeats before triggering convergence?

   A. 60

   B. 30

   C. 5

   D. 32

5. You are in the process of configuring an 8-node NLB cluster that will be used to host an important Web site. You want to be able to connect to each node in the cluster separately using a computer located on a remote subnet using RDP so that you can perform administrative duties. One administrative duty is using *robocopy* to replicate Web site data from one server to other servers in the cluster. Each server has a single network card. Which of the following must you do? (Choose two. Each answer forms a part of the solution.)

   A. Configure NLB port rules.

   B. Configure the cluster to use multicast.

   C. Configure the cluster to use unicast.

   D. Configure the cluster to use IPv6.

   E. Configure the cluster to use DNS Round Robin.

Lesson 2: Windows Server 2008 Cluster Tools

Whereas DNS Round Robin and NLB are appropriate for applications with their own data stores, Failover Clustering in Windows Server 2008 is the availability strategy of choice for applications with shared data that can be spread across multiple systems. Failover Clustering is managed through the Failover Cluster Management interface in Windows Server 2008. Through this MMC snap-in you can create, validate, and manage Failover Clusters in Windows Server 2008.

Failover Clustering, formerly known as server clustering, is available in Windows Server 2008 Enterprise and Datacenter editions and is not available in Windows Server 2008 Standard or Web editions.

After this lesson, you will be able to:
- Understand Failover Clustering.
- Configure Failover Clustering.

Estimated lesson time: 25 minutes

Selecting Redundancy Strategies

A primary characteristic of a server cluster in Windows Server 2008 is that it utilizes shared storage of application data. In this way, server clusters are more advanced than their NLB counterparts. Server clusters differ from NLB in that with a server cluster, data is shared among cluster participants, whereas NLB clusters must each have a copy of the data.

A typical configuration for a cluster would use a shared disk technology such as RAID (Redundant Array of Inexpensive Disks) or SAN (Storage Area Network) to share back-end data stores. Because of this constraint, clusters are usually physically located close to one another because of the high cost of instant data replication across Wide Area Network (WAN) links. However, Windows Server 2008 no longer requires cluster members to be located on the same subnet—instead, they can be located in different subnets, thus simplifying the creation of geographically dispersed clusters.

A Closer Look at RAID

RAID is a well-tested method for providing data protection and enabling multiple physical disks to be combined into one larger logical disk. RAID has several levels, which represent the resulting configuration. Each level has its own set of requirements.

- **RAID 0**   This level combines two or more disks into one larger unit. It provides no redundancy or data protection. Losing one disk of a RAID 0 set will result in loss of all data.

- **RAID 1**   RAID 1 is commonly known as a mirror. RAID 1 uses two or more disks and maintains exact copies of the data from each on each disk. Unlike RAID 0, the size of a RAID 1 set is equal to that of its smallest member.

- **RAID 5**   RAID 5 uses a striping technique to spread parity information across the disks within the configuration. RAID 5 uses at least three disks and provides a higher amount of fault tolerance than RAID 1 because one disk in the array can fail and the array can still remain online. Additionally, many RAID controllers enable the use of hot spare disks, meaning that four or more disks can be used. If one fails, one of the hot spares can take over with no downtime.

- **RAID 6**   RAID 6 provides two sets of parity information rather than one (as with RAID 5). This is important because it can still continue to operate even in the event of two simultaneous disk failures.

- **RAID 10**   RAID 10 combines the mirroring of RAID 1 with the striping of RAID 0 to create a larger, fault tolerant array than would be possible by otherwise just using separate RAID 1 arrays.

Exam Tip   When considering RAID options for redundancy, remember that RAID 1 can operate on two disks while RAID 5 needs at least three. RAID 1 is frequently used as a system volume, providing basic redundancy for the operating system, while RAID 5 or 6 is used for data volumes.

Several concepts must be understood when considering Failover Clusters, including the failover model to be used, the type of application to be deployed, and the clustering strategy.

The Type of Application to Be Deployed

Two types of applications can be run within a cluster: single-instance and multiple-instance. This section looks at each.

- **Single-instance application**   A single-instance application can run on one server at a time. An example of this is an authentication server. If an authentication server service is running on multiple servers simultaneously, the client might receive multiple answers to a request for authentication, and some of those answers might conflict, with one answer sending successful authentication and another server sending an answer of a failed authentication attempt. When running in a cluster, single-instance applications must operate on one server while operating in standby mode on the other members of the cluster.

■ **Multiple-instance application**   Multiple-instance applications can either share data or partition the data in such a way that one node in the cluster can provide an answer for a particular part of the data. Advanced database servers and some e-mail servers can operate in this fashion.

Running Applications on Failover Clusters

Although a chosen application might run on a Windows Server 2008 Failover Cluster, that application might not be optimized for clustering or supported as a clustered application by the software vendor or Microsoft. In the production environment, you need to choose applications carefully. An unsupported application might seem to meet an immediate need but cause you a great deal of trouble and expense in the future. You need to work with the software vendor to determine the requirements, functionality, and limitations of an application.

The following criteria need to be met to ensure that an application can benefit from and adapt to running on a cluster:

■ The cluster application must use an IP-based protocol.

■ Applications that require access to local databases must allow you to configure where data can be stored.

■ If an application needs to have access to data regardless of the cluster node on which it is running, the data needs to be stored on a shared disk resource that will failover with the Services And Applications group.

■ If an application can run and store data only on the local system or boot drive, you should choose the Node Majority Quorum or the Node and File Share Majority Quorum model. You will also need a separate file replication mechanism for the application data.

■ If an application encounters a network disruption or fails over to an alternate cluster node, client sessions must be able to reestablish connectivity. No client connectivity exists during the failover process until an application is brought back online. If the client software does not try to reconnect and instead times out when a network connection is broken, the application is not suited for failover (or NLB) clusters.

If a cluster-aware application meets all the required criteria, you can typically deploy it in a Windows 2008 Failover Cluster with some degree of confidence. However, you should test all applications on a non-production network before deploying them in a production scenario. Many services built in to Windows 2008 can also be clustered and will failover efficiently and properly. If a particular application is not cluster-aware but you want to use it anyway, you need to be especially careful to investigate all the implications of installing the application on a Windows Server 2008 Failover Cluster before first prototyping and then deploying the solution.

NOTE Designed for Windows Server 2008

If you plan to purchase a third-party software package to use in a Windows Server 2008 Failover Cluster, make sure that both Microsoft and the software manufacturer certify that it will work on Windows Server 2008 Failover Clusters.

Understanding Cluster Concepts

Setting up a cluster in Windows Server 2008 has few requirements. Like Windows Server 2003, Windows Server 2008 requires the same processor architecture—32-bit or 64-bit. These cannot be mixed within a cluster. Unlike Windows Server 2003, Windows Server 2008 clustering will no longer support direct SCSI connections to shared storage. Connections using Fibre Channel, SAS, and iSCSI are supported, however. All servers within a cluster must be within the same Active Directory domain.

NOTE Hardware configurations

Microsoft recommends that you use the same hardware configurations for all nodes within a cluster.

What's New in Failover Clustering?

Windows Server 2008 offers several enhancements for Failover Clustering. Not only has the name changed (from server clustering) but it also has new validation tests including node, network, and storage tests. Cluster creation is much less prone to error thanks to the new validation tests. Cluster managment has been improved, making it much easier to configure and add nodes to clusters. You can use the Volume Shadow Copy service to create cluster backups, and new Quorum models have been added to increase availability. See *http://www.microsoft.com/windowsserver2008/failover-clusters.mspx* for more detail on new clustering features in Windows Server 2008.

Understanding Cluster Quorum Models

Quorums are used to determine the number of failures that can be tolerated within a cluster before the cluster itself has to stop running. This is done to protect data integrity and prevent problems that could occur because of failed or failing communication between nodes.

Quorums describe the configuration of the cluster and contain information about the cluster components such as network adapters, storage, and the servers themselves. The quorum exists as a database in the registry and is maintained on the witness disk or witness share. The witness disk or share keeps a copy of this configuration data so that servers can join the cluster at any time, obtaining a copy of this data to become part of the cluster. One server manages the quorum resource data at any given time, but all participating servers also have a copy. You can use the following four quorum models with Windows Server 2008 Failover Clusters:

- **Node Majority** Microsoft recommends using this quorum model in Failover Cluster deployments that contain an odd number of cluster nodes. A cluster that uses the Node Majority quorum model is called a Node Majority cluster and remains up and running if the number of available nodes exceeds the number of failed nodes—that is, half plus one of its nodes is available. For example, for a seven-node cluster to remain online, four nodes must be available. If four nodes fail in a seven-node Node Majority cluster, the entire cluster shuts down. You should use Node Majority clusters in geographically or network-dispersed cluster nodes. To operate successfully this model requires an extremely reliable network, high-quality hardware, and a third-party mechanism to replicate back-end data.

- **Node and Disk Majority** Microsoft recommends using this quorum model in clusters that contain even numbers of cluster nodes. Provided that the witness disk remains available, a Node and Disk Majority cluster remains up and running when one-half or more of its nodes are available. A six-node cluster will not shut down if three or more nodes plus its witness disk are available. In this model, the cluster quorum is stored on a cluster disk that is accessible to all cluster nodes through a shared storage device using Serial Attached SCSI (SAS), Fibre Channel, or iSCSI connections. The model consists of two or more server nodes connected to a shared storage device and a single copy of the quorum data is maintained on the witness disk. You should use the Node and Disk Majority quorum model in Failover Clusters with shared storage, all connected on the same network and with an even number of nodes. In the case of a witness disk failure, a majority of the nodes need to remain up and running.

For example, a six-node cluster will run if (at a minimum) three nodes and the witness disk are available. If the witness disk is offline, the same six-node cluster requires that four nodes are available.

Exam Tip   If the 70-646 examination asks which quorum model is the closest to the traditional single-quorum device cluster configuration model, the answer is the Node and Disk Majority quorum model.

- **Node and File Share Majority**   This configuration is similar to the Node and Disk Majority model, but the quorum is stored on a network share rather than on a witness disk. A Node and File Share Majority cluster can be deployed in a similar fashion to a Node Majority cluster, but as long as the witness file share is available the cluster can tolerate the failure of half its nodes. You should use the Node and File Share Majority quorum model in clusters with an even number of nodes that do not utilize shared storage.

- **No Majority: Disk Only**   Microsoft recommends that you do not use this model in a production environment because the disk containing the quorum is a single point of failure. No Majority: Disk Only clusters are best suited for testing the deployment of built-in or custom services and applications on a Windows Server 2008 Failover Cluster. In this model, provided that the disk containing the quorum remains available, the cluster can sustain the failover of all nodes except one.

MORE INFO   **Quorum models webcast**

Four quorum models are available with Windows Server 2008. For more information on the models, view the TechNet webcast at *http://msevents.microsoft.com/CUI/WebCastEventDetails .aspx?EventID=1032364841&EventCategory=4&culture=en-US&CountryCode=US*.

Before you deploy a Failover Cluster you need to determine whether to use shared storage, ensuring that each node can communicate with each LUN the shared storage device presents. When the cluster is created, you add all nodes to the list and ensure that the correct cluster quorum model is selected for the new Failover Cluster.

When you configure the cluster, Windows Server 2008 will suggest the most appropriate quorum model for that cluster. For example, when you create a single-node cluster, the configuration wizard will suggest the Node Majority quorum model. However, if you do not agree with the model chosen, you can change this from within the Failover Cluster Management interface. If the chosen model utilizes shared storage and a witness disk, the smallest available LUN will be selected for this disk. If needed, you can change this after the cluster is created.

When a failure occurs within the cluster, such as a network card failure, the cluster can become partitioned or split, because the nodes of the cluster might no longer be able to communicate. In such an event, the quorum model dictates that the node owning the quorum copy will be the active node.

Using Clustering to Meet Business Requirements

Services and applications are deployed on failover and NLB clusters because they are critical to business operations. Clustering can increase reliability, provide failover, and increase the availability of data and business-critical operations. It is essential that the clusters are themselves highly reliable and do not introduce any single points of failure. For example, as you learned earlier in this lesson, the No Majority: Disk Only quorum model is not recommended for a production environment because its disk storage represents a single failure point.

Windows Server 2008 Enterprise and Datacenter Editions support Failover Clusters that provide fault tolerance. If a system or node in the cluster fails and cannot respond to client requests, the services or applications that were running on that node are taken offline and moved to another available node where functionality and access is restored to the client. To meet business requirements, Failover Clusters are typically used with the following types of server:

■ **File servers**   When you deploy file servers as nodes on a Failover Cluster, clients can access a single data-storage repository through the currently assigned and available cluster node without replicating the file data.

■ **Print servers**   If a node in a print server Failover Cluster fails, each of the cluster's shared printers continues to remain available to clients that continue to use the same print server name. Although you can use Group Policy to redeploy printers when a non-clustered print server fails, the switchover is seldom seamless.

■ **Database servers**   Typically, large organizations deploy line-of-business (LOB) applications and other critical services and applications that require a highly available back-end database system. Deploying database servers in Failover Clusters is the preferred method of providing high availability and failover support. If you use stand-alone, unclustered database servers and one goes down, configuring a replacement can take several hours, as can recovering the database from backup. A Failover Cluster provides seamless access to data in the event that a cluster node fails. Note that you still need a regular and efficient backup regime.

■ **Back-end messaging systems**   Enterprise messaging services are business-critical in many organizations and are best deployed in failover clusters to provide seamless failover and mailbox access.

NLB provides fault tolerance for front-end Web applications and Web sites, Terminal Servers, VPN servers, streaming media servers, and proxy servers by having each server in the cluster run the network services or applications individually. This removes any single points of failure. Depending on the particular needs of the service or application deployed on an NLB cluster, you can configure settings such as affinity options to determine how clients connect to back-end NLB cluster nodes. For example, client requests to access a Web site could be directed to any of the NLB cluster nodes that host the site.

On the other hand if a user accesses a secure Web site on an NLB cluster to purchase goods or services, the client session should be initiated and serviced by a single cluster node, because the session will most likely be using Secure Sockets Layer (SSL) encryption and will also contain specific session data, including the contents of the user's shopping cart and other user-specific information.

Configuring Failover Clustering

This section examines how to configure Failover Clustering in Windows Server 2008. Failover Clustering is considered a feature and can be installed through Server Manager in Windows Server 2008. You use the Add Features Wizard to install Failover Clustering.

MORE INFO   **More on installing Failover Clustering**

You can find more information on installing Failover Clustering at *http://technet2.microsoft.com/ windowsserver2008/en/library/ebd1d3bc-d5b6-4c82-b233-615512fba44f1033.mspx?mfr=true.*

You configure Failover Clustering using the Failover Cluster Management MMC snap-in, shown in Figure 11-14.

Within the Failover Cluster Management interface you can perform several tasks related to configuration of Failover Clusters including validation, creation, and management.

Validating a Failover Cluster Configuration

Prior to creating a cluster it is recommended that you validate the configuration of the computers that will become nodes in the cluster. Windows Server 2008 includes new

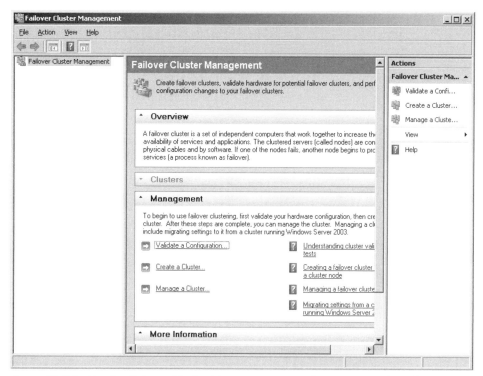

Figure 11-14 Use the Failover Cluster Management console to manage clustering

cluster validation tests. You validate component configuration like storage, network, and the server itself within the Validate A Configuration Wizard. Validating the servers that will be part of the cluster will perform several tests on those servers to ensure compatibility and functionality to ensure that the cluster will operate properly.

Other changes to Windows Server 2008's Failover Clustering include the cluster .exe command-line tool for working with Failover Clusters and improvements in the management of clusters.

It is recommended that you deploy similar components, including matching computers, as part of a cluster. Hardware such as network cards and storage must be explicitly marked "Certified for Windows Server 2008" to be supported in a Failover Cluster. Other considerations for Failover Clustering include:

■ Remove single points of failure such as nodes with one network connection or more than one network connection both going to the same switch. Failure to do so may result in a warning during validation, though the tests will pass.

- Parallel SCSI cannot be used for storage and NTFS is recommended for cluster partitions. NTFS is required for the witness disk.

- Any storage using multipath I/O must be verified with the vendor to ensure that it is appropriate for Windows Server 2008 Failover Clusters.

Validation contains four types of tests:

- **Inventory Test** Creates an inventory of components and settings in the node.

- **Network Test** Ensures that network settings are appropriate for clustering.

- **Storage Test** Examines storage for compatibility with clustering.

- **System Configuration Test** Validates system settings across servers.

MORE INFO **Learn more about validation**

For more information about cluster validation, consult the following TechNet link:

http://technet2.microsoft.com/windowsserver2008/en/library/e7877a17-bd60-4d64-9f2a-3b6f4fc6221c1033.mspx?mfr=true.

Creating a Failover Cluster

Cluster creation depends on the cluster service being installed through Server Manager and the cluster configuration being validated. After you complete these steps, a cluster is created using the Failover Cluster Management console. Within Failover Cluster Management, selecting Create A Cluster will start the Create Cluster Wizard, shown in Figure 11-15.

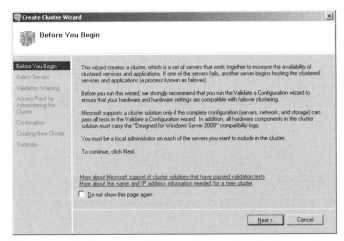

Figure 11-15 Creating a Failover Cluster using the Create Cluster Wizard

You will need the following information:

- The server names you want to include in the cluster.
- The name of the cluster.
- The IP address information for the network, if not already provided.

A report located in SystemRoot\Cluster\Reports displays the steps taken by the wizard during cluster configuration.

You also use the Failover Cluster Management console to add a node to an existing cluster. With the cluster selected, choosing Add Node from the Action menu will start the Add Node Wizard.

MORE INFO **More on adding nodes to Failover Clusters**

See *http://technet2.microsoft.com/windowsserver2008/en/library/616dee74-62c3-47ff-ae2d-cb41b97aa84c1033.mspx?mfr=true* for more information on creating a cluster and adding a node to an existing cluster.

Configuring Services for High Availability

You can configure several services and applications for use in a Failover Cluster. Use the High Availability Wizard to configure these services and applications. Several applications and services have specific settings and can be selected within the High Availability Wizard. Services and applications not listed within the wizard should use the Generic Service, Generic Application, or Generic Script options. Services and applications specifically listed include:

- DFS Namespace Server
- DHCP Server
- Distributed Transaction Coordinator (DTC)
- File Server
- Internet Storage Name Service (iSNS)
- Message Queuing
- Other Server
- Print Server
- WINS Server

MORE INFO   **More on services in Failover Clusters**

For more information on generic services in Failover Clusters, see *http://technet2.microsoft.com/ windowsserver2008/en/library/b064689c-7111-435b-b00c-4e40d8e17a791033.mspx?mfr=true.*

To start the High Availability Wizard from the Failover Cluster Management interface, select the cluster, select Services And Applications, and then select Configure A Service Or Application from the Action menu.

Managing a Failover Cluster

This section examines common tasks involved in managing Failover Clusters. Included in this discussion are pausing and resuming cluster nodes, the basics of backup and recovery, and bringing a clustered service offline.

Cluster management is performed within the Failover Cluster Management console located in Administrative Tools. Within Failover Cluster Management, the available clusters are shown on the left. Expanding a cluster reveals available options for that cluster, including nodes. You can expand the Nodes item to reveal the nodes in the cluster. Figure 11-16 shows a single-node cluster with a node named MONTREAL.

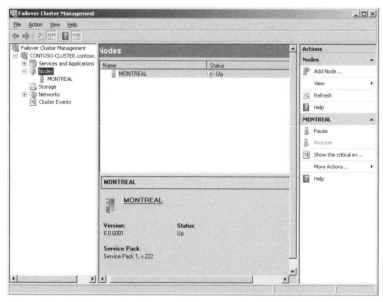

Figure 11-16   The node of a small cluster as seen through Failover Cluster Management

To pause a node, select Pause from the Action menu. To resume the node, select Resume. You can also use the cluster.exe command-line tool to pause and resume nodes. To pause the MONTREAL node of the CONTOSO-CLUSTER using the command line, open the

Command Prompt window by clicking Start and selecting Command Prompt. Type the following at the command prompt:

```
cluster CONTOSO-CLUSTER node MONTREAL /pause
```

Type the following to resume the node:

```
cluster CONTOSO-CLUSTER node MONTREAL /resume
```

Backups of Failover Clusters can include everything from the configuration of the cluster to the data itself. You can find more information on backing up Failover Clusters *at http://technet2.microsoft.com/windowsserver2008/en/library/b064689c-7111-435b-b00c-4e40d8e17a791033.mspx?mfr=true.*

Clustered services and applications can be taken offline. This might be necessary for maintenance or to apply updates. Clustered services and applications are managed through the Failover Cluster Management console. Within the management console, expanding the cluster node reveals the Services And Applications node, as shown in Figure 11-16. When you take a clustered application offline, a warning appears, confirming that all active connections will be disconnected when this operation occurs.

MORE INFO Managing clustered applications

You can find more information on bringing clustered applications online and taking them offline in the following TechNet article: *http://technet2.microsoft.com/windowsserver2008/en/library/056a73ef-5c9e-44d7-acc1-4f0bade6cd751033.mspx?mfr=true.*

Practice: Validating a Node

In this exercise, you will validate that a server is capable of performing within a Failover Cluster. You need to complete the exercise in Lesson 1 before attempting this exercise. If you cannot add a member server to your network, treat this exercise as optional.

▶ **Exercise: Validate Your Member Server Can Perform Within A Failover Cluster**

To carry out this exercise you need to log on at your member server with the Kim_Akers account.

1. Open Failover Cluster Management by clicking Start, clicking Administrative Tools, and then clicking Failover Cluster Management.

2. In the Failover Cluster Management console, select Validate A Configuration from the Action menu. Doing so will open the Validate A Configuration Wizard, shown in Figure 11-17. Click Next.

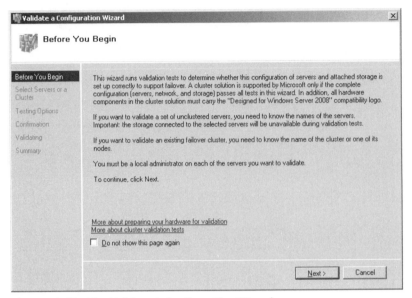

Figure 11-17 The Validate A Configuration Wizard

3. On the Select Servers Or A Cluster page, enter the name of the Windows Server 2008 server and click Add. Figure 11-18 shows the server named MONTREAL being added to the list of Selected Servers. After you add the server, click Next.

4. Next choose which tests to run. It is recommended that you run all tests. Click Next.

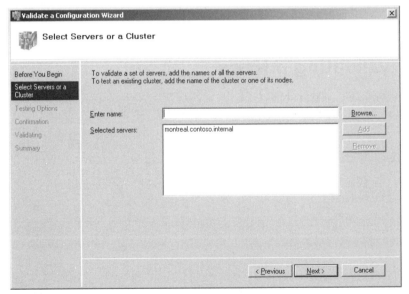

Figure 11-18 Adding a server to the list of Selected Servers

5. Click Next on the Confirmation page, as shown in Figure 11-19. The tests will now run, beginning the validation process. The wizard will display the progress of each test along with overall progress.

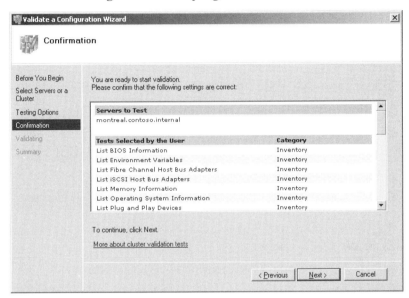

Figure 11-19   Confirming the settings

6. When the tests are complete, a Summary page appears, similar to Figure 11-20. (If any tests fail, your Summary may look different.) Click Finish to complete the validation.

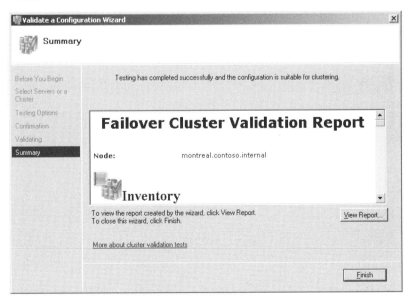

Figure 11-20   Summary page

Lesson Summary

- Failover Clustering is used for session-aware applications that have the need for shared data storage and are capable of using shared data storage.

- DHCP servers, e-mail servers, and SQL Server servers, among others, are all good candidates for Failover Clustering.

- The four quorum models in Windows Server 2008 are Node Majority, Node and Disk Majority, Node and File Share Majority, and No Majority: Disk Only.

- Failover Clustering is managed through the Failover Cluster Management snap-in or with the cluster.exe command-line tool.

- You use wizards for validation of clusters, nodes, network, and storage, and for configuration of clusters.

- Failover Clustering can be combined with NLB and DNS Round Robin.

Lesson Review

The following questions test your knowledge of Lesson 2, "Windows Server 2008 Clustering Tools." The questions are also available on the companion CD if you prefer to review them in electronic form.

1. Choose the quorum model recommended for clusters with an odd number of nodes.

   A. Node and File Share Majority

   B. Node Majority

   C. No Majority: Disk Only

   D. Node and Disk Majority

2. When considering RAID options, which of the following levels could be used with two disks? (Choose all that apply.)

   A. 0

   B. 1

   C. 5

   D. 10

3. You have a two-node cluster operating with a file share located on a different server and running in Node and File Share Majority mode. What happens

to the application and cluster when one of the servers in the cluster has a hardware failure?

A. The application will still run because the quorum model allows it to continue.

B. The application will fail because the witness disk is no longer available.

C. The answer depends on which server housed the cluster resource at the time.

D. The application will fail because the quorum model used requires that it stop servicing requests if half of the nodes become unavailable.

Chapter Review

To further review this chapter and learn the skills within, you can:

- Review the Chapter Summary.
- Review the list of key terms and their definitions.
- Complete the case scenario in this chapter.

Chapter Summary

- Windows Server 2008 uses three key methods for providing high availability and redundancy: DNS Round Robin, NLB, and Failover Clustering.
- DNS Round Robin and Network Load Balancing are used for applications that can utilize their own data store, such as Web sites. Failover Clustering is used for applications that have a shared data store.
- NLB and Failover Clustering use management tools in Windows Server 2008, whereas DNS Round Robin can be used with any DNS server, including Windows Server 2008.
- NLB creates a virtual network adapter and has two modes of operation, unicast and multicast. In multicast mode, the routers within the network must understand multicast MAC addressing.

Key Terms

- DNS round robin
- Failover clustering
- Network load balancing
- Quorum model

Case Scenario

In the following case scenario, you will apply what you have learned about Windows Server 2008 management, monitoring, and delegation. You can find answers to these questions in the "Answers" section at the end of this book.

Case Scenario: Choosing the Appropriate Availability Strategy

You are the administrator for a company running a network with 98 percent Windows Server 2008 servers along with two percent Linux servers. The business has just deemed three applications business-critical, meaning that the applications need to have minimal downtime. These three applications include Exchange Server running on two Windows Server 2008 servers; the company's main Web site that contains just static, informational pages; and an internal customer service application that utilizes Web servers running on Linux. Answer the following questions:

1. Which availability strategies can be used for these applications and why? Include what could be done to improve the application availability based on what you know about the environment.

2. Which Windows Server 2008 availability strategies are not available for each of these applications and why not?

3. If you choose Failover Clustering for any of the applications, which quorum model should be used, and why?

Suggested Practices

To help you successfully master the exam objectives presented in this chapter, complete the following tasks.

Create a DNS Round Robin

Do all of the practices in this section.

- **Practice 1: Create a New DNS Zone**   Using the DNS Manager, create a DNS zone for the contoso.internal domain.

- **Practice 2: Create a Load Balance**   Using the DNS Manager, create two A records pointing to the same www resource.

- **Practice 3: Test the Configuration**   Use the nslookup command-line tool to test the DNS lookups for the records you just created.

Create a Failover Cluster

Do all of the practices in this section.

- **Practice 1: Validate a Cluster Configuration**   From within the Failover Cluster Management tool, validate the node that you are using.

- **Practice 2: Create a Cluster**   After you have validated the node, create a single node cluster using the Failover Cluster Management tool.

Take a Practice Test

The practice tests on this book's companion CD offer many options. For example, you can test yourself on just one exam objective, or you can test yourself on all the 70-646 certification exam content. You can set up the test so that it closely simulates the experience of taking a certification exam, or you can set it up in study mode so that you can look at the correct answers and explanations after you answer each question.

MORE INFO   Practice tests

For details about all the practice test options available, see "How to Use the Practice Tests" in this book's Introduction.

Chapter 12
Backup and Recovery

Backup and recovery have always been a core component of a systems administrator's job. With more reliable hardware, the amount of time that a systems administrator spends on backup and recovery has decreased, but management's expectations about server availability have also changed. Users who accepted that a file server might have been out of action for 24 hours in the late 1990s are unwilling to accept several hours of downtime a decade later. In this chapter, you will learn what is new in terms of the process of backing up Windows Server 2008 and the data and services that it hosts for your organization. You will also learn how to plan and implement the disaster recovery for your organization's Windows Server 2008 environment. You will learn how to recover everything from single Active Directory objects through to files, folders, roles, volumes, and even entire servers.

Exam objectives in this chapter:
- Plan for backup and recovery.

Lessons in this chapter:

Before You Begin

To complete the lesson in this chapter, you must have done the following:

- Installed and configured the evaluation edition of Windows Server 2008 Enterprise Edition in accordance with the instructions listed in the first practice exercise of Lesson 1 in Chapter 1, "Installing, Upgrading, and Deploying Windows Server 2008."

- The practices in this chapter require that you have access to an extra disk that is able to store 25 gigabytes (GB) of data and attach it to server Glasgow. This disk can be an extra virtual disk if you are using virtual machine software, a physical disk, or an attached USB 2.0 or IEEE 1394 disk if you are using real hardware. This disk will be used to store backup data.

Real World

Orin Thomas

In my experience, the most important factor in recovering from a disaster is keeping a cool head. In some ways, disaster recovery is like putting together a puzzle. If you are calm and methodical about it, everything fits into the right place and before you know it you are back to where you were before the disaster occurred. If you are flustered or freaked out, you are going to run into problems. Stressed-out people make mistakes. I have seen recovery operations go awry because someone was nervous and rushed. People have to start all over again because they did not take a few moments to take a few deep breaths and remember to keep a clear head.

Lesson 1: Backing Up Data

The backup tools built into Windows Server 2008 have changed significantly from those that were included in Windows Server 2003. Backup techniques that you may have been familiar with over the course of your career have changed. One example of this is that you can no longer write scheduled backups to tape drives. In this lesson, you will learn how to use the new Windows Server 2008 backup utility to back up your servers; you will learn how to use the wbadmin.exe command-line backup utility; and you will learn how to back up files, folders, and Active Directory. You will also learn how to configure Shadow Copies of Shared Folders, a technology that allows you to move the process of recovering deleted or corrupted shared files away from the help desk and onto the individual user.

> **After this lesson, you will be able to:**
> - Understand how to use the wbadmin.exe utility to back up servers.
> - Perform a complete server backup.
> - Back up Active Directory and Server Role data.
> - Back up System State data.
> - Perform remote backup operations.
>
> **Estimated lesson time: 40 minutes**

Shadow Copies of Shared Folders

Implementing Shadow Copies of Shared Folders will reduce an administrator's restoration workload dramatically because it almost entirely eliminates the need for administrator intervention in the recovery of deleted, modified, or corrupted user files. Shadow Copies of Shared Folders work by taking snapshots of files stored in shared folders as they exist at a particular point in time. This point in time is dictated by a schedule and the default schedule for Shadow Copies of Shared Folders is to be taken at 7:00 A.M. and 12:00 P.M. every weekday. Multiple schedules can be applied to a volume and the default schedule is actually two schedules applied at the same time.

To enable Shadow Copies of Shared Folders, open Computer Management from the Administrative Tools menu, right-click the Shared Folders node, click All Tasks and then click Configure Shadow Copies. This will bring up the Shadow Copies dialog box, shown in Figure 12-1. This dialog box allows you to enable and disable Shadow Copies on a per-volume basis. It allows you to edit the Shadow Copy of Shared Folder settings for a particular volume. It also allows you to create a shadow copy of a particular volume manually.

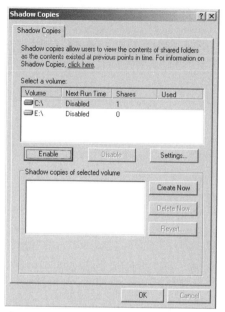

Figure 12-1   Enabling Shadow Copies

Enabling Shadow Copies on a volume will automatically generate an initial shadow copy for that volume. Clicking Settings launches the dialog box shown in Figure 12-2. From this dialog box, you can configure the storage area, the maximum size of the copy store, and the schedule of when copies are taken. Clicking Schedules allows you to configure how often shadow copies are generated. On volumes hosting file shares that contain files that are updated frequently, you would use a frequent shadow copy schedule. On a volume hosting file shares where files are updated less frequently, you should configure a less frequent shadow copy schedule.

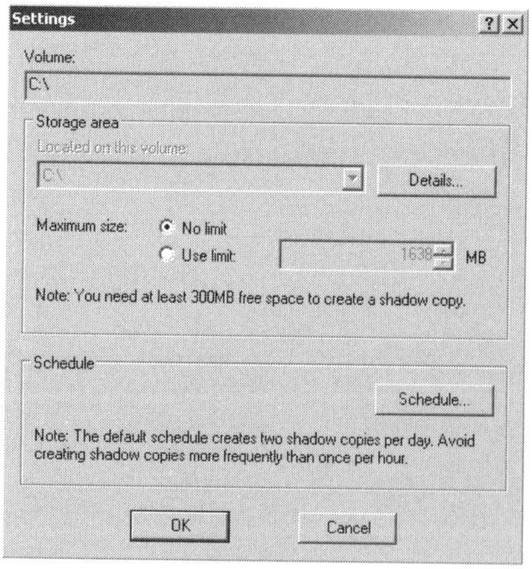

Figure 12-2   Shadow Copy settings

When a volume regularly experiences intense read and write operations, such as a commonly used file share, you can mitigate the performance impact of Shadow Copies of Shared Folders by storing the shadow copy data on a separate volume. If a volume has less space available than the set limit, the service will remove the oldest shadow copies that it has stored as a way of freeing up space. Finally, no matter how much free space is available, a maximum of 64 shadow copies can be stored on any one volume. When you consider how scheduling might be configured for a volume, you will realize how this directly influences the length of shadow copy data retention. Where space is available, a schedule where shadow copies are taken once every Monday, Wednesday, and Friday allows shadow copies from 21 weeks previously to be retrieved. The default schedule allows for the retrieval of up to 6 weeks of previous shadow copies.

When planning the deployment of Shadow Copies of Shared Folders, it is important to remember that you configure settings on a per-volume basis. This means that the storage area, maximum size, and schedules for different volumes can be completely separate. If you plan shares in such a way that each volume hosts a single share, you can optimize the shadow copy settings for that share based on how the data is used, rather than trying to compromise in finding an effective schedule for very different shared folder usage patterns.

Quick Check

1. On what basis (server, volume, share, disk, or folder) are Shadow Copies of Shared Folders enabled?
2. What happens to shadow copy data when the volume that hosts it begins to run out of space?

Quick Check Answers

1. Shadow Copies of Shared Folders are enabled on a per-volume basis.
2. The oldest shadow copy data is automatically deleted when volumes begin to run out of space.

Windows Server Backup

The Windows Server Backup tool is significantly different from ntbackup.exe, the tool included in Windows Server 2000 and Windows Server 2003. Administrators familiar with the previous tool should study the capabilities and limitations of the new

Windows Server Backup utility because many aspects of the tool's functionality have changed.

Exam Tip   **What the tool does**

The Windows Server 2008 exams are likely to focus on the differences between NTBACKUP and Windows Server Backup.

The key points to remember about backup in Windows Server 2008 are:

- Windows Server Backup cannot write to tape drives.

- You cannot write to network locations or optical media during a scheduled backup.

- The smallest object that you can back up using Windows Server Backup is a volume.

- Only local NTFS-formatted volumes can be backed up.

- Windows Server Backup files write their output as VHD (Virtual Hard Disk) files. VHD files can be mounted with the appropriate software and read, either directly or through virtual machine software such as Hyper-V.

MORE INFO   **Recovering NTbackup backups**

You cannot recover backups written using ntbackup.exe. A special read-only version of ntbackup.exe that is compatible with Windows Server 2008 can be downloaded from *http://go.microsoft.com/fwlink/?LinkId=82917*.

Windows Server Backup is not installed by default on Windows Server 2008 and must be installed as a feature using the Add Features item under the Features node of the Server Manager console. When installed, the Windows Server Backup node becomes available under the Storage node of the Server Manager Console. You can also open the Windows Server Backup console from the Administrative Tools menu. The wbadmin.exe command-line utility, also installed during this process, is covered in "The wbadmin Command-Line Tool" later in this lesson. To use Windows Server Backup or wbadmin to schedule backups, the computer requires an extra internal or external disk. External disks will need to be either USB 2.0 or IEEE 1394 compatible. When planning the deployment of disks to host scheduled backup data, you should ensure that the volume is capable of holding at least 2.5 times the amount of data that you want to back up. When planning deployment of disks for scheduled backup, you should monitor how well this size works and what sort of data retention it allows in a trial before deciding on a disk size for wider deployment throughout your organization.

When you configure your first scheduled backup, the disk that will host backup data will be hidden from Windows Explorer. If the disk currently hosts volumes and data, these will be removed to store scheduled backup data. Note that this only applies to scheduled backups and not to manual backups. You can use a network location or external disk for a manual backup without worrying that data already stored on the device will be lost. The format and repartition only happens when a device is first used to host scheduled backup data. It does not happen when subsequent backup data is written to the same location.

It is also important to remember that a volume can only store a maximum of 512 backups. If you need to store a greater number of backups, you will need to write these backups to a different volume. Of course given the amount of data on most servers, you are unlikely to find a disk that has the capacity to store so many backups. So that scheduled backups can always be executed, Windows Server Backup will automatically remove the oldest backup data on a volume that is the target of scheduled backups. You do not need to manually clean up or remove old backup data.

Performing a Scheduled Backup

Scheduled backups allow you to automate the backup process. After you set the schedule, Windows Server Backup takes care of everything else. By default, scheduled backups are set to occur at 9:00 P.M. If your organization still has people regularly working on documents at that time, you should reset this. When planning a backup schedule you should ensure that the backup occurs at a time when the most recent day's changes to data are always captured. Only members of the local Administrators group can configure and manage scheduled backups.

To configure a scheduled backup, perform the following steps:

1. Open Windows Server Backup. Click Backup Schedule in the Actions pane of Windows Server Backup. This will start the Backup Schedule Wizard. Click Next.

2. The next page of the wizard asks whether you want to perform a full server backup or a custom backup. Select Custom and click Next. As you can see in Figure 12-3, volumes that contain operating system components are always included in custom backups. Volume E is excluded in this case, because this is the location where backup data will be written.

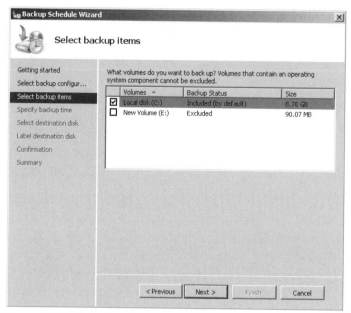

Figure 12-3   Selecting backup items

3. The default backup schedule is once a day at 9:00 P.M. You can configure multiple backups to be taken during the day. You are most likely to do this in the event that data on the server that you are backing up changes rapidly. On servers where data changes a lot less often, such as on a Web server where pages are only updated once a week, you would configure a more infrequent schedule.

4. On the Select Destination Disk page, shown in Figure 12-4, you select the disk that backups are written to. If multiple disks are selected, multiple copies of the backup data are written. You should note that the entire disk will be used. All existing volumes and data will be removed and the backup utility will format and hide the disks prior to writing the first backup data.

5. On the Label Destination Disk page, note the label given to the disk you have selected to store backups. When you finish the wizard, the target destination is formatted and then the first backup will occur at the scheduled time.

An important limitation of Windows Server Backup is that you can only schedule one backup job. In other words, you cannot use Windows Server Backup to schedule jobs that you might be used to scheduling in earlier versions of Windows, such as a full backup on Monday night with a series of incremental backups every other day of the week. You can configure Windows Server Backup to perform incremental backups, but this process is different from what you might be used to with other backup applications.

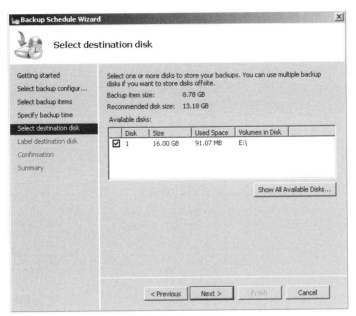

Figure 12-4   Selecting a destination disk

Performing an Unscheduled Single Backup

Unscheduled single backups, also known as manual backups, can be written to network locations, local and external volumes, and local DVD media. If a backup encompasses more than the space available on a single DVD media, you can span the backup across multiple DVDs. Otherwise, if the calculated size of a backup exceeds the amount of free space available on the destination location, the backup will fail. You will perform a manual backup in a practice exercise at the end of this lesson.

When performing a manual backup, you must choose between using one of the following two types of Volume Shadow Copy Service backup:

- **VSS Copy Backup**   Use this backup option when another backup product is also used to back up applications on volumes in the current backup. Application log files are retained when you perform this type of manual backup. This is the default when taking a backup.

- **VSS Full Backup**   Use this backup option when no other backup products are used to back up the host computer. This option will update each file's backup attribute and clears application log files.

When performing a single backup, you can also back up a single volume without having to back up the system or boot volumes. This is done by clearing the Enable System Recovery option when selecting backup items. You might use this option to back up a specific volume's data when you are going to perform maintenance on the volume or suspect that the disk hosting the volume might fail, but do not want to wait for a full server backup to complete.

Optimizing Backup Performance

Incremental backups work slightly differently than they did in earlier versions of Windows. Although incremental backups still only back up data that has changed since the last backup, in Windows Server Backup you do not choose whether to make an individual backup full, differential, or incremental when you create the backup job. Whether full backups or incremental backups are taken is configured separately as a general backup performance option. All backups are configured as either full or incremental. The first backup image taken in a schedule will be the equivalent of a full backup.

You can configure backup performance by clicking Configure Performance Settings in the Actions pane of the Windows Server Backup Console. When you do this you can select from the options shown in Figure 12-5. These options are straightforward, with

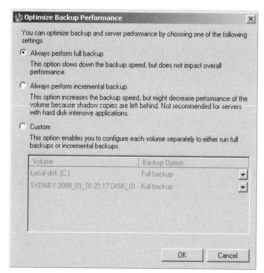

Figure 12-5   Optimizing backup performance

the Custom Backup option allowing you to choose full or incremental backups on a per-volume basis. Selecting the incremental backup option will allow you to store more scheduled backups on the same media, and in general you should use this option because it will give you a greater window from which you can restore data. A benefit of the way that Windows Server Backup works is that you will not have to hunt around for specific incremental backup sets when performing a restore. When you perform a restore, the appropriate backup images are located based on your restoration selections. Restoration is covered in more detail by Lesson 2, "Disaster Recovery."

The wbadmin Command-Line Tool

The wbadmin utility is available on both the Standard and Server Core installations of Windows Server 2008 and allows you to do everything you can do with Windows Server Backup and more. The wbadmin utility is installed on a Standard installation of Windows Server 2008 when you install the Windows Server Backup feature and choose to install the command-line tools option, as shown in Figure 12-6.

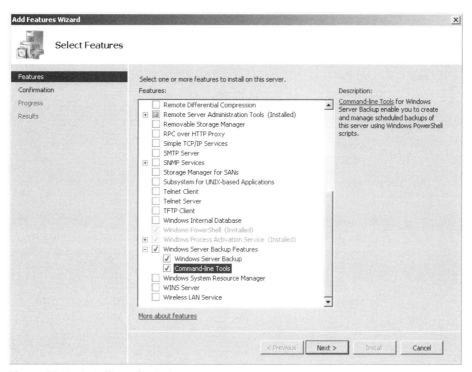

Figure 12-6   Installing wbadmin

The wbadmin utility is the only direct backup utility that you can use on a server in the Server Core configuration, although it is possible to connect to such a computer remotely using the Windows Server Backup console. You can install wbadmin on a computer running in the Server Core configuration by issuing the following command:

```
Ocsetup WindowsServerBackup
```

The following wbadmin.exe commands are useful for backing up Windows Server 2008 files:

- **wbadmin enable backup**   This command allows you to create and manage scheduled backups.

- **wbadmin start systemstatebackup**   This command allows you to perform a system state data backup.

- **wbadmin start backup**   This command allows you to start a single manual backup.

- **wbadmin get versions**   This command allows you to view details of backups that have already been taken.

- **wbadmin get items**   This command allows you to determine which items are contained in a specific backup image.

Most administrators will be interested in the *wbadmin start backup* command because it allows the performance of manual backups to shared folders. This is done using the syntax *–backuptarget:\\Share\Folder* where the shared folder location is expressed as a UNC pathname. In the event that you need to provide authentication credentials to write data to the shared folder, you can use the *–user:* and *–password:* options. For example, to back up volumes E, F, and G of a server to the shared folder Store on the server Glasgow using Kim Aker's credentials, you would issue the following command:

```
Wbadmin start backup -backuptarget:\\Glasgow\Store -include:E:,F:,G: -
User:Kim_Akers@contoso.internal -Password:P@ssw0rd
```

Because you can call wbadmin.exe from a batch file, and you can call batch files from the Scheduled Tasks utility, you can schedule the execution of more precisely configured backups than you can using Windows Server Backup's scheduling options. You can use this method to configure scheduled backups to network locations. For example, the command:

```
Echo wbadmin start systemstatebackup -backupTarget:\\Server\Share -user:RemoteUser -
password:RemotePassword -quiet >> c:\scripts\ssbackup.bat
```

will create a batch file named ssbackup.bat in the c:\scripts directory that will perform a system state backup to the network share \\Server\Share using the credentials of user RemoteUser. Using Scheduled Tasks, you can configure this batch file to run according to a schedule, mimicking Windows Server Backup's backup schedule functionality. When you plan backups using this method, keep the following points in mind:

- The *–quiet* option is necessary in the wbadmin command because you do not want a scheduled task halting because it is waiting for input.

- The scheduled task must be run using the local Administrator account because wbadmin.exe must be run with elevated privileges.

- If the scheduled task is writing to a network share, you will need to put user account credentials into the script called by the scheduled task. You can protect these credentials by using EFS to encrypt the file so that only the local Administrator account can view the script contents.

- The primary drawback to scripted backups is that they will fail if the target location is full. Backups scheduled using wbadmin.exe will automatically remove the oldest backup when not enough space exists for the current backup.

MORE INFO **Full list of wbadmin options**

You can learn about more about wbadmin syntax at *http://technet2.microsoft.com/ windowsserver2008/en/library/4b0b3f32-d21f-4861-84bb-b2eadbf1e7b81033.mspx?mfr=true.*

Backing Up Server Roles and Applications

In general, backing up a particular server role, such as the DHCP or DNS roles and their associated data, is simply a matter of backing up System State data. System State data is automatically included in backups any time you perform a full server backup or any type of scheduled backup. System State data is also backed up when you perform a manual backup using Windows Server Backup and choose the Enable System Recovery option when selecting backup items. The only method by which you can back up only System State data is to use wbadmin.exe with the *start systemstatebackup* option. An important limitation when using wbadmin.exe with this option is that System State data can only be written to a local volume, even when performing a manual backup. To perform a System State data backup, open a command prompt with elevated privileges and issue the following command, where F: is the volume identifier:

```
Wbadmin start systemstatebackup –backuptarget:F: –quiet
```

Performing a System State data recovery will be covered in detail in Lesson 2, "Disaster Recovery."

Backing Up Applications

Windows Server Backup will take special note of applications that are Volume Shadow Copy Service (VSS) and Windows Server Backup–aware, allowing you to restore just the application and its associated data from a full server or volume backup. For you to be able to use this functionality, an application must be registered with Windows Server Backup, which would occur automatically during the application's installation process. This limits this functionality to applications that are designed to run on Windows Server 2008. You can still back up and restore data related to applications if your application does not register itself with Windows Server Backup. The benefit of this feature is that it vastly simplifies the application restoration process, ensuring that all application data—from executable files through to registry settings—is packaged in such a way that you can restore just that application, its dependencies, and data.

Backing Up Active Directory

Active Directory is automatically backed up whenever you back up the critical volumes on a domain controller. You can also perform an Active Directory backup by performing a System State backup. A copy of the Active Directory database is stored on all DCs within a domain, so that in the event that one is lost and you do not have access to backup data, you can perform a recovery by reinstalling from scratch and replicating the database back from other domain controllers.

Although performing a System State backup does back up all Active Directory objects, the nature of Active Directory replication makes the recovery of some objects more difficult than the recovery of others. While the process of performing an authoritative restore is covered in detail by Lesson 2, the technique for restoring a deleted Group Policy Object is significantly different from restoring a user account or OU tree. Group Policy Objects are backed up using the Group Policy Management Console, and you should use this console, rather than Directory Services Restore Mode, to recover deleted GPOs.

To back up Group Policy Objects, open the Group Policy Management Console so that the Group Policy Objects container is visible. Right-click the Group Policy Objects item, shown in Figure 12-7, and then click Back Up All. As a part of this process you will need to specify a location and a description for the backup. It should be a location that is normally backed up as a part of the Windows Server Backup routine.

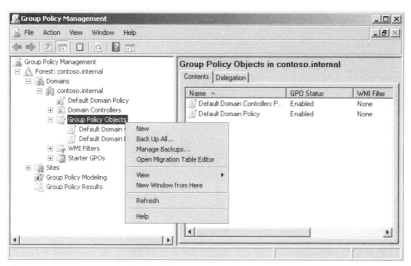

Figure 12-7   Group Policy backup

MORE INFO   **Active Directory backup**

For more information on backing up Active Directory, consult the following Microsoft TechNet article: *http://technet2.microsoft.com/windowsserver2008/en/library/1ac7f330-7283-453d-bbf4-f748fbc0ec4a1033.mspx?mfr=true.*

> ## Quick Check
>
> 1. What command is used to install wbadmin.exe on a Windows Server 2008 computer that is running the Server Core configuration?
> 2. What happens to any volumes and data stored on a disk that you select as a target to store backup data generated by Windows Server Backup?
>
> ## Quick Check Answers
>
> 1. *Ocsetup WindowsServerBackup*
> 2. All volumes and data on the target disk are removed before Windows Server Backup writes its first set of backup data.

Remotely Backing Up Computers

The Windows Server Backup tool can be used to connect to another Windows Server 2008 computer and perform backup tasks as though the backup were being performed on the local computer. This allows users that have the Remote Systems Administration Tools installed on their Windows Vista workstations to connect to Windows Server 2008 computers and perform backup operations as though they were logged on locally. To perform this operation, the user making the connection must be a member of the Backup Operators or local Administrators group on the Windows Server 2008 computer to which she is making the connection.

The same limitations that apply to a locally run instance apply to remote connections using the Windows Server Backup console. A user that is only a member of the Backup Operators local group will be unable to schedule backups and will only be able to perform unscheduled backups. A user that is a member of the local Administrators group on the server that is the target of the remote Windows Server Backup connection will be able to perform all normal backup tasks.

Windows Server Backup does not allow you to schedule backup data generated on remote computers to be written to a local source. You can write to a local source when performing an unscheduled backup only if the computer you are attempting to write data to has a shared folder configured. You cannot use the wbadmin.exe utility to manage backups on remote computers.

Further Considerations for Planning Backups

The smallest unit of backup using Windows Server backup is the volume, as opposed to the ability to back up individual files and folders in Windows Server 2003. This limitation will significantly impact how you configure servers prior to their deployment. When planning the deployment of file servers you need to consider how they are going to be backed up and restored. Because backup works on a per-volume level, you might be more inclined to create separate volumes for each share rather than placing several shares on each volume because this makes it easier to perform per-volume backup and restoration. It is also easier to mount a per-volume backup image within a virtual machine if you cannot immediately restore it to its original server in the event of a hardware failure.

Another consideration in the planning of backups is how frequently particular volumes need to be backed up. Using Storage Reports, you can gain some insight as to how often files on a particular volume are altered. A shared folder that hosts HR policy documents that are only updated on an occasional basis does not need to be backed up nightly. By moving this shared folder to its own partition, you can configure backups for its contents to occur less frequently. Alternatively, you might locate a particular shared folder where data is updated so frequently and is so mission-critical that you might need to back that volume up every few hours. Ultimately you should develop a backup strategy for your organization that best meets your organization's needs, not the limitations of the specific tools that you have to work with.

A final consideration in the planning of backups is developing an offsite strategy. Offsite backups ensure that if the building that hosts your servers is destroyed by flood, fire, or earthquake, your organization can still recover its data. When planning an offsite backup strategy, consider the following points:

- Offsite backups must be stored in secure locations. You should avoid having staff members take backup data home because this environment is not secure.

- Ensure that if data is encrypted, the recovery keys are included in the offsite backup data set.

- Ensure that you have enough equipment at your recovery site so that you can recover your servers.

System Center Data Protection Manager

System Center Data Protection Manager 2007 (DPM 2007) is an advanced backup solution that is available from Microsoft. Whereas Windows Server Backup is suitable for most simple backup and restore situations, DPM 2007 is targeted at more complex backup scenarios such as the backing up of production Exchange Server 2007 servers or SQL Server 2008 instances. DPM 2007 has the following primary benefits:

- Provides byte-level backups. In an incremental backup, only files that have changed since the most recent backup are written to the backup. In a byte-level backup, only those bytes in the files that have changed are written to the backup, significantly reducing the amount of data that needs to be written to a backup.

- Can be used to provide zero data loss restoration of Exchange, SQL Server, and Office SharePoint Server. This works through integrating point-in-time database backups with existing application logs. When combined, application data can be restored to the point in time where the failure occurred, not just to the point where the last backup was taken.

- Agent software can be installed on branch office servers, allowing backup data to be forwarded over WAN links. Agent software can also be used to forward backup data over the LAN, allowing remote backups to be written to local media.

- Supports backup to direct attached storage, Fibre Channel SAN, and iSCSI SAN. Does not support USB and IEEE 1394 devices.

- Comprehensive reporting including protection success and failure as well as backup media utilization.

- Management Pack is available for System Center Operations Manager 2007. This allows centralized management of the state of data protection and recovery for multiple DPM 2007 servers and servers with DPM 2007 agent software installed. Best used in environments with many DPM 2007 servers and clients.

NOTE   DPM 2007 FAQ

To learn more about DPM 2007, consult the DPM 2007 FAQ at *http://technet.microsoft.com/en-us/library/bb795549.aspx*.

Exam Tip   Manual versus scheduled backup

Take care with questions involving scheduled backups, because the locations that you can write backup data to are more restricted than the locations that you can write backup data to when performing a manual backup.

Practice: Backing Up Windows Server 2008

In this set of practice exercises, you will perform three separate types of backup on Windows Server 2008 computer Glasgow. The first type of backup will be a normal Windows Server Backup operating system backup. The second type of backup involves using wbadmin.exe to perform a simple volume backup. The final type of backup will be a system state–only backup.

NOTE   Extra disks

As noted in the introduction to this chapter, the practices in this chapter require that you have access to an extra disk and attach it to server Glasgow. This disk can be an extra virtual disk if you are using virtual machine software, a physical disk, or an attached USB 2.0 or IEEE 1394 disk if you are using real hardware. This disk will be used to store backup data. The disk should be approximately 25 GB in size so that it can store all of the backup data generated in these practice exercises.

▶ **Exercise 1: Performing a Manual Backup Using Windows Server Backup**

In this exercise, you will install the Windows Server Backup feature and then perform a manual backup of server Glasgow. At the start of the exercise you will create a set of Active Directory objects that will be backed up. These objects will be removed and later restored as a part of the practice exercises at the end of Lesson 2.

To complete this practice, perform the following steps:

1. Log on to server Glasgow using the Kim_Akers user account.

2. In the Server Manager console, click the Features node and then click Add Features. On the Select Features page of the Add Features Wizard, expand the Windows

Server Backup Features node. Select Windows Server Backup And Command-Line Tools, click Next, and then click Install. When the feature has been installed, click Close to exit the Add Features Wizard.

NOTE   Needs Windows PowerShell

Depending on which other practice exercises you have completed, you may be prompted to confirm the installation of the Windows PowerShell feature.

---

3. Open Active Directory Users And Computers. Create a new OU called **Planets** under the Contoso.internal domain. Within the Planets OU create four computer accounts named **Saturn, Jupiter, Neptune,** and **Uranus.** Close Active Directory Users And Computers.

4. Verify that the extra disk is connected to your computer and that you know its volume name. If the disk is not formatted, format it using the NTFS file system, although a manual backup can be written to a FAT32 file system.

5. Open Windows Server Backup from the Administrative Tools menu. In the Actions pane, click Backup Once. This will open the Backup Once Wizard.

6. Ensure that the Different Options item is selected and then click Next.

7. On the Select Backup Configuration page, shown in Figure 12-8, select Custom and then click Next.

Figure 12-8   Choose custom backup configuration

8. Ensure that the Enable System Recovery option is selected, as shown in Figure 12-9. This will automatically select all volumes that contain operating system components. Click Next.

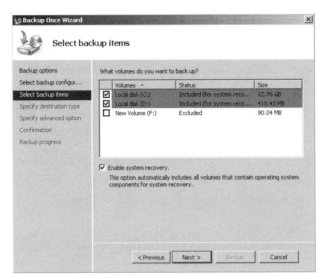

Figure 12-9   Selecting backup items

9. On the Specify Destination Type page, ensure that Local Drives is selected and then click Next.

10. On the Select Backup Destination page, use the drop-down menu to select the new disk that you added to the server and then click Next.

11. On the Specify Advanced Option page, select VSS Full Backup and then click Next.

12. On the Confirmation page, click Backup. The backup process will now begin. When the backup process completes, click Close.

▶ **Exercise 2: Performing a System State and Volume Backup Using wbadmin.exe**

In this exercise, you will perform a System State backup using the wbadmin.exe command-line utility and then create a scheduled task. To complete this exercise, perform the following steps:

1. Ensure that you are logged on to Windows Server 2008 computer Glasgow with the Kim Akers user account.

2. Create a folder on volume c: named **Continents**. Create five text files within this volume named **Europe.txt**, **Antarctica.txt**, **Africa.txt**, **Australia.txt**, and **Asia.txt**. The content of each text file should be its name.

3. Open a command prompt with administrative privileges.

4. Issue the command *wbadmin start backup –backuptarget:f: -include:c: -vssFull –quiet*.

NOTE **Backup target volume**

If the extra disk is located on volume e:, you would use *–backuptarget:e:*

---

5. After the backup has completed, delete the c:\Continents folder.

6. Issue the command *wbadmin start systemstatebackup –backuptarget:f: -quiet*.

7. When the command completes, issue the command *wbadmin get versions*.

8. Verify that three backup jobs have been created, as shown in Figure 12-10.

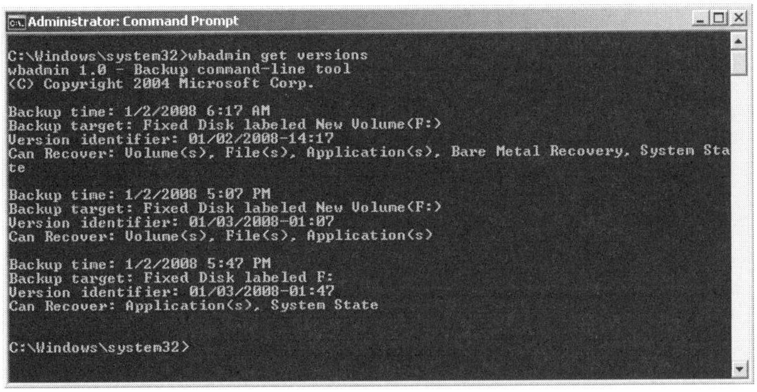

Figure 12-10   Verifying that items have backed up

Lesson Summary

■ Windows Server Backup is a feature that allows the creation of scheduled and manual backups on Windows Server 2008.

■ Only members of the Administrators local group can schedule backups on Windows Server 2008, although members of the Backup Operators group can take manual backups.

■ The wbadmin.exe command-line tool provides more functionality than Windows Server Backup, but can only be used from an elevated command prompt.

■ Scheduled backups can only be written to local disks or externally attached USB 2.0 or IEEE 1394 disks. Manual backups can be written to these locations as well as network shares and local DVD writers.

■ You can create scheduled backups to network locations by placing a wbadmin.exe command within a script and scheduling it using the Scheduled Tasks tool. A script that calls the wbadmin.exe command must be run using the local Administrator account.

- Backing up Active Directory involves taking a System State data backup. Taking a System State data backup is generally all that is required to back up Windows Server 2008 roles.

Lesson Review

You can use the following questions to test your knowledge of the information in Lesson 1, "Backing Up Data." The questions are also available on the companion CD if you prefer to review them in electronic form.

NOTE   Answers

Answers to these questions and explanations of why each answer choice is correct or incorrect are located in the "Answers" section at the end of the book.

---

1. You want to enable a user at a remote site to take manual backups of a file server once a week to a removable USB 2.0 device that will be then transported by courier to your organization's head office location. Which local group on the file server should you add this trusted staff member's domain user account to so that he can accomplish this task without being granted unnecessary administrative privileges?

   A. Power Users

   B. Backup Operators

   C. Administrators

   D. Remote Desktop Users

2. You want to schedule a daily system state backup to be written to a network location. Which of the following should you do to accomplish this? (Each correct answer presents part of the solution. Choose two.)

   A. Create a batch file that contains the *wbadmin start systemstatebackup* command that targets the UNC path of the network share with credentials that have access to the share.

   B. Create a batch file that contains the *wbadmin start systemstatebackup* command that targets a local volume using the local Administrator account credentials.

   C. Use the Scheduled Tasks tool to configure a job that runs the batch file using the local Administrator account credentials once a day.

    D. Use the Scheduled Tasks tool to configure a job that runs the batch file using credentials that have access to the share once a week.

    E. Use the Scheduled Tasks tool to configure a job that runs the batch file using the local Administrator account credentials once a week.

3. Which of the following locations can be the target of backups scheduled with Windows Server Backup? (Each correct answer presents a complete solution. Choose three.)

    A. USB 2.0 External Disk

    B. IEEE 1394 External Disk

    C. IDE Internal disk

    D. iSCSI SAN

4. Which of the following applications and services can you use to mount a Windows Server Backup backup file? (Each correct answer presents a complete solution. Choose two.)

    A. Virtual Server 2005 R2

    B. Hyper-V

    C. Storage Explorer

    D. Disk Management

    E. Storage Manager for SANs

5. You are developing organizational policy with respect to modifications to Active Directory. You want to ensure that a full System State backup is taken prior to any modifications being made to Active Directory. You only want to back up System State data and will be doing this using the *wbadmin.exe start systemstatebackup* command. Which of the following targets can you specify when executing this command manually? (Each correct answer presents a complete solution. Choose three.)

    A. Network Share

    B. DVD writer

    C. External USB 2.0 HDD

    D. External IEEE 1394 HDD

    E. Internal SCSI HDD

Lesson 2: Disaster Recovery

Part of the disaster recovery process is determining the cause of the original failure. If you do not deal with the cause of the original failure, the failure might occur again. For example, if a disk drive has failed because of a problem on the motherboard and you are unable to correctly diagnose this problem, a replacement disk might suffer the same fate as the original. In this lesson, you will learn how to recover from disaster using backups that you have already taken. You will learn how to recover an entire server using the bare metal recovery process and how to recover System State data, and you will learn about the process of authoritatively restoring deleted items from Active Directory.

After this lesson, you will be able to:

- Recover servers.
- Recover Role Services.
- Recover data.
- Recover Active Directory.

Estimated lesson time: 40 minutes

Windows Server Backup Recovery Modes

If you are going to perform recovery operations using Windows Server Backup, your user account must be a member of the Backup Operators or Administrators group or must have been delegated the appropriate permissions. As mentioned at the start of the chapter, backups taken with ntbackup.exe cannot be restored using Windows Server Backup or wbadmin.exe. You can obtain a read-only version of ntbackup.exe from Microsoft; the link for this utility is provided in the first lesson of this chapter.

Although servers might be protected by BitLocker when they are backed up, when you perform a volume, operating system, or full server restore, BitLocker settings are not restored. You will have to reapply BitLocker after the restoration is complete to ensure that volumes are encrypted. The process of applying BitLocker to a computer running Windows Server 2008 was covered in Chapter 1.

Recovering Files and Folders

Although Windows Server Backup only allows the backup at the volume level, you can perform recovery at the file and folder level. As Figure 12-11 shows, this functionality allows you to restore a set of files and folders, or even just an individual file.

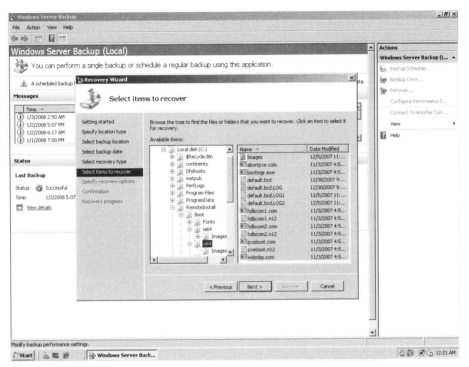

Figure 12-11   Selecting items to recover

When planning to restore a file or folder you need to know the following things:

- The date that the file or folder was backed up

- The file or folder's location

- Whether you want to restore the file or folder's security settings

- The location to which you want to restore the file or folder

- What to do if a duplicates are found in the restoration location

If a duplicate is found in the restoration location, the options are to automatically have a copy created, to overwrite the existing files with recovered files, or to not recover those specific files where duplicates exist.

A great advantage of Windows Server Backup over earlier versions of the Windows Server Backup utility is that it manages your existing backup files so that if backup data needs to be read from several different backup files—such as when several volumes on a folder that has been backed up incrementally need to be restored—the process occurs automatically. Determining which backups were required when performing a restoration was the greatest drawback to performing a restore from incremental backups.

You will perform a file and folder recovery during the first practice exercise at the end of this lesson.

MORE INFO   **More on restoring files and folders**

For more information on restoring files and folders, consult Scenario 3 in the following Microsoft TechNet link: *http://technet2.microsoft.com/windowsserver2008/en/library/00162c92-a834-43f9-9e8a-71aeb25fa4ad1033.mspx?mfr=true.*

Recovering Applications and Application Data

A new feature of Windows Server Backup is the ability to perform application-specific restorations. An application-specific restoration only restores an application, its settings, and associated application data. You can only use Windows Server Backup to perform an application restoration on an application that has been registered with Windows Server Backup, a process that occurs during application installation.

When you perform an application recovery you will be given a list of applications registered with Windows Server Backup that can be recovered based on the backup date that you have selected. If the backup that you are performing the restore from is the most recent backup taken of that application according to the data stored in the backup catalog, you will have the option of rolling forward the application database. The default option is to allow roll-forward. You should only select the Do Not Perform A Roll-Forward Recovery Of The Application Database if you want to block roll-forward. You would use this option if the change you are trying to undo was made after the backup was taken, such as if an important table in a SQL Server database was dropped.

MORE INFO   **More on recovering applications**

To learn more about recovering Windows Server Backup-aware applications, consult the following link on Microsoft TechNet: *http://technet2.microsoft.com/windowsserver2008/en/library/00162c92-a834-43f9-9e8a-71aeb25fa4ad1033.mspx?mfr=true.*

Recovering Volumes

Volume recovery is a straightforward recovery of all volume contents. Volume recovery is useful in situations where you might have lost a volume because of the failure of a disk but you do not need to go to the stage of performing a full operating system or server recovery. The most important thing to remember about performing a volume recovery is that all existing data at the destination location will be lost when you perform the recovery. You can recover one or more volumes during a volume recovery.

MORE INFO   **More about volume recovery**

To learn more about volume recovery, including a list of detailed steps required to perform the recovery, consult the following Microsoft TechNet article: *http://technet2.microsoft.com/windowsserver2008/en/library/00162c92-a834-43f9-9e8a-71aeb25fa4ad1033.mspx?mfr=true.*

Full Server and Operating System Recovery

Also known as Bare Metal Recovery, full server recovery allows you to completely restore the server by booting from the Windows Server 2008 installation media or Windows Recovery Environment. See the note on building a recovery solution for more information on how to set up a local Windows Recovery Environment on a Windows Server 2008 computer. Full server recovery goes further than the Automated System Recovery (ASR) feature that was available in Windows Server 2003 because full server recovery will restore all operating system, application, and other data stored on the server. ASR did not provide such a complete recovery and it was necessary to further restore data from backup after the ASR process was complete.

NOTE   **Building a recovery solution**

You can learn how to create a recovery solution for installation on another disk on your Windows Server 2008 computer by following the instructions at *http://technet2.microsoft.com/WindowsVista/en/library/61e08b15-82d8-46bd-a5f1-7947193e6ed81033.mspx?mfr=true.* (These instructions reference Windows Vista but will work for Windows Server 2008.)

An operating system recovery is similar to a full server recovery except that you only recover critical volumes and do not recover volumes that do not contain critical data. For example, if you have a file server where the disks that host critical operating system volumes are separate from the disks that host shared folder volumes and the disks that host the critical operating system volumes fail, you should perform an operating system recovery.

When performing either a full server or operating system recovery you must ensure that the disk you are recovering to is at least as large as the disk that contained the volumes you backed up, regardless of the size of the volumes on that disk. For example, if you performed a full server backup on a server that was configured to only use a 30 GB partition on a 100 GB disk and that disk failed, you will need to perform the restore to a disk that is at least 100 GB in size when performing a full server or operating system recovery.

Operating system and full server recovery is performed by booting from the Windows Server 2008 installation media or into the recovery environment and using the computer repair options. To perform a full operating system or server recovery, perform the following steps:

1. Boot from the Windows Server 2008 installation media.

2. In the Language Settings dialog box, click Next.

3. On the Install Windows page, shown in Figure 12-12, click Repair Your Computer.

Figure 12-12 Repairing your computer

4. If you are recovering your computer onto new hardware, the System Recovery Options list will be empty. Otherwise it will contain any detected operating systems on the computer, even if they are corrupted. Either way, click Next.

5. In the System Recovery Options dialog box, shown in Figure 12-13, click Windows Complete PC Restore.

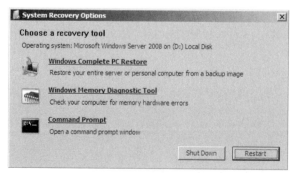

Figure 12-13 Select Windows Complete PC Restore

6. When you select the Complete PC Restore option, the utility will scan all local and attached storage devices for the most recent complete backup. You can choose to restore from the most recent available backup detected, or specify a different backup by choosing the Restore A Different Backup option. Figure 12-14 shows several different backups that can be restored from the same removable USB 2.0 device. Clicking the Advanced option allows you to search for a backup on the network or to install a driver for a locally attached disk, such as a SCSI drive, that is not visible because the appropriate software has not been loaded.

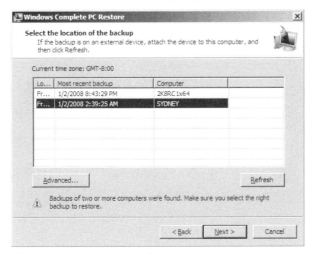

Figure 12-14   Selecting a backup to restore

7. On the Choose How To Restore The Backup page you can select the Format And Repartition Disks option if you have not already prepared the disks for restoration. Select the Exclude Disks option if there are disks that you do not want formatted and repartitioned. The disk hosting the backup data is automatically excluded. If there are disks that do not contain critical data you can select the Only Restore System Disks option to perform a system-only recovery. At this point you can also install extra drivers if the disks that you are recovering data to require extra drivers to function. Selecting Advanced Options allows disks to be checked for errors immediately after recovery is complete.

MORE INFO   **More on operating system recovery**

To learn more about operating system and full server recovery, consult the following link on Microsoft TechNet: *http://technet2.microsoft.com/windowsserver2008/en/library/f06b5935-4d50-456a-a249-8212d0bd26c71033.mspx?mfr=true.*

System State Recovery

Performing a System State recovery is the most common method of recovering corrupt server role data or restoring Active Directory. It is not possible to perform a partial System State recovery. System State recovery must occur in its entirety. To perform a System State recovery using the wbadmin utility, perform the following steps:

1. Open an administrative command prompt and enter the command **wbadmin get versions**. This will produce a list of backups, with the most recent backup listed first.

2. Make a note of the backup version identifier, which will be in the format MM/DD/YYYY-HH:MM. It is necessary to provide the entire backup version identifier when performing the restore.

3. Enter the command **wbadmin Start SystemStateRecovery −version:MM/DD/YYYY-HH:MM**. Type **Y** to accept the System State Recovery and then press Enter to start the recovery process. When the process completes, reboot the server.

4. The server may need to reboot several times, depending on which server roles were installed on Windows Server 2008 when the system state backup was taken.

Quick Check

1. Under what conditions can you perform an application recovery?
2. How do you access the tool that allows you to perform a full server recovery?

Quick Check Answers

1. The application needs to be registered with Windows Server Backup. An application that is registered with Windows Server Backup can be restored without requiring the restoration of any other non-application-related data.

2. To access the tool that you use to perform a full server recovery, it is either necessary to boot from the Windows Server 2008 installation media or boot into the Windows Recovery Environment.

Recovering Active Directory

Active Directory is recovered when you recover a domain controller's System State data. When you recover the System State data you perform what is termed a *nonauthoritative restore*. A nonauthoritative restore brings the Active Directory database on the server back to the point it was at when the backup was taken. When you restart the DC at the end of the System State replication process the DC replicates with other DCs in the domain and the Active Directory database is updated with changes that have occurred since the backup was taken. If, rather than just wanting to recover the DC, you want to recover specific Active Directory objects that have been deleted from the database, you need to perform what is known as an *authoritative restore*. Authoritative restores are covered in the next section.

MORE INFO   **More on performing nonauthoritive restores**

For more on performing nonauthoritative restorations of Active Directory, consult the following Microsoft TechNet article: *http://technet2.microsoft.com/windowsserver2008/en/library/fd79a503-dfe7-483a-9de1-a7b39dae76aa1033.mspx?mfr=true.*

Authoritative Restore

When a nonauthoritative restore is performed, objects deleted after the backup was taken will again be deleted when the restored DC replicates with other servers in the domain. On every other DC the object is marked as deleted so that when replication occurs the local copy of the object will also be marked as deleted. The authoritative restore process marks the deleted object in such a way that when replication occurs, the object is restored to active status across the domain. It is important to remember that when an object is deleted it is not instantly removed from Active Directory, but gains an attribute that marks it as deleted until the tombstone lifetime is reached and the object is removed. The tombstone lifetime is the amount of time a deleted object remains in Active Directory and has a default value of 180 days.

To ensure that the Active Directory database is not updated before the authoritative restore takes place, you use the Directory Services Restore Mode (DSRM) when performing the authoritative restore process. DSRM allows the administrator to perform the necessary restorations and mark the objects as restored before rebooting the DC and allowing those changes to replicate out to other DCs in the domain.

NOTE   **Only DC in the domain**

Authoritative restores are not necessary if there is only one DC in the domain because there is no other copy of the Active Directory database.

Booting into Directory Services Restore Mode

You can use three methods to boot into DSRM. The first method is to press F8 during the boot process and then select Directory Services Restore Mode from the prompt, as shown in Figure 12-15.

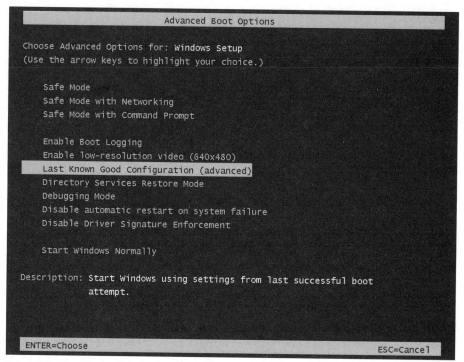

Figure 12-15   Using F8 to boot into DSRM

The amount of time that you have to use the F8 method is short and many administrators are frustrated to find that they press the key too late, meaning that they have to boot all the way into Windows Server 2008 normally. To second method involves opening an administrative command prompt and issuing the following command:

```
Bcdedit /set safeboot dsrepair
```

This changes the boot option so that Windows Server 2008 automatically boots into DSRM. This option is generally used on DCs that are configured to run in the Server Core configuration. To remove this boot option, open an administrative command prompt and issue the following command:

```
Bcdedit /deletevalue safeboot
```

If you do not remove this option, the server will always boot into DSRM. The third method of starting a Windows Server 2008 DC in Directory Services Restore Mode is to open the System Configuration console from the Administrative Tools menu and select the Active Directory Repair Safe Boot option, as shown in Figure 12-16.

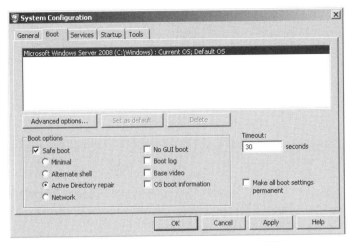

Figure 12-16   Configuring a server to restart in DSRM

Logging into DSRM requires that you have the DSRM password. The DSRM password is set on an individual basis for each domain controller during the domain controller promotion process. Because it can be some time between a domain controller being promoted and an administrator needing to utilize DSRM, this password is often forgotten. If the DSRM password has been forgotten, you can reset it by performing the following actions, also shown in Figure 12-17:

1. Log on to the domain controller with an account that is a member of the Domain Admins group.

2. Open an administrative command prompt and type **ntdsutil**.

3. At the Ntdsutil command prompt, type **set dsrm password**.

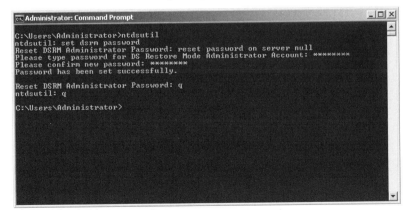

Figure 12-17   Resetting the DSRM password

4. At the DSRM command prompt do one of the following:

- ❑ If resetting the DSRM password on the local DC, enter the command **reset password on server null**. Type and confirm the new password.

- ❑ If resetting the DSRM password for another DC, enter the command **reset password on server** *servername* where *servername* is the FQDN of the server for which you are resetting the password.

5. At the DSRM prompt, type **q**. At the Ntdsutil command prompt, type **q** to exit.

After a DC has been rebooted into DSRM and you have logged on using the Administrator account and the DSRM password, you need to perform a nonauthoritative restore by restoring the System State data using the wbadmin.exe utility. This process was covered earlier in "System State Recovery" earlier in the chapter. If you need to perform an authoritative restore of SYSVOL, perform the System State recovery using the –*AuthSysVOL* option. You should only use this option when it is necessary to roll SYSVOL back to an earlier version than the one that currently exists. This option is not commonly used as a part of the authoritative restore process.

Once the System State recovery process has completed, you need to use the NTDSUTIL utility to enter the Authoritative Restore mode. From here you can restore objects by making reference to their distinguished names.

To restore an object, type **Restore Object** and then the object's distinguished name. To restore a container and everything located under it, type **Restore Subtree** and then the container's distinguished name. For example, to restore the Platypus OU and all of its contents in the Tailspintoys.com domain, issue the following command:

```
Restore Subtree "OU=Platypus,DC=Tailspintoys,DC=COM"
```

If objects have back links, an LDIF file will be generated in the directory from which you have performed the authoritative restore operation. A back link includes information such as group memberships that the restored object had that are not automatically included when you perform the authoritative restore operation. You must run the LDIF file in each domain that might have group objects that may have included the restored object at the time of its deletion. To perform this operation, execute the following command on a DC in each necessary domain:

```
Ldifde -I -k ldif.filename
```

You will perform the authoritative restoration of Active Directory objects during the second practice exercise at the end of this lesson.

MORE INFO More on authoritative restoration

For more information on performing an authoritative restoration of Active Directory objects, consult the following article on Microsoft TechNet: *http://technet2.microsoft.com/windowsserver2008/ en/library/f4e9ee21-ee35-4650-acca-798555c0c32c1033.mspx*.

Recovering Deleted Group Policy Objects

You cannot use an authoritative restore to restore deleted GPOs. They must be recovered using the Group Policy Management Console. To do this, open the GPMC, right-click the Group Policy Objects container, and then click Manage Backups. Browse to the location where backed-up GPOs are stored, select the GPO that you want to recover in the dialog box shown in Figure 12-18, and then click Restore.

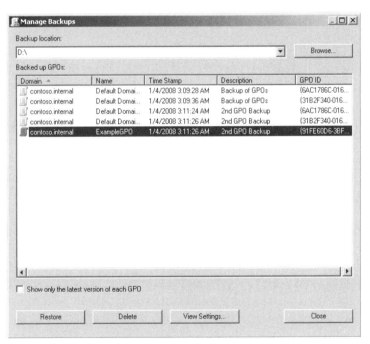

Figure 12-18 Restoring a GPO

Performing Full Server Recovery on a Domain Controller

When you perform a full server recovery of a domain controller you automatically perform a nonauthoritative restore of Active Directory. Because of the nature of the full server recovery process, it is difficult to use it to perform an authoritative restore because the server will most likely reboot and replicate before you have a chance to force it into DSRM to perform the authoritative restoration process. This might be technically possible for an administrator who is quick at pressing F8 at the appropriate time, but performing a full server recovery on a DC should not be considered a viable method of restoring deleted Active Directory object data. Of course after the full server recovery is complete, nothing is stopping you from then performing a more traditional authoritative restore using the methods outlined earlier in this lesson. Performing a full server recovery on a domain controller follows the steps outlined earlier in the lesson on performing a standard full server recovery.

MORE INFO   **More on full server recovery of a DC**

For more information on performing a full server recovery of a domain controller, consult the following article on Microsoft TechNet: *http://technet2.microsoft.com/windowsserver2008/en/library/ fd79a503-dfe7-483a-9de1-a7b39dae76aa1033.mspx.*

Active Directory Database Mounting Tool

The Active Directory Database Mounting Tool (dsamain.exe) allows for the creation and viewing of data stored within Active Directory Directory Services without needing to restart the domain controller in Directory Services Restore Mode. You can use the dsamain.exe tool to compare the state of Active Directory as it exists in different snapshots without having to restore multiple backups. This can be very useful if you are trying to determine whether a particular backup of Active Directory contains the objects that you want to restore.

You can use dsamain.exe with both the ntdsutil snapshot operation and with a Windows Server 2008 System State data backup. The process involves using ntdsutil to mount the snapshot of the directory and then using dsamain.exe to view and modify the snapshot. For security reasons, only members of the Domain Admins and Enterprise Admins group are able to view these snapshots. Although you can use the dsamin.exe tool to re-create deleted objects, this process is tricky and laborious. Microsoft recommends that you use DSRM and an authoritative restore as your primary method of restoring deleted directory objects rather than attempting manual recreation through dsadmin.exe.

NOTE   **More on dsamain.exe**

To learn more about the Active Directory Database Mounting Tool and how it can be used in Windows Server 2008 disaster recovery scenarios, consult the following Microsoft TechNet article: *http://technet2.microsoft.com/windowsserver2008/en/library/4503d762-0adf-494f-a08b-cf502ecb76021033.mspx?mfr=true.*

NOTE   Tombstone reanimation

If you want to learn even more about recovering deleted objects from Active Directory, you should read the article "Reanimating Active Directory Tombstone Objects" at *http://www.microsoft.com/ technet/technetmag/issues/2007/09/Tombstones/default.aspx.*

Hyper-V and Disaster Recovery

Windows Server Backup writes backup data as image files in VHD format. Using Windows Server Backup and wbadmin.exe you can perform a full operating system recovery or recover a volume or individual files and folders to the original (or different) server hardware. Another option is to perform a recovery to a virtual machine hosted under Hyper-V or Virtual Server 2005 R2 (although you cannot use the latter product to recover an x64 version of Windows Server 2008).

From the perspective of disaster recovery planning, this means that you can use Windows Server 2008 Datacenter Edition as a recovery platform when you need to bring servers back up but you do not have the available hardware because your head office site has burned down or was hit by a meteor. Alternatively, if an important server's hardware fails and it will take some time before the components can be replaced, you can run the recovered server in a virtualized environment as a stopgap measure. Figure 12-19 shows a complete PC restore of server Sydney to a virtual machine running under Hyper-V.

You can also mount the backup images as volumes on an existing virtual machines by editing the virtual machine properties and adding the VHD image as a new virtualized hard disk drive. In general, though, it is easier to use Windows Server Backup's restore functionality to perform this type of operation, although this technique can be useful as a quick method of migrating a partition from a real to a virtual server without having to go through the file copy process.

MORE INFO   32-bit VHD mounting

To mount virtual hard disks on 32-bit Windows Server 2008 computers, download Virtual Server 2005 from the Microsoft Web site and then extract the vhdmount.exe utility from the setup files. You can learn how to do this by following the instructions at *http://technet2.microsoft.com/ windowsserver/en/library/22c042cd-9029-407f-9866-3288fe2ad2d61033.mspx?mfr=true.*

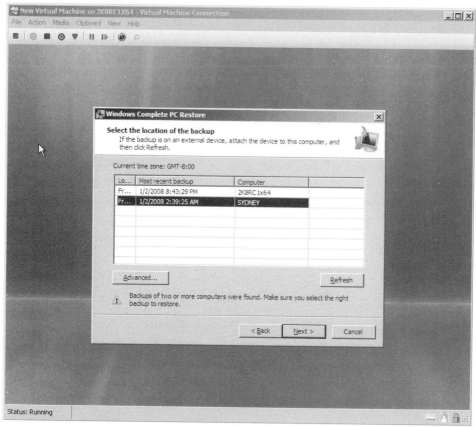

Figure 12-19 Restoring a server using Hyper-V

Practice: Restoring Windows Server 2008

This practice exercise requires that you have completed all of the practice exercises at the end of Lesson 1. In this set of exercises, you will restore files and folders that were backed up and then deleted. You will reset your DSRM password. You will perform an authoritative restore of Active Directory objects and you will restore a backup catalog.

▶ **Exercise 1: Restore Files and Folders**

In this exercise, you will restore the deleted Continents directory and the files that it hosted. You will also prepare for the second practice by deleting several important Active Directory objects. To complete this exercise, perform the following steps:

1. Log onto server Glasgow with the Kim_Akers user account. Verify that the C:\Continents directory is not present.

2. Start Windows Server Backup from the Administrative Tools menu. Click Continue when prompted by the UAC dialog box.

3. In the Actions pane, click Recover. This will launch the Recovery Wizard. On the Getting Started page, select This Server (Glasgow) and click Next.

4. On the Select Backup Date, select the date when you performed the second practice exercise in Lesson 1 and then click Next.

5. On the Select Recovery Type page, choose Files And Folders and then click Next.

6. On the Select Items To Recover page, expand Glasgow, Local Disk (C:) and select the Continents folder, shown in Figure 12-20, and then click Next.

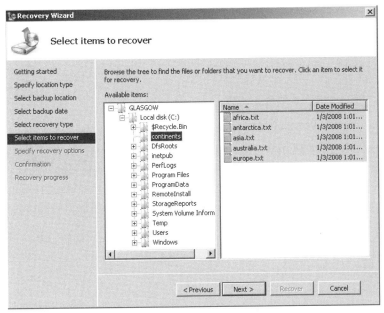

Figure 12-20   Select Items to Recover

7. On the Specify Recovery Options page, shown in Figure 12-21, set the Recovery Destination to the Original Location and ensure that security settings are restored. Click Next.

8. On the Confirmation page, click Recover. When the recovery is complete, click Close.

9. From the Administrative Tools menu, open Active Directory Users And Computers. In the View menu, ensure that the Advanced Features option is selected.

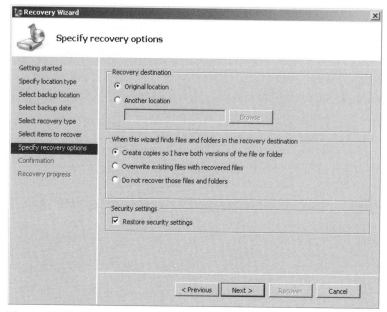

Figure 12-21 Recovery options

10. Right-click the Planets OU and select Properties. On the Object tab, clear the Protect Object From Accidental Deletion option and then click OK. Right-click the Planets OU and then click Delete. Click Yes to confirm the deletion and then click Yes to confirm that you want to delete all of the objects contained within the Planets OU.

11. Close Active Directory Users And Computers.

▶ **Exercise 2: Perform an Authoritative Restore**

In this exercise, you will use the System State backup of server Glasgow that you took during the practice exercises at the end of Lesson 1 and use it as the basis of an authoritative restore of specific objects within the deleted Planets OU. You will also need your DSRM password to perform this action. If you have forgotten this password, you can reset it using the instructions provided earlier in "Booting into Directory Services Restore Mode."

1. When logged on to server Glasgow with the Kim_Akers user account, open the System Configuration console from the Administrative Tools menu. Click Continue when prompted by the User Account Control dialog box.

2. On the Boot tab, select Safe Boot and then choose the Active Directory Repair option. Click OK to close the System Configuration console.

3. When prompted, click Restart. Server Glasgow will now restart.

4. When the server restarts, log on as Administrator with the DSRM password.

5. Verify that the server has rebooted in safe mode. The desktop background should be black and the words Safe Mode should appear in the corners of the screen. If the computer has not rebooted in safe mode, start again from step 1.

6. Open a command prompt with elevated privileges and then type **wbadmin get versions.**

7. The final backup in the list should state that you can recover only Application(s), System State. Make a note of the version identifier. In Figure 12-22, the version identifier for the System State backup is 01/03/2008-01:47.

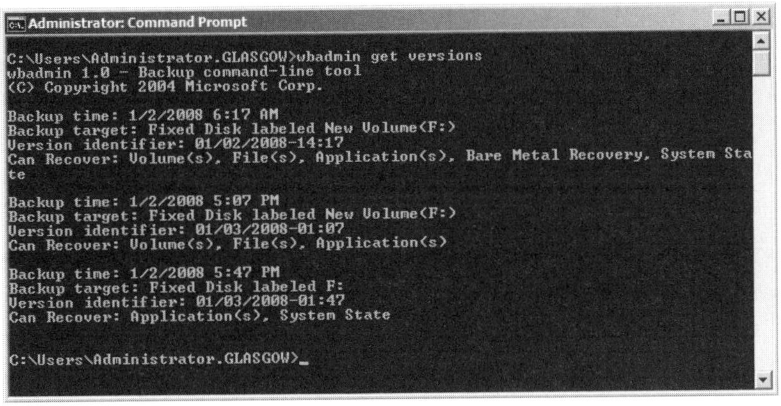

```
Administrator: Command Prompt

C:\Users\Administrator.GLASGOW>wbadmin get versions
wbadmin 1.0 - Backup command-line tool
(C) Copyright 2004 Microsoft Corp.

Backup time: 1/2/2008 6:17 AM
Backup target: Fixed Disk labeled New Volume(F:)
Version identifier: 01/02/2008-14:17
Can Recover: Volume(s), File(s), Application(s), Bare Metal Recovery, System Sta
te

Backup time: 1/2/2008 5:07 PM
Backup target: Fixed Disk labeled New Volume(F:)
Version identifier: 01/03/2008-01:07
Can Recover: Volume(s), File(s), Application(s)

Backup time: 1/2/2008 5:47 PM
Backup target: Fixed Disk labeled F:
Version identifier: 01/03/2008-01:47
Can Recover: Application(s), System State

C:\Users\Administrator.GLASGOW>_
```

Figure 12-22   Locating the backup version identifier

8. Issue the command *wbadmin Start SystemStateRecovery −version:01/03/2008-01:47 −backupTarget:f:* substituting the appropriate version identifier and backup location from your own System State backup. When prompted press Y to start the System State recovery operation.

9. Once the System State recovery process has completed, issue the *NTDSUTIL* command.

10. Type **Activate Instance NTDS** and then press Enter.

11. Type **Authoritative Restore** and then press Enter.

12. Type **Restore Object "OU=Planets,dc=Contoso,dc=internal"** and press Enter. Click Yes at the prompt to confirm that you want to perform the restore. Verify that ntdsutil reports that the Authoritative Restore Completed Successfully, as shown in Figure 12-23.

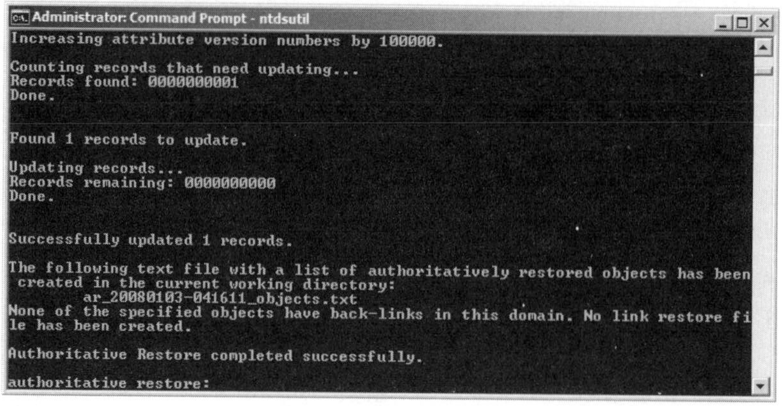

Figure 12-23 Successful authoritative restore

13. Type **Restore Object** "**ou=Saturn,ou=Planets,dc=Contoso,dc=internal**" and press Enter. Click Yes at the prompt to confirm that you want to perform the restore.

14. Type **Quit** twice to exit the NTDSUTIL tool. Type **Exit** to close the command prompt.

15. From the Administrative Tools menu, open the System Configuration console. On the Boot tab, clear the Safe Boot option and click OK. When prompted, click Restart to restart the server.

16. The server may reboot several times as a part of the recovery process.

17. When the server completes the reboot process, log on with the Kim_Akers user account. Press Enter in the Command Console window to acknowledge that System State recovery operation has completed.

▶ **Exercise 3: Recover a Backup Catalog**

In this exercise, you will simulate the process of deleting a corrupted backup catalog and restoring a new catalog from the current set of backups. To complete this exercise, perform the following steps:

1. While logged on to server Contoso with the Kim_Akers user account, open an elevated command prompt.

2. Type the command **wbadmin delete catalog** and press Enter.

3. When prompted about catalog deletion, press Y.

4. Type the command **wbadmin restore catalog –backupTarget:f:** where f: is the volume that backups are stored on.

5. When prompted about catalog restoration, press Y.

6. Type **wbadmin get versions** to confirm the contents of the catalog.

Lesson Summary

- To perform a recovery, you must ensure that the user's account is a member of the local Backup Operators or Administrators group.

- When performing an operating system or full server recovery to a new hard disk, you must ensure that the disk is as big as the original disk that contained the volumes that were backed up.

- Application restore can only be used on applications that are registered with Windows Server Backup.

- Recovering the System State data restores most server roles, including Active Directory.

- An authoritative restore is performed after rebooting a domain controller into Directory Services Restore Mode. Active Directory authoritative restores are used to recover deleted Active Directory objects.

Lesson Review

You can use the following questions to test your knowledge of the information in Lesson 2, "Disaster Recovery." The questions are also available on the companion CD if you prefer to review them in electronic form.

NOTE Answers

Answers to these questions and explanations of why each answer choice is correct or incorrect are located in the "Answers" section at the end of the book.

---

1. You have rebooted a domain controller in the Contoso.internal domain into Directory Services Restore Mode, performed a System State recovery, and put NTDSUTIL into the Authoritative Restore mode. Which of the following commands would you use to authoritatively restore the accidentally deleted Pluto computer account to the Solar OU?

   A. Restore Object "cn=Solar,OU=Pluto,dc=Contoso,dc=internal"

   B. Restore Computer "cn=Pluto,OU=Solar,dc=Contoso,dc=internal"

   C. Restore Object "cn=Pluto,OU=Solar,dc=Contoso,dc=internal"

   D. Restore Computer "cn=Solar,OU=Pluto,dc=Contoso,dc=internal"

2. Kim Akers is a member of the local Administrators group on Windows Server 2008 computer Sydney. Sydney hosts a network share to which Sam Abolrous, a member of the local Administrators group on Windows Server 2008 computer Melbourne, uses as a target location when he performs manual backups of the

data on server Melbourne's volumes. Sam is on a training course this week and the users of server Melbourne need Kim to restore some deleted folders that they cannot access through VSS. Which group membership must Kim have to use the Windows Server Backup tool from Sydney to restore data on Melbourne while keeping to the principle of least privilege?

A. Power Users group on Sydney

B. Power Users local group on Melbourne

C. Backup Operators group on Melbourne

D. Administrators group on Melbourne

3. All RODCs deployed at your branch office sites have all volumes protected by BitLocker. Full server backups of each RODC are taken once a month to DVD. The hard disk drive on the Traralgon branch office RODC fails. You replace the component and perform a full server recovery. What other steps must be taken to return the RODC to its original condition?

A. Perform an authoritative restore.

B. Perform a nonauthoritative restore.

C. Reapply BitLocker.

D. Perform a full server backup.

4. The motherboard of an important intranet server at one of your organization's remote branch offices has just failed. The motherboard is the only component that needs replacement, but because of the branch office's remote location, it will be several days before a replacement can be obtained. A full server backup was manually performed on the server 12 hours before the failure occurred. This backup was written to removable USB disk drive. A Windows Server 2008 x64 Enterprise Edition computer with Hyper-V is also located at the site and hosts a virtualized domain controller. Which of the following steps could be taken to ensure that the intranet server is available until the replacement components arrive while not disrupting existing services?

A. Perform a bare metal restore on the Windows Server 2008 x64 Enterprise Edition's computer.

B. Mount the backup images on the Windows Server 2008 x64 Enterprise Edition computer as extra volumes.

C. Perform a full server recovery to a Hyper-V virtual machine.

D. Restore the System State data from the backup images to the Windows Server 2008 x64 Enterprise Edition computer.

Chapter Review

To further practice and reinforce the skills you learned in this chapter, you can perform the following tasks:

- Review the chapter summary.
- Review the list of key terms introduced in this chapter.
- Complete the case scenarios. These scenarios set up real-world situations involving the topics of this chapter and ask you to create a solution.
- Complete the suggested practices.
- Take a practice test.

Chapter Summary

- Windows Server Backup scheduled backups can only be written to local internal or external disks. Windows Server Backup manual backups can be written to DVD writers and network locations.
- Wbadmin.exe is the command-line utility that you can use to backup and restore Server Core as well as standard deployments of Windows Server 2008. Wbadmin.exe is the only utility that can be used to perform a System State backup without backing up other items.
- To perform recoveries using Windows Server Backup, you must ensure that an account is a member of the Backup Operators or Administrators group, or have been delegated the appropriate authority.
- When performing an operating system or full server recovery to a new hard disk, you must ensure that the disk is as big as the original disk that contained the volumes that were backed up.

Key Terms

Do you know what these key terms mean? You can check your answers by looking up the terms in the glossary at the end of the book.

- Authoritative restore
- Bare metal restore
- Directory services restore mode
- System state backup

Case Scenarios

In the following case scenarios, you will apply what you have learned about backup and recovery. You can find answers to these questions in the "Answers" section at the end of this book.

Case Scenario 1: Wingtip Toys Backup Infrastructure

You are planning the backup strategy for Wingtip Toys in light of their soon-to-be-completed migration from all servers running Windows 2000 Server to running the Windows Server 2008 operating system. The current strategy at Wingtip Toys was developed in an ad-hoc manner, and part of your job is to ensure some consistency to backup procedures. With that in mind, you must find answers to the following questions:

1. Thirty file servers that use NTBACKUP to write backup data to DLT tapes are to be upgraded to Windows Server 2008. What steps must be taken to ensure that scheduled daily backups can still be taken using the Windows Server Backup utility?

2. You are considering your organization's offsite backup strategy for scheduled backups using Windows Server Backup. What types of hardware devices should you consider deploying to support this strategy?

3. Currently 23 percent of all help desk jobs involve restoring documents to shared folders that were accidentally deleted by the people working on them. What steps can you take to reduce the impact this problem has on help desk staff?

Case Scenario 2: Disaster Recovery at Fabrikam

On Saturday evening at 11:00 P.M., the Fabrikam head office building was destroyed by a massive fire. The Fabrikam head office hosted the Fabrikam.internal forest root domain DCs and the hq.fabrikam.internal child domain. The Fabrikam.internal forest has 15 domains. The following backups exist at an offsite location:

- Full server backups of the forest root domain controllers taken on Friday

- System State data backups of the hq.fabrikam.internal domain controllers taken on Wednesday

- Full server backups of the hq.fabrikam.internal domain controllers taken on Friday

- Full server backup of fileserv.hq.fabrikam.internal file server taken on Wednesday

- Full backup of volumes hosting shared folders on fileserve.hq.fabrikam.internal taken on Friday

On Thursday night, several important Active Directory objects were accidentally removed from the hq.fabrikam.internal domain during a software upgrade. These objects were restored on Saturday morning prior to the fire. You are now at the disaster recovery site and have replacement servers.

1. Which DCs should you restore first and why?

2. What steps should you take to ensure that the objects that were present within Active Directory on Saturday afternoon are restored as completely as possible?

3. What steps should you take to restore shared files on fileserve.hq.fabrikam.internal as completely as possible?

Suggested Practices

To help you successfully master the exam objectives presented in this chapter, complete the following tasks.

Plan for Backup

Do all the practices in this section.

- **Practice 1: Remote Backup** Use Windows Server Backup console to perform a full system backup on a member server of the Contoso.internal domain that is deployed in the Server Core configuration.

- **Practice 2: Server Core System State Backup** Perform a System State backup locally on a computer that is deployed in the Server Core configuration.

Plan for Recovery

Do all the practices in this section.

- **Practice 1: Server Core Restore** Boot using the Windows Server 2008 installation media and perform full server recovery on a computer that was originally deployed in the Server Core configuration. Use the full server backup data that was generated in the Remote Backup practice.

- **Practice 2: Server Core System State Recovery** Perform a System State recovery on a computer deployed in the Server Core configuration. Use the System State backup data that was generated in the Server Core System State Backup practice.

Take a Practice Test

The practice tests on this book's companion CD offer many options. For example, you can test yourself on just one exam objective, or you can test yourself on all the 70-646 certification exam content. You can set up the test so that it closely simulates the experience of taking a certification exam, or you can set it up in study mode so that you can look at the correct answers and explanations after you answer each question.

MORE INFO   **Practice tests**

For details about all the practice test options available, see the "How to Use the Practice Tests" section in this book's Introduction.

Answers

Chapter 1: Lesson Review Answers

Lesson 1

1. **Correct Answers: C and D**

   A. **Incorrect:** Only Windows Server 2003 Datacenter Edition can be upgraded to Windows Server 2008 Datacenter Edition.

   B. **Incorrect:** Only Windows Server 2003 Web Server Edition can be upgraded to Windows Web Server 2008.

   C. **Correct:** Windows Server 2003 Standard Edition can be upgraded to Windows Server 2008 Enterprise Edition.

   D. **Correct:** Windows Server 2003 Standard Edition can be upgraded to Windows Server 2008 Standard Edition.

   E. **Incorrect:** Although Windows Server 2003 Standard Edition can be upgraded to Windows Server 2008 Standard Edition, it is not possible to upgrade any edition of Windows Server 2003 to a Server Core version of Windows Server 2008.

2. **Correct Answer: A**

   A. **Correct:** The 32-bit version of Windows Server 2003 Standard Edition can be upgraded only to a 32-bit version of Windows Server 2008 Standard or Enterprise Editions.

   B. **Incorrect:** It is not possible to upgrade a 32-bit version of Windows Server 2003 to a 64-bit version of Windows Server 2008.

   C. **Incorrect:** It is not possible to upgrade Windows Server 2003 Standard Edition to Windows Server 2008 Datacenter Edition.

   D. **Incorrect:** It is not possible to upgrade a 32-bit version of Windows Server 2003 to a 64-bit version of Windows Server 2008.

3. **Correct Answer: B**

   A. **Incorrect:** To implement BitLocker, it is necessary to have a 1.5-GB system volume that is active. You do not need to configure Group Policy if a TPM 1.2 or later chip is available.

B. **Correct:** BitLocker requires a non-encrypted volume to start from in the event that the operating system itself is going to be encrypted.

C. **Incorrect:** Although it is possible to implement BitLocker without a TPM chip, deactivating the chip will not enable you to implement BitLocker on this computer.

D. **Incorrect:** The TPM chip does not need to be upgraded to implement Bit-Locker.

4. **Correct Answer: C**

A. **Incorrect:** If a TPM chip is not present, it is possible to enable BitLocker with a USB key through the local policy. The removable USB memory device does not have to be present to start the activation of BitLocker, although it will be necessary to insert it during the activation process.

B. **Incorrect:** Although a computer's BIOS must support starting from a USB device, the lack of a compatible BIOS will not block the start of the BitLocker Wizard. It is possible, though not mandatory, to perform a system check for USB support prior to hard disk encryption.

C. **Correct:** If a TPM chip is not present, you can enable BitLocker with a USB key through the local policy. Until this policy is configured, you cannot activate BitLocker.

D. **Incorrect:** The BitLocker Control Panel item is not present if the BitLocker feature is not installed.

5. **Correct Answer: C**

A. **Incorrect:** Clustering is supported only in the Enterprise and Datacenter Editions of Windows Server 2008.

B. **Incorrect:** Clustering is supported only in the Enterprise and Datacenter Editions of Windows Server 2008.

C. **Correct:** The question specifies that a Failover Cluster needs to be present before an Exchange Server 2007 clustered mailbox server can be deployed. Failover Clustering is supported only on the Enterprise and Datacenter Editions of Windows Server 2008.

D. **Incorrect:** Clustering is supported only in the Enterprise and Datacenter Editions of Windows Server 2008. Although this is knowledge that is not directly relevant to the 70-646 exam, you should be aware that Exchange Server 2007 will only install on x64 versions of Windows Server 2003 and Windows Server 2008.

Lesson 2

1. **Correct Answers: A, B, and C**

   A. **Correct:** A Windows Server 2008 computer must be a member of an existing Active Directory domain prior to the deployment of Windows Deployment Services.

   B. **Correct:** A DHCP server that is authorized in Active Directory must be present for Windows Deployment Services to function correctly.

   C. **Correct:** A properly configured DNS server must be present for Windows Deployment Services to function correctly.

   D. **Incorrect:** Windows Deployment Services is not dependent on the Application Server role.

2. **Correct Answer: A**

   A. **Correct:** An unattended installation can be initiated from the Windows PE 2.0 environment.

   B. **Incorrect:** An unattended installation cannot be initiated from a Windows NT boot disk.

   C. **Incorrect:** An unattended installation cannot be initiated from an MS DOS boot disk.

   D. **Incorrect:** An unattended installation can be started only from the Windows PE 2.0 environment, or from within Windows Server 2003.

3. **Correct Answer: A**

   A. **Correct:** When collocating DHCP and WDS, you must ensure that the WDS server is configured not to listen on port 67 and that the DHCP option 60 is set to PXEClient. This is done through the DHCP Settings tab of the Windows Deployment Services server properties.

   B. **Incorrect:** You cannot configure WDS to listen on an alternate port through the DHCP Server console. By default DHCP and PXE servers listen on the same port, so if both services are collocated on the same server, you must get WDS to listen on an alternate port and update DHCP—which you can do through the WDS server properties—to inform PXE clients to look on an alternate port through DHCP option 60.

   C. **Incorrect:** The DNS server is not the problem. The problem in this situation is a conflict between the DHCP and WDS servers.

   D.   **Incorrect:** The clients settings are used to set up unattended installation
        settings. The problem in this case is that WDS cannot listen on the port that
        DHCP is already listening on and must be configured to use an alternative.

4. **Correct Answer: D**

   A.   **Incorrect:** DNS information does not need to be modified to support WDS.

   B.   **Incorrect:** It is not necessary to configure a special IPv6 DHCP scope for
        PXE clients.

   C.   **Incorrect:** It is not necessary to configure a special IPv4 DHCP scope for
        PXE clients.

   D.   **Correct:** Routers that support multicast transmissions are required when
        using Windows Deployment Services multicast transmission functionality.
        The question indicates that the WDS server and the clients are located on
        different subnets, which hints that the router might be the problem.

5. **Correct Answer: C**

   A.   **Incorrect:** Although placing an unattended XML answer file on a shared
        folder could be made to work, it would require significant intervention
        because the servers would need to network boot into Windows PE so that
        the correct setup argument could be issued.

   B.   **Incorrect:** Unattended XML answer files are configured on a per-WDS
        server basis, not on a per-multicast transmission basis.

   C.   **Correct:** Default unattended XML answer files can be configured on a
        per-WDS server basis.

   D.   **Incorrect:** Although placing an unattended XML answer file on a removable
        USB device could work, this would require significantly greater manual
        intervention than locating the unattended XML file on the WDS server.

Case Scenario 1: Contoso's Migration to Windows Server 2008

1. Because it is not possible to upgrade to a core edition of Windows Server 2008,
    you will need to perform a migration where data is backed up, a clean installa-
    tion is performed on the existing hardware, and then the data is restored.

2. Prior to the installation of the operating system, you will need to correctly parti-
    tion the hard disk drive so that it starts from a separate system volume that does
    not host the operating system. It is also beneficial, though not necessary, to
    ensure that the server hardware includes a TPM 1.2 or later chip.

3. Windows Web Server 2008 would be the appropriate edition of Windows Server 2008 to deploy given that the server's only function will be to host the company Web site.

Case Scenario 2: Tailspin Toys Automates Windows Server 2008 Deployment

1. It is important to check that all of the older routers support multicast transmissions.

2. During WDS setup it is important to stop WDS from listening on port 67 and to ensure that all DHCP scopes have option 60 set.

3. Create a multicast transmission that will not start until 10 clients have connected to the WDS server.

Chapter 2: Lesson Review Answers

Lesson 1

1. **Correct Answer: B**

    A. **Incorrect:** ARP is a broadcast-based protocol used by IPv4 to resolve MAC addresses to IPv4 addresses. ND uses ICMPv6 messages to manage the interaction of neighboring nodes.

    B. **Correct:** ND uses ICMPv6 messages to manage the interaction of neighboring nodes.

    C. **Incorrect:** DHCPv6 assigns stateful IPv6 configurations. ND uses ICMPv6 messages to manage the interaction of neighboring nodes.

    D. **Incorrect:** EUI-64 is not a protocol. It is a standard for 64-bit hardware addresses.

2. **Correct Answer: A**

    A. **Correct:** The solicited mode address consists of the 104-bit prefix ff02::1:ff (written ff02::1:ff00:0/104) followed by the last 24 bits of the link-local address, in this case a7:d43a.

    B. **Incorrect:** Although the 104-bit prefix is written ff02::1:ff00:0/104, the /104 indicates that only the first 104 bits (ff02::1:ff) are used. Hence the solicited mode address is ff02::1:ffa7:d43a.

C. **Incorrect:** Addresses that start with fec0 are site-local, not solicited node.

D. **Incorrect:** This answer is incorrect for the reason given for answer C.

3. **Correct Answer: C**

A. **Incorrect:** A site-local unicast IPv6 address identifies a node in a site or intranet. It is the equivalent of an IPv6 private address, for example 10.0.0.1.

B. **Incorrect:** A link-local unicast IPv6 address is autoconfigured on a local subnet. It is the equivalent of an IPv4 APIPA address, for example 169.254.10.123.

C. **Correct:** A global unicast address (or aggregatable global unicast address) is the IPv6 equivalent of an IPv4 public unicast address and is globally routable and reachable on the 6Bone.

D. **Incorrect:** Two special IPv6 addresses exist. The unspecified address :: indicates the absence of an address and is equivalent to the IPv4 unspecified address 0.0.0.0. The loopback address ::1 identifies a loopback interface and is equivalent to the IPv4 loopback address 127.0.0.1. Neither is the IPv6 equivalent of an IPv4 public unicast address.

4. **Correct Answer: A**

A. **Correct:** In configured tunneling, data passes through a preconfigured tunnel using encapsulation. The IPv6 packet is carried inside an IPv4 packet. The encapsulating IPv4 header is created at the tunnel entry point and removed at the tunnel exit point. The tunnel endpoint addresses are determined by from configuration information.

B. **Incorrect:** Dual stack requires that hosts and routers provide support for both protocols and can send and receive both IPv4 and IPv6 packets. Tunneling is not required.

C. **Incorrect:** ISATAP connects IPv6 hosts and routers over an IPv4 network using a process that views the IPv4 network as a link layer for IPv6, and other nodes on the network as potential IPv6 hosts or routers. This creates a host-to-host, host-to-router, or router-to-host automatic tunnel. A preconfigured tunnel is not required.

D. **Incorrect:** Teredo is an enhancement to the 6-to-4 method. It enables nodes that are located behind an IPv4 NAT device to obtain IPv6 connectivity by using UDP to tunnel packets. Teredo requires the use of server and relay elements to assist with path connectivity. It does not require a preconfigured tunnel.

5. **Correct Answer: D**

   A. **Incorrect:** This command displays the IPv6 configuration on all interfaces. It does not configure an IPv6 address.

   B. **Incorrect:** You can use this command to add the IPv6 address of, for example, a DNS server to an IPv6 configuration. You use *netsh interface ipv6 set address* to configure a static IPv6 address.

   C. **Incorrect:** This command lets you change IPv6 interface properties but not an IPv6 address. You use *netsh interface ipv6 set address* to configure a static IPv6 address.

   D. **Correct:** You use *netsh interface ipv6 set address* to configure a static IPv6 address.

6. **Correct Answers: A, D, F, and G**

   A. **Correct:** IPv4 and IPv6 are both supported by Trey's network hardware and service provider. Dual stack is the most straightforward transition strategy.

   B. **Incorrect:** Trey does not need to encapsulate IPv6 packets inside IPv4 packets. Configured tunneling transition is typically employed if IPv6 is not currently available.

   C. **Incorrect:** Trey saw no need to configure NAT and use private IPv4 addresses. The organization is unlikely to use site-local addresses, which are the IPv6 equivalent of private addresses.

   D. **Correct:** Trey uses public IPv4 addresses throughout its network. It is likely to use global unicast addresses in its IPv6 network.

   E. **Incorrect:** Trey's clients run Windows Vista Ultimate edition and its servers run Windows Server 2008. All Trey's clients and servers support IPv6 and the protocol is installed by default.

   F. **Correct:** There is no guarantee that Trey's network projectors and network printers support IPv6, although they probably do because the company believes in investing in cutting-edge technology.

   G. **Correct:** Network management systems need to be checked for IPv6 compatibility.

   H. **Incorrect:** High-level applications are typically independent of the Internet protocol used.

Lesson 2

1. **Correct Answer: B**

   A. **Incorrect:** The zone is AD DS integrated so you need to use the */DsPrimary* switch. You specify */Primary* for file-based DNS, in which case you also need to specify a filename.

   B. **Correct:** This creates the correct type of zone and the address prefix is in the correct format.

   C. **Incorrect:** The in-addr.arpa designation is used for IPv4 Reverse Lookup zones. Also the zone type is specified incorrectly.

   D. **Incorrect:** You need to use 4-bit nibbles in reverse order to specify the address prefix. You cannot use slash notation in the *dnscmd* command.

2. **Correct Answer: A**

   A. **Correct:** You cannot list DNS records by using *nslookup* unless you have allowed zone transfers, even when the records are on the same computer.

   B. **Incorrect:** You run the Command Console as an administrator when using configuration commands such as *dnscmd*. You do not need to do so when you are displaying but not changing information.

   C. **Incorrect:** You can enter **nslookup ls –d adatum.internal** directly from the command prompt. However you can also enter **nslookup** and then enter **ls –d adatum.internal** from the nslookup> prompt.

   D. **Incorrect:** You can perform most operations on a server, including nslookup, by logging on through a Remote Desktop connection. Logging on to servers interactively is bad practice and should be avoided.

3. **Correct Answer: D**

   A. **Incorrect:** There is no problem with the host record for the Web server. Other users can access the internal Web site.

   B. **Incorrect:** You do not need to flush the DNS cache on the DNS server. The problem is at the user's client computer.

   C. **Incorrect:** The client computer is registered in DNS and can access other Web sites.

   D. **Correct:** A DNS cache entry on the client computer has marked the Web site URL as not resolvable. Flushing the DNS cache solves the problem.

Case Scenario 1: Implementing IPv6 Connectivity

1. Site-local IPv6 addresses are the direct equivalent of private IPv4 addresses and are routable between VLANs. However, you could also consider configuring every device on your network with an aggregatable global unicast IPv6 address. NAT and CIDR were introduced to address the problem of a lack of IPv4 address space, and this is not a problem in IPv6. You cannot use only link-local IPv6 addresses in this situation because they are not routable.

2. Both IPv4 and IPv6 stacks are available. In this scenario, dual stack is the most straightforward transition strategy.

3. As with DHCP for IPv4, you should configure a dual-scope DHCPv6 server on each subnet. The scope for the local subnet on each server should include 80 percent of the full IPv6 address range for that subnet. The scope for the remote subnet on each server should include the remaining 20 percent of the full IPv6 address range for that subnet.

Case Scenario 2: Configuring DNS

1. You can configure secure dynamic updates. This ensures that only authenticated users and clients can register information in DNS.

2. You can configure zone replication to occur only with DNS servers that have NS records and are on the Name Server list. Alternatively, you can manually specify a list of servers and configure zone replication so that zone information is replicated only to these servers.

3. When a Windows Server 2008 server is configured as an RODC it replicates a read-only copy of all Active Directory partitions that DNS uses, including the domain partition, ForestDNSZones, and DomainDNSZones. Therefore DNS zone information on RODCs updates automatically.

4. Create an IPv6 Reverse Lookup zone.

Chapter 3: Lesson Review Answers

Lesson 1

1. **Correct Answers: A and B**

   A. **Correct:** Typically you apply a PSO to a global security group.

B. **Correct:** You can apply a PSO to a domain user account, although it is better practice to apply it to a global security group and place the domain user account in that group.

C. **Incorrect:** You cannot apply a PSO directly to an OU. If you want to apply it to user accounts in an OU you need to create a special group, which is a global distribution group that contains all the user accounts in the OU.

D. **Incorrect:** A global distribution group is used to create an Exchange mail list. You cannot associate a PSO with a global distribution group.

E. **Incorrect:** You cannot associate a PSO with a computer account.

2. **Correct Answer: C**

A. **Incorrect:** You can control which AD DS operations you want to audit by modifying the system access control list (SACL) of an object. The SACL is not a tool and you cannot use it to view AD data stored in snapshots.

B. **Incorrect:** The Password Settings Container (PSC) object is created by default under the System container in the domain. It stores the Password Settings Objects (PSOs) for that domain. The PSC is not a tool and you cannot use it to view Active Directory data stored in snapshots.

C. **Correct:** You can use the AD DS data mining tool to view Active Directory data stored in snapshots online, compare data in snapshots that are taken at different times, and decide which data to restore without having to restart the DC.

D. **Incorrect:** The AD DS Installation tool (or wizard) lets you specify whether you are installing a writable DC or an RODC. You cannot use it to view Active Directory data stored in snapshots.

3. **Correct Answer: B**

A. **Incorrect:** Forest trusts are between forests. Windows NT4 does not recognize the concept of a forest.

B. **Correct:** External trusts are used when migrating resources from Windows NT domains. Windows NT does not use the concept of forests; a Windows NT4 domain is a self-contained, autonomous unit. You would use an external trust when you plan to migrate resources from a Windows NT4 domain into an existing Active Directory forest.

C. **Incorrect:** You use a realm trust when accessing resources in a UNIX realm. You would not use a realm trust if you plan to migrate resources from a Windows NT4 domain into an existing Active Directory forest.

D. **Incorrect:** If users in one child domain frequently need to access resources in another child domain in another forest, you might decide to create a shortcut trust between the two domains. You would not use a shortcut trust if you plan to migrate resources from a Windows NT4 domain into an existing Active Directory forest.

4. **Correct Answer: D**

A. **Incorrect:** Password Replication Policy is configured by connecting Active Directory Users And Computers to a writable DC, not an RODC. Your branch office colleague does not have the rights required to configure this policy.

B. **Incorrect:** Password Replication Policy cannot be configured in Server Manager. Also, it is very bad practice to add users who may not have the appropriate skills to the Domain Admins group.

C. **Incorrect:** Password Replication Policy cannot be configured in Server Manager.

D. **Correct:** A domain administrator can configure Password Replication Policy by opening Active Directory Users And Computers and ensuring that the tool is connected to a writable DC.

5. **Correct Answer: C**

A. **Incorrect:** Windows 2000 forest functional level does not support forest trusts.

B. **Incorrect:** Windows 2000 native is a domain functional level, not a forest functional level. It does not support forest trusts,

C. **Correct:** Windows Server 2003 forest functional level supports forest trusts.

D. **Incorrect:** Windows Server 2008 forest functional level supports forest trusts. However, the minimum forest functional level that supports forest trusts is Windows Server 2003.

6. **Correct Answer: B**

A. **Incorrect:** Windows 2008 domain functional level supports *netdom.exe*. However, it does not support Windows Server 2003 DCs.

B. **Correct:** Windows Server 2003 domain functional level supports Windows Server 2003 DCs, Windows Server 2008 DCs, and *netdom.exe*.

C. **Incorrect:** Windows Server 2000 native domain functional level does not support *netdom.exe*.

D.   Incorrect: Windows 2000 mixed domain functional level is not available in a domain that contains Windows Server 2008 DCs. Also, it does not support *netdom.exe*.

Lesson 2

1.   **Correct Answers: A and E**

   A.   Correct: The Disk Diagnostic: Configure Execution Level Computer-Based Policy setting requires that Desktop Experience be installed on a Windows Server 2008 server. It determines the execution level for SMART-based disk diagnostics.

   B.   Incorrect: The Do Not Allow Clipboard Redirection user-based policy setting specifies whether to prevent the sharing of clipboard contents between a remote computer and a client computer during a Terminal Services session. It does not require that Desktop Experience be installed on a Windows Server 2008 server.

   C.   Incorrect: The Enforce Removal Of Remote Desktop Wallpaper user-based policy setting specifies whether desktop wallpaper is displayed on remote clients connecting via Terminal Services. It does not require that Desktop Experience be installed on a Windows Server 2008 server.

   D.   Incorrect: The Set Update Interval To NIS Subordinate computer-based policy setting allows you to set an update interval for pushing Network Information Service (NIS) maps to NIS subordinate servers. It does not require that Desktop Experience be installed on a Windows Server 2008 server.

   E.   Correct: The Disk Diagnostic: Configure Custom Alert Text computer-based policy setting requires that Desktop Experience be installed on a Windows Server 2008 server. It substitutes custom alert text in the disk diagnostic message shown to users when a disk reports a SMART fault.

2.   **Correct Answers: A, C, and D**

   A.   Correct: The Allow Time Zone Redirection user-based policy setting determines whether the client computer redirects its time zone settings to the Terminal Services session.

   B.   Incorrect: The Disk Diagnostic: Configure Execution Level computer-based policy setting determines the execution level for SMART-based disk diagnostics. It is not associated with Terminal Services.

    C. **Correct:** The Do Not Allow Clipboard Redirection user-based policy setting specifies whether to prevent the sharing of clipboard contents (clipboard redirection) between a remote computer and a client computer during a Terminal Services session.

    D. **Correct:** The Enforce Removal Of Remote Desktop Wallpaper user-based policy setting specifies whether desktop wallpaper is displayed on remote clients connecting via Terminal Services.

    E. **Incorrect:** The Turn On Extensive Logging For SNIS DCs computer-based policy setting allows you to manage the extensive logging feature for SNIS DCs. It is not associated with Terminal Services.

3. **Correct Answers: B, C, and E**

    A. **Incorrect:** Although having too many GPOs (often with the same settings) is a common mistake, it is also a bad idea to have too few. If a GPO has a lot of policy settings configured in different areas it can be difficult to understand everything it does or to give it a descriptive name. Linking GPOs to OUs across sites can slow replication and increase traffic over slow WAN links.

    B. **Correct:** If you put ADMX files in a central store on a DC, they can be replicated to other DCs in your domain. The Group Policy Object Editor does not copy ADMX files to each edited GPO but instead reads them from a single domain-level location or central store. This speeds up the process and reduces network traffic. Also, if you decide to generate custom ADMX files you can put them in the central store and they will be read (or consumed) by the Group Policy Object Editor.

    C. **Correct:** Both GPOs and OUs should have descriptive names. You might know what GPO06 does right now, but will you remember in three months' time? If you had called it (for example) Kiosk Policy, its function would be much clearer. Similarly, an OU named Human Resources is more helpful than OU23.

    D. **Incorrect:** Features such as block inheritance, no override, security filtering, and loopback policies can be useful in the situations for which they were designed. However, they add complexity and make your Group Policy design more difficult to understand. You should use these exceptions only where you can identify a real advantage in doing so.

E.   **Correct:** Even if changes to a GPO have been replicated across the domain they do not take effect until the next time Group Policy is refreshed. The *gpupdate* command forces a policy refresh. You can use the command on a DC or on any member server or client on the domain where you want Group Policy changes to take effect immediately.

4.   **Correct Answer: D**

A.   **Incorrect:** The *Policies* element contains the individual policy setting definitions. It does not contain version number or encoding information.

B.   **Incorrect:** The *SupportedOn* element specifies references to localized text strings defining the operating systems or applications affected by a specific policy setting. It does not contain version number or encoding information.

C.   **Incorrect:** The *PolicyNamespaces* element defines the unique namespace for the ADMX file. It does not contain version number or encoding information.

D.   **Correct:** The XML declaration is required to validate the file as an XML-based file. It contains version number and encoding information.

Case Scenario 1: Planning a Windows Server 2003 Upgrade

1.   Windows Server 2008 introduces fine-grained password policies that enable settings other than the default to be set for specified users or security groups. In Windows 2003 domains, variations in password policy typically require additional domains.

2.   There is no need to raise the forest functional level to Windows Server 2008 during this upgrade because the Windows Server 2003 forest functional level supports all the new features. The eventual plan is to raise the domain functional level to Windows Server 2008 to take advantage of (for example) fine-grained password policies, but this need not be done until all DCs are running Windows Server 2008. Domain and forest functional levels do not affect member severs. A Windows 2000 Server member server can operate in a domain with a Windows Server 2008 domain and forest functional level.

3.   Windows Server 2008 RODCs can be installed at branch offices, possibly on the servers that currently host the secondary DNS servers. This improves logon speed while avoiding the security and administration issues that would result from placing writable DCs at these locations.

Case Scenario 2: Planning and Documenting Troubleshooting Procedures

1. The first thing to check is whether the user should have access to the facilities. The colleagues he mentions could, for example, work in another department. The next procedure is to determine the resultant set of policy (RoSP) for that user. This can be done through GPMC or by using the *GPResult.exe* tool. Finally, look at factors that might delay the application of policy changes to that particular user. For example, the policy change might have been applied recently and the user needs to log off and back on again, or it might be necessary to run *gpupdate* on the user's computer.

2. If problems are computer-related rather than user-related, the first thing to check is the network infrastructure. Is the computer plugged into the network? Are services running? Has the computer received the correct configuration through DHCP? Are there DNS problems? Next, check that the computer is in the correct OU. If recent changes have been made to Group Policy settings, run *gpupdate* on the computer.

3. Does Group Policy Results list the GPO as applied? Is the setting listed in Group Policy Results Report? Is the GPO listed in the Denied List?

Chapter 4: Lesson Review Answers

Lesson 1

1. **Correct Answer: B**

    A. **Incorrect:** ASF adds the .NET Framework 3.0 features to the .NET Framework 2.0, which is included in Windows Server 2008. IIS7 does not use ASF to implement message-based activation over HTTP.

    B. **Correct:** WAS is a new process activation mechanism for the Windows Vista and the Windows Server 2008 operating systems. IIS7 uses WAS to implement message-based activation over HTTP.

    C. **Incorrect:** The Net.TCP Port Sharing Service makes it possible for multiple applications to use a single TCP port for incoming communications. IIS7 does not use Net.TCP port sharing to implement message-based activation over HTTP.

D. **Incorrect:** Distributed transactions makes the MS DTC available to the Application Server server role. Applications that connect to and perform updates on multiple databases or other transactional resources distributed across a network may require that these updates are performed on an all-or-nothing basis. MS DTC provides this functionality. IIS7 does not use distributed transactions to implement message-based activation over HTTP.

2. **Correct Answers: A, B, and C**

A. **Correct:** WCF is a .NET Framework 3.0 component. It is the Microsoft programming model for building service-oriented applications that use Web services to communicate with each other.

B. **Correct:** WPF is a .NET Framework 3.0 component. It is the Microsoft programming model that developers use to build Windows smart-client applications.

C. **Correct:** WF is a .NET Framework 3.0 component. It is the Microsoft programming model that enables developers to build workflow-enabled applications on Windows Server 2008.

D. **Incorrect:** WAS is not a .NET Framework 3.0 component. It is a feature of the Application Server server role that IIS7 uses to implement message-based activation over HTTP.

E. **Incorrect:** MS DTC is not a .NET Framework 3.0 component. It is installed by the distributed transactions feature of the Application Server server role and enables applications that connect to and perform updates on multiple databases or other transactional resources distributed across a network to perform these updates on an all-or-nothing basis.

3. **Correct Answer: D**

A. **Incorrect:** The Accessibility Wizard, used in earlier Windows operating systems, is replaced in Windows Server 2008 by the questionnaire provided by the Ease Of Access Center.

B. **Incorrect:** The Ease Of Access Center replaces the Utility Center that was provided by earlier Windows operating systems.

C. **Incorrect:** The Windows Server 2008 Ease Of Access Center provides a centralized location for accessibility settings and programs that were found in Accessibility Options in previous Windows operating systems.

   D. **Correct:** Windows Server 2008 introduces the Ease Of Access Center, which provides a centralized location for accessibility settings and programs that used to be found in Accessibility Options and implements the functionality previously provided by Utility Center and the Accessibility Wizard.

4. **Correct Answer: A**

   A. **Correct:** Newer applications typically use WCF to support remote invocation because WCF provides loose coupling, which makes integrated systems less dependent on each other and provides interoperability across multiple platforms.

   B. **Incorrect:** WF is the Microsoft programming model that enables developers to build workflow-enabled applications on Windows Server 2008. It does not support remote invocation.

   C. **Incorrect:** WAS is not an ASF component. It is a feature of the Application Server server role that IIS7 uses to implement message-based activation over HTTP. It does not support remote invocation.

   D. **Incorrect:** WPF is the Microsoft programming model that developers use to build Windows smart-client applications. It does not support remote invocation.

5. **Correct Answer: C**

   A. **Incorrect:** If you assign the software at logon to all users in the OU, the software installs on a per-user basis the first time that a user logs on at the computer, not at power on. If a user who is not in that OU logs on, the software does not install for that user. This is not what is required.

   B. **Incorrect:** Publishing the software to all users in the OU lets a user choose whether to install (or uninstall) the software by using Programs And Features in Control Panel. The software also installs through document invocation.

   C. **Correct:** When you assign the software to all computers in the OU, the software (and any subsequent update) is installed when the computer turns on. The software is available to any user that logs on at the computer.

   D. **Incorrect:** You cannot publish software to a computer.

Lesson 2

1. **Correct Answers: A, C, and D**

   A. **Correct:** The wizard prompts you for the applications and versions you want to update, such as Exchange Server 2007, the 2007 Office system, and so on.

   B. **Incorrect:** An image file is used when installing an operating system and sometimes also pre-staged applications that are installed on all clients that run the operating system. It is not used for updates.

   C. **Correct:** The wizard prompts you for your update language or languages.

   D. **Correct:** The wizard prompts you for the types of updates you want to install, such as critical and security updates.

   E. **Incorrect:** The wizard prompts you for update installation preferences. However, installation settings, such as silent install, are specified for application and operating system installation, not for update.

2. **Correct Answers: B, D, and E**

   A. **Incorrect:** For security reasons the System Center Configuration Manager 2007 site needs to be in native mode when you manage clients over the Internet.

   B. **Correct:** Targeting software distribution to users relies on Active Directory information. You cannot do this when you manage clients over the Internet.

   C. **Incorrect:** You can distribute updates, including security updates, to clients over the Internet.

   D. **Correct:** NAP is not appropriate to a public network. You cannot use this feature when managing clients over the Internet.

   E. **Correct:** Wake On LAN is not appropriate to a public WAN. You cannot use this feature when managing clients over the Internet.

   F. **Incorrect:** You can create both hardware and software inventories for clients that you manage over the Internet.

3. **Correct Answers: D, E, and F**

   A. **Incorrect:** If the server operating system meets the prerequisite for installing System Center Configuration Manager 2007, the Wake On LAN feature can be used. Wake On LAN does not depend upon the server operating system.

B.   **Incorrect:** This is a prerequisite for NAP, not for Wake On LAN.

C.   **Incorrect:** USMT 3.0 provides user state migration. It is not associated with Wake On LAN.

D.   **Correct:** System Configuration Manager 2007 client software must be installed on the computer to enable you to use the tool to manage the computer, including using the Wake On LAN feature.

E.   **Correct:** The client network card must support magic packet format to enable it to receive and interpret the Wake On LAN packet.

F.   **Correct:** The client BIOS must be configured for wake-up packets on the network card. Otherwise the client will not respond to the wake-up packet.

4.   **Correct Answer: A**

A.   **Correct:** The Summary Information Of Clients In Native Mode report identifies clients that have successfully switched their site mode configuration.

B.   **Incorrect:** You can use the Client Assignment Failure Details report to help you track and monitor client deployment for Configuration Manager 2007 clients. It does not tell you which clients have successfully switched their site mode configuration.

C.   **Incorrect:** Summary Information Of Clients Capable Of Native Mode report identifies clients that can be switched to native site mode. It does not identify clients that have successfully switched their site mode configuration.

D.   **Incorrect:** The Clients Incapable Of Native Mode report identifies clients that cannot be switched to native site mode. It does not identify clients that have successfully switched their site mode configuration.

Case Scenario 1: Planning LOB Application Resilience

1.   You need assurances that Windows Installer entry points are provided when any LOB application in the suite is accessed through a shortcut, through invocation, or through COM advertising.

2.   Windows Installer checks the Darwin Descriptor for a COM component. This is stored in the InprocServer32 registry value.

3.   You should be concerned about the following:

   ❑   Scheduled applications

   ❑   Applications that run from the command line

❑ Applications that run as system services

❑ Applications that initially access the operating system

❑ Applications that call other applications

Case Scenario 2: Managing Clients and Deploying Software

1. In this situation you would recommend System Center Configuration Manager 2007. Although System Center Essentials 2007 meets the specification and will operate on the current network, the organization is expanding and is likely to have more than 30 servers or 500 clients in the near future. In addition, System Center Configuration Manager 2007 will manage Pocket PCs and will manage remote laptops over the Internet. The tool provides features such as NAP, Wake On LAN, and software metering that will help make client management more efficient. Also, the main prerequisites for installing System Center Configuration Manager 2007 have already been met.

2. The software metering feature in System Center Configuration Manager 2007 will indicate what software is used on client computers, rather than what software is installed. This will enable software licensing to be rationalized when licenses are due for renewal.

3. The NAP feature of System Center Configuration Manager 2007 will allow only restricted network access to noncompliant client computers. If the software updates feature is configured and enabled, remediation can bring such computers into a compliant state and then permit full network access. NAP requires that a Windows Server 2008 server configured with the Network Policy Server role exists on the network. It is probably a bad idea to install this role on a DC, so a real or virtual Windows Server 2008 member server is required on the network.

Chapter 5: Lesson Review Answers

Lesson 1

1. **Correct Answer: A**

    A. **Correct:** The Equal_Per_User WSRM policy ensures that a user connected to a Terminal Server with two concurrent sessions is assigned the same resources as a user connected with a single session.

B. **Incorrect:** The Equal_Per_Session WSRM policy ensures that each session connected to a Terminal Server is allocated equal resources. When this policy is enforced, a user connected with two sessions will be allocated more system resources than a user connected with a single session.

C. **Incorrect:** Resource allocation cannot be configured by editing the properties of a server in Terminal Server Management Console. Resource allocation can only be managed using Windows System Resource Manager.

D. **Incorrect:** Resource allocation cannot be configured by editing the RDP-Tcp properties. Resource allocation can only be managed using Windows System Resource Manager.

2. **Correct Answer: A**

A. **Correct:** If a license server's discovery scope is set to domain, only computers within the local domain will be able to request CALs from that server.

B. **Incorrect:** If a license server's discovery scope is set to forest, it is possible that clients from other domains in the forest will acquire licenses from it even if there is a server closer to them—for example, when their local server runs out of CALs.

C. **Incorrect:** A license server located in the root domain with a scope set to forest will provide CALs to clients in the forest, but will not do so in a way that meets with the location requirements of the scenario.

D. **Incorrect:** A license server located in the root domain with a scope set to domain will only provide CALs to clients in the root domain, not in the specific branch office locations mentioned in the question.

3. **Correct Answers: A and C**

A. **Correct:** It is necessary to set the license server scope prior to installing CALs on a TS license server.

B. **Incorrect:** It is not necessary to set the domain functional level to Windows Server 2008 to install licenses on a Terminal Server license server.

C. **Correct:** It is necessary to activate the TS license server prior to the installation of CALs.

D. **Incorrect:** Terminal Server license servers can issue both per-device and per-user CALs.

E. **Incorrect:** It is not necessary to install IIS on a TS license server.

4. **Correct Answer: D**

    A. **Incorrect:** Using WSRM policies will not enable capacity to be added as needed.

    B. **Incorrect:** Hyper-V would not work as a solution because there is an upper limit to processor capacity on the virtual host. This solution requires the ability to add processor capacity as required.

    C. **Incorrect:** Although adding Terminal Servers would meet emerging capacity needs, it would not meet the requirement that clients do not need to be reconfigured.

    D. **Correct:** Planning the deployment of a Terminal Server farm allows you to add and remove servers from the farm as necessary without altering client configuration.

5. **Correct Answer: C**

    A. **Incorrect:** OneCare Live and other anti-virus solutions can check for viruses and malware after a client connection has been made, but cannot block unhealthy clients from connecting.

    B. **Incorrect:** TS Session Broker is used to manage sessions that connect to Terminal Server farms—you cannot use it to ensure that connecting clients pass health checks.

    C. **Correct:** A TS Gateway Server can be used in conjunction with Network Access Protection to disallow computers that have not passed a health check to connect to the Terminal Server.

    D. **Incorrect:** ISA Server 2006 cannot be used to block clients from connecting to a Terminal Server if they do not pass a health check. It is possible to use Network Access Protection in conjunction with ISA Server 2006 but not specifically to block access to Terminal Services clients.

Lesson 2

1. **Correct Answer: B**

    A. **Incorrect:** Virtual Server Migration Toolkit is a more appropriate tool to virtualize a small number of existing servers.

    B. **Correct:** System Center Virtual Machine Manager 2007 can be used to move virtualized servers between virtual hosts over a Fibre Channel SAN.

Because you cannot use other types of tools to accomplish this type of migration, it presents the most compelling case for the deployment of System Center Virtual Machine Manager 2007.

C. **Incorrect:** You can use System Center Virtual Machine Manager 2007 to manage and monitor thousands of virtual machines. Although it is possible to manage just 10 virtual machines using this product, the built-in Hyper-V tools are more than adequate to such a task. Because one answer in this set requires System Center Virtual Machine Manager 2007, this answer is not the most compelling.

D. **Incorrect:** Automating server deployment is accomplished through Windows Deployment Services rather than System Center Virtual Machine Manager.

2. **Correct Answer: A**

A. **Correct:** It is only possible to install the Hyper-V role on an x64 version of Windows Server 2008. It is possible to install Hyper-V on a Server Core computer.

B. **Incorrect:** It is only possible to install the Hyper-V role on an x64 version of Windows Server 2008.

C. **Incorrect:** It is only possible to install the Hyper-V role on an x64 version of Windows Server 2008.

D. **Incorrect:** It is only possible to install the Hyper-V role on an x64 version of Windows Server 2008.

3. **Correct Answers: A, B, and C**

A. **Correct:** It is possible to access RemoteApp applications through a Web page and you can deploy Web page bookmarks through Group Policy.

B. **Correct:** It is possible to create Windows Installer Packages for RemoteApp applications and to deploy these packages through Group Policy.

C. **Correct:** It is possible to create RDP shortcuts and to place these on accessible shared folders to allow users to access RemoteApp applications.

D. **Incorrect:** RemoteApp does not work by executing applications on shared folders, but by executing the applications on the Terminal Server. Applications can be deployed using TS Web Access pages, through Windows Installer Packages, and through RDP shortcuts.

4. **Correct Answer: C**

   A. **Incorrect:** You should use Microsoft Application Virtualization—TS RemoteApp will not resolve the problem of applications conflicting when installed on the same Terminal Server.

   B. **Incorrect:** You should use Microsoft Application Virtualization—a TS Gateway Server will not resolve the problem of applications conflicting when installed on the same Terminal Server.

   C. **Correct:** Microsoft Application Virtualization allows applications that would normally conflict—including different versions of the same application—to be deployed from the same Terminal Server.

   D. **Incorrect:** You should use Microsoft Application Virtualization—TS Web Access will not resolve the problem of applications conflicting when installed on the same Terminal Server.

5. **Correct Answer: C**

   A. **Incorrect:** The problem is caused by the most recent version of the RDC software not being installed. Installing Internet Explorer 6.0 will not resolve this problem.

   B. **Incorrect:** Disabling the Windows XP firewall will not resolve this problem—it is necessary to install the most recent version of the RDC software, which is included in Windows XP SP3.

   C. **Correct:** Windows XP clients need the version of the RDC software shipped with Windows XP SP 3 to connect to RemoteApp applications using TS Web Access.

   D. **Incorrect:** Installing Windows Defender will not resolve this problem. It will be necessary to install the most recent version of the RDC software, which is included with Windows XP SP3.

Case Scenario 1: Tailspin Toys Server Consolidation

1. Install the 64-bit version of Windows Server 2003 Enterprise Edition and deploy Hyper-V. Virtualize the server that hosts the domain controller, DNS, and DHCP services on one virtual server. Virtualize the server that hosts the SQL Server 2000 database and individually virtualize each of the servers hosting the business application. This would require one physical server. It would also be possible to upgrade the existing servers to Windows Server 2008 without requiring

extra licenses because the Enterprise Edition includes four licenses for virtualized instances of Windows Server 2008.

2. Although it would be possible to virtualize each Terminal Server, this would not meet the goal of reducing the number of Terminal Servers–though it would meet the goal of minimizing the amount of server hardware. In this situation, you can reduce the amount of hardware and Terminal Servers by deploying Microsoft Application Virtualization, which allows applications to run in virtualized silos so that they do not conflict with each other. Rather than virtualizing the server, this solution virtualizes the applications.

Case Scenario 2: Planning a Terminal Services Strategy for Wingtip Toys

1. Deploy a TS license server in each state office. Set the server to use the domain discovery scope.

2. Create a Terminal Service farm using TS Session Broker.

3. To access RemoteApp applications through TS Web Access it is necessary to upgrade Windows Vista clients to SP1 and Windows XP clients to SP3.

Chapter 6: Lesson Review Answers

Lesson 1

1. **Correct Answers: A and C**

   A. **Correct:** You access the Provision A Shared Folder Wizard from the Share And Storage Management console.

   B. **Incorrect:** You access the New Namespace Wizard from Namespaces in the DFS Management console.

   C. **Correct:** You access the Provision Storage Wizard from the Share And Storage Management console. The wizard starts only if the server can access disks with unallocated space or storage subsystems with available storage for which a VDS hardware provider is installed.

   D. **Incorrect:** You do not use a wizard to create quotas. You can access the Create Quota dialog box from Quotas in the File Server Resource Manager console.

E. **Incorrect:** You do not use a wizard to create file screens. You can access the Create File Screen dialog box from File Screens in the File Server Resource Manager console.

2. **Correct Answers: A, B, and D**

A. **Correct:** You can use the Provision A Shared Folder Wizard to share an existing folder.

B. **Correct:** You can use the Provision A Shared Folder Wizard to create and share a folder.

C. **Incorrect:** You have not installed the Services For Network File System (NFS) role service. Therefore, SMB is the only network sharing protocol available and you cannot change it.

D. **Correct:** Provided that the shared resource is on (or is) an NTFS-formatted volume, you can configure local NTFS permissions with the Provision A Shared Folder Wizard.

E. **Incorrect:** You have not installed the Distributed File System (DFS) server role. Therefore, you cannot publish the shared resource to a DFS namespace.

3. **Correct Answer: D**

A. **Incorrect:** You can use the Print Management console to change printer ports for a printer on a remote server. However, you could previously change ports on a local server, so this task is not new to the Print Management console.

B. **Incorrect:** You can use the Print Management console to view the printer status for a printer on a remote server. However, you could previously view the printer status on a local server, so this task is not new to the Print Management console.

C. **Incorrect:** You can use the Print Management console to add or modify forms for a printer on a remote server. However, you could previously add or modify forms on a local server, so this task is not new to the Print Management console.

D. **Correct:** Custom printer filters allow you and other administrators to view and manage selected printers based on their site, rights, and roles. This task is new to the Print Management console.

4. **Correct Answer: C**

   A. **Incorrect:** In Windows Server 2008, quotas can be typically applied to both volumes and shared folders. In previous Windows Server releases they could be applied only to volumes. The 100 MB Limit template creates a hard quota (cannot be exceeded) that can be applied to both volumes and shared folders.

   B. **Incorrect:** In Windows Server 2008, quotas can be typically applied to both volumes and shared folders. In previous Windows Server releases they could be applied only to volumes. The 200 MB Limit Reports To User template creates a hard quota (cannot be exceeded) that can be applied to both volumes and shared folders.

   C. **Correct:** In Windows Server 2008, quotas can be typically applied to both volumes and shared folders. In previous Windows Server releases they could be applied only to volumes. However, the Monitor 200 GB Volume Usage template creates a soft quota (can be exceeded and is used for monitoring) that can be applied to volumes only.

   D. **Incorrect:** In Windows Server 2008, quotas can be typically applied to both volumes and shared folders. In previous Windows Server releases they could be applied only to volumes. However, the Monitor 50 MB Share Usage template creates a soft quota (can be exceeded and is used for monitoring) that can be applied to shared folders only.

Lesson 2

1. **Correct Answers: B and C**

   A. **Incorrect:** Windows Server 2008 Standard can support only a single DFS namespace. It can support Windows Server 2008 mode.

   B. **Correct:** Windows Server 2008 Enterprise can support multiple DFS namespaces. It can also support Windows Server 2008 mode.

   C. **Correct:** Windows Server 2008 Datacenter can support multiple DFS namespaces. It can also support Windows Server 2008 mode.

   D. **Incorrect:** Windows Server 2003 R2, Datacenter Edition can support multiple DFS namespaces. However, it cannot support Windows Server 2008 mode.

E. **Incorrect:** Windows Server 2003 R2, Enterprise Edition can support multiple DFS namespaces. However, it cannot support Windows Server 2008 mode.

2. **Correct Answers: A, B, and D**

A. **Correct:** A stand-alone namespace can support more than 5000 DFS folders regardless of whether it is on a Windows Server 2008 server.

B. **Correct:** A stand-alone namespace can support more than 5000 DFS folders regardless of whether it is on a Windows Server 2008 server.

C. **Incorrect:** In a domain-based namespace in Windows 2000 Server mode the size of the namespace object in AD DS should be fewer than 5 MB (approximately 5,000 folders with targets).

D. **Correct:** A domain-based namespace in Windows Server 2008 mode can support more than 5,000 DFS folders.

3. **Correct Answer: B**

A. **Incorrect:** A file screen controls the types of files that users can save, and generates notifications when users attempt to save unauthorized files.

B. **Correct:** Access-based enumeration allows users to see only files and folders on a file server that they have permission to access.

C. **Incorrect:** A soft quota is a storage quota that a user can exceed. Soft quotas are used for monitoring.

D. **Incorrect:** A folder target in DFS is a physical shared folder that holds the data a user wants to access. DFS folders are logical entities that point to folder targets.

4. **Correct Answer: C**

A. **Incorrect:** The storage quota is 4,096 MB. However, when this limit is reached DFSR deletes old files from the staging folder to reduce the disk usage. If necessary the staging folder can also increase in size. In Windows Server 2008, the staging folder is not a hard allocation on the disk but instead uses only the disk resource it requires.

B. **Incorrect:** The quota size of each Conflict And Deleted folder is 660 MB. The quota size of a staging folder is 4,096 MB.

C. **Correct:** The storage quota is 4,096 MB. When this limit is reached DFSR deletes old files from the staging folder to reduce the disk usage. If necessary the staging folder can also increase in size. In Windows Server 2008, the staging folder is not a hard allocation on the disk but instead uses only the disk resource it requires.

D. **Incorrect:** The quota size of each Conflict And Deleted folder is 660 MB. The quota size of a staging folder is 4,096 MB.

5. **Correct Answer: D**

A. **Incorrect:** This option specifies that the user chooses the files that are synchronized and available offline. The Optimize For Performance check box is not available for this option.

B. **Incorrect:** This option specifies that the user chooses the files that are synchronized and available offline. The Optimize For Performance check box is not available for this option.

C. **Incorrect:** This option specifies that whenever a user accesses the shared folder or volume and opens a user or program file, that file or program is automatically made available offline to that user. The Optimize For Performance check box is available for this option but you need to select and not clear it to ensure that executable files that a client runs from the shared resource are automatically cached on that client, and that the next time the client needs to run one of those executable files it will access its local cache instead of the shared resource on the server.

D. **Correct:** This option specifies that whenever a user accesses the shared folder or volume and opens a user or program file, that file or program is automatically made available offline to that user. The Optimize For Performance check box is available for this option. Selecting this option ensures that executable files that a client runs from the shared resource are automatically cached on that client, and that the next time the client needs to run one of those executable files it will access its local cache instead of the shared resource on the server.

Case Scenario: Planning a Windows Server 2003 Upgrade

1. You can advise the Technical Director that multiple domain-based DFS namespaces can be configured on the company's DCs. Because the source of domain-based namespaces is hidden there is little security risk, although if hosting the namespaces puts too much load on the DCs the company might consider upgrading one or more of its member servers to Windows Server 2008

Enterprise. Because the DCs all run Windows Server 2008 Enterprise, multiple namespaces in Windows Server 2008 mode can be implemented and DFSR can be configured.

2. If you set up DFSR you can ensure that the same data can be held in several folder targets throughout the corporate network and that the files in these folder targets are consistent and up to date. This ensures failover and spreads the load on servers. Because you are using domain-based namespaces, the client computer does not need to be configured with the UNC path to a folder target. The folder targets can be moved to other servers but the DFS folders that point to these targets are accessed in a consistent fashion.

3. Windows Server 2008 lets you create and manage file screens that control the types of files users can save, and lets you generate notifications when users attempt to save unauthorized files. You can define file screening templates that you can apply to new volumes or folders and use across your organization. You can create screening exceptions so that while users cannot save video or music files on server shares, storage of specific types of media files (such as training files) is permitted. You could also create an exception that allows members of the senior management group to save any type of file they want to save.

Chapter 7: Lesson Review Answers

Lesson 1

1. **Correct Answers: A and E**

   A. **Correct:** RSAT can be installed on Windows Vista Business, Enterprise, or Ultimate editions as long as Service Pack 1 has also been deployed.

   B. **Incorrect:** The RSAT tools are not available for Windows XP at the time of Windows Server 2008's release. Administration of Windows Server 2008 from Windows XP must be performed using tools such as Remote Desktop.

   C. **Incorrect:** The RSAT tools are not available for Windows Server 2003 at the time of Windows Server 2008's release.

   D. **Incorrect:** RSAT tools cannot be installed on Windows Vista Home Basic or Windows Vista Home Premium.

   E. **Correct:** The RSAT tools can be installed as a feature on Windows Server 2008 Enterprise Edition, unless the Server Core installation option has been chosen.

2. **Correct Answers: A and B**

   A. **Correct:** By default, members of the Administrators group are able to connect to a stand-alone Windows Server 2008 computer using Remote Desktop.

   B. **Correct:** Members of the Remote Desktop Users group can connect to a stand-alone Windows Server 2008 computer even if they are not members of the Administrators local user group.

   C. **Incorrect:** Members of the Print Operators group are not automatically granted the ability to log on to a stand-alone computer using Remote Desktop.

   D. **Incorrect:** Members of the Backup Operators group are not automatically granted the ability to log on to a stand-alone server using Remote Desktop.

3. **Correct Answer: C**

   A. **Incorrect:** Remote Desktop cannot be used if the network adapters on a Windows Server 2008 computer have failed.

   B. **Incorrect:** Telnet cannot be used if the network adapters on a Windows Server 2008 computer have failed.

   C. **Correct:** Emergency Management Services provides a method of managing a server that is still operational after the failure of core hardware components.

   D. **Incorrect:** Microsoft Management Consoles either require the use of a graphics card for local management tasks or active network connections for remote management tasks.

4. **Correct Answer: A**

   A. **Correct:** Terminal Services Gateway Servers allow Remote Desktop sessions to be tunneled through a firewall on port 443. Placing a TS Gateway Server at the subsidiary office location will allow you to connect to the remote office Windows Server 2008 servers to perform administrative tasks.

   B. **Incorrect:** You should not place a Terminal Services Gateway Server at the local office because this will not grant you access to the remote office servers.

   C. **Incorrect:** Port 25 is not used for Remote Desktop Protocol.

   D. **Incorrect:** Port 25 is not used for Remote Desktop Protocol, and even if you could use port 25, your head office private IP address range would be the incorrect configuration for the firewall.

5. **Correct Answer: B**

A. **Incorrect:** Filters must be created each time they are used. Custom views are persistent and can be saved.

B. **Correct:** Custom views can be saved and will allow you to achieve the goal of viewing critical events from the Forwarded Events log that have occurred within the last 24 hours.

C. **Incorrect:** Although subscriptions can be configured only to extract critical event data, the question asked for the ability to view only critical events, not to collect only critical events. The difference is that with a subscription you can collect all types of events and then apply a custom view to show only specific events.

D. **Incorrect:** You should not configure a Windows System Resource Manager Policy. WSRM policies are unrelated to Event Logs.

Lesson 2

1. **Correct Answer: C**

A. **Incorrect:** Microsoft System Center Operations Manager 2007 cannot be used to configure policies that bind device interrupts to specific processors on multiprocessor computers.

B. **Incorrect:** Windows System Resource Manager cannot be used to configure policies that bind device interrupts to specific processors on multiprocessor computers.

C. **Correct:** The Interrupt-Affinity Policy Tool can be used to bind device interrupts to particular processors on multiprocessor computers. This can maximize performance and scaling by allowing specific tasks to be assigned to specific processors.

D. **Incorrect:** The device manager cannot be used to bind device interrupts to particular processors on multiprocessor computers.

2. **Correct Answer: B**

A. **Incorrect:** Applying a policy manually once will leave it active. It might be possible to manually apply the policy using the appropriate schedule.

B. **Correct:** Configuring a WSRM policy that is applied during the appropriate times using the calendar best achieves this goal.

   C. **Incorrect:** Interrupt-Affinity policies allow you to bind hardware device interrupt requests to a specific processor in a multiprocessor system. They cannot be used to grant one group of users priority access to resources.

   D. **Incorrect:** Interrupt-Affinity policies allow you to bind hardware device interrupt requests to a specific processor in a multiprocessor system. They cannot be used to grant one group of users priority access to resources.

3. **Correct Answer: B**

   A. **Incorrect:** An average logical disk queue length of 1 is not a cause for concern.

   B. **Correct:** A Memory Pages /Sec above 50 is cause for concern.

   C. **Incorrect:** A Processor % Processor Time of 65 % is not cause for concern.

   D. **Incorrect:** On a 1 GBit network, a Network Total Bytes/Sec is not a cause for concern.

4. **Correct Answer: B**

   A. **Incorrect:** Changing the schedule will not increase the period over which data is gathered.

   B. **Correct:** Creating a User Defined Data Collection Set based on the System Performance Data Collector Set allows you to set a longer data collection duration.

   C. **Incorrect:** You should use the System Performance Data Collector Set rather than the System Diagnostics Data Collection Set.

   D. **Incorrect:** Configuring the existing schedule will not alter the duration of the data collection. The schedule only dictates when the collection starts. It does not dictate when the collection ends. This is done on the Stop Condition tab, which is separate from the Schedule tab.

Lesson 3

1. **Correct Answer: A**

   A. **Correct:** Feature delegation at the global level is only possible when the built-in Administrator account is logged on directly or invoked through the *runas* command.

   B. **Incorrect:** Feature delegation at the global level is only possible with the built-in Administrator account. It is not possible to perform IIS feature delegation at the global level with an account that is a member of the local Administrators group unless that account is the built-in Administrator account.

C. **Incorrect:** Feature delegation at the global level is only possible with the built-in Administrator account. Adding a domain account to the Domain Admins group will not resolve this problem.

D. **Incorrect:** Adding a local account to the local Administrators group will not resolve the problem because the only way to perform feature delegation at the global level is by using the built-in Administrator account.

2. **Correct Answer: D**

A. **Incorrect:** Delegating the ability to manage groups will not allow trusted users to change passwords.

B. **Incorrect:** Delegating the ability to create user accounts will provide branch office users with more rights than are necessary and will also not allow them to actually change passwords.

C. **Incorrect:** Allowing a trusted user at each branch office to read user information will not allow them to change passwords.

D. **Correct:** Delegating the Reset User Passwords And Force Password Change At Next Logon task to a trusted user at a branch office site will allow that user to perform basic password management tasks without granting other unnecessary permissions.

3. **Correct Answer: D**

A. **Incorrect:** Although this would technically work, Sam would be granted the ability over all groups located in the OU, not just the Interns group. This violates the principle of least privilege, which requires that you assign only those rights that are necessary.

B. **Incorrect:** The Delegation Of Control Wizard cannot be used directly on security groups.

C. **Incorrect:** The Delegation Of Control Wizard cannot be used directly on security groups.

D. **Correct:** Using the Managed By tab to set Sam's user account, the group manager also confers the ability to modify group membership.

4. **Correct Answers: A and B**

A. **Correct:** The dsacls command, targeted at the appropriate OU, with the /resetDefaultDACL option, will reset an OU's permissions to the default state.

B. **Correct:** Clicking the Restore Defaults button on an OU's Advanced Security Settings for Delegation dialog box will reset an OU's permissions to the default state.

C. **Incorrect:** The Managed By tab on an OU's properties is for information, rather than administrative, purposes.

D. **Incorrect:** The Managed By tab on an OU's properties is for information, rather than administrative, purposes.

E. **Incorrect:** The dsquery command only provides information about objects in Active Directory. It cannot be used to reset an errant delegation.

Case Scenario 1: Fabrikam Event Management

1. Ensure that the Windows Event Collector service is configured to start automatically. Configure a source computer initiated subscription on the collector computer.

2. Use Group Policy to configure the 30 servers to forward events to the computer that you have configured as a collector.

3. Attach a task to the event using the Event Log Viewer and set the task as the PowerShell script that you created.

Case Scenario 2: Server Performance Monitoring at Blue Yonder Airlines

1. Although a number of counters record this data, Processor\% Processor Time, Memory\Available Mbytes, and LogicalDisk\Current Disk Queue Length provide a good overview of the processor usage, amount of available RAM, and the load on the disk subsystem.

2. Ensure that your reading is taken over a period of normal use. The period should be long enough to generate good average values. If you record a set of baseline performance statistics in the middle of the night, you will not have an accurate picture of how the server performs under a normal load.

3. One compelling argument that the current hardware is inadequate is a set of reports—taken over a reasonable amount of time—that shows that server performance has reached a plateau because of hardware limitations. Simply taking one performance snapshot is not as compelling because the conditions under which the snapshot was taken could be unusual and not part of a consistent performance trend.

Case Scenario 3: Delegating Rights to Trusted Users at Wingtip Toys

1. You need to separate user accounts into an OU structure that represents existing departmental organization. After user accounts are placed into new OUs, you can use the Delegation Of Control Wizard to grant departmental administrative assistants the right to change and reset passwords.

2. Although team leaders should be able to modify group membership, they have no reason to actually be able to create or delete groups. To prepare for the implementation of this plan, create the specified team groups and then, by using the Managed By tab on each security group's properties, specify the corresponding manager's user account.

Chapter 8: Lesson Review Answers

Lesson 1

1. **Correct Answers: B and C**

   A. **Incorrect:** Network Load Balancing is only used to balance traffic between WSUS servers; it will not help ensure that clients connecting at any office will use the local WSUS server.

   B. **Correct:** Enabling DNS Round Robin and netmask ordering allows clients to be provided with the IP address of their closest WSUS server.

   C. **Correct:** For this method to work, all clients need to access the WSUS server using the same FQDN. This allows the DNS server to return the "closest" result to the querying DNS client.

   D. **Incorrect:** BIND secondaries allow non-Windows DNS servers to host zone data from Windows DNS servers. This setting is not related to WSUS deployment.

   E. **Incorrect:** Configuring a large host file will not solve the problem. Queries to host files do not return results based on the querying host's IP address.

2. **Correct Answer: C**

   A. **Incorrect:** Because each faculty's IT department needs the ability to approve updates, you should not configure downstream servers as replicas.

B. **Incorrect:** Replica servers do not allow for local administrators to approve updates.

C. **Correct:** Configuring one upstream server to retrieve updates from the Internet and five downstream autonomous servers—one for each faculty—meets the question objectives of minimizing bandwidth use and allowing each faculty's IT department to approve or disapprove updates.

D. **Incorrect:** Although five autonomous servers would allow faculty IT departments to approve updates, it would not minimize the amount of traffic between the university and Microsoft Update.

3. **Correct Answers: A and C**

A. **Correct:** You need to create computer groups on the WSUS server and then assign clients to these computer groups using GPOs applied to departmental OUs.

B. **Incorrect:** The GPOs need to be assigned to OU rather than to the domain.

C. **Correct:** You need to create computer groups on the WSUS server and then assign clients to these computer groups using GPOs applied to departmental OUs.

D. **Incorrect:** You do not need to create a security group. It is necessary to create a WSUS computer group.

E. **Incorrect:** You do not need to create a security group. It is necessary to create a WSUS computer group.

4. **Correct Answer: C**

A. **Incorrect:** Although it may be possible with a significant amount of effort, creating a scheduled task is not the best way to deploy updates using WSUS. You should create an Automatic Approval rule that uses the PatchTest WSUS computer group as a target.

B. **Incorrect:** An Automatic Approval rule that deploys updates to the All Computers group will deploy updates to all computers, not the PatchTest WSUS group as specified in the question text.

C. **Correct:** Automatic Approval rules use WSUS computer groups as targets for update deployment.

D. **Incorrect:** Automatic Approval rules do not use security groups as targets for update deployment.

5. **Correct Answer: C**

    A. **Incorrect:** Update Status Summary will provide information about the number of computers the update did not install on, but will not provide detailed information about specific computers.

    B. **Incorrect:** Computer Status Summary will provide summary information about computers and updates, but will not provide detailed information about specific computers.

    C. **Correct:** The Update Detailed Status report provides a per-update report with a list of computers and update status. Navigating to the page that holds information about the problematic update will allow you to quickly locate the necessary computers.

    D. **Incorrect:** A Computer Detailed Status report will give you one-computer-per-page information about the status of particular updates. Although it would be possible to check every page of such a report to determine which computers did not have the update, this requires significantly more effort than having a single page that lists each computer's status for a particular update.

Lesson 2

1. **Correct Answer: A**

    A. **Correct:** The Audit Account Logon Events policy records logon events authenticated by a domain controller. Forwarding these events to server records from all domain controllers will allow you to get a full picture of account logon activity at the site.

    B. **Incorrect:** Account management relates to the creation or modification of user accounts or groups. It does not relate to recording domain authentication events.

    C. **Incorrect:** Audit Logon Events only writes local logon events to the event log. If instituted, it would only provide data about people logging on to the domain controller rather than logon events authenticated by the domain controller when users log on using another computer in the domain.

    D. **Incorrect:** The Audit Directory Service Access policy is used to enable auditing on the access to Active Directory objects that have System Access Control Lists applied.

2. **Correct Answer: C**

   A. **Incorrect:** Although shared folders can be protected using BitLocker, BitLocker works on a per-volume basis and cannot be used to restrict access on a per-user account basis.

   B. **Incorrect:** EFS works only with user accounts. Group accounts cannot be assigned EFS certificates.

   C. **Correct:** Encrypting the confidential data to each of the five accountant's user accounts will meet this goal.

   D. **Incorrect:** Although shared folders can be protected using BitLocker, BitLocker works on a per-volume basis and cannot be used to restrict access on a per-user account basis.

3. **Correct Answer: A**

   A. **Correct:** Domain isolation restricts communication so that computers that are members of the domain are only accessible to other computers that are members of the domain.

   B. **Incorrect:** VPNs are used for remote access. VPNs are not used to restrict access to computers on a Local Area Network.

   C. **Incorrect:** EFS is used to encrypt local files. It cannot be used to restrict network access.

   D. **Incorrect:** NAP restricts access to the network based on client health, not domain membership.

4. **Correct Answer: D**

   A. **Incorrect:** You should not place file servers on a perimeter network. Because the contractor computers are DHCP clients, it will be difficult to configure an internal firewall to block access to these servers.

   B. **Incorrect:** A domain isolation policy would block contractor access to all domain hosts including those hosts that they should have access to.

   C. **Incorrect:** Because the contractor computers are DHCP clients, it will be difficult to configure an internal firewall to block access to these servers. Although this might be possible with DHCP reservations, the fact that different contractors are present each week would make it hard to implement.

   D. **Correct:** Server isolation policies allow you to limit network access to a specific group of servers on the basis of whether a host computer is a member of an Active Directory domain.

Case Scenario: Deploying WSUS 3.0 SP1 at Fabrikam

1. You should add the CIO's account to the WSUS Reporters local group. This will allow the CIO to run reports without assigning unnecessary administrative privileges.

2. You should configure the downstream WSUS servers at the Fabrikam satellite offices as WSUS replicas. This way the update approvals and the computer group configuration at the head office WSUS server will automatically be inherited by the downstream servers.

3. You should generate an Update Detailed Status report. This will allow you to bring up an update's report page which will list the specific computers that the update failed to install on.

Chapter 9: Lesson Review Answers

Lesson 1

1. **Correct Answer: B**

   A. **Incorrect:** L2TP over IPsec uses port 1701. SSTP uses port 443, the port used for HTTP over SSL (also known as HTTPS).

   B. **Correct:** SSTP uses port 443, the port used for HTTP over SSL (also known as HTTPS).

   C. **Incorrect:** PPTP uses port 1723. SSTP uses port 443.

   D. **Incorrect:** SLIP (Serial Line Internet Protocol) is an old dial-up protocol and cannot be used as a VPN tunnel.

2. **Correct Answer: D**

   A. **Incorrect:** DHCP reservations are used to assign particular IP addresses to particular clients on the basis of client MAC address.

   B. **Incorrect:** DHCP exclusions ensure that a range of IP addresses in the scope are not added to the DHCP pool.

   C. **Incorrect:** Configuring the Default Class on a DHCP server will assign those options to all DHCP clients, not just remote access clients.

   D. **Correct:** The Default Routing And Remote Access Class is a feature new to the DHCP service in Windows Server 2008 that allows separate DHCP options to be assigned to remote access clients.

3. **Correct Answer: D**

   A. **Incorrect:** Windows 2000 Professional clients cannot connect to an SSTP VPN server.

   B. **Incorrect:** Windows XP Professional clients cannot connect to an SSTP VPN server.

   C. **Incorrect:** A Windows Vista RTM client cannot connect to an SSTP VPN. Windows Vista must have Service Pack 1 installed before this VPN connection is possible.

   D. **Correct:** Windows Vista clients can only connect to an SSTP VPN if they have Service Pack 1 installed.

4. **Correct Answer: D**

   A. **Incorrect:** NPS accounting data is generated on the NPS server, which is also the RADIUS server, rather than on the RADIUS client.

   B. **Incorrect:** NPS accounting data is generated on the NPS server, which is also the RADIUS server, rather than on the RADIUS client.

   C. **Incorrect:** The SQL Server computer will not be forwarding RADIUS accounting data to the NPS server, the NPS server will be forwarding RADIUS accounting data to the SQL Server.

   D. **Correct:** It is possible, using the accounting node in the NPS console, to configure all NPS accounting data to be written to a SQL Server database rather than the local log files.

5. **Correct Answer: A**

   A. **Correct:** A TS-RAP (Resource Authorization Policy) specifies which internal network resources that a client connecting through the TS Gateway Server can connect to.

   B. **Incorrect:** A TS-CAP (Connection Authorization Policy) specifies which user accounts are able to connect through a TS Gateway Server.

   C. **Incorrect:** You have no need to use a TS Session Broker because the question does not mention the need to reconnect to the same Terminal Server in a Terminal Server farm.

   D. **Incorrect:** You do not need to use a TS Session Broker because the question does not mention the need to reconnect to the same Terminal Server in a Terminal Server farm.

Lesson 2

1. **Correct Answer: A**

   A. **Correct:** IPsec enforcement can be configured to allow and deny access on a port-by-port basis. This means that you can allow access only to computers with valid health certificates on the RDP port while allowing access to HTTP and HTTPS for computers without valid health certificates.

   B. **Incorrect:** 802.1X places clients on VLANs according to their health. A healthy client will be placed on a different VLAN from an unhealthy one. Although it may change in future, as OSI Layer 2 devices, switches cannot be configured to block specific TCP/UDP ports (although some switches can prioritize particular traffic). In general, the term *port* on a switch refers to an interface.

   C. **Incorrect:** DHCP enforcement places clients on different IP networks based on their health and cannot be configured to allow traffic on one port and block it on another.

   D. **Incorrect:** VPN enforcement works on remote clients and is not appropriate in an intranet scenario because it will not influence non-remote clients.

2. **Correct Answers: A and D**

   A. **Correct:** Using the operating system as a condition allows you to apply different rules to Windows XP and Windows Vista clients.

   B. **Incorrect:** You should not create a VLAN; you should create a conditional policy based on client operating system.

   C. **Incorrect:** You should configure the policy to allow Windows XP, not Windows Vista, to bypass the health check.

   D. **Correct:** Configuring a policy that allows Windows XP computers to bypass the health check means that Windows Vista computers will still be checked.

   E. **Incorrect.** You should not create a VLAN; you should create a conditional policy based on client operating system.

3. **Correct Answer: C**

   A. **Incorrect:** The Windows Server 2003 DC does not need to be upgraded to support DHCP NAP enforcement.

   B. **Incorrect:** The DNS server does not need to be upgraded to support DHCP NAP enforcement.

    C. **Correct:** The DHCP ES (Enforcement Service) is only available on Windows Server 2008. The existing Windows Server 2003 computer must be upgraded to Windows Server 2008 to use DHCP NAP enforcement.

    D. **Incorrect:** The Network Policy Server does not need to be upgraded to support DHCP NAP enforcement.

4. **Correct Answers: A and B**

    A. **Correct:** IPsec enforcement requires a Health Registration Authority and a Windows Server 2008 CA.

    B. **Correct:** IPsec enforcement requires a Health Registration Authority and a Windows Server 2008 CA.

    C. **Incorrect:** A Windows Server 2008 DHCP server is not necessary for IPsec enforcement because statically configured addresses can be used.

    D. **Incorrect:**. HCAP Servers are used in conjunction with Cisco Network Access Control and is not implemented as a part of the IPsec enforcement program.

    E. **Incorrect:** An NPS Server configured as a RADIUS proxy is not a necessary component of NAP IPsec Enforcement.

5. **Correct Answers: A and C**

    A. **Correct:** A Windows Server 2008 computer must host the NPS server role in an environment where 802.1X NAP enforcement is to be deployed.

    B. **Incorrect:** A RADIUS proxy server is not necessary to implement 802.1X NAP enforcement.

    C. **Correct:** Clients must have the EAPHost EC (Enforcement Client) for 802.1X NAP enforcement to be deployed.

    D. **Incorrect:** HCAP is only necessary when you are using Cisco Network Access Control clients. Although you might use Cisco switches, 802.1X NAP enforcement does not require the HCAP server role be installed.

    E. **Incorrect:** A DHCP server is not necessary when using 802.1X enforcement.

Case Scenario: Remote Access at Wingtip Toys

1. At the Sydney site, you would use a TS-CAP (Terminal Services Connection Authorization Policy).

2. SSTP should be used at the port 443, which SSTP uses, is already open.

3. You should use VPN enforcement in the Melbourne location.

Chapter 10: Lesson Review Answers

Lesson 1

1. **Correct Answer: B**

   A. **Incorrect:** You should not deploy an Enterprise Root CA because the question indicates that one has already been deployed.

   B. **Correct:** As the question indicates, an Enterprise CA is already present in some capacity at the head office location. You should deploy an Enterprise Subordinate CA.

   C. **Incorrect:** The question mentions support for autoenrollment policies, meaning that an Enterprise CA is required.

   D. **Incorrect:** The question mentions support for autoenrollment policies, meaning that an Enterprise CA is required.

2. **Correct Answers: A and B**

   A. **Correct:** To deploy autoenrollment, you must enable autoenrollment within Active Directory.

   B. **Correct:** Autoenrollment permissions must be applied to certificate templates before certificates can be automatically enrolled.

   C. **Incorrect:** CRL publication settings do not need to be modified from their defaults to support the deployment of autoenrollment.

   D. **Incorrect:** An Online Responder is not necessary for the deployment of autoenrollment.

   E. **Incorrect:** Web enrollment is not necessary for the deployment of autoenrollment.

3. **Correct Answers: B, C, and E**

   A. **Incorrect:** The OCSP Response Signing certificate needs to be installed on the Online Responder, not the CA.

   B. **Correct:** You need to configure the OCSP Response Signing certificate template on the CA.

   C. **Correct:** You need to install the OCSP Response Signing certificate on the server that will perform the Online Responder function.

D. **Incorrect:** You need to configure the AIA extension on the CA with the URL of the Online Responder.

E. **Correct:** You need to configure the AIA extension on the CA with the URL of the Online Responder rather than the URL of the CA.

4. **Correct Answer: D**

A. **Incorrect:** Installing an Enterprise Subordinate CA in the branch office will not reduce problems associated with revocation checks that currently occur across WAN links.

B. **Incorrect:** Although it is possible to publish CRL data to alternate locations such as a branch office file share, by default, the deployment of an Enterprise Subordinate CA does not include CRL information of certificates issued by a CA further up the PKI hierarchy. This task is best suited to Online Responders.

C. **Incorrect:** Standalone Subordinate CAs cannot help in servicing revocation checks for certificates issued by enterprise root CAs.

D. **Correct:** Online Responders can speed up certificate verification because they hold a copy of the CRL and can reply to requests on an individual basis about the status of specific certificates. Having a satellite office local Online Responder reduces traffic over WAN links.

5. **Correct Answer: C**

A. **Incorrect:** The Certification Authority console can view the status of one CA at a time. The Enterprise PKI tool can be used to view the status of all CAs in an Active Directory forest at a time.

B. **Incorrect:** The Online Responder Management Console is used to manage Online Responders. Even though the console can be used to manage Online Responder Arrays, Online Responders do not have to be installed on servers that function as CAs.

C. **Correct:** The Enterprise PKI tool can be used to view the status of a network's PKI environment, including all CA hierarchies that exist within an Active Directory forest.

D. **Incorrect:** The Certificates snap-in allows you to view certificates for a user, computer, or service account. It cannot be used to view the status of Certificate Authorities.

Lesson 2

1. **Correct Answer: C**

    A. **Incorrect:** Remote Differential Compression is related to the transfer of data using minimal bandwidth. It is not directly related to Fibre Channel storage devices.

    B. **Incorrect:** UDDI is used by Web services and is not related to Fibre Channel storage devices.

    C. **Correct:** Multipath I/O (MPIO) must be installed on a server if it will access a LUN through multiple Fibre Channel ports or iSCSI initiator adapters.

    D. **Incorrect:** RPC over HTTP Proxy is not directly related to Fibre Channel storage devices.

2. **Correct Answer: D**

    A. **Incorrect:** The spanned LUN type does not provide improved I/O performance and is not fault tolerant.

    B. **Incorrect:** The striped LUN type provides improved I/O performance over the simple type but is not fault tolerant.

    C. **Incorrect:** The simple LUN type does not provide I/O improvements and is not fault tolerant.

    D. **Correct:** The Striped with Parity LUN type (also known as RAID-5) provides improved I/O performance over the simple, spanned, and mirrored LUN types and also is fault tolerant.

3. **Correct Answer: B**

    A. **Incorrect:** The Failback MPIO policy uses a preferred path, only shifting I/O to an alternate path when the preferred path fails.

    B. **Correct:** The Round-Robin MPIO policy uses all available paths between the server and the SAN array.

    C. **Incorrect:** The Weighted Path MPIO policy directs I/O to the path that has been assigned the least weight by the administrator that configured it.

    D. **Incorrect:** The Dynamic Least Queue Depth MPIO policy directs I/O to the path with the least number of outstanding requests. It does not distribute requests equally across all paths, but directs requests taking into account a path's current load.

4. **Correct Answer: A**

   A. **Correct:** Storage Manager for SANs is used to create LUNs.

   B. **Incorrect:** Storage Explorer is used to manage Fibre Channel and iSCSI fabrics. It cannot be used to create LUNs on storage arrays.

   C. **Incorrect:** Device Manager cannot be used to create LUNs on a Fibre Channel Array.

   D. **Incorrect:** Disk Management cannot be used to create LUNs on a Fibre Channel array.

Case Scenario: Deploying Certificate Services and a SAN Array at Coho Vineyard and Winery

1. Configure autoenrollment in Active Directory and on the IPsec certificate template.

2. Deploy an Online Responder.

3. The RAID-5 LUN type offers the best mix of performance and fault tolerance.

Chapter 11: Lesson Review Answers

Lesson 1

1. **Correct Answer: B**

   A. **Incorrect:** The Network Load Balancing Manager handles NLB clusters, not DNS Round Robin.

   B. **Correct:** The DNS Manager is used to create and manage DNS records in Windows Server 2008.

   C. **Incorrect:** You can use the nslookup utility to query much useful information, but not to create or manage DNS.

   D. **Incorrect:** The Server Manager in Windows Server 2008 is used to manage the server as a whole, not DNS settings in particular.

2. **Correct Answers: C and D**

   A. **Incorrect:** This is not a limitation of DNS Round Robin. These configurations are frequently used successfully on the Internet.

   B. **Incorrect:** The DNS administrator has complete control over the TTL for domains and DNS records. Though they do not always do so, clients and other DNS servers should honor your TTL.

C. **Correct:** This is a disadvantage of DNS Round Robin. Because you cannot control which server will receive or serve a request, stateful applications have problems with DNS Round Robin configurations.

D. **Correct:** This is a disadvantage of DNS Round Robin. The administrator cannot control or give extra weight to certain servers to make sure that they receive or serve more requests.

3. **Correct Answer: A**

A. **Correct:** The MAC and IP addresses are shared among all cluster participants with NLB.

B. **Incorrect:** Although the IP address is shared, the MAC address is as well.

C. **Incorrect:** Although the MAC address is shared, the IP address is also shared among participants.

D. **Incorrect:** The MAC and IP addresses are shared.

4. **Correct Answer: C**

A. **Incorrect:** Sixty is not the correct number of heartbeats.

B. **Incorrect:** Thirty is not the correct number of heartbeats.

C. **Correct:** Five is the correct number of heartbeats. If five heartbeats are missed, convergence is triggered among the remaining participants.

D. **Incorrect:** Thirty-two is not the correct number of heartbeats.

5. **Correct Answers: A and B**

A. **Correct:** It is necessary to configure NLB port rules to ensure that traffic to the Web server uses NLB but other traffic types do not.

B. **Correct:** Multicast is required because the cluster hosts have one adapter and must communicate with each other during the robocopy replication of Web site data.

C. **Incorrect:** Unicast mode does not support communication between cluster nodes.

D. **Incorrect:** IPv6 is not necessary in this configuration.

E. **Incorrect:** DNS Round Robin is not necessary in this situation.

Lesson 2

1. **Correct Answer: B**

   A. **Incorrect:** This model is recommended for an even number of nodes.

   B. **Correct:** This is the recommended model for clusters with odd numbers of nodes.

   C. **Incorrect:** This model is not recommended.

   D. **Incorrect:** This model is recommended for an even number of nodes.

2. **Correct Answers: A and B**

   A. **Correct:** RAID 0 creates one larger logical disk out of two or more smaller disks.

   B. **Correct:** RAID 1 creates a mirror from one disk to another.

   C. **Incorrect:** RAID 5 requires three disks.

   D. **Incorrect:** RAID 10 combines the mirroring of RAID 1 along with the striping available in RAID 0 and requires a minimum of 4 disks.

3. **Correct Answer: A**

   A. **Correct:** The Node and File Share Majority uses a file share to store the configuration data and can continue if half of the nodes fail.

   B. **Incorrect:** The witness disk is stored on a file share.

   C. **Incorrect:** The use of a file share means that the cluster resource remains available on the file share thus making this answer incorrect.

   D. **Incorrect:** This quorum Model allows half of the nodes to fail and it will still run.

Case Scenario 1: Choosing the Appropriate Availability Strategy

1. The Exchange Server computers should use Failover Clustering. Exchange is cluster-aware. Based on the information given, the company's main Web site appears to run from one server. An additional server should be added. Because the site has static, informational pages, this implies that simple Network Load Balacing can be used. The Web sites running on the Linux server should use DNS Round Robin because no other option is available with Windows Server 2008. Other factors to consider include the connectivity and physical and environmental factors involved in providing high availability.

2. The Exchange Server computers could use NLB or Failover Clustering but not DNS Round Robin. DNS Round Robin is not session-aware and requests could go to different servers. The company's Web site in its current state, using only one server, cannot use any of the high-availability options. At least one additional server with a copy of the Web site would be necessary to provide redundancy. Finally, the Linux servers can only use DNS Round Robin because none of the Windows Server 2008 high-availability options supports Linux.

3. The most likely quorum model would be Node and File Share because it enables the witness disk to be on a file share. Because there are only two servers in this scenario, it would be best to store witness disk information in a separate location.

Chapter 12: Lesson Review Answers

Lesson 1

1. **Correct Answer: B**

   A. **Incorrect:** Members of the Power Users group cannot perform manual backups.

   B. **Correct:** Members of the Backup Operators group cannot configure Windows Server Backup schedules, but can perform manual backups on Windows Server 2008 computers.

   C. **Incorrect:** Although members of the Administrators group can perform manual backups, adding the trusted staff member to this group will provide unnecessary administrative privileges because this task can also be accomplished by members of the Backup Operators group.

   D. **Incorrect:** Members of the Remote Desktop Users group cannot perform manual backups.

2. **Correct Answers: A and C**

   A. **Correct:** Because the script will run with the local Administrator account credentials, it will be necessary to place extra credentials for the remote share in the script.

   B. **Incorrect:** Local Administrator account credentials will not enable access to a remote shared folder (unless the remote computer uses the same Administrator password).

   C. **Correct:** It is necessary to run the script using the local Administrator account because wbadmin.exe can only be executed with elevated privileges.

   D. **Incorrect:** It is necessary to run the script using the local Administrator account credentials because wbadmin.exe can only be executed with elevated privileges.

   E. **Incorrect:** The question specifies that the task must run daily.

3. **Correct Answers: A, B, and C**

   A. **Correct:** Windows Server Backup can write scheduled backups to local external USB 2.0 disks.

   B. **Correct:** Windows Server Backup can write scheduled backups to local external IEEE 1394 disks.

   C. **Correct:** Windows Server Backup can write scheduled backups to IDE Internal disks.

   D. **Incorrect:** Windows Server Backup cannot be used to write scheduled backups to iSCSI SANs.

4. **Correct Answers: A and B**

   A. **Correct:** Virtual Server 2005 R2 can be used to mount VHD files.

   B. **Correct:** Hyper-V can be used to mount VHD files.

   C. **Incorrect:** Storage Explorer cannot be used to mount VHD files.

   D. **Incorrect:** Disk Management cannot be used to mount VHD files.

   E. **Incorrect:** Storage Manager for SANS cannot be used to mount VHD files.

5. **Correct Answers: C, D, and E**

   A. **Incorrect:** Although generally when performing a manual backup you are able to write backup data to a network share, this is not the case with a System State data backup created using wbadmin.exe.

   B. **Incorrect:** Although generally when performing a manual backup you are able to write backup data to a local DVD writer, this is not the case with a System State data backup created using wbadmin.exe.

   C. **Correct:** You can write a System State-only backup using wbadmin.exe to an external USB 2.0 HDD.

   D. **Correct:** You can write a System State-only backup using wbadmin.exe to an external IEEE 1394 HDD.

E. **Correct:** You can write a System State-only backup using wbadmin.exe to a local internal SCSI hard disk drive.

Lesson 2

1. **Correct Answer: C**

   A. **Incorrect:** This command recovers the object named Solar located in the Pluto OU.

   B. **Incorrect:** You must use the Restore Object command to restore an object, whether it is a user or computer account.

   C. **Correct:** You need to issue the command Restore Object "cn=Pluto,OU=Solar,dc= Contoso,dc=internal" to restore the Pluto computer account to the Solar OU in the domain Contoso.internal.

   D. **Incorrect:** You must use the Restore Object command to restore an object, whether it is a user or computer account.

2. **Correct Answer: C**

   A. **Incorrect:** Members of the Power Users local groups cannot restore backup data.

   B. **Incorrect:** Members of the Power Users local groups cannot restore backup data.

   C. **Correct:** To perform a restoration it is necessary to be a member of the Backup Operators or local Administrators group on the server that the restoration is being performed on. Because user accounts that are members of the Backup Operators group have fewer privileges than user accounts that are members of the local Administrators group, when following the principle of least privilege, you should use the former.

   D. **Incorrect:** Although membership of the local Administrators group will allow for restoration of files and folders to be performed, this task can also be performed by members of the Backup Operators group. The Backup Operators group is assigned fewer privileges than the local Administrators group.

3. **Correct Answer: C**

   A. **Incorrect:** It is not possible to perform an authoritative restore using an RODC.

   B. **Incorrect:** By performing a full server recovery on the RODC you have already performed a nonauthoritative restore.

C. **Correct:** Performing a full server recovery does not reapply BitLocker settings. You will need to reapply BitLocker settings to a server after the full server recovery process is complete.

D. **Incorrect:** Although performing backups is always prudent, it is not necessary to perform a full server backup after performing a full server recovery. Remember, if you have just performed a full server recovery, any backup taken will be identical to the backup data you already have on the recovery media.

4. **Correct Answer: C**

A. **Incorrect:** You should not perform a bare metal recovery because this will remove the existing operating system and applications from the server.

B. **Incorrect:** You should not mount the backup images as volumes because this will not restore the intranet server's functionality without further intervention.

C. **Correct:** In this case, mounting the backup images as a virtual machine under Hyper-V will work as an effective stopgap measure until the replacement component arrives and the server can be restored normally.

D. **Incorrect:** Restoring the system state data from one server to another will not resolve this problem and may even cause stability problems.

Case Scenario 1: Wingtip Toys Backup Infrastructure

1. An internal or external USB 2.0 or IEEE 1394 storage device must be attached to the servers so that scheduled backup data can be written.

2. Windows Server Backup can only write to local or externally connected volumes. Offsite backup necessitates that backup media be moved to an offsite location. This means that removable external devices, such as USB 2.0 or IEEE 1394 storage devices, must be used because these devices can easily be transported to offsite locations.

3. Configure Shadow Copies of Shared Folders on each shared folder and instruct users how to access it. This will allow users to recover their own files and reduce the amount of time that help desk staff must spend on this task.

Case Scenario 2: Disaster Recovery at Fabrikam

1. You should restore the forest root domain controllers first because these must be in place to perform some operations on the domains that make up the rest of the forest.

2. Recover the domain controllers using the Friday full server backups. Perform an authoritative restore of the objects that were deleted on Thursday using the Wednesday system state backups.

3. To restore fileserve.hq.fabrikam.com as completely as possible, restore the full server backup and then restore the shared volume backups. When you perform volume backups, volumes that contain the operating system are automatically backed up.

Glossary

The .NET framework A software component that is included in Windows operating systems. It provides precoded solutions to common program requirements, and controls the execution of programs written for the Framework. Most new applications created for the Windows platforms use the .NET Framework.

ACID properties A set of properties that guarantee that single logical operations (in particular database transactions) are processed reliably. Atomicity guarantees that either all of the tasks of a transaction are performed or none of them is. Consistency requires that the data is in a legal state when the transaction begins and when it ends. Isolation guarantees that the application makes operations in a transaction appear isolated from all other operations. Durability guarantees that after the user has been notified of success, the transaction will persist, and not be undone.

Access control A combination of share and NTFS permissions and user rights that should ensure that users can access the resources they require but prevent inappropriate access to resources that users are not entitled to access.

Access control entry (ACE) An assignment of permissions to a security principal.

Access control list (ACL) A list of ACEs. ACLs are sometimes known as permission sets.

Address space The total number of addresses (theoretically) available with an Internet protocol.

Anycast address An IPv6 address that can identify a number of hosts. Packets addressed to an anycast address are delivered to the closest interface (in terms of routing distance) that is identified by the address.

Application accessibility Refers to the features that permit a wide range of users to run an application. Direct accessibilty requires that an application be designed so that the greatest number of people possible can use it without needing special adaptive software or hardware. Further accessibility is provided by interfaces specifically designed to improve accessibility for (for example) physically impaired users or users with sight or hearing impairment.

Application availability The readiness of an application (and the service it runs under) to handle customer requests and to return timely and accurate responses.

Application resilience   Ensures that if an installed application is corrupted or if its executable file is deleted, the application automatically reinstalls. It also ensures that applications are kept up to date and new updates, service packs, and application revisions install as required.

ASP.NET   A Microsoft Web application framework that programmers use to build dynamic Web sites, Web applications, and extensible markup language (XML) Web services.

Authoritative restore   A technique by which objects deleted from Active Directory can be recovered.

Autoenrollment   A process by which a digital certificate is automatically assigned without administrator or user intervention.

Autonomous mode   A downstream WSUS server administration mode that uses different approvals to the upstream server.

Bare metal restore   When a restore is performed without loading an operating system.

Boot partition   The boot partition hosts the operating system files. The easiest way to remember this when considering the system partition is that the labels are counterintuitive.

BootP-enabled   A BootP-enabled router or layer-3 switch can pass DHCP or DHCPv6 traffic to remote subnets so that a DHCP server can allocate addresses from different scopes to different subnets.

Collector computer   A computer that is sent Event Log data or a computer that polls a set of computers for Event Log data. The Event Log data of multiple computers can be viewed on a collector computer.

Component object model (COM)   A Microsoft platform for component-based software engineering (CBSE). COM is used to enable dynamic object creation and interprocess communication in any programming language that supports the technology.

CA   Certificate Authority. A special server that issues digital certificates to users, computers, and services.

CRL   Certificate Revocation List. A list of certificate serial numbers for certificates that are no longer considered valid by the issuing authority.

DFS namespace   A hierarchy of DFS folders.

DFS replication (DFSR)   Fast, efficient multimaster replication that ensures that data within a DFS namespace is consistent and up to date. In Windows Server 2008, DFSR also replicates Active Directory information.

DHCP   Dynamic Host Configuration Protocol. This protocol is used to provide IPv4 and IPv6 addressing information dynamically to clients on the network.

DFS root   In stand-alone DFS, the root is the namespace server. In domain-based DNS, the root is the domain.

DNS round robin   This technique, not limited to Windows Server 2008, creates multiple answers for an individual host in the DNS to create a primitive form of load balancing.

Data collector set   Can include performance monitor data, event trace data, and computer configuration information.

Delegation   The assigning of administrative privileges to non-administrative users.

Directory services restore mode   A special operating mode of a Windows Server 2008 domain controller that allows for the restoration of Active Directory objects.

Distributed file system (DFS)   An arrangement in which resources can be distributed in folder targets on one or more servers and users can access resources via virtual DFS folders without needing to know where they are stored physically.

Domain isolation policy   A policy that restricts computers to only accepting incoming communication from other computers that are members of the same domain.

Downstream server   A server that receives approvals and/or updates from another WSUS server in the organization.

EFS   Encrypting File System. A technology that allows individual files and folders to be encrypted.

EAP-TLS   Extensible Authentication Protocol-Transport Layer Security is an authentication protocol that supports advanced authentication mechanisms such as digital certificates and smart cards.

Failover clustering   Formerly known as server clustering, Failover Clustering creates a logical grouping of servers, also known as nodes, that can service requests for applications with shared data stores.

Forward lookup zone   A DNS zone that enables a host name to be resolved to an IP address.

Functional levels   The levels at which a domain and forest operate. Higher functional levels provide more functionality but support fewer operating system versions.

Group policy object (GPO)   An AD DS object that contains Group Policy settings. GPOs are typically linked to one or more OUs.

Group policy setting   A configurable setting that determines the security and resource access applied to a user or computer account that is held in an OU.

Hyper-V   The name of the Windows Server Virtualization feature. This feature was known as Viridian in early Windows Server Longhorn documentation.

Indexing   Creating an index of the most common file and non-file data types on a server. You can index on file content in addition to data type.

L2TP/IPsec   A VPN protocol that uses IPsec to encrypt data and verify its integrity.

LUN   Logical Unit Number. A LUN is a logical reference to a portion of a storage sub-system. A LUN can be a partition on a single disk, an entire disk, or even a group of disks.

Line-of-business (LOB) application   A custom application that addresses operational requirements for a specific organization (or group of organizations).

Multicast   A transmission type where multiple hosts are sent data from one host across the network, but the data is transmitted only once to the hosts in the multicast groups rather than being transmitted in full to each host individually.

Multicast address   An address (IPv4 or IPv6) that identifies several hosts. Packets addressed to a multicast address are delivered to all interfaces that are identified by the address.

Network access protection (NAP)   A management feature that determines whether a client computer joining a network meets predefined configuration conditions, such as whether security updates have been applied and the operating system is up to date. If the client is not compliant, network access is restricted until remediation takes place.

Network load balancing   A high-availability feature of Windows Server 2008 that creates a virtual network adapter between two or more servers and sends requests to the servers based on administrator-defined criteria.

Offline file   A file that is automatically downloaded from a server so that a user can work on it offline and automatically uploaded to the server when the user's client computer is again online. The process of uploading and downloading offline files is known as synchronization.

Organizational unit (OU)   An AD DS container that can hold user accounts, computer accounts, or both.

PPP   Point-to-Point Protocol is a data-link protocol that is used for transmitting data.

PPTP   Point-to-Point Tunneling Protocol is a VPN protocol based on PPP.

PXE   Preboot Execution Environment. Allows compatible network clients to start an operating system from a network source rather than from local media such as a hard disk or CD-ROM.

Password settings container (PSC)   An object class in AD DS that contains PSOs.

Password settings object (PSO)   An AD DS object that contains security settings that can be different from the security settings for the domain.

Privilege   The ability to perform an administrative action, such as change a user password or create an Active Directory object.

Quorum model   The technique by which a Windows Server 2008 Failover Cluster determines the minimum number of cluster members to continue operating. Windows Server 2008 has four such models.

Quota   A setting that determines the amount of storage space in a shared folder or volume that an individual user is entitled to use. Soft quotas can be exceeded. Hard quotas cannot.

RADIUS   An authenticating, authorizing, and accounting protocol used with remote access traffic.

Read-only domain controllers (RODC)   A domain controller that holds AD DS information and can authenticate users and resolve DNS inquiries, but which does not permit connected user to make any changes to AD DS structure. RODCs contain only a small subset of the domain's user name and password information (if any).

Reliability   A measurement of how stable a computer's operating system, applications, services, and hardware are.

Remediation   The process of updating a client computer so that it becomes compliant and can be granted full network access. Automatic remediation through System Center Configuration Manager 2007 requires that the tool's software updates feature is installed and enabled.

Replica mode   A downstream WSUS server administration mode where all configuration information is inherited from the upstream server.

Reverse lookup zone   A DNS zone that enables an IP address to be resolved to a host name.

Route aggregation   A property of Internet protocol addresses that permits a number of contiguous address blocks to be combined and summarized as a larger address block.

SSTP   A VPN protocol that uses SSL to encrypt PPP traffic.

Scope   A range of contiguous addresses that can be allocated by a stateful address allocation protocol such as DHCP or DHCPv6.

Shadow group   A security group that contains all the user accounts in an associated OU. You cannot apply a PSO to an OU, so you apply it to the shadow group instead.

Silo   In Microsoft Application Virtualization, a silo is a virtualized partition in which an application executes.

Softgrid   Previous name of Microsoft Application Virtualization.

System partition   The system partition is the disk partition that the computer starts from. The easiest way to remember this when considering the boot partition is that the labels are counterintuitive.

System state backup   Backs up all Windows Server 2008 configuration data, such as the registry, Active Directory, and server role data.

Two-stage installation   A procedure where an administrator creates a computer account and a non-administrative user installs the operating system on the computer. Two-stage installation is typically used to install RODCs.

Unicast address   An address (IPv4 or IPv6) that uniquely identifies a host on a network.

VPN   Virtual Private Network allows hosts to the Internet to use encrypted tunnels to communicate with each other in such a way that it appears that the hosts are all on the same local network.

Virtualized   A virtualized server or application runs in its own separate environment under the management of a host or parent computer.

Volume shadow copy service (VSS)   A set of application program interfaces (APIs) that enable the capture of shadow copies of disk volumes while applications on a system continue to write to the volumes.

Wake on LAN   A feature that wakes a client computer from sleep mode so that (for example) updates can be applied. The computer's network adapter needs to be capable of receiving and processing wake-up packages.

Windows PE   The Windows Preinstallation Environment is a stripped-down, bootable environment that allows maintenance tasks to occur. It is most often used in network installations where a computer does not have a PXE-compliant network adapter.

Index

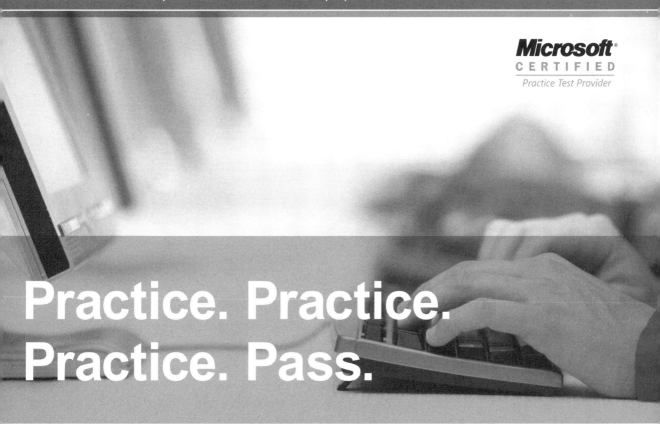

System Requirements

We recommend that you use a test workstation, test server, or staging server to complete the exercises in each lab. The following are the minimum system requirements your computer needs to meet to complete the practice exercises in this book. For more information, see the Introduction.

Hardware Requirements

You can complete almost all practice exercises in this book using virtual machines rather than real server hardware. The following hardware is required to complete the lab exercises:

- Personal computer with minimum 1GHz (x86) or 1.4GHz (x64) processor (2GHz or faster recommended)

- 512 MB of RAM or more (2 GB recommended; 4 GB enables you to host all the virtual machines specified for all the practice exercises in the book.)

- 15 GB free hard disk space (40 GB recommended; 60 GB enables you to host all the virtual machines specified for all the practice exercises in the book.)

- CD-ROM drive or DVD-ROM drive

- Super VGA (1,024 x 768) or higher resolution video adapter and monitor

- Keyboard and Microsoft mouse or compatible pointing device

Software Requirements

The following software is required to complete the lab exercises:

- Windows Server 2008 Enterprise Edition. An evaluation edition is available from the TechNet Evaluation Center at *http://technet.microsoft.com/en-us/evalcenter/ cc137123.aspx*.

- To perform the optional exercises in Chapter 4, "Application Servers and Services," you need an additional Windows Server 2003 member server. (This can be a virtual machine.) You can download an evaluation version of Windows Server 2003 from the following address: *http://technet.microsoft.com/en-us/ windowsserver/bb430831.aspx*.

- To perform the optional exercises in Chapter 11, "Clustering and High Availability," you need an additional Windows Server 2008 Enterprise member server. (This can be a virtual machine.)

To minimize the time and expense of configuring physical computers, we recommend that you use virtual machines. To run computers as virtual machines within Windows, you can use one of the following

- Microsoft Virtual PC 2007. You can download Virtual PC 2007 for free from *http://www.microsoft.com/windows/downloads/virtualpc/default.mspx.*

- Virtual Server 2005 R2 SP1. You can download a free evaluation edition from *http://www.microsoft.com/technet/virtualserver/evaluation/default.mspx.*

What do you think of this book?

We want to hear from you!

Do you have a few minutes to participate in a brief online survey?

Microsoft is interested in hearing your feedback so we can continually improve our books and learning resources for you.

To participate in our survey, please visit:

www.microsoft.com/learning/booksurvey/

...and enter this book's ISBN-10 or ISBN-13 number (located above barcode on back cover*). As a thank-you to survey participants in the United States and Canada, each month we'll randomly select five respondents to win one of five $100 gift certificates from a leading online merchant. At the conclusion of the survey, you can enter the drawing by providing your e-mail address, which will be used for prize notification only.

Thanks in advance for your input. Your opinion counts!

* Where to find the ISBN on back cover

ISBN-13: 000-0-0000-0000-0
ISBN-10: 0-0000-0000-0

Example only. Each book has unique ISBN.

Microsoft®
Press

www.microsoft.com/learning/booksurvey/